Microsoft®

Word 2010
IN DEPTH

Faithe Wempen

800 East 96th Street

Indianapolis, Indiana 46240

MICROSOFT® WORD 2010 IN DEPTH

Copyright © 2011 by Que Publishing

ISBN-13: 978-0-7897-4311-4

ISBN-10: 0-7897-4311-6

Library of Congress Cataloging-in-Publication Data:
Wempen, Faithe.
  Microsoft Word 2010 in depth / Faithe Wempen.
    p. cm.
  Includes index.
  ISBN-13: 978-0-7897-4311-4
  ISBN-10: 0-7897-4311-6
  1. Microsoft Word. 2. Word processing. I. Title. II. Title: Word 2010 in depth.
  Z52.5.M52W4643 2011
  005.52—dc22
                              2010029001

Printed in the United States of America

First Printing: August 2010

Trademarks

All terms mentioned in this book that are known to be trademarks or service marks have been appropriately capitalized. Que Publishing cannot attest to the accuracy of this information. Use of a term in this book should not be regarded as affecting the validity of any trademark or service mark.

Microsoft is a registered trademark of Microsoft Corporation.

Warning and Disclaimer

Every effort has been made to make this book as complete and as accurate as possible, but no warranty or fitness is implied. The information provided is on an "as is" basis. The author and the publisher shall have neither liability nor responsibility to any person or entity with respect to any loss or damages arising from the information contained in this book.

Bulk Sales

Que Publishing offers excellent discounts on this book when ordered in quantity for bulk purchases or special sales. For more information, please contact

  U.S. Corporate and Government Sales
  1-800-382-3419
  corpsales@pearsontechgroup.com

For sales outside the United States, please contact

  International Sales
  international@pearson.com

Associate Publisher
Greg Wiegand

Acquistions Editor
Michelle Newcomb

Development Editor
Joyce Nielson

Technical Editors
Joyce Nielson
Doug Holland

Managing Editor
Sandra Schroeder

Senior Project Editor
Tonya Simpson

Copy Editor
Gill Editorial Services

Indexer
Publishing Works, Inc.

Proofreader
Water Crest Publishing, Inc.

Publishing Coordinator
Cindy Teeters

Book Designer
Anne Jones

Compositor
Bronkella Publishing

CONTENTS AT A GLANCE

CONTENTS

III Tables and Graphics

9 Creating and Formatting Tables 335

ABOUT THE AUTHOR

Faithe Wempen, M.A., is a Microsoft Office Master Instructor and the author of more than 100 books on computer hardware and software. An adjunct instructor of computer information technology at Purdue University, she specializes in Office applications and PC hardware architecture. In addition, she writes and teaches online courses in Office applications and Microsoft Windows for Powered.com; her online courses in Office applications for corporate clients including Hewlett-Packard, CNET, and Sony have educated more than a quarter of a million students. Faithe is an A+ certified PC technician and the author of several textbooks on PC repair and maintenance. In her spare time (!), she owns and operates a small bed and breakfast in central Indiana.

About the Contributing Author

Patrice-Anne Rutledge is a business technology author and consultant who specializes in teaching others to maximize the power of new technologies. She has authored or coauthored several books for Pearson Education on Microsoft Office applications, including *Using Microsoft PowerPoint 2010*. You can reach her through her website at www.patricerutledge.com.

Dedication

To Margaret, who makes it all possible.

— Faithe Wempen

Acknowledgments

Thanks to my wonderful editors at Que for another job well done. Que is a great publishing company to work for, and I'm always proud of the work that we turn out together.

— Faithe Wempen

TELL US WHAT YOU THINK!

As the reader of this book, *you* are our most important critic and commentator. We value your opinion and want to know what we're doing right, what we could do better, what areas you'd like to see us publish in, and any other words of wisdom you're willing to pass our way.

As an associate publisher for Que Publishing, I welcome your comments. You can email or write me directly to let me know what you did or didn't like about this book—as well as what we can do to make our books better.

Please note that I cannot help you with technical problems related to the topic of this book. We do have a User Services group, however, where I will forward specific technical questions related to the book.

When you write, please be sure to include this book's title and author as well as your name, email address, and phone number. I will carefully review your comments and share them with the author and editors who worked on the book.

Email: feedback@quepublishing.com

Mail: Greg Wiegand
Associate Publisher
Que Publishing
800 East 96th Street
Indianapolis, IN 46240 USA

READER SERVICES

Visit our website and register this book at quepublishing.com/register for convenient access to any updates, downloads, or errata that might be available for this book.

Introduction

Welcome to *Microsoft Word 2010 In Depth*! This book is designed to
be your one-stop reference for *Microsoft* Word 2010, from the basics of
Ribbon usage to the intricacies of forms, fields, and customization tools.
Whether you're just getting started, are upgrading, or are already a
Word whiz, this book can help you move up to the next level in exper-
tise.

How This Book Is Organized

Microsoft Word 2010 In Depth is organized into these parts.

Part I: Working with Text

This part explains how to create a basic document by typing and editing
text, saving in various formats, correcting your mistakes, and printing
your work. These basic skills will pave the way to more extensive editing later in the book.

Part II: Formatting a Document

In this part, you'll learn how to format documents on several levels:
character, paragraph, and document-wide. You'll discover how to automate formatting with styles and themes; how to set up sections that
enable different margin, column, and header/footer information in different parts of a document; and how to use and create project templates
that streamline the process of formatting documents that you frequently
re-create. You'll also learn how to create some nonstandard documents,
such as banners, envelopes, and greeting cards.

Part III: Tables and Graphics

This part explains how to create and format data in tabular format and
how to insert and format a variety of special-purpose graphical elements

including clip art, drawings, charts, SmartArt, and mathematical equations. Most of these graphics types have formatting controls in common, so after you've learned how to format one type of object, the other types become much easier.

Part IV: Collecting and Managing Data

In this part, you'll learn how to use Word to collect data and to use data to automate tasks. You'll see how to mail-merge labels, letters, envelopes, and catalogs and how to use fields and data entry forms to display and collect information.

Part V: Working with Long Documents

This part covers the many tools Word provides for managing lengthy manuscripts, such as research papers and books. You'll learn how to outline and summarize documents, how to create master documents that combine several files into a single unit, and how to generate tables of contents and other listings. This part also includes information about the new citation management features in Word 2010 and explains how to create effective indexes.

Part VI: Collaboration and Online Sharing

In this part, you'll learn about the tools that Word 2010 provides for sharing your work with others, both while it is in the development stages and when it is finalized. You'll find out how to collaborate on documents with a team, how to protect and secure your files, and how to use Office Live and SharePoint Team Services. This part also covers developing online content via Word and generating XML content.

Part VII: Customizing and Extending Word

This part explains how you can make Word easier to use by adding features such as macros and add-ins and by customizing the Word interface.

Part VIII: Appendixes

The appendixes for this book provide an assortment of reference guides, including help for recovering and repairing problems, converting from other word processing systems, and setting up and modifying Office 2010.

Conventions Used in This Book

Here's a quick look at a few structural features designed to help you get the most out of this book. To begin with, you'll find Tips, Notes, and Cautions.

 tip

Tips are designed to point out especially quick ways to get the job done, good ideas, or techniques you might not discover on your own.

Troubleshooting Tips

Troubleshooting boxes provide advice for getting back to normal when things go wrong.

Often, when a subject is covered in greater detail, you'll find a marker like this, which points you to the location where the topic can be found:

 For more information about Word's automated spelling and grammar checker, see "Performing an Interactive Spelling and Grammar Check," p. 98.

Que's *In Depth* conventions are designed to be completely predictable. It's easy to understand what you're reading and what you're supposed to do.

For example, whenever you should press multiple keys together, in this book they are written separated by a plus sign, like this: Ctrl+B. That means hold down the Ctrl key, press the B key, and then release both keys.

Terms introduced and defined for the first time are formatted in italic.

Text that you are supposed to type is formatted in bold type, as in the following example:

Run Setup using a command such as **setup.exe /q1 /b1**.

That's all you need to know to get the most out of this book. Now fire up your copy of Word 2010 and let's have a go at it.

 note

Notes offer even more insight into features or issues that may be of special interest, without distracting you from the meat-and-potatoes answers you're looking for.

 caution

As you'd expect, cautions warn you about potential pitfalls and problems and point out fixes for common issues.

CREATING AND SAVING DOCUMENTS

Understanding the Word 2010 Interface

Word 2010 is an amazing, powerful program that can meet all your word processing needs, from 1000+ page dissertations to family newsletters. But at first glance, it might seem a bit intimidating. There are hundreds of features, and although the program is well organized, it is not always obvious where to find them and what they offer.

If you've upgraded from Word 2007, you'll be glad to know that the interface has not changed substantially. What you knew before about using tabs and the Ribbon will carry over to 2010 easily. If you are upgrading from an even earlier version, though, such as 2003, you're in for more of a challenge. Word 2007 and 2010 both use a Ribbon interface rather than a traditional menu system, and it takes some getting used to.

In this chapter, I'll explain some of what makes Word 2010 so special—and so different from any other word processing system. You'll learn about the user interface, and you'll find out how to change the view and access the Help system—essential survival skills for the rest of the book. I'll also explain how to save your work in various formats and how to open documents.

Word 2010 is part of the Microsoft Office 2010 suite, and most of the applications in the suite use the same basic type of user interface. Therefore, if you spend the time to learn the new Word 2010 interface, you're 80 percent of the way to learning other applications, such as Excel 2010 and PowerPoint 2010.

Tabs and the Ribbon

The Ribbon—a thick toolbar full of buttons and other controls—replaces the traditional menu system. The Ribbon consists of multiple toolbars, each one on a separate tab. Each of the words running across the top of the screen is a tab name; click a tab name to bring its controls to the fore-front. In Figure 1.1, the Home tab is displayed, for example. Within a tab, commands are organized into groups. The Home tab has these groups: Clipboard, Font, Paragraph, Styles, and Editing.

The Quick Access toolbar floats above the tab names. You can customize the content of the Quick Access toolbar so that it contains buttons for the activities you most frequently perform. For example, if you frequently do a spell check, you could add the button for spell checking there. The commands and buttons that appear on the Ribbon depend on which tab you have selected, but the Quick Access toolbar always appears the same, no matter what tab you're using.

Quick Access Toolbar   Ribbon

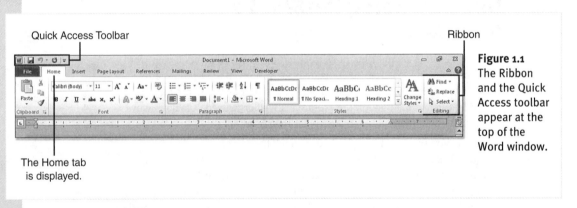

Figure 1.1
The Ribbon and the Quick Access toolbar appear at the top of the Word window.

The Home tab
is displayed.

To add any command or button from any tab to the Quick Access toolbar, right-click the button or command and choose Add to Quick Access Toolbar from its shortcut menu. To remove a button from the Quick Access toolbar, right-click it on the Quick Access toolbar and choose Remove from Quick Access Toolbar.

Some tabs are always available, such as Home and View. Others come and go depending on what you're doing. Those are *contextual tabs*. For example, when you're working with a table, two addi-tional tabs appear—Design and Layout—under a Table Tools heading (see Figure 1.2). When you move the insertion point out of the table, those tabs go away.

The contents of the tabs change somewhat depending on the size of the Word window. All the con-trols are always available, but not always in the same format.

For example, when the Word window is fairly wide (say, around 1100 or more pixels), each of the items in the Page Background group on the Page Layout tab appears as a large button, as shown on the left side of Figure 1.3. When the window decreases a bit (say, to around 1024 pixels), each of those buttons becomes a smaller, horizontal one, as shown on the right side of Figure 1.3.

Figure 1.2
Contextual tabs appear only when an object is selected that requires them.

Table Tools Tab Group

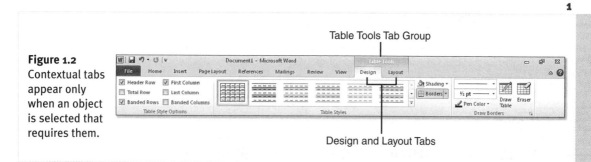

Design and Layout Tabs

Figure 1.3
Certain groups on certain tabs change their look as the window changes width.

Not only do the sizes and shapes of buttons change based on the window width, but some groups actually change their content. All the items are still available, but instead of them being separate buttons, they become a single button with a menu. For example, on the Review tab, the Proofing group could be quite expanded (see Figure 1.4, left), moderately compressed but still with separate buttons for everything (see Figure 1.4, center), or completely compressed with just a Proofing button that opens a menu (see Figure 1.4, right).

Figure 1.4
Some groups collapse completely, except for a single button when the window is very narrow.

 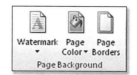

It's important to know about this collapsing of groups because if you are running Word in a window size other than what was used to create the graphics in this book (1024×768), sometimes your tabs will not look exactly like the ones shown in the book, and occasionally a step-by-step procedure might be slightly different. For example, you might have an extra step where you have to click a collapsed group's button to access a button, or you might not have to click a collapsed group's button when the book shows that you do. It's not a big deal, but be aware.

Backstage View: the File Menu

A blue File tab appears to the left of the other Ribbon tabs. Clicking it opens the File menu, also called Backstage View (see Figure 1.5), from which you can perform various file-based activities like saving, opening, printing, and sending your work to others.

Click any tab to leave Backstage view.

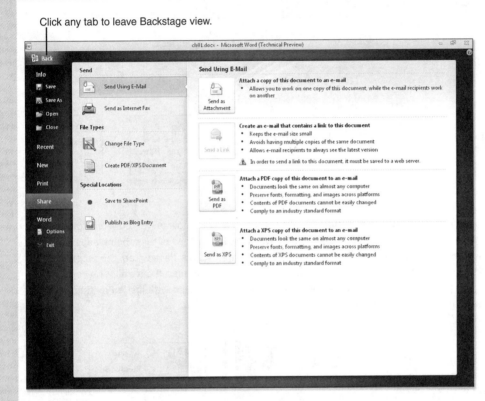

Figure 1.5
Backstage View contains commands for working with document files.

When you open the File menu, a multilayered menu system appears. Many of the commands along the left side of the screen are categories that open submenus when you click them. For example, in Figure 1.5, the Save & Send command has been selected, revealing additional choices.

The top-level categories on the File menu are as follows:

- **Save**—Saves the active document under its existing name.

- **Save As**—Saves the active file and prompts you for a new name and/or location.

- **Open**—Opens a saved document.

- **Close**—Closes the active document.

- **Info**—Displays information about the current document, including its properties. Commands are available for working with versions, permissions, and distribution.

- **Recent**—Displays a list of recently opened documents, from which you can quickly reopen one.

- **New**—Displays a list of templates available for starting a new document.

- **Print**—Provides access to printing options, including setting a print range, choosing a printer, and specifying settings like color and collation. Shows a preview of the current document in the right pane.

- **Save & Send**—Offers access to features for distributing the document via email or fax, saving to an online location, or posting to a blogging site.

- **Help**—Opens the Help system.

- **Options**—Click here to open a dialog box where you can customize the interface.

- **Exit**—Choose this command to exit Word.

The Mini Toolbar

When you select some text in your document, a pop-up Mini Toolbar appears next to it, providing easy access to common formatting commands. To display the Mini Toolbar, select some text and then hover the mouse over the selection. The Mini Toolbar appears as a semitransparent "ghost" above and to the right of the selected text. If you then move the mouse pointer over the ghosted image, the Mini Toolbar appears full-strength, as in Figure 1.6. This floating toolbar enables you to apply some of the most common formatting changes to text, including selecting a font, size, and color and applying highlighting. (Those text-formatting commands can also be applied from the Home tab on the Ribbon.)

Another way to display the Mini Toolbar is to right-click the selected text. A shortcut menu appears, but so does the Mini Toolbar, above the shortcut menu.

➥ *To learn about the specific buttons and lists on the Mini Toolbar, see Chapter 4, "Applying Character Formatting."*

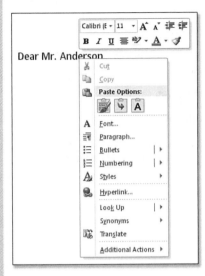

Figure 1.6
The Mini Toolbar provides quick access to common formatting tools.

Galleries, Dialog Boxes, and Panes

Dialog boxes prompt you for more information when you issue certain commands. Some of the buttons on the Ribbon open dialog boxes. For example, the Picture button on the Insert tab opens the Insert Picture dialog box, prompting you to select a picture to insert.

In cases in which you choose from a short list of options, Word provides a drop-down list from the button rather than a dialog box. For example, on the Page Layout tab, the Orientation button opens a menu containing Portrait and Landscape, as shown in Figure 1.7.

Some buttons' menus contain *galleries*, which are collections of presets you can apply. In some cases, you can also save custom settings to create your own presets that appear on these menus. For example, on the Insert tab, the Footer button opens a Footer Gallery from which you can select a preformatted document footer. Notice also the command at the bottom of that menu—you can add the selected text in the document to the gallery as a new footer preset, which will then appear on this menu.

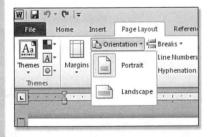

Figure 1.7
Many buttons, such as this one, open drop-down lists containing the most common settings.

Figure 1.8
Some buttons open galleries of presets.

Some galleries—or at least the first line of them—appear directly on a tab. If you want to select one of the items that appears in that first row, you simply click it from the tab. For example, in Figure 1.9, you can apply one of the style examples from the Styles group on the Home tab by clicking it. To see the rest of the gallery, you can either click the single down-pointing arrow to scroll down to the next row of the gallery, or you can open the full gallery by clicking the More button (the down arrow with the line over it).

Click here for the next
row of gallery entries.

Figure 1.9
Some galleries appear directly on a tab.

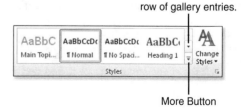

More Button

Some buttons that have drop-down lists have a command at the bottom for opening an associated dialog box. For example, in Figure 1.10, notice that the Columns button not only contains some presets, but also a More Columns command. Clicking More Columns opens the Columns dialog box, from which you can choose less common column settings, such as unequal widths.

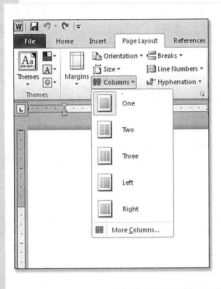

Figure 1.10
Select the More command from a button's list to open its dialog box.

In addition, some of the tab groups have dialog boxes associated with them. Look in the bottom-right corner of a group for a dialog box launcher icon. If a group has one of these, you can click the icon to open a dialog box from which you can control settings applicable to that group. For example, in Figure 1.11, notice that most of the groups on the Home tab have these. Each one opens a different dialog box.

Despite the name, not all of the dialog box launcher icons open actual dialog boxes. For example, the one in the Clipboard group in Figure 1.11 opens the Clipboard task pane, and the one in the Styles group opens the Styles task pane.

Some dialog boxes are *modal*, which means you can't do anything else while they are open. For example, while the Save As dialog box is open, you can't continue working on the document. You either have to save your work by clicking Save, or you have to close the dialog box by clicking Cancel. Other dialog boxes are *nonmodal*, meaning you can leave them open as you work. For example, when you're formatting a shape, you can leave the Format Shape dialog box open as you drag the shape around, resize it, add text, and so on.

Certain commands open task panes along the left or right side of the document. For example, the Clip Art button on the Insert tab opens the Clip Art pane. There are also panes for working with the Clipboard and finding text strings, among other things. You can close a task pane by clicking the X in its upper-right corner. To move the pane, click the down arrow in its title bar to open a menu (see Figure 1.12), and then choose Move; then drag the pane to a different location.

Figure 1.11
Dialog box
launcher but-
tons open
dialog boxes
pertaining to
the group.

Dialog Box Launchers

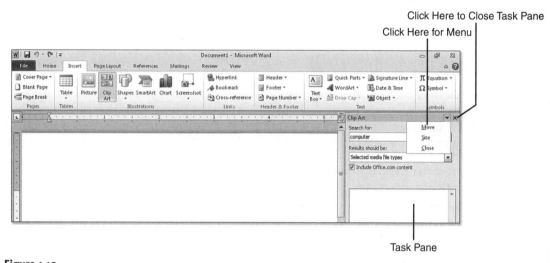

Click Here to Close Task Pane
Click Here for Menu

Task Pane

Figure 1.12
Task panes can be moved or resized.

Working with Views

Setting an optimal view for your needs can make a tremendous difference in Word's usability. Not only can you choose among various document views (such as Draft, Print Layout, and so on), but you can zoom in and out within those views. You can also display or hide onscreen elements such as rulers and gridlines and display multiple document windows simultaneously. The following sections explain these viewing options.

Switching Document Views

Word 2010 offers five views:

- **Print Layout view**—Shows most document features as they will print, including headers, footers, graphics, and columns. You see the entire page, all the way to the edges of the paper, so you can gauge the margins visually.

Print Layout is not always completely accurate in showing the way the document will print. For a fully accurate picture, use Print Preview (File, Print, and then look on the right side of Backstage View for a preview of the print job).

- **Full Screen Reading view**—Shows the document in two book-style columns, with large font, and with the Ribbon and other screen elements hidden. You can use the right- and left-arrow keys to move between pages. There is also a variety of special reading tools available here, as explained in the section "Working in Full Screen Reading View" of Chapter 20, "Collaborating with Others."

- **Web Layout view**—Shows the document as it will appear in a web browser. This view is suitable for creating web pages and email messages.

- **Outline view**—Shows the document as collapsible levels of headings, so you can see the document's structure at a glance. To learn more about the tools available in this view, see the "Outline Basics" section of Chapter 17, "Outlining and Combining Documents."

- **Draft view**—Shows just the main text of the document; you don't see graphics, headers, footers, or multiple columns. Also, page breaks and section breaks are represented by horizontal lines rather than actual breaks. This view uses less memory than others to draw the display and can make a performance difference on a slow PC.

If you try to create graphics or work with other document elements that aren't supported in Draft view, Word automatically switches to Print Layout view.

The quickest way to switch views is to click one of the view buttons in the bottom-right corner of the Word window (see Figure 1.13).

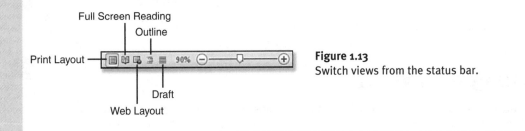

Figure 1.13
Switch views from the status bar.

You can also switch views from the View tab; each view has its own button in the Document Views group (see Figure 1.14). (This View tab also figures heavily into the view customizations described in the following sections.)

Figure 1.14
The View tab provides a variety of viewing options, including Document Views.

Showing or Hiding Onscreen Elements

The Show group of the View tab has several check boxes that turn special elements on and off:

- **Ruler**—In Print Layout, Web Layout, and Draft views, this option displays a horizontal ruler across the top of the document, with markers for margins, indents, and tab stops. If you're in Print Layout view, you also get a vertical ruler along the left side of the document.

- **Gridlines**—A nonprinting grid of squares that fills the area within the margins. It can be useful to help align graphic objects more precisely.

- **Navigation Pane**—A multitabbed pane from which you can view an outline, thumbnail images of each page, or a search interface.

> ➡ *To learn more about thumbnails, see "Locating Specific Content," p. 71.*

Changing the Zoom

The zoom is the size of the document within the document window. It is an onscreen setting only; it has no effect on the printed version. A higher zoom percentage (such as 400 percent) makes everything very large, and you can't see very much at once. A lower zoom percentage (such as 50 percent) makes everything small so you can see entire pages at once (but you'll probably find them harder to read).

The easiest way to adjust the zoom is to drag the Zoom slider on the status bar or to click the minus or plus button at either end of the Zoom slider (see Figure 1.15).

Drag the Slider

Figure 1.15
Change the zoom by dragging the Zoom slider or incrementing its setting by clicking a button at one end or the other.

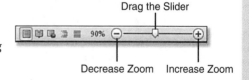

Decrease Zoom   Increase Zoom

You can also adjust the zoom from the View tab, shown in Figure 1.14. The One Page, Two Pages, and Page Width buttons do just what their names imply: They adjust the zoom level for optimal viewing depending on the size of your Word window. For example, if your Word window is maximized on a 1024×768 resolution display, a One Page zoom would be 55 percent. On a higher-resolution display, a One Page zoom would be a higher percentage than that.

The Zoom button on the View tab opens a Zoom dialog box, in which you can enter an exact zoom percentage (see Figure 1.16).

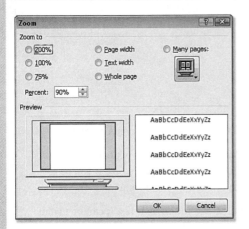

Figure 1.16
Use the Zoom dialog box to set an exact zoom amount.

Displaying Multiple Documents and Windows

Word allows multiple documents to be open at once, each in its own window. By default, only one window appears at once, but you can arrange the windows so that several are visible at once, as you would arrange any other windows. Each document has its own Ribbon and other controls in its window.

To switch between open Word documents, select the desired document from the Windows taskbar, or click the Switch Windows button on the View tab in Word and choose from the list of open documents (see Figure 1.17).

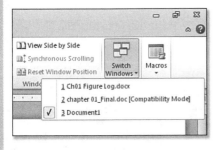

Figure 1.17
The Switch Windows button lists all the open documents so you can switch between them.

In addition to manually arranging document windows onscreen, you can use some arrangement shortcuts that are built into Word (on the View tab):

- **New Window**—Opens a second window containing a copy of the active document. The copies are joined, so changes made in one copy are automatically reflected in the other copy. You can use the second copy to scroll to a different spot in the document, so you can view multiple locations simultaneously.

- **Arrange All**—Arranges all open Word document windows so that each one takes up an equal amount of space onscreen.

- **Split**—Creates a split line within the active document and provides separate scroll bars on each side of the split. That way, you can scroll to two different parts of the documents at once without opening a whole separate Word window.

- **View Side by Side**—Arranges the active document and one other document of your choice, side by side. If there are only two documents open, it uses those two; if there are more, a dialog box appears asking what you want the second document to be.

- **Synchronous Scrolling**—When View Side by Side is active, this option locks the scrolling of the two documents so that scrolling in one also scrolls in the other an equal amount (if possible).

- **Reset Window Position**—When View Side by Side is active, this option resets the arrangement of the two windows to the original size and shape—with each window side by side, taking up half the available space each.

Using the Help System

The entryway to the Help system in Word 2010 is the Help icon, the small blue circle with a question mark in the upper-right corner of the Word window. Either click it or press F1 to open the Word Help window. You can also choose File, Help to get there.

Help is context-sensitive, so depending on what you were doing when you asked for help, a different listing might appear. If you were not doing anything that triggers a certain section of help, a general Microsoft Office Word Help window appears, as in Figure 1.18. From here you can click a topic to see subtopics, and eventually you'll arrive at specific instructions for doing something.

If the Help window takes a long time to display its content, try switching it offline. To do so, click Connected to Office.com in the status bar to open a menu. On the menu, click Show Content Only from This Computer. Only the basic Word help information will be available, but it'll be available more quickly.

The following buttons are available in the Word Help window:

 Use the Back arrow button to move back to the previous Help screen.

 After using Back, use the Forward arrow button to move forward again.

 Click Stop to stop a page from loading (for example, if it is loading from the web and is taking too long).

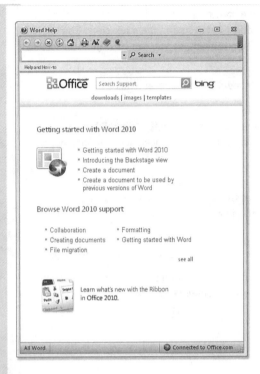

Figure 1.18
Browse help topics from the main Word Help window.

 Click Refresh to refresh the display of the page (for example, if it is located online and did not load properly the first time).

 To return to the general index of topics, click the Home button.

Click the Print button to print the displayed topic.

 Click the Change Font Size button to open a list of font sizes, and select the one that works best for your vision.

Click Show Table of Contents to open a Table of Contents pane at the left, from which you can browse a list of Help topics without leaving the current page.

 Click the Keep on Top button to toggle the Word Help window between always being on top and being an ordinary stackable window.

Another way to get help is to search for topics or keywords of interest. To do this, type a word in the Search box at the top of the Word Help window and then press Enter or click Search. For example, Figure 1.19 shows the list of topics when searching for "numbering."

Figure 1.19
Search the help system for the topic you need help with.

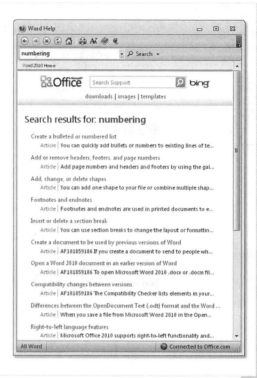

Within a help article, blue or purple words are hyperlinks. Point at one and it becomes underlined. Click it to go to a different topic. The color of the hyperlink depends on whether it has been visited (that is, previously clicked on).

Help Searches Are Slow or Provide Too Many Results

Sometimes Word can be *too* helpful when it comes to finding help information. Every time you search for even the simplest thing, it does a full-scale search, including web resources.

If you just want the basic steps for performing tasks, restrict the help search to only Word Help. To do so, in the Word Help window, click the down arrow to the right of the Search button, and on the menu that appears, choose Word Help.

Starting a New Document

When Word starts, it displays a single blank document, ready for editing. This blank document is set up with generic settings that are appropriate for a variety of uses; it has 1.15 line spacing, 11-point text, and standard margins of 1 inch on all sides. You can use this document or create another one.

New Documents Are Using Nondefault Settings

On a new install of Word or Office 2010, the default font is set for +Body (Calibri), 11 point, and the margins are set for 1 inch on all sides. If you have upgraded from Word 2003 or earlier, however, or if you chose to leave Word 2003 installed on your PC alongside Word 2010, the default settings for the earlier version might remain in effect.

This happens because Word 2010 does not delete old versions of the default template (Normal. dot). Furthermore, if such a template exists, Normal.dotm copies its settings.

If you want to continue using the default settings from Word 2003, just let it be. If you don't, however, here's how to fix it:

1. Close all versions of Word.

2. Navigate to the folder containing user templates:

   C:\Users*username*\AppData\Roaming\Microsoft\Templates (Windows Vista or Windows 7) or C:\Documents and Settings*username*\Application Settings\Microsoft\Templates (Window XP), where *username* is the logged-in Windows user.

3. Delete Normal.dot and Normal.dotm.

4. Restart Word. The settings will now be the defaults described in this chapter.

Creating a Blank Document

To create a new, blank document with the same settings as the one that appears automatically when Word starts, press Ctrl+N or do the following:

1. Choose File, New. The blue File tab is located in the top-left corner of the Word window.

2. Under Available Templates (see Figure 1.20), click Blank Document, and then click Create.

   ➡ *To learn how to add a button to the Quick Access toolbar that starts a new document, see "Customizing the Quick Access Toolbar," p. 863.*

Blank documents are based on the Normal.dotm template. Notice the *m* at the end of the template name; this stands for "macro-enabled." In Word 2010, there are three types of Word templates: Word 97–2003 templates for backward compatibility (.dot extension), regular Word templates (.dotx extension) that work with Word 2007 and Word 2010, and macro-enabled templates (.dotm extension). You will learn more about these in Chapter 8, "Working with Templates and Nonstandard Layouts."

Figure 1.20
The New section of Backstage View contains a Blank Document icon for creating a new blank document.

Normal.dotm is a hidden file. Depending on your Windows version, it is stored either in Users*username*\\AppData\\Roaming\\Microsoft\\Templates (Windows Vista or Windows 7) or in Documents and Settings*username*\\Application Data\\Microsoft\\Templates (Windows XP), where *username* is the currently logged in Windows user. A separate copy is maintained for each local user of the PC (based on Windows login).

➤ *To learn more about template types, see "About Templates," p. 289.*

Adding a Toolbar Button for a New Blank Document

In Word 2003 and earlier, there was a New button on the toolbar that created a new blank document based on Normal.dot, without going through a dialog box. Word 2010 does not have that button by default, although its shortcut key combination remains usable (Ctrl+N). Here's how to add it to the Quick Access toolbar:

1. Click the down arrow at the right end of the Quick Access toolbar.
2. Click New.

➤ *To learn more about customizing the Quick Access toolbar, see "Customizing the Quick Access Toolbar," p. 863.*

Creating a Document Based on a Template

In addition to the basic blank document template, Word offers dozens of specialized templates for items such as resumes, newsletters, and business cards. Most of the templates have sample text and graphics in them, as well as styles and other formatting set up to facilitate the chosen document type.

➥ *For more information about styles, see "Understanding Styles," p. 217.*

Word 2010 installs a few simple templates on your hard disk for items such as letters and reports, and it makes many other templates available via Office.com. Here are the steps to access these templates:

1. Choose File, New. Icons for available templates appear.

2. To access the locally stored templates, click Sample Templates.

   To access the online Office.com templates, click one of the categories listed under Office.com Templates.

3. Click the desired template. (For some Office.com template categories, you might need to click through one or more layers of subcategories to get to the templates.) Figure 1.21 illustrates selecting one of the sample templates.

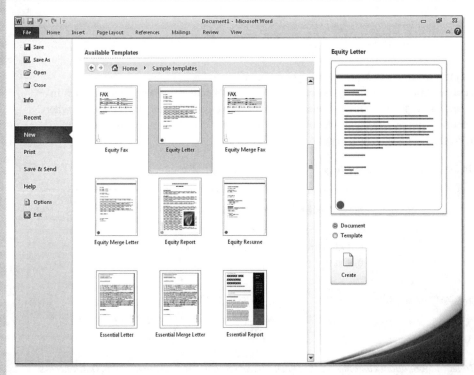

Figure 1.21
Select one of the sample templates to see a preview of it.

4. Click Create or Download to start the document. The command differs depending on the template's location; a local template shows Create, whereas a template from Office.com shows Download.

One of the installed templates, Office Word 2003 Look, creates documents with the same settings as the default blank document from Word 2003. It's essentially the same as the Normal.dot file from Word versions 2003 and earlier. It uses Times New Roman font and single spacing for paragraphs.

Templates you create yourself are stored in the default template folder, which is Users*username*\AppData\Roaming\Microsoft\Templates if you are running Windows Vista or Windows 7, or Documents and Settings*username*\Application Data\Microsoft\Templates if you are running Windows XP.

To access these local templates, follow these steps:

1. Choose File, New. Icons for available templates appear.

2. Click My Templates. The New dialog box opens (see Figure 1.22). Icons appear for the templates stored in the default template folder.

Figure 1.22
Use templates you've created by selecting My Templates.

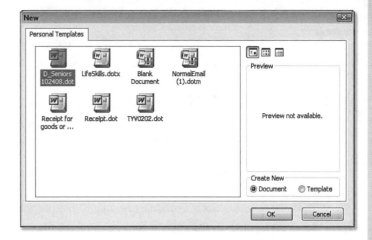

3. Click a template, and then click OK to create a new document based on it.

➡ *To create your own templates, see "Creating Your Own Templates," p. 301.*

The templates stored in the default template storage location are specific to the user logged into Windows. If some other user logs into the same PC, that user will not have access to these templates. To make a template available to all users on the local PC, place it in the workgroup template folder.

➡ *To set up a workgroup template folder, see "Accessing Workgroup Templates," p. 298.*

Saving a Document

"Save early, save often," as the saying goes, to avoid losing work due to unexpected power outages or program crashes. Word 2010 offers many saving options, including saves in different formats and to different locations.

The basic save is the same as in other Office programs. Use any of these methods:

- Click the Save button on the Quick Access toolbar.

- Press Ctrl+S.

- Choose File, Save.

- Exit Word (File, Exit) without saving the document and then click Save when asked if you want to save your changes.

For an unsaved document, the Save As dialog box opens and you specify the file's name, location, and type. For a previously saved document, the changes are automatically saved. (No dialog box opens.) The Save As dialog box differs depending on the version of Windows you are running, especially when it comes to navigating between locations. The following sections explain the procedures in the various Windows versions.

The navigation techniques explained in the following sections also apply to the Open dialog box, as well as to almost all other dialog boxes in which you select files within Word 2010.

Changing the File Save Location (Windows Vista or Windows 7)

With Windows Vista or Windows 7, the Save As dialog box has a navigation bar across the top with breadcrumbs on it that point to the path of the location shown. You can click the arrow to the right of one of those folder names to open a menu of other locations you can jump to at that level, as shown in Figure 1.23. To see a top-level list of locations (such as Computer, Network, and so on), click the arrow to the right of the leftmost item. (In Figure 1.23, the leftmost item is a folder icon.)

The Save As dialog box is resizable; just drag its bottom-right corner.

Select the desired save location, enter a name for the file, select a file type, and then click Save. After a document has been saved, you can resave it with different settings using the File, Save As command.

Save Thumbnail saves a preview of the first page of the document so that the preview will appear rather than a generic icon when browsing for files to open in the Open dialog box.

Notice that the Save As dialog box contains many of the same elements you would expect to see in a Windows Explorer window (such as the Computer window). Some of these are pointed out in Figure 1.24, including these:

- A Navigation pane, from which you can select among common locations including any Favorites you have set up, any libraries, your computer, your desktop, or your network.

- A toolbar containing an Organize menu, a Views menu, and a New Folder button.

Open a Menu of Top-Level Locations

Go Back to Previous Location   Open a Menu of Other Folders at That Level

Figure 1.23
The Save As dialog box under
Windows Vista and Windows
7 displays a breadcrumb-style
path.

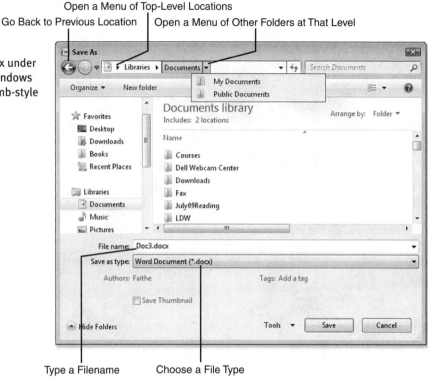

Type a Filename   Choose a File Type

Managing Files in the Save As Dialog Box

While you're in the Save As dialog box (or the Open dialog box, for that matter), you can do some simple file management tasks. Most of these work in all Windows versions.

The Organize menu (in Windows Vista and Windows 7 only) contains commands for many common file operations; click the Organize button shown in Figure 1.24 to access it.

You can also use shortcut keys or right-click operations to work with files. To copy a file or folder, select it and press Ctrl+C (or right-click it and choose Copy). Then move to the desired location and press Ctrl+V (or right-click an empty area and choose Paste).

To move a file or folder, select it and press Ctrl+X (or right-click it and choose Cut), move to the desired location, and press Ctrl+V (or right-click an empty area and choose Paste).

To delete a file or folder, select it and press Delete (or right-click it and choose Delete).

Manage files from
the Organize menu.

Use the Views menu to change
the file listing appearance.

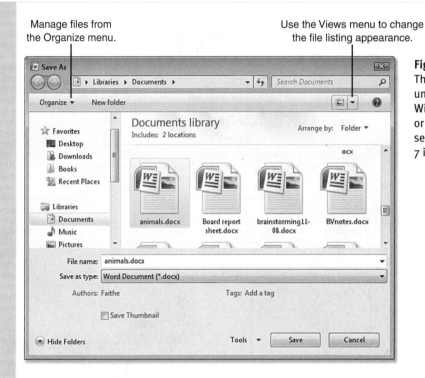

Figure 1.24
The Save As dialog box
under Windows Vista or
Windows 7 can display
or hide the content of the
selected location. (Windows
7 is shown here.)

Changing the File Save Location (Windows XP)

Under Windows XP, Word 2010's Save As dialog box is very much the same as it was in earlier
Word versions. To display a different location in the Save As dialog box, open the Save In drop-
down list and select the desired location. If it doesn't appear on the list, select the drive and then
drill down until you get to the desired folder within it (see Figure 1.25).

Saving to Remote Locations

The preceding sections covered saving to your local hard disk or other local drives, but what about
when you need to save to drives on other systems, such as network drives, web servers, or FTP
locations? The following sections address some of these special situations.

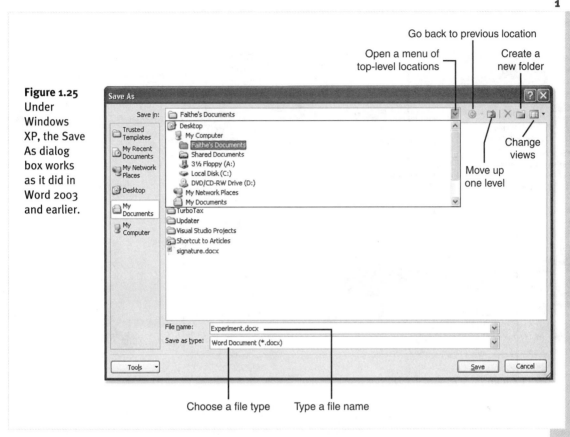

Figure 1.25
Under Windows XP, the Save As dialog box works as it did in Word 2003 and earlier.

Go back to previous location

Open a menu of top-level locations

Create a new folder

Change views

Move up one level

Choose a file type   Type a file name

Saving to a Network Location

A *network location* is one that's accessible from your personal or business LAN, without connecting to the Internet. You can either choose a network favorite shortcut that has already been set up on the system, or you can browse the entire network for valid locations to which to save.

For Windows 7:

- To browse the entire network, click Network in the Navigation pane at the left. Then browse the entire network via the icons that appear for available network resources. See Figure 1.26.

- To browse your Homegroup (a Windows 7 peer-to-peer network, if you have one set up), click Homegroup in the Navigation pane at the left.

For Windows Vista:

- To choose an existing network shortcut, click Browse Folders to display the Favorite Links list, select Network Shortcuts from that list, and then select the desired shortcut's icon.

Double-click the computer you want.

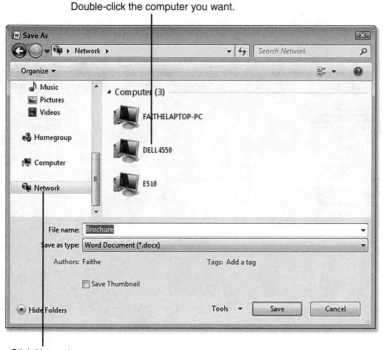

Figure 1.26
Select Network from the Navigation pane in Windows 7 to browse all network resources.

Click Network.

- To browse the entire network, click the arrow to the left of the leftmost (topmost) level in the path and choose Network from the menu that appears (see Figure 1.27). Then browse the entire network via the icons that appear for available network resources.

For Windows XP, start out by clicking My Network Places on the Favorites bar or selecting My Network Places from the Save In list. After that, do this:

- To choose an existing network shortcut (called a Network Favorite under XP), double-click any of the shortcuts that appear on the My Network Places list.

- To browse the entire network, double-click the Entire Network icon and then navigate to the desired network location.

Some networks have mapped drives, so certain network locations appear as drive letters on the local PC. Treat these like any other drive.

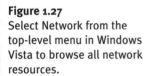

Figure 1.27
Select Network from the top-level menu in Windows Vista to browse all network resources.

Click here to open the top-level menu

Choose Network

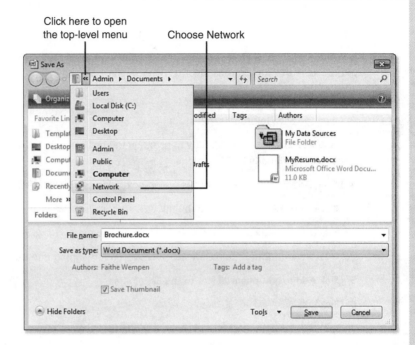

Saving to a Web Location

To save to a web location, type the URL in the File Name text box and press Enter. A prompt appears for your username and password. Enter them, and the folders on that web server appear like local folders on your hard disk. Check with the hosting company to make sure you know the correct folder in which to save.

Saving to an FTP Site

FTP stands for *File Transfer Protocol*, an older way of transferring files on the Internet. Word 2010 can save directly to an FTP server using Windows' built-in FTP protocols.

In Windows Vista or Windows 7, follow these steps to save to an FTP location:

1. Choose File, Save As.

2. In the File name box, type the complete path to which you want to save. For example, if the server is ftp.wempen.com and the file name to use is myfile.docx, the path would be ftp://ftp.wempen.com/myfile.docx.

3. Click Save. The FTP Log On dialog box opens.

4. Click the User button, and enter your username and password for the FTP server.

5. Click OK.

In Windows XP, the FTP capabilities are actually a bit more robust than in Windows Vista/7, in that you can save FTP locations as favorites. Follow these steps:

1. Click File, Save As.

2. Open the Save In drop-down list.

3. If the FTP site you want already appears on the list, select it and skip to step 7. Otherwise, choose Add/Modify FTP Locations.

4. In the Add/Modify FTP Locations dialog box, fill in the information needed for the connection:

   - Name of FTP site—Include the full FTP address here, such as ftp.que.com.

   - Log on as—Click User and then type the username.

   - Password—Enter the password given to you for logging into this server.

5. Click Add to add this FTP site to the list of sites.

6. Click OK.

7. On the FTP server, navigate to the folder where you want to save and then continue saving normally.

Changing the Favorite Locations

Depending on the Windows version you have, there is either a Favorites list (Windows 7), a Favorite Links List (Windows Vista), or a Favorites bar (Windows XP) available for providing quick access to the most common file locations.

Changing the Favorites or Favorite Links List (Windows Vista or 7)

If you have Windows Vista or 7, a Favorites or Favorite Links List appears in the Save As and Open dialog boxes, as well as most other related dialog boxes that browse for files to open. This list provides shortcuts for the locations to which you most frequently save. You can add a folder to it by dragging any folder from the folder list into the Navigation pane under the Favorites or Favorite Links heading, or you can remove a folder from it by right-clicking its shortcut and choosing Remove Link (Windows Vista) or Remove (Windows 7).

Changing the Favorites Bar (Windows XP)

If you have Windows XP, a Favorites bar appears to the left of the file listing in the Save As and Open dialog boxes. It contains shortcuts to commonly selected locations.

The Windows XP Favorites bar starts out with six shortcuts: Trusted Templates, My Recent Documents, My Network Places, Desktop, My Documents, and My Computer. You can add your own favorite locations to this list. Here's how:

1. Display the location for which you want to create an icon.

2. Right-click the Favorites bar and choose Add Location, where Location is the folder name.

To remove a shortcut from the Favorites bar, right-click it and choose Remove. To rename an item, right-click it and choose Rename. Then type the new name. Both of those activities work only with items you have added to the bar yourself, not with the default items there.

To rearrange the order of the items in the Favorites bar, right-click an item and choose Move Up or Move Down. You can rearrange any of the items, even the default ones.

You can fit more items on the Favorites bar at once if you display them as small icons, but they look more like they did in earlier versions of Word if you display them as large icons. To switch the icon size, right-click the Favorites bar and choose Large Icons or Small Icons.

Selecting an Appropriate File Format

Word 2010's file format is the same as Word 2007. Like those in other Office 2010 applications, it is based on eXtensible Markup Language (XML). XML is a type of markup language in which plain-text is used to express both the literal text of the document and the coding that specifies what to do with that text. It is a close cousin to Hypertext Markup Language (HTML), the markup language used on the web. (In fact, the latest version of HTML, called XHTML, is actually created with XML.)

There are many good reasons for Word 2007 and 2010's adoption of a new file format based on XML:

- The files are smaller than in previous version formats.

- When a file is corrupted, it is easier to extract the data from it because the content can be separated from the formatting.

- Using XML makes it possible for third-party developers to build application solutions that can work with Office data.

- Files can include many types of objects, such as graphics and charts, and still be fully XML-compatible. In Office 2003, an XML format was available, but it didn't fully support all the graphics object types that the applications could create or import.

Experimenting with WordML

When I first encountered the Word 2007/2010 format, known as WordML, I tried to open the file in a text editor. After all, I thought, regular XML files open in a text editor, and these are XML, so why shouldn't it work?

Well, it didn't work, and here's why. WordML files are not plain XML files. They are actually compressed archives (ZIP files, to be exact) that contain multiple XML files. You can open one using a plaintext editor, but first you have to extract the files from it.

If you want to give it a try, follow these steps:

1. Create a new Word 2010 document. Type a few lines of text in it, and then save it and exit Word.

2. In Windows, browse to the folder where you saved the file. Select the file, copy it (Ctrl+C), and paste the copy (Ctrl+V).

3. Make sure the display of file extensions is enabled.

4. Right-click the copy of the file and choose Rename. Rename the file to test.zip. A warning appears; click Yes. Now the file has a different icon.

5. Double-click the file to open it in a Windows Explorer window. There'll be a [Content_Types].xml file, plus three folders: _rels, docProps, and word.

6. Double-click the word folder, and then double-click document.xml. The document opens in Internet Explorer showing the XML markup. Scroll down through the file and locate the text you typed in the document. Figure 1.28 shows an example.

7. Close Internet Explorer and delete the copy you created.

Besides being an interesting exercise that helps you understand the new format, the preceding steps can be used to help you recover text from a corrupted file. You can always open a Word 2010 document this way and manually copy and paste text out of it.

I Can't See the File Extensions

By default, Windows does not display the file extensions for file types that it recognizes. This is ostensibly to shield the beginning user from the scary-looking extensions, but it's a hindrance to advanced users who want to see what they're doing. Here's how to turn on the display of all file extensions:

Windows Vista or Windows 7—Open Computer (or any file management window) and choose Organize, Folder and Search Options. On the View tab, clear the Hide Extensions for Known File Types checkbox and click OK.

Windows XP—Open My Computer (or any file management window) and choose Tools, Folder Options. On the View tab, clear the Hide Extensions for Known File Types checkbox and click OK.

Figure 1.28
The XML source
code behind the
document text for
a Word 2010 docu-
ment.

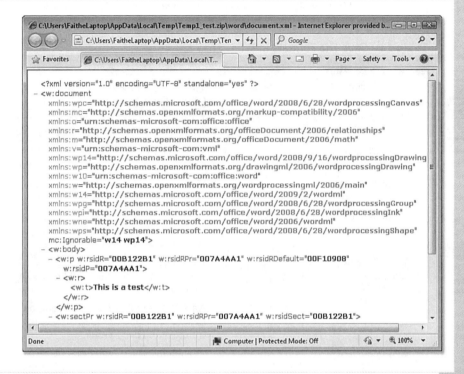

➡️ *To learn other ways of recovering the content of corrupted files, see Appendix A, "Recovering Files and Repairing Word."*

Microsoft did something revolutionary with file extensions in Office 2007 and 2010: It broke out of the three-character extension limit. The original limit was imposed by MS-DOS's 8-3 naming convention; files were limited to eight characters for the name and three characters for the extension. To maintain backward compatibility with MS-DOS systems, files had to adhere to that limitation. Backward compatibility with such systems is still possible by using one of the older formats, but the new formats will work only under operating systems that support long filenames. (Both Windows 9x forward and the Mac OS do.)

For many previous versions, Word used the same file format for its documents, which made it easy to transfer files between PCs of different versions. That format is called Word 97–2003, a nod to the fact that the format didn't change over all those versions: Word 97, Word 2000, Word XP, and Word 2003.

However, Word 2007 and 2010's XML-based file format changes all this. The new format is not backward-compatible with earlier Word versions—or for that matter, with any other word processing application. (Microsoft does offer a compatibility pack for free download that can enable earlier Word versions to open Word 2007/2010 files, but you can't assume that everyone—or even most people—will have it.) Therefore, it's important to choose an appropriate file format for a document based on the needs of others who might be working with it.

Table 1.1 lists a summary of the file format options that Word 2010 provides.

Table 1.1   Save File Formats in Word 2010

Format	Extension	Notes
Word Document	.docx	The default format for Word 2010, supporting all the latest features of the program.
Word Macro-Enabled Document	.docm	A Word document that supports macro usage; the new .docx format does not, for security reasons.
Word 97–2003 Document	.doc	A backward-compatible document format for exchanging documents with earlier versions of Word.
Word Template	.dotx	The new Word 2010 format for full-featured document templates.
Word Macro-Enabled Template	.dotm	The same as .dotx, but macros can be stored in it. As with the regular Word files, the standard template does not store macros for security reasons.
Word 97–2003 Template	.dot	A backward-compatible template format, useful when creating templates that will be used across multiple Word versions.
PDF	.pdf	An Adobe Acrobat file, which can be opened with Adobe Reader or Adobe Acrobat. Widely used on the web to distribute static documents.
XPS Document	.xps	The Microsoft equivalent of a PDF file, which can be opened with an XPS reader (included with Windows Vista and Windows 7).
Single-File Web Page	.mhtml, .mht	A web page in which all the graphics and other helper files are embedded. Useful for creating HTML-based email.
Web Page	.html, .htm	A web page that retains all the coding it needs for full use in Word plus all the coding it needs for full use on the web; graphics and other helper files are placed in a support folder.
Web Page, Filtered	.html, .htm	A web page that contains only standards-compliant HTML code and no Word coding. Graphics and other helper files are placed in a support folder.
Rich Text Format	.rtf	A widely accepted generic word processing format supported by almost any word processing program (including WordPerfect). Retains basic features such as tables and text formatting.
Plain Text	.txt	As the name implies, this format saves the text only, with no formatting at all.
Word XML Document	.xml	A document in eXtensible Markup Language, easily integrated with XML projects.
Word 2003 XML Document	.xml	A document in the Word 2003 version of XML.

Table 1.1   Continued

Format	Extension	Notes
OpenDocument Text	.odt	A new XML-based standard for file sharing between programs, developed by OASIS (Open Document Format for Office Applications).
Works 6–9 Document	.wps	Another really old document format, this one for swapping data with early versions of the Microsoft Works word processor.
Works 6.0 and 7.0	.wps	Another version of the preceding, specifically for versions 6.0 and 7.0.

Image Writer Is Not Available

Earlier versions of Microsoft Office included a printer driver called Microsoft Document Image Writer that enabled you to save a document page as a graphics file. It was not installed by default in Office 2007, but it was available as an optional component. This feature is not part of Office 2010. If you upgraded from a previous version of Office, you might still have the Microsoft Document Image Writer printer driver installed; if so, you can use it.

If you upgraded to Word 2010 from an earlier version, you might have other file formats available besides the ones shown in the preceding table.

If backward compatibility is not an issue, use the default Word document format. The files will open only in Word 2007 and 2010, but you'll have access to all of Word 2010's features.

To save a file as a different file type, you can change the type from the Save as Type drop-down list in the Save As dialog box, but there's also another way. You can choose File, Save & Send, Change File Type and then choose one of the popular file types. The Save As dialog box then appears with that chosen file type already filled in.

Saving in Web Format

Word 2010 is not a full-featured web development tool, but it does save in three different web-based formats:

- **Web Page**—The default web format is a *round-tripping* format. In other words, it not only contains all the codes needed to display as HTML in a browser, it contains all the codes needed to retain its status as a full-fledged Word document. You can save it as a web page and then open it in Word again and save it as a document file, without losing Word functionality. As you might expect, such a file is much larger than either a pure Word version or a pure HTML version.

- **Web Page, Filtered**—For files that will be exported to HTML and not reimported into Word, Word provides a pure-HTML save format. This format consists only of standards-compliant HTML coding, and the file size is dramatically smaller. Such a file is also much easier for someone accustomed to working with HTML code to understand and modify in a text editor.

- **Single-File Web Page**—Web pages are text-only files that do not contain graphics. Instead, they have hyperlinks to the graphics files, which the web browser pulls in when the page is displayed. Therefore, when you save in either of the aforementioned web formats, Word pulls out any graphics as separate files and stores them in a support folder. That's fine if the page will be published on a web server, but it's a problem for pages that will be distributed via email. To solve this problem, Word offers the Single-File Web Page format, aka MIME-encoded HTML (MHTML). This file type embeds the graphics into the web page for easy transport. The drawback of using MHTML is that old browsers (pre-Internet Explorer 4.0) cannot view the files. As time goes by, however, it becomes less and less likely that anyone viewing a page will have a browser that old.

The only difference between saving in regular Word format and saving in one of these web-based formats is the addition of the Page Title option in the Save As dialog box. The *page title* is the text that appears in the title bar.

By default, Word chooses a page title based on the first line of text in the document. Click the Change Title button in the Save As dialog box to change it to something else, as shown in Figure 1.29.

To learn how to customize how Word saves web pages to support a specific web browser, see "Options for Web Page Saving," p. 816.

Figure 1.29
Set a page title when saving a document in a web format.

Click here to set the page title.

Converting a Document to Word 2007/2010 Format

When a Word document created in Word 2003 or earlier is open in Word 2010, a Convert command appears in Backstage View when Info is selected. Use this command to update the file to Word 2007/2010 format. The downside, of course, is that the file won't be usable in Word 2003 or earlier or in any other non–Office application.

Although you can't by default open Word 2007/2010 files in earlier Word versions, there's a work-around. Microsoft has a free compatibility pack available at http://office.microsoft.com that will install Office 2007/2010 filters in earlier versions to enable people to open Office 2007 and 2010 files.

When you issue the Convert command, a confirmation box appears explaining that upgrading will enable you to use new Word 2010 features and will decrease the size of the document file. Click OK to perform the upgrade. If you don't want to see the confirmation box in the future, mark the check box labeled Do Not Ask Me Again About Converting Documents. To find out more about the conversion process, click the Tell Me More button.

Opening a Document

The purpose of saving a file, of course, is to open it at some point in the future. This section discusses ways of opening files, looks at the types of files you can open, and more.

Opening a Recently Used Document

If you have recently saved a new document or opened an existing one in Word, it appears on the Recent list in Backstage View. "Recent" here is a relative term; the list shows the 20 files you most recently worked on, regardless of how long ago that was. To open a recently used file, select it from the Recent Documents section in Backstage View, as shown in Figure 1.30.

You can customize the number of files that appear on the Recent Documents list; the default is 20. To change this setting, choose File, Options, click Advanced, scroll down to the Display section, and set a Show This Number of Recent Documents value.

You can "pin" a recently used file to the listing so that it never disappears from the list even if other files were more recently used. Notice the little pushpin icon next to each filename in Figure 1.30? Click a pushpin to lock the corresponding file onto the top of the list.

Another way to access recently used documents is by selecting File, Open and then clicking the My Recent Documents shortcut in the Favorites bar (Window XP), the Recently Changed shortcut in the Favorite Links list (Windows Vista), or Recent Places in the Favorites list (Windows 7). This listing shows all files that Word can open (including HTML files, document templates, and so on) according to their Last Modified dates, whereas the File menu's list shows only the files you have actually opened and edited with Word. A Recent Places list appears in the right pane when viewing recent documents; you can use it to quickly browse locations you have previously accessed.

At the bottom of the Recent Documents list on the File menu, you can optionally mark the Quickly Access This Number of Recent Documents check box and then enter a number. The last documents you have worked with then appear immediately below the Close command on the File menu.

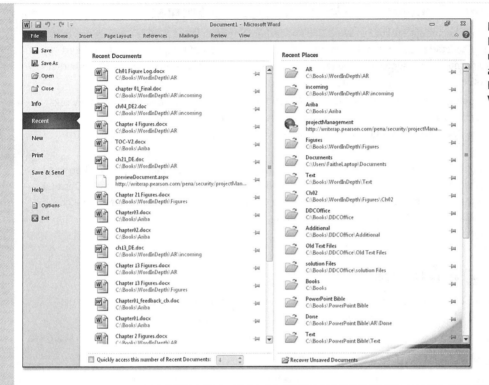

Figure 1.30
Recently
used files
appear in
Backstage
View.

And one more way: From the Start menu in Windows 7, you can point to the Microsoft Word short-cut and then choose a recent document from a fly-out menu.

Opening a Document with the Open Dialog Box

If the file you want doesn't appear on one of the recently used lists, use the Open dialog box to locate and select it. Choose File, Open, and then navigate to the folder containing the file. The navigational controls are the same for the Open dialog box as for the Save As dialog box, covered earlier in this chapter. There are major differences in the dialog box depending on whether Word 2010 is running under Windows 7, Windows Vista, or Windows XP.

> *To review file navigation techniques for the Open and Save As dialog boxes, see "Changing the File Save Location (Windows Vista or Windows 7)", p. 30, or "Changing the File Save Location (Windows XP)", p. 26, depending on your Windows version.*

Figure 1.31 shows the Open dialog box under Windows 7 (which is similar to the way it is under Windows Vista). Navigate to the desired location, and then click the desired file and click Open, or just double-click the file you want.

Figure 1.31
The Open dialog box shares many features with the Save As dialog box.

To open more than one file at once, select multiple files in the Open dialog box. To select a contiguous group, click the first one and hold down Shift as you click the last one.

To select a noncontiguous group, hold down Ctrl as you click each one you want. This works only if all the files are stored in the same folder.

You can also open files from a network or web location, the same as with saving files to those locations. Refer to "Saving to a Network Location" or "Saving to a Web Location" earlier in this chapter; the same information applies to opening as to saving.

➡ *To save or open a file on an Office Live document workspace, see "Using Microsoft Office Live Workspace," p. 777.*

➡ *To save or open a file on a SharePoint team site, see "Collaborating with Microsoft SharePoint WorkSpace 2010," p. 788.*

Changing the File List View in the Open Dialog Box

Sometimes changing the View setting in the Open dialog box can help you locate the file you need.

Under Windows Vista and Windows 7, a Views button appears near the top of the Open dialog box. Click the Views button and then select a view from the list by dragging the slider, as in Figure 1.32.

Views Button

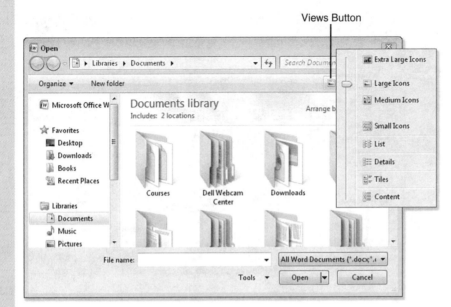

Figure 1.32
Drag the slider to change the view of the file listing.

The icon that appears for each file is either a generic Word icon or a preview of the document, depending on whether you saved a thumbnail with the document when you saved the document. In the Save As dialog box, when the Browse Folders area is expanded, a Save Thumbnails check box appears. If you mark this check box, the file's preview is created during the save operation. Files that were saved this way show their preview as the icon in the Open dialog box; files that were not saved this way show a generic Word icon.

Under Windows XP, there is also a Views button, but its menu contains different options. The various icon sizes are split out separately and given different names, and there is a separate view for seeing previews of the documents that is not dependent on whether a preview has been saved with the document or not.

Opening Other File Types

The file type in the Open dialog box is set by default to show all supported file types (All Word Documents) for maximum flexibility. The file type appears to the right of the File Name box under Windows Vista and Windows 7, or on a separate Files of Type line beneath the filename under Windows XP.

Word 2010 can open several more file types than it can save in; for example, it can open files from many different WordPerfect versions. This enables users to convert from other word processors to Word. (But conveniently for Microsoft's sales of Word, it can't convert back to WordPerfect again!)

The Files of Type selection merely serves as a filter based on file extension; it does not prevent you from opening files. If you are working with a folder containing hundreds of files and you want to quickly find just the ones with the .wps extension (Microsoft Works word processor files), you could set the Files of Type selection to Works 6–9 Document and all the other files would be hidden on the listing. Similarly, the default setting of All Word Documents filters out files with extensions that Word doesn't recognize.

By default, Word converts from other file types silently, without asking for confirmation. If you would rather know when a conversion is occurring, choose File, Options. Click Advanced, and in the General section, mark the Confirm File Format Conversion on Open check box.

I Need to Open a Nonsupported File Type

If Word doesn't appear to support the file type you want to open, you have several options. One is just to try opening it anyway by changing the Files of Type setting to All Files. Another is to go back to the original application and resave it in a format that Word can recognize. Rich Text Format (RTF) is supported in almost all word processing programs, for example. If all else fails, save it as a plain text file, or open the original program alongside Word 2010 and then copy and paste the text from one application to another.

If the file's extension does not represent the file type accurately, rename that file in Windows before attempting to open it in Word. Word's converter works much better when it knows what type of document it should expect. If you don't want to take the time to do that, though, you can set the Files of Type setting to All Files so that all file types are displayed in the dialog box, and then either rename that file on the fly (right-click it and choose Rename) or just try to open it as is.

If none of that does the trick, consider a third-party file conversion application such as DataViz Conversions Plus.

 *For more information about opening different file types, see Appendix B, "Converting from Other Word Processing Systems."*

Opening Files in Special Modes

The Open button in the Open dialog box has a drop-down list (see Figure 1.33) from which you can choose any of several special modes. Instead of clicking the face of the Open button, open the list and choose the desired mode.

Open Read-Only restricts you from overwriting the original file with your changes. You are still free to use Save As to save it with a different name, type, or location. Read-Only mode is useful if it's important that the original file be retained in its current state and you don't trust yourself not to get trigger-happy with the Save button.

Open as Copy also preserves the original, but Open as Copy actually creates a copy of the original file in the same location as the original and then opens the copy for editing. The file is not read-only.

Figure 1.33
The Open button has a menu that enables you to open a file in special modes.

Open in Browser, available only when opening web content, opens the file in your default web browser rather than in Word.

Open with Transform, available only when opening an XML file, tells Word to prompt you for a transform file after opening this file.

Open in Protected View opens the document in an uneditable form. Documents from untrusted sources, such as from email attachments, open in this mode automatically. To enable editing, you must click Enable Editing in the warning bar that appears across the top of the document.

Open and Repair opens the document and repairs any corruption in it. Use this if you have gotten an error message previously when trying to open the document.

Show Previous Versions enables you to retrieve older versions of the file that do not contain the latest edits, in case you need to retrieve previously deleted text, for example. You can access previous versions only if your operating system is Windows Vista or Windows 7.

Making a Document Read-Only

The special modes you learned about in the previous section are useful only if the person opening the files knows to utilize them, of course. If you are concerned about people making changes to a file and you don't trust them to remember to use Open Read-Only or Open as Copy, consider making the document itself read-only. You can do this from outside of Word, or you can do it from the file listing in the Save As or Open dialog box:

1. Right-click the filename and choose Properties.

2. In the Properties dialog box (see Figure 1.34), mark the Read-Only check box.

3. Click OK.

➡️ *To learn more about protecting a file from changes, see "Restricting What Users Can Do to a Document," p. 796.*

Figure 1.34
To set a file to be read-only, modify its properties.

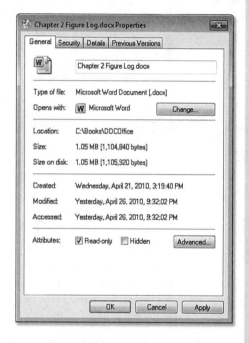

Working with File Properties

All files have properties, such as their size, their type, their extension, the date they were last modified, and whether or not they are read-only. You can see a file's properties in Windows by right-clicking the file and choosing Properties, as you did in the preceding section.

But in Word, the term *properties* has a separate meaning. A document's Properties settings in Word store information that users can enter and edit, such as subject, category, and keywords. You can then use this information to organize and find files on a document management server or even on your own hard disk.

There are two levels of properties in Word: Standard and Advanced. The Standard properties consist of some text boxes into which you can enter information that will be helpful for filing purposes, such as author, title, and category. To access the Standard properties, click the File tab, and then click the Properties button to open its drop-down list and choose Show Document Panel. A Document Properties bar appears across the top of the document, as shown in Figure 1.35.

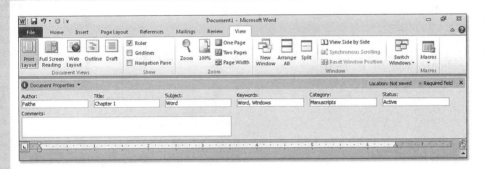

Figure 1.35
The standard properties for a document.

A few notes about some of the Standard properties:

- The Author field is filled in automatically for you if you specified a username when you set up Word. If you did not, you can do so at any time. Choose File, Options, click General, and enter your name and initials in the text boxes provided for them. The Author name will then be pre-entered for all new documents you create.

- The Title property is not the same as the filename. The document title is used when you're creating a web page; it's the text that appears in the title bar of the web browser when the page is displayed. If you have ever saved this document as a web page, the Title field is filled in with the title you used then.

- The Subject, Keywords, Category, and Status fields are all freeform fields; you can put whatever you want in them. However, if you are participating in a corporate document server, or if you share files with others on your network, you might want to find out if there are established conventions for using these fields in your company.

To see the Advanced properties, click the down arrow next to Document Properties in the Document Panel, and click Advanced Properties. (Or, to go directly there if the Standard properties are not already displayed, choose File, Properties, Advanced Properties.) A Properties dialog box appears for the document. It is similar to the Properties dialog box accessible from Windows, but it has more tabs and more detail:

■ **General**—Contains the same basic information as in the Windows version of the Properties dialog box (refer to Figure 1.34). The file attributes (read-only, hidden, and so on) are not editable from within Word.

MS-DOS Names

One interesting and unique piece of information on the General tab is the MS-DOS name. Earlier in the chapter, I mentioned that MS-DOS limited filenames to eight characters for the name and three for the extension. If a file that does not meet that specification is placed on an MS-DOS system, it won't be accessible. To get around this problem, Windows stores an MS-DOS name for each file along with its long name that strips out any spaces and trims the name to eight and three (8-3) characters. If the long name is already 8-3 or less, the MS-DOS name is the same as the long name. Otherwise, the MS-DOS name consists of the first six letters of the filename (or as many letters as it has, if less than six) followed by a tilde symbol (~) and a number starting with 1 for the first file with this name, then 2, and so on. The number helps account for the fact that several files might begin with the same six letters in their names. If you plan on using the file on an MS-DOS system, it might be helpful to know what its name will be when it gets there, for easier retrieval.

■ **Summary**—Contains the same text boxes as the Standard view of the properties, plus a few additional text boxes such as Manager and Company. It also tells what document template is assigned to the document. The Save Thumbnails for All Word Documents check box generates a thumbnail of the first page of the document and shows it as the file's icon in the Open dialog box (under Windows Vista or Windows 7) or places it in the Preview pane of the Open dialog box (under Windows XP).

■ **Statistics**—Lists the dates and times of the file's creation, modification, and last access and printing. It also tells who last saved the file, how many revisions there have been, and how much time has been spent editing it. Finally, document statistics appear here, such as the number of pages, paragraphs, lines, words, and characters (see Figure 1.36).

■ **Contents**—If you marked the Save Thumbnails for All Word Documents check box on the Summary tab, the Contents tab shows a snapshot of the document headings here. Otherwise, it shows only the document title.

■ **Custom**—On this tab, you can define values for less commonly stored facts about the document, again useful for doing searches on document servers and in large collections of documents.

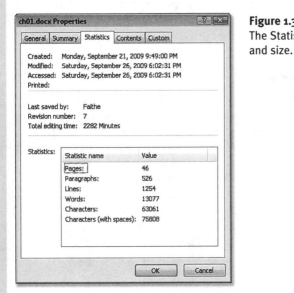

Figure 1.36
The Statistics tab summarizes the document's editing history and size.

Defining Custom Properties

Custom properties are special-purpose fields that you can choose to use in managing your documents on an as-needed basis. You can enter and edit them on the Custom tab of the Properties dialog box.

Here are the steps to follow to define a custom property:

1. Click the Custom tab in the Properties dialog box.

2. On the Name list, click the property you want to use.

3. Select the type of data to be stored in that field from the Type drop-down list. The most generic type is Text; it accepts everything. You might use a more specific type, such as Date, to prevent invalid entries.

4. In the Value field, enter the value for that property for the current document.

5. Click the Add button. The property, type, and value appear in the Properties list, as shown in Figure 1.37.

To edit a custom property, select it from the Properties list at the bottom of the dialog box and then change the value in the Value box.

Figure 1.37
Add a custom property to the document.

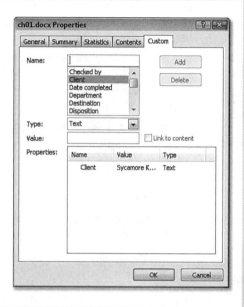

Automatically Updating Custom Properties

Custom properties are usually static; their values remain set at whatever you specify for them. To create a custom property that automatically updates based on some text in the document, define that text as a bookmark, as you'll learn in Chapter 15, "Copying, Linking, and Embedding Data," and then mark the Link to Content check box on the Custom tab. (That check box isn't available unless the document has at least one bookmark in it.)

The Value field changes to the Source field, which is a drop-down list of all the bookmarks in the document.

Setting File-Handling Preferences

One of Word 2010's strengths is its customization capability. If you don't like the way something works, you can change it. Here are some tips for configuring Word to better reflect the way you want to save and open files.

Setting the Default Save Location and File Type

Word's default save location is Documents on a Windows Vista or Windows 7 system, or My Documents on Windows XP. That folder appears by default in the Save As and Open dialog boxes. Beginners should leave this at the default so that they never have to remember where they stored a file—it's always in that location. More advanced users may want to save files in other locations, though, and might even want one of those other locations to be the default.

The default save location in Office 2010 is the Documents or My Documents folder for the currently logged-in user. That folder's path is Users*username*\Documents (in Windows Vista or 7) or

Documents and Settings*username*\\My Documents (in Windows XP), where *username* is the user. Therefore, when a different person logs into the computer, another location will be accessed in Office 2010 applications.

You can also change the default file format in which files are saved. If you are using only Word 2010, leave the default file format set to Word Document, but if you frequently need to exchange files with people using earlier versions, set the default format to one that's compatible with those other users' PCs.

Both of these defaults are set in the same location.

To set up file location preferences, follow these steps:

1. Choose File, Options.

2. Click Save.

3. Open the Save Files in This Format drop-down list and choose the desired file format (see Figure 1.38).

4. In the Default File Location box, enter the path to the desired location, or use the Browse button to locate it.

5. (Optional) To set the file locations for other types of files, such as templates, do the following:

   a. Click Advanced, and scroll all the way to the bottom.

   b. Click File Locations. The File Locations dialog box opens.

   c. Click a file type, and click Modify. The Modify Location dialog box opens.

   d. Navigate to the desired location, and then click OK. The location changes in the Location column for that file type.

   e. Repeat steps c and d for other file types, or click OK to return to Word Options.

6. Click OK to close the Word Options dialog box.

Setting an AutoRecover Interval

Word automatically saves a temporary copy of each document every 10 minutes (that's the default interval). This way, if Word crashes or your computer shuts down unexpectedly, you won't have lost more than 10 minutes' worth of work. When you restart Word after such a crash, the saved backup file(s) open automatically.

To change the interval at which Word saves backups or to turn off the feature entirely, do the following:

1. Choose File, Options.

2. Click Save, and then mark or clear the Save AutoRecover Information Every ___ Minutes check box to turn the feature on or off. To change the save interval, type a different number in the text box (refer to Figure 1.38).

 tip

The File, Recent, Recover Unsaved Documents command opens a dialog box from which you can recover data from temporary files left behind when Word crashed before you had a chance to save your work.

Figure 1.38
Set the default file location and type here.

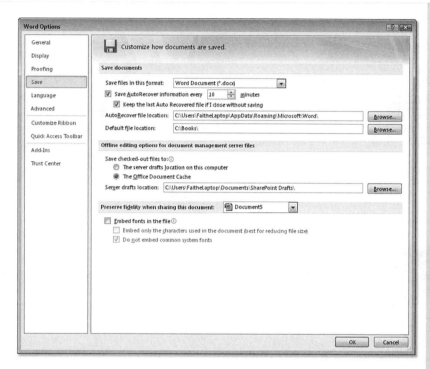

3. To change the location where Word stores these temporary backup files, click the Browse button and browse to a different location, or type a new path directly into the AutoRecover File Location text box.

4. Click OK to close the Word Options dialog box.

2

TYPING AND EDITING TEXT

Text Entry and Editing Basics

A blank document starts out with a flashing insertion point, which looks like a small vertical bar. In addition, if you're working in Draft or Outline view, a horizontal bar (not flashing) appears as an end-of-file marker (see Figure 2.1). Initially the two markers are together because there's nothing in the file, but the end-of-file marker moves further down on the page as you add more text to your document.

➡️ *To switch between views, such as Draft and Print Layout, see "Switching Document Views," p. 13.*

Text you type always appears at the insertion point. (You can move it around, as you will learn later in the chapter.) To enter text, just type as you would in any program. The following keys have specific functions:

- **Enter**—Press this key to start a new paragraph.

- **Shift+Enter**—Press this key combination to start a new line within the same paragraph.

- **Ctrl+Enter**—Press this key combination to start a new page.

- **Tab**—Press this key to move to the next tab stop (by default, every 0.5 inches).

- **Backspace**—Press this key to delete a single character to the left of the insertion point.

- **Delete**—Press this key to delete a single character to the right of the insertion point.

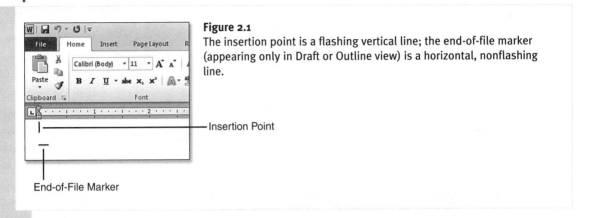

Figure 2.1
The insertion point is a flashing vertical line; the end-of-file marker (appearing only in Draft or Outline view) is a horizontal, nonflashing line.

— Insertion Point

End-of-File Marker

You can also delete a text selection of any size, including text or other objects, by pressing the Delete or Backspace key.

Line Breaks Versus Paragraph Breaks

A surprising number of people have trouble understanding the difference between a new paragraph and a new line. Yes, starting a new paragraph does also start a new line, so on the surface they seem to be doing the same thing. But if you turn on the Show/Hide (¶) feature (on the Home tab), you'll see that two completely different symbols are inserted.

A paragraph break (¶ symbol) creates a whole new paragraph, which can have its own indentation, bullets and numbering, line spacing, and other paragraph-level settings.

A line break (symbol) is like any other character of text within the paragraph, except instead of printing a letter on the screen, it moves the insertion point to the next line. The text after the line break has the same paragraph-level formatting as the text before the break, because it's all one paragraph.

Line breaks come in handy whenever you don't want the stylistic attributes of multiple paragraphs. For example, suppose you want to create a bulleted list of mailing addresses, with each complete address as a separate bullet point. If you press Enter between the lines in each address, each line will have its own bullet character, like this:

- John Smith
- 240 W. Main Street
- Macon, IL 62544

By using line breaks instead, you can create a single bulleted item with multiple lines, like this:

- John Smith
  240 W. Main Street
  Macon, IL 62544

Switching Between Insert and Overtype Modes

When editing text, Insert mode is on by default, meaning that any text you type to the left of existing text causes the existing text to scoot over to the right to make room for it. The alternative, Overtype mode, types over any existing text to the right of the insertion point.

To toggle between Insert and Overtype mode, follow these steps:

1. Choose File, Options.

2. Click Advanced.

3. Under Editing Options, mark or clear the Use Overtype Mode check box.

4. Click OK.

If you find yourself frequently switching between Insert and Overtype, you might want to set up an easier method for performing the switch. There are two such methods available: remapping the Insert key, and adding an Insert/Overtype indicator to the status bar.

By default, the Insert key works as a shortcut for the Paste command on the Home tab. If you prefer, you can change its mapping so that it instead switches between Insert and Overtype modes.

➡ *To learn about using the Insert key as a pasting shortcut, see "Keeping or Discarding Formatting When Pasting," p. 66.*

To make the Insert key toggle between Insert and Overtype views, follow these steps:

1. Choose File, Options.

2. Click Advanced.

3. Under Editing Options, mark the Use the Insert Key to Control Overtype Mode check box.

4. Click OK.

Now the Insert key functions as a toggle between Insert and Overtype modes. To make it more obvious which mode you are in, you might want to turn on the Insert/Overtype mode indicator on the status bar.

To add the indicator to the status bar:

1. Right-click the status bar.

2. Click to place a check mark next to Overtype.

Insert (or Overtype) appears in the status bar. You can then click that word to toggle between them.

Undoing, Redoing, and Repeating

Whenever you make a mistake, such as accidentally deleting or overwriting something, you can easily reverse it with Word's Undo feature. To undo, press Ctrl+Z, or click the Undo button on the Quick Access toolbar.

The Undo feature retains a list of actions you've recently taken, and you can undo any number of them. The effect is cumulative. In other words, you can undo, for example, the previous five actions you took, but you can't pick and choose among those five; you must undo the intervening four to undo the fifth one. To undo multiple levels, repeat Ctrl+Z or repeatedly click the Undo button on the Quick Access toolbar, or click the down arrow to the right of the Undo button to open a menu and then select the actions to undo from that list. The most recent actions appear at the top of the list.

After you have undone one or more actions, the Redo button becomes available on the Quick Access toolbar. It reverses undo operations and comes in handy when you accidentally undo too much. Ctrl+Y is its keyboard shortcut. Figure 2.2 shows the Undo and Redo buttons.

Redo

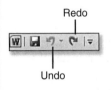

Undo

Figure 2.2
The Undo button undoes the last action when clicked. Redo restores an action that has been undone.

The Repeat feature enables you to repeat an operation such as typing, formatting, or inserting. The Repeat button looks like a U-turn arrow and appears in place of the Redo button on the Quick Access toolbar, when available. Its shortcut is also Ctrl+Y; this works because Repeat and Redo are not available at the same time (see Figure 2.3).

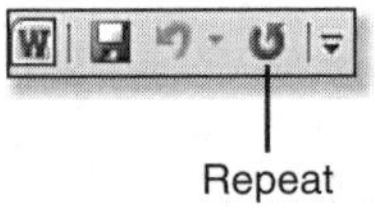

Repeat

Figure 2.3
The Repeat button makes it easy to repeat the last action you took.

Inserting Symbols and Special Characters

The computer keyboard is limited in the characters it can produce, and people often need other characters to produce typeset-quality documents. For example, the copyright (©) and trademark (™) symbols are frequently used in business documents, and an attractively typeset page uses em dashes (—) rather than two hyphens together (--) to represent dashes in sentences.

Inserting Symbols with Keyboard Shortcuts or AutoCorrect

Some of the most popular symbols have keyboard shortcuts or AutoCorrect shortcuts. AutoCorrect is a feature used most often for correcting common spelling errors, but it is also useful for generating certain common symbols on the fly. To use an AutoCorrect shortcut, type the text shown and press the spacebar once, and Word converts the shortcut text to the specified symbol. Table 2.1 summarizes both the keyboard shortcuts and the AutoCorrect entries for some common symbols.

Table 2.1 Keyboard and AutoCorrect Shortcuts for Symbols

Symbol	Keyboard Shortcut	AutoCorrect Shortcut
— (em dash)	Ctrl+Alt+Num – (Minus sign on the numeric keypad)	
– (en dash)	Ctrl+Num – (Minus sign on the numeric keypad)	
© (copyright)	Ctrl+Alt+C	(c)
® (registered trademark)	Ctrl+Alt+R	(r)
™ (trademark)	Ctrl+Alt+T	(tm)
... (ellipsis)	Ctrl+Alt+. (period)	...
' (single opening quote)	Ctrl+`,` Hold down Ctrl and press the grave accent key (`) twice. It is above the Tab key.	
' (single closing quote)	Ctrl+',' Hold down Ctrl and press the apostrophe key twice. It is to the left of the Enter key.	
" (double opening quote)	Ctrl+`,"    Hold down Ctrl and press the grave accent key (`) once, and then type a quotation mark.	
" (double closing quote)	Ctrl+'," Hold down Ctrl and press the apostrophe key once, and then type a quotation mark.	
← (typographical left arrow)	None	<--
→ (typographical right arrow	None	-->
← (thick typographical left arrow)	None	<==
→ (thick typographical right arrow)	None	==>
↔ (double-headed arrow)	None	<=>

Notice that in Table 2.1, there are no AutoCorrect entries for the dashes and the quotation marks. That's because they're not needed. Word automatically converts straight quotes to typographical ones (Word calls these "smart quotes") and two hyphens in a row to a dash. If you don't want that change to occur, use Undo (Ctrl+Z) immediately after Word makes the change to reverse it. Undo also reverses any of the AutoCorrect conversions if you catch them immediately after they occur.

➥ *To disable an AutoCorrect entry, see "Automating Corrections with AutoCorrect," p. 110.*

➥ *To learn how to disable the automatic conversion of straight quotes to smart quotes, or two hyphens to a dash, see "Setting AutoFormat As You Type Options," p. 176.*

> **note**
>
> The single and double quotation marks in Table 2.1 are typographical—that is, they differ depending on whether they are at the beginning or end of the quoted phrase. This is different from the straight quotation marks and apostrophes that you can directly type from the keyboard.

Inserting Symbols with the Symbol Dialog Box

Another way to insert a symbol is with the Symbol button on the Insert tab. Click Symbol to open a drop-down list of some common symbols (see Figure 2.4). (This list has some overlap with the ones in Table 2.1, but it is not the same list. This list changes depending on your usage; when you insert a symbol, that symbol appears on this list in the future for easy reinsertion.)

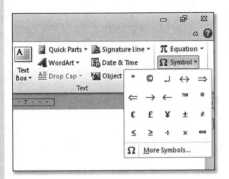

Figure 2.4
Symbols can be inserted from the Symbol drop-down list on the Insert tab.

If the symbol you want doesn't appear, click More Symbols to open the Symbol dialog box, shown in Figure 2.5. From here, you can select any character from any installed font, including some of the alternative characters that don't correspond to a keyboard key, such as letters with accent symbols over them.

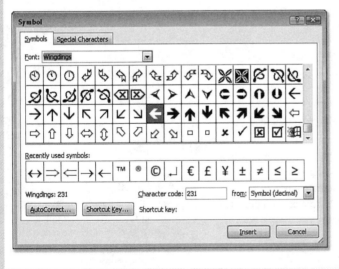

Figure 2.5
The Symbol dialog box can be used to insert any character from any font.

You can also find a symbol by its character code, which is a numeric identifier of a particular symbol in a particular coding system. The two main coding systems are ASCII and Unicode. ASCII is the older system, and characters can be identified using either decimal or hexadecimal numbering. Unicode is the Windows standard for character identification, and it uses only hex numbering. Select the desired coding system from the From drop-down list, and then type the character code in the Character Code box.

On the Special Characters tab of the dialog box are some of the most common typographical characters, along with reminders of their keyboard shortcuts. If you need to insert one of these common characters, finding it on the Special Characters tab can be easier than trying to wade through all the characters in a font for it.

Automating Symbol Entry

To make it easier to insert the same symbol again later, you might want to set up an AutoCorrect entry or a shortcut key combination for it.

To create an AutoCorrect entry, follow these steps:

1. From the Symbol dialog box, click the symbol for which you want to create the entry.

2. Click AutoCorrect. The AutoCorrect dialog box opens with a new entry already started.

3. Type the text that should represent the symbol. It is customary to enclose one or two characters in parentheses for AutoCorrect symbol insertion, but this is not required. For example, to create an entry for the ± sign, you might choose (+) as the text to enter (see Figure 2.6).

4. Click Add. The new entry appears on the list.

5. Click OK to return to the Symbol dialog box.

To assign a shortcut key combination to a symbol, follow these steps:

 tip

If you want a special character, such as an accented letter or copyright symbol, to blend in smoothly with the rest of the paragraph, make sure (normal text) is selected from the Font drop-down list in the Symbol dialog box. You won't always be able to do this, though, because not all symbols are available in all fonts. When you select symbols from the Special Characters tab, they are automatically in the (normal text) font.

 tip

For a wide choice of interesting and unique symbols, check out the Wingdings fonts, which you can select from the Font drop-down menu.

1. From the Symbol dialog box, click the symbol for which you want to create the shortcut.

2. Click Shortcut Key. The Customize Keyboard dialog box appears.

3. Click in the Press New Shortcut Key text box, and then type the key combination you want to use. If that key combination is currently assigned to something else, a Currently Assigned To line appears, as in Figure 2.7. (You can overwrite a default shortcut key assignment if desired.)

4. By default, the change is saved to the Normal.dotm template; if you want it saved only to the open document, open the Save Changes In list and choose the document.

5. Click the Assign button.

6. Click Close to return to the Symbol dialog box.

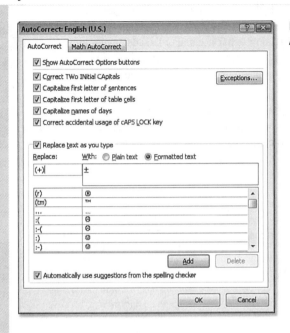

Figure 2.6
Add an AutoCorrect entry for a symbol.

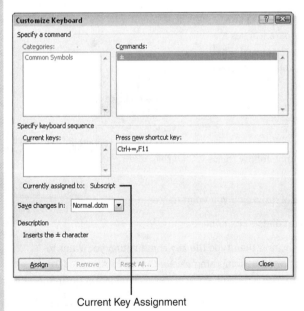

Figure 2.7
Map a keyboard shortcut to a symbol.

Current Key Assignment

To learn more about creating AutoCorrect entries, see "Automating Corrections with AutoCorrect," p. 110.

Moving Around in a Document

In a short document, moving around is easy. You can use the keyboard's arrow keys to move the insertion point, or click the mouse to place the insertion point where you want it.

But when a document grows to several pages or more, those basic methods can be insufficient. In the following sections, you'll learn some shortcuts and alternative methods for moving around in a document.

Scrolling

Vertical and horizontal scroll bars are available at the right and bottom of the Word window, respectively, whenever there is more content than will fit in the window. You're probably already familiar with these from other applications, but here's a quick review:

- **Arrows**—Click an arrow to scroll a small amount in that direction, or click and hold on an arrow to scroll quickly.

- **Scroll box**—This is the boxed portion of the bar; drag it to scroll quickly without moving through each page on the way there. The scroll box is context sensitive; the more the undisplayed content, the smaller the bar will be. For example, if 50 percent of the document appears onscreen and the other 50 percent is not shown, the scroll box takes up approximately 50 percent of the scroll bar.

- **Scroll bar**—This is the empty area behind the scroll box. Click above the scroll box to move up one screenful, or click below the scroll box to move down one screenful.

Many mice and trackballs have a wheel between the left and right buttons. Roll this toward you or away from you to scroll vertically in the document. Some of these wheels can also be pushed to the left or right to scroll horizontally.

Moving the Insertion Point with Click and Type

The Click and Type feature enables you to place text anywhere on the page. If the location you choose is outside the current document, extra tab stops or empty paragraphs are added to allow the insertion point to reach that spot.

So what does "outside the current document" mean? Recall from the beginning of this chapter that each document has an end-of-file marker, a small horizontal line that marks where the last line of the document ends. This marker is visible only in Draft and Outline view, but it's always there, enforcing the boundary of the document. As you type lines of text, this marker moves further down the page.

Before the days of Click and Type, you could not move the insertion point past this end-of-file marker via normal methods (such as by pressing the arrow keys or by clicking). That meant if you wanted to place text further down on the page than the end-of-file marker, you had to press Enter, adding blank paragraphs, until the document had sufficiently expanded so that the desired area was part of the document.

Click and Type provides an alternate method for placing text outside the document's current borders—and for starting text at horizontal locations other than the left margin. With Click and Type, you simply double-click to place the insertion point, rather than the usual single-clicking.

If the location you chose is outside the end-of-file marker (whether displayed or not in the view you are using), Word automatically inserts the needed blank paragraphs so that the area is within the document.

 note

If you find yourself accidentally enabling Click and Type when you don't want it, turn the feature off. To do so, choose File, Options, click Advanced, and in the Editing Options section, clear the Enable Click and Type check box.

You can get different text alignments on those tab stops that Word creates with Click and Type. Notice that the mouse pointer changes as you move over different areas of the page. When you are in an area where Click and Type can be used, the mouse pointer has a text alignment symbol on it. Over the left side of the page, it's a left-align symbol, as in Figure 2.8. In the center it's a center-align symbol, and as you approach the right margin, it's a right-align symbol. Whatever symbol is shown when you double-click determines the horizontal alignment of the paragraph that's created.

If the location you chose is not at the left or right margin, or directly in the center of the page, Word inserts a tab stop at the chosen spot and tabs over to it for you. If the text you type is longer than can fit on one line, Word wraps the next line to the left margin. To make all the text line up under the first line you typed, select the paragraph and press Ctrl+T to create a hanging indent.

Figure 2.8
The alignment symbol on the mouse pointer depends on the area of the page in which you are using Click and Type.

Navigating with Keyboard Shortcuts

Table 2.2 lists some keyboard shortcuts for moving the insertion point in Word 2010.

Table 2.2   Keyboard Shortcuts for Navigation

Keyboard Shortcut	Moves to:
Alt+ ↓	Next object
Alt+End	End of the row
Alt+F1 (or F11)	Next field
Alt+F6	Next window
Alt+F7	Next misspelled word
Alt+Home	Start of the row
Alt+Page Down	Bottom of the current column
Alt+Page Up	Top of the current column
Alt+Shift+F1 (or Shift+F11)	Previous field

Table 2.2 Continued

Keyboard Shortcut	Moves to:
Alt+Shift+F6	Previous window
Alt+ ↑	Previous object
Ctrl+Alt+Page Down	Bottom of the window
Ctrl+Alt+Page Up	Top of the window
Ctrl+Alt+Z (or Shift+F5)	Previous location of the insertion point
Ctrl+ ↓	Next paragraph or next table cell
Ctrl+End	End of the document
Ctrl+F6 (or Alt+F6)	Next window
Ctrl+Home	Beginning of the document
Ctrl+ ←	One word to the left
Ctrl+Page Down	Next item (based on the Browse Object setting)
Ctrl+Page Up	Previous item (based on the Browse Object setting)
Ctrl+ →	One word to the right
Ctrl+Shift+F6	Previous window
Ctrl+ ↑	Previous paragraph
End	End of the current line
F6	Next pane or frame
Home	Beginning of the current line
Page Down	Next screen
Page Up	Previous screen
Shift+F6	Previous pane or frame
Shift+Tab	Previous cell in a table
Tab	Next cell in a table, or starts a new table row if already in the last cell

Selecting Text and Other Objects

Like most applications, Word works using the selection/action system. First you select some text or other data, and then you act upon that selection by issuing a command. For example, first you select text to be copied, and then you issue the command to copy it.

There are many ways of selecting text and other objects in a Word document, and you can use any combination of methods. However, some methods are much more convenient and well suited for certain situations.

The most basic way to select text with the mouse is to drag across the text (with the left mouse button down). The selected text becomes highlighted.

I Don't Want Word to Extend Selections

By default, Word extends your selection to the nearest entire word, and it includes the paragraph marker at the end of a selected paragraph. In other words, if you drag across a paragraph to select it, Word automatically includes the hidden end-of-paragraph marker in the selection area. This is for your own good, because it prevents you from leaving behind the paragraph's marker inadvertently. Word also automatically selects an entire word when you drag across selections, so your selection doesn't stop in the middle of a word.

If you dislike either of these features, you can turn them off. Choose File, Options, click Advanced, and in the Editing Options section, clear the Use Smart Paragraph Selection check box or the When Selecting, Automatically Select Entire Word check box.

There are also shortcuts for selecting certain objects or amounts of text with the mouse and keyboard, as described in Tables 2.3 and 2.4, respectively. To use keyboard shortcuts, first position the insertion point at the starting point for the selection, and then use the keys indicated to extend the selection.

Table 2.3   Mouse Shortcuts for Selecting

To select...	Do This:
From the insertion point to any other point	Position the insertion point, and then hold down Shift and click the end point for the selection.
The entire document	Triple-click in the left margin.
A word	Double-click the word.
A sentence	Ctrl+click the sentence.
A paragraph	Triple-click the paragraph, or double-click in the left margin next to it.
A line	Click in the left margin next to it.
A table	Click in the table, and then click the Table Selection box (looks like a four-headed arrow) in the top-left corner of the table grid.
A table cell	Click the left edge of the cell.
A table row	Point the mouse pointer to the left of the row so the pointer turns into a white arrow, and then click.
A table column	Point the mouse pointer at the top gridline of the column so the pointer turns into a black arrow, and then click.
A graphic	Click the graphic.

Table 2.3 Continued

To select...	Do This:
A text box	Click any outer edge of the text box.
A rectangular block (unrelated to paragraph or column divisions)	Hold down Alt and drag across the area to select.
Multiple noncontiguous selections	Make the first selection, and then hold down Ctrl as you drag across additional selections.
Multiple graphics or nontext objects	Click the first object, and then hold down Ctrl as you click additional objects.

Table 2.4 Keyboard Shortcuts for Selecting

To select...	Press This:
The entire document	Ctrl+A
The bottom of the window	Ctrl+Alt+Shift+Page Down
The top of the window	Ctrl+Alt+Shift+Page Up
The end of the paragraph	Ctrl+Shift+ ↓
The beginning of the paragraph	Ctrl+Shift+ ↑
The end of the document	.Ctrl+Shift+End
The beginning of the document	Ctrl+Shift+Home
A rectangular block (unrelated to paragraph or column divisions)	Ctrl+Shift+F8+arrow keys
The beginning of the word	Ctrl+Shift+ ←. Press the left arrow key again, still holding Ctrl+Shift, to extend to subsequent words.
The end of the word	Ctrl+Shift+ →. Press the right arrow key again, still holding Ctrl+Shift, to extend to subsequent words.
The entire line above	Shift+ ↑
The entire line below	Shift+ ↓
The end of the line	Shift+End
The beginning of the line	Shift+Home
One character, line, or table cell in any direction	Shift+arrow keys

Moving and Copying Text and Objects

Perhaps the most important benefit of word processing over typewriter use is the ability to move and copy objects and blocks of text. There are many ways of accomplishing move and copy operations in Word, so you can select whatever method is most comfortable for you or makes the most sense in a particular situation. The following sections explain the various move and copy operations and the differences between them.

Moving or Copying Text with Drag-and-Drop

Drag-and-drop operations are popular because they most closely resemble the way you do things outside the computer. (Yes, there really is life outside the computer!) When you want to move something in your living room, you pick it up and reposition it. Or if it's heavy, like a piece of furniture, you drag it and drop it. You can do the same thing with objects and with blocks of selected text in Word.

For a standard drag-and-drop operation, follow these steps:

1. Select the text or object(s) you want to move or copy.

2. (Optional) To copy, hold down the Ctrl key. You don't have to hold anything down if you want to move.

3. Position the mouse over the selection, and then click and hold down the left mouse button on it.

4. Still holding down the left mouse button, drag the selection to a new location. Then release the mouse button.

There are additional drag-and-drop options; to see them, use the right mouse button rather than the left one in the preceding steps. (Don't hold down the Ctrl key if you are using the right mouse button.) When you release the mouse button in step 4, a shortcut menu appears with these choices on it:

- **Move Here**—The default operation; the same as regular dragging with the left mouse button.

- **Copy Here**—The same as holding down the Ctrl key with the left-mouse-button drag.

- **Link Here**—Creates a copy that retains a link to the original location, such that if the original changes, this copy changes, too.

- **Cancel**—Cancels the current drag-and-drop operation.

 tip

Here's a trick you can do with the F8 key for selecting: Press F8 to turn Extend mode on, and then press it again to select the current word. Pressing it a third time selects the current sentence, pressing it a fourth time selects the current paragraph, and pressing it a fifth time selects the entire document. You can also use F8 with the arrow keys to extend the selection one character or line at a time in the arrow's direction. Use Shift+F8 to reduce the size of the selection. Press Esc to turn Extend mode off.

 note

There are actually two Clipboards—the Windows Clipboard and the Office Clipboard. The Windows Clipboard holds only one item at a time; when you place a second item on that Clipboard, the first item is erased from it. The Office Clipboard has multiple slots for holding content. It uses the Windows Clipboard for one slot, but it can also hold 23 other items at the same time. I explain more about the Office Clipboard later in this chapter.

Using Cut, Copy, and Paste

One of the complaints that many people have with drag-and-drop is that they are simply not coordinated enough to manage positioning the mouse pointer in exactly the right spot while holding down keys and mouse buttons. People who have this problem may prefer to use the Cut, Copy, and Paste commands instead.

 tip

Experienced users generally end up using the keyboard shortcut methods most frequently because they are the fastest.

Cut and Copy are similar operations. Cut removes the selection from the document and places it on the Clipboard, which is a hidden holding area; Copy leaves the selection as is and places a copy of it on the Clipboard. After a Cut or Copy operation, you can then use Paste to place the Clipboard's content at the insertion point location.

Word offers Ribbon, keyboard, and right-click methods for issuing the Cut, Copy, and Paste commands. Table 2.5 summarizes them.

Table 2.5   Cut, Copy, and Paste Methods

	Cut	Copy	Paste
Click these buttons on the Home tab:	✂	📑	📋
Press these shortcut keys:	Ctrl+X	Ctrl+C	Ctrl+V
Right-click your selection, and then choose one of these commands:	Cut	Copy	Paste (may be multiple types of paste available)

I'd Like to Save Clipboard Content for Later Use

By far the easiest way to save something from the Clipboard is to paste it into Word (or some other application) and then save it in that application's native file format. But you can also save, organize, and recall items from the Windows Clipboard.

With a default installation of Office, a utility is installed called Microsoft Clip Organizer. It is primarily for managing clip art, but you can also use it to save items to and from the Clipboard.

You'll find it on the Start, All Programs, Microsoft Office, Microsoft Office 2010 Tools folder. Start it up, and then choose Edit, Paste to copy the current contents of the Windows Clipboard into the organizer. The pasted item appears as a thumbnail image there. You can drag it into any of the various collections on the Collection List, assign keywords to it, place it back on the Clipboard (with Edit, Copy), and more.

Continued...

One thing you can't do with the Microsoft Clip Organizer, however, is to save the clip as a separate file. To do this, you need a different utility—the ClipBook Viewer. This is a Windows XP utility, not Office. (It is not available in Windows Vista or Windows 7.) In Windows XP, you can find it at this path: Windows\System32\clipbrd.exe. (Use the Run command to run it.)

The ClipBook Viewer starts out with a single, minimized window called Clipboard that contains the current contents of the Windows Clipboard. Restore this window and then choose File, Save As to save that clip as an NT Clipboard File (with a .clp extension). To recall a saved Clipboard item, use File, Open. This places the content of the file onto the Windows Clipboard, displacing what was there before.

Keeping or Discarding Formatting When Pasting

You can optionally specify whether or not the formatting of the cut or copied source is transferred when you paste. For example, if the cut or copied text was bold, italic, or a certain color, you can choose whether or not to transfer those attributes.

To do so, instead of clicking the face of the Paste button, click the down arrow under it, opening its menu. From there, click one of these icons (labeled in Figure 2.9):

- **Keep Source Formatting**—Transfers all formatting from the cut or copied text.

- **Merge Formatting**—Changes the formatting so that it matches the text that surrounds it.

- **Keep Text Only**—Does not transfer formatting from the cut or copied text; the pasted text takes on whatever formatting is in effect in the new location.

Depending on what you are pasting, you might see additional icons for other pasting options as well.

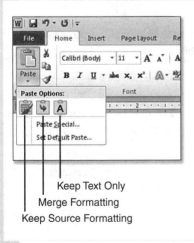

Figure 2.9
Use the Paste button's menu to specify whether formatting is transferred in a Paste operation.

Keep Text Only
Merge Formatting
Keep Source Formatting

You can also access these same options *after* doing a regular Paste, by clicking the Paste Options floating icon that appears next to the pasted object. Click it to open a menu containing the paste options, as shown in Figure 2.10.

Figure 2.10
Paste formatting options can also be accessed via the Paste Options floating icon in the text.

The Set Default Paste command opens the Word Options dialog box (same as File, Options) and displays the Advanced options. From here you can set a variety of paste options in the Cut, Copy, and Paste section, as shown in Figure 2.11.

Options for Controlling Paste Behavior

Figure 2.11
Paste options are controlled in the Word Options dialog box.

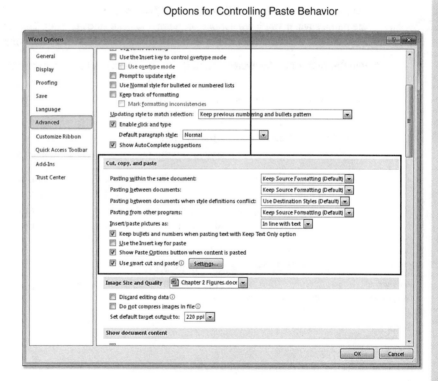

- **Pasting Within the Same Document**—Choose how formatting is applied to the copy when copying within a document. You can choose Keep Source Formatting, Merge Formatting, or Keep Text Only.

- **Pasting Between Documents**—Choose how formatting is applied to the copy when styles are not an issue (for example, when both the source and destination use the same style defined the same way).

- **Pasting Between Documents When Style Definitions Conflict**—Choose how formatting is applied to the copy when you are copying between documents and the style applied in the source document differs from that applied at the insertion point location in the destination document.

- **Pasting from Other Programs**—Choose how formatting is applied to the copy when the text is coming from some other application than Word.

- **Insert/Paste Pictures As**—Choose how nontext objects are placed in the document. In Line with Text means the object is treated as a text character at the insertion point and will move with the surrounding text. The other options are various wrapping settings for floating objects.

> *For more on picture/text wrap settings, see "Setting Text Wrap," p. 386.*

- **Keep Bullets and Numbers When Pasting Text with Keep Text Only Option**—This is just like the name says. If you have set one of the previous settings to Keep Text Only but you are copying a bulleted or numbered list, this setting determines whether the bullet or number is preserved.

- **Use the Insert Key for Paste**—Mark this if you want the Insert key on the keyboard to be remapped to be a shortcut for the Paste command. This check box is paired with the Use the Insert Key to Control Overtype Mode check box (on the same tab); only one or the other can be chosen at once.

- **Show Paste Options Button When Content Is Pasted**—Clear this check box if you don't want that Paste Options button to appear next to pasted selections. (Sometimes it can get in the way.)

- **Use Smart Cut and Paste**—This enables Word to apply a rather complex set of rules to determine how selections should be pasted. To fine-tune these rules, click the Settings button to display the Settings dialog box (see Figure 2.12). Note that you can choose default options for Word 2002–2010 or for Word 97–2000, or you can go your own way with custom settings.

Figure 2.12
Fine-tune the paste options here.

Pasting with Paste Special

The Paste Special command enables you to define the format of the pasted copy, and in some circumstances also create a dynamic link to the original. In this context, "format" does not mean the appearance-based formatting that you learned about copying in the previous section (bold, italic, and so on), but the actual type of the pasted content (text, graphics, spreadsheet cells, etc.).

To use Paste Special, open the drop-down menu below the Paste button (refer to Figure 2.9) and select Paste Special from the menu.

Doing so opens the Paste Special dialog box, shown in Figure 2.13.

Figure 2.13
Use the Paste Special dialog box to paste in a different way than the default.

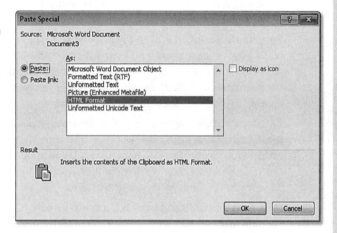

For a normal (nonlinked) paste, select a paste format from the As list. The choices on the list depend on the type of content you cut or copied. For example, if you copied some text from another document that had some unusual formatting, you could choose to keep that formatting by selecting Formatted Text (RTF), or you could choose to discard that formatting by selecting Unformatted Text.

Pasting in a format whose name ends with "Object" creates an embedded copy that retains its link to the original program. This is not especially relevant for copying text within and between Word documents because the original program is Word itself, but it makes a difference when copying multimedia content, such as graphics from a graphics program, into Word, for example. When you choose an "Object" format, the selection is placed in its own separate frame from the rest of the document, and you can edit that object in its native program later by double-clicking it.

 caution

Don't use Paste Link unless you can actually benefit from it, because it makes the file size larger, and if the original file is ever deleted or moved, an error message appears in the file containing the copy.

caution

If you paste text in one of the Picture formats, it is no longer editable as text; you can edit it only with a picture-editing program.

For Paste Link to be available, the selection must have been copied from some other document or file than the one in which it is being pasted. Paste Link creates a dynamic link between the original and the copy so that when the original changes, the copy also changes.

➡ *To learn more about linking and embedding, see "Embedding Data," p. 599, and "Linking to Data in Other Files," p. 604.*

Using the Office Clipboard

The Office Clipboard is an expanded version of the Windows Clipboard. It can hold up to 24 selections, and you can choose which item to paste with each operation.

To access any clips other than the last one stored, you must display the Office Clipboard task pane. To view the Office Clipboard task pane, click the dialog box launcher for the Clipboard group on the Home tab. The Office Clipboard appears to the left of the main document window.

Each time you copy something to the Clipboard, it is added to the Clipboard task pane's list, with the most recently added items at the top. To paste an item from it, position the insertion point and then click that item in the Clipboard task pane. To paste all the items at once, click Paste All.

To remove a single item from the Clipboard task pane, right-click the item and click Delete (see Figure 2.14). (Alternatively, you can point at the item until a down arrow appears to its right. Click that down arrow to open the same menu as with right-clicking; then click Delete.)

To clear the entire Clipboard at once, click the Clear All button at the top. Clearing the Office Clipboard also clears the Windows Clipboard.

To fine-tune the way the Office Clipboard works, click the Options button. A menu appears with these options on it:

 note

If you are copying or cutting between an Office application and a non-Office application, the two Clipboards talk to each other, but only via the first position on the Office Clipboard. The other 23 possible positions on the Office Clipboard are simply ignored.

 note

By default, the Clipboard pane is fixed in location and size, but you can click the down arrow in its top-right corner for a menu from which you can move and resize it.

- **Show Office Clipboard Automatically**—Displays the Office Clipboard automatically when copying items.

- **Show Office Clipboard When Ctrl+C Pressed Twice**—Displays the Office Clipboard when Ctrl+C is pressed twice.

- **Collect Without Showing Office Clipboard**—Copies items to the Office Clipboard but does not show the task pane unless you specifically call for it (by pressing Ctrl+C twice, for example).

- **Show Office Clipboard Icon on Taskbar**—Displays an Office Clipboard icon in the notification area of the taskbar (near the clock) whenever the Office Clipboard is active. You can double-click that icon to display the Office Clipboard in the active application. (Remember, all Office apps share the Office Clipboard.)

- **Show Status Near Taskbar When Copying**—Pops up a message near the Office Clipboard icon when something has just been copied to the Clipboard.

Figure 2.14
Delete an item from the Clipboard.

Locating Specific Content

Word offers many ways of jumping quickly to certain content in a document. This content can be actual data that you've typed, or it can be an object such as an image, a caption, a bookmark, or even a certain type of formatting. In the following sections, you'll learn about several ways to browse or search a document to find specific items.

Finding and Replacing

The Find feature in Word helps locate instances of a specified text string. That text string can be anything you care to look for—a product name, a person, a string of numbers, or whatever. You can even use it to find specific formatting or a nonprinting symbol or code, such as a tab or a paragraph break. For example, suppose you are looking for a phone number in a document. You don't remember what page it's on, but you know it starts with a (317) area code. You could search for (317) to locate it.

 note

There are two Find interfaces in Word 2010. The newer one works with the Navigation pane, listing all instances of the found text at once; you can jump between instances by clicking them on that list. The older, more traditional one works with the Find and Replace dialog box, as in earlier versions of Word.

The Replace feature works hand-in-hand with Find; it performs a Find operation but then replaces the found item with a different text string you specify. As with Find, you can also use Replace with formatting and with nonprinting symbols and codes. For example, suppose you are drawing up a contract for a Ms. Smith when you find out that she has recently become Mrs. Brown. You can perform a Replace operation to change all instances of Smith to Brown and all instances of Ms. to Mrs. (Be careful with that one, though, because there might be more than one person in the document who uses Ms. as a prefix.)

Finding a Text String with the Navigation Pane

New in Word 2010, you can use the Navigation pane to find text in a document. All instances of the found text string appear listed in the Navigation pane, and you can click any one of them to jump to that place in the document.

To search with the Navigation pane:

1. Press Ctrl+F, or click Find on the Home tab. The Navigation pane opens.

2. Type the search string in the text box, and press Enter. The document display jumps to the first found instance. See Figure 2.15.

3. (Optional) Click another instance in the Navigation pane to jump to it.

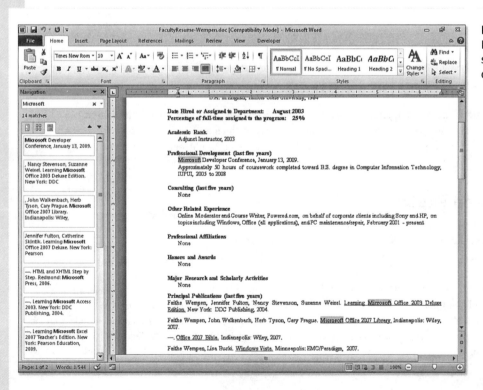

Figure 2.15
Find a text string in a document.

Finding a Text String with the Find and Replace Dialog Box

Some people prefer the legacy Find interface in Word, the one that came with previous versions. It works within the Find and Replace dialog box. It has more options available, and it lets you do special types of searches that the Navigation pane method does not.

The old style of Find operation cannot be initiated directly from the Ribbon in Word 2010, but it's easy enough to get to it—click Replace on the Home tab. This opens the Find and Replace dialog box with the Replace tab displayed. Then click the Find tab to access the legacy version of the Find feature. Another way of getting to it is to click the down arrow on the Search box in the Navigation pane and then click Find. See Figure 2.16.

Figure 2.16
The Search box's drop-down list provides an alternate way of opening the Find and Replace dialog box.

Click here for menu.

To add a button for the legacy-style Find feature to the Quick Access Toolbar, see "Customizing the Quick Access Toolbar," p. 863.

To find a text string with the Find tab of the Find and Replace dialog box:

1. Press Ctrl+H, or click Replace on the Home tab.

2. Click the Find tab.

3. Type the text string into the Find What box. (To find other things besides text strings, such as special characters or formatting, see the next several sections.)

4. Click Find Next. The display jumps to the first instance of that text (see Figure 2.17).

5. Keep clicking Find Next until you find the instance you are interested in or until a message appears that Word has finished searching the document.

Found Text

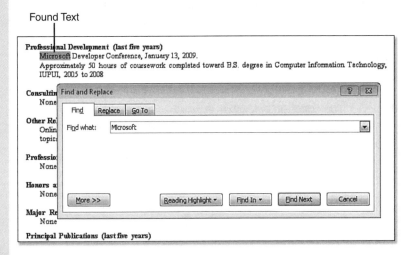

Figure 2.17
Find a text string in a document.

Selecting All Instances of Found Text

When you use the Navigation pane method of finding, all instances of the found string are temporarily highlighted in yellow; you can scroll through the document to examine them.

You can also use the Find and Replace dialog box to select all instances at once. This method selects the text strings, as if you had held down Ctrl and dragged across them to select them yourself with the mouse. Clicking anywhere in the document deselects them, so you can't do editing of individual instances here without disturbing the selection. However, what you *can* do is perform some global formatting command upon them all, such as making them all bold or a different font or color.

To select all instances of the found text using the Find and Replace dialog box, follow these steps:

1. Press Ctrl+H, or click Replace on the Home tab, and then click the Find tab.

2. Type the text string into the Find What box.

3. Click Find In. On the menu that opens, click Main Document. Word selects each instance of the text string.

4. Without closing the Find and Replace dialog box, scroll through the document to examine all the instances. If desired, apply a formatting command to them as a group.

   ➡ *To learn more about text formatting, see Chapter 4, "Applying Character Formatting."*

5. When you are finished, click Cancel to close the Find and Replace dialog box.

Highlighting All Instances of Found Text

The preceding procedures select the instances only for as long as the Find and Replace dialog box or Navigation pane is open and you have not clicked to select anything else. If you want more durable marking of each found instance, try this instead:

1. Press Ctrl+H, or click Replace on the Home tab, and then click the Find tab.

2. Type the text string into the Find What box.

3. Click Reading Highlight. On the menu that opens, click Highlight All.

4. Close the Find and Replace dialog box and examine all the found instances at your leisure.

5. When you are finished examining all the found instances, reopen the Find and Replace dialog box (Ctrl+H; then click the Find tab).

6. Click Reading Highlight. On the menu that opens, click Clear Highlighting. This clears the highlighting applied from the Find and Replace dialog box, but it does not clear highlighting applied with the Highlight feature on the Home tab.

7. Close the Find and Replace dialog box.

Customizing a Find Operation

The Find operation has many options available for customizing the search. To access them, click the More >> button in the Find and Replace dialog box. The dialog box that appears is shown in Figure 2.18.

Figure 2.18
Customize the Find command using these search options.

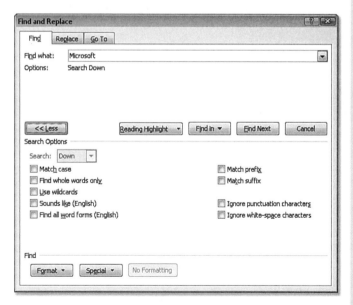

You can set any of these options as needed:

- **Search**—Choose Down, Up, or All to determine in what direction from the insertion point the Find operation will proceed.

- **Match Case**—The search is limited to the letter case you used for typing the Find What entry. For example, if you are searching for *butter*, Word will not find *Butter*.

- **Find Whole Words Only**—The search is limited to whole words that match the search string. For example, if you are searching for *butter*, Word will not find *butterfly*.

- **Use Wildcards**—You can use wildcard designators in your searches to find any character (^?), any digit (^#), or any letter (^$). If you forget these codes, you can select them from the Special menu.

- **Sounds Like (English)**—The search will include words that are pronounced similarly to the word you are searching for. This is good to have if you aren't sure how to spell a word but you know how it sounds.

- **Find All Word Forms (English)**—The search will contain forms of a word even if they are not spelled the same. For example, a search for *is* will find words such as *am, is, are, was, were,* and *be*.

- **Match Prefix**—Finds the string only if it appears at the beginning of a word.

- **Match Suffix**—Finds the string only if it appears at the end of a word.

- **Ignore Punctuation Characters**—Omits punctuation from the search. For example, a search for *three and* will find *three, and* (note the comma) if this option is turned on.

- **Ignore White-Space Characters**—Omits whitespace from the search. For example, a search for *living room* will find *livingroom*.

With all these options showing, the Find and Replace dialog box becomes rather large and cumbersome. You can shrink it again by clicking the <<Less button.

Replacing a Text String

Click the Replace tab in the Find and Replace dialog box for access to the Replace tools. If the dialog box is not already open, you can open it and display that tab on top by pressing Ctrl+H or selecting Replace on the Home tab.

After entering text in the Find What and Replace With boxes, click Find Next to find the first instance of the string, and then click Replace to replace that instance, or click Find Next again to skip that instance (see Figure 2.19).

If you're really brave, click Replace All to change all instances at once. Be aware, though, that this can have unintended consequences if there are instances you didn't anticipate. For example, suppose you are replacing all instances of *White* with *Brown*. But somewhere in your document you talk about the whitening power of a laundry product. The word *whitening* would become *browning*, which is clearly not what you want.

Figure 2.19
Replace one text string with another on the Replace tab.

Finding and Replacing Formatting

In addition to finding text strings, Find and Replace can find formatting. You can use this to find certain strings that are formatted in a certain way, or you can simply find the formatting itself and not include text in the search.

To find (and optionally replace) certain formatting, follow these steps:

1. Make sure the additional controls are displayed in the Find and Replace dialog box. Click the More >> button to display them if they are not.

2. Click in the Find What box to place the insertion point in it. (Optional) If you want to limit the search to certain text, type that text.

3. Click the Format button. A menu opens.

4. Click the type of formatting you want to specify. For example, to specify character formatting such as a font, click Font.

5. In the dialog box that appears, specify the formatting you want to find and then click OK. The dialog box will be different depending on the type of formatting you chose in step 4. For example, in Figure 2.20, the Find Font dialog box is shown.Notice that the Effects check boxes have a solid fill in them, meaning that their setting will not be an issue in the search. If you click one of them, it becomes selected with a check mark, meaning the search will find text only with that attribute on. Click it again and it becomes cleared, meaning the search will find text only with that attribute off. Click it a third time to cycle back to the solid fill again.

 note

If you make a mistake in specifying formatting, click in either the Find What or the Replace With text box and click No Formatting to clear it.

Back in the Find and Replace dialog box, a line now appears beneath the Find What text box stating the formatting that has been chosen.

6. (Optional) Repeat steps 3–5 to specify more formatting criteria for the text to be found.

7. (Optional) If you want to specify formatting for the replacement, click in the Replace With box and then repeat steps 3–5.

8. Continue the find operation normally. You can use the Find Next button for an interactive find, or use Replace, Replace All, Find In, or Reading Highlight. (The latter two are available only on the Find tab.)

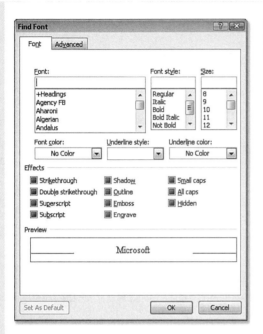

Figure 2.20
Find Font is just one example of the dialog boxes for specifying formatting to find.

Finding and Replacing Special Characters

Sometimes the text you need to find is not really text at all, but a layout character such as a paragraph break, page break, or tab. It's actually a fairly common need. For example, suppose you download some unformatted text from the Internet in a plaintext file that uses two paragraph breaks per paragraph—one to end a paragraph and one to create an extra line break between paragraphs. You want to get rid of the extra paragraph breaks, but it's a 100-page document. No problem. For the Find What field, enter two paragraph breaks by selecting Paragraph Mark from the Special menu twice in a row. In the Replace With box, enter a single paragraph mark. In other words, you're replacing every instance of two paragraph marks with one paragraph mark.

As you select a symbol from the Special menu, a caret code is entered into the Find What or Replace With box. It's called a caret code because each of these codes begins with a caret (^) symbol. If you happen to remember the code for what you want, feel free to type it in manually. Table 2.6 lists the codes for all the available special characters. Some of these are available only to find, not to replace, so they will not be available on the list when the insertion point is in the Replace With box.

Table 2.6 Caret Codes for Special Characters in Find and Replace Operations

Symbol	Code	Where Available
Paragraph break	^p	Find What/Replace With
Tab character	^t	Find What/Replace With
Any character	^?	Find What
Any digit	^#	Find What
Any letter	^$	Find What
Caret character	^^	Find What/Replace With
Section character (§) (not an actual section break)	^%	Find What/Replace With
Paragraph character (¶, not an actual paragraph break)	^v	Find What/Replace With
Clipboard contents	^c	Replace With
Column break	^n	Find What/Replace With
Em dash (—)	^+	Find What/Replace With
En dash (–)	^=	Find What/Replace With
Endnote mark	^e	Find What
Field	^d	Find What
Find What text	^&	Replace With
Footnote mark	^f	Find What
Graphic	^g	Find What
Manual (hard) line break	^l	Find What/Replace With
Manual (hard) page break	^m	Find What/Replace With
Nonbreaking hyphen	^~	Find What/Replace With
Nonbreaking space	^s	Find What/Replace With
Optional hyphen	^-	Find What/Replace With
Section break	^b	Find What
White space	^w	Find What

In addition to the "caret codes" that refer to individual symbols, there are special codes that can refer to multiple characters. Table 2.7 lists the available codes and their usage.

Table 2.7   Text String Codes for Find and Replace Operations

To find...	Use This:	Example
Text at the beginning of a word	<	<(new) finds newton but not renew; same as Match Prefix.
Text at the end of a word	>	>(new) finds renew but not newton; same as Match Suffix.
Any single character of a list of characters	[ ]	f[ai]n finds fan and fin, but not fun.
Any single character in a range	[-]	s[a-o]ng finds sang, sing, and song, but not sung.
Any single character except the specified character range	[!]	s[!a-o]ng finds sung but not sang, sing, or song.
An exact number of occurrences of the preceding character or expression	{n}	we{2}d finds weed but not wed.
At least a number of occurrences of the preceding character or expression	{n,}	we{1,}d finds both weed and wed.
Any single character	{n,m}	5{1,4} finds 50, 500, 5000, and 50000.
One or more occurrences of the preceding character or expression	@	50@ finds 50, 500, 5000, and higher numbers of zeros.

Using Select Browse Object

The Select Browse Object feature provides an efficient way to scroll through a document when you are looking for a specific type of content. For example, suppose you want to scroll through a large document so you can check the captions on the graphics. You could use Select Browse Object to scroll to the graphics, skipping over any screens that don't contain graphics.

Start by clicking the Select Browse Object button, which is the round icon below the lower arrow on the vertical scroll bar. (Alternatively, press Ctrl+Alt+Home.) A fly-out palette of choices appears. You can point to each choice to see a description. (Table 2.8 also describes each one.) Click one of the choices to specify what to browse for (see Figure 2.21).

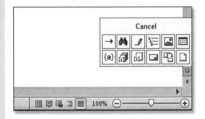

Figure 2.21
Choose what Word should browse for.

After selecting the browse type, use the blue double arrows above and below the Select Browse Object button (or press Ctrl+Page Down or Ctrl+Page Up) to move to the next or previous instance of the chosen item.

Table 2.8 Select Browse Object Types

Button	Object Type
→	Opens the Go To tab in the Find and Replace dialog box
🔍	Opens the Find tab in the Find and Replace dialog box
✏	Browse by edits (if tracking changes)
☰	Browse by heading
🖼	Browse by graphic
▦	Browse by table
{a}	Browse by field
📑	Browse by endnote
🗒	Browse by footnote
💬	Browse by comment
▥	Browse by section
▢	Browse by page

Using Go To

Go To is useful when you want to go to a particular instance of a content type, not just browse all instances. For example, perhaps you don't want to go through the document page by page, but instead want to jump immediately to page 100. Go To lets you enter the desired page number and go to it. It does this not just with pages, but with many other types of items as well, such as comments, bookmarks, and graphics.

As you saw in Table 2.8, you can access the Go To tab of the Find and Replace dialog box via the Select Browse Object feature, or by pressing Ctrl+G. You can also access it by clicking the down arrow on the Find button on the Home tab and selecting Go To.

On the Go To tab, select the item type and then enter the information about it. Depending on the type of item, either a text box or a drop-down list appears. Figure 2.22 shows an example of browsing for a particular section, for example.

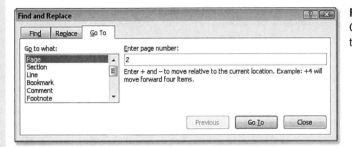

Figure 2.22
Go to a specified instance of a particular type of item with the Go To tab.

To learn about the other tabs of the Find and Replace dialog box, see *"Finding and Replacing,"* *p. 71.*

Displaying a Document Map

In a document that uses heading styles, you can display a document map that lists the headings, like a mini-outline view. You can click a heading in the document map to jump quickly to that heading within the document.

The document map is on a tab in the Navigation pane. To display the document map, display the Navigation pane (clicking the Find button on the Home tab is one way; another is to mark the Navigation Pane check box on the View tab). Then click the leftmost tab, Browse the Headings in Your Document. You can then click a heading to jump to it in the document.

You can expand and collapse levels of the outline in the document map by clicking the arrows to the left of the headings there. A diagonally pointing arrow indicates the level is expanded; a right-pointing arrow indicates it's collapsed. See Figure 2.23. Point to the arrow, so it turns yellow, and then click it to change its status.

To learn about heading styles, see *"Understanding Styles,"* *p. 217.*

To change the outline level at which a style appears in the document map, see *"Setting a Style's Outline Level,"* *p. 668.*

Displaying Page Thumbnails

Thumbnails are small images of each page. They are useful when you want to move to a certain page based on what it looks like. (Maybe it has a distinctive graphic on it, for example.) Page thumbnails appear on the middle tab of the Navigation pane. Jump to a page by clicking its thumbnail. See Figure 2.24.

Figure 2.23
A map of the document, based on its headings, appears in the Navigation pane.

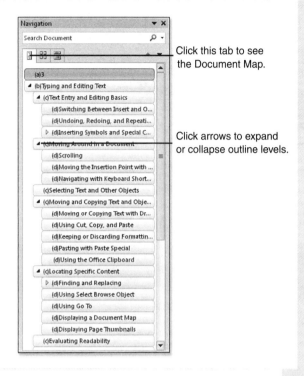

Click this tab to see the Document Map.

Click arrows to expand or collapse outline levels.

Figure 2.24
View page thumbnails from the Navigation pane.

Click this tab to view thumbnails.

Evaluating Readability

Readability refers to the ease with which people can read what you have written. It's determined using some basic statistics about the document, such as counts (word, character, paragraph, sentence) and averages (sentences per paragraph, words per sentence, characters per word). Those counts and averages are then fed into formulas that provide numeric evaluations of your writing.

Word supports two types of readability evaluation:

- **Flesch Reading Ease**—A number between 0 and 100. The higher the number, the easier it is to comprehend.

- **Flesch-Kincaid Grade Level**—An estimate of the approximate grade level of education someone would need to be able to understand your writing with ease. For example, a score of 9 means someone who can read at a ninth-grade level or higher should be able to read it.

How Is Readability Calculated?

Word does the calculation for you, so you don't have to worry about calculating the readability yourself. Just in case you are interested, though, here's how it's done. For each of the following formulas, ASW refers to average syllables per word, and ASL refers to average sentence length (in words).

For the Flesch Reading Ease scale:

$206.835 - (1.015 \times ASL) \times (8.46 \times ASW)$

For the Flesch-Kincaid Grade Level:

$(0.39 \times ASL) + (11.8 \times ASW) - 15.59$

To get readability statistics for a document, turn on the feature as follows:

1. Choose File, Options.

2. Click Proofing.

3. Scroll down to the When Correcting Spelling and Grammar in Word section and mark the Show Readability Statistics check box.

4. Click OK.

From that point on, every interactive spelling and grammar check will end with a Readability Statistics dialog box being displayed, as shown in Figure 2.25.

➡ *To learn how to do an interactive spelling and grammar check, see "Correcting Spelling and Grammatical Errors," p. 95.*

Figure 2.25
Display readability statistics about a document at the end of the
spelling and grammar check.

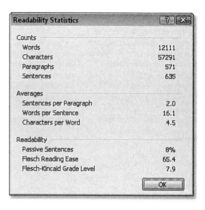

Viewing Word Count

Many a student struggling to come up with a 1,000-word essay has appreciated Word's ability to do
a quick word count!

Word count statistics are similar to readability statistics, in that they have some measurements in
common. However, whereas readability statistics are evaluative, word count statistics are simply
numeric counts of various items (pages, words, characters excluding spaces, characters including
spaces, paragraphs, and lines). See Figure 2.26.

To display the document's statistics, display the Review tab and click the Word Count button.

Figure 2.26
Word count statistics.

Controlling Hyphenation

When a long word does not quite fit at the right edge of a paragraph, it wraps to the next line, and
you end up with a short line of text. In a paragraph where some lines are dramatically shorter than
others, the right margin can look distractingly ragged.

Employing hyphenation can help. When the word is allowed to break at a hyphenation point, the
paragraph's right edge looks more uniform, and you can fit more text on the page. Figure 2.27
shows the difference.

When designing science experiments for middle school students, it is important that activities be not only educational and utilize modern scientific methods, but also fun and interesting to the average young teenager. Experiments that involve everyday objects combined in unusual ways are often very successful.

When designing science experiments for middle school students, it is important that activities be not only educational and utilize modern scientific methods, but also fun and interesting to the average young teenager. Experiments that involve everyday objects combined in unusual ways are often very successful.

Figure 2.27
A paragraph with hyphenation (left) and without hyphenation (right).

Word has two types of hyphenation: automatic and manual. Automatic hyphenation applies a uniform set of hyphenation rules, whereas manual hyphenation provides more control on a case-by-case basis.

Enabling or Disabling Automatic Hyphenation

To turn on automatic hyphenation for a document, display the Page Layout tab and then choose Hyphenation, Automatic. To turn hyphenation off, choose Hyphenation, None.

To fine-tune the hyphenation settings, choose Hyphenation, Hyphenation Options. The Hyphenation dialog box appears, shown in Figure 2.28. From here you can set the following:

- **Automatically Hyphenate Document**—This is the same as choosing Hyphenation, Automatic from the menu.

- **Hyphenate Words in CAPS**—Many times all-caps words are acronyms, which should not be hyphenated. (By default this setting is off.) Mark this check box to override the default behavior.

- **Hyphenation Zone**—The default zone is one-quarter-inch from the right margin. If the last word of the line ends further to the left than that, it becomes a candidate for hyphenation. You can adjust that measurement to allow more or less leniency in applying hyphenation.

- **Limit Consecutive Hyphens To**—When multiple lines in a row have hyphenated words at the end, that's called stacking, and most professional layout/typesetting people try to avoid it because it looks bad. You can set this value to the maximum number of consecutive lines that can be hyphenated if desired.

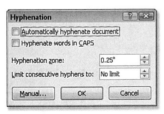

Figure 2.28
Fine-tune automatic hyphenation settings here.

Turning Off Automatic Hyphenation for Specific Text

If there is a specific part of the document that you *don't* want to hyphenate, do the following to exclude a paragraph (or more) from the hyphenation setting:

1. Select the paragraph(s) to affect.

2. On the Home tab, click the dialog box launcher in the bottom-right corner of the Paragraph group, opening the Paragraph dialog box.

3. On the Line and Page Breaks tab, mark the Don't Hyphenate check box (see Figure 2.29).

4. Click OK.

Figure 2.29
You can exclude certain paragraphs from hyphenation via the Paragraph dialog box.

Click here to turn off hyphenation for the selected text.

Hyphenating a Document Manually

Manual hyphenation works by inserting discretionary hyphens in certain words. A discretionary hyphen is one that *can* appear if the word happens to fall near the end of a line and needs to be hyphenated, but otherwise does not appear. Discretionary hyphens are better than hyphens you would type with the minus key because if you happen to add or remove text that makes the paragraph line breaks shift, you aren't stuck with extraneous hyphens to try to track down and delete.

To manually hyphenate a document, follow these steps:

1. On the Page Layout tab, choose Hyphenation, Manual. The Manual Hyphenation dialog box appears, showing the first word that is a candidate for hyphenation.

   In the Hyphenate At box (shown in Figure 2.30), all the available hyphen points for the word are shown with hyphens in them; the suggested hyphenation point is highlighted.

Figure 2.30
Evaluate the hyphenation suggestion for the word.

2. Do one of the following:

   - Click Yes to accept the default hyphenation point for the word.

   - Click one of the other hyphens in the word to select it as the preferred hyphenation point, and then click Yes.

   - Click No to decline to hyphenate that word.

3. Continue evaluating words until the Hyphenation Is Complete message appears; then click OK.

You can also insert discretionary hyphens into words as symbols, unrelated to the hyphenation feature. To do so, click where you want to place a discretionary hyphen in a word and then press Ctrl+– (that is, hold down Ctrl and type a minus sign). Alternatively, on the Insert tab, choose Symbol, More Symbols. On the Special Characters tab, click Optional Hyphen and then click Insert.

 caution

Words that have been manually hyphenated might be flagged as possible spelling errors (wavy red underline). They are not really errors, of course, and "correcting" them removes the discretionary hyphens.

Inserting Dummy Text

Dummy text is generic text that is inserted so that you can see the document's formatting. This is especially useful when creating multicolumn frame-based layouts such as in a brochure or newsletter.

Different applications use different words for dummy text; some programs repeat the same sentence over and over, use nonsense words, or use Greek phrases. (The latter is an inside joke born of the fact that in typesetting, when lines are placed where text will eventually go, it's called *greeking*, as in "It's all Greek to me.")

Word 2010, however, has real English language paragraphs that it uses, and they even make sense! Word uses three paragraphs with text that discusses the galleries feature. If you insert more than three paragraphs, they start repeating.

To insert dummy text, you use a random function such as the following, where p represents the desired number of paragraphs:

=rand(*p*)

You just type this directly into the document, and when you press Enter, Word replaces what you typed with the paragraphs.

By default, each paragraph has three sentences in it. If you want more or fewer sentences per paragraph, add another argument to the function, like this:

=rand(*p,s*)

Here, s is the desired number of sentences. For example, to get eight paragraphs with four sentences each, use

=rand(8,4)

 caution

This function works only when it is typed as a paragraph all to itself. It doesn't work when typed as part of an existing paragraph or at any position other than the beginning of a paragraph.

Working with Building Blocks

Building blocks are stored snippets that can contain formatted text, graphics, and other objects. You can insert them into any document at any time. Another name for building blocks is *AutoText*, and some sections of the program use that term instead; both refer to the same thing.

Building blocks are categorized by their function and are organized in *galleries*. The gallery in which a building block is stored is a matter of preference, but different galleries do show up in different places in the program. For example, if you place a building block in the Quick Parts category, it appears on the Quick Parts drop-down list on the Insert tab.

Building blocks are stored in templates. To make a block accessible to all new documents based on Normal.dotm, you can store it in that template. Alternatively, you can store a building block in a template called Building Blocks.dotx, designed specifically for holding them. The Building Blocks.dotx template is always available, no matter what template is applied to the body of the document.

 note

The difference in file extensions between the two templates is part of Word 2010's system of file naming. A .dotm template supports macros; a .dotx template does not.

Creating a Building Block

A building block can contain text (formatted or unformatted); graphics; objects such as text frames, diagrams, or WordArt; and more. Anything you create in Word can be saved in a building block.

To create a building block, first create the content and then do the following:

1. Select all the content that should be included in the document part.

2. On the Insert tab, choose Quick Parts, Save Selection to Quick Part Gallery. The Create New Building Block dialog box opens (see Figure 2.31).

 tip

If you choose Quick Parts, AutoText, Save Selection to AutoText Gallery instead in step 2, the same procedure applies except that in step 4, the gallery is set to AutoText rather than Quick Parts.

Figure 2.31
Create a new
building block
and specify
which gallery it
belongs to.

3. In the Name box, change the default name if desired. This name appears on lists of building blocks. By default, the name is the first few words of the text.

4. Change the Gallery setting if desired.

   By default, the Gallery is set to Quick Parts. Items placed in this gallery are accessible via the Quick Parts menu, so they are convenient. However, if you add too many items to the Quick Parts gallery, it might become unwieldy to work with the list. Various galleries are used for features you will learn about in other chapters throughout the book, including headers and footers, page numbers, and cover pages.

5. (Optional) Assign a category to the item. You can stick with the default General category or choose Create New Category to build your own system of categories.

6. Type a description of the building block in the Description box if desired.

7. Change the Save In setting if desired. The default is Building Blocks.dotx.

8. Select the desired insertion method from the Options list:

   - **Insert content only**—Places the item at the insertion point.

   - **Insert content in its own paragraph**—Places the item in a separate paragraph.

   - **Insert content in its own page**—Places the item on a new page.

9. Click OK to create the new building block entry.

The new building block is now available for insertion, as explained in the next section.

> **tip**
> The items in Building Blocks.dotx are available via the Building Blocks Organizer regardless of what template is in use.

Inserting a Building Block

A building block's insertion method depends on the gallery in which you placed it when you created it. If you chose to place it in the Quick Parts gallery, it appears on the Quick Parts list. If you chose to place it in the AutoText gallery, point to AutoText and then select it from the AutoText submenu's list. See Figure 2.32.

Items you add to the AutoText gallery
appear on that command's submenu.

Items you add to the Quick Parts gallery
appear on the top level of the menu.

Figure 2.32
Building blocks
appear on dif-
ferent menus
depending on
the gallery in
which they
were placed.

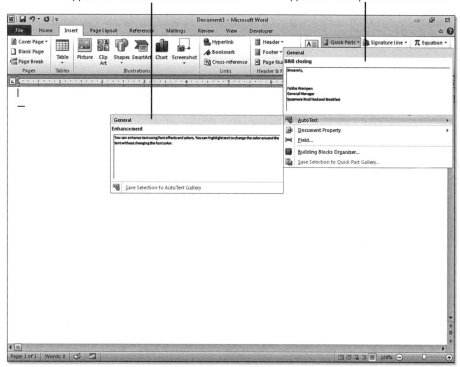

If the desired building block does not appear in either location,
you can select it from the Building Blocks Organizer, as follows:

1. From the Insert tab, click Quick Parts and then click Building
   Blocks Organizer. The Building Blocks Organizer dialog box
   appears.

2. Click an item to preview it (see Figure 2.33).

3. When you find the item you want to insert, click Insert.

4. When you are finished inserting blocks, click Close.

 note

You might have some different
building blocks than shown in Figure
2.33. If you upgraded from Word
2003 or earlier, for example, you will
have some of the Microsoft-supplied
AutoText entries from your old version available.

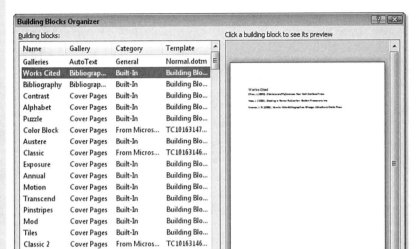

Figure 2.33
Insert an item from the Building Blocks Organizer.

The Building Blocks.dotx File Is Corrupted

If you see a warning about the Building Blocks.dotx file being missing or corrupted, click OK. If asked whether you want to recover the data from the file, choose No. Then close Word, and use Windows to search for the file Building Blocks.dotx. Delete all instances of that file and reopen Word. Word then regenerates a fresh copy of the file. You lose any building blocks you have created, however.

Deleting Building Blocks

You can delete any building blocks, both those that you have created and those stored in the Building Blocks.dotx template that comes with Word. To delete a building block, follow these steps:

1. From the Insert tab, choose Quick Parts, Building Blocks Organizer. The Building Blocks Organizer dialog box appears.

2. Click the item to delete.

3. Click the Delete button.

4. When you are finished deleting blocks, click Close.

Changing a Building Block's Properties

All of a building block's properties are editable, including its gallery and its template location. Follow these steps to edit building block properties:

1. From the Insert tab, choose Quick Parts, Building Blocks Organizer. The Building Blocks Organizer dialog box appears.

2. Click the item and then click Edit Properties. The Modify Building Block dialog box opens. It is much the same as the dialog box you used to create the building block initially (refer to Figure 2.31).

3. Make any changes as needed, and then click OK.

4. A confirmation box appears; click Yes.

3

CORRECTING AND PRINTING DOCUMENTS

Correcting Spelling and Grammatical Errors

Word has a built-in, automatic spelling and grammar checker that compares every word and sentence to a built-in dictionary and grammar guide and then lets you know which words, phrases, and sentences are questionable—not necessarily wrong, but worthy of a second look.

There are two ways of checking spelling and grammar in a document. You can check individual words and phrases on a case-by-case basis, or you can run a complete spelling and grammar check of the entire document. Each technique is explained separately in the following sections.

Checking the Spelling of an Individual Word

In an open text document, a wavy red or blue underline (nonprinting) indicates a word that Word can't identify. It might be misspelled, or it simply might not be in Word's dictionaries for some reason.

The difference between the red and the blue underlines is context. A red underlined word is not in the dictionary at all. For example, in the following sentence, *luse* would be red-underlined:

> You've got nothing to luse.

A blue underline represents a word that is in the dictionary but might be used improperly in its current context. For example, in the following sentence, *loose* would be blue-underlined:

> You've got nothing to loose.

Right-click a red-underlined or blue-underlined word to see a menu, as shown in Figure 3.1, that contains these options:

- **Spelling corrections**—These are suggestions for the spelling correction. Click a suggestion to apply it. If the correct spelling for the word does not appear on the list, you can manually edit the word, as you would any other text in the document.

- **Ignore**—Ignores only this instance in the current document. The word is still flagged elsewhere in the document.

- **Ignore All**—Ignores this and all other instances of the word within the current document only. The word is still flagged in other documents.

- **Add to Dictionary**—Adds the word to the custom dictionary so that it is not flagged in future documents (or in any instances in the current document). This one is not available for blue-underlined words.

- **AutoCorrect**—Opens a submenu containing all the words that were suggested at the top of the menu so that you can quickly set up an AutoCorrect entry that always changes your misspelling to that word. This option does not appear if there are no spelling suggestions on the list or if the word is blue-underlined.

➡ *To learn more about AutoCorrect settings, see "Automating Corrections with AutoCorrect," p. 110.*

Word Marks Passages of Text as the Wrong Language

This is actually fairly common. Word decides for some reason that a passage of text in U.S. English is actually in UK English and marks it as such. It's not a huge problem, but it does prevent the spelling checker from identifying words that use British spellings rather than American.

One way around this problem is to mark the entire document as U.S. English and then prevent Word from identifying the language of future passages. Here's how:

1. Select the entire document.

2. On the Review tab, choose Language, Set Proofing Language.

3. In the Language dialog box, choose the desired language—in this case, English (U.S.).

4. Click the Set as Default button. A confirmation box appears.

5. Click Yes to confirm that you want the chosen language to be the default.

6. Clear the Detect Language Automatically check box.

7. Click OK.

Figure 3.1
Right-click a red-underlined word to get spelling assistance for it.

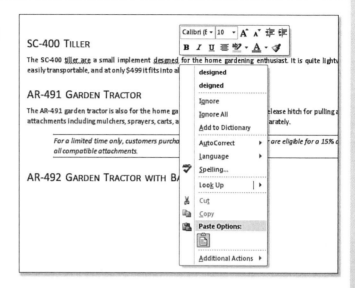

- **Language**—Enables you to set a different language for the word so that it will be evaluated using a different dictionary (if you have multiple language dictionaries installed).

- **Spelling**—Opens the Spelling dialog box, discussed fully in the next section.

- **Look Up**—Opens the Research pane, which provides information from various reference sources such as dictionaries.

> *To learn more about the Research tools in Word, see "Using Research Tools," p. 117.*

It's important to note that a red-underlined word is not always wrong. It's just not in any of the dictionaries that Word consulted. It could be a proper name, such as the name of a person or product, or it could be a model number, serial number, or some other type of code.

Fixing Individual Grammatical Errors

A possible error in grammar or punctuation appears with a green wavy underline. Word finds many types of grammatical errors, ranging from double punctuation (such as two commas in a row) to a lack of subject/verb agreement.

Right-clicking a green-underlined phrase produces a shortcut menu with one or more grammar suggestions or options. The exact content of the menu depends on the type of error, but as shown in Figure 3.2, here are some of the options you might see:

- **Grammar corrections**—These are suggestions for the grammar correction. Click a suggestion to apply it.

- **Ignore Once**—Ignores the grammar rule in this instance but continues to check for this grammar rule elsewhere in the document.

Figure 3.2
Right-click a green-underlined phrase to get grammar help.

- **Grammar**—Opens the Grammar dialog box, described in the next section.

- **About This Sentence**—Opens a Help window explaining the grammar rule that is (perhaps) being violated.

- **Look Up**—Opens the Research pane, which provides information from various reference sources such as dictionaries.

Word is good at finding possible errors and suggesting corrections, but it can't substitute for a human proofreader. Grammar is a lot more subjective than spelling, and Word makes more mistakes with grammar. In some cases, it even suggests changes that will make the grammar out-and-out wrong. If you don't know whether something is grammatically correct, don't take Word's word for it; look it up or ask a friend.

Performing an Interactive Spelling and Grammar Check

An interactive spelling and grammar check can save some time when you have a large document to check. It uses a dialog box interface to jump to each possible spelling and grammatical error, one by one, so you don't have to scroll through the document looking for the red and green underlines.

To perform an interactive check, follow these steps:

1. Display the Review tab and click Spelling & Grammar to open the Spelling and Grammar dialog box. (F7 is a shortcut.)

2. (Optional) To perform only a spell check (not grammar too), clear the Check Grammar check box.

3. If a spelling error is found, examine the word that appears in red in the Not in Dictionary box (see Figure 3.3). Then do one of the following to respond to it:

- Click Ignore Once to skip this instance but continue to flag other instances in the current document.

- Click Ignore All to ignore this and all instances of the word in the current document.

- Click Add to Dictionary to add the word to the custom dictionary.

- Click a word on the Suggestions list and then click Change to change this one instance only to the chosen word, or click Change All to change all instances.

- Click in the Not in Dictionary box to move the insertion point into it, type a correction there manually, and then click the Change button.

- Click a word on the Suggestions list and then click AutoCorrect to create an AutoCorrect entry for it.

Figure 3.3
Check spelling via the Spelling and Grammar dialog box.

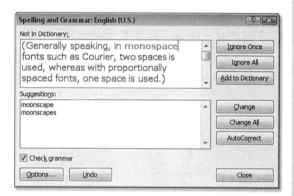

4. If a grammatical error is found, examine the phrase that appears in green in the Grammatical Error box (see Figure 3.4) and then do one of the following to respond to it:

- Click Ignore Once to skip this instance but continue to flag other instances in the current document.

- Click Ignore Rule to ignore this and all instances of the grammar rule in the current document.

- Click Next Sentence to skip this sentence, not making changes.

- Click a suggestion in the Suggestions list and then click Change to change this instance as recommended. If no automatically applicable suggestion is available (for example, if the suggestion is to revise the sentence so that it is no longer a fragment), the Change button is unavailable.

- Click Explain to see a Help window with a description of the error found.

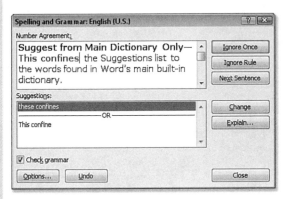

Figure 3.4
Check grammar via the Spelling and Grammar dialog box.

5. Continue the spelling and grammar check until you've checked the entire document, or click Cancel or Close to end the check early.

Finding Proofing Errors

When a document contains one or more spelling errors, the Proofing Errors icon appears in the status bar, as shown in Figure 3.5. Click that icon to jump to the first error (starting at the current insertion point position) and display a shortcut menu with suggestions of how to deal with it. It's like doing a Search for red and green wavy underlines.

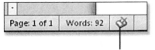

Proofing Errors Icon

Figure 3.5
Click the Proofing Errors icon on the status bar to jump to an error and see suggestions for correcting it.

When no more proofing errors exist in the document, the button changes to a No Proofing Errors one (a blue check mark).

Customizing Spelling and Grammar Options

The spelling and grammar checker is customizable. For example, you can choose not to check certain types of words (such as words in all uppercase or those that contain numbers), you can turn the wavy red and green underlines on and off, and much more. You can even specify a level of "strictness" for the grammar checker to enforce.

To access the spelling and grammar options, choose File, Options and then click Proofing (see Figure 3.6).

Figure 3.6
Control spelling and grammar settings in the Word Options dialog box.

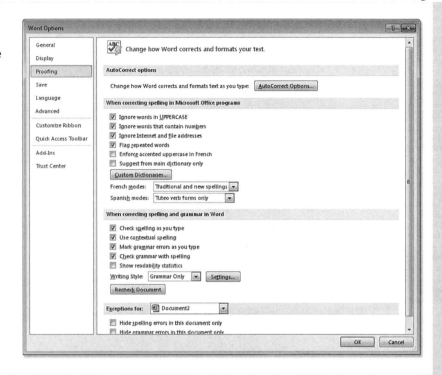

 To learn more about AutoCorrect settings, see "Automating Corrections with AutoCorrect," p. 110.

Basic spelling options are found in the When Correcting Spelling in Microsoft Office Programs section. These are applied globally in all Office applications (Word, Excel, PowerPoint, and so on):

> **tip**
> You can also access the spelling and grammar options from the Spelling and Grammar dialog box (or the individual Spelling or Grammar boxes) by clicking the Options button.

- **Ignore Words in UPPERCASE**—This refers to words that are all-uppercase, not just words that begin with a capital letter.

- **Ignore Words That Contain Numbers**—This refers to words that contain digits, such as *BR549*, not words that spell out numbers, such as *sixteen*.

- **Ignore Internet and File Addresses**—This excludes URLs, email addresses, and file paths (such as C:\Windows) from being checked.

- **Flag Repeated Words**—This marks a possible misspelling when the same word appears twice in a row.

- **Enforce Accented Uppercase in French**—This marks a possible misspelling in text marked as French when uppercase letters that normally require accents do not have them.

- **Suggest from Main Dictionary Only**—This confines the Suggestions list to the words found in Word's main built-in dictionary. Any words you have added to the custom dictionary are not suggested.

- **Custom Dictionaries**—This opens the Custom Dictionaries dialog box.

- **Modes**—You can customize French and Spanish modes via their corresponding drop-down lists.

➡ *To learn how to mark a passage of text as French or any other language, see "Checking Spelling and Grammar in Multiple Languages," p. 109.*

➡ *To work with custom dictionaries, see "Managing the Spelling Dictionaries," p. 104.*

The When Correcting Spelling and Grammar in Word section's options are specific to Word only:

- **Check Spelling As You Type**—Turn this off to stop Word from checking spelling (and red-underlining words) on the fly. To check spelling when this is turned off, you must use the interactive spelling and grammar check (F7).

- **Use Contextual Spelling**—Turn this off to stop Word from blue-underlining words that might be used improperly in the current context.

- **Mark Grammar Errors As You Type**—Turn this off to stop Word from checking grammar (and green-underlining words and phrases) on the fly. To check grammar when this is turned off, you must use the interactive spelling and grammar check (F7).

- **Check Grammar with Spelling**—Turn this off to stop Word from checking grammar when using the Spelling and Grammar dialog box.

- **Show Readability Statistics**—Turn this on to display a box with readability information at the end of a spelling and grammar check with the Spelling and Grammar dialog box.

- **Writing Style**—Set the level of grammar check you want here; you can have it check for grammar only, or also check stylistic conventions. Examples of style issues include contractions, clichés, commonly misspelled words, and unclear phrasing. (To fine-tune these settings, see the next section.)

- **Recheck Document**—Click this button to run the spelling and grammar check again after changing the grammar settings to see if any additional errors or concerns are flagged.

The Exceptions For section enables you to select any open document from the drop-down list and then set these options:

- **Hide Spelling Errors in This Document Only**—This does not turn off the spell checking as you type, but it does prevent the wavy red underlines from appearing onscreen.

- **Hide Grammar Errors in This Document Only**—Same thing. It does not turn off the grammar checking as you type, but it suppresses the green underlines.

Customizing Grammar and Style Rules

It can be really annoying when Word insists on marking a certain grammatical or stylistic convention as "wrong" when you know it's right. To avoid situations like that, you can adjust the grammar and style rule application settings to match the way you want to write.

The grammar settings are controlled from the Proofing tab of the Word Options dialog box, which you saw in Figure 3.6. Choose File, Options, click Proofing, and then scroll down to the When Correcting Spelling and Grammar in Word section, and click the Settings button. The Grammar Settings dialog box appears, as in Figure 3.7.

Figure 3.7
Fine-tune the grammar and style settings to your specifications here.

In the Grammar Settings dialog box, open the Writing Style list and select the writing style to customize—either Grammar Only or Grammar & Style.

Then in the Require section, turn on any of the checks you want to use:

- **Comma Required Before Last List Item**—This is called the "serial comma" in the professional editing world. When you have three or more items in a list, some writing styles (such as in academic writing) prescribe a comma between the last two, like this: *bread, butter, and milk.* In other writing styles (such as journalism), the comma is omitted, like this: *bread, butter and milk.* Because style conventions vary, Word's default is not to check this. Your other choices are Always and Never.

- **Punctuation Required with Quotes**—Some writing styles prescribe that punctuation should fall within the quotation mark when both occur at the end of a sentence, like this: Tom is "angry at his father." In other writing styles, the punctuation falls outside the quotes. Your choices here are Don't Check, Inside, and Outside. (Inside is the more common convention.)

- **Spaces Required Between Sentences**—Some writing styles prescribe one blank space between sentences; others prescribe two. (Generally speaking, in monospace fonts such as Courier, two spaces is used, whereas with proportionally spaced fonts, one space is used.) You can choose 1 or 2 here to make Word enforce one convention or the other.

In the Grammar section, clear the check boxes for any of the options you don't want. They are all marked by default.

In the Style section, mark or clear check boxes as desired. They are almost all marked if you chose Grammar & Style as the writing style setting; they are all cleared if you chose Grammar Only.

After making the changes to the settings, click OK to close the Grammar Settings dialog box. Then, back in the Word Options dialog box, click the Proofing tab and click Recheck Document to check it using the new settings you just specified.

Managing the Spelling Dictionaries

The main dictionary in Word is not editable, so when you add words to the dictionary, those words have to be stored somewhere else. That's where custom dictionaries come into the picture.

The default custom dictionary is a plaintext file called custom.dic, stored in the \Users\ *username*\ AppData\Roaming\Microsoft\UProof folder (Windows Vista or Windows 7) or the \Documents and Settings\ *username*\Application Data\Microsoft\UProof folder (Windows XP). Because it is stored in the folder set for the individual user logged into the PC, it is available only to that one user; each user has his own custom.dic file.

If you happen to have a custom.dic file in the \Users\ *username*\AppData\Roaming\Microsoft\ Proof folder (Windows Vista or Windows 7) or the \Documents and Settings\ *username*\Application Data\Microsoft\Proof folder in Windows XP (that's Proof, not UProof), it's a leftover file from an earlier version of Word. The custom.dic file for Word 2010 was created based on that older file when you upgraded, but any changes you've made to the custom dictionary in Word 2010 since then are reflected only in the copy in the UProof folder.

Adding Flagged Words to the Custom Dictionary

To add a word that has been identified as a possible error to Custom.dic, right-click the red-underlined word and choose Add to Dictionary, or in the Spelling and Grammar dialog box, click Add to Dictionary.

Editing a Custom Dictionary's Word List

You can also add words to a custom dictionary (such as Custom.dic) without having them appear in the document. Here's how to do this:

1. Choose File, Options.

2. Click Proofing.

3. Click Custom Dictionaries.

4. Select the desired custom dictionary from the list. As shown in Figure 3.8, only one dictionary appears (custom.dic).

Figure 3.8
Edit custom dictionaries from the Custom Dictionaries dialog box.

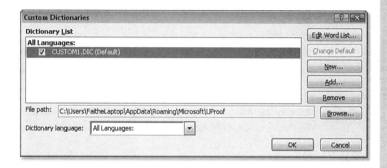

5. Click Edit Word List. A dialog box appears listing all the words currently in that dictionary.

6. To add a new word, type it in the Word(s) box and click Add. Words can be no longer than 64 characters.

7. To delete a word, select it and click Delete. To clear the entire dictionary, click Delete All.

8. Click OK three times to close all open dialog boxes when you are finished editing the custom dictionary.

Changing the Associated Language for a Custom Dictionary

By default, a custom dictionary's language is set to All Languages, meaning that Word uses it no matter what language is specified for the text. You can limit a dictionary's use to a certain language by changing its Dictionary Language setting in the Custom Dictionaries dialog box (refer to Figure 3.8).

> *To specify the language to be used when checking a block of text, see "Checking Spelling and Grammar in Multiple Languages," p. 109.*

Adding Many Words at Once to a Custom Dictionary

The procedure in the preceding section adds only one word at a time. If you have a lot of words to add, the process can be really tedious. You might instead prefer to manually edit the custom dictionary file from outside of Word. Dictionary files are plaintext files with one word per line, so they are

---

⚠ caution

Type only one word per entry; multiword entries are accepted but are entered that way in the list, and spellings consisting of only part of the entry are not recognized. For example, you could enter Roberto Sanchez, but the spell-checker would not recognize Roberto or Sanchez by itself. On the other hand, if you enter them as separate words, Word accepts them either separately or together

easy to edit in the Windows Notepad. You can even combine two or more dictionary files into a single file by copying and pasting lists of words between them.

To manually edit a dictionary file, follow these steps:

1. Exit Word and use Windows Explorer (click Start, Computer) to browse to the folder containing the dictionary files:

   In Windows XP: \Documents and Settings*username*\Application Data\Microsoft\UProof.

   In Windows Vista or Windows 7: \Users*username*\AppData\Roaming\Microsoft\UProof.

2. Right-click the dictionary file to edit (such as CUSTOM.DIC) and choose Open. (If needed, select Notepad as the program with which to open it.) The file opens in Notepad (see Figure 3.9). The word list will be different from what's shown in Figure 3.9 depending on what words you have added.

3. Edit the list, deleting and adding words as desired. Copy words from other files if needed.

4. Choose File, Exit. When prompted to save your changes, click Yes (or Save).

Figure 3.9
If you have a lot of words to add or delete, you can often edit custom dictionary files more expediently in Notepad.

Creating a New Custom Dictionary

A custom dictionary can contain a maximum of 5,000 words and can be no larger than 64KB in file size. If you need a larger custom dictionary, create another dictionary.

You might also want to create additional custom dictionaries to keep sets of words separate for different projects. For example, suppose you are doing work for a client that uses an alternative spelling for certain words. You don't want those words marked in documents for that client, but you do want them marked in documents for all other clients. You can create a custom dictionary just for that client and then enable/disable that dictionary as appropriate for the current document. You might even write a macro that enables and disables that custom dictionary, and you can assign a shortcut key combination to it.

➡ To enable or disable a dictionary, see "Enabling and Disabling Custom Dictionaries," p. 107. To record a macro, see "Recording a Macro," p. 836.

Follow these steps to create a custom dictionary:

1. Choose File, Options.

2. Click Proofing and then click Custom Dictionaries.

3. Click New.

4. When the Create Custom Dictionary dialog box appears, navigate to the location where you want to store the dictionary. Here are some recommendations:

   - To make the dictionary accessible to all users of the PC, store it in C:\Program Files\ Microsoft Office\Office14\Dictionaries. If the folder does not already exist, create it.

   - To make the dictionary accessible to only the current Windows user, store it here:

     In Windows XP: \Documents and Settings*username*\Application Data\Microsoft\UProof.

     In Windows Vista or Windows 7: \Users*username*\AppData\Roaming\Microsoft\UProof.

     As long as Word knows where you have stored the dictionary, you can put it anywhere you like; the preceding locations are just suggestions.

5. Type a name for the dictionary in the File Name box.

6. Click Save.

The new dictionary now appears on the Dictionary List in the Custom Dictionaries dialog box.

> To add someone else's dictionary file to your copy of Word, see "Adding an Existing Custom Dictionary to Word," 108.

Enabling and Disabling Custom Dictionaries

All spell checks use the main dictionary plus all the dictionaries that are selected on the Dictionary List. To disable a certain dictionary from being used, clear its check box in the Custom Dictionaries dialog box (refer to Figure 3.8).

Setting the Default Custom Dictionary

All enabled custom dictionaries are checked automatically during the spell-checking process, but newly added words are placed only in the default custom dictionary. To set the default dictionary, select a custom dictionary in the Custom Dictionaries dialog box and then click the Change Default button.

Using an Exclusion Dictionary

With an exclusion dictionary, you can specify words that appear in the main dictionary that you nevertheless want to be flagged as possible misspellings. An exclusion dictionary is the opposite of a custom dictionary, in that it forces normally correct words to be considered incorrect.

For example, perhaps your company has a product with an unusual spelling that's similar to a common word in the dictionary, like *Tek*. Because your employees commonly forget about the unusual spelling and write *Tech* instead, you might add *Tech* to the exclusion dictionary so Word will flag it as a potential misspelling. That way the writer can take a second look at each instance to ensure that it is correct.

The default exclusion dictionary is named ExcludeDictionaryEN0409.lex (for U.S. English versions). If you delete this file, Word re-creates it the next time you start the program. By default, the file is empty, but you can add words to it as follows:

1. From Windows, navigate to this folder:

   In Windows XP: \Documents and Settings*username*\Application Data\Microsoft\UProof.

   In Windows Vista or Windows 7: \Users*username*\AppData\Roaming\Microsoft\UProof.

2. Open ExcludeDictionaryEN0409.lex in Notepad. (See the following sidebar for help with that if needed.) If you haven't already modified this file, it is empty.

3. Type the words you want to exclude, one per line.

4. Save and close the file.

Opening a .lex File in Notepad

If you have previously opened .lex files in Notepad on this computer, you can simply right-click the ExcludeDictionaryEN0409.lex file and choose Edit.

If the Edit command does not appear on the right-click menu, you need to set up Notepad as the default application for editing .lex files. To do this:

1. On the right-click menu, choose Open With.

2. Click Select a Program from a List of Installed Programs and click OK.

3. Click Notepad and click OK.

Adding an Existing Custom Dictionary to Word

You can download new dictionaries from the Microsoft Office website and also buy them from third-party sources. For example, you can purchase dictionaries for medical, pharmaceutical, legal, and academic writing, sparing you the trouble of adding the many words unique to that profession individually to custom dictionaries.

When you get a new dictionary, you must then integrate it into Word. You must also do this for each Word user if you want to share a dictionary among multiple users. For example, log in as one local Windows user, make the change in Word, log out, log in as someone else and repeat, and so on.

To add an existing dictionary to Word, follow these steps:

1. Outside of Word, copy the custom dictionary file where you want it. If only one user should be able to access it, copy it here:

   In Windows XP: \Documents and Settings*username*\Application Data\Microsoft\UProof.

   In Windows Vista or Windows 7: \Users*username*\AppData\Roaming\Microsoft\UProof.

   If it should be accessible to multiple users, copy it to C:\Program Files\Microsoft Office\Office14\Dictionaries. (If the folder is not already there, add it.)

2. In Word, choose File, Options.

3. Click Proofing and then click Custom Dictionaries.

4. Click Add. The Add Custom Dictionary dialog box opens.

5. Navigate to the folder containing the dictionary to be added and select it.

6. Click Open. The dictionary appears on the Dictionary List in the Custom Dictionaries dialog box.

To remove a custom dictionary from the list, select it and click Remove. This does not delete the dictionary file; it only removes it from the listing in Word.

Checking Spelling and Grammar in Multiple Languages

By default, the spelling and grammar check is performed in the native language for your copy of Word. For example, if you bought your copy of Word in the United States, English (U.S.) is the default language.

The country designation is significant because many languages have slightly different spelling and grammar rules in other countries. For example, in the United Kingdom (UK), words such as *realize* and *customize* are spelled with an *s* instead of *z* (*realise* and *customise*). Word 2010 has default AutoCorrect entries that change those words (and others) to the U.S. spellings, so if you specifically need the UK spellings, you need to mark the text as being in a different national language.

When you right-click a spelling error, one of the choices on the menu is Language. It opens a sub-menu from which you can select the desired language module to check the word. At first there is only one language module on the list, but you can easily add others.

To add a language, follow these steps:

1. Select the text that should be checked in a different language.

2. On the Review tab, click the Language button and then click Set Proofing Language.

3. In the Language dialog box, select the desired language. Languages for which support is installed on your PC are indicated by a check mark icon, as shown in Figure 3.10. (The English-language versions of Word include support for all variants of English, Spanish, and French; you can buy additional language packs separately.)

Figure 3.10
Choose a language to be made available for spell checking.

4. (Optional) If you want Word to simply ignore the selected text, mark the Do Not Check Spelling or Grammar check box. Otherwise, Word attempts to check the text using the rules defined for the chosen language.

5. (Optional) If you want Word to try to detect languages and mark text passages with the correct language automatically, leave the Detect Language Automatically check box marked.

6. (Optional) To make a different language the default for future spell checks (including those in all new documents based on the Normal.dotm template), select it and click the Default button.

7. Click OK.

 tip

Detect Language Automatically sounds like a good idea, but Word makes mistakes in identification. If you find that passages in U.S. English are not getting properly checked because Word is misidentifying them as some other variant of English, for example, you might want to turn that option off.

The text is now marked as being in the chosen language.

Automating Corrections with AutoCorrect

AutoCorrect is a service that automatically replaces all instances of a certain text string with another. There are many uses for AutoCorrect, several of which you've seen in previous chapters. For example, you can quickly insert symbols with AutoCorrect, such as by typing (r) for the ® symbol. AutoCorrect also works with the spelling checker to automatically fix common misspellings, as you saw earlier in the chapter.

AutoCorrect isn't a command you need to explicitly issue; it happens automatically. You can set its options or turn it off, though, and you can manage the list of AutoCorrect entries.

Rejecting an Automatic Correction

When an automatic correction occurs, a small blue box appears when you rest your mouse pointer near the text. Point to the blue box, and an AutoCorrect Options button appears. Click that button, and a menu opens, as shown in Figure 3.11. From here, you can do the following:

- Change back to the original usage for this instance only.

- Stop correcting this particular word or phrase. Choosing this adds the word or phrase to the Exceptions list, covered in the next section.

- Open the AutoCorrect Options dialog box, also covered in the next section.

You might see other options too, depending on the type of correction that was made.

There are also shortcut keys you can use for rejecting an automatic correction. They all appear to do the same thing, but there is a difference:

- Ctrl+Z (Undo) undoes the correction, but Word does not remember that preference.

- Backspace or the left-arrow key undoes the correction and adds it to the Exceptions list.

Figure 3.11
The AutoCorrect Options button appears next to an automatic correction in the document.

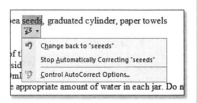

For Backspace or the left-arrow key to add items to the Exceptions list, you must mark the Automatically Add Words to List check box in the AutoCorrect Exceptions dialog box on the tab for the applicable error type. You'll learn about this in the next section.

Setting AutoCorrect Options

To access the AutoCorrect options (see Figure 3.12), choose File, Options. Click Proofing and then click the AutoCorrect Options button.

Figure 3.12
The AutoCorrect Options button appears next to an automatic correction in the document.

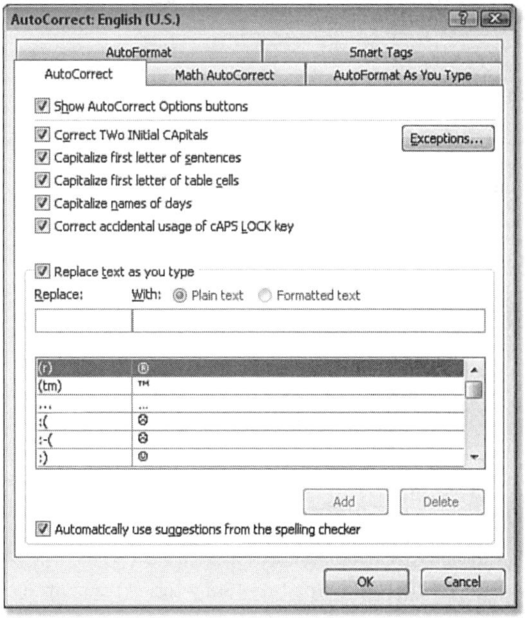

The top portion of the AutoCorrect tab contains check boxes for enabling or disabling certain features:

- **Show AutoCorrect Options Buttons**—Clear this to prevent the AutoCorrect Options button from appearing after an AutoCorrect action (as in Figure 3.11).

- **Correct TWo INitial CApitals**—In a word that starts out with two capital letters and then switches to lowercase, AutoCorrect lowercases the second letter.

- **Capitalize First Letter of Sentences**—AutoCorrect capitalizes the first letter of the first word that comes at the beginning of a paragraph or after a sentence-ending punctuation mark.

- **Capitalize First Letter of Table Cells**—AutoCorrect capitalizes the first letter of the first word in each table cell.

- **Capitalize Names of Days**—AutoCorrect capitalizes days of the week, such as Monday, Tuesday, and so on.

- **Correct Accidental Usage of cAPS LOCK Key**—When this feature is enabled, AutoCorrect notices when you have left the Caps Lock on; it turns it off and corrects the text that was erroneously capitalized.

To set up exceptions to some of the features, click the Exceptions button. The AutoCorrect Exceptions dialog box opens (see Figure 3.13).

Figure 3.13
Manage the exceptions list for automatic corrections.

For each tab, use Add and Delete to manage the list of exceptions. You can type new words or phrases and click Add, or you can select existing items on the lists and click Delete.

- **First Letter tab**—Sometimes the first letter after a sentence-ending punctuation mark (such as a period) should not be capitalized. For example, you would not always want a capitalized first letter after an abbreviation such as *etc.*

- **INitial CAps tab**—Sometimes two initial caps in a row should be left alone. For example, when talking about student *IDs*, it is perfectly proper to capitalize the first two letters.

- **Other Corrections tab**—These are words that Word should not automatically correct, even though they appear on the Replace Text as You Type list. For example, perhaps you want to accept UK spellings of certain words as well as U.S. spellings.

For each tab, mark or clear the Automatically Add Words to List check box. When this is marked, words are added to the appropriate list whenever you press Backspace or the left-arrow key to undo an AutoCorrect operation immediately after it occurs.

The bottom part of the AutoCorrect tab contains a list of AutoCorrect entries. Word comes with a large list of common spelling corrections and symbol insertions. You can add or remove entries from it on your own as well, as the following sections explain.

Changing or Removing an AutoCorrect Entry

Most of the time, the AutoCorrect entries that come with Word are useful, but occasionally you might find one that interferes with your writing. For example, by default (c) is the AutoCorrect entry for the copyright symbol, but Que Corporation, the publisher of this book, happens to use (c) to indicate a heading in a manuscript. Someone working for that employer would want to remove or change the copyright symbol's AutoCorrect entry.

To edit an entry, open the AutoCorrect dialog box, as you learned in the preceding section, and then scroll through the Replace Text as You Type list to locate the desired entry. (You can type the first few letters of the entry in the Replace box to jump to that portion of the list quickly.) When the entry appears in the Replace and With boxes, you can edit the text in either box to change the entry. To remove an entry entirely, select it and click the Delete button.

Adding a Plain Text AutoCorrect Entry

You saw earlier in the chapter how to add an AutoCorrect entry via the Spelling and Grammar checker. When you're correcting the spelling on a word, the AutoCorrect entry appears, offering to make that correction an automatic one.

An alternative is to manually type a new text entry in the AutoCorrect dialog box. Type the text into the Replace box, deleting whatever is already there, and type the desired replacement into the With box (also deleting what is already there). Then click Add to add the entry to the list. This type of entry is a plain text one and is limited to 255 characters.

You can use AutoCorrect not only for simple spelling corrections, but also for inserting blocks of text that you type frequently. For example, you could set up an AutoCorrect entry that replaces your initials in parentheses with your full name. You don't have to use the parentheses, but they help prevent regular typing from unintentionally triggering the automatic correction.

Adding a Formatted or Graphical AutoCorrect Entry

When typing text into the With box for an AutoCorrect entry, there's no way to include formatting, graphics, or line/paragraph breaks. However, using an alternative method, you can create formatted entries that include all these things, plus special characters and symbols that you cannot directly type into the With box.

Follow these steps to create a formatted entry:

1. In a document, type the full text that you want to paste into the With box in an AutoCorrect entry.

2. Select the text (and graphics if desired). There's no need to copy it to the Clipboard.

3. Open the AutoCorrect dialog box (File, Options, Proofing, AutoCorrect Options). The text you selected appears in the With box, as formatted text. (If the Formatted Text option button is not already selected, select it.)

4. In the Replace box, enter the code that should represent the selection. (Avoid using anything that you might type for other reasons.)

5. Click Add.

Configuring Math AutoCorrect

Word 2010 has a whole separate AutoCorrect database for mathematical entries. These entries serve as shortcuts for creating various math-related symbols. For example, instead of hunting around in the Symbol dialog box for the not-equal-to symbol ($\neq$), you could simply type \neq, and Word would automatically AutoCorrect it into that symbol.

To work with math AutoCorrect options, click the Math AutoCorrect tab in the AutoCorrect dialog box (see Figure 3.14).

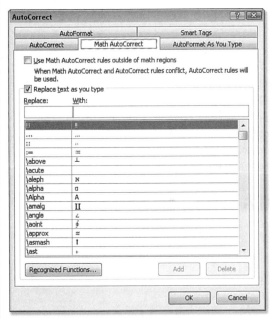

Figure 3.14
Math AutoCorrect is a separate set of AutoCorrect entries that create math symbols.

By default, Math AutoCorrect is in effect only within what Word calls *math regions*, which are areas the Equation Editor creates. You can change this behavior so that Math AutoCorrect entries are universally applied by marking the Use Math AutoCorrect Rules Outside of Math Regions check box. This would be useful, for example, if you were writing a document on the subject of mathematics and needed to discuss certain principles in sentence form.

You can add and remove entries from the Math AutoCorrect tab in the same way you do on the regular AutoCorrect tab.

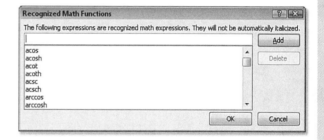 *For more information about the Equation Editor, see "Creating Math Formulas with the Equation Editor," p. 538.*

Within the Equation Editor, any text you type is assumed to be a variable and is therefore italicized. When you are referencing a function, however, you won't want that automatic italicizing to occur. Word maintains a list of recognized functions that are not italicized when they appear as text in an equation. To edit that list, click the Recognized Functions button on the Math AutoCorrect tab. Then in the Recognized Math Functions dialog box (see Figure 3.15), add or remove functions from the list. To add a function, type it and click Add. To remove a function, select it and click Delete.

Figure 3.15
Add or remove function names from the list.
Items on this list are not italicized when used
in the Equation Editor.

Working with Actions

An *action* is an activity you can perform on certain types of selected text in a document. Depending on the text, Word might offer to perform any of a variety of services on that text, such as looking up an address, scheduling a meeting, or getting a stock quote. Actions were called Smart Tags in previous versions of Office.

Here are some of the types of data that can have actions assigned:

- **Addresses**—You can add a contact to Outlook or display a map or driving directions.

- **Dates and times**—You can schedule a meeting in Outlook or display the Outlook calendar.

- **Financial symbols**—You can retrieve stock quotes from MSN MoneyCentral, get company reports, and read news about the company.

- **People**—You can send email or instant messages, schedule meetings, open contact information in Outlook (or create new contact information), and insert addresses.

- **Places**—You can display a map or driving directions.

- **Telephone numbers**—You can add a phone number to an Outlook Contact list entry.

Performing an Action

When you right-click some text, an Additional Actions command appears at the bottom of the context menu. Point to that command to see a fly-out menu that tells you whether any actions are available for that text. For example, in Figure 3.16, a person's name has been right-clicked and Word offers a variety of actions suitable for a person.

Figure 3.16
Right-click some text and choose Additional Actions, and then the appropriate action.

Configuring Action Settings

The specific actions displayed are controlled via the AutoCorrect dialog box. Here you can choose what type(s) of recognizers to use. A *recognizer* is a type of data, such as Date, Financial Symbol, Place, and so on. Follow these steps to configure action settings:

1. Choose File, Options.

2. On the Proofing tab, click AutoCorrect Options.

3. In the AutoCorrect dialog box, click the Actions tab.

4. To turn the action labels on or off as a whole, mark or clear the Enable Additional Actions in the Right-Click Menu check box. (It is on by default.)

5. Place a check mark next to each recognizer type you want to use (see Figure 3.17).

6. Click OK.

Figure 3.17
Choose which recognizers you want to use as actions in your documents.

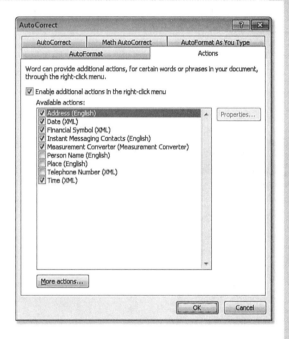

Using Research Tools

In addition to the spelling- and grammar-checking features, Word has a variety of research and translation features that can help you improve your document. These tools are significant because they represent a shift from mechanics to meaning. Not only is Word helping you with the mechanics of your document (such as spelling and punctuation), but it is actually helping you write stronger and more accurate content by helping you choose the right words and present accurate facts and figures.

All the research tools use the same Research pane, and you can switch between them freely within that pane.

You can also use the Research pane in Internet Explorer. From IE, choose View, Explorer Bars, Research.

Checking a Word's Definition with a Dictionary

Word's Research tools include the Encarta Dictionary, which you can use to look up quick definitions of words. Most of Word 2010's research tools, including the dictionaries, rely on the Internet
for their data; these tools do not work very well (or at all in some cases) unless you are online.

To look up a word in the dictionary, follow these steps:

1. Select the word in the document. If you select more than one word, the dictionary looks up only
   the first one.

2. On the Review tab, click Research. The Research pane opens.

3. Open the drop-down list under the Search For box and choose Encarta Dictionary: English
   (North America). Or, if you are in some other part of the world, choose whatever is applicable to
   your location and language.

   Information about the word appears, including its definition, its pronunciation, and its hyphenation, as shown in Figure 3.18.

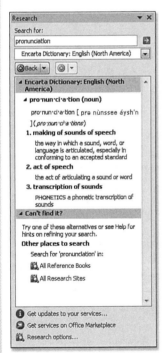

Figure 3.18
Look up a word's definition in the dictionary.

To learn how to add other dictionaries to the Research pane, see "Adding and Removing
Research Providers," p. 125.

The default dictionary depends on the language and country set as your default. To use a different dictionary, click Research Options at the bottom of the Research pane and select a different dictionary from the Reference Books list.

Finding Words with a Thesaurus

A *thesaurus* is a book (or service) that lists the synonyms and antonyms of common words to help you improve and diversify your word choices. A *synonym* is a word that means roughly the same thing as another word (such as *happy* and *glad*); an *antonym* is a word that means the opposite of another word (such as *happy* and *sad*).

One way to look up a synonym is to right-click it and use the shortcut menu. To look up a word from your document in the thesaurus, follow these steps:

1. Select the word.

2. Right-click the word and point to Synonyms. A quick list of synonyms for the word appears (see Figure 3.19).

3. To substitute any of the found words for the selected word, click the desired word.

Figure 3.19
Get quick synonyms.

Another way to look up a synonym is with the Research pane:

1. Select the word.

2. On the Review tab, click Thesaurus.

   The Research pane appears to the right of the document, with synonyms and antonyms for the word. (Antonyms are clearly marked as such, as in Figure 3.20.)

3. (Optional) To replace the instance in the document with one of the found words, right-click the found word and click Insert.

note

Live Search is an older Microsoft search tool; Bing is the newer model. If the Research pane shows Live Search rather than Bing, try updating your services. To do so, click Research Options at the bottom of the Research task pane, and then click Update/Remove.

4. (Optional) To copy the word to the Clipboard, right-click the found word and click Copy.

5. (Optional) To look up synonyms and antonyms for one of the found words, double-click it. (Use the Back button on the Research pane to return to the results for the previous word.)

Figure 3.20
Look up synonyms and antonyms in the thesaurus.

By default, the thesauruses are enabled for each of the languages you have enabled in the Set Language tool. You can enable/disable the various thesauruses, such as for different languages and different nationalities within a language, by clicking Research Options at the bottom of the Research pane and marking/clearing check boxes in the Reference Books list.

Looking Up Information at a Research Site

Word offers several very good research sites at no additional charge to users:

- **Factiva iWorks**—A Dow Jones/Reuters service with business news and information collected from more than 9,000 authoritative sources. This is a good source of accurate, up-to-date information.

- **HighBeam Research**—A research library of more than 3,000 library publications, including 35 million magazines, journals, and other resources you might find at an academic library.

- **Bing (or Live Search)**—This is the web search engine associated with the popular MSN portal. (Note that data from a search engine is not authoritative or even necessarily correct; it just finds what's out there on the web.)

Live Search is an older Microsoft search tool; Bing is the newer model. If the Research pane shows Live Search rather than Bing, try updating your services. To do so, click Research Options at the bottom of the Research task pane, and then click Update/Remove.

All of these require Internet connectivity for use.

To look up a word or phrase at one of these sites, start the process the same as with the dictionary lookup, but specify one of the research sites instead of the dictionary as the site:

1. Select the word or phrase in the document.

2. On the Review tab, click Research. The Research pane opens, with results from all reference books.

3. Open the drop-down list under the Search For box and choose any site within the All Research Sites portion of the list (see Figure 3.21).

Figure 3.21
Look up a word or phrase with a research tool.

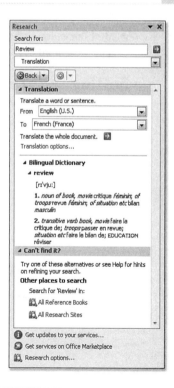

Translating Text into Other Languages

Word 2010 can translate from almost any language to almost any other language, a real boon for those who need to communicate internationally. Of course, the translation won't be as good as if a real person did it, and it might even be unintentionally hilarious to its recipient! But in most cases, you can at least make yourself understood.

Word has two different means of translation available, depending on the languages you are translating to/from. The U.S. English version of Word has built-in bilingual dictionaries and translates word for word between English and several languages, including French, Spanish, Italian, German, Japanese, Chinese, and Korean. More languages are being added periodically, so by the time you read this, even more may be available.

For all other language pairs, Word uses online machine translation by a website called WorldLingo. Using this service, Word can translate between less common languages such as Arabic, Hebrew, Czech, Polish, Danish, Dutch, Swedish, Greek, and Thai.

The Translate button on the Review tab has a drop-down menu, from which you can select one of these options:

- **Translate Document**—This translates the entire document using the most recently selected To and From languages. See "Translating the Entire Document," later in this chapter.

- **Translate Selected Text**—This translates only the text you have selected, and it does so in the Research pane, as explained in the next section.

- **Mini Translator**—This is an on/off toggle for a feature that provides a quick translation for an individual word or phrase in the document when you point at it.

Setting the Translation Language

Some of the translation features assume certain To and From languages. To specify the languages to use, click Review, Translate, Choose Translation Language. In the Translation Options dialog box that appears, select the languages you want. There are two sections: one for the mini translator, and one for general translation.

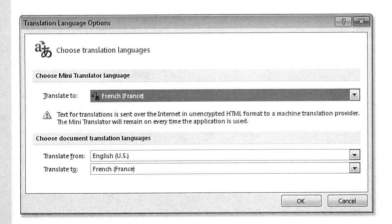

Figure 3.22
Choose the languages you want to use.

Translating the Entire Document

You can also translate an entire document:

1. On the Review tab, choose Translate, Choose Translation Language. Choose the languages you are going from and to, and click OK.

2. On the Review tab, click Translate, and then click Translate Document.

3. A warning box appears. Click Send. A web page opens, showing the translated text.

4. (Optional) Select the translated text, copy it (Ctrl+C), and paste it into Word (Ctrl+V).

Translating with the Research Pane

The Research pane provides full-service access to the translation services in Word. From there, you can choose different languages, set translation options, and more.

There are two ways of opening the Research pane and displaying the Translation services:

- Alt+click any word in the document to open that word in the Research pane; then select Translation from the drop-down list at the top of the pane. (By default, it is set to the most recently used reference tool.)

- Select the word or phrase to translate, and then on the Review tab, click Translate, Translate Selected Text.

Once the translation services are displayed, you can select the desired From and To languages, and the translation appears in the Research pane (see Figure 3.23). Depending on the languages you chose, the translation appears from the bilingual dictionaries in Word or from the WorldLingo service.

Using the Mini Translator

The Mini-Translator is new in Office 2010. You can set it up to pop up a ScreenTip containing a quick translation for whatever word (or whatever selected phrase) you point at.

First, make sure the Mini Translator is set for a language other than the one the document is written in. See "Setting the Translation Language," earlier in this chapter. For example, if the document is primarily in English, you might want the mini translator to show certain words in French.

Then choose Review, Translate, Mini Translator to turn on the feature. From that point on, you can simply point at a word, and a translation will pop up. The toolbar in the pop-up box has a Play button (right-pointing triangle); clicking this plays an audio clip of the word, so you can learn its pronunciation (see Figure 3.24). To turn off the feature, choose Review, Translate, Mini Translator again.

Figure 3.23
Translate text into any of several language choices.

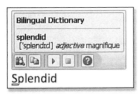

Figure 3.24
The Mini Translator pops up a quick translation of a word or phrase.

Setting Translation Options

Click Translation Options in the Research pane to see a list of dictionaries and services available, as shown in Figure 3.25.

In the Bilingual Dictionary section, these options are available:

- **Use Online Dictionary**—Enables Word to access the web for dictionary lookups.

- **Use Only When the Installed Dictionary Is Unavailable**—Uses local dictionaries whenever possible, relying on the web version only when the local dictionary is not available.

■ **Available Language Pairs**—Each bilingual dictionary installed in Word is listed here. Clear a check box to disable a dictionary. Doing so forces Word to use machine translation (such as WorldLingo) for that language pair.

Figure 3.25
Select dictionaries and translation services for each language pair.

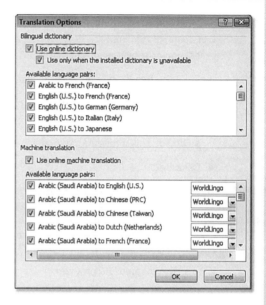

In the Machine Translation section, you can choose whether to use online machine translation when bilingual dictionaries are not available (or when you are translating more than a few words at a time). Mark or clear the check box for each language pair as desired.

By default, Word is set up to access only one translation service: WorldLingo. If you install other translation services through third-party vendors, you can choose which service should be employed for each language pair by changing its drop-down list setting to the desired service.

Customizing and Extending the Research Tools

The Research tools in Word are fully customizable. You can choose exactly which services you want to use. You can even add new services and implement parental control limits.

Adding and Removing Research Providers

One thing that really separates Microsoft Word from the competition is the full array of tools included with it. At no extra charge, you get access to valuable research and reference services such as, HighBeam Research, Factiva iWorks, dictionaries, translation services, and more. No other word processor offers anywhere near that much.

Even with all these tools, however, there's still more to wish for. For example, legal offices might want to add FindLaw, an online version of the West Legal Directory, and LexisNexis's lexisONE research service, covering state and federal case law and other legal news. Many third-party research tools are available for academic, business, and professional use.

Typically, these for-pay providers have their own setup utility that copies the needed files to your hard disk and sets up the link to the Research pane in Office. After running the setup utility for a tool, restart Word, and the new tool appears on the list of services in the Research pane. In some cases, however, you need to point Word to the new service. To do so, follow these steps:

1. From the Research pane, click Research Options.

2. In the Research Options dialog box, click Add Services.

3. Type the URL of the provider in the Add Services dialog box. (The service provider should have given you this information when you signed up for the service.)

4. Click Add.

5. Follow the prompts that appear for the selected service.

You can also remove a provider from the list. Removing a provider removes all the research services from that provider; you can't pick and choose. (However, you can enable or disable individual services, as you'll learn in the next section.)

Here's how to remove a provider:

1. From the Research pane, click Research Options.

2. In the Research Options dialog box, click Update/Remove.

3. Select a provider. All the services for that provider are automatically selected.

4. Click Remove and then follow the prompts for removal.

Added Research Service Does Not Appear in the Research Pane

Exit and restart Word. Any changes you make to the research services do not show up until you do so.

Enabling or Disabling Research Services

Some research services are not enabled by default because they are for some other language or nationality. For example, you might have access to the North American version of Encarta Dictionary by default, but not the UK and Canadian versions. You can enable any of these additional services by following these steps:

1. From the Research pane, click Research Options.

2. In the Research Options dialog box, mark the check boxes for any additional services you want to use.

3. Clear the check boxes for any services you don't want.

4. Click OK.

Updating Installed Services

Sometimes a service provider adds or changes its service offerings. To get the latest information and set up any additional services that might be available, do the following:

1. From the Research pane, click Research Options.

2. In the Research Options dialog box, click Update/Remove.

3. Select a provider. Word automatically selects all the services for that provider.

4. Click Update. Word checks for updates via the web, downloads them, and offers to install any updates or additions it finds.

5. Follow the prompts to update the service. When the update is complete, click OK at the confirmation message.

Using Parental Controls to Limit a Research Service

You can configure parental controls to prevent the research services from delivering any search results that might be offensive. This can be useful for parents with children who use the Research pane and for people who just want to make sure they don't accidentally encounter anything that offends them.

To set up parental controls for research, follow these steps:

1. From the Research pane, click Research Options.

2. In the Research Options dialog box, click Parental Control. The Parental Control dialog box appears.

3. Mark the Turn on Content Filtering check box.

4. (Optional) Type a password for parental control setting changes. (If you don't do this, anyone can turn off the parental controls.)

5. Click OK. A Confirm Password dialog box appears.

6. Retype the password and click OK. A notice now appears in the Research Options dialog box stating that parental controls are active and that some of the services on the list are now unavailable. (The unavailable services are those that do not use content filtering.)

7. Click OK to close the Research Options dialog box.

 note

The tools used in the Research pane are already pretty well scrubbed, generally speaking. Most are business and research oriented, so there won't be much sex or violence in the results. The only exception might be the general MSN search tool, which searches the entire web, not just research sites.

Most of the research sites become unavailable if you turn on parental controls. Even though these research services contain little or no material that anyone might object to, the filtering programs block the sites because their content constantly changes and cannot be guaranteed to be completely sanitized at all times. This can be a hindrance to children trying to do research reports for school because the research services contain good information on the topics that students are frequently assigned to cover.

Printing a Document

Even in this age of electronic communication, the best way to distribute a document is still often the hard-copy printout. Most legal contracts are valid only when printed and signed, for example, and printouts help you reach audiences that don't have computer access.

Printing a document can be as simple or as complex as you make it. You can do a quick print job with default settings with just a single mouse click, or you can delve deep into the print setup options to get special effects, custom ranges, and more.

Printing Quickly with Default Settings

For a quick printout consisting of a single copy of the entire active document on the default printer, choose File, Print, and click the Print button without making changes to the settings.

You can also do a quick print from *outside* of Word. In Windows, browse to the folder containing the document to print and then right-click the document and choose Print. The document opens in Word, prints, and then closes again, all in the blink of an eye.

Printing the Current Document

To specify basic properties of the print job, such as number of copies, page range, printer to use, and so on, choose File, Print. Then change any print settings desired before clicking the Print button. (see Figure 3.26).

Several shortcut key combinations open Backstage View with the Print settings displayed: Ctrl+P, Ctrl+F2, and Ctrl+Alt+I all work. The latter two were for displaying Print Preview in earlier versions of Word, but in Word 2010, Print Preview is integrated into the printing options section of Backstage View. Therefore, all three key combinations now go to the same place.

Selecting the Printer

The default printer appears under the Printer heading. To choose a different printer, click the current printer to open a drop-down list of available printers, and pick one. For example, you might have a color printer that has a rather expensive per-page cost of ink, so for drafts, you might want to print instead to a monochrome laser printer.

Click here after changing
any settings as needed.   Print Preview

Figure 3.26
Use the Print
settings in
Backstage View
to specify how
you want the
document to be
printed.

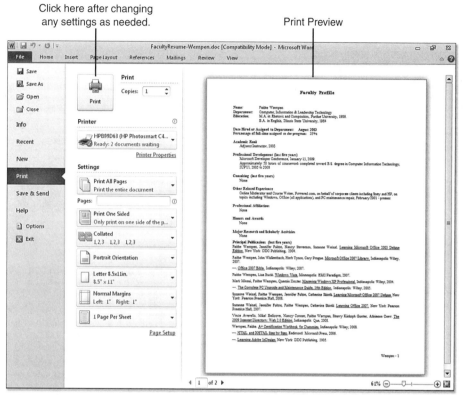

The default printer gets that designation from Windows, not from Word. To change the default printer, follow these steps:

- **In Windows 7**—Choose Start, Control Panel. Choose View Devices and Printers (under Hardware and Sound). Right-click a printer and choose Set as Default Printer.

- **In Windows Vista**—Choose Start, Control Panel. Choose Printer (under Hardware and Sound). Right-click a printer and choose Set as Default Printer.

- **In Windows XP**—Choose Start, Printers and Faxes. Right-click a printer and choose Set as Default Printer.

Choosing Copies and Collation

The number of copies defaults to 1; you can type a value here or increment the current value up or down with the arrow buttons.

If you set the number of copies to greater than 1, collation becomes an issue. When collation is off, all the copies of page 1 print, followed by all the copies of page 2, and so on. When collation is on, full sets print, ready to be stapled. Change this setting with the Collated button under Settings.

Choose What to Print

In the first list under the Settings heading (Print What), the default setting is Print All Pages. You can click the default setting to open a menu from which you can instead specify some other print range:

- **Print Selection**—The content that was selected when you opened the Print section of Backstage View. If no content was selected beforehand, this option is unavailable.

- **Print Current Page**—The page in which the insertion point lies.

- **Print Custom Range**—A page range that you specify. Choose Print Custom Range and then enter the page numbers in the Pages text box:

  - For a contiguous page range, use a hyphen between the first and last number, as in 1-4.

  - For noncontiguous pages or ranges, separate them by commas, as in 2, 5, 7-10.

  - For sections, precede the number by an *s* to indicate you are talking about sections, not pages, as in s2-s4.

  - For pages within sections, use *p* for page and *s* for section, as in p1s2.

- **Document Properties**—Instead of the document itself, you can print any of several information sheets about the document by selecting them from the list, as in Figure 3.27.

  - **Document Properties**—Prints the property information such as author, title, subject, keyword, date created, and so on.

  - **List of Markup**—Prints only a list of marked changes to the document (done with the Track Changes feature). Note that this does not print the marked-up document. If you want to print the marked-up document, open the menu to choose what to print and make sure that the Print Markup option is enabled (see Figure 3.27).

  - **Styles**—Prints a list of the styles in use in the document.

  - **AutoText Entries**—Prints the AutoText entries available in this document.

  - **Key Assignments**—Prints a list of the custom shortcut key assignments saved with this document.

- **Print Markup**—Select this option to print the marked-up document.

- **Only Print Odd Pages**—Select this option to print only the odd pages.

- **Only Print Even Pages**—Select this option to print only the even pages.

Printing AutoText entries prints not only your own entries you've created, but all the entries provided in Building Blocks.dotx, so it takes many pages to print them all.

Figure 3.27
Choose what to print.

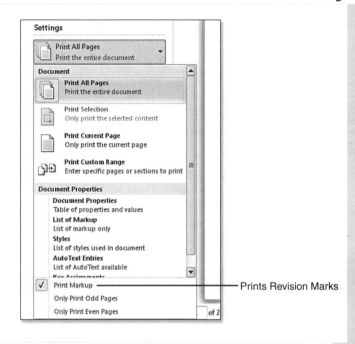

Prints Revision Marks

To learn about sections, see "Working with Sections," p. 253.

To learn about document properties, see "Working with File Properties, p. 43.

To learn about markup with the Track Changes feature, see "Using Revision Tracking," p. 764.

To learn about styles, see "Understanding Styles," p. 217.

To learn about building blocks, see "Working with Building Blocks," p. 89.

To learn how to set custom shortcut key assignments, see "Defining Shortcut Keys," p. 872.

Printing on Both Sides of the Paper

Most printers can print on only one side of the paper, so if you need two-sided printouts, you must reinsert the printed pages for printing on the second side. This is known as *manual duplexing*. Word enables you to specify whether you want two-sided printing, and if so, whether the printer should do the flipping itself (if it is capable) or whether you will flip the paper yourself.

Click the Print One Sided entry under Settings, and select one of the following from its menu:

- **Print on Both Sides**—Flip pages on the long edge (available only if your printer has duplex capability).

- **Print on Both Sides**—Flip pages on the short edge (available only if your printer has duplex capability).

- **Manually Print on Both Sides**—Reload the paper when prompted to print on the second side.

If you use the latter option, to manually print on both sides, only the odd-numbered pages print, and a message appears onscreen telling you to reinsert the pages and click OK. Do so, and Word prints the reverse sides of the pages.

An alternative to manual duplexing is to print only the odd- or even-numbered pages from the Print What list (Figure 3.27, at the bottom of the menu). Printing only the odd or even pages might be helpful if you eventually want to do a duplex print but you want to wait until later to print the second half of the job.

Orientation

Choose between Portrait Orientation and Landscape Orientation for the print job. The default is whatever the document itself is set up for (from the Orientation button on the Page Layout tab).

➡ *To learn about page orientation, see "Setting Page Orientation," p. 259.*

Paper Size

You can quickly change the paper size before printing. The choices are the same as with the Size button on the Page Layout tab. The default is Letter.

You can also scale the printout to fit a particular paper size, even if the document is not set up for that paper size. For example, perhaps all you have is legal-sized paper at the moment, but you want to print a document that will eventually be copied onto letter-sized paper with a copier. To set a scale, click the 1 Page per Sheet setting, and on the menu that appears, point to Scale to Paper Size and choose the paper you want to use. See Figure 3.28.

➡ *To learn about paper sizes, see "Setting Paper Size," p. 260.*

 tip

The trick to manual duplexing is making sure you understand how paper feeds into your printer. One good way to determine this is to draw an up-pointing arrow on a blank page with a marker or pencil, and then insert it into the paper tray face-up, with the arrow facing into the printer. Then print the first page of your document on it. This shows you the relationship between how the paper goes in and how the printout is made. You can then adjust the paper orientation accordingly to make sure you are printing the second side of your duplex job on the correct side, and that it's not upside-down on the second side.

Figure 3.28
Scale to a different paper size than the document is set up for if needed.

Margins

You can change the margins before printing, too. The choices mirror the ones from the Margins button on the Page Layout tab.

To learn about paper sizes, see "Changing Page Margins," p. 256.

Pages Per Sheet

To get multiple pages per sheet, simply set the number of Pages Per Sheet to the desired value in the Print section of Backstage View. The pages are shrunk to fit automatically; you do not have to specify a shrinkage amount.

Using Print Preview

Print Preview helps you save paper—and wear and tear on your printer—by showing you onscreen exactly how the printout will appear on paper. It's great for catching unattractive page breaks, awkward placement of headings and artwork, inconsistent indentation, unbalanced columns, and more.

In Word 2010, Print Preview is built into the Print section of Backstage View. Your document appears previewed on the right side of the screen, and the print options appear along the left side. Figure 3.29 points out the controls available:

- **Page**—Use the right and left arrow keys to move between the pages.

- **Zoom**—Drag the slider to increase or decrease the zoom on your view of the page(s).

- **Zoom to Page**—Click this button to change the zoom so that one page exactly fits in the allotted space.

Preview of Document

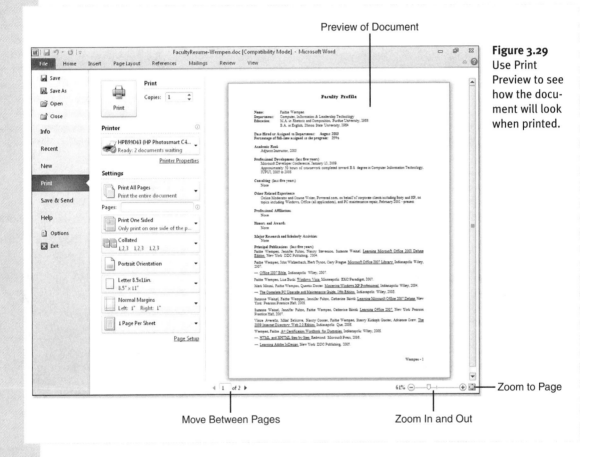

Figure 3.29
Use Print Preview to see how the document will look when printed.

Move Between Pages

Zoom In and Out

Zoom to Page

Setting Print Options for Word Documents

The settings in the Print section of Backstage View apply only to the current document. To set options that affect all documents printed in Word, choose File, Options and click Display. At the bottom are printing options. Mark or clear any of these check boxes to control what happens when you execute the Print command:

- **Print Drawings Created in Word**—This option includes drawings created using Word's drawing tools, including AutoShapes, in the printout. They are printed by default. The option to exclude them is available because sometimes people use those drawing tools to create annotations (circles, arrows, and so on) that they don't want to print.

- **Print Background Colors and Images**—A dark page background that looks great onscreen can look terrible on a printout, especially a black-and-white one. Background colors and images are not printed by default for this reason.

- **Print Document Properties**—When this is marked, the document properties print in addition to the document. (This is in contrast to the Print What setting in the Print section of Backstage View, through which you can choose to print the document properties *or* the document.)

- **Print Hidden Text**—One of Word's text-formatting options is the Hidden attribute. You can set hidden text to be displayed or hidden onscreen, independent of its print setting. Here, you can choose whether to print hidden text as well.

- **Update Fields Before Printing**—This is applicable only if the document contains fields (which are covered in Chapter 16, "Working with Fields and Forms"). It ensures that the fields contain the most recent values available.

- **Update Linked Data Before Printing**—This is applicable only if the document contains links (covered in Chapter 15, "Copying, Linking, and Embedding Data"). It retrieves a fresh copy of the linked data before printing.

Additional printing options are found on the Advanced tab of the Word Options dialog box. Click Advanced, scroll down to the Print section, and configure these controls:

- **Use Draft Quality**—Prints the document at a lower resolution, resulting in a smaller, faster print job.

- **Print in Background**—Returns control to Word after you've started a print job, so you can continue working while you are waiting for it to finish. If you disable this option, Word is locked up until the print job has finished spooling.

> **caution**
>
> In some cases, you might not want links and fields updated. For example, if you are reprinting an archival copy of a memo that used a date field code, you would not want the date updated to today when printing the document; you would want the field value to stay at its original value.

- **Print Pages in Reverse Order**—This is useful for printers that spit out the pages face-up rather than face-down; it ensures that the printout pages will be in the same order as in the document.

- **Print XML Tags**—When you're working with an XML document, this option includes the tags in the printout. They are hidden by default.

> **caution**
>
> Don't reverse the page order both in Word and in the printer's driver properties, or the two settings will cancel each other out. (The reverse of the reverse is the same as the original.)

- **Print Field Codes Instead of Their Values**—When you're working with a document containing fields (Chapter 16), by default the values in those fields print. Marking this option makes the field codes print instead of the values.

- **Allow Fields Containing Tracked Changes to Update Before Printing**—When you have combined change-tracking with field codes, this allows them to update.

- **Print on Front of the Sheet for Duplex Printing**—Enables printing on the front of a sheet on a printer that supports duplex.

- **Print on Back of the Sheet for Duplex Printing**—Enables printing on the back of the sheet on a printer that supports duplex printing.

- **Scale Content for A4 or 8.5 ×11 Paper Size**—Scales the document content to the appropriate size if the printer paper doesn't match the paper size specified in Word.

- **Default Tray**—This setting specifies which paper tray to use for the document, if more than one is available. For example, for a letter, you might want the tray that contains your letterhead stationery.

These last two options are applicable only for individual documents. Select the document from the When Printing This Document list and then mark or clear these check boxes:

- **Print PostScript over Text**—This option enables watermarks or other PostScript-specific content to be printed. When this option is not selected, PostScript overlays are printed beneath the text rather than on top of it. This option is applicable only when printing on a PostScript-compatible printer.

- **Print Only the Data from a Form**—This setting is applicable only if the document contains form controls (covered in Chapter 16). When this option is marked, only the data from the filled-in fields appears on the printout. When cleared, both the text labels and the data print.

Setting Options for a Certain Printer

Each printer has its own set of properties in Windows. These properties affect all print jobs from all applications, not just Word. You can access these properties from within Word, but it's important to remember that these are not Word settings.

To access a printer's properties, first select the printer from the Printer list in Backstage View and then click the Printer Properties hyperlink. A dialog box for that printer appears.

Figure 3.30 shows one example, but there is little standardization in these dialog boxes because the printer's manufacturer (or whoever wrote the printer driver) provided their options. Color printers have different options from black-and-white; ink-jet printers have different options from lasers; PostScript printers have different options from non-PostScript.

Here are a few settings that almost all printers have, though:

- **Copies**—Like the setting in the Print section of Backstage View, this controls the number of copies of the print job. Be aware, however, that this is a separate setting, and it functions as a multiplier with the Copies value in the Print section of Backstage View. If you set them both to 2, for example, you end up with four copies.

- **Orientation**—This switches between portrait and landscape modes. The orientation set in Word overrides the orientation set here. This setting is applicable mainly in programs that don't enable you to set the orientation.

Figure 3.30
Each printer has its own set of properties you can adjust.

- **Paper Size**—Choose the paper size that's in the printer's input tray. For printers that have multiple trays, you can choose which tray to pull paper from, or you can leave it set to Automatically Select. (In Figure 3.30, there's a Paper/Quality tab for this and the next two options.)

- **Paper Type**—Most printers have a paper type setting, but it's an important issue mostly on ink-jet printers, which print at different resolutions depending on the paper type. On such printers, setting a paper type also sets the print quality.

- **Print Quality**—If the printer has a separate setting for this from the paper type, specify a value in dots per inch (dpi). The lower the dpi (down to about 300 dpi), the faster the printing; the higher the dpi, the better the quality.

- **Color Adjustment**—Most color printers have color adjustments you can make, such as color correction, balance, and matching.

- **Utilities (or Tools)**—Ink-jet printers typically have utilities built into their printer drivers for cleaning and aligning the print heads. Unless you are experiencing color problems, such as stripes or missing colors, you can ignore these.

Do your own quality comparison. Print a page containing both text and graphics at various dpi settings that your printer supports. (You won't notice much difference on the text; the graphics are usually the deciding factor.) If you can't tell a difference between them, go with the lower setting and get faster printing.

Storing Different Properties for a Single Printer

What Windows calls a "printer" is actually a printer driver. You can have multiple drivers installed that refer to the same printer, making it possible to quickly switch among printer settings. For example, if you have a color laser printer, you could have two copies of its driver—one that prints in black-and-white only and one that prints in color. Then depending on the demands of the print job at hand, you could choose one or the other.

To set up additional drivers for a printer that is already installed, use the Add Printer Wizard in Windows (from the Devices and Printers window in Windows 7, or Printers and Faxes in Windows XP or Vista). Do not automatically detect the printer, though; instead, select it from the list provided or insert the driver disk that came with the printer. After setting up a duplicate copy of the same printer, change the properties for one of the copies.

Printing Iron-On Transfers

Iron-on transfer paper is available at any office supply or computer store. It enables you to create your own transfers for T-shirts, hats, tote bags, and anything else made of cloth. There's just one gotcha, though—everything on a transfer is backward, a mirror image of the final design.

What you need, then, is a way to create a mirror image of your design in Word. If your printer supports mirroring (flipping), that's the easy way to go. Open the Printer Properties dialog box for the printer (File, Print, and then click the Printer Properties hyperlink near the top) and look for a Mirror Image (or similar) check box.

If your printer does not have a Mirror feature, but your design is graphics-only (no text), you can flip it by selecting all the objects and then using the Flip Horizontal command in Word. This doesn't work with text, though, because Word does not mirror text. (It does work with WordArt, however.)

➡ *To learn how to flip objects, see "Rotating and Flipping Objects," p. 427.*

If having text on your transfer is important, consider using some other application to create the transfer, such as Photoshop or Paint Shop Pro. These programs let you create text as a graphic; then you can rotate or flip it as freely as you would any other graphic.

Managing a Print Queue

Each printer installed in Windows has its own print queue, in which documents wait their turn to be printed (from all applications, not just Word). Although this is not part of Word per se, it does affect your work in Word. A print spooler service in Windows manages this queue.

The print spooler accepts the print job from Word and holds it in the queue until the job can be sent to the printer. The spooler communicates with the printer and sends the job as quickly as the printer can accept it. If the printer reports a problem, it tells the print spooler, which in turn displays a message to you in Windows. The print spooler relieves the applications of the responsibility of ensuring that the print job has completed, so the application can be freed up to continue working. If the print spooler did not exist or were turned off, Word would lock up until the document had finished printing.

Most of the time, the print spooler does its job in the background, and users don't even notice it's there. You might notice a printer icon flash briefly in the notification area in Windows, as the job enters and exits the queue. It's only when a problem occurs that the print queue gets attention.

When there is a problem with a print job, an icon appears in the notification area (by the clock) indicating that the printer is waiting for help. Usually it is a printer icon with a question mark on it. A pop-up balloon is usually also present, reporting an error condition.

To open a print queue, double-click its icon in the notification area. Or, if the icon does not appear there, open Devices and Printers (Windows 7), Printers (Windows Vista), or Printers and Faxes (Windows XP) from the Control Panel and double-click the printer in question.

The print queue window lists the jobs that are waiting to be printed. Normally jobs come and go quickly here—almost instantaneously—so most of the time when you open the print queue window, it is completely empty.

If you want to get a good look at a print job, pause the print queue and then submit a print job. To pause the queue, choose Printer, Pause Printing. Figure 3.31 shows a print queue that has been paused. To resume the queue, choose Printer, Pause Printing again.

When an error occurs, the job's status shows Error. Usually you cannot recover from such an error; you need to delete the print job. To do so, select the print job and press the Delete key, or choose Document, Cancel.

However, sometimes deleting a print job can leave extraneous codes in the printer that also doom all the print jobs coming after it to pages of gibberish. Therefore, when other jobs are waiting to be printed behind the one with the error, it's best to pause those other jobs until the problem can be cleared. To pause a print job, select the job and choose Document, Pause. To resume it, repeat this selection.

To delete all the print jobs in the queue, choose Printer, Cancel All Documents. This is a quick way to delete all jobs at once instead of canceling each one individually.

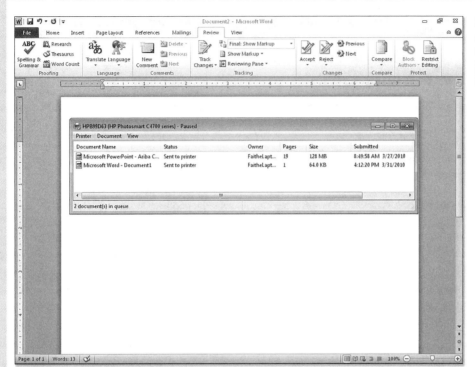

Figure 3.31
A paused print queue with one job waiting to be printed.

Have you ever accidentally printed a huge document? Rather than eating up all that paper unnecessarily, cancel the print job. To do so, first take the printer offline. (Click its Online button, or pull out the paper tray to interrupt it.) Then cancel the print job from the print queue. Finally, on the printer itself, use its LED panel (if it has one) to issue the command to cancel the current print job, or just unplug it, wait a few seconds, and plug it back in.

An Extra Blank Page Prints at the End

It's possible that you simply have an extra page in your document composed of nothing but empty paragraph breaks. Switch to Draft view and then position the insertion point immediately after the final text in your document and press the Delete key until you see the end-of-file marker (horizontal line).

You can also turn on the display of paragraph markers (on the Home tab) and look for extraneous paragraph marks to delete.

While you're in Draft view, look also for any extra hard page breaks you might have inserted at the end of the document. These appear as horizontal lines running across the whole width of the page in Draft view. (In Print Layout view, you see the actual pages rather than break markers.)

Faxing Documents

For quick document delivery, faxing is an attractive alternative to mailing a hard copy. (So is email, discussed in Chapter 22, "Developing Online-Delivered Content.")

Faxing is an old technology, but it's still viable. The standard fax method is to use a fax modem on both ends of the conversation, connected via a dial-up telephone connection. The sending and receiving fax machines send codes that negotiate a mutually acceptable speed and protocol, and then the pages are transferred. With standard faxing, the pages are black-and-white only (no gray-scale, no color), and herein lies the primary drawback of faxing. Because all colors and gray tones are reduced to either black or white (whichever they are nearest to), most artwork ends up as shapeless blobs. Color and grayscale-compatible fax machines and services are available, but the machines at both ends need to have that capability.

There are also Internet-based faxing services that can deliver black-and-white or color faxes to any fax machine (or any other Internet faxing service) without your having to actually own a fax modem.

Faxing a Document with a Fax Modem

A fax modem is the same thing as a regular dial-up modem that you might use for a dial-up Internet connection. Faxing services have been included with dial-up modems for more than a decade now, so if you have a dial-up modem, you have a fax modem. However, if you have a cable or DSL modem, you do *not* have faxing capabilities built into it. These are not really modems, but rather terminal adapters that connect you to Internet services.

Most fax modems come with basic faxing software that you can install in Windows. Windows also has a faxing client you can use.

Faxing with Windows Vista or Windows 7

A Windows Fax and Scan utility is built into Windows Vista and Windows 7; you do not have to do anything special to set it up. A Fax driver is automatically installed as a printer; just print to it to start faxing.

The first time you print to the Fax driver, a Fax Setup dialog box opens; work through the prompts provided to set up your fax account.

After you set up the fax account, a New Fax window opens with the current document shown as an attachment. Create your cover sheet in the New Fax window by filling in the fields provided, and then click Send to send the fax (see Figure 3.32).

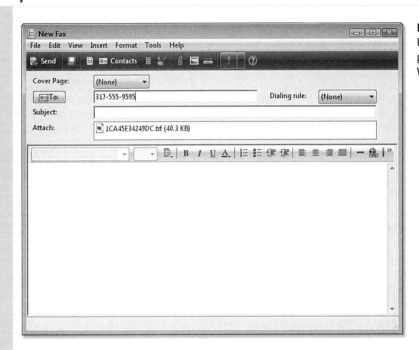

Figure 3.32
Use the New Fax window to prepare and send a fax in Windows Vista or Windows 7.

Faxing with Windows XP

Windows XP has a fax client called Microsoft Fax. It is not installed by default, but you can easily add it.

To add Microsoft Fax to your system in Windows XP, follow these steps:

1. Open the Control Panel and open Add or Remove Programs.

2. Click Add/Remove Windows Components.

3. If Fax Services does not have a check mark next to it already, mark it, and then click Next.

4. Follow the prompts to install the faxing service. You will probably be prompted to insert your Windows CD.

5. After installing Fax Services, choose Start, All Programs, Accessories, Communications, Fax Console. The Fax Configuration Wizard runs.

6. Work through the wizard to configure the fax settings on your PC, including entering your contact information and selecting the modem to use.

After fax services have been configured in Windows XP, you can send a fax from Word by printing to the Fax printer driver that was set up when you installed Fax Services. Follow these steps:

1. Choose File, Print.

2. Open the Name list and choose Fax as the printer name.

3. Click OK. The Send Fax Wizard runs.

4. Work through the wizard, entering the recipients and other information required to send the document as a fax.

Distributing Documents via Internet Fax

If you don't own a fax machine or fax modem and don't want to buy one, you might want to consider an Internet faxing service. These services send your faxes over the Internet, for delivery to regular fax machines or to other Internet fax service accounts. (Such services are not free; they typically charge monthly or per-fax fees.)

To get started, choose File, Save & Send, Send as Internet Fax, Internet Fax. If you have not yet signed up with a fax provider, a message to that effect appears; click OK. You are then redirected via a web browser interface to a page at Microsoft.com that describes the available fax providers and offers links through which you can sign up for them.

APPLYING CHARACTER FORMATTING

Changing Text Font, Size, and Color

Character formatting is formatting that you can apply to individual characters of text. There are other types of formatting too, which I address in other chapters. *Paragraph formatting* is formatting that applies to entire paragraphs (for example, line spacing), and *page formatting* is formatting that applies to entire pages (for example, page margins and paper size).

Each character has a certain font (typeface) and size applied to it that govern how the letter appears. You can change the font or the size for a single character or any size block of text, often dramatically changing the look of the document.

Understanding How Fonts Are Applied

When you type some text in Word, how does Word know what font to use for it? And how can you change that font choice? The answers to those questions are surprisingly complex.

 note

In Microsoft Office and Windows, the term *font* is synonymous with *typeface*; it refers to a style of lettering, such as Arial or Times New Roman. (Windows also uses this definition; if you add or remove fonts, you are actually adding/removing typefaces.) This usage is not universal, however. Some programs refer to a typeface as a *font family*, and a typeface at a certain size with certain attributes (such as bold) as a *font*. Modifiers such as bold and italic are called *font styles*.

There are three ways that you can assign a font to text:

- You can apply the font manually to the text. You select the text and then choose a font from the Home tab or the Font dialog box. Manual font choices override styles and themes.

- You can modify the font definition in the style applied to the text. Each paragraph has a paragraph style assigned to it; the default paragraph style is called Normal. The style's definition can include a font, such that any paragraphs with that style applied appear in the specified font unless manual formatting has been applied to override it.

- In Word 2007 and 2010 documents (not backward-compatible ones), instead of assigning a specific font to a style, you can assign a Body or Heading placeholder. Then you can specify a theme on the Page Layout tab that changes what font those placeholders represent, or you can choose a Style Set from the Home tab (Change Styles, Style Set).

> *To learn how to change the font assigned to a style, see "Modifying a Style Definition," p. 239.*

> *To change to a different set of fonts by changing the document's theme, see "Working with Themes," p. 246.*

> *To change to a different set of fonts by applying a Style Set, see "Changing the Style Set," p. 221.*

In the default Normal.dotm template, the default paragraph font is defined using the Body placeholder. The default theme applied is called Office, and it defines the Body placeholder as Calibri 11-point text. As a result, Calibri 11-point is the default font and size in new documents. You can change this by switching to a different theme, by redefining the Normal style to use a specific font, or by selecting the desired text and manually applying a font.

In most cases, it is best to change the font at the style or theme level and let the change trickle down to the individual instances. This helps ensure consistency throughout a document. However, sometimes you just want one block of text to change, independently of the rest of the document. For that type of formatting, you must select the text and make the change manually.

If you select a block of text and then change the font, Word places invisible beginning and ending codes around that block of text.

For example, suppose you type ACME Industries and then select it and apply Arial font. Codes are inserted at the beginning and end of the selection to indicate what font to use, like this:

[begin font Arial]ACME Industries**[end font Arial]**

That's just a conceptual example; the actual codes are hidden deep within the file's coding and are not available to end users except by manually deconstructing the XML coding.

 tip

WordPerfect users may be accustomed to that program's Reveal Codes feature, which shows you the actual codes that mark the beginning and ending of the formatting. Word does not have such a feature, but it does have a Reveal Formatting task pane that displays information about selected text. To display it, press Shift+F1.

How WordML Applies Font Formatting

If you would like to see the actual codes that WordML (Word XML) uses to apply manual formatting, make a copy of your document file and rename the copy with a .ZIP extension. Then double-click it to open it as a folder. Locate the word\document.xml file and open it in Internet Explorer to view its contents.

In WordML, there are two parts to the process of applying a font manually. First, a code sets up Arial to use:

```
<w:rFonts w:ascii="Arial" w:hAnsi="Arial" w:cs="Arial" />
```

Then the text to be formatted is surrounded by a pair of codes that call the font specified:

```
<w:t>ACME Industries</w:t>
```

If you change the font without first selecting any text, Word puts beginning and ending font codes around the insertion point, so that whatever you type next appears in that font (as long as you don't move the insertion point outside the codes):

[begin font Arial](insertion point)[end font Arial]

It's important to understand the placement of those codes, because if you move the insertion point outside the coded area (by clicking or by using the arrow keys, for example), the font choice is no longer in effect.

 To learn more about the Reveal Formatting feature, see "Revealing and Comparing Formatting," *p. 174.*

Changing the Font and Size

As I mentioned earlier, the default font assigned to the Normal style in the Normal.dotm template is Calibri. It is a clean, easy-to-read font, suitable for a variety of document types, but you are free to change any or all text to another font at any point in the document-creation process.

To manually change the font, position the insertion point or select the block of text to affect, and then choose from the Font drop-down list on the Home tab (see Figure 4.1). You can also right-click or point to the selection to display the Mini Toolbar and then select a font from there instead.

Notice that each font appears in its actual lettering style on the menu (where possible), making it easy to browse the available choices. For some fonts, it is not possible to view the names in the actual fonts because the fonts contain no letters; Wingdings is a symbols-only font, for example.

 **note**

The Mini Toolbar, which you learned about in Chapter 1, "Creating and Saving Documents," is available only in Word 2007 and 2010 documents; it does not work in a Word 97–2003 document. You can display it in two ways: You can right-click the selection, which displays both the Mini Toolbar and a shortcut menu, or you can point at the selection. When you point at it, a faint version of the Mini Toolbar appears; move your mouse onto it to make it bright (and available).

Figure 4.1
Select a font from the Font drop-down list on the Home tab.

The Font drop-down list displays fonts in three areas:

- **Theme Fonts**—When you choose Body or Headings as the font choice rather than selecting a specific font, you allow the chosen theme (selected from the Page Layout tab) to control the font choices. Selecting one of the fonts in this section of the list sets the text to draw its font choice from those placeholders; changing the theme (on the Page Layout tab) changes the font.

  ➡ *To apply and modify themes, see "Working with Themes," p. 246.*

- **Recently Used Fonts**—Fonts that you have recently applied appear here, for easy reselection. This section does not appear if you have not selected any fonts.

- **All Fonts**—A complete list of the available fonts appears here.

The fonts appear in alphabetical order in the All Fonts part of the list. To quickly jump to a certain area of the list, start typing the first few letters of the font's name.

Only One or Two Fonts Appear in the Font List

This problem is usually caused by not having a default printer selected in Windows or by having a corrupt driver for the default printer. Make sure you have set a default printer. If you have two or more printers, try a different printer as the default. If that helps, remove and reinstall the driver for the printer that was formerly the default.

Font sizes are measured in points. A *point* is 1/72 of an inch on the printed page. (Because zoom settings and monitor sizes vary, the font size has no fixed relationship to the size of the text onscreen.)

To change the font size, select from the Font Size drop-down list. You are not limited to the sizes that appear on this list, though; you can type any size (including decimal numbers, such as 10.5) into the text box at the top of the list area (see Figure 4.2). You can enter a font size of up to 1638 points here. In addition, the Home tab has Grow Font and Shrink Font buttons that increase and decrease, respectively, to the next larger or smaller size on the Font Size list. (Depending on the font and the current size, this could be 1 point or it could be more. Notice, for example, that there are big jumps between the larger sizes, such as 48 and 72.)

Figure 4.2
Choose a font size from the list, or type a custom font size.

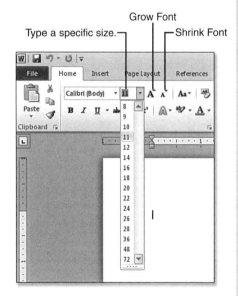

Type a specific size.

Grow Font

Shrink Font

There are also shortcut keys for changing the font size (see Table 4.1).

Table 4.1   Shortcut Keys for Adjusting the Font Size

Shortcut	Effect
Ctrl+]	Increases the font size by 1 point.
Ctrl+[	Decreases the font size by 1 point.
Ctrl+Shift+>	Increases the font size to the next larger size in the Font Size list. Sometimes this is 1 point; sometimes it's more.
Ctrl+Shift+<	Decreases the font size to the next smaller size in the Font Size list.
Ctrl+Shift+P	Opens the Font dialog box with the Size list selected; you can then use the up and down arrow keys to select a font size and press Enter to close the dialog box.

In Word 2007/2010 documents, you can also access font and size controls by right-clicking or pointing at a text selection. When you do so, the Mini Toolbar appears, containing a Font drop-down list, a Size drop-down list, and the Grow Font and Shrink Font buttons (see Figure 4.3).

Grow Font ——   ┌─Shrink Font

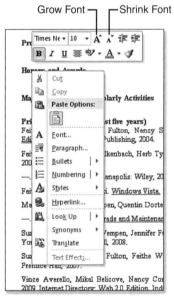

Figure 4.3
Use the Mini Toolbar for quick access to the Font and Size lists and to the buttons for increasing and decreasing font size.

There is one more method: You can use the Font dialog box to change both the font and the size. To display the Font dialog box shown in Figure 4.4, do any of the following:

- Press Ctrl+D.

- Click the dialog box launcher in the bottom-right corner of the Font group on the Home tab.

- Right-click the selected text and choose Font from the shortcut menu that appears.

Figure 4.4
The Font dialog box offers a variety of character-formatting options, including font and size choices.

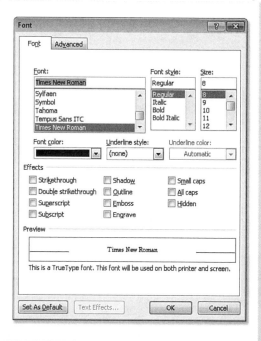

The Font dialog box is useful as a one-stop shop for all types of character formatting—not only fonts and sizes, but attributes such as bold, italic, underline, strikethrough, and so on, as well as character spacing. You'll learn about all these things as this chapter progresses. For font and size selection, however, the Font dialog box offers little benefit over the tab method, and in fact it has several drawbacks. Fonts appear on the dialog box's list in plaintext, rather than as the actual fonts, so you must look to the Preview area to see a sample of the font you have chosen. The Font list in the dialog box also does not pull out theme fonts or recently used fonts separately, making them more difficult to find. Finally, the Font list here does not show icons indicating the font types.

The Font Onscreen Is Not the Font That Prints

Some printers that have many built-in fonts (such as PostScript printers) have font-substitution tables built into their drivers. Such tables enable the printer to use one of its built-in fonts rather than a soft font (that is, one that the PC sends to the printer as needed) whenever there is a close match between one of the Windows fonts and one of the printer's own fonts. It is advantageous to use a printer-resident font rather than a soft font because it makes the job print faster. However, if the substituted font is not exactly the font you want, it can cause a problem.

Continued...

Open the Devices and Printers folder in Windows 7 (or Printers and Faxes in Windows XP, or Printers in Windows Vista), and then right-click the printer icon and choose Printer Properties (if using Windows 7) or Properties (if using Windows XP or Vista). Then locate the font substitution information for your printer and modify it. Font substitution data is stored in different locations depending on the printer model. There might be a Fonts tab on which it is displayed, for example, or there might be a Device Settings tab on which there is a Font Substitution Table entry. Some printers do not have a font substitution o ption. (This option is more common on lasers than on ink-jets because lasers have more fonts built in.)

Setting the Default Font

If you don't like the default font of Calibri, you can easily change it. You make this change to the Normal.dotm template, so that all new documents are affected.

There are two ways to set a default font. If you always want a certain font, you can set the default definition of the Normal style to a fixed choice. If you prefer to maintain the flexibility of working with the Body and Heading placeholders, so you can use themes to format the fonts later if desired, you can define a set of theme fonts and then set them as the default.

Specifying a Fixed Default Font

Notice in the Font dialog box (refer to Figure 4.4) that a Set As Default button appears in the bottom-left corner. Select the desired default font and size, and then click the Set As Default button. In the resulting confirmation box, you can choose between making the change to this document only or to all documents based on the Normal.dotm template. Choose an option and then click OK. Your choice of font and size becomes the default.

Here's another way of doing the same thing: Apply the desired font to some text, and select that text. Then on the Home tab, click Change Styles and click Set as Default. (With that method, you don't get the confirmation dialog box, and the default is applied only to the current document, not to the Normal.dotm template.)

Setting Different Default Theme Fonts

You'll learn about themes in Chapter 6, "Creating and Applying Styles and Themes," but here's a quick walkthrough of how to change the default definition for Body and Heading by creating a new theme font set and then setting it to be the default:

1. On the Home tab, click Change Styles, point to Fonts, and click Create New Theme Fonts.

2. In the Create New Theme Fonts dialog box, specify a Heading Font and Body Font.

3. Type a name for the new font theme in the Name box.

4. Click Save.

5. Click Change Styles again, and click Set as Default.

 For more information about theme font sets, see "Working with Themes," p. 246.

Accidentally Modified Normal.dotm, and Now All New Documents Are Messed Up

If you just want to change the default font, open the Font dialog box, choose the font settings you want, and click the Set As Default button. That should overwrite the settings in Normal. dotm.

If you've really messed things up and just want to go back to the way Normal.dotm was originally, delete it. Normal.dotm is custom-created for each user, and if Word doesn't find a copy when it starts up, it creates a new copy with the default settings.

Close Word and then navigate to C:\Documents and Settings*username*\Application Data\ Microsoft\Templates (Windows XP) or C:\Users*username*\AppData\Roaming\Microsoft\ Templates (Windows Vista or Windows 7), where *username* is the name under which you are logged into Windows. Select Normal.dotm and press the Delete key on the keyboard—or, if you're feeling a little timid about the process, rename the file to something like Normal.old. The next time you start Word, Normal.dotm will be re-created anew.

By the way, don't be shocked if you browse for the newly created Normal.dotm and can't find it. Unless you make a change to Normal.dotm, it doesn't actually exist as a separate file from Word; Word simply uses its internal version of this file. Make a change to the default settings, however, and a file named Normal.dotm will appear.

If you've deleted Normal.dotm and things still haven't gone back to normal, go back in and look for Normal.dot, a leftover template from a previous version of Word. Delete it, too, to prevent its settings from carrying over.

More About Font Types

The majority of the fonts used in Windows are scalable OpenType or TrueType fonts. These are *outline fonts*, which means they consist of unfilled mathematically created outlines of each character. When you assign a size, you are sizing the outline; then the outline is filled in with black (or whatever color you choose) to form each character. Such fonts look good at any size.

TrueType fonts, which Microsoft and Apple jointly developed, have been around since the late 1980s; they're good basic scalable fonts that you can use on any printer. OpenType was created as a joint venture between Microsoft and Adobe (the makers of PostScript), so OpenType fonts have many of the characteristics and benefits of both TrueType fonts and Adobe Type 1 fonts, including the capability of storing more than 65,000 characters in a single font file. For example, OpenType fonts typically store ligatures, alternative characters, typeset-style ordinals, and built fraction sets, as well as characters for different written languages.

Not all fonts are created equal, however. The simple fact of a font being OpenType does not necessarily make it better than a TrueType font, because both amateurs and experts create both types. In the end, the quality and versatility of a font depends in large part upon who created it. The best commercial OpenType fonts, such as those that Adobe has produced, have several alternative character sets in them, plus alternative characters for superscript and subscript numbers, fractions, ligatures, and so on. (See the Advanced tab of the Font dialog box to control the available options.) And although Word cannot access this feature, most commercial OpenType fonts have several weights of lettering, such as light, normal, semibold, bold, and extra bold. A free, amateur-created font might have only the basic keyboard letters, numbers, and symbols.

Word's Font list shows icons to the left of the fonts that indicate their type. An O indicates an OpenType font, and a TT indicates TrueType.

caution

Try not to use printer-resident fonts when creating documents that you intend to save in PDF format. PDF documents might not be searchable when created using printer fonts. This relates to the way the PDF file format embeds the font information; PDF files know how to handle TrueType, OpenType, and Adobe Type 1 fonts, but not printer-resident fonts.

Depending on the default printer, you might also have some printer-resident fonts available. The printer driver tells Windows (and Word) about their existence, and the fonts become available on Word's list. (They do not appear in the Fonts folder in the Windows Control Panel, as other fonts do.) For example, most PostScript-compatible printers have 35 or more printer-resident fonts. In Word, printer-resident fonts appear with a printer icon to their left. The available printer-resident fonts on the Fonts list change when you set a different printer to be the default in Windows. Don't use these fonts in documents that you plan on printing on a different printer than the default one currently connected to your computer, because the other printer may not have them available.

Figure 4.5 shows examples of each of the three font type icons on the Font menu. You might not have these same fonts.

Printer-resident fonts do not usually have Windows equivalents, so the version you see onscreen may not exactly match the version you see printed. With a TrueType or OpenType font, on the other hand, what you see onscreen is what you get on the printout.

Adding More Fonts to Your System

Fonts, like printers, are installed Windows-wide. Different word processing and desktop publishing applications come with different fonts, so your font choices depend on what other programs you have installed besides Word.

Figure 4.5
TrueType,
OpenType, and
printer-resident
icons in the
Font list in
Word.

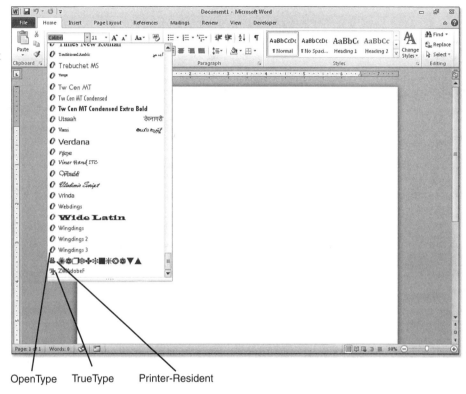

OpenType   TrueType   Printer-Resident

Office 2010 comes with a large selection of fonts, but you can also buy more (or acquire them for free online in many cases). After acquiring one or more new fonts, install them in Windows to gain access to them in all applications (including Word).

The installation process for fonts depends on your Windows version.

Installing Fonts in Windows 7

Windows 7 handles font installation differently than previous Windows versions. For Windows 7, you simply open the Fonts window and drag and drop the font files into it.

1. Open the Start menu and click Control Panel.

2. Click Appearance and Personalization.

3. Click Fonts.

4. Open Windows Explorer and navigate to the folder containing the font files.

5. Drag and drop the font files into the Fonts window.

Installing Fonts in Windows Vista

In Windows Vista, here are the steps to follow:

1. Open the Start menu and click Control Panel.

2. Click Appearance and Personalization.

3. Click Fonts.

4. Press the Alt key to display a menu bar.

5. On the menu bar, choose File, Install New Font.

 tip

If you are using the Classic view of the Control Panel, you can skip step 2 and double-click instead of single-click Fonts.

6. If needed, open the Drives list and change to the drive containing the fonts.

7. In the Folders list, navigate to the folder containing the fonts. The available fonts appear under List of Fonts.

8. In the list of fonts, click the font(s) to install. To select more than one, hold down the Ctrl key as you click each one, or hold down Shift as you click the first and then the last one in a contiguous group. To select all the fonts in that location, click Select All (or press Ctrl+A).

9. Click Install. Windows Vista installs the fonts.

Installing Fonts in Windows XP

Here are the steps to take in Windows XP:

1. Open the Control Panel. If you're not already in Classic view, click Switch to Classic View.

2. Double-click Fonts. The Fonts folder opens.

3. Choose File, Install New Font. The Add Fonts dialog box opens.

4. If needed, open the Drives list and change to the drive containing the fonts.

5. In the Folders list, navigate to the folder containing the fonts. The available fonts appear under List of Fonts (see Figure 4.6).

6. In the list of fonts, click the font(s) to install. To select more than one, hold down the Ctrl key as you click each one, or hold down Shift as you click the first and then the last one in a contiguous group. To select all the fonts in that location, click Select All (or press Ctrl+A).

7. Click OK. Windows XP installs the fonts.

Figure 4.6
Add new fonts to your system in Windows XP.

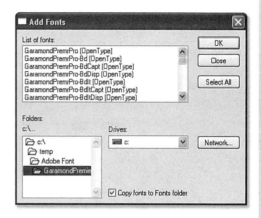

Embedding and Substituting Fonts

One potential problem when sharing documents with other people is that not everyone has the same fonts installed on their PCs. When a document is opened on a PC that does not have the correct font, the name of the font appears in the Font box on the Home tab, but the actual font does not appear; instead the text appears in whatever Word considers to be a close match for the font. (Often it is not a close match at all, but a generic-looking font such as Courier.) The text remains marked as using the missing font, so if the document is later opened on a different PC with the correct font installed, it appears as originally intended.

To get around this problem, in some cases you can embed the font in the document so that the font travels with it. This works only if there is no prohibition against embedding built into that font. (Some font designers disallow embedding to keep the font from being distributed without their permission.)

To embed fonts in a document, follow these steps:

1. Choose File, Save As. The Save As dialog box opens.

2. Click Tools and choose Save Options. The Word Options dialog box opens.

3. Mark the Embed Fonts in the File check box.

4. Select either or both of the options provided:

- **Embed only the characters used in the document**—This embeds only the letters in use; do not do this if the document will be edited later.

- **Do not embed common system fonts**—This prevents fonts from being embedded that come with Windows, such as Times New Roman and Arial.

5. Click OK.

6. Continue saving normally.

If the person who created the document did not have the foresight to embed the needed fonts, you aren't completely stuck; you can change the font substitution table so that the missing fonts are at least displayed in a font of your choice. To modify the font substitution table for the document, follow these steps:

1. Choose File, Options. The Word Options dialog box opens.

2. Click Advanced.

3. Scroll down to the Show Document Content section and click Font Substitution.If no fonts need to be substituted, a message appears to that effect and you're done. Otherwise, the Font Substitution dialog box opens, listing the missing and substituted fonts (see Figure 4.7).

4. Click a font on the list, and then select a different font from the Substituted Font drop-down list. Repeat for each font.

5. (Optional) To permanently convert all instances of the missing font to the chosen substitution, click Convert Permanently and then click OK to confirm.

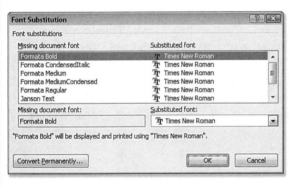

Figure 4.7
View and change font substitutions.

6. Click OK to close the Font Substitution dialog box, and then OK to close the Word Options dialog box.

Changing Font Color

The default setting for font color in Word is Automatic (not black, as many people assume). Automatic makes the text appear either black or white, depending on which would most sharply contrast with the background on which it is placed. By default, the background is white, so text appears black.

 caution

If you are sharing the document with others, be wary of converting fonts permanently. You might be the only one who is missing the chosen font, and the original font choice might be important to maintain (for example, to match the company's official document-formatting standards).

However, if you change the background to a dark color (or to black), the text changes to white. You can change the font color to any color you like—including fixed black or fixed white.

To understand the font color choices in Word 2010, you must know something about themes. A *theme* is like a style that applies to the entire document. Themes include colors, fonts, and object effects (for formatting drawn lines and shapes). There are 12 color placeholders in a theme. By changing the theme, you can change what colors are populated into those placeholders.

➡ *To change themes, see "Applying a Theme," p. 247.*

➡ *To learn more about object effects, see "Changing the Theme Effects for the Entire Document," p. 532.*

When specifying the color for text (or for an object), you can either choose a fixed color or a theme color. A fixed color does not change, regardless of the theme applied. A theme color does not actually apply a color to the selection, but rather a link to one of the theme's color placeholders. Then whatever color happens to be assigned to that placeholder trickles down to the selection. That way, you can have elements in your document that change color automatically when you switch themes.

You do not necessarily have to apply a theme color at full strength; you can instead apply a *tint* or *shade* of it. A tint is a scaled-back version of a color, derived by blending the color with white. Tints are described in percentages, such as a 25 percent tint, a 50 percent tint, and so on. Shades are darkened versions, derived by blending the color with black. Shades are also described in percentages, such as a 50 percent shade.

Color formatting works like font formatting, in that if you select the text first, it applies only to the selected block. If you do not select anything, the formatting applies to the insertion point's current position.

To change the font color, do the following:

1. If you want, select text to affect. Otherwise, the change applies to new text typed at the insertion point's current location.

2. On the Home tab, open the Font Color button's drop-down list (see Figure 4.8).

3. Do one of the following:

   ▪ Click Automatic.

   ▪ Click a theme color (top row).

   ▪ Click a tint or shade of a theme color.

   ▪ Click a standard (fixed) color.

   ▪ Click Gradient and define a color gradient for the font color (not common).

➡ *To learn more about gradients, see "Applying a Gradient Fill," p. 439.*

 tip

This same Font Color list is also available in the Font dialog box. You can also point to or right-click the selected text and use the Font Color button on the Mini Toolbar.

Theme Colors

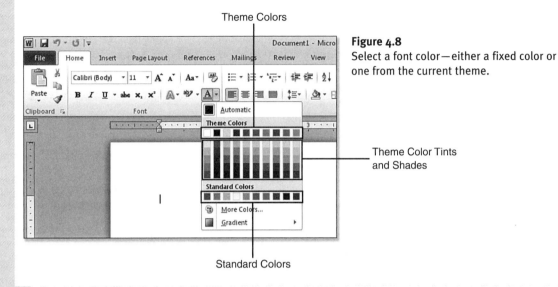

Figure 4.8
Select a font color—either a fixed color or one from the current theme.

Theme Color Tints and Shades

Standard Colors

If none of the color choices please you, choose More Colors from the Color drop-down list and select a color from the Colors dialog box. This dialog box has two tabs: Standard and Custom.

On the Standard tab, you can click any of the colored hexagons, as shown in Figure 4.9.

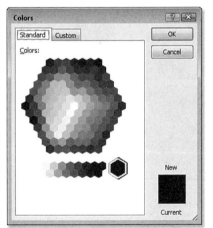

Figure 4.9
Select one of the standard colors from the Standard tab.

On the Custom tab, you can define a color precisely using its numeric value from either the RGB or the HSL color model. These numeric color models can be useful when you are trying to match a color exactly; for example, many corporations have official colors to be used in all company correspondence and publications.

RGB stands for Red/Green/Blue; colors are defined with values ranging from 0 to 255 for each of those three colors. Equal amounts of each color result in varying shades of black-gray-white.

HSL stands for Hue/Saturation/Luminosity. These are also values from 0 to 255, but H is for all hues (0 and 255 are both red; the numbers in between are the other colors of the rainbow), S is for saturation (the intensity of the color, as opposed to neutral gray), and L is for the lightness/darkness (white to black). As you can see in Figure 4.10, you can click any spot on the color grid to select that color, or you can drag the vertical slider up or down.

Figure 4.10
Define a color numerically on the Custom tab.

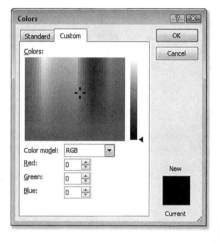

Bold and Italic: Applying Font Styles

Font styles are modifiers that affect the shape or thickness of the characters. In Word, a font's style can be set to Regular, Italic, Bold, or Bold Italic. The way font styles are applied depends on the particular font. Some fonts that appear as single entries in Word's Font list are actually four separate font files behind the scenes—one for each style. This is the ideal, because the shapes of the letters can be subtly different for each style. Other fonts have only one font definition, and Word must simulate "bold" by fattening up the characters or "italic" by skewing them to the right slightly. In some programs, this skewing is called *false italics*.

> **caution**
> Do not confuse font styles with character styles. A *character style* is a Word-defined style that applies to individual characters, covered in Chapter 6.

Word makes no distinction between true italics and false ones, or between true bold and simulated bold, but you can see the difference for yourself by experimenting with the various fonts on your system. For example, in Figure 4.11, the Broadway and Times New Roman fonts are shown in both regular and italic. Notice that the Broadway font's letters are simply tilted to the right, but the Times New Roman letters are actually different in shape and thickness.

Broadway Regular
Broadway Italic

Times New Roman Regular
Times New Roman Italic

Figure 4.11
Some fonts are merely tilted for italic; others have completely different character shapes.

You can also tell which fonts have separate files for the various styles by opening the Fonts folder from the Control Panel. In the Fonts folder:

- In Windows XP or Vista, open the View menu and make sure that Hide Variations is not marked. Then browse the font icons that appear, looking for fonts that have separate icons for regular, bold, italic, and bold italic.

- In Windows 7, open the View menu and choose Details. Then look in the Font Style column; fonts with separate files for the styles have multiple entries in this column.

Some professional-quality fonts might even have more styles than just the standard four; they might have separate sets for light, normal, demibold, bold, and so on. Word recognizes and uses only one level of bold, however.

As with other formatting, you can select the text first and then apply bold or italic, or you can apply the font style to the insertion point position.

To quickly apply bold or italic to text, use one of these methods:

- Click the Bold or Italic button on the Home tab, as shown in Figure 4.12.

- Right-click the selected text and use the Bold or Italic button on the Mini Toolbar.

- Use shortcut keys: Ctrl+B for bold or Ctrl+I for italic.

All these *methods* are on/off toggles. To remove bold or italic, click the button again or use the shortcut key again. (You can also strip off all formatting from text, including bold and italic, by selecting it and pressing Ctrl+spacebar.)

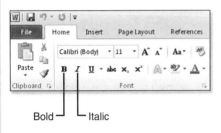

Bold — Italic

Figure 4.12
Apply bold or italic from the Home tab.

➡ *To learn about clearing text formatting, see "Clearing Formatting," p. 173.*

You can also apply bold or italic from the Font dialog box:

1. On the Home tab, click the dialog box launcher in the lower-right corner of the Font group, or press Ctrl+D. The Font dialog box opens.

2. On the Font Style list, click your preference: Regular, Italic, Bold, or Bold Italic.

3. Click OK.

Underlining Text

Word enables you to apply a variety of underline styles and colors to text. Unlike bold and italic, underlining does not modify the basic shape or weight of the text; it's an additive element.

To apply the default underline style (a plain, solid single line, Automatic color), click the Underline button on the Home tab. The Underline button on the Home tab also has a drop-down menu associated with it for choosing alternate underline styles, as shown in Figure 4.13. To pick an underline color from the menu, point to Underline Color for a fly-out menu of color choices.

Figure 4.13
Apply underlining from the Home tab.

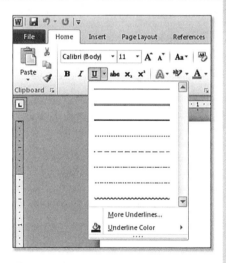

For even more underline options, choose More Underlines from the menu to display the Font dialog box (see Figure 4.14). From here, open the Underline Style drop-down list and select a style. A variety of line styles are available, including solid, dotted, dashed, single, double, and wavy. While you're here, open the Underline Color list and select a color. (The choices for underline colors are the same as for font colors.)

 note

There are shortcut keys for some of the most popular underline styles:

- Single plain underline—Ctrl+U
- Words Only underline—Ctrl+Shift+W
- Double underline—Ctrl+Shift+D

Select an underline style.

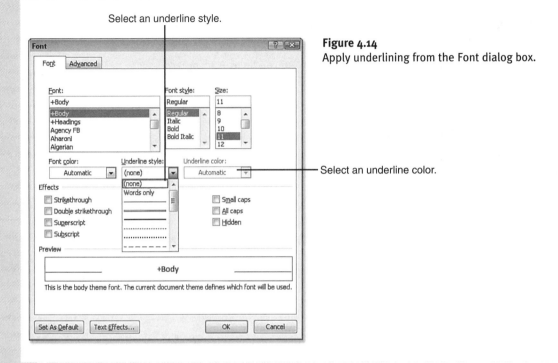

Figure 4.14
Apply underlining from the Font dialog box.

Select an underline color.

Applying Font Effects and Text Effects

Font effects are additives or modifiers applied to the text, such as strikethrough, shadow, or superscript. Some of these are available from the Home tab; others must be applied via the Font dialog box (refer to Figure 4.14). Table 4.2 summarizes the effects and shows the Home tab buttons or the shortcut keys where applicable.

Table 4.2 Font Effects

Effect	Home Tab Button	Shortcut Key	Usage Example(s)
Strikethrough	abc	—	Text to be marked for deletion.
Double strikethrough	—	—	Text to be marked for deletion.
Sub$_{script}$	x₂	Ctrl+=(equal sign)	Chemical formulas.
Super^{script}	x²	Ctrl+Shift++(plus sign)	Exponents, footnotes.

Table 4.2   Continued

Effect	Home Tab Button	Shortcut Key	Usage Example(s)
SMALL CAPS	—	Ctrl+Shift+K	Headings, emphasis. Let ters already capitalized appear full size; letters not already capitalized appear capitalized in shape but about 20% smaller than normal capitals.
ALL CAPS	—	Ctrl+Shift+A	Headings, emphasis. All letters appear in full-size caps regardless of their previous state. This does not actually change the letters; if you remove the All Caps effect, the letters go back to their previous capitalization.
Hidden	—	Ctrl+Shift+H	Text that should not appear in printed copies (makes text non-printing).

As the name implies, the Hidden effect hides the text. Marking text as hidden is useful when you don't want it in the current draft, but you might eventually want it again. For example, in a boilerplate contract, you could hide text that doesn't apply to a certain client. Hidden text does not print under any circumstances, but you can choose whether it should appear onscreen. The easiest way to do this is to click the Show/Hide (¶) button on the Home tab; this turns on the display of all hidden text and characters. If you don't want all the other hidden characters, but just hidden text, customize the viewing options as follows: Choose File, Options, and on the Display tab, mark the Hidden Text check box if you want hidden text to show onscreen.

Font effects can be combined, but there are a few exceptions. The following are mutually exclusive:

- Strikethrough and double strikethrough

- Superscript and subscript

- Small caps and all caps

Text Effects are an extra type of character formatting that you can apply when working in Word 2007/2010 documents. (They are not available in Compatibility Mode.) In Word 2007 they were part of the WordArt effects, but Word 2010 has made them available for any and all text in the document. Click the Text Effects button in the Font dialog box to open the Text Effects dialog box, shown in Figure 4.15.

Text Effects include

- **Text Fill**—You can apply a solid or gradient fill color to the text that replaces its regular font color.

- **Text Outline**—You can outline the letters in a different color than the fill. (This is useful mainly with extremely large and thick letters.)

- **Outline Style**—If you choose to use a text outline, you can control the type of line used for it (dashed, dotted, solid, and so on).

- **Shadow**—You can apply a graphics-style shadow to the text.

- **Reflection**—You can make the text appear to have a reflection, as if it were on a shiny surface.

- **Glow and Soft Edges**—You can blend the edges of the text to various degrees of softness or apply a fuzzy halo effect (a glow) around it.

- **3D Format**—You can tilt and rotate the text to make it appear 3-D.

Figure 4.15
You can apply text effects to any text in a Word 2007/2010 document.

You will learn more about these effects in Chapter 11, "Working with Drawings, WordArt, and Clip Art." All these effects also apply to drawings and WordArt and are covered in detail there. You can experiment with these effects on your own in the meantime if you like; each has fairly self-explanatory controls.

Changing Text Case

In the ASCII character set, which is the basic set of characters used in English-language writing (as well as many other languages), upper- and lowercase versions of the same letter are considered two completely separate characters. For example,

 caution

The Capitalize Each Word option is not "smart" or contextual. It simply capitalizes the first letter in every word. Modern English usage dictates that certain words such as *of* and *in* should not be capitalized in titles, so you need to edit what Word has done to conform to that standard usage. However, the grammar checker can also fix such problems, so running a grammar check immediately after changing text to Title Case should do the trick.

a capital *A* has no inherent relationship to a lowercase *a*. Therefore, generally speaking, if you accidentally type *A* instead of *a*, you must retype it.

There are cases in which you don't have to retype text to change its case, however. As you learned in Chapter 3, "Correcting and Printing Documents," Word's AutoCorrect feature turns off the Caps Lock feature and corrects any text that you have accidentally typed with it on. AutoCorrect also fixes instances of two capital letters at the beginning of an otherwise-lowercased word.

Alternatively, you can use Word's Change Case feature to change the case of some text. Here are the choices:

- **Sentence case**—Text is capitalized as in an English-language sentence (first letter of the first word only).

- **Uppercase**—All letters of all words are capitalized.

- **Lowercase**—All letters of all words are lowercased.

- **Capitalize Each Word**—The first letter of each word is capitalized.

- **Toggle Case**—The current case of each letter is reversed.

To change the text case of some text, select the text and then click the Change Case button on the Home tab. Select the desired case from the menu, as shown in Figure 4.16. Alternatively, you can toggle through uppercase, lowercase, and sentence case by pressing Shift+F3.

 note

The All Caps font effect covered in the preceding section does make the text *appear* to be in all caps, but this is just an illusion. The letters have not changed; they have just had a mask placed over them that makes them appear as their uppercase cousins. That's not the same thing as actually changing the text's case. It's useful, for example, if you want to make a heading all caps for a certain appearance effect, but you want to retain the flexibility of going back to the original capitalization later without retyping.

Figure 4.16
Change case from the Home tab.

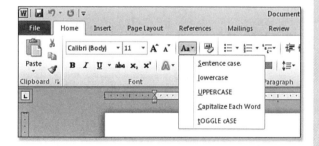

Highlighting Text

Students have long known that a highlighter marker can be of great help in marking important passages of a textbook. Word's highlighting feature lets you do the same thing to Word documents. You can use highlighting to call attention to text or to color-code various passages (for example, to mark text that's the responsibility of a certain writer or reviewer).

There are two ways to highlight text:

- Select the text, and then select a highlight color from the Text Highlight Color button's drop-down list on the Home tab (see Figure 4.17).

- Select a highlight color, and then drag across text to be highlighted with that color. Press Esc to turn off the highlight when finished.

 note

Highlighting is the one type of character formatting that is *not* removed by the Clear Formatting command (Ctrl+spacebar or the Clear Formatting button on the Home tab). Highlighting can be removed only with the Text Highlight Color button.

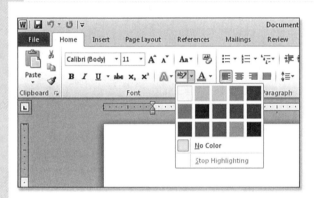

Figure 4.17
Select a highlight color.

To remove a highlight, select the text and then open the Text Highlight Color button's list and choose No Color.

Adjusting Character Spacing and Typography

Have you ever wondered why ordinary word processing documents don't look as polished and professional as book or magazine pages? It's the spacing. A professional designer knows how to subtly manipulate spacing and typography settings to create more readable and attractive pages.

Word enables you to adjust text spacing to achieve the same professional-looking effects that professionals enjoy who use expensive page layout programs. Although Word's controls are perhaps not as exhaustive in function, they are adequate for most projects.

To change character spacing and typography settings, use the Font dialog box. Follow these steps:

1. Select the text to affect, or position the insertion point where you will type new text that will have this formatting.

2. On the Home tab, click the Font dialog box launcher to open the Font dialog box.

3. Click the Advanced tab.

4. Adjust any of the character spacing settings, as described following these steps and as shown in Figure 4.18.

5. Click OK.

Figure 4.18
Set spacing options on the Advanced tab of the
Font dialog box.

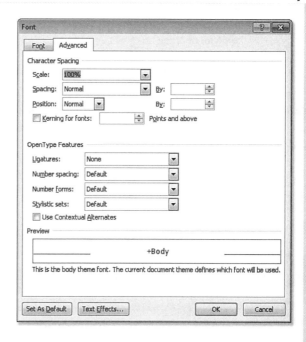

Here are some details about the options on the Advanced tab:

- **Scale**—This is the size of the text in relation to its baseline size (as specified via the Font Size setting). Scale can
  be used to subtly adjust the size of certain characters—for
  example, to make an @ sign or punctuation mark slightly
  larger or smaller than the surrounding text. A drop-down list
  of common percentages is provided, but you can manually
  enter any value from 1 percent to 600 percent.

- **Spacing**—This is an increase or decrease of the space
  between letters compared to a baseline size of Normal. This
  setting does not change the letters themselves, but only the
  space between the letters. In some programs, this is called
  tracking. You choose either Expanded or Condensed and
  then specify a number of points. (One point is 1/72 of an
  inch.) The increment arrows move the value up one point at
  a time, but you can manually type values in as fine a detail
  as 1/20 of a point (for example, 1.05 points).

- **Position**—This is a raising or lowering of the characters compared to the baseline of Normal. This setting is called *baseline shift* in some desktop publishing programs. You choose

 tip

To redefine the defaults in Normal.
dotm, click the Set As Default button
in the Font dialog box.

 tip

Setting scaling for a character is
preferable to setting its font size
because its size shifts proportionally if you later change the font size
definition for the style on which it is
based. For example, suppose that
the Body style is defined as 12 point,
and you choose to make a particular
character 120 percent of that size.
That character ends up 14.4 point in
size. If you redefine the Body style
to be 10 point, the character changes
to 12 point (120 percent of 10 point).

either Raised or Lowered and then specify a number of points. As with spacing, you can use the increment arrows to go up or down one point at a time or manually enter values in as fine a detail as 1/20 of a point. You can use this to make a manual adjustment to the height of a superscript or subscript character, for example.

caution

Kerning may cause spacing to shift, and in some cases it might cause text to float from one page to another.

- **Kerning**—This is a spacing adjustment between certain pairs of letters based on their shapes. For example, when the letters *A* and *V* appear adjacent to one another, they can afford to be closer together because their shapes fit into one another: AV. You can turn kerning on or off, and you can specify a minimum font size at which kerning should occur.

Kerning is more useful at larger sizes; with small text, however, kerning can actually backfire and make letters look like they are *too* close together. Kerning also slows down the computer's performance somewhat, especially noticeable on a PC that is slow to begin with. If you notice a difference in performance with kerning turned on for body text sizes (say, 10 point and up), but you want to kern text that size, consider doing all the editing on the document with kerning turned off and then turning it back on right before you print.

tip

High-end desktop publishing programs enable you to manually adjust the kerning values between specific letter pairs. Word does not offer this feature, but you can simulate such an adjustment by changing the spacing between two letters with the Spacing setting. For example, if you think a particular *A* and *V* are too close to each other, select the *V* and change its spacing to Expanded by a certain value (perhaps 0.5 point to start with), and then adjust up or down as needed.

Many OpenType and TrueType fonts have kerning tables built into them that determine how much space should be left between letters when kerning is turned on for maximum readability and attractiveness. This table can contain as many as 500 *kerning pairs* (pairs of letters with rules established for kerning them when they appear together). If the font has such a table, Word uses it; otherwise, Word tries to kern based on the letter shapes.

Creating Your Own Built Fractions

A *built fraction* is one that looks typeset, like this:

¹/₂

as opposed to a regular typed fraction, like this:

1/2

Most fonts have built fractions for ¹/₂ and ¹/₄ ; you can access them via the Symbol command (on the Insert tab). However, when you have some odd fraction such as 23/54, the font can't realistically be expected to have a built-in symbol for it.

To create a built fraction manually in Word, use a combination of font size, superscript, and position:

1. Type the fraction normally. You might want to zoom in on it to see it more clearly.

2. Select the numerator and make it superscript (from the Home tab).

Continued...

3. Select the divider line (/) and the denominator and change their font size to two-thirds of the original size. For example, if the original size was 12, set the size to 8.

4. Select the divider line and change its Position to Raised by 1 point.

The result won't fool a professional typesetter, but it'll be good enough that casual readers won't be able to tell the difference, especially at body text size.

If the selected text uses an OpenType font, you can adjust additional options on the Advanced tab. This is a new feature in Word 2010, allowing Word to use some of the powerful extra features of some OpenType fonts, in the same way that professional-quality desktop publishing programs such as Adobe InDesign do. For example, you can control *ligatures* (which are letters that run together typographically), number spacing, number forms, and stylistic sets. See Figure 4.19.

Figure 4.19
You can set advanced options for OpenType fonts on the Advanced tab of the Font dialog box.

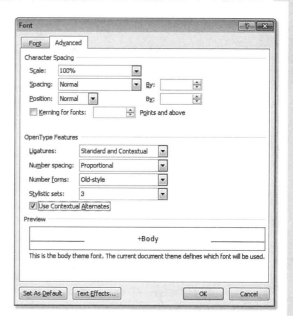

Creating a Drop Cap

A *drop cap* is an enlarged capital letter at the beginning of a paragraph, "dropped" down into the paragraph. Drop caps are used to call attention to the beginning of a chapter, section, or article; they say to the reader "begin here."

There are two basic styles of drop cap: Dropped and In-Margin. The Dropped style places the letter in the paragraph, so that the lines move over to accommodate its presence. An In-Margin drop cap places the letter to the left of the paragraph and does not interfere with line positions (see Figure 4.20).

Dropped style
(inside left margin)

oxes everywhere. Boxes in the hallways. Boxes in the kitchen. Piles and piles of
them, stacked like children's blocks, with narrow pathways between them leading
from room to room. How in the world did we accumulate so much stuff in that
little 3-bedroom ranch we left behind?

oxes everywhere. Boxes in the hallways. Boxes in the kitchen. Piles and piles of them,
stacked like children's blocks, with narrow pathways between them leading from room to
room. How in the world did we accumulate so much stuff in that little 3-bedroom ranch
we left behind?

In-margin style
(outside left margin)

Figure 4.20
Dropped-style drop cap
versus in-margin style.

To create a drop cap for a paragraph, click in the paragraph. Then on the Insert tab, click the Drop Cap button and choose the type of drop cap you want: Dropped or In Margin (see Figure 4.21). To remove a drop cap from a paragraph, choose None.

Figure 4.21
Apply a simple drop cap from the Drop Cap button's menu.

For a drop cap with custom settings, choose Drop Cap Options. The Drop Cap dialog box opens (see Figure 4.22). From here, you can select the following options:

- **Font**—By default, whatever font was previously applied to that letter is used. Sometimes a different font can make for a more interesting drop cap, though; for example, an Old English or handwriting style font can be attractive.

- **Lines to Drop**—The default is three lines. The larger the value here, the larger the drop cap will be and the further down into the paragraph it will drop.

tip

If you increase the Distance from Text setting, the drop cap appears somewhat indented compared to the rest of the paragraph. To counteract this, adjust the first-line indent for the paragraph. A quick way to do this is to drag the first-line indent marker to the left on the horizontal ruler.

- **Distance from Text**—The default is 0 inches. Increase this value to increase the spacing around the drop cap.

Figure 4.22
Create custom drop caps with the Drop Cap dialog box.

 To learn about adjusting paragraph indentation, see "Indenting Paragraphs," p. 187.

Clearing Formatting

Sometimes it's easier to format text by starting from scratch rather than wondering what formatting has been applied to it. To quickly strip off all the character formatting from some text (except for highlighting), select the text and press Ctrl+spacebar, or click the Clear Formatting button on the Home tab.

> **note**
>
> Ctrl+spacebar is an old trick that Word has offered for many versions now, but few people knew about it because there was no menu command for it. The Clear Formatting button just makes the feature more obvious.

Copying Formatting with Format Painter

You can copy formatting from one block of text to another, which can save a tremendous amount of time if text has multiple formatting actions applied to it. For example, instead of individually making multiple blocks of text 16 point *and* bold *and* italic *and* red, you can format one block of text that way and use Format Painter to copy all that formatting to other blocks.

To copy the formatting from one block of text to another, follow these steps:

1. Select the text that is already formatted correctly. You can select as little as a single character. If you do not select any text, Format Painter copies the text settings that are in effect at the insertion point's current location.

2. Click the Format Painter button on the Home tab (see Figure 4.23), click the Format Painter button on the Mini Toolbar, or press Ctrl+Shift+C. The mouse pointer changes to show a paintbrush.

3. Drag across the text to receive the formatting.

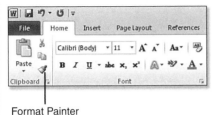

Figure 4.23
Use Format Painter to copy formatting.

Format Painter

Format Painter turns itself off automatically when you release the mouse button. If you want Format Painter to stay on so you can copy the same formatting to additional selections, double-click instead of single-clicking the button in step 2.

Revealing and Comparing Formatting

The Reveal Formatting task pane is Word's partial response to requests from WordPerfect users who missed that program's Reveal Codes feature after moving to Word. To display the Reveal Formatting pane, press Shift+F1. The pane describes the formatting applied to the currently selected text or to the insertion point's current location (see Figure 4.24).

Figure 4.24
The Reveal Formatting task pane describes the formatting of the selected text.

Notice the underlined headings in the Reveal Formatting task pane, in sections such as Font, Language, Alignment, and Indentation. Each of those headings is a hyperlink to the dialog box in which that setting can be changed.

The Reveal Formatting task pane also has two check box options:

- **Distinguish Style Source**—When this is marked, information appears about where the formatting comes from. For example, if the font choice comes from the paragraph style applied to it, that source is noted. It's good to know that a particular formatting attribute is part of the style (or not) so you know whether to change the style's definition or apply manual formatting over it.

- **Show All Formatting Marks**—When this is marked, nonprinting characters such as end-of-paragraph markers appear. This can be helpful in sorting out where one paragraph ends and the other begins, and where manual line breaks (Shift+Enter) have been inserted.

You can also use the Reveal Formatting pane to compare the formatting between two blocks of text. Here's how to do this:

1. With the Reveal Formatting task pane open, select the first block of text to compare.

2. Mark the Compare to Another Selection check box.

3. Select the second block of text to compare. The differences appear on the Formatting Differences list in the task pane, as shown in Figure 4.25.

The differences are indicated with -> arrows. For example, under Font, it indicates that the first text uses 13 pt, whereas the second text uses 14 pt.

Figure 4.25
You can also use the Reveal Formatting task pane to compare formatting.

If you want to select different text for the initial selection, clear the Compare to Another Selection check box and then start the steps over again.

Using AutoFormat

There are actually two different features called AutoFormat in Word:

- **AutoFormat As You Type**—Automatically makes formatting changes for you, such as changing two minus signs in a row to a dash and converting straight quotes to curly ones (smart quotes). These options work behind the scenes in every document. You can turn individual options on or off.

- **AutoFormat**—Sets up headings and lists and applies some styles automatically. AutoFormat can be done all at once (in a single pass) or interactively (you confirm or decline each change).

The latter AutoFormat has been deemphasized in Word 2007 and 2010, to the point where there is not even a button for it on any of the tabs. You have to know the shortcut key combo for it (Ctrl+Alt+K) or add a button for it to the Quick Access toolbar. It's still around, however, and still useful.

Setting AutoFormat As You Type Options

Most AutoFormat As You Type options are enabled by default in Word, so setting options consists mostly of turning off the ones you don't want. To access these options and make your selections, follow these steps:

1. Choose File, Options. The Word Options dialog box opens.

2. Click the Proofing tab, and then click AutoCorrect Options.

3. Click the AutoFormat As You Type tab (see Figure 4.26).

4. Mark or clear check boxes to make your selections.

5. Click OK to close the AutoCorrect dialog box, and then click OK to close the Word Options dialog box.

As shown in Figure 4.26, the options are broken down into three major categories:

- **Replace As You Type**—A set of options for inserting typographical symbols to substitute for plain typing. These provide shortcuts for items such as ordinals, fractions, quotation marks, and dashes.

- **Apply As You Type**—A set of options for applying automatic formatting at the paragraph level, including bulleted and numbered lists, borders, headings, and tables.

- **Automatically As You Type**—A set of options for tidying up text as you type, including formatting list items in a parallel fashion and defining styles based on formatting.

As in many other dialog boxes in Word, you can click the Help button in the top-right corner to get detailed information about its options, so I won't belabor each of the options here. However, I do want to point out a couple of things that are especially useful.

With the Tables option under Apply As You Type, you can create a table by typing plus and minus signs. Type a row that begins with a plus sign, and use minus signs for spaces and plus signs

Figure 4.26
Set AutoFormat As You Type options.

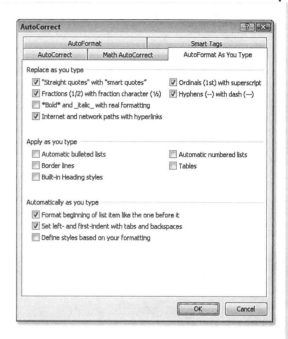

where column breaks should occur. When you press Enter at the end of the line, Word creates a table with the columns in the spots you indicated.

Another item of interest is Format Beginning of List Item Like the One Before It. When this option is on, Word pays attention to special formatting you apply at the beginning of a list item, such as a bold word or phrase preceding the rest of the text in a bullet point. When you press Enter to start a new bulleted paragraph, Word automatically formats the first words of the paragraph to match whatever formatting you applied in the previous item.

 tip

You might also want to experiment with Define Styles Based on Your Formatting. (This is one of the few settings that's off by default.) It generates new styles based on the manual formatting you apply as you work. Some people find that it results in too many unwanted styles being created, but try it for yourself and see what you think.

Formatting a Document with AutoFormat

All those AutoFormat As You Type options apply only to new text that you type. If you import existing text, such as from a plaintext version of a document, AutoFormat As You Type won't help you. Instead, you must rely on the regular AutoFormat command.

There are two types of AutoFormat you can run—an automated type (by pressing Ctrl+Alt+K) and an interactive type. We'll look at each of these in more detail shortly, but first you need to know how to access them.

Making AutoFormat Available on the Quick Access Toolbar

As mentioned earlier, Word 2010 still includes AutoFormat, but it has been deemphasized. There's no way to launch either the automated or interactive AutoFormat command from any of the tabs.

The automated AutoFormat still retains its shortcut key combo, Ctrl+Alt+K. However, there is no keyboard shortcut for the interactive AutoFormat. Fortunately, you can customize the Quick Access toolbar to add buttons for either or both.

To add the button(s) to the Quick Access toolbar, follow these steps:

1. Choose File, Options. The Word Options dialog box opens.

2. Click the Quick Access Toolbar tab.

3. Open the Choose Commands From list and choose All Commands.

4. Scroll through the list and locate AutoFormat. There are four AutoFormat entries on the list:

   - **AutoFormat**—The interactive (dialog box-based) AutoFormat.

   - **AutoFormat As You Type**—The AutoFormat As You Type options from the AutoCorrect dialog box.

   - **AutoFormat Now**—The Ctrl+Alt+K automatic version of AutoFormat.

   - **AutoFormat Options**—The AutoFormat options from the AutoCorrect dialog box.

   Click the one you want (probably the first one, AutoFormat), and then click Add to add it to the Quick Access toolbar.

5. Repeat step 4 for another button if desired.

6. Click OK.

 note

If you add both AutoFormat and AutoFormat Now to the Quick Access toolbar, they arrive there with identical icons. However, you can hover the mouse over them to see ScreenTips that differentiate between them.

Setting AutoFormat Options

The AutoFormat options are similar to the AutoFormat As You Type ones (refer to Figure 4.26). They are all turned on by default, so setting options consists mainly of disabling any you don't want.

To access the AutoFormat options, follow these steps:

1. Choose File, Options. The Word Options dialog box opens.

2. On the Proofing tab, click AutoCorrect Options.

3. Click the AutoFormat tab.

 tip

If you placed the AutoFormat button on the Quick Access toolbar in the preceding section, then as an alternative to steps 1–3 here, you can open the AutoFormat dialog box (from the button) and click Options.

4

4. Mark or clear check boxes to make your selections. As shown in Figure 4.27, the options are broken down into four categories:

- **Apply**—Various types of styles that can be automatically applied, such as headings, lists, and bullets.

- **Replace**—Typographical symbols, formatting, and hyperlinks that can replace plaintext.

- **Preserve**—Only one option here: Styles. Leave this marked to leave any styles that are already applied to the text.

Figure 4.27
AutoFormat options govern what happens when you issue the AutoFormat command.

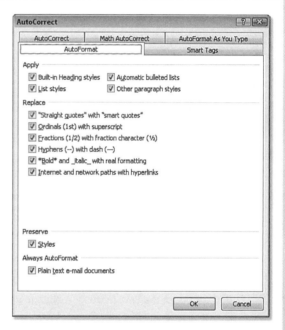

- **Always AutoFormat**—Only one option here: Plain Text E-Mail Documents. Leave this marked to let AutoFormatting occur when using Word as an email editor.

5. Click OK twice to close both dialog boxes.

Applying AutoFormat (Automated Mode)

In automated mode, AutoFormat applies all the selected options (from the preceding section) to the entire document as best it can. There is no prompt. To AutoFormat a document, press Ctrl+Alt+K, or if you placed a button on the Quick Access toolbar for the command, click that button.

If there's anything AutoFormat does that you don't like, undo the operation (press Ctrl+Z or click the Undo button on the Quick Access toolbar). Then open up the AutoFormat options again, deselect any options you want to omit, and then try the AutoFormat again.

Applying AutoFormat (Interactive Mode)

In interactive mode, you can review each AutoFormat change. As mentioned earlier, you must add the AutoFormat command to the Quick Access toolbar to get access to this feature in Word 2010.

Follow these steps to AutoFormat interactively:

1. Click the AutoFormat button on the Quick Access toolbar (assuming you placed it there in the earlier section). The AutoFormat dialog box appears (see Figure 4.28).

Figure 4.28
Perform an interactive AutoFormat.

2. Click AutoFormat and Review Each Change.

3. The default document type is General Document. If you are composing a letter or email, open the drop-down list and select one of those types instead.

4. Click OK. A message appears that the formatting is completed.

5. Click Review Changes. A markup of the document appears. Additions appear red and underlined; deletions appear red and strikethrough.

6. Click one of the Find buttons. A change appears and is described in the Review AutoFormat Changes dialog box (see Figure 4.29).

Figure 4.29
Review each AutoFormat change.

7. To accept the change, click a Find button to move past it. To reject the change, click the Reject button. Continue through the document until you have reviewed all changes.

8. Click Cancel to close all open dialog boxes as needed.

FORMATTING PARAGRAPHS AND LISTS

How Word Handles Paragraphs

A *paragraph* is a block of text that ends with a paragraph marker (¶), which you create by pressing the Enter key on the keyboard. The marker symbol does not print, and it does not show up onscreen unless you have configured Word to display nonprinting characters.

Pressing Enter starts a new paragraph (and ends the previous one), but not all line breaks are paragraph breaks. You can create a line break that does *not* start a new paragraph by pressing Shift+Enter. A line break is represented by the nonprinting symbol. (Again, the symbol doesn't appear onscreen unless Word is displaying non-printing characters.) Figure 5.1 shows examples of paragraph breaks and line breaks.

 tip

To toggle between displaying non-printing characters, such as the paragraph marker, click the Show/Hide (¶) button on the Home tab or press Ctrl+* (that's Ctrl+Shift+8).

Click here to toggle the display of nonprinting characters.

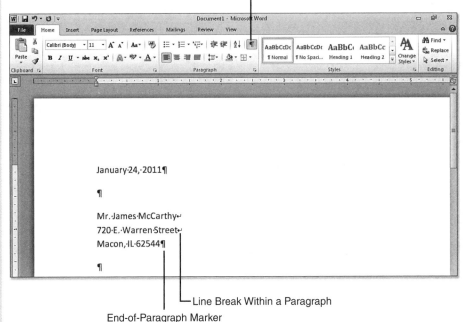

Figure 5.1
Paragraph and line breaks are nonprinting characters; they can be displayed or hidden onscreen.

Line Break Within a Paragraph
End-of-Paragraph Marker

Customizing Which Nonprinting Characters Appear

When you click the Show/Hide (¶) button on the Home tab, it toggles all the nonprinting characters on and off, including the little dots representing each space. If you want to see only certain nonprinting characters, use this method instead:

1. Toggle *off* all the nonprinting characters with the Show/Hide (¶) button.

2. Choose File, Options and click Display.

3. Mark the check boxes for the nonprinting characters you want to see: tab characters, spaces, paragraph marks, hidden text, optional hyphens, and object anchors. (Notice that you cannot separately control line breaks created with Shift+Enter. They are lumped in the paragraph marks for this setting.)

4. Click OK. Now only the marks you've selected appear, and they appear regardless of the Show/Hide (¶) toggle setting.

Generally speaking, starting a new paragraph by pressing Enter carries over the same paragraph settings as were in the preceding paragraph. So, for example, if the preceding paragraph has a 1-inch left indent, the new paragraph will, too. (An exception would be if the style assigned to that paragraph was set up to use a different style on subsequent paragraphs.)

Paragraph formatting is stored as part of the end-of-paragraph marker. Deleting the paragraph marker between two paragraphs combines them into a single paragraph that has the paragraph formatting settings of the first of the two paragraphs. Any settings that were stored in the second paragraph's marker are deleted, along with the marker.

It's important to remember that paragraph formatting is stored in the marker because when you are copying or moving text, you might or might not also want to copy or move the paragraph formatting along with it. To preserve the paragraph formatting, make sure the end-of-paragraph marker is included in your selection. To make the pasted text conform to the paragraph settings in its new destination, do *not* include the paragraph marker in the selection.

Each paragraph has a paragraph style applied to it from which it inherits its basic properties. These basic properties include not only paragraph characteristics such as line spacing and indentation, but character-formatting defaults such as font, size, and color.

To change a paragraph's appearance, you can apply a different paragraph style to it, change the definition of the paragraph style that's applied, or apply manual paragraph formatting that overrides the style's formatting.

In this chapter, you'll learn how to apply manual paragraph formatting that overrides the paragraph's style. Learning these techniques enables you to format paragraphs without worrying about style definitions. These techniques also familiarize you with the basic paragraph controls you can use to make changes to the paragraph styles in Chapter 6, "Creating and Applying Styles and Themes."

Setting Line Spacing

Line spacing is the vertical spacing of the paragraph's lines. It can be expressed as a fixed amount in points or as a percentage of the line height. You can set line spacing to any amount you like, as described in the following sections. You can also set different line spacing for different paragraph styles. (Paragraph styles are discussed in Chapter 8, "Working with Templates and Nonstandard Layouts.")

Choosing a Line Spacing Multiplier

You can quickly switch a paragraph among a few common line-spacing settings with the Line and Paragraph Spacing button on the Home tab. The choices are measured in multiples of the text height: 1.0, 1.15, 1.5, 2.0, 2.5, or 3.0.

Because line spacing depends on the font size, it changes as the font size does. For example, if the text in the paragraph is 12 points in size, a setting of 1.5 would add 6 points of extra space between lines (see Figure 5.2). (The 1 is the line itself, and the .5 is the extra space.)

 note

When a paragraph has multiple font sizes, each line of the paragraph controls its own height independently based on the size needed for the largest font used on that line.

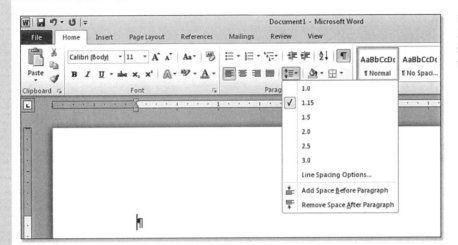

Figure 5.2
Make quick line
spacing selections
from the Home tab.

Setting a Precise Line-Spacing Value

The Line Spacing Options command on the Line and Paragraph Spacing button's menu opens the Paragraph dialog box (see Figure 5.3).

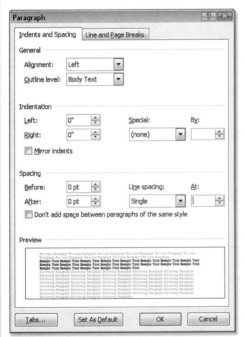

Figure 5.3
More spacing options are available in the Paragraph dialog box.

The Line Spacing drop-down list in the Paragraph dialog box offers these choices:

- **Single**—Single spacing. There's no extra space between lines. It's the same as 1.0 on the button's menu.

- **1.5 Lines**—One-and-a-half spacing. There's an extra half-height blank line between each printed line of the paragraph. It's the same as 1.5 on the button's menu.

- **Double**—Double-spacing. There's an extra blank line between each printed line of the paragraph. It's the same as 2.0 on the button's menu.

- **At Least**—A minimum line height to be used. (You specify the amount.) If the single-space line height is greater than the amount specified, single spacing is used for that line. Otherwise, the At Least value is used.

- **Exactly**—A precise line height to be used. (You specify the amount.) Be careful with this setting; if you specify a size that's smaller than the largest font size used in the paragraph, the large letters become truncated on top.

- **Multiple**—A multiple of single spacing. (For example, enter 3 for triple spacing.) You can enter any value from 0 to 132, in decimal increments of 0.01. This is how the default setting of 1.15 is created.

Desktop publishing programs typically call line spacing by another name: leading (rhymes with *bedding*). The term *leading* technically refers to the amount of blank space between the lines, not to the total line height. For example, in a desktop publishing program, a leading value of 4 points would add 4 points of vertical space between each line of the paragraph, regardless of the total line heights.

In Word, you cannot directly set leading. The At Least and Exactly settings are the closest things to it, but they're calculated differently. The At Least and Exactly values are expressed in total line height, not blank space height. For example, an Exactly setting of 16 pt, when used on a paragraph that has 12-point text in it, would result in a 4-point vertical space between lines. However, that same setting, when used with 10-point text, would have a 6-point vertical space between lines. And when used with 20-point text, there would be no vertical space between lines, and the tops of the larger letters would be cut off.

When the line spacing setting specifies more height than is needed for a line of text (given its largest font size), the extra spacing appears *below* the text. This is useful to keep in mind because it affects the amount of space that follows the paragraph. If you have two consecutive double-spaced paragraphs, there will also be double spacing between them because the extra space for the last line of the first paragraph will appear at its bottom. However, if a double-spaced paragraph follows a single-spaced one, there will only be single spacing between them because the single-spaced paragraph specified no extra space below each line.

Setting Spacing Before or After a Paragraph

The quickest way to add spacing before or after a paragraph is to choose Add Space Before Paragraph or Remove Space After Paragraph from the Line and Paragraph Spacing button's menu on the Home tab (refer to Figure 5.2). This adds the same amount of space, either before or after the paragraph, as the paragraph's font size. For example, if the font size is 12, choosing Add Space Before Paragraph adds 12 points of space before it.

If you need different spacing than that, use the Paragraph dialog box (refer to Figure 5.3). It has Before and After settings that add space before and after the paragraph, respectively. Enter the number of points of extra space you want.

The After setting is cumulative with the line-spacing setting. For example, if you have a paragraph with 12-point text and its line spacing is set to Double, and then you add an After value of 5 pt, there will be 17 points of space between that paragraph and the next one.

Before and After values are also cumulative with one another. If two consecutive paragraphs have Before values of 10 and After values of 10, they will have 20 points of space between them (not counting any extra space coming from the Line Spacing setting).

The Page Layout tab also has Before and After boxes that work the same as their counterparts in the Paragraph dialog box. Use the increment arrows or type values directly into the text boxes there (see Figure 5.4).

 tip

Because all these cumulative effects can be potentially confusing, I recommend using only After spacing (not Before spacing) when creating space between paragraphs. That's a somewhat arbitrary decision; you could just as easily stick with the Before setting and never use the After setting. However, because line spacing applies itself below each line of a paragraph (including the last line), it makes marginally more sense to go with After.

Spacing Before and After Paragraphs

Figure 5.4
Set Before or After spacing from the Page Layout tab.

If you're in a hurry, it can be tempting to simply create extra space between paragraphs by pressing Enter a few extra times. That technique backfires in longer documents, however, because it results in spacing that is inflexible and difficult to modify. Each time you press Enter, you get exactly one line of space—what if you want more or less than that? And each of the spaces between the paragraphs is actually its own blank paragraph, so you can't change the spacing by applying paragraph styles to the text.

On the other hand, by applying spacing to a paragraph with the After setting (or Before, whichever you like), you make the spacing an integral part of the paragraph. That way, you can easily define that paragraph's settings as a new style and apply that style to other paragraphs to achieve a consistent look. You can also modify the style at any time to change the amount of spacing between paragraphs to tighten up or spread out a page as needed.

➥ *To change the line spacing for a paragraph style, see "Modifying a Style Definition," p. 239.*

Indenting Paragraphs

Indentation is the amount of horizontal space between the margin and the paragraph. It is used for a variety of stylistic purposes. For example, left and right indents often set off long quotations, and first-line indents are commonly used in newspapers and magazines to help readers' eyes track the beginnings of paragraphs.

You can set paragraph indentation with keyboard shortcuts, with buttons on the Home tab, with the Paragraph dialog box, or with the ruler. Although these methods achieve the same basic results, you create them somewhat differently.

Setting Precise Indent Values

For maximum control and precise numeric entry, use the Paragraph dialog box method. Select the paragraph(s) and then open the Paragraph dialog box by clicking the dialog box launcher icon in the bottom-right corner of the Paragraph group on either the Home tab or the Page Layout tab.

As you can see in Figure 5.5, the Paragraph dialog box offers three types of indents:

- **Left**—The indentation between the left margin and the left side of the paragraph.

- **Right**—The indentation between the right margin and the right side of the paragraph.

- **Special**—A list from which you can select one of two types:

  - **First Line**—The indentation of only the first line of the paragraph, in relation to the general left indent. For example, if the paragraph has a 1-inch left indent and a 0.5-inch first-line indent, the first line starts at 1.5 inches and all other lines start at 1 inch.

  - **Hanging**—The indentation of all the lines of the paragraph except the first one. Like First Line, this setting is cumulative with the Left indent setting.

The Page Layout tab also has Left and Right indent controls that correspond with the Left and Right settings in the Paragraph dialog box. Enter amounts or use the increment arrow buttons (see Figure 5.6).

Indents can be either positive or negative numbers. A negative indent forces the paragraph outside of the document margins. For example, in a document with a 1-inch left margin, a setting of –0.25 inches would place the paragraph 0.75 inches from the edge of the paper.

You can specify each indent type in increments as small as 0.01 inches. Note that indents are measured in inches, not points, as with vertical spacing. There is no fixed limit for the maximum amount of indentation you can specify, but if the indents are so large that they squeeze out the text entirely, an error message appears telling you that you have chosen indents that are too large.

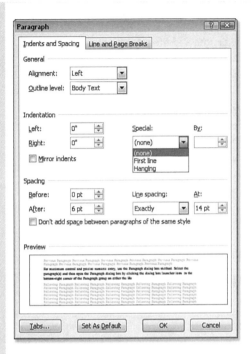

Figure 5.5
Set indents in the Paragraph dialog box.

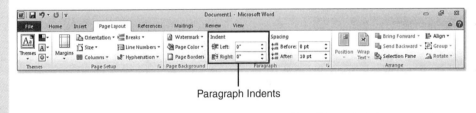

Paragraph Indents

Figure 5.6
You can set left and right indents from the Page Layout tab.

Quick Indenting with Buttons and Shortcuts

To quickly increase or decrease the left indent of a paragraph by 0.5 inches, select the paragraph(s) to affect and then click the Increase Indent or Decrease Indent button on the Home tab (see Figure 5.7).

There are corresponding shortcut keys for these buttons: Ctrl+M for Increase Indent and Ctrl+Shift+M for Decrease Indent.

 note

You can only decrease an indent to 0 with the Home tab buttons or the shortcut keys; you cannot force the paragraph outside the document margins. If you need to do that, for example, to create a one-time hanging indent, use the Paragraph dialog box method described in the preceding section or the ruler method described next.

Decrease Indent ¬   ¬ Increase Indent

Figure 5.7
Use the Indent buttons on the Home tab to quickly increase or decrease a paragraph's left indent.

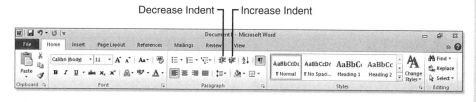

There are also shortcut keys for increasing or decreasing hanging indents, although there are no corresponding buttons on the tab: Ctrl+T is used to increase the hanging indent 0.5 inches, and Ctrl+Shift+T is used to decrease it.

Visually Indenting with the Ruler

Sometimes it is easier to set an indent by "eyeballing it" with drag-and-drop. By dragging the indent markers on the ruler, you can do just that.

The ruler has four indent markers on it (see Figure 5.8). At the left end are these three:

- **Left indent**—Controls the left indent for all lines of the paragraph.

- **Hanging indent**—Controls all lines except the first line. On the ruler, it is inseparable from the left indent marker.

- **First-line indent**—Controls the first line of the paragraph.

At the right end is a single marker:

- **Right indent**—Controls the right indent for all lines of the paragraph.

tip

If the ruler does not appear across the top of the document, turn it on by marking the Ruler check box on the View tab.

Hanging ¬   ¬ First Line   Right

Figure 5.8
Indent markers on the ruler.

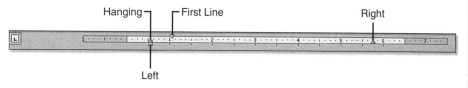

Left

Indent changes apply only to the selected paragraph(s), so make your selection before working with the indent markers.

You can drag the first-line indent marker separately from the others to create a different first line from the rest, just like when you enter a hanging indent value in the Paragraph dialog box. The zero mark on the ruler represents the document's left margin; you can drag the first-line marker to the left of 0 to create a negative indent that forces the paragraph past the margin.

The hanging indent works differently on the ruler than it does in the Paragraph dialog box. With the ruler method, dragging the hanging indent marker also moves the left indent marker, so the hanging indent is not cumulative with the left indent. A paragraph's left indent is always the same as its hanging indent; the first-line indent can either match up with them or can be offset to the left or the right.

When you drag the left indent marker (the rectangle), the first-line and hanging markers move along with it, without losing their relationship to each other. So, for example, if the hanging and left indent markers are at 1 inch and the first-line indent marker is at 0 inches, moving the left indent marker to 2 inches moves the first-line indent marker to 1 inch.

There is also an alternative method of setting the first-line indent and left indent on the ruler: Use the tab stop controls. (You'll see these in detail in the next section.) Here's how that works:

1. Select the paragraph(s) to affect.

2. At the far-left end of the ruler is the Tab Stop Type button. Click it until the first-line indent marker appears on the button's face, as shown in Figure 5.9.

3. Click on the ruler where you want to move the first-line indent marker.

4. Click the Tab Stop Type button again. Now the left indent marker appears on its face.

5. Click on the ruler where you want to move the left indent marker (and the hanging indent marker; remember that they move together).

note

The ScreenTip calls the marker in step 4 the hanging indent marker, but that's not wrong; it's just that the left indent marker and the hanging indent marker function as a single entity when setting them this way.

Click on the ruler where you
want to set the first line indent.

Click here until the first-line indent symbol appears.

Figure 5.9
You can set the first-line and left indents using a tab stop method.

Working with Tab Stops

Tab stops are nonprinting markers that tell the insertion point where to stop when you press the Tab key. By default, a paragraph has tab stops every 0.5 inches in Word, but you can create your own custom tab stops to replace or supplement these.

Back in the days of the typewriter, the best (and only) way to create a multicolumn layout was to use tab stops. In Word 2010, there are many alternatives to that, such as creating newspaper-style columns with the Columns feature and creating a multicolumn tabular layout with the Tables feature. Nevertheless, tab stops remain a viable option for simple multicolumn lists, and they even have some advantages that those other options can't match.

 tip

Each paragraph maintains its own tab stop settings, just like it does with line spacing and indentation. If you want the entire document to have the same tab stops, select the entire document (Ctrl+A) before setting the tab stops, or better yet, include tab stops in the definitions of the styles you apply to the paragraphs.

➡ *To create a document with newspaper-style columns, see "Working with Multiple Columns," p. 280.*

➡ *To create a document with tabular columns, see "Creating a Table," p. 335.*

➡ *To modify a style's tab stop settings, see "Modifying Styles," p. 238.*

When setting up a tabbed list, many beginners end up pressing Tab multiple times, moving through the default tab stops until they reach the desired position. With nonprinting characters displayed, that might look something like Figure 5.10.

 ## Tab Stops Don't Work in a Table

You can have tab stops in table cells, but how do you move the insertion point to them? Pressing the Tab key within a table cell moves the insertion point to the next cell, not to the tab stop. Try using Ctrl+Tab instead.

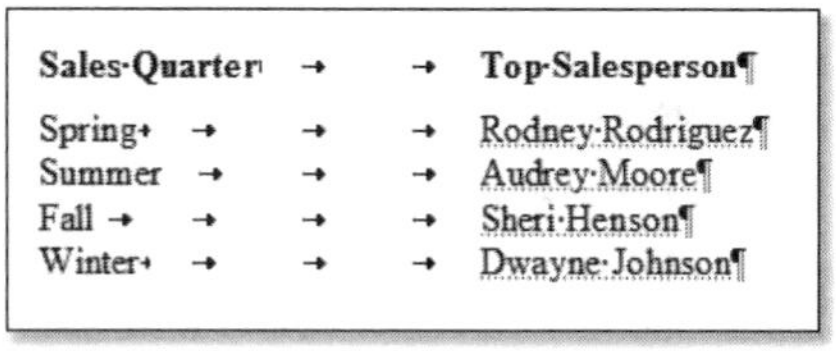

Figure 5.10
Some people press Tab multiple times to move through the default tab stops.

Sales·Quarter	→	→	Top·Salesperson¶
Spring⁺	→	→	→ Rodney·Rodriguez¶
Summer	→	→	→ Audrey·Moore¶
Fall →	→	→	→ Sheri·Henson¶
Winter⁺	→	→	→ Dwayne·Johnson¶

A better way, though, is to simply set a custom tab stop where you want the insertion point to stop and then press Tab only once to get to it. (When you set a custom tab stop, all the default tab stops to its left disappear.) With a single tab stop creating the full amount of space, as in Figure 5.11, it's easy to modify the list later by adjusting that one tab stop's position.

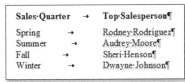

Figure 5.11
A better use of tab stops is to create a single stop exactly where you want it.

Types of Tab Stops

The default tab stop type is Left, the traditional "typewriter-style" stop. That's not the only type of stop available, though; here is a full list of the tab stop types. Figure 5.12 shows examples of several types.

Left—Text is left-aligned and extends to the right of the stop. This general-purpose tab stop is the staple of most lists.

Center—Text is center-aligned with the tab stop so that half of it extends to the left of the stop and half to the right. Center tab stops work well for centering headings over columns of data.

Right—Text is right-aligned and extends to the left of the tab stop. This type is good for aligning text at the right margin, for example.

Decimal—The first decimal (period) in the text is aligned at the tab stop position; anything that comes before it is right-aligned, and anything that comes after it is left-aligned. This one is great for lining up columns of numbers that have differing numbers of digits before and after the decimal point.

Bar—This one is not really a tab stop in the same sense as the others. When a bar stop is set at a particular position, pressing Tab to move to that spot places a vertical line there, the height of that line of text. When several of these appear in consecutive lines, they form a solid vertical divider line, making the tabbed list resemble a table.

Placing and Removing Tab Stops on the Ruler

Each time you click the Tab Stop Type button (to the far left of the ruler), the button cycles through the tab stop types listed in the preceding section. (There are actually two other items within the cycle—First Line Indent and Left Indent—but they are for setting indents, not tabs.)

> ➡ *To learn about setting the first-line and left indents using the Tab Stop Type button, see "Visually Indenting with the Ruler," p. 189.*

Figure 5.12
Tab stop examples.

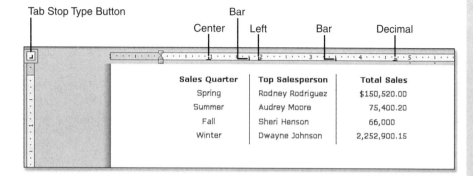

I Can't Place a Tab Stop Over an Indent Marker

When you click on the ruler to place a tab stop, it doesn't work if there is already an indent marker at that spot. To get around this, temporarily drag the indent marker to another location, place the tab stop, and then drag the indent marker on top of the tab stop. Alternatively, place the tab stop in a different location and then drag it on top of the indent marker.

When the Tab Stop Type button face shows the type of stop you want, click on the ruler to place it at the desired location. To remove a tab stop from the ruler, drag the stop off the ruler (up or down) and drop it.

To reposition a tab stop on the ruler, drag the stop to the left or right. As you drag, a dotted vertical line appears to help you line up the stop appropriately with the content in your document.

Defining Tab Stops with the Tabs Dialog Box

The Tabs dialog box is useful for setting tab stops when you need precise positions or when you need a leader character. A *leader* is a repeated character that extends from typed text to the next tab stop. Leaders are commonly used in tables of contents, for example, as shown in Figure 5.13.

 To generate tables of contents in Word, see "Creating a Table of Contents," p. 723.

> **tip**
>
> As you are dragging a stop to reposition it, hold down the Alt key to see measurements of the current tabbed column widths. This is useful if you need to create tabbed columns with exact width measurements. That's different from the exact positions on the ruler you get when creating tab stops with the Tabs dialog box (covered next), because this feature tells you the width of each column individually, whereas the Tabs dialog box tells you the ruler position of each stop. (Sure, you could calculate the width of a column from the ruler positions, but why bother when Word does it for you?)

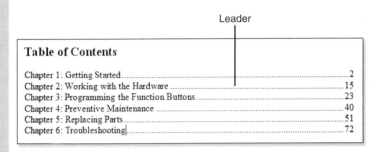

Figure 5.13
A tab leader example.

There are two ways to open the Tabs dialog box:

- Double-click any custom tab stop on the ruler.

- Open the Paragraph dialog box and click the Tabs button.

The Tab Stop Position list shows all the custom tab stops that are set for the selected paragraph(s). Tab stops are identified by their position on the ruler, in inches. The ruler begins with 0 inches as the left margin.

To remove a single tab stop from the list, click it and click Clear. To remove them all, click Clear All.

To create a new tab stop, enter a new value in the Tab Stop Position box, select an Alignment for it, and optionally select a leader for it (see Figure 5.14). Then click the Set button to create the tab stop.

Figure 5.14
Control custom tab stops in the Tabs dialog box.

You can change every aspect of a tab stop. Select the stop from the Tab Stop Position list and then change its numeric value (position), its alignment, or its leader setting.

I Don't See Some of My Custom Tab Stops on the Ruler

When multiple paragraphs are selected and they don't all have the same tab stops, tab stops do not appear on the ruler. You can set new tab stops that then apply to all selected paragraphs, but any tab stops that are specific to only certain paragraphs within the selection are inaccessible.

Changing the Default Tab Stop Interval

Word provides soft tab stops every 0.5 inches in a paragraph. By "soft," I mean they exist only when necessary—that is, when you press the Tab key. Otherwise, you would never know they're there.

You can change this interval for the entire document by doing the following:

1. Display the Tabs dialog box (refer to Figure 5.14).

2. In the Default Tab Stops box, increase or decrease the value.

3. Click OK to close the Tabs dialog box.

 tip

A change to the default tab stop interval affects all paragraphs in the current document. To make the change to all new documents, open the Normal.dotm template and make the change there.

Converting a Tabbed List to a Table

Tabbed lists work great when they contain small amounts of text, but what if some text in one of the columns needs to wrap to an additional line or two? In cases like that, you're faced with the thorny task of manually splitting up lines of text and trying to figure out how much text will fit between the tab stops.

When items of text must wrap to multiple lines in the list, go for a table instead. Fortunately, you don't have to start from scratch when you make the discovery that you should have used a table; you can convert a tabbed list to a table easily:

1. Select the entire tabbed list.

2. On the Insert tab, click the Table button. A menu appears.

3. On the menu, click Convert Text to Table. The Convert Text to Table dialog box opens (see Figure 5.15).

4. Confirm the number of columns. If the number is not what you expected, click Cancel, check that you have an equal number of tab stops in each line, and then try again.

5. Click OK. The tabbed list is now a table, and the Table Tools tab appears.

➡ *To control the table's size or adjust row heights or column widths, see "Sizing a Table," p. 349.*

➡ *To format the table, see "Formatting a Table," p. 354.*

Figure 5.15
Converting a tabbed list to a table.

Copying Tab Stop Settings Between Paragraphs

Because tab stops are somewhat time-consuming to set up, you will probably want to reuse the settings wherever possible rather than reset the stops for each paragraph. One way to facilitate this is to select multiple paragraphs before you set the tab stops in the first place. But let's suppose for the moment that you forgot to do that.

When you start a new paragraph by pressing Enter at the end of a paragraph, the tab stops carry over automatically.

To manually copy the tab stop settings (and other paragraph formatting too) from one paragraph to another, use the Format Painter tool you learned about in Chapter 4, "Applying Character Formatting," but instead of selecting specific text, follow these steps:

1. Click anywhere within the paragraph that contains the tab stops to be copied.

2. On the Home tab, click the Format Painter button.

3. Click anywhere within the paragraph to receive the tab stops.

If you need to copy the stops to more than one paragraph, double-click the button in step 2 rather than single-clicking, and then you can click multiple paragraphs, one by one, in step 3. Alternatively, you can drag over a group of paragraphs in step 3 instead of clicking within one.

Setting Paragraph Alignment

Alignment, also called *justification*, is the way that text aligns horizontally within its assigned area. In a regular paragraph, that area is the space between the right and left margins (or between the right and left indent markers, if set). In a table or text box, that area is the cell or the box.

The choices for paragraph alignment are as follows:

 Left

 Centered

 Right

 Justified

All are self-explanatory except perhaps that last one. *Justified,* also called *Full* in some programs, aligns the text at both the right and left margins. To accomplish this, Word inserts small amounts of space between words and characters so that shorter lines come out the same length as longer ones.

Left alignment is usually the best choice for business letters, reports, booklets, and other print publications. Left alignment results in the easiest-to-read text.

To set a paragraph's alignment, select the paragraph(s) to affect and then click one of the alignment buttons on the Home tab.

You can also select paragraph alignment from the Paragraph dialog box, although there is no advantage to doing so unless you already happen to have that dialog box open. Use the Alignment drop-down list on the Indents and Spacing tab.

 caution

Some people use Justified alignment for all their documents, thinking it makes the documents look more polished. Well, it does make for a pretty page, which is nice in a brochure or glossy handout, but it often impedes readability. For text-heavy documents such as letters, business reports, and research papers, stick with Left alignment.

Creating Numbered and Bulleted Lists

Bulleted and numbered lists help break up text into more manageable chunks and make it easier to read and skim. Just take a look at the text in this book! Regular paragraphs and headings are interspersed liberally with lists to better help you understand the material being presented.

Bulleted and numbered lists almost always use hanging indents, so that the bullet or number character "hangs" to the left of the rest of the paragraph. Back in the days of the typewriter, such formatting was done rather awkwardly with tab stops, but Word's Bullets and Numbering feature makes list making as simple as clicking a button.

 tip

Some people use bulleted and numbered lists interchangeably, but that's not always appropriate. When the order of the items is significant, such as in step-by-step driving directions, use numbering. When the order is not significant, such as in a grocery list, use bullets.

➡ *To number an outline, see "Numbering Outline Items," p. 671.*

Typing a Quick Numbered or Bulleted List

For a quick and simple bulleted or numbered list, use the Bullets or Numbering button on the Home tab, as shown in Figure 5.16.

Bullets ─┐   ┌─ Numbering

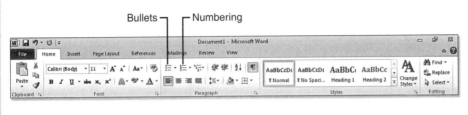

Figure 5.16
The Bullets and Numbering buttons on the Home tab quickly turn list formatting on and off.

There are two ways to use these buttons:

- Type the entire list, select all the text, and then click the Bullets button or the Numbering button.

- Click one of the buttons first and then start typing the list. Each time you press Enter, a new bulleted or numbered paragraph is created. Press Enter twice in a row to turn off the list formatting and return to normal text.

The bullet character or numbering style applied with these buttons is whatever you most recently used. The default is a plain round black bullet or Arabic numerals (1, 2, 3) in the same font and size as the paragraph text. Later in this chapter, you will learn how to change the bullet character or number style. After you make such a change, Word will remember your setting and will use that new setting for all future lists.

Creating Lists with AutoFormat As You Type

Recall from Chapter 4 that AutoFormat As You Type allows Word to apply certain types of formatting for you, on the fly, as you work. The feature includes help for creating bulleted and numbered lists, too.

First, make sure the options are enabled for numbered and bulleted lists by doing the following:

1. Choose File, Options. The Word Options dialog box opens.

2. Click Proofing, and then click AutoCorrect Options. The AutoCorrect dialog box opens.

3. Click the AutoFormat As You Type tab.

4. In the Apply As You Type section, make sure Automatic Bulleted Lists and Automatic Numbered Lists are marked.

5. Click OK to close the AutoCorrect dialog box, and then click OK to close the Word Options dialog box.

Then just start typing a list in Word. For a bulleted list, type an asterisk followed by a tab, and then the text for the paragraph. Or for a numbered list, type a number followed by a tab or period. Word automatically converts the list to use its own Bullets and Numbering feature.

To the left of the new number or bullet, an AutoCorrect Options icon appears. Open its menu and choose Undo Automatic Numbering or Undo Automatic Bullets if you did not intend for AutoFormat As You Type to kick in for that instance (see Figure 5.17). You can also press Ctrl+Z or click Undo to undo the autoformatting immediately after it occurs.

If you decide you do not like the automatic bullets and numbering, you can turn off either or both. Use the preceding steps to go back to the AutoCorrect Options dialog box and clear one or both check boxes, or on the AutoCorrect Options icon's menu shown in Figure 5.17, choose Stop Automatically Creating Numbered Lists (or Bulleted Lists, as the case may be).

➡ *To learn more about AutoFormat As You Type, see "Setting AutoFormat As You Type Options,"*
p. 176.

Figure 5.17
The AutoCorrect Options icon's menu lets you reverse an
AutoFormatting action.

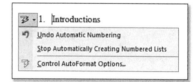

Restarting or Continuing List Numbering

When one paragraph of a numbered list immediately follows another, Word continues the list without incident. But when there is intervening text, Word can sometimes get confused.

Fortunately, Word *knows* it can get confused, so it asks for your help in the form of an AutoCorrect Options icon. In Figure 5.18, Word has guessed that the third numbered item is actually a new list, and it has restarted the numbering at 1. But whatever Word guesses, it gives you the option of sending it the other way. Click the AutoCorrect Options icon, and on its menu, click Continue Numbering.

Figure 5.18
Word gives you the option of continuing the preceding numbered list.

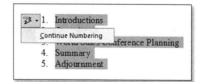

The AutoCorrect Options icon remains next to the paragraph after you switch to Continue Numbering, but its menu choice changes to Restart Numbering so you can go back if needed.

If you don't see an AutoCorrect Options icon, there's an alternate way. Follow these steps:

1. Do one of the following to open the Set Numbering Value dialog box (see Figure 5.19):

   ■ Click in the paragraph to affect. Then on the Home tab, click the down arrow to the right of the Numbering button, opening a menu, and then click Set Numbering Value.

   ■ Right-click the paragraph to affect, and on the menu that appears, point to Numbering and then click Set Numbering Value.

Figure 5.19
Control numbering by starting a new list, continuing a list, or setting a specific value.

2. Click Start New List or click Continue from Previous List.

3. Click OK.

Starting a List at a Certain Number

Besides starting or continuing a list, you can assign a specific number to a numbered list item. A list need not start with 1; it can start with any number you want, including 0. That can be useful when you are enumerating items that have unusual numbering or when you're continuing a list from another document.

To set a specific number, display the Set Numbering Value dialog box (refer to Figure 5.19), as in the preceding section, and then enter a specific number in the Set Value To box.

 caution

If you are using some other style of numbering, such as letters or roman numerals, don't enter that style in the Set Value To box; enter simple Arabic numbers there (1, 2, 3, and so on).

Changing the Number Format

A *number format* is the specification that defines how the numbering for the numbered list will appear. A number format consists of the following aspects:

■ **Number style**—What type of number characters will you use? Choices include Arabic (1, 2, 3), uppercase or lowercase roman (I, II, III or i, ii, iii), and uppercase or lowercase letters (A, B, C or a, b, c).

■ **Font**—In what font, size, and color will the numbers appear? By default, they appear in whatever way is defined by the paragraph's style, but you can modify that.

- **Extra text or symbols**—What text or symbols will precede or follow the number character? Common symbols to follow a number include a period or a closing parenthesis. Some numbered lists also have text preceding the number, as in Chapter 1, Chapter 2, Chapter 3.

- **Alignment**—What type of tab stop will be used to separate the numbers from the paragraph? The choices are left, right, and centered. The choice determines the way the numbers align.

Alignment is not much of an issue when all the numbers are the same length (such as an Arabic list of fewer than 10 items), but it's a big issue in longer lists or lists that use roman numerals. Figure 5.20 illustrates the difference between Left and Right number alignment.

Figure 5.20
Alignment governs the tab stop type at which the numbers align.

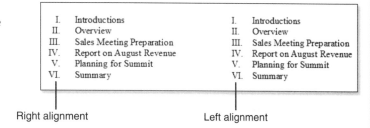

Right alignment   Left alignment

Selecting from the Numbering Library

The quickest way to change number formats is with the Numbering Library, available from the Numbering button's drop-down list on the Home tab (see Figure 5.21). You can also access the Numbering Library by right-clicking the selected list and pointing to the Numbering command. Just click the number format you want.

Your number format choice remains in effect (within the current document only) until you select a different number format. Subsequent numbered lists within the document use your chosen format automatically when you create them by clicking the Numbering button on the Home tab.

When you move to a different document (or start a new one), the default numbering reverts to regular Arabic style, but your previous choice remains easily accessible from the Recently Used Number Formats area of the Numbering button's drop-down list.

Defining a Custom Number Format

If none of the choices in the Numbering Library is right, you can define a custom number format instead. Follow these steps:

1. Select the numbered list to affect.

2. Open the drop-down menu for the Numbering button on the Home tab and click Define New Number Format. (Alternatively, right-click the numbered list and choose Numbering, Define New Number Format.) The Define New Number Format dialog box opens (see Figure 5.22).

3. Open the Number Style list and select the desired style. Notice that this list contains some additional options that were not in the Numbering Library, such as ordinals (1st, 2nd, 3rd) and text numbering (One, Two, Three).

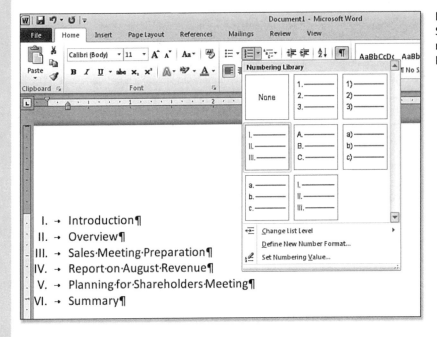

4. Click the Font button. The Font dialog box appears.

It is just like the regular Font dialog box, except some of the Effects check boxes are filled with solid squares. These squares indicate "no selection" for those effects. In other words, for those effects, the numbers will inherit the settings from the style. Leave these alone unless you need one of the effects to always be on or off for the numbers; if so, then click the check box to cycle through its settings (see Figure 5.23).

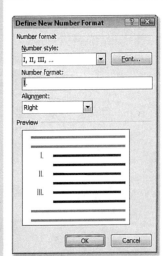

Figure 5.22
Define your own number format here.

Figure 5.23
Specify different font formatting for the numbers if desired.

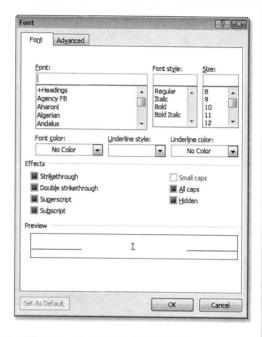

5. If desired, select a different font, font style, size, color, and so on for the numbers; then click OK to return to the Define New Number Format dialog box.

6. In the Number Format box, a code for the number appears shaded in gray. You can't change that. Click in the Number Format box, though, and place any extra text on either side of that code, such as a period or parenthesis after it or some text such as *Chapter* or *Section* before it.

7. Open the Alignment list and select an alignment for the numbering.

8. Click OK. The new numbering format is applied to the numbered list in your document.

After you've defined a new number format, it appears in the Numbering Library. It continues to appear there even if you start a new document or close and reopen Word. To remove it from the gallery, right-click it and choose Remove.

Changing the Bullet Character

With numbering formats, there's a limit to the creativity because numbers have to be...well, *numbers*. And there are only so many ways of expressing them. However, with bullet characters, the sky's the limit. Virtually *anything*, text or graphic, can be used as a bullet character.

The Bullets button on the Home tab has a drop-down list containing a small library of bullet characters. To apply one of these bullets to your list, select the list and then open the button's drop-down list and click a bullet (see Figure 5.24).

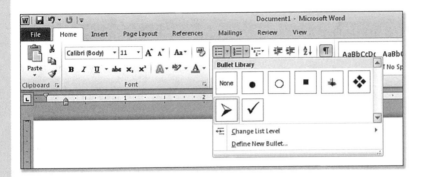

Figure 5.24
Select a bullet from the Bullet Library.

If you don't like any of the bullets in the Bullet Library, choose Define New Bullet from the menu. This opens the Define New Bullet dialog box, shown in Figure 5.25. From here, you can choose one of two types: Symbol or Picture.

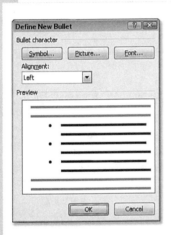

Figure 5.25
Create a new bullet.

Creating a Symbol (Text) Bullet

Symbols are text characters. You can select any character from any font installed on your PC—even one of the characters that doesn't correspond to any of the keyboard keys. To select a symbol bullet, click the Symbol button and then select from the Symbol dialog box (see Figure 5.26). First choose the desired font from the Font list, and then click the desired character within that font.

 note

If you happen to know the numeric code for a particular symbol, you can enter it in the Character Code box to locate and select it quickly.

Any font is a potential source of symbols, but some are much better suited than others. You wouldn't typically want to use a regular letter or number as a bullet, for example, and most fonts are primarily letters and numbers. Look instead at the specialty fonts such as Symbol, Wingdings, Webdings, and Marlett. Not sure which fonts contain potential bullet characters? Open the Font drop-down list on the Home tab and scroll through, looking for fonts where sample characters appear to the right of the name. Such fonts are good candidates.

After selecting a symbol as your bullet, click the Font button to change the font formatting for it. You can make all the same changes as for numbers, as you saw back in Figure 5.23. One of the most common changes is to increase or decrease the font size for the bullet, for example.

Figure 5.26
Select a symbol to use as a bullet.

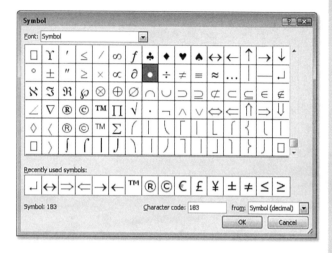

The Default Bullet Character Appears as a Clock Face

The default bullet character comes from the Symbol font (symbole.fon). If that font is damaged or has been removed from the system, Word falls back on the Wingdings font.

Each character within a font has a certain numeric value; when you change to a different font, the numeric value stays the same but the character changes. (That's why, for example, you get a different-looking capital *F* when you change to a different font, but it doesn't change to a capital *Z*.) Between fonts that contain letters and numbers, there is little difference between the characters represented by the same number, but within fonts designed primarily for use as symbols and bullet characters, there is a great difference.

As you might surmise by all that, the clock symbol in the Wingdings font happens to correspond to the plain bullet symbol in the Symbol font. So if Symbol isn't available, all your bullets look like clocks.

To fix the problem, look in the Fonts folder for the Symbol font (symbole.fon). To access the Fonts folder, go through the Control Panel or browse to C:\Windows\Fonts. If the Symbol font is there, delete it. If it's not there, someone has already deleted it. Replace it by copying the font file from the Windows CD, or from another PC that has Windows installed, into the Fonts folder.

➡ *To install a font, see "Adding More Fonts to Your System," p. 154.*

Creating a Picture Bullet

To use a picture bullet, click the Picture button in the Define New Bullet dialog box. The Picture Bullet dialog box opens (see Figure 5.27). This dialog box is actually a filtered version of the Clip Organizer, set up to show only clip art images that are suitable for use as bullet characters. Click one of the bullet pictures to select it, and then click OK.

A few notes on the picture bullet selection process:

- Some bullets have a little yellow star icon in the bottom-right corner. These are animated bullets; when they appear on a web page, they will have some type of animation associated with them.

- By default, the Picture Bullet dialog box does not access Office.com (a source of additional bullets) because on PCs with slow Internet connections, it makes the list slow to scroll. If you have a fast connection and want additional bullet choices, mark the Include Content from Office.com check box.

- The Search Text box at the top of the Picture Bullet dialog box lets you search for a bullet picture by keyword. However, in practice, most of the bullets have the same keywords, so this feature is of limited usefulness.

- To use a graphic of your own design for a bullet, click the Import button in the Picture Bullet dialog box, and then select the graphics file and click Add. You can add any graphic this way, of any size. Valid graphic formats for bullets are .gif, .bmp, and .jpg (or .jpeg). Simple graphics work best because of the small size.

- Unlike with a symbol bullet, you cannot directly modify the size of a picture bullet. The paragraph's font size determines the picture bullet's size.

 tip

Here's a workaround for picture bullet size. Global settings for a paragraph are stored in its end-of-paragraph marker, so by changing the formatting on that marker, you can affect the bullet character size. Make sure end-of-paragraph markers are displayed onscreen, so you can see what you're doing, and then select the marker only. (Position the insertion point to the left of the marker, hold down Shift, and press the right arrow key once.) Then change the font size from the Font Size list on the Home tab. The picture bullet's size will change.

Changing the List Level

Word supports up to nine levels of list nesting—that is, placing a subordinate list within a list. You can combine bulleted lists and numbered lists within the same nested structure, too. For example, in Figure 5.28, a numbered procedure has a bulleted list nested under one of the steps, and one of those bullet points has its own nested numbered list.

Here's the easiest way of creating a nested list: Start typing the main list normally, and press Enter for a new paragraph, and then press the Tab key. An indented, subordinate list item is created, ready for the text to be typed.

 note

Tab and Shift+Tab control list levels only if you press them when the insertion point is at the beginning of the paragraph, and only when bullets or numbering is turned on. Otherwise, pressing Tab simply tabs over to the next tab stop.

Figure 5.27
Select a picture bullet.

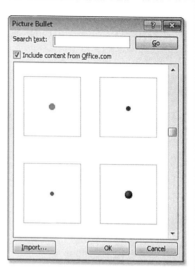

When the subordinate list is complete and you want to go back to the main list level, press Enter again to start a new paragraph, and then either press Enter again or press Shift+Tab. Both do the same thing: They promote that paragraph to the next-higher level.

Figure 5.28
Word supports up to nine levels of list nesting.

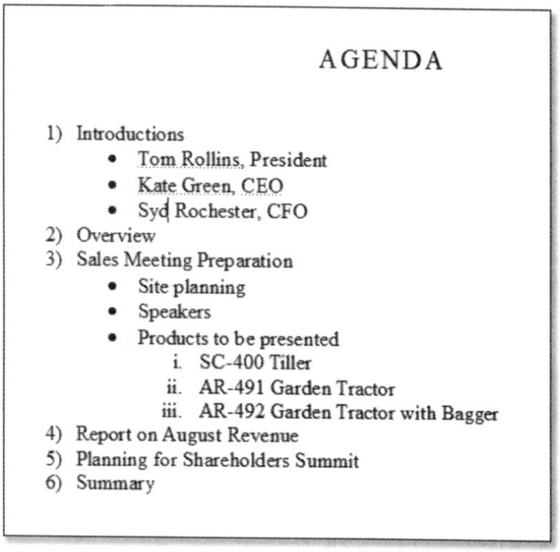

AGENDA

1) Introductions
   - Tom Rollins, President
   - Kate Green, CEO
   - Syd Rochester, CFO
2) Overview
3) Sales Meeting Preparation
   - Site planning
   - Speakers
   - Products to be presented
       i. SC-400 Tiller
       ii. AR-491 Garden Tractor
       iii. AR-492 Garden Tractor with Bagger
4) Report on August Revenue
5) Planning for Shareholders Summit
6) Summary

Another way to switch among list levels is with the Change List Level submenu, found on the drop-down list for both the Bullets and the Numbering buttons on the Home tab. Open the submenu and click the desired level for the selected paragraph(s), as shown in Figure 5.29.

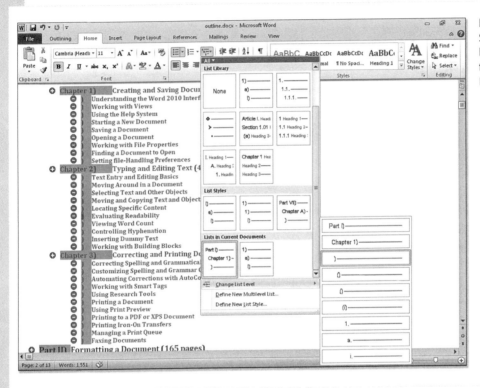

Figure 5.29
Switch among list levels via the Change List Level submenu.

 For more information about multilevel numbered lists, especially when used in outlines, see "Numbering Outline Items," p. 671.

Adjusting Bullet or Number Spacing and Indents

In earlier versions of Word, you could customize bullet and number formats by specifying a bullet position and text position. These positions defined the left indents and tab stop positions for the first line and subsequent lines.

You can still define bullet and text indents in Word 2010, but not as part of the bullet or number format. Instead, you make those changes as you would with any other paragraph, through the Paragraph dialog box or with the ruler.

To review the procedures for controlling indents, see "Indenting Paragraphs," p. 187.

> **tip**
>
> Although you can manually apply borders to individual paragraphs, as you will learn in this section, it is often more efficient to create a paragraph style that includes the desired border and apply that paragraph style to the desired text.

Applying Paragraph Borders

A *border* is a visible line around one or more sides of a paragraph (or around a group of paragraphs). Borders help create separations in the text to make it easier to read and skim. You can see borders at work in this book, for example, in the tips, notes, and cautions.

A border can be placed on any or all sides of a paragraph. The most common usage is to place the border around all sides, creating a box, but you can also achieve interesting effects by applying the sides more selectively. For example, in Figure 5.30, a bottom-only border is used under each heading, and notes are marked with top and bottom borders.

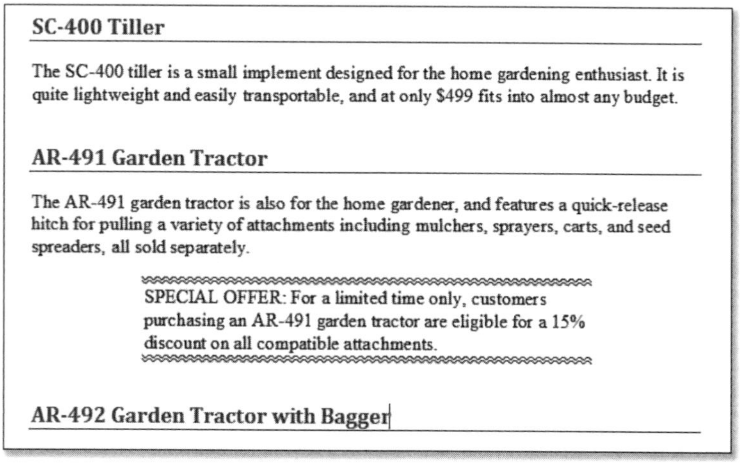

Figure 5.30
Examples of borders applied to only certain sides of paragraphs.

SC-400 Tiller

The SC-400 tiller is a small implement designed for the home gardening enthusiast. It is quite lightweight and easily transportable, and at only $499 fits into almost any budget.

AR-491 Garden Tractor

The AR-491 garden tractor is also for the home gardener, and features a quick-release hitch for pulling a variety of attachments including mulchers, sprayers, carts, and seed spreaders, all sold separately.

SPECIAL OFFER: For a limited time only, customers purchasing an AR-491 garden tractor are eligible for a 15% discount on all compatible attachments.

AR-492 Garden Tractor with Bagger

To create a paragraph style, see *"Creating a New Style by Example,"* p. 231.

I Wanted a Border on a Single Paragraph Only, But the Border Keeps Expanding as I Type

Remember, by default when you press Enter to start a new paragraph, Word continues the same settings into the new paragraph. Therefore, if the original paragraph had a border, the new ones do, too. This is by design.

To stop this, select the paragraph containing the unwanted border and then, on the Home tab, open the Borders button's drop-down list and click No Border.

Applying and Removing Borders

For a basic border (solid, black, thin), select the paragraph(s) and then use the Borders drop-down menu on the Home tab. It contains options for borders on various sides of the selection (see Figure 5.31).

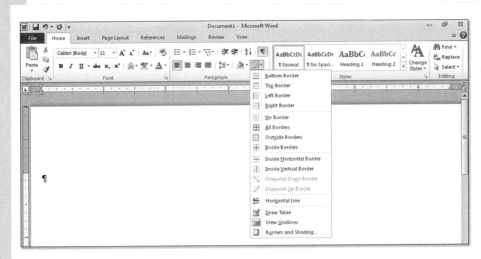

Figure 5.31
Apply a basic border to one or more sides of the selected paragraph(s).

Table 5.1 provides a summary of the border choices, along with some notes on their usage.

Table 5.1   Border Types

Menu Selection	Notes
No Border	Removes all borders from all sides of the selected paragraph(s).
All Borders	Turns on all borders on all available sides of the selected paragraph(s). This includes the borders between each pair of paragraphs in a multi-paragraph selection.
Outside Borders	Turns on all borders on all outer sides of the selection. If the selection is a single paragraph, the effect is the same as with All Borders. If the selection is multiple paragraphs, no lines will appear between the paragraphs.
Inside Borders	In a single-paragraph selection, this does nothing. In a multiparagraph selection, it places borders between the paragraphs but not around the outsides.
Top, Bottom, Left, and Right Border	These settings individually turn on each side. Settings can be combined; select Top and then reopen the menu and select Bottom, for example.
Inside Horizontal Border	In regular paragraphs, this is the same as Inside Borders. In a table, this adds the inside borders between rows only, not between columns.
Inside Vertical Border	In regular paragraphs, this does nothing. In a table, this adds the inside borders between columns only, not between rows.
Diagonal Down and Diagonal Up Border	In regular paragraphs, these settings do nothing. In a table, they draw diagonal lines through the selected cell(s).

Formatting Borders

The Borders button enables you to turn borders on and off, but it doesn't help you format them. So, if you want a border that's a different thickness, color, or line style (such as dotted or dashed), you must use the Borders and Shading dialog box.

To format a border, follow these steps:

1. Select the paragraphs(s) to affect. They can already have a border applied to them or not—it doesn't matter.

2. Open the Borders button's drop-down list and click Borders and Shading. The Borders and Shading dialog box opens with the Borders tab displayed (see Figure 5.32).

3. Select a border type from the Setting icons along the left side of the dialog box:

   - **None**—Turns off all borders.

   - **Box**—Places an outside border in which all sides are the same thickness.

   - **Shadow**—Places an outside border, and places a shadow effect along the bottom and right sides.

   - **3-D**—Places an outside border with a 3D effect—in theory, anyway. In most cases, there is no difference in the result between Box and 3D.

   - **Custom**—Enables you to select and format each side individually. (You can start with any of the other settings, and when you start to change individual sizes, the setting changes to Custom automatically.)

 tip

The Shadow effect that the Borders and Shading dialog box applies is quite limited. You can't change its size or color, and you can't shift it to other sides of the paragraph. If you need a more complex shadow, consider placing the text in a text box and then applying a shadow to the text box. That way you get a full range of shadow-formatting tools.

Figure 5.32
Format paragraph borders from the Borders tab of the Borders and Shading dialog box.

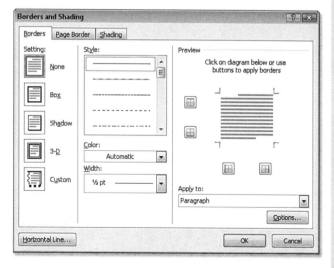

4. On the Style list, select a line style.

5. On the Color list, select a line color. (Color selection works the same here as with any other colored object.)

➡️ *For an explanation of Word's color choices, see "Changing Font Color," p. 158.*

6. On the Width list, select a line thickness.

7. (Optional) If you want to remove the border on certain sides, click the corresponding button in the Preview area. (There is a button for each of the four sides.)

8. (Optional) To control how far the border appears from the text on each side, click the Options button and then enter values (in points) in the Border and Shading Options dialog box (see Figure 5.33). Then click OK to return to the Borders tab.

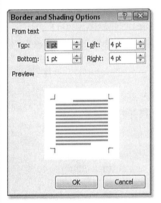

Figure 5.33
Adjust spacing between the text and the border if desired.

9. Click OK to accept the new border.

After having applied border formatting as in these steps, the next border(s) you apply with the Border button's drop-down list are formatted in the same way. For example, if you chose a light-green double border in the preceding steps, all new borders you apply will be light green and double until you change to something else (within the current document only).

Applying Different Formatting on Each Side

You can create some interesting effects by varying the borders on certain sides. To do this, first turn off the sides in the Preview area of the Borders and Shading dialog box by clicking them. Next, change the formatting selected in the Style, Color, or Width lists, and then click those sides again in the Preview area to reenable them with the new formatting.

For example, for a (somewhat) 3-D effect, apply a thick solid border to the bottom and right sides, and then apply the same style and thickness to the top and left sides but in a lighter color (perhaps a tint of the same theme color you used on the bottom and right).

Applying Paragraph Shading

Paragraph shading places a colored background behind the entire paragraph. Shading—like borders—helps make the text stand out from the crowd. You might make the shading on an important warning bright orange, for example, to point out its urgency.

To apply a simple solid-fill shading, follow these steps:

1. Select the paragraph(s) to affect.

2. On the Home tab, open the Shading button's drop-down list and click the desired color (see Figure 5.34). To try out different colors before committing, point to a color to see a preview of it.

 note

Don't confuse paragraph shading with highlighting (from Chapter 4). Highlighting is applied to individual characters within a paragraph; highlighting cannot exist in areas where there is no text (for example, at the ragged right margin of a paragraph). Paragraph shading, on the other hand, extends all the way to the edges of the paragraph on all sides in a neat rectangular form.

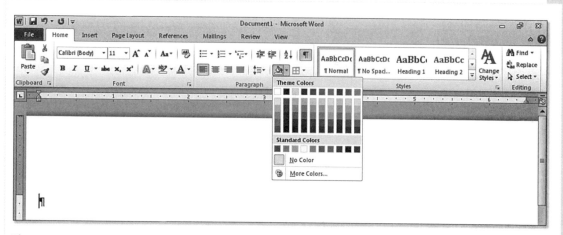

Figure 5.34
Select a solid shading color.

➡ *For an explanation of Word's color choices, see "Changing Font Color," p. 158.*

Patterned shading is another option. A *pattern* is a two-tone background that consists of one basic color (the Fill color) overlaid with a pattern of the second color. That pattern can be subtle, such as a spray of fine dots, or dramatic, such as strong stripes. The two colors can sharply contrast for a strong effect or can be very nearly the same for a subtle one.

To create a pattern fill, follow these steps:

1. Select the paragraph(s) to affect.

2. On the Home tab, open the Borders button's drop-down list and click Borders and Shading. The Borders and Shading dialog box opens.

3. Click the Shading tab.

4. Open the Fill drop-down list and choose the desired color.

5. Open the Style drop-down list and select the pattern style desired (see Figure 5.35).

6. Open the Color drop-down list and choose the color for the pattern.

7. Click OK to apply the pattern.

 caution

Patterns make the text more difficult to read, especially the bold ones with strongly contrasting colors. Use patterned shading sparingly and strategically.

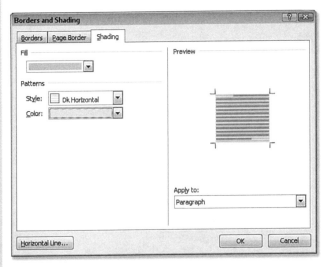

Figure 5.35
Select a pattern for the shading if desired.

Preventing Paragraphs from Breaking

In multipage documents, paragraphs don't always break gracefully. Sometimes a single line of a paragraph appears either at the bottom or the top of a page. These stray lines are called *widows* and *orphans*, and you can easily prevent them from occurring.

Follow these steps to examine and change the break settings for a paragraph:

1. Select the paragraph(s) to affect. To affect the entire document, press Ctrl+A.

2. Open the Paragraph dialog box and click the Line and Page Breaks tab (see Figure 5.36).

 note

There is debate over which situation constitutes a "widow" and which an "orphan." If a single line is left behind at the bottom of a page, is it orphaned, or is it widowed? The point is mostly moot because Word uses a single setting for avoiding single lines at both the top and the bottom of a page. However, Word Help defines an orphan as a single line at the bottom of a page, and a widow as a single line at the top. Word has several settings for controlling how (or if) paragraphs are allowed to break between pages. All are found in the Paragraph dialog box, on the Line and Page Breaks tab.

3. Mark or clear any of these check boxes as desired:

- **Widow/Orphan Control**—Ensures that if a paragraph breaks across pages, at least two lines of the paragraph will appear on each page. If this is not possible, the paragraph floats completely to the next page.

- **Keep with Next**—Ensures that the paragraph will not be on a different page from the paragraph that follows it.

> 🔍 **note**
>
> If you want to change the widow/orphan setting for all text, including any new text you type later, modify the paragraph style, as you'll learn to do in Chapter 6. You can specify line and page breaks in style definitions just like any other paragraph formatting.

Figure 5.36
Specify options for keeping lines together.

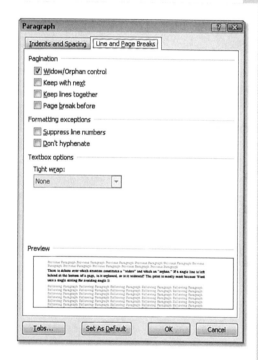

This is useful for keeping a heading with the body paragraph that follows it.

- **Keep Lines Together**—Prevents a paragraph from breaking at all. If it will not fit at the bottom of a page, the whole paragraph moves to the next page. This is especially useful in tables, where a page break that interrupts the text in a table cell can create confusion.

- **Page Break Before**—Starts the paragraph on a new page. This is useful for chapter and section titles, for example.

4. Click OK.

➡ *To create styles, see "Creating a New Style by Example," p. 231.*

 tip

Why use Page Break Before when you could just insert a hard page break before the paragraph? Well, if it's a one-time instance, that would be fine, but if you are setting up a paragraph style to be reused for multiple headings, all of which should start on a new page, you can save some time by adding the formatting to the style.

6

CREATING AND APPLYING STYLES AND THEMES

Understanding Styles

Styles are named formatting definitions that you can apply to text to ensure consistency within a document. For example, you could apply the Heading 1 style to all headings in the document, and all the headings would be formatted in the same way.

Styles also make it easier to make global changes to the formatting in a document; when you modify the style, all text based on that style is automatically updated. Suppose you decide you want all the headings to be underlined—just turn on underlining for the Heading 1 style and you're done.

Word uses styles not only to standardize document formatting, but to control the organization in outlines, tables of contents, and master documents. Investing time in learning about styles will pay off many times over as you explore Word's advanced features later in this book.

Types of Styles

Word supports several types of styles, each suitable for a specific formatting task.

The most common style type is *paragraph style*, which can apply both paragraph and character formatting to entire paragraphs. All paragraphs have a paragraph style; the default one is called Normal, and it carries the default settings for body paragraphs in the document. There are also built-in paragraph styles for headings, such as Heading 1, Heading 2, and Heading 3, each presenting a different heading level.

A *character style* is a style that contains only character-level formatting and that applies to individual characters. The default character style is Default Paragraph Font, which is derived from the character formatting defaults from the Normal paragraph style.

Two popular built-in character styles are Strong and Emphasis. By default, Strong makes text bold, and Emphasis makes text italic. At first it might seem strange that there are character styles that basically do the same thing as Bold and Italic manual formatting. The benefit in using them is not in the initial application, but in the possibility they create for easy change later. For example, suppose you know that you want to set off certain new vocabulary words in a document in some way, but you haven't decided on the exact formatting yet. If you've made them all bold with the Bold button and then later decide to use italic instead, you would have to manually change each instance. (Using the Replace feature could help somewhat.) On the other hand, suppose you format all the vocabulary words as Strong using the character style. Then if you decide to make the words italic, you simply modify the definition of Strong so that it is italic rather than bold.

In addition to character and paragraph styles, there are *linked styles*. Linked styles are nearly identical to paragraph styles, except for their behavior when applied to a selection of text (rather than to an entire paragraph). Suppose you select one sentence within a paragraph, and then you apply a paragraph style. The entire paragraph receives that style's character and paragraph formatting equally. If you apply a linked style, however, the character aspects of the style apply only to the selected text. (The paragraph aspects of the style apply to the entire paragraph as usual.) Throughout this chapter, everything you learn about paragraph styles also applies to linked styles, unless otherwise noted.

You can apply paragraph styles to text within table cells, but not to the cells themselves. To format table cells, use a *table style*. Table styles store table cell formatting such as background color, vertical and horizontal alignment, and cell border.

➡ *To format tables, see "Formatting a Table," p. 354.*

A *list style* applies settings specific to bulleted and numbered lists. List formatting, such as bullet and numbering styles, can also be stored in paragraph styles, but the List type has the advantage of storing up to nine levels of numbering or bullet formatting in a single named style. That way, if a list item changes in level, it need not have a different style applied to it.

Order of Style Application

When multiple types of styles are applied to the same text and one layer contradicts another, the formatting is determined by the last-applied style. Styles are applied in this order: table, list, paragraph, character. Therefore, any conflict between a paragraph style and a character style always results in the character style winning. However, attributes that the later-applied style does not specify are inherited from the earlier-applied style.

For example, suppose the Heading 1 style (a paragraph style) is set for Arial font, italic, 14-point, and red. Further, suppose the Emphasis style (a character style) is set for bold and green. If you apply the Emphasis style to a word within a Heading 1 paragraph, that word appears in Arial, bold, italic, 14-point, and green. Notice that because the Emphasis style doesn't specify the font type, italicization, or size of the lettering, the word instead inherits those attributes from the Heading 1 style.

Methods of Applying Styles

There are many ways of applying styles in a document, and much of the first half of this chapter is devoted to explaining those methods. Here's a quick summary:

- **Select a Quick Style from the Home tab**—This is a fast and easy way to use styles, but not all the available styles are represented. See "Working with Quick Styles," p. 220. To change which styles appear on the Quick Style Gallery, see "Removing or Adding a Style in the Quick Style Gallery," p. 222.

- **Choose a style from the Apply Styles pane**—Use a handy floating pane to access a drop-down list of styles. See "Using the Apply Styles Pane," p. 224.

- **Choose a style from the Styles pane**—Use the full-size Styles pane, as in earlier versions of Word, for full access to all styles. See "Using the Styles Pane," p. 222.

- **Press a shortcut key combination assigned to a style**—You can assign keyboard shortcuts to any style for quick application; see "Applying a Keyboard Shortcut to a Style," p. 237.

Methods of Creating and Modifying Styles

The built-in styles are useful, but most people find that they need more or different styles for their projects. You can create new styles or modify the definitions of existing ones. Here's a quick reference to those skills I cover in this chapter:

- **Change the Quick Style set**—You can quickly change the look of the paragraphs that have the built-in Quick Styles applied by changing the Quick Style set. These sets alter the definitions of the built-in styles automatically for you. See "Changing the Style Set," p. 221.

- **Create a new style based on existing formatting**—You can quickly define a new style that mimics some manual formatting that's already applied in the document; see "Creating a New Style by Example," p. 231.

- **Define a new style**—You can precisely define every aspect of a new style—everything from the font choice to the spacing and indentation. It takes longer, but you have more control. See "Creating a New Style by Definition," p. 233.

- **Make a style change automatically**—If you like, you can set up styles such that, when you apply manual formatting to text that has those styles applied, change their definition to match, so there is no manual formatting in your document. See "Updating a Style Automatically," p. 238.

- **Change a style to match a selection**—You can apply manual formatting to some text and then update the text's style to match it. See "Updating a Style to Match a Selection," p. 239.

- **Modify a style definition**—You can precisely define the changes you want to make to the style. See "Modifying a Style Definition," p. 239.

Working with Quick Styles

The Quick Styles feature enables you to apply certain styles from a sample-based menu system called the Quick Style Gallery on the Home tab. (In some parts of Word, it is called the Quick Styles list; it's the same thing.)

The first row of styles appears on the tab without opening the menu. Click a style there to apply it (see Figure 6.1).

If the style you want doesn't appear, click the down arrow to open the full menu (see Figure 6.2).

Quick Styles Gallery

Click here to open full gallery and menu.

Figure 6.1
The Quick Style Gallery is located on the Home tab.

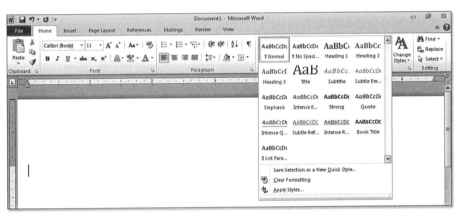

Figure 6.2
Select a style from the Quick Style Gallery.

In Print Layout or Web Layout view, as you roll the mouse over the various styles, the text in the document changes to show a preview of that style, so you can experiment with the various styles before you commit to one.

➡ *To create your own styles, see "Creating a New Style by Example," p. 231.*

➡ *To designate whether or not a style appears on the Quick Styles list, see "Removing or Adding a Style in the Quick Style Gallery," p. 222.*

 tip

To quickly apply one of the built-in heading styles (Heading 1 through Heading 3), press Ctrl+Alt plus the number corresponding to the heading level. For example, for Heading 1, press Ctrl+Alt+1. To quickly apply the Normal style, press Ctrl+Shift+N.

Changing the Style Set

In earlier versions of Word, each style had only one definition per template. If you wanted to change the definition of the Normal style, for example, you had to either change the style manually or apply a different template to the document.

In Word 2007 and 2010, however, you can apply style sets that redefine the built-in styles in various ways, all within the current template. You can quickly switch among the various style sets to create different looks without having to modify styles or change templates.

Here's how to select a different style set:

1. From the Home tab, click the Change Styles button.

2. Point to Style Set and then point to one of the style sets (see Figure 6.3). The document is previewed in that style set.

Figure 6.3
Browse the style sets.

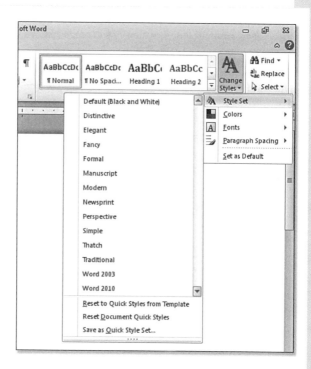

3. When you find a style set that you like, click it to apply it. The built-in styles change to reflect the new choice.

If you have any styles you've created yourself, they will not be updated by changing to a different style set unless they are based on one of the built-in styles. For example, if you have a Big Normal style that is based on the Normal style but is 14

 tip

You can create your own style sets by setting up the formatting the way you want it and then choosing Change Styles, Style Set, Save as Quick Style Set.

point, and the style set redefines the font and size of Normal, the font change cascades down to Big Normal, but the size change does not because Big Normal has its own size definition.

 To learn more about basing one style on another, see "Working with Cascading Styles," p. 241.

Removing or Adding a Style in the Quick Style Gallery

Ideally, the Quick Style Gallery should show only the styles you use most often. Keeping the list streamlined makes it easier to apply your favorite styles without wading through a large assortment. For example, if you never use heading levels deeper than Heading 1, you could remove the other heading levels.

To remove a style from the Quick Styles list, open the list and right-click a style; then choose Remove from Quick Style Gallery.

If you change your mind and want to re-add the style to the list later, display the Styles pane (as you'll learn in the next section) and then right-click the style and choose Add to Quick Style Gallery.

Using the Styles Pane

The Styles pane shows a list of the available styles (optionally with a preview). You can click a style to apply it to the selected text.

To display the Styles pane, click the dialog box launcher in the bottom-right corner of the Styles group on the Home tab. You can dock it, as shown in Figure 6.4, or drag it by its title bar into the center to turn it into a floating window.

To see a complete description of a style's definition, point at the style with the mouse (see Figure 6.5).

Each style has its own drop-down list in the Styles pane, which you can access either by right-clicking the style name or by pointing at it and then clicking the down arrow that appears to its right. On this menu are these options:

- **Update *stylename* to Match Selection**—Changes the style's definition to match the formatting of the currently selected text or the formatting at the insertion point's current location if no text is selected.

 tip

You can prevent users from switching style sets in a document by doing the following: Click the Styles dialog box launcher in the bottom-right corner of the Styles group (on the Home tab) to display the Styles pane. Click the Manage Styles button at the bottom (the third button from the left). In the Manage Styles dialog box, click the Restrict tab and then mark the Block Quick Style Set Switching check box.

note

Why use the Styles pane, when the Quick Style Gallery is so much more convenient? The Quick Style Gallery is somewhat limited in the styles it shows, for one thing. Not all styles are Quick Styles—nor should they be. Quick Style designation is reserved for the few most frequently used styles that you need to keep closest at hand. Heavy-duty style work is best done in the Styles pane.

Figure 6.4
The Styles
pane.

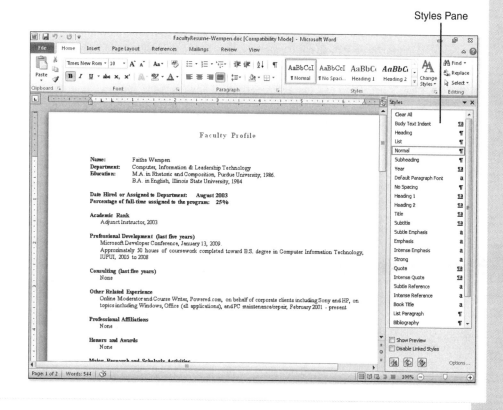

Styles Pane

Figure 6.5
View a description of the style's formatting.

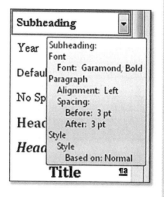

■ **Modify**—Opens the Modify Style dialog box, where you can edit the style's definition. (More on this later in the chapter.)

- **Select All x Instances**—Enables you to quickly select all instances of the style in the entire document. This makes it easy to apply manual formatting to all instances at once (although that's not really a good idea; it would be better to update the style definition to make such a global change). If the style is not currently in use, this option will be unavailable and will read Select All: Not Currently Used.

- **Clear Formatting of x Instances**—Strips off any manually applied formatting to text formatted with this style, re-establishing the consistency of the formatting. This option does not appear unless you have manually applied formatting.

- **Delete** *stylename*—Deletes the style. Works only on user-created styles; you cannot delete built-in styles.

- **Remove from Quick Style Gallery**—Keeps the style on the Styles pane's list but removes it from the list on the Home tab. If the style is not currently in the Quick Style Gallery, the command appears as Add to Quick Style Gallery.

Using the Apply Styles Pane

An abbreviated version of the Styles pane is also available: the Apply Styles pane. To display it, open the Quick Style Gallery menu and click Apply Styles, or press Ctrl+Shift+S.

The Apply Styles pane is a small floating pane where you can choose styles from a drop-down list (see Figure 6.6). Its buttons are described in the following list:

- **Reapply**—After selecting a style from the list, click this button to apply it to text. It's equivalent to clicking a style on the Styles pane.

- **Modify**—Click this button to modify the style's definition (which you'll learn to do later in this chapter). It's equivalent to right-clicking a style and choosing Modify on the Styles pane.

Figure 6.6
The Apply Styles pane.

➡ *Another way to avoid moving the mouse to apply styles is to use shortcut key assignments for common styles. See "Applying a Keyboard Shortcut to a Style," p. 237.*

Customizing the Styles Pane

The controls at the bottom of the Styles pane offer several ways of customizing its appearance and functionality.

When Show Preview is enabled, the style names appear in the actual styles they represent, as nearly as possible. This makes it easier to remember what a style represents, but it makes the list somewhat less compact and can slow down performance somewhat on a slow PC.

When Disable Linked Styles is enabled, linked styles behave like paragraph styles. For example, when you select some characters of text and then apply a linked style, only those characters receive the character-level formatting from the style. If you disable linked styles, however, that character-level formatting applies to the entire paragraph regardless of the selection.

Click the Options hyperlink to display the Style Pane Options dialog box (see Figure 6.7).

Figure 6.7
The Style Pane Options dialog box.

The Select Styles to Show setting controls which styles appear on the Styles pane and Apply Styles pane. Here are the choices:

- **Recommended**—Only styles marked as Recommended appear.

  ➡ *To choose which styles are marked as Recommended, see "Sorting the Styles List," p. 243.*

- **In Use**—Only styles that are currently in use appear.

- **In Current Document**—Only styles that have been applied in this document appear. (Heading 1 through Heading 3 and Normal always appear even if they are not in use.)

- **All Styles**—All available styles appear.

The Select How List Is Sorted setting controls how styles will be arranged on the list. You can choose from the following options:

- **Alphabetical**—From A to Z by name.

- **As Recommended**—Styles marked as Recommended appear first, followed by the others, alphabetically within each section of the list.

- **Font**—Arranged according to the font choice, alphabetically by font.

- **Based On**—Arranged according to the style on which each is based, and alphabetically within that list.

- **By Type**—Arranged according to paragraph style versus character style, and alphabetically within those categories.

In the Select Formatting to Show as Styles section, specify how you want entries to appear in the Styles pane for manual formatting that has occurred but has not yet been officially designated as a style. This can be handy because it can help you create styles more quickly out of existing formatting.

In the Select How Built-In Style Names Are Shown section, specify whether you want built-in names to appear only if the previous level is used (for example, show Heading 5 only if Heading 4 is in use), and whether to hide built-in names when an alternate name exists.

Finally, you can choose to have these options apply Only In This Document or in New Documents Based on This Template. If you choose the latter, these settings are saved with the template; otherwise, they are saved with the document.

Clearing Styles and Formatting

There are several ways of clearing formatting, depending on how extreme you want the removal to be:

- To clear all manual formatting and remove all styles, reverting the text to Normal style, choose Clear All from the Styles pane's list.

- To remove the manual formatting from text, leaving only the style's formatting, do any of the following:

  - Click the Clear Formatting button on the Home tab.

  - In the Apply Styles pane, select the style name and click Reapply.

  - Open the Quick Style Gallery menu and click Clear Formatting.

- To remove all the manual formatting and all the character styles, leaving only the paragraph formatting, select the text and press Ctrl+spacebar.

- To strip any manually applied paragraph formatting, leaving only the paragraph formatting specified by the paragraph style, select the text and press Ctrl+Q.

You can also use a feature called the *Style Inspector*, a floating pane that can help you examine the formatting for text and strip anything you don't want. To activate the Style Inspector, click the Style Inspector button in the Styles pane.

The Style Inspector consists of two sections: Paragraph Formatting and Text Level Formatting. Each section has two eraser buttons. The upper button in each section removes the style (paragraph style and character style, respectively), and the lower button in each section strips any manual formatting but leaves the style intact (see Figure 6.8).

Figure 6.8
Use the Style Inspector to examine and remove formatting.

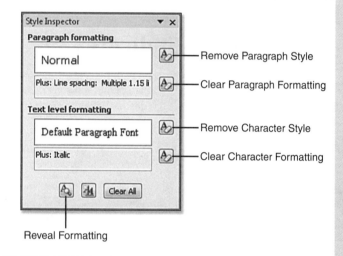

Reveal Formatting

Each of the areas in the Style Inspector also has a menu, similar to the menus available by right-clicking the style names in the Styles pane or the Quick Style Gallery (see Figure 6.9). What's different here is that you can access the paragraph style and the character style separately for the same text; this is useful when manual formatting has been overlaid over character styles that have in turn been overlaid on paragraph styles.

 tip
You can drag the Style Inspector window to the far left or right edge of the Word window to dock it there as a full-size pane.

Figure 6.9
All the usual menu commands for the styles appear here.

The Reveal Formatting button, pointed out in Figure 6.8, opens the Reveal Formatting pane that you learned about in Chapter 4, "Applying Character Formatting." It shows the exact formatting applied to the selected text.

⮕ *For more information about the Reveal Formatting pane, see "Revealing and Comparing Formatting," p. 174.*

Viewing the Style Area

In Draft or Outline view, you can optionally display a Style area to the left of the document. Next to each paragraph, the assigned paragraph style name appears, so you can easily locate any paragraphs that do not have the desired styles applied (see Figure 6.10).

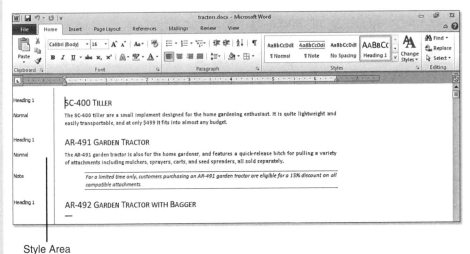

Style Area

Figure 6.10
The Style area.

To turn on the Style area, do the following:

1. Choose File, Options.

2. Click Advanced.

3. Scroll down to the Display section, and in the Style Area Pane Width in Draft and Outline Views box, enter a value greater than 0, in inches. The larger the number, the wider the Style area will be (see Figure 6.11). Figure 6.10 shows a width of 1 inch, which is typical.

4. Click OK.

⮕ *To switch to different views such as Draft and Outline, see "Working with Views," p. 13.*

Set the width of the style area.

Figure 6.11
Display the Style area
by specifying a width
for it.

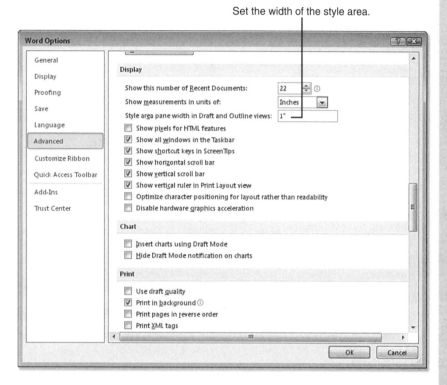

Creating and Deleting Styles

There are several ways to create styles, ranging from simple example-based techniques to powerful and specific definitions. The following sections look at the ins and outs of style creation, naming, and deletion.

Style Naming and Alternate Names

Before you start creating styles, spend some time thinking about the rules you will use for deciding on the names. Many a beginner has started out with a naming scheme that proved unwieldy, only to have to rename dozens of styles later to fix the problem.

Create style names based on the intended usage for the style, not based on the formatting. For example, *Article Title* is a much better name than *Arial 16-point* because you might decide later that the title should be a different font or size.

To create clusters of styles, name them with the same first few characters so that they appear together in alphabetically sorted listings. For example, to keep several bulleted and numbered list styles together alphabetically, you might name them List Bullet A, List Bullet B, List Number A, and List Number B.

Strategic naming is an issue only for the new styles you create yourself, because Word does not allow you to rename a built-in style. You can, however, create *alternate names* (aliases) for them.

To create an alternate name, follow these steps:

1. From the Styles pane or the Quick Styles list, right-click a style and choose Modify.

2. In the Name box, click to place the insertion point at the end of the current name. Then type a comma and the alternate name. For example, to alias Heading 1 as H1, type the following:

   Heading 1,H1

3. Click OK. The style name now appears in all listings with both names.

note

With built-in styles, you can actually just delete the name that appears in the Name box and replace it entirely with the alternate name. When you click OK, Word reinserts the original name before the name you typed, with a comma separator.

Creating the alternate name is in itself not that useful because lists continue to be sorted by the real names. However, you can then set up the Styles list to show the alternate names of styles *instead of* the real names. Follow these steps:

1. In the Styles pane, click Options. The Style Pane Options dialog box opens.

2. Mark the Hide Built-In Name When Alternate Name Exists check box (see Figure 6.12).

3. Click OK. Now, if a style has an alternate name, that name appears instead of the real name in the Styles list.

— Mark this checkbox to use alternate names.

Figure 6.12
Set the Styles list to show only alternate names when they exist.

Creating a New Style by Example

Creating a style by example is useful if you already have some text that's formatted in the correct way and you want to apply that same formatting consistently throughout the document.

Here's how to create a new style and place it on the Quick Style Gallery list:

1. Format text the way you want the style to be, and select that text. If creating a paragraph style, select the entire paragraph.

2. On the Home tab, open the Quick Style Gallery and choose Save Selection as a New Quick Style. Alternatively, right-click the selected text and choose Styles, Save Selection as a New Quick Style. The Create New Style from Formatting dialog box opens.

3. In the Name box, type a name for the style (see Figure 6.13).

4. Click OK. The new style appears on the Quick Styles list.

 note

The Modify button in Figure 6.13's Create New Style from Formatting dialog box opens a larger version of the same dialog box. This larger version opens by default when you create the new style from the Styles pane, as in the next set of steps. In it, you can make changes to the style definition. You'll learn about these changes later in the chapter.

Figure 6.13
Create a new style by example.

You can also create a new style by example with the Styles pane:

1. If the Styles pane is not already open, display it by clicking the dialog box launcher in the bottom-right corner of the Styles group in the Home tab.

2. Format text the way you want the style to be, and select that text. If you're creating a paragraph style, select the entire paragraph.

3. In the Styles pane, click the New Style button. The Create New Style from Formatting dialog box opens (see Figure 6.14).

4. In the Name box, type a name for the style.

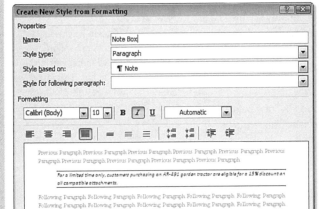

Figure 6.14
This dialog box is a more complex version of the one in Figure 6.13.

5. (Optional) Make any changes desired to the style definition. (You'll learn about such changes in the next section.)

6. (Optional) If you want this to be a Quick Style, mark the Add to Quick Style List check box.

7. (Optional) If you want the style to automatically update, mark the Automatically Update check box.

8. (Optional) If you want the new style to be saved in the template, click New Documents Based on This Template.

9. Click OK. The new style appears in the Styles pane.

 caution

You probably don't want to use Automatically Update because it can get you into unintended messes. This feature updates the style's definition whenever you make manual formatting changes to text that has that style applied. For example, if you have a heading level that is bold but not italic, and you apply italic to one instance, the style itself changes so that it includes italic and changes all instances.

A Style Changed Itself Automatically

This can happen when you have Automatically Update turned on for a style. That feature inter-prets any manual formatting applied to text as an invitation to update the style's definition to match that formatting.

To turn this off, right-click the style name, click Modify, and clear the Automatically Update check box.

Creating a New Style by Definition

Creating a style by definition means constructing the style's specifications based on dialog box settings rather than based on an example. That's somewhat misleading as a definition, though, because technically *every* new style definition starts out as a "by example." When you open the dialog box for constructing a new style, the default settings within it come from whatever style was in effect at the insertion point position when you opened the dialog box. The main point of differ-entiation, then, is whether you make modifications to the settings or just accept what the example provided.

To define a style, you use many of the skills you acquired in Chapter 4, "Applying Character Formatting," and Chapter 5, "Formatting Paragraphs and Lists," for applying character and para-graph formatting to individual blocks of text. The same controls—or at least similar ones—are used for the style definition in many cases.

To create a new style by definition, it is preferable to start out with as much of a "blank slate" as possible example-wise, so click in an area of the document that has the Normal style applied, or apply that style to an area. (Ctrl+Shift+N is a shortcut for applying the Normal style.) Then do the following:

1. If the Styles pane is open, click the New Style button. If not, on the Home tab open the Quick Styles list and click Save Selection as a New Quick Style. Then click the Modify button. Either way, the larger version of the Create New Style from Formatting dialog box appears.

2. Type a name for the new style in the Name box.

3. Select a style type from the Style Type list. The dialog box controls change to show formatting appropriate for the type chosen:

   - **Paragraph**—Contains paragraph-level formatting and can optionally contain character-level formatting that applies to the entire paragraph.

   - **Character**—Contains character-level formatting only.

   - **Linked (paragraph and character)**—Contains both paragraph-level and character-level for-matting and can be applied as either a Paragraph or Character style.

- **Table**—Contains formatting specific to tables and can include elements of paragraph and character formatting, as they apply to table cells.

- **List**—Contains formatting specific to bulleted or numbered lists, somewhat like an outline numbered list.

 note

A List style contains paragraph formatting for up to nine levels of bulleted or numbered list elements in a single style. This is useful because you can use the same style for an entire multilevel list, and you can promote and demote items without changing their styles.

4. Select a parent style from the Style Based On list. Anything that is not specifically defined for the new style is copied from this style. The most common style to base other styles on is Normal. This option is not available for List styles.

5. (Paragraph and Linked types only) Make a selection in the Style for Following Paragraph list. This determines the style of the next paragraph that appears when you press Enter at the end of a paragraph. For a heading style, it would be appropriate for the next paragraph to be a body style such as Normal; for a body style, it would be appropriate to have another paragraph of the same style.

6. In the Formatting section, use the controls to define formatting for the style. The controls are different for each style type. Figure 6.15 shows them for a Paragraph style, for example.

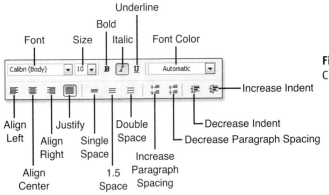

Figure 6.15
Creating a new Paragraph type of style.

The Linked style type's controls are the same as in Figure 6.15, and the Character type's controls are a subset of those. (The Character type includes only the controls that apply to individual characters, such as font, size, and color.)

The Table style type's controls are shown in Figure 6.16, and the List style type's in Figure 6.17.

 tip

If you want to be able to change the text appearance by applying formatting themes, don't specify a certain font or color for a style. Instead, set the font to the (Body) font for a body style or the (Heading) font for a heading style, and set the color to Automatic.

7. For the List type only, open the Apply Formatting To list and choose a list level (1st through 9th). Then specify the formatting for that level, and go on to the next level until you have set up all levels (refer to Figure 6.17).

Figure 6.16
Creating a new Table type of style.

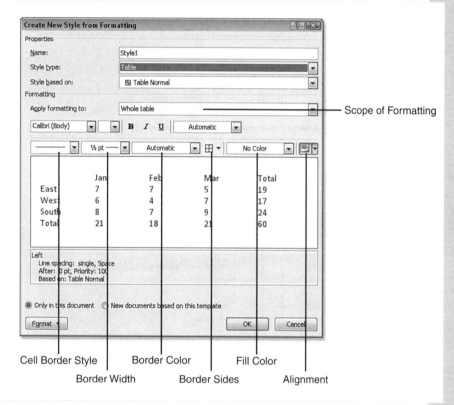

Scope of Formatting

Cell Border Style

Border Width

Border Color

Border Sides

Fill Color

Alignment

8. If any formatting is needed that isn't available in the Formatting section, click the Format button to open a menu of formatting categories, and then click the appropriate category.

Then set up the formatting in the dialog box that appears and click OK to return to the Create New Style from Formatting dialog box. The dialog boxes are the same as the ones you learned about in Chapters 4 and 5 for the individual formatting categories (Font, Paragraph, Tabs, and so on).

For example, to create a hanging indent for the style, you would need to select Paragraph and then set the Special indent on the Indents and Spacing tab.

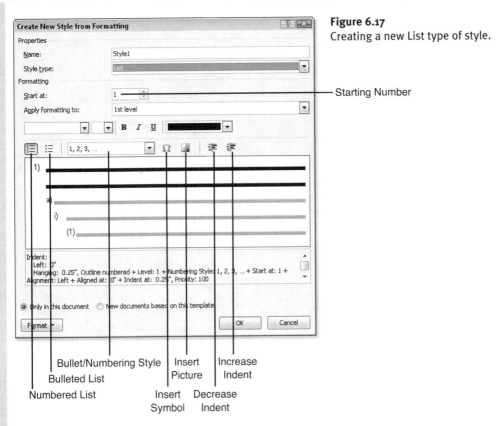

Figure 6.17
Creating a new List type of style.

Starting Number

Bullet/Numbering Style
Bulleted List
Numbered List

Insert
Picture
Insert
Symbol

Increase
Indent
Decrease
Indent

Each of the choices on the Format button's menu corresponds to a dialog box covered elsewhere in the book:

➡ For Font, see "Changing the Font and Size," p. 147.

➡ For Paragraph, see "Setting Line Spacing," p. 183.

➡ For Tabs, see "Working with Tab Stops," p. 191.

➡ For Border, see "Applying Paragraph Borders," p. 209.

➡ For Language, see "Checking Spelling and Grammar in Multiple Languages," p. 109.

➡ For Frame, see "Setting Text Wrap," p. 386.

➡ For Numbering, see "Creating Numbered and Bulleted Lists," p. 197.

9. If you want this style to appear on the Quick Styles list (gallery), mark the Add to Quick Style List check box. (This is not available for Table or List styles.)

10. If you want the style to automatically update its definition when you reformat text in the document that has that style applied, mark the Automatically Update check box. (This option is for Paragraph and Linked styles only.)

11. Select how the new style will be available: either Only in This Document or New Documents Based on This Template.

12. Click OK to create the new style.

Applying a Keyboard Shortcut to a Style

Keyboard shortcuts make style application much faster and easier because you don't have to take your hands off the keyboard to use them.

Certain built-in styles already have keyboard shortcuts assigned to them:

- **Normal**—Ctrl+Shift+N.

- **Heading 1 through Heading 3**—Ctrl+Alt+*number* (for example, Ctrl+Alt+1 for Heading 1).

You can assign keyboard shortcuts to other styles as desired. You can assign keyboard shortcuts as you are creating the styles or add them later.

To assign a shortcut key combination, follow these steps:

1. Do one of the following:

- To assign while creating a new style, start the new style as you learned in the preceding section, so that the large version of the Create New Style from Formatting dialog box is open.

- To modify an existing style, right-click the style on the Quick Styles list or in the Styles pane and choose Modify.

2. Click the Format button and then choose Shortcut Key. The Customize Keyboard dialog box opens.

3. Click in the Press New Shortcut Key box and then press the key combination to assign (see Figure 6.18).Key combinations usually involve some combination of the Ctrl or Alt key plus one or more numbers or letters, or a function key (F1 through F12). Many key combinations are already assigned; if you pick one that is taken, the Currently Assigned To indicator shows its existing assignment. You can assign an already-assigned combination, but the new assignment overrides the old one.

4. Open the Save Changes In list and choose where to store the keyboard shortcut—either in the current template or the current document.

5. Click Assign to assign the keyboard shortcut.

6. Click Close.

 note

You cannot assign shortcut keys to Table styles.

 note

Different dialog boxes open when you're creating a new style versus modifying an existing one, but they are virtually identical except for their names.

 note

To remove a keyboard shortcut from a style, repeat steps 1 and 2, select the shortcut in the Current Keys list, and then click Remove.

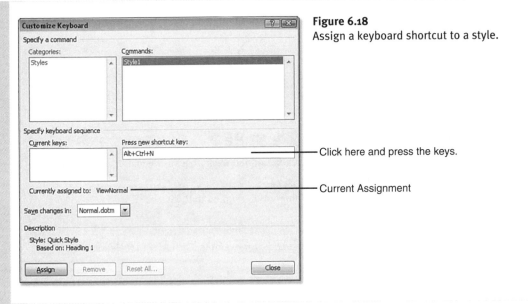

Figure 6.18
Assign a keyboard shortcut to a style.

— Click here and press the keys.

— Current Assignment

Deleting a Style

You cannot delete built-in styles, such as Normal and Heading 1 through Heading 9. (You can rede-fine them, though, as you'll learn in the next section.)

To delete a user-created style, right-click it (either from the Quick Styles list or the Styles pane) and choose Delete *name*, where *name* is the style name.

If the style is based on some other style than Normal, rather than a Delete command, you'll see a Revert To command. This command not only deletes the style but converts the formatting on any text to which it is assigned to the parent style. For example, if you have a style called Modified Heading 1 that is based on the Heading 1 style, selecting Revert to Heading 1 deletes Modified Heading 1, and all text that was formatted with it becomes formatted with Heading 1 instead.

Modifying Styles

Styles can be modified in several ways. You can set styles to update automatically, update a style by example, or revisit the style's definition using dialog box interfaces.

Updating a Style Automatically

As you saw when creating styles earlier in the chapter, an Automatically Update option is available. This option changes the style's definition whenever you apply manual formatting to text with that style applied. So, for example, suppose you select a Heading 1–styled paragraph and change the font for it. If the Automatically Update check box is marked for the Heading 1 style, the definition of

Heading 1 changes to reflect the new font choice, and all instances of Heading 1 used in the document also change.

It sounds like a good idea, but in practice, Automatically Update can cause problems because it takes away your ability to apply manual formatting to individual instances within a document. Therefore, be cautious with this option.

Here's how to turn on/off Automatically Update for a style:

1. Right-click the style on the Quick Style Gallery or in the Styles pane and choose Modify.

2. Mark or clear the Automatically Update check box.

3. Click OK.

Updating a Style to Match a Selection

As long as Automatically Update is not enabled (see the preceding section), you retain the ability to manually format some text in a manner that's different from its style's definition. If you then choose to incorporate that new formatting into the style's definition, you can use Update to Match Selection to do so.

To update a style to match the formatting of selected text, right-click the style on the Quick Styles list or in the Styles pane and choose Update *name* to Match Selection, where *name* is the style name.

Modifying a Style Definition

The same process you learned earlier in "Creating a New Style by Definition" can be used to modify the style later. This method uses a set of dialog boxes for defining the formatting.

To access the Modify Style dialog box, right-click the style and choose Modify. The Modify Style dialog box is identical to the Create New Style from Formatting dialog box, except for the name. Then use the same controls as when creating a style. You can set the basic formatting in the Formatting section; for more options, click the Format button to open a menu of categories.

Redefining the Normal (Default) Style

The Normal style is the basis for most other styles in the document, so modifying it trickles down changes throughout many styles.

You can modify the Normal style the same as you can any other style, but there is also a special location in which you can set a definition of Normal, either for the document or for the template. This is a rather basic definition, but it includes the essentials: font, size, color, paragraph position and indentation, and paragraph spacing (before, after, and between lines).

To modify the default settings for the Normal style, follow these steps:

1. Display the Styles pane and then click the Manage Styles button. The Manage Styles dialog box appears.

2. Click the Set Defaults tab.

3. Change any settings as desired (see Figure 6.19).

4. (Optional) If you want the changes to apply to the template, click New Documents Based on This Template.

5. Click OK.

 tip

If you want to retain the ability to have a theme change the body text's font, make sure you set the Font to +Body rather than a specific font. The same goes for color: If you want themes to be able to specify body color, set the Font Color to Automatic.

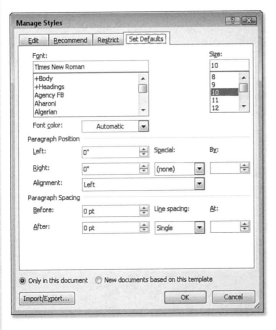

Figure 6.19
Redefine the default Normal style settings for the document or template.

Renaming Styles

To rename a style, open the Modify Style dialog box (right-click the style and choose Modify) and type a different name in the Name box. You cannot rename the built-in styles, only the user-created ones. (However, see the section "Style Naming and Alternate Names" earlier in the chapter to learn how to assign an alternate name to a built-in style.)

Style name changes are automatically populated throughout the document. Any text that is formatted with the renamed style remains so, but the style name associated with it changes to match the new name.

Working with Cascading Styles

Documents look best when all the styles are coordinated to give a unified impression. (That's the basic idea behind the Themes feature, covered later in this chapter.) When you make a change to one style in your document, you might end up needing to make the same change to all the styles to keep the document's look consistent, and this can be time-consuming.

To avoid having to make changes to multiple styles, consider setting up all the styles in the document as cascading versions of one central style, such as Normal. Then if you want to change a certain aspect of the formatting, you make the change to Normal, and the change trickles down to all styles based on it. This is known as *cascading* style definitions. You could even have multiple levels of cascading. Style C could be based on Style B, and Style B based on Style A, and Style A based on Normal.

Or, at the other end of the spectrum, perhaps you don't want every style to update based on your changes to Normal. Perhaps there's a certain style that should never change. You can set up such a style to be based on No Style, locking it into its own definition.

To set the style's basis, follow these steps:

1. Right-click the style and choose Modify.

2. Open the Style Based On list and select a style, or choose (No Style) from the top of the list.

3. Click OK.

Changing the basis does not change the style's definition, but it changes whether and how it *will* (or *will not)* change later. For example, if a style is no longer based on Normal, changes to Normal will not affect it in the future.

Modifying the Styles in the Current Template

Word 2010 makes it easy to modify the styles in the template. You do not even have to open the template for editing to do so—just work from within any document based on that template.

To modify the style definitions in the current template, start modifying a style and make sure you select the New Documents Based on This Template option in the Modify Style dialog box. This saves the style change to the template, not just to the current document.

You can also open the template file itself (File, Open and then select All Word Templates as the file type to open), but there's not much advantage in that in Word 2010 because you can so easily save styles to the current template from within any document.

Modifying Styles in the Manage Styles Dialog Box

If you need to modify a lot of styles, you might find the Manage Styles dialog box to be a more efficient interface for doing so than the Quick Style Gallery or the Styles pane.

To access the Manage Styles dialog box, display the Styles pane and click the Manage Styles button at the bottom.

The Manage Styles dialog box has four tabs. We're most interested in the Edit tab at the moment, shown in Figure 6.20. It lists all available styles in the document.

From the Edit tab, you can do the following:

- **Specify that changes be saved in the template**—Click New Documents Based on This Template before making changes.

- **View style definitions**—Click a style and examine the Preview area's sample and definition.

- **Modify a style's definition or name**—Click the style and click Modify, and use the Modify Style dialog box.

- **Delete a style (except built-in styles)**—Click the style and click Delete.

- **Create a new style**—Click the New Style button and use the Create New Style from Formatting dialog box.

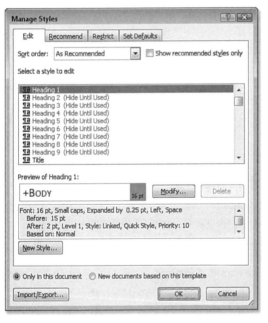

Figure 6.20
Manage the entire Styles list from one interface in the Manage Styles dialog box.

One handy feature of the Manage Styles dialog box is that it identifies styles that are set for Automatically Update with an (AutoUpdate) indicator following their names. This is a good way to see at a glance which styles are being automatically updated and to remove that designation if needed.

➡ To import or export styles, see "Copying Styles Between Documents," p. 245.

➡ To learn about the Recommend tab in the Manage Styles dialog box, see "Sorting the Styles List," p. 243.

Sorting the Styles List

An alphabetical list of styles, such as the one that appears in the Styles pane, is perhaps not the most efficient list. If a frequently used style happens to begin with a *Z*, for example, and the Styles list is long, you end up needing to scroll through the Styles pane's list every time you want to apply that style. It would be much nicer to be able to prioritize the list so that your favorite styles appear near the top of the list, for easy selection.

The Recommend feature enables you to do just that. You can set up a Recommend level for a style between 1 and 99 and then set the list's sort order to As Recommended. Within a certain level, entries are sorted alphabetically.

To view the current Recommend level assignments, follow these steps:

1. From the Styles pane, click the Manage Styles button. The Manage Styles dialog box opens.

2. Click the Recommend tab. All the styles available in the current document appear. (This includes both styles inherited from the template and styles you might have created uniquely in this document.)

3. Scroll through the list. The number that appears to the far left is the Recommend level (see Figure 6.21).

 note

If you set the Recommend level to greater than 99, the style is set for Last, which means it appears at the bottom of the list.

Figure 6.21
Set a Recommend level for each style.

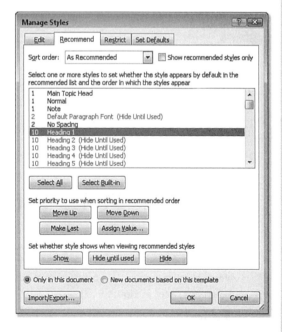

4. To change a level, select the style and then click one of the following buttons:

- **Move Up**—Promotes it one level (if not already 1).

- **Move Down**—Demotes it one level (if not already Last).

- **Make Last**—Sets it to Last.

- **Assign Value**—Opens a dialog box where you can type the number desired.

5. Click OK.

 tip

You can set the level for more than one style at once. Select multiple styles by holding down Ctrl as you click each one, or use the Select All or Select Built-In button. Be aware, however, that if either All or Built-In includes one or more unchangeable styles, you won't be able to change the value for that group.

Now make sure the Styles list is set to be sorted by the Recommend level. Here's how to do this:

1. On the Styles pane, click Options. The Style Pane Options dialog box opens (see Figure 6.22).

2. On the Select How List Is Sorted list, make sure As Recommended is selected.

3. Click OK.

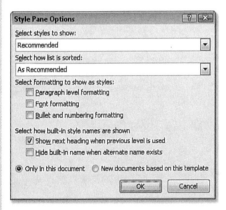

Figure 6.22
Set viewing options for the Styles list.

Filtering the Styles List

Besides the style sort order, the Recommend list controls which styles appear on a list that is filtered to show only recommended styles. The term *Recommended* in this context has nothing to do with the Recommend level number you assigned in the preceding section. Instead, it has to do with which of three statuses are configured for the style on the Recommend tab of the Manage Styles dialog box (refer to Figure 6.21):

- **Show**—The style appears on the list whether the list is filtered or not.

- **Hide Until Used**—The style appears on the list whether the list is filtered or not, but only if the style is in use in the document.

- **Hide**—The style does not appear on a filtered list.

To set a style's status, follow these steps:

1. From the Styles pane, click the Manage Styles button. The Manage Styles dialog box opens.

2. Click the Recommend tab. All the styles available in the current document appear.

3. Select a style, and then click the Show, Hide Until Used, or Hide button.

4. Repeat for each style to control whether it appears on a filtered list.

5. Click OK.

Next, filter the Styles list to show only the recommended styles by doing the following:

1. On the Styles pane, click Options. The Style Pane Options dialog box opens (refer to Figure 6.22).

2. In the Select Styles to Show list, choose Recommended.

3. Click OK.

Copying Styles Between Documents

One way to transfer the styles between documents is to save the styles to the template and then use the same template for the other document. That's the simplest and most-used method—and in fact, that's what templates are for.

If you can't do this for some reason, though, perhaps because the two documents must have different templates or because you didn't save the styles to the template and don't have the patience to go back and modify each style, you might find the Import/Export feature useful.

To transfer styles from one document to another or to transfer the styles from the document to the template, follow these steps:

1. Display the Styles pane and then click the Manage Styles button. The Manage Styles dialog box opens.

2. Click the Import/Export button. The Organizer dialog box opens.

3. Click the Styles tab. A list of the styles in the current document appears on the left, and a list of styles in the current template appears on the right (see Figure 6.23).

4. Select styles from the list at the left, and then click the Copy button to copy them to the list at the right.

What if the files you want to copy to/from don't appear in the right spots in the Organizer? Not a problem. Click the Close File button under the area to change, and the button changes to Open File. Then click it again and an Open dialog box appears. From here, you can select any file you like from which to copy styles.

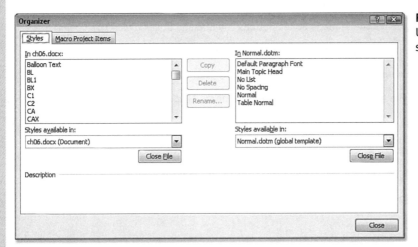

Figure 6.23
Use the Organizer to copy styles between documents.

Working with Themes

Themes enable you to change the look of the entire document at once by applying color, font, and effect changes that apply globally.

In Chapter 1, "Creating and Saving Documents," you learned that Word's native file format is based on eXtensible Markup Language (XML), and one of the benefits of XML is its ability to apply definitions to the various tags in a document. For example, if a certain paragraph is tagged as a Heading 1 style, you can use an XML-based theme to redefine certain aspects of what Heading 1 looks like, without actually modifying the Heading 1 style. This is useful if you want to change the look of a style in only one document and not all the documents you have that might use that style.

The Themes feature provides two main attributes to the text: font choice and color. A font theme defines two font choices: Heading and Body. A color theme defines about a dozen color swatches. These placeholders, when they are assigned to styles instead of fixed values, enable those attributes to be changed by changing the theme.

 note

Exactly how many colors are there in a theme? Technically there are 12, but two of those are for hyperlinks only and can't be applied to normal text. When selecting colors for text or objects in Word, you have 10 choices available. However, when you're selecting a color theme from the Page Layout tab, the samples show only 8 swatches.

If you want to use themes to control formatting, you must set the style's Font setting to either Body or Heading, depending on the type of element it represents. Also, you must set the Font Color to Automatic. Otherwise, the Theme setting cannot affect the text.

Applying a Theme

When you apply a theme, it affects the whole document, and it changes the font, font color, and effect settings. (Don't worry about effect settings yet; they don't affect text. They're for graphic object formatting.)

To apply a theme, display the Page Layout tab and then select a theme from the Themes list (see Figure 6.24).

When you point at a theme on the Themes list, a box pops up telling you its filename (for example, Flow). Sometimes it can be useful to know the filename of a theme if you want to copy it to another computer or delete it from your computer.

To go back to the default theme in the template, open the Themes list again and choose Restore Template Theme.

> **note**
>
> Themes are files with .thmx extensions. (They're binary files, not straight XML, so you can't browse them in a text editor.) The built-in themes are stored in C:\Program Files\Microsoft Office\Document Themes 14.

Figure 6.24
Select a theme.

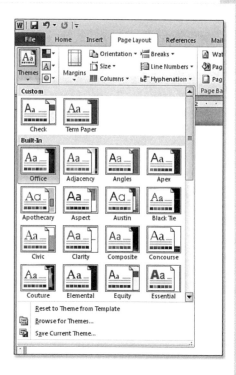

Setting the Default Theme

The default theme in the Normal template as it ships from Microsoft uses Calibri as the body text font and Cambria as the heading font. The headings are in various tints of blue or black. This default theme is called Office.

To change the default theme in the Normal template to some other theme, select that other theme from the Themes list and then reopen the Themes list (refer to Figure 6.24) and click Set as Default Theme.

Creating New Themes

A *theme* is a combination of fonts, colors, and effects, so to create your own new theme, first select all three of those elements. (Use the three drop-down list buttons to the right of the Themes button. You'll learn more about each of these later in the chapter.)

> For information about effects, see "Changing the Theme Effects for the Entire Document," p. 532.

Then after you have made your selections, choose Themes, Save Current Theme. In the Save Current Theme dialog box, enter a name for the theme and click Save.

User-created themes are saved in the C:\Documents and Settings*username*\ApplicationData\Microsoft\Templates\Document Themes folder (on Windows XP systems) or the C:\Users*username*\AppData\Roaming\Microsoft\Templates\Document Themes folder (on Windows Vista and Windows 7 systems). Each local user has a separate set of user-created themes, so your saved themes will be available only to you. If you need to make a theme available to all users on the local PC, save them instead to C:\Program Files\Microsoft Office\Document Themes 14. (The 14 refers to Microsoft's own numbering convention of version numbers; Office 2007 was 12. Don't worry too much about it.)

If you need to integrate a theme into Word that is not stored in either of those locations, browse for it. To browse for a theme, open the Themes menu and choose Browse for Themes.

Applying a Color Set

In addition to the full-blown themes, you can apply a variety of color sets. Use these when you're already happy with your fonts and just want the colors. Theme color sets are stored in C:\Program Files\Microsoft Office\Document Themes 14\Theme Colors, and they are stored in files with an .xml extension. (Again, you can copy these from PC to PC.)

To choose a different color set, open the Theme Colors menu on the Page Layout tab and click the desired color set (see Figure 6.25).

Creating a New Color Set

You can create your own color set, defining the exact colors that should appear in each of the color theme placeholder spots. You can then apply it to any document from the Theme Colors drop-down list, or you can use it as part of a new custom theme you create.

Figure 6.25
Select a color set.

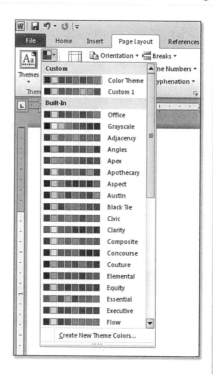

User-defined color sets are saved by default to C:\Documents and Settings\ *username*\
Application Data\Microsoft\Templates\Document Themes\Theme Colors (Windows XP) or C:\
Users\ *username*\AppData\Roaming\Microsoft\Templates\Document Themes\Theme Colors
(Windows Vista and Windows 7) as .xml files. As with themes files, these are available only to the
current user; to make sets available to all users, store them instead in C:\Program Files\Microsoft
Office\Document Themes 14\Theme Colors.

Color sets consist of 12 placeholders, each one populated with a certain color. There are four Text/
Background colors (two each for Light and Dark), six accent colors, and colors for visited and unvisited hyperlinks. Those are just the default purposes for the colors, though; you can assign any
placeholder to any object.

Follow these steps to create a color set:

1. If you want to base the new set on an existing one, apply that set to the document.

2. From the Page Layout tab, open the Theme Colors menu and choose Create New Theme Colors.
   The theme colors from the current theme are filled into the placeholders in the Create New
   Theme Colors dialog box (see Figure 6.26).

3. Click a placeholder to open a color menu for it and then click one of the colored squares, or click
   More Colors to select a color that is not shown.

4. Repeat step 3 for each of the colors you want to change.

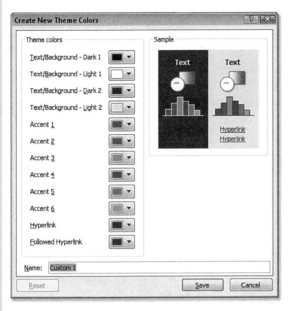

Figure 6.26
Create a new set of theme colors.

5. In the Name box, type a name for the color scheme. This is also the filename assigned to the scheme file saved to the hard disk.

6. Click Save to create the new color set.

Applying a Font Set

You can apply font sets to change the theme font without changing the color or effects. Any text that has a font choice of Body or Heading is eligible for formatting via the font set. These font changes work only if no specific font has been designated for the text, either through a style or through manual formatting.

To choose a different font set, open the Theme Fonts menu on the Page Layout tab and click the desired font set (see Figure 6.27).

Creating a New Font Set

To create a new font set, open the Theme Fonts menu (Page Layout tab) and choose Create New Theme Fonts. Then in the Create New Theme Fonts dialog box (see Figure 6.28), use the drop-down lists to select Heading and Body fonts. Give the set a name in the Name box and click Save.

 tip

Technically, you could also create a new color set by copying one of the existing color .xml files and editing it in a text editor such as Notepad. But the method from within Word is so much easier that there's little reason to do so.

Figure 6.27
Select a font set.

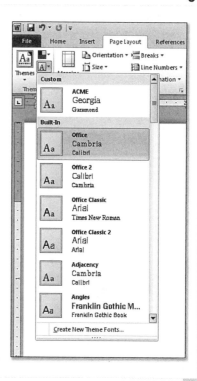

Figure 6.28
Create a new font theme.

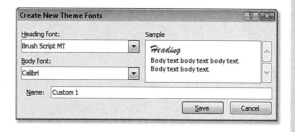

User-defined font sets are saved by default to C:\Documents and Settings*username*\ Application Data\Microsoft\Templates\Document Themes\Theme Fonts (Windows XP) or C:\ Users*username*\AppData\Roaming\Microsoft\Templates\Document Themes\Themes Fonts (Windows Vista and Windows 7) as .xml files. As with themes files, these are available only to the current user; to make sets available to all users, store them instead in C:\Program Files\Microsoft Office\Document Themes 14\Theme Fonts.

I Copied a Theme from Another PC and the Fonts Don't Look Right

A theme does not contain the fonts; it only references them. Therefore, if the new PC does not have the same set of fonts as the one from which the theme was copied, there could be a problem. When Word cannot find a font that is referenced in the document, it makes a substitution, which could be similar to the original or could be way out there in left field. See "Embedding and Substituting Fonts" in Chapter 4 for more information.

7

FORMATTING DOCUMENTS AND SECTIONS

Working with Sections

This chapter is about the types of formatting that affect entire documents or sections. So before getting too far into that, let's review what those terms mean.

A *document*, obviously, is the entire document file. Document-wide settings affect every page in the document and include vertical alignment, margins, line numbering, newspaper-style columns, page watermarks, and headers and footers. The settings that affect the entire document are stored in the hidden, nonprinting end-of-file marker for the document.

However, sometimes it's useful to have different "document-wide" settings in various parts of a single document, such as unique margin settings for certain pages or diverse column types. A *section* is an area of a document that can have its own separate values for settings that are otherwise document-wide.

You create sections with *section breaks*. Inserting a single section break can divide a document into two sections—one before the break and one after. One dramatic example of a document with a section break, for example, is a letter with its envelope. The envelope, in its own section, has a different paper size and page orientation.

➡ *To create envelopes, see "Addressing Envelopes," p. 322.*

The section break stores the same types of settings as an end-of-file marker, so the section can have its own set of "document-wide" settings.

Types of Section Breaks

There are five types of section breaks:

- **Next Page**—Starts the new section on a new page. Useful when you want different margins, headers/footers, or paper sizes (such as plain paper and an envelope).

- **Continuous**—Starts the new section without beginning a new page. This is useful when you want different numbers of columns on a page, for example, such as with a newsletter. You can't use this type of break between sections that have varied page orientations or paper sizes.

- **Even Page**—Starts the new section on the next even page number. This is useful when you want to make sure that the section starts on the *verso* (on the left side) of a two-sided spread.

- **Odd Page**—Starts the new section on the next odd page number. If the current page is odd, a blank page is inserted between the current page and the new one. This is useful when you want to make sure that each new chapter starts on the *recto* (on the right side) of a two-sided spread, for example.

- **New Column**—Starts the section in a new column, applicable only in a multiple-column document layout. This one isn't on the menu in Figure 7.1, but you can select it by inserting one of the other types of section breaks and then changing the type.

Figure 7.1
Insert a section break.

➡️ *To set up multiple columns, see "Working with Multiple Columns," p. 280.*

Inserting a Section Break

To create a section break, display the Page Layout tab and click the Breaks button. On the menu that appears, select the desired type of section break (see Figure 7.1).

You can also create section breaks indirectly by selecting a block of text and then applying some formatting to it that would normally apply to the entire document, such as changing the number of columns. When you do this, Word creates two continuous section breaks—one before the selected text and one after it.

Section breaks are nonprinting characters, like paragraph breaks. You can display them by switching to Draft or Outline view (see Figure 7.2).

Figure 7.2
A section break
is a nonprinting
character.

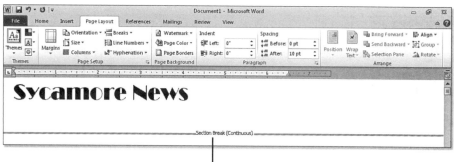

Section Break Marker (Appears Only in Draft View)

Deleting a Section Break

To delete a section break, select it or click immediately before it and press Delete.

Deleting a section break combines the text that was previously above the break with the section that follows it. For example, if you deleted the section break between the envelope and its letter, assuming the envelope was above the section break and the letter below it, the envelope's layout would change to that of a regular 8.5-inch × 11-inch portrait-orientation sheet.

Changing a Section Break's Type

You can switch section breaks among all the types listed earlier. One type in particular, New Column, can be set up only by changing the type of an existing section break; it does not appear on the Breaks menu.

To change a break type, open the Page Setup dialog box. Either of these methods will work:

- Double-click the section break line in Draft view.

- Move the insertion point into the section (anywhere above the break line) and then click the dialog box launcher in the Page Setup group on the Page Layout tab.

In the Page Setup dialog box, display the Layout tab, open the Section Start list, and select the desired break type (see Figure 7.3).

Select a section break type.

Figure 7.3
Insert a section break.

Changing Page Margins

Margins are the areas between the text and the edge of the paper on each side. The document's initial margin settings come from the template (for example, from Normal.dotm). Word 2010's default margin settings are 1 inch on all sides.

Selecting a Margin Preset

The Margins button on the Page Layout tab offers quick access to a few of the most popular margin settings, including Normal, Narrow, Wide, and Mirrored (see Figure 7.4). The Mirrored setting changes the Right and Left margin settings to Inside and Outside, so you can have a larger margin on the inside if desired to account for the binding taking up part of the space. If you have previously created custom margin settings, Last Custom Setting also appears on the menu.

 *For more information about adjusting margins for binding, see "Setting Up Gutters and Book Folds," p. 258.*

Figure 7.4
Select a margin preset.

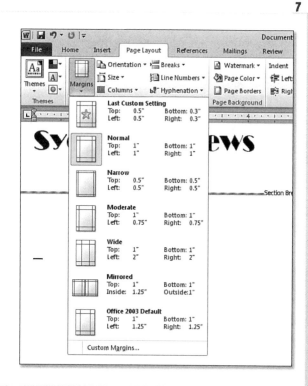

To set the margins for each section separately in a multisection document, click in the section to affect before setting the margin. The shortcuts from the Margins button apply only to the current section. Conversely, to apply the same margin setting in every section in a multisection document, select the entire document (Ctrl+A) before changing the margins.

Entering Precise Margin Values

For more control over margins, open the Margins button's menu and choose Custom Margins. The Page Setup dialog box opens (see Figure 7.5). From here, you can set individual margins for Top, Bottom, Left, and Right in inches (down to 1/100 of an inch of precision).

By default, margin settings apply only to the current section (if the document contains multiple sections). To change this, open the Apply To list and select either This Point Forward (to affect the current section and all sections that come after it) or Whole Document.

 tip

There can be two or more continuous sections on the same page, each with different margin settings. For example, if most of the document has a 1-inch left margin but a certain section has a 2-inch left margin, that section appears indented 1 inch compared to the rest of the document. (That's worth remembering if you are ever trying to figure out why some paragraphs appear indented but no indents are set for them.)

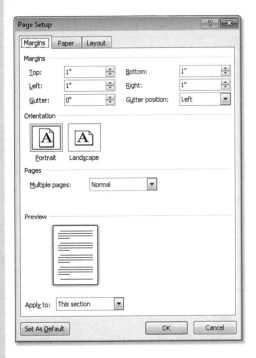

Figure 7.5
Enter margin settings in inches

Setting Up Gutters and Book Folds

When pages are bound into a booklet, you lose a certain amount of space in the center area, called the *gutter*. Therefore, when printing pages that you know will be bound this way, it makes sense to make the margin a little bit larger on the side of the binding. That's the principle behind the Gutter margin setting (refer to Figure 7.5). You can specify a gutter amount (that is, an amount of additional space to use) and a gutter position (either Left or Top).

In a two-sided publication, though, you can't simply add extra space on the left, because every other page will actually be on the right. The Multiple Pages setting takes care of this issue; you can choose from among these settings:

- **Normal**—No adjustment.

- **Mirror Margins**—Odd-numbered pages will add the Gutter value on the left; even-numbered pages will add it on the right.

- **Two Pages per Sheet**—Use this when printing two pages on one sheet of paper, either side by side (if Landscape orientation) or top and bottom (if Portrait orientation).

- **Book Fold**—This is the same thing as Two Pages per Sheet, except Landscape is the only orientation available, and you can specify how many sheets there will be per booklet. This is useful because Word automatically reorders the pages when printing so that they will come out right when printed two-sided and stapled in the center (see Figure 7.6).

- **Reverse Book Fold**—Available only when a language pack is installed for a language written right to left, such as Arabic or Hebrew, or a language that is read vertically, such as Chinese. It's the same as Book Fold, but the pages are oriented for that language's pagination.

Figure 7.6
Setting up a Book Fold page layout.

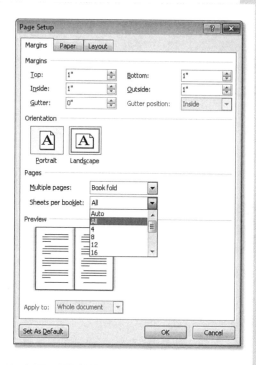

Setting Page Orientation

The *orientation* of a page is the direction the text runs on it. When text runs across the narrow edge of the paper, that's called *Portrait*. When it runs across the wide edge, that's *Landscape*.

To set page orientation, from the Page Layout tab, click the Orientation button and choose either Portrait or Landscape.

You can also set orientation in the printer driver, but in most cases, the orientation in Word overrides it.

Printouts Are Not Printing in the Correct Page Orientation

Word has a page orientation setting (on the Page Layout tab), but each printer's driver also has print properties that contain this setting. If the orientation is not what you think it should be based on Word's setting, look at the printer's properties. To do so, choose File, Print and click the Printer Properties hyperlink next to the printer's name. The page orientation set in Word is supposed to override any orientation set in the printer's driver, but sometimes this doesn't happen; changing the orientation in the printer driver can be a workaround.

Setting Paper Size

Word supports a variety of common paper sizes, and you can set up custom sizes as well. To pick one of the paper size presets, open the Size list on the Page Layout tab and select a size (see Figure 7.7).

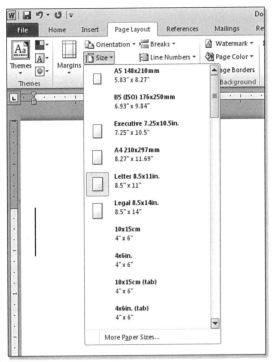

Figure 7.7
Select a paper size.

For more choices, click More Paper Sizes at the bottom of that menu to open the Paper tab of the Page Setup dialog box, shown in Figure 7.8. From here, you can select from a more extensive list of presets or enter exact Width and Height settings for a custom size.

Figure 7.8
More paper size options are available in the Page Setup dialog box.

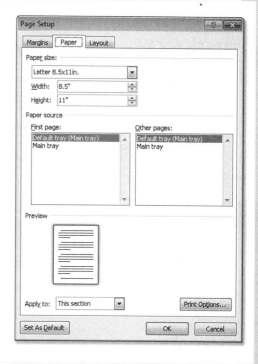

Setting Vertical Alignment

Every document and section starts out with vertical alignment set to Top by default, which means that if you type less than a full page of text, it is top-aligned. Most of the time that's good, but if you are trying to perfectly center a business letter vertically, you might prefer a Center vertical orientation.

To change the vertical alignment for a section, follow these steps:

1. On the Page Layout tab, click the dialog box launcher in the Page Setup group. The Page Setup dialog box opens.

2. Click the Layout tab.

3. Open the Vertical Alignment list and select a vertical alignment: Top, Center, Justified, or Bottom.

4. Click OK.

 note

There are lots of alternative ways of opening this dialog box. For example, you can click Margins on the Page Layout tab and choose Custom Margins, or click Line Numbers and then choose Line Numbering Options.

Justified vertical alignment spreads everything out vertically so the first line is at the top margin and the last line is at the bottom, on every page except the last one. (On the last page, Top alignment applies.) This might be useful, for example, if you are using widow/orphan control and a certain page is looking a little "short" because of it. It can cause inconsistencies in line spacing, however, and if you forget justification is turned on, it can turn into a tough-to-troubleshoot puzzle.

Using Line Numbering

Line numbering is a section-wide option that places a small number to the left of each line. People sometimes use it in legal documents or in documents that a committee is reviewing, for ease of referring participants to a specific spot in the document. It's much easier for people to find "line 20, page 10" than "the second line of the paragraph that begins about halfway down page 10."

To number the lines, click in the section and then click the Line Numbers button on the Page Layout tab. A menu of line-numbering options appears (see Figure 7.9). Select one of these options.

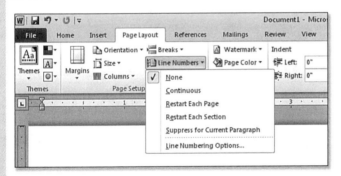

Figure 7.9
Choose a line-numbering method.

To access more line-numbering choices, do the following:

1. From the Line Numbers menu shown in Figure 7.9, click Line Numbering Options. The Page Setup dialog box opens with the Layout tab displayed.

2. Click the Line Numbers button. The Line Numbers dialog box opens.

3. Mark the Add Line Numbering check box. Line numbering options become available (see Figure 7.10).

4. Set numbering options as needed:

   ▪ **Start At**—Specify a starting number, or leave it set to 1.

   ▪ **From Text**—Specify a number in inches (the increment buttons increment by 1/10 of an inch with each click), or leave it set to Auto.

Figure 7.10
Set line-numbering options.

- **Count By**—Specify an amount to increment the value for each line (for example, 5 to count 5, 10, 15, 20, and so on), or leave it set to 1.

- **Numbering**—Choose to restart the numbering in each page or each section, or let it run continuously throughout the document.

5. Click OK two times to close both dialog boxes.

Inserting Page Breaks

Soft page breaks occur whenever Word runs out of room at the bottom of a page. You don't have to create or delete them; they come and go as needed. A soft page break occurs whenever there is no room in the main document area for the next line. Usually that's at the bottom margin, but it could be earlier than that due to various other factors, such as a page footer, footnotes, or widow/orphan control.

 To create page footers, see "Creating Headers and Footers," p. 266.

 To create footnotes, see "Working with Footnotes and Endnotes," p. 708.

 To set widow/orphan control, see "Preventing Paragraphs from Breaking," p. 214.

To end a page early—that is, before any of the conditions kick in that would trigger a soft page break—create a *hard page break* by inserting a Page Break code.

To insert a page break, position the insertion point where you want the page break to occur, and do any of the following:

- Press Ctrl+Enter.

- On the Insert tab, click Page Break.

- On the Page Layout tab, click Breaks and then click one of the page break types shown:

> **⚠ caution**
>
> Remember from Chapter 1, "Creating and Saving Documents," that the layout of certain groups changes depending on the window size. For example, when the Word window is fairly narrow, the Cover Page, Blank Page, and Page Break buttons disappear and are replaced by a generic Pages button representing their entire group. You must click the Pages button to access those other three buttons in a drop-down list.

- **Page**—Inserts a hard page break but does not create a new section.

- **Next Page**—Inserts a section break that is also a page break.

- **Even Page**—Inserts a section break that is also a page break, and includes an additional page break if needed so that the new section starts on an even-numbered page.

- **Odd Page**—Same as Even Page except the new section starts on an odd-numbered page.

Creating a page break does not really insert a new page; it just creates a break at the insertion point. For example, if you position the insertion point between two paragraphs and press Ctrl+Enter, the first paragraph appears on the first page and the second paragraph on the second page. You haven't really inserted anything (well, except for the page break marker). Instead, you've just created a split. However, Word 2010 does have a feature that actually inserts a new page: the Blank Page button on the Insert tab. It's the same as if you had created two hard page breaks and then moved the insertion point between them.

Inserting Cover Pages

The Cover Page feature lets you insert various sample page layouts for document cover pages. It always inserts the new content at the beginning of the document regardless of the insertion point position, and it creates a hard page break between the newly added content and the existing content.

On the Insert tab, click Cover Page and then select the desired cover page style (see Figure 7.11).

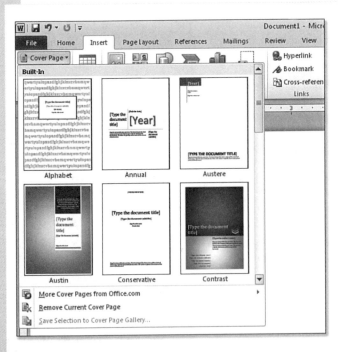

Figure 7.11
Insert a cover page.

Switch to Print Layout view, if necessary, to view the cover page layout. The resulting page contains ordinary content, in a mixture of regular paragraphs and text boxes. Some of the text boxes have background colors, but they are not fixed colors; they are placeholders from the theme color set. To change the colors, apply a different theme or theme color set.

 To work with themes and color sets, see "Working with Themes," p. 246.

 To learn how to manipulate text boxes, see "Creating Text Box Layouts," p. 307.

Saving Content as a New Cover Page

Here's where the cover page insertion feature becomes really useful: You can save your own formatted content as a new cover page and make it available for insertion in any document.

If this sounds familiar, it should—it's a continuation of the Building Blocks feature from Chapter 2, "Typing and Editing Text." In fact, the pages you create are actually stored as building blocks, exactly the same way the text-based blocks you created were stored.

To save content as a new cover page, follow these steps:

1. Create the content you want to save as a cover page.

2. Select everything you want to include on the page.

3. Click the Cover Page button, and select Save Selection to Cover Page Gallery. The Create New Building Block dialog box appears.

4. Fill in the blanks to describe the new building block:

   - **Name**—Give it a descriptive name of your choice.

   - **Gallery**—Leave this set to Cover Pages.

   - **Category**—Stick with General or create your own categories by choosing Create New Category.

   - **Description**—You can use this optional field to hold more information.

   - **Save In**—You can save in the current template (probably Normal.dotm) or in Building Blocks.dotm, the central library for building blocks in Word 2010.

   - **Options**—This setting controls how the insertion interacts with any existing text in the document. To make

> **note**
>
> After inserting a cover page, you can remove it by reopening the Cover Page menu and choosing Remove Current Cover Page. (That works for cover pages only, not other sample pages.)

> **note**
>
> To quickly review: A *building block* is a formatted snippet of text, graphics, or other objects, with complete formatting, stored as a reusable object within a template. The built-in building blocks in Word are stored in a template called Building Blocks. dotm. You can store your own custom building blocks there too, or you can store them in Normal.dotm (or whatever template is currently in use) if you prefer.

> **note**
>
> Don't worry if Word doesn't appear to let you simultaneously select regular text and a text box or graphic. If the anchor for the text box or graphic is included in the text selection, the object travels along with it.

the inserted text run in with existing text, choose Insert Content Only. The other choices are Insert Content in Its Own Paragraph and Insert Content in Its Own Page (the default, recommended for pages).

5. Click OK to create the new cover page. It now appears at the top of the Cover Page menu, ready for your use.

➡ *To learn more about building blocks, see "Working with Building Blocks," p. 89.*

Creating Headers and Footers

A *header* is an area at the top of a page, outside of the document margin, where repeated text is placed, such as a title, page number, or date. A *footer* is the same thing except at the bottom of the page.

Each section can have its own unique header and footer, or a section can continue the same header/footer from the previous section. It's up to you which way you want to set it up. In addition, each document or section can have a different first-page header/footer than in the rest of its pages. This enables you to have a different first page (for example, no page numbering on the first page) without having to set up multiple sections.

It is common to place *field codes* in headers and footers. These codes are placeholders that pull their information from the document or from the system. For example, a Date code inserts the current date, and a Page code inserts the current page number.

All those attributes of headers and footers are fairly ordinary and have been available for many Word versions. What makes Word 2010 special in the header/footer department is its ability to use *building blocks* (yes, the same as in the previous section) to insert and save custom-formatted header and footer layouts.

Understanding the Header and Footer Areas

The header and footer areas themselves are not "inserted." They are always there; they're just empty by default so you don't notice them. To type some text into one of them, do the following:

1. On the Insert tab, click Header (or click Footer).

2. On the menu that appears, click Edit Header (or click Edit Footer).

An empty header is shown in Figure 7.12. A blue dotted divider line separates it from the main document. You can type anything you like into it. Notice that it has two tab stops set on the ruler: a center-aligned tab in the middle and a right-aligned tab at the right margin. These tab stops make it easy to type text that is centered or right-aligned.

When the header or footer is active, the Design tab is available. On it, you can switch between the header and footer boxes by clicking the Go To Header and Go To Footer buttons on that tab. (You can also manually scroll the page to access the header and footer areas.)

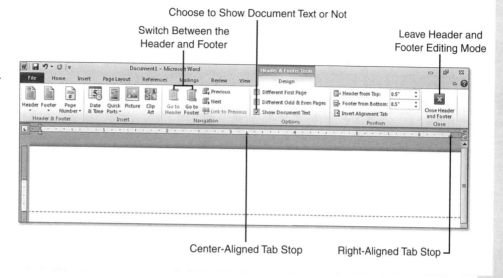

Figure 7.12
The header area on a document.

By default, the text in the document is displayed as you work on headers and footers, but it appears in gray to indicate it is not editable at the moment. It is often useful to see how the text will interact with the header or footer so you can gauge how much space to leave for it. To hide the document text, clear the Show Document Text check box on the Design tab.

When you are finished working with the header and footer, click the Close Header and Footer button on the Design tab to return to normal editing, or double-click the regular text in the document to activate it for editing (and deactivate the header and footer).

Inserting a Header or Footer Building Block

Building blocks are available for headers and footers, offering a variety of formatting and layout ideas. Their use is optional; you are free to manually create your own header/footer designs from scratch if you prefer.

To insert a header or footer building block, follow these steps:

1. From the Insert tab, click Header or click Footer.

2. Click a sample from the menu that appears (see Figure 7.13).

To switch to a different layout, repeat the preceding steps. To remove everything from the header or footer so that it goes back to "empty," choose Remove Header (or Remove Footer) from the Header or Footer button's menu. (The Header and Footer buttons appear on the Design tab, in the Header & Footer group, so you don't have to switch back to the Insert tab to access them.)

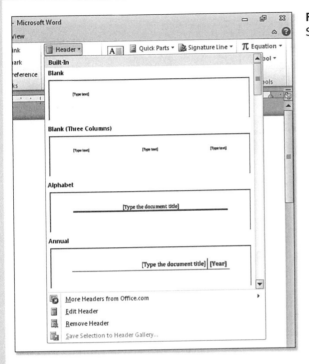

Figure 7.13
Select a header (or footer) building block.

Some of the building block headers and footers simply place text and codes in the header or footer area. Others create their own layout using drawing objects (rectangles, lines, and so on) and text boxes.

➥ *To learn how to manipulate text boxes, see "Creating Text Box Layouts," p. 307.*

➥ *To modify drawn lines and shapes, see "Modifying Drawn Objects," p. 423.*

Understanding Header/Footer Field Codes

Most of the building blocks include field codes for inserting certain information from the document or the system. You can tell a field code because when you click it, its background turns gray.

The text in Figure 7.14 is a mixture of regular text and codes. The words *Confidential* and *Page* are regular text; the *1* and the date are field codes.

Field codes are easier to see if you toggle their display to show the actual codes rather than the code results. To do so, right-click the field code and choose Toggle Field Codes. (Even though the command says *codes*, it actually only toggles the one code you clicked.) Field codes are contained in curly braces. Figure 7.15 shows the same header as in Figure 7.14, but with the field codes displayed.

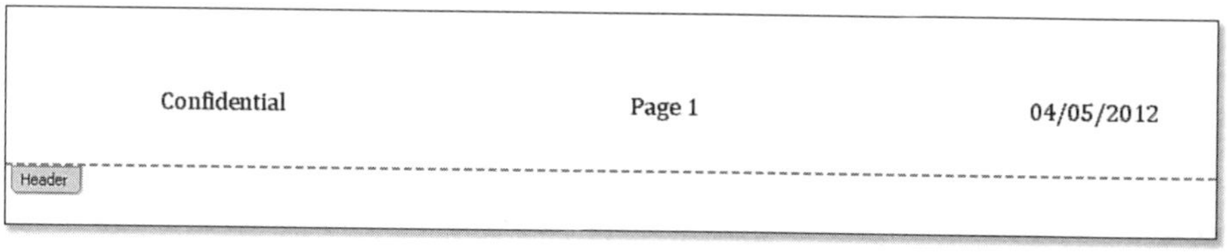

Figure 7.14
Field codes in a header.

Confidential   Page 1   04/05/2012

Header

Figure 7.15
Field codes with the codes showing rather than their results.

Confidential   Page { PAGE * MERGEFORMAT } { DATE \@ "M/d/yy" }|

Header

Deleting a Field Code

To delete a field code, click the icon that appears above it, which selects the entire code block, and press the Delete key on the keyboard.

Adding and Formatting a Page-Numbering Code

To insert a page numbering code, you can use the Page Number button's menu system either from the Insert tab or the Header & Footer Tools Format tab. The menu contains four location choices, each with its own submenu:

- **Top of Page**—Choosing from this submenu inserts a sample header of your choice, replacing whatever was previously there.

- **Bottom of Page**—Choosing from this submenu inserts a sample footer of your choice, replacing whatever was previously there.

If you use Top of Page or Bottom of Page, make sure you do it as the first step in constructing a header or footer, so you don't accidentally wipe out any work on it.

- **Page Margins**—The choices on this submenu place a floating text box in the header. It is "in" the header in the sense that it is selectable and movable only when the header and footer are active, but it can actually be placed anywhere on the page, such as along the left or right side.

- **Current Position**—This inserts a page numbering code wherever the insertion point is. If it's in the header or footer, that's where the code goes. If it's in the body of the document, it goes there instead (and appears only on that one page in the document, not repeating itself on each page). The Current Position choice works well in situations when you already have a header or footer you like, and you just want to add a page number to it.

After opening one of the submenus, select the Building Block sample that best represents the positioning and style you want. Figure 7.16 shows some of the choices for Top of Page; the others are similar.

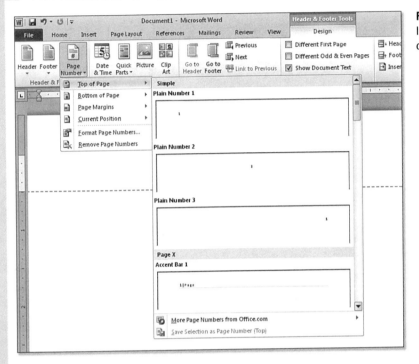

Figure 7.16
Insert a page-numbering code.

Setting the Format for a Page-Numbering Code

When you think about "formatting" a page number, the first thing that might spring to mind is its font, size, color, and so on. You can apply all those formatting attributes to the code as if it were regular text.

When Word talks about formatting a page number, it means something else—it means specifying the numbering style (1, 2, 3 versus I, II, III) and the starting number. To set up those attributes, follow these steps:

1. With the page number code selected, click the Page Number button (Insert or Design tab), and choose Format Page Numbers. The Page Number Format dialog box opens (see Figure 7.17).

2. Select a number format from the Number Format list.

Figure 7.17
Format page number codes.

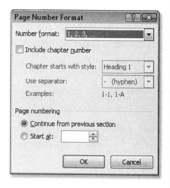

3. (Optional) If you want the numbering to restart with each page that includes a certain heading level, do the following:

    a. Mark the Include Chapter Number check box.

    b. Select the style that denotes a numbering restart from the Chapter Starts with Style list.

    c. Select a separator character from the Use Separator list.

    d. Check the Examples section to make sure the result is as you want it; adjust if needed.

4. To start the page numbering with 1 or continue from the previous section if this is not the first section in the document, leave Continue from Previous Section selected. Otherwise, click Start At and enter a number at which to start.

5. Click OK.

Inserting a Date or Time Code

A date or time code automatically pulls in the date or time from the PC's real-time clock and displays it in a format of your choice.

Many different formats are available for dates and times, ranging from short dates such as Nov-12, to long, complete date-and-time combinations such as Monday, November 15, 2012 09:30 PM. There are field codes that generate each of these formats, but you don't have to memorize the syntax because Word inserts it for you.

To insert a date or time code in a header or footer, follow these steps:

1. Place the insertion point where you want the code to appear.

2. On the Design tab, click Date & Time. The Date and Time dialog box opens (see Figure 7.18).

3. Mark the Update Automatically check box. (Important! If you don't do this, you'll get a static date, not an automatically updated one.)

 tip

To set the chosen format as the default format, click the Default button and then click Yes to confirm.

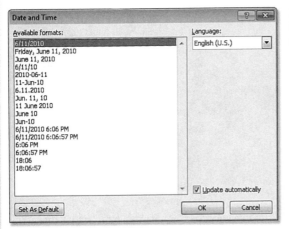

4. Click the desired format from the Available Formats list.

5. Click OK. The code is inserted. By default, it looks like any other text, showing the current information.

If you are curious about the code syntax that was inserted, toggle the field code on by right-clicking the code and choosing Toggle Field Codes. For example, the syntax for a date such as 3/22/2011 would look like this:

{ DATE \@ "M/d/yyyy" }

The \@ portion of the code is called a Date-Time Picture field switch. It tells Word to display the date using the "picture" (that is, the format) that you specify.

That's good to know because if none of the date/time codes in the Date and Time dialog box are in the format you want, you can manually create your own code syntax. Table 7.1 provides the syntax rules.

Table 7.1   Syntax Rules for Constructing Custom Date/Time Fields

Type	Usage	Result
Month (M) (must be uppercase)	M	Month as a number without a leading zero (examples: 6, 12)
	MM	Month as a number with a leading zero (examples: 06, 12)
	MMM	Month as a three-letter abbreviation (examples: Jan, Feb)
	MMMM	Month as full name (examples: January, February)

Table 7.1 Continued

Type	Usage	Result
Day (d or D)	d	Day of the month as a number without a leading zero (examples: 6, 12)
	dd	Day of the month as a number with a leading zero (examples: 06, 12)
	ddd	Day of the week as a three-letter abbreviation (examples: Mon, Wed)
	dddd	Day of the week as a full name (examples: Monday, Wednesday)
Year (y or Y)	yy	Year as two digits with leading zero (examples: 2009 as 09, 1999 as 99)
	yyyy	Year as four digits (examples: 1999, 2012)
Hour (h or H)	h	Hour without a leading zero (examples: 6, 12)
	hh	Hour with a leading zero (examples: 06, 12)
Minutes (m) (must be lower-case)	m	Minutes without a leading zero (examples: 6, 12)
	mm	Minutes with a leading zero (examples: 06, 12)
A.M. and P.M.	am/pm or AM/PM	Displays AM or PM in uppercase

To use this syntax, start with the {DATE \@} code and then put the desired format after the \@. For example, here's how to produce a date such as 06/09:

{ DATE \@ MM/yy }

If there are spaces, punctuation, or text in the syntax, you must enclose the syntax in quotation marks. (It's good to get into the habit of always using the quotation marks so you don't run into problems later if you add any of those elements.) For example, here's how to produce a date such as June 8:

{ DATE \@ "MMMM d" }

To include constant (unchanging) text in the syntax, enclose it in single quotes, making sure to include spaces on both sides of it inside the quotation marks. For example, here's how to produce a date/time such as June 8 at 9 AM:

{ DATE \@ "MMMM d' at 'h AM/PM" }

Word automatically inserts a space after the opening bracket and before the closing one.

Inserting a Document Property

You can also insert codes that represent various properties of the file, such as Author, Category, Comments, Keywords, and so on. To insert one of these, click Quick Parts, and then point to Document Property on the Design tab. Then click the desired property on the menu.

➡ To modify file properties, choose View, Properties. For more information, see "Working with File Properties," p. 43.

Adjusting Header and Footer Positioning

By default, the top of the header box is 0.5 inches from the edge of the paper, and ditto for the bottom of the footer box. Because the default top and bottom margin settings are 1 inch each, that leaves approximately 0.5 inches of space each for the header and the footer, allowing for a small amount of whitespace buffer between the header/footer and the document.

To adjust the header or footer position, use the Position controls on the Header & Footer Tools Design tab. The Header from Top measurement sets the position of the top of the header, and the Footer from Bottom measurement sets the position of the bottom of the footer (see Figure 7.19).

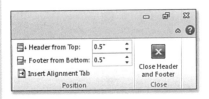

Figure 7.19
Adjust the header or footer position.

The header and footer positioning can affect the document margins, but only indirectly. The header and footer must be of adequate size to hold whatever text you have placed in their boxes, and if you increase their positions to the point where that content starts to encroach on the main document, the main document margins shift inward so there is no overlap. However, as long as the header and footer positions are such that they don't interfere with the main document, they move independently of it.

 tip

Some of the building block headers and footers do not use the header and footer boxes; they create their own text boxes. Therefore, these settings do not affect them.

The header and footer boxes are flexible in size; they hold whatever you place in them. Therefore, to increase the size of a header or footer area, add more content to it. (Blank paragraphs are fine.) For example, if you think the header is crowding the main document too much, press Enter at the bottom of the Header box to create more space.

Inserting a Picture in a Header or Footer

A small picture such as a company logo or a decorative line in a header or footer can sometimes add to a page's attractiveness. Don't go overboard and place huge pictures there, though, because they will crowd out the document text.

To insert a picture from the Header & Footer Tools Design tab, click either the Picture or the Clip Art button and then insert the artwork as you normally would for those graphics types.

A picture placed in a header or footer is set up as an inline image by default; in other words, it is treated as a character of text (albeit a large character perhaps). That's fine if you want the picture to be part of a well-defined header or footer area, but you can also break the picture out of the box and position it anywhere on the page.

To make a picture "floatable," drag it outside the header or footer box. Then on the Format tab, open the Text Wrapping button's menu and select a text wrap type. For example, use Tight to allow the text of the main document to wrap around the picture, or use Behind Text to make the main document's text run over the top of the picture.

After you've set the text wrapping for the graphic to anything other than Inline with Text, you can then drag the picture anywhere on the page, including outside the header and footer areas.

➡ *For more information about inserting pictures from files, see "Inserting Pictures from Files," p. 384.*

➡ *For more information about inserting clip art images, see "Finding and Inserting Clip Art," p. 451.*

➡ *To learn more about acquiring images directly from a scanner or camera, see "How Word Handles Pictures," p. 383.*

➡ *To learn more about repeating items such as pictures on every page of a document, see "Repeating Elements on Every Page," p. 276.*

Working with Multiple Headers/Footers

By default, a document has only one header and one footer, but there are many ways to get around that.

It is common to want a different header and footer on the first page of the document than on subsequent pages. Header and footer text on a cover page of a report often looks out of place, for example. To arrange this, mark the Different First Page check box on the Design tab. This creates two sets of headers/footers: a First Page set and a regular set.

Similarly, when creating a document destined for multisided printing, you might want different headers and footers on the left (even) and right (odd) pages. To do this, mark the Different Odd & Even Pages check box on the Design tab. This creates two sets of headers/footers, too: an Odd set and an Even set. (If you combine this option with the First Page one, you end up with three sets: First Page, Odd, and Even.)

To move between the boxes for the various header/footer sets in a document, use the Show Next and Show Previous buttons on the Design tab (see Figure 7.20).

Move between header and footer sections.

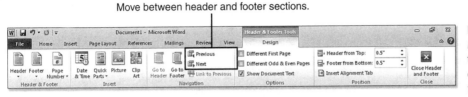

Figure 7.20
Move between the various sets of headers and footers in the document.

But that's not all. Remember that each section can have its own set of headers and footers. So potentially, you could have different First Page, Odd, and Even footers for every section in your document. If you have three sections, that's a total of nine separate headers and footers you could have.

Does all that make your head spin? It does mine. With all those different headers and footers, there's big potential for confusion and inconsistency, but Word helps out by making the headers and footers between sections "Same as Previous." In other words, by default each section's headers and footers are linked to those of the section that precedes it. When that feature is turned on, "Same as Previous" appears at the right side of the header and footer boxes when you're viewing the headers/footers in sections other than the first one.

To turn off this linking, click the Link to Previous button on the Header & Footer Tools Design tab so that you can configure the selected section's header/footer separately.

Repeating Elements on Every Page

To repeat elements on every page, attach them to the header or footer. Because the header and footer place their content on every page in which they are in effect, you can control which pages an item repeats on by controlling which header/footer set is associated with that page. For example, to make a picture repeat on the first four pages of a document, display the Section 1 header and place the picture on the page (floating, so it can be moved outside the header area), and then on the fifth page, start a new section and do not link its header/footer to the previous ones.

You saw earlier in the chapter how to place a picture in a header and then how to free it up so that it can float outside the header box. You can use a similar technique to insert any type of content. You can insert pictures, clip art, WordArt, text boxes, and more.

 tip

Why insert a text box when you've got a perfectly good place to type text in the Header or Footer box itself? It's primarily an issue of positioning. The Header and Footer boxes are not manually movable and resizable; a floating text box is. You might have noticed that many of the header and footer building blocks use text boxes, rather than text entered directly into the Header and Footer boxes, for this very reason.

Here's how to associate content with a header or footer but place it outside the header/footer boxes:

1. On the Insert tab, click Footer, Edit Footer (or Header, Edit Header). Word switches to the header/footer editing mode without placing header/footer content.

2. The Design tab is currently displayed; click Insert to display the Insert tab instead.

3. Use the Insert tab to insert content on the page. The details of each type of insertable content are covered in later chapters, but for example, suppose you want to insert a text box:

   a. Click Text Box.

   b. Click Draw Text Box.

   c. Drag the mouse to draw a text box anywhere on the page. It will be associated with the footer (or header), but it does not have to rest anywhere near it.

   d. Click in the text box and type some text.

   e. Format the text box as needed.

4. Insert other types of content on the page as desired.

5. Double-click the main document area to exit from header/footer editing mode.

> To insert text boxes, see "Creating Text Box Layouts," p. 307.

> To insert clip art, see "Finding and Inserting Clip Art," p. 451.

> To insert photos or other graphics stored in files on your hard disk, see "Inserting Pictures from Files," p. 384.

> To create WordArt, see "Creating and Modifying WordArt," p. 446.

> To draw your own lines or shapes, see "Drawing a Shape," p. 417.

Applying a Page Watermark

A *watermark* is text that appears behind the main text of a document, like a faint image. Sometimes a watermark is stamped into the paper in fine stationery, but more often a watermark is actually printed on the page. For example, a watermark could denote each page of a document as CONFIDENTIAL or DRAFT (see Figure 7.21).

You can create your own watermarks using the technique you learned in the preceding section for associating objects with the header/footer. You can create some WordArt containing the desired text, for example, and color it pale gray so it looks washed out. However, Word 2010 offers a Watermark feature that does all that work for you automatically.

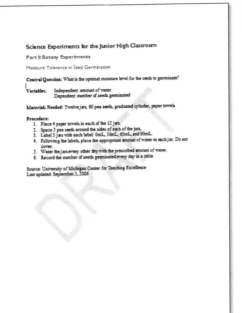

Figure 7.21
A watermark example.

Inserting a Built-In Watermark

To use the built-in Watermark feature, open the Watermark menu (from the Page Layout tab) and click one of the samples. To remove a watermark, reopen the Watermark menu and click Remove Watermark.

If none of the samples is exactly what you want, try one of the custom watermarks, described in the next few sections. (Custom text and custom picture watermarks are covered separately because their procedures are quite different.)

Inserting a Custom Text Watermark

A custom text watermark can contain any text you like. You can format it using any font, size, and color and orient it either diagonally or horizontally. Follow these steps to create a custom text watermark:

1. Make sure the insertion point is in the section where you want to insert the watermark if the document has multiple sections.

2. From the Page Layout tab, click Watermark and then click Custom Watermark. The Printed Watermark dialog box opens.

3. Click Text Watermark. The controls for creating a text watermark become available (see Figure 7.22).

Applying a Page Watermark **279**

CHAPTER

7

Figure 7.22
Create a custom text watermark.

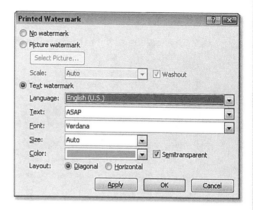

4. In the Text box, either select a phrase from the drop-down list or type your own custom text.

5. Select Font, Size, and Color settings from these drop-down lists.

6. If you want the watermark to appear faint (recommended) rather than full-strength, make sure the Semitransparent check box is marked.

7. Select Diagonal or Horizontal for the layout.

8. Click OK to place the watermark into the document.

Creating a Picture Watermark

>
> ## caution
>
> Watermarks are applied only to the current section, because they are placed in the header/footer and each section has its own. If a section is set up to continue the same settings as in the previous section, any watermark from the previous section carries over. This doesn't go backwards, though, so if you are in section 3 when you insert the watermark, sections 1 and 2 will not have it.

A picture watermark places a picture of your choice behind the main document, in a washed-out form (unless you specify otherwise) so it does not impede text readability. Follow these steps to create a picture watermark:

1. Make sure the insertion point is in the section where you want to insert the watermark if the document has multiple sections.

2. From the Page Layout tab, click Watermark and then click Custom Watermark. The Printed Watermark dialog box opens.

3. Click Picture Watermark. The controls for creating a picture watermark become available.

4. Click Select Picture. The Insert Picture dialog box opens.

5. Select the desired picture and click Insert.

6. In the Scale list, select a percentage of the original size or click Auto to allow Word to choose the size (recommended).

7. To allow the picture to appear as a washout (recommended), leave the Washout check box marked.

8. Click OK to place the watermark into the document.

Using a Clip Art Image as a Watermark

The Picture Watermark feature does not allow you to select clip art from the Clip Organizer to use as a watermark, but there are ways around that. You can insert the clip art into the header or footer and then float it outside the header/footer box. (You'll need to set its coloring to Washout manually.)

Follow these steps to use a clip-art image as a watermark:

1. Insert the clip art into the header.

2. Select the image. The Format tab appears.

3. Click the Position button on the Format tab, and select a position that shows the image centered vertically and horizontally on the page.

4. Click Wrap Text, and then choose Behind Text.

5. Click the Color button in the Adjust group and choose Washout (in the Recolor section).

6. Display the Header & Footer Tools Design tab and click Close Header and Footer.

Working with Multiple Columns

There are two types of multicolumn layouts: tabular columns and newspaper-style columns. It's important to choose the right type for the job at hand.

A multicolumn tabular layout is the same thing as a table. Use a tabular layout whenever there are varying amounts of data in each column and you need the data to align horizontally across multiple columns. Tables have their own chapter in this book (Chapter 9, "Creating and Formatting Tables"). Figure 7.23 shows information that is best presented in a tabular layout.

A newspaper-style column layout is appropriate when you want the text to "snake" from one column to the next, like in a newsletter or magazine. The text in one column does not need to have a relationship to the text in adjacent columns in such a layout. Figure 7.24 shows an example.

In this section, you'll learn how to create newspaper-style columns. Tabular column layouts are covered in Chapter 9.

Figure 7.23
A tabular layout keeps items in the various columns aligned with one another.

Exam #	Title	Chapters Covered	Notes
1	Hardware Basics	1-6	Includes binary/decimal/hexadecimal conversions, determining CPU speeds, setting jumpers, and installing motherboards
2	Disk Drives	7-10	Covers disk drive installation and troubleshooting, determining cable positions, and calculating drive capacity based on CHS values
3	Operating Systems	11-14	Includes operating system selection and installation, determining system requirements, and describing the step-by-step sequence of the boot process

Figure 7.24
A newspaper-column layout runs text from one column to the next without worrying about relationships between columns.

Test Question Writing Tips

By Faithe Wempen

When writing fill-in-the-blank questions, make sure the word they fill in is an important vocabulary word, and that there is only one possible correct answer. For example, compare these two questions:

In Table Design view, the setting in the Type column indicates the kind of _____ that will be stored in it.

In Table Design view, the setting in the _____ column indicates the kind of data that will be stored in it.

The first one is problematic because there are several words that could potentially fit: data, information, etc. The second one has been constructed so that they must supply a specific column onscreen—no gray area—and they must supply an important term they need to know for mastery of the program.

The problem here is that the student is not sure what you mean by "how a field appears." Do you mean its format? If so, the correct answer could be B. But A is also a possibility in a generic sense, because technically all fields in a query, form, or report are known as "controls." You could also argue for C, because when you change a query, you are changing the "design." Finally, D could also be right because when you change a field's label, you do change how it appears in the query, in the sense that you change the column heading in the results datasheet.

Here's a corrected version. Notice how it gets much more specific about what you want from them, and gives wrong answers that could not possibly be correct in any interpretation:

To apply a different number format to a field in a query, you must display the _____ box for the field and make a selection from the _____ list.

Applying a Column Preset

Columns are set for entire sections (or documents); to set the number of columns, click anywhere within the document or section to affect. Then open the Columns menu from the Page Layout tab and select a column preset (see Figure 7.25). The presets include One, Two, and Three (all equal column widths), as well as Left and Right (two columns, but a narrower one on the left or right, respectively).

To go back to a single-column layout, choose the One preset.

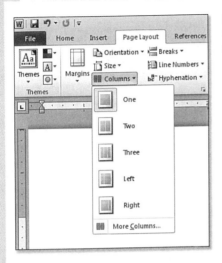

Figure 7.25
Use one of the column presets to select a number of columns for the current section.

Creating Manual Column Breaks

In a multicolumn layout, the text starts automatically in the next column when it fills up the preceding one. To end a column early, insert a manual column break.

To insert a manual column break, on the Page Layout tab, click Breaks. Then choose Column from the menu that appears.

Applying Custom Column Settings

For more control over column widths, open the Columns menu (from the Page Layout tab) and choose More Columns, opening the Columns dialog box.

 tip

If you are trying to balance the text between columns, a manual column break is not the best way to go because it won't shift automatically if you add or delete text later that unbalances the layout. Instead, insert a continuous section break at the end of the document; this forces the columns on the last page to balance.

In the Columns dialog box, all the same presets are available as on the menu, but you can customize the settings (see Figure 7.26).

Here's what you can do with the custom column settings:

- **Number of Columns**—Enter a number or use the increment buttons. There's no fixed limit, but the higher you get, the thinner the columns get until they become not-so-useful.

- **Line Between**—This places a vertical divider between each column, like in a newspaper. It helps readability.

Figure 7.26
Customize column settings in the Columns dialog box.

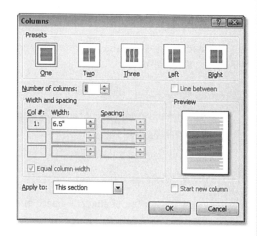

- **Width and Spacing**—Specify an exact width for each column as well as an amount of spacing between columns. The Spacing setting refers to the spacing to the *right* of the column. Set these up individually for each column, or equalize everything by marking Equal Column Width.

- **Apply To**—By default, column settings apply only to the current section. You can change this to This Point Forward or Whole Document.

Using Different Column Settings for Selected Text

Word has a strict one-column-setting-per-section policy, so you can't have two different column layouts within a single section. That's okay, though, because you can use Continuous section breaks to create sections wherever you need them. A section can be as small as a single paragraph.

There are two ways to set off a small amount of text in its own section with custom column settings. One is to manually insert the section breaks above and below the text to be included; then click anywhere within the newly defined section and change the number of columns.

An easier way is to select the text and then change the number of columns. Word automatically creates the needed section breaks and changes the column setting within the new section.

Applying a Page Background

A *page background* appears behind everything on the page (including behind the watermark, if present). It can be a solid color or a *fill effect*.

Fill effects are covered fully in Chapter 11, "Working with Drawings, WordArt, and Clip Art" so we'll reserve the main discussion of them until then, but briefly here are the types to choose from:

- **Gradient**—Gradual transition from one color to another

- **Texture**—Repeating tiled graphic that resembles a surface such as wood, marble, or fabric

- **Pattern**—Repeating two-color repetition of dots, lines, and so on

- **Picture**—Repeating tiled graphic using any graphics image file you specify

note

The page background appears onscreen only in certain views: Print Layout, Full-Screen Reading, and Web Layout. It's hidden in Outline and Draft views.

To select a page background, follow these steps:

1. From the Page Layout tab, click Page Color. The Color menu appears (see Figure 7.27).

2. Do one of the following:

   - Click one of the theme colors.

   - Click a tint or shade beneath one of the theme colors.

   - Click one of the standard colors.

   - Click Fill Effects and then select from the Fill Effects dialog box.

➡ *For a full description of how to use each of the fill effects, see "Applying a Picture Fill," p. 438.*

➡ *To review the difference between theme colors, tints and shades, and standard colors, see "Changing Font Color," p. 158.*

➡ *To change to a different color set for the theme colors, see "Applying a Color Set," p. 248.*

The Page Background Doesn't Print at All

The page background does not print by default. (On a black-and-white printer, the background usually just looks muddy, and on a color printer, the background wastes expensive color ink.) If you want it to print, do the following:

1. Choose File, Options, and click Display.

2. Mark the Print Background Colors and Images check box.

3. Click OK.

4. Continue printing normally.

The Page Background Doesn't Print All the Way to the Edge of the Paper

Almost all printers have a nonprinting range around the outer 1/4 inch or so of the paper. You can't avoid this except with special printers that advertise borderless printing (also called *full bleed printing*). Such printers are usually either very expensive or print only very small prints (like 4-inch × 6-inch photos).

A common workaround is to print a page on a paper slightly larger than needed and then trim the paper afterward to remove the unprintable area. In fact, that's how most magazines and other professional print jobs are done.

Figure 7.27
Select a page background color or choose Fill Effects to use an effect.

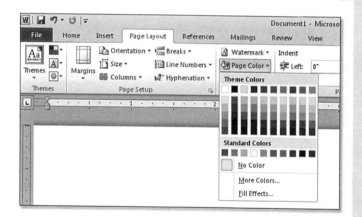

Using Page Borders

Page borders are much like paragraph borders; the main difference is that they apply to entire pages rather than individual paragraphs. A page border can apply to individual sections or to the entire document, as you specify.

To apply a basic page border, follow these steps:

1. On the Page Layout tab, click Page Borders. The Borders and Shading dialog box opens with the Page Border tab displayed (see Figure 7.28).

2. Set up a border style, color, and width, as you did with paragraph borders in Chapter 5, "Formatting Paragraphs and Lists."

➡ To review paragraph border options, see "Applying Paragraph Borders," p. 209.

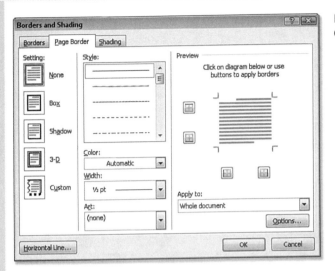

Figure 7.28
Create a page border.

3. If you do not want the page border to apply to the entire document, open the Apply To box and select some other range.

4. Click OK.

The one difference between a page border and a paragraph border is that you can specify art for a page border. For example, Figure 7.29 shows part of a page with the Apple art clip.

To use border art, follow these steps:

1. On the Page Layout tab, click Page Borders. The Borders and Shading dialog box opens.

2. Open the Art list and select an art clip.

3. In the Width box, select a width. This determines the height of the artwork in points. (1 point is 1/72 of an inch.)

4. On the Apply To list, select the scope to which the border should be applied (the whole document or just one section).

5. Click OK.

 note

The choices here are somewhat different from other section-wide formatting: This Section, This Section - First Page Only, and This Section - All Except First Page.

Figure 7.29
An example of
page border
art.

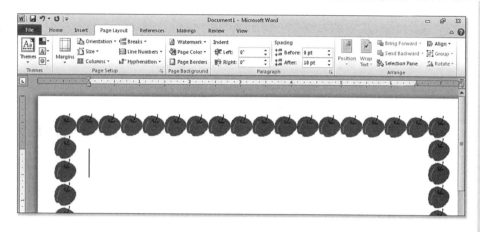

8

WORKING WITH TEMPLATES AND NONSTANDARD LAYOUTS

About Templates

Templates are specifications on which documents are based. So far you have been working with Normal.dotm, the default template for Word documents. If you don't specify otherwise, Word always bases new documents on that template. It consists of a blank document (no default content) with 1-inch margins on all sides, no extra spacing between paragraphs, and Calibri 11-point text. But a template is much more than just formatting setup; a template can also store styles to be applied to the document, and in some cases, sample or boilerplate text.

One way to think about a template is that it's the starting point for a document. Suppose you want to make 100 documents, all basically the same but with some small changes to each one. You would put the standard parts in a template and base each new document on it. Then all you would need to do to each one is insert the unique content.

Word installs several templates on your hard disk, and you can access Microsoft's library of templates online for additional choices. You can also create your own templates or modify

 note

In Word 2002 and 2003, you could store custom toolbars and menus in templates, but you can't do that in Word 2007 or 2010. Any customization you do of the Ribbon applies to all documents using all templates, so application customization is no longer storable in a template. When you open a document based on a Word 97–2003 template that contains custom menus or toolbars, they appear on the Add-Ins tab.

any of the preinstalled ones and save the modified copy as your own template.

You can apply template files to a document in several ways:

- You can start a new document based on a template. See "Starting a New Document Based on a Template," p. 291.

- You can switch an open document to a different template. See "Changing a Document's Template," p. 302.

- You can apply a template globally, so that its features are available to all documents. See "Applying Global Templates," p. 303.

note

However, in Word 2010, there is a way to export Ribbon customizations to a file that you can share with others; it just isn't attached to a particular template. See Chapter 24, "Customizing the Word Interface," for details about exporting and importing Ribbon customization.

Before diving into those skills, however, take a moment to read the next section to learn more about the types of template files you might encounter.

Types of Template Files

Word 2010 accepts three types of templates. When you are using templates to create new documents, the distinction between them is not very important, but as you move into modifying and creating them, the template type becomes a major issue:

- **Word 97-2003 template (.dot)**—These templates work in any version of Word (97 through 2010). If you have templates you created in Word 2003 or earlier, they'll be in this format. It's also the format you'll want to use if you are creating templates that you'll share with others who don't have Word 2007 or Word 2010. Documents created with these templates do not support any of the new features in Word 2007 and 2010. When working with a document based on one of these templates, Compatibility Mode appears in the Word window's title bar.

- **Word template (.dotx)**—These are the standard templates for Word 2007 and 2010. They support all Word 2007 and 2010 features, but they do not store macros. Not storing macros is a security feature, because macros can carry viruses.

- **Word Macro-enabled template (.dotm)**—These are just like regular Word templates except they *do* store macros. Create and use these templates whenever you need to store macros in the template.

➥ *For more information about macros, see "Understanding Macros," p. 833.*

Determining What Template a Document Is Using

To see what template a document is using, follow these steps:

1. Click the File tab to open Backstage View.

2. Click Properties, and choose Advanced Properties. The Properties dialog box for the document opens.

3. Click the Summary tab. The Template name is reported near the bottom of the dialog box (see Figure 8.1).

4. Click OK to close the Properties dialog box.

Click here and select Advanced Properties.

Figure 8.1
Check a document's template usage from its Properties dialog box.

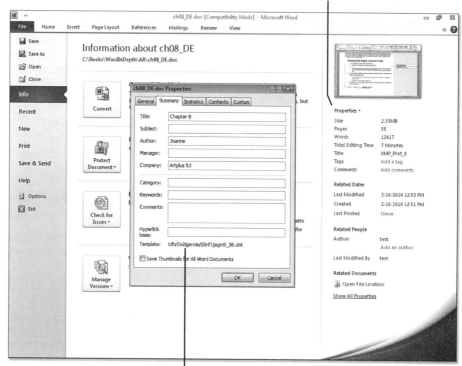

See the template name here.

Starting a New Document Based on a Template

Technically, there is no way to create a new document without basing it on some form of template, because blank documents themselves are based on a template (Normal.dotm). However, generally when we refer to basing a document on a template, we mean something other than Normal.dotm.

As you learned in Chapter 1, "Creating and Saving Documents," dozens of templates are available. A template can hold any settings that a document can, as well as any type and length of text. The most common uses for a template are to provide page-layout settings, custom definitions for document styles, and boilerplate text.

For more information about styles, see "Understanding Styles," p. 217.

Using Installed Templates

A *sample template* is one that comes with Word and is stored on your local hard disk. There are more than 30 of these, ranging from letters and faxes to reports and resumes.

If you've upgraded from Word 2003, one of the most useful templates might be the Office Word 2003 Look template. It creates a blank document with the same settings as the default blank document in Word 2003.

Some templates set up various types of merges, for items such as lists, labels, and envelopes. A merge combines a document with a database or list to create customized copies of the document. Merging will make more sense after you have read Chapter 14, "Performing Mail and Data Merges." Such templates can be identified by the word *Merge* in the name.

➡️ *For more information about merge fields, see "Inserting Merge Fields," p. 564.*

To start a new document based on a sample template, follow these steps:

1. Choose File, New. An Available Templates pane appears.

2. Click the Sample Templates icon. Thumbnail images appear for each of the installed samples.

3. Click the desired template (see Figure 8.2). A preview of it appears at the right.

4. Make sure that the Document option button is selected in the bottom-right corner of the pane.

5. Click the Create button to start the document.

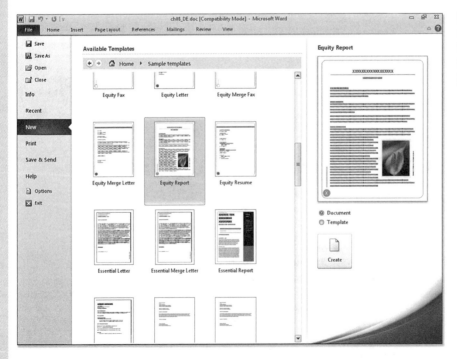

Figure 8.2
Create a document based on a Word template stored on your hard disk.

Using Office Online Templates

Microsoft Office Online provides hundreds of additional templates free to Word users. These templates are professionally designed, and they contain complex combinations of clip art, drawn shapes, text formatting, text boxes, and more. The templates available are changing constantly as Microsoft adds new templates and retires old ones. For access to these, ensure that an Internet connection is available.

You can access some of the templates online directly from within Word. To see what's available, follow these steps:

1. Choose File, New. The Available Templates pane appears.

2. In the Office.com Templates section, click a category. A list of templates (or subcategories) appears. If a subcategory appears, click the desired subcategory.

3. Click the desired template. In Figure 8.3, a Fax template is selected.

4. Click Download to download and open the template.

You can type a keyword here to search for templates.

Figure 8.3
Select online templates from Backstage View.

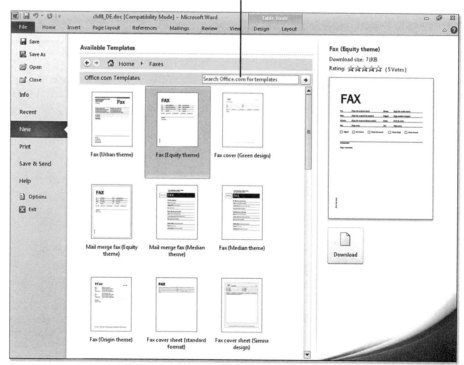

You can search the Office Online templates by keyword, rather than browsing by category. To do this, click in the Search Office.com for Templates box, type a keyword, and click the arrow button or press Enter.

Many more templates are available from http://office.microsoft.com, accessed via web browser. By downloading templates with your browser, you can make them available offline, so you don't have to be connected to the Internet to use them. Follow these steps to explore Microsoft's full template library:

1. Open a web browser (such as Internet Explorer) and navigate to http://office.microsoft.com.

2. In the navigation bar at the top of the window, click Templates.

3. Click the All Template Categories hyperlink and browse the templates available.OrIn the Search Templates box, type a keyword and press Enter to search for templates. Figure 8.4 shows the page for a newsletter template.

4. Examine the information about the template.

   - **Version**—Check what versions of Word the template will work with. Templates for one Word version will work with all higher versions, too. For example, a Word 2007 template will work with Word 2010.

   - **Download size**—See how long the template will take to download and how much disk space it will consume.

   - **Feedback**—Click the stars to rate the template (ostensibly after you have used and evaluated it). Ratings can help other users choose among similar templates.

   - **Download**—Click this button to begin the download.

5. Click Download.

6. If a user agreement appears, click Accept to continue. You might also be prompted to install an ActiveX component; if so, follow the onscreen prompts to do so.

7. If the Save As dialog box appears, accept the default template location and click Save.

> 🔍 **note**
>
> The rating is determined by people just like you who have downloaded a template and then voted on it. You can't rate templates from the Available Templates pane, but you can from the Office Online website.

If you get a message that the template could not be downloaded automatically, directions will appear on the error message page that explain how you can manually download it. This involves downloading a compressed file (.cab) and then extracting the template file from it.

If the template does download successfully, a new document opens based on it in Word. From here, save the file as a template to an appropriate folder. Here are the folders to use:

- **Personal user template**—If using Windows Vista or Windows 7, save to Users*username*\AppData\Roaming\Microsoft\Templates.

  If using Windows XP, save to \Documents and Settings*username*\Application Data\Microsoft\Templates, where *username* is the name with which you have logged into Windows.

Figure 8.4
Locate a template that you want to download.

Template Information

- **Workgroup user template**—Save to the folder you have designated as the workgroup template folder, if any. See "Accessing Workgroup Templates" later in this chapter for more information about this location.

- **Microsoft-installed template**—Save to \Program Files\Microsoft Office\Templates\1033.

 note

1033 is the country code for the United States. If you have a version for some other country, the country code will be different. You will find only one folder with a four-digit number as the name, however, so that'll be the one.

Using a User Template

A *user template* is one that you or another user has created. Templates you create are stored in the default template folder:

- **In Windows Vista or Windows 7**—Users*username*\AppData\Roaming\Microsoft\Templates.

- **In Windows XP**—Documents and Settings*username*\Application Data\Microsoft\Templates, where *username* is the name with which you have logged in to Windows. To make a template available that you have received from someone else, place it in that folder.

Here's how to access these local templates:

1. Choose File, New.

2. Click My Templates. The New dialog box opens (see Figure 8.5). Icons appear for the templates stored in the default template folder. The templates that appear in the list will be different depending on what templates you have already created, if any.

3. Click a template and then click OK to create a new document based on it.

➡ To create your own templates, see "Creating Your Own Templates," p. 301.

⚠ caution

If you log in to Windows as a different user, you will not have access to your user templates. See "Accessing Workgroup Templates" later in this chapter to learn how to share templates with all the local users of the PC and how to change the default storage location for both workgroup and user templates.

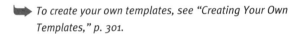
Click here for a dialog box.

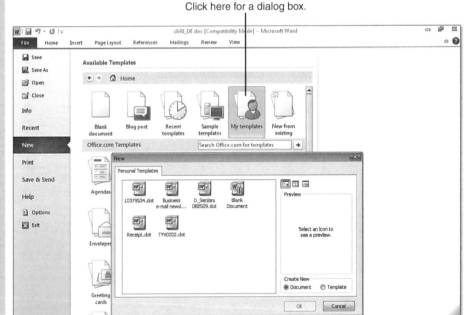

Figure 8.5
Use templates you've created yourself by selecting My Templates.

Using an Existing Document

You do not have to convert a document to a template to create other documents based on it. Any document can function as a makeshift template. When you start a new document based on a template, Word makes a copy of the document and opens that copy in an unsaved document window.

To base a new document on an existing one, follow these steps:

1. Choose File, New.

2. Click New from Existing. The New from Existing Document dialog box opens. It's just like the Open dialog box except for the name.

3. Select the document on which to base the new one.

4. Click Create New. The new document is created, with all the same settings and text as the document you chose.

Modifying Templates

The easiest way to get comfortable with creating templates is to modify an existing template. For example, suppose Word provides a calendar template that you really like, but you wish the colors were different. You can make the color changes and then save your work, either overwriting the previous version or creating a new file.

Template Storage Locations

To open a template, you must know where it's stored. As you learned earlier, a template can potentially be stored in several locations, depending on the type of template it is:

- **Personal user templates**—For Windows Vista or 7, Users*username*\AppData\Roaming\Microsoft\Templates.

  For Windows XP, Documents and Settings*username*\Application Data\Microsoft\Templates, where *username* is the name with which you have logged into Windows.

- **Workgroup user templates**—The folder you specified in Options, if any. See "Accessing Workgroup Templates" later in this chapter for details of how to do that.

- **Microsoft-installed templates**—\Program Files\Microsoft Office\Templates\1033.

Opening a template is like opening any other Word file. By default, the Open dialog box displays all files that Word can open, including templates, but you might find it easier to filter the files to show only a certain type of template. To do that, change the Files of Type setting in the Open dialog box, as shown in Figure 8.6.

 caution

When you edit an existing template, you're making a permanent change to it, so do this with caution. Even if you open the template with intentions of saving it under another name, it's easy to forget and click the Save button and accidentally overwrite the original version. For this reason, the safest route is to create a backup folder into which you can put copies of the original template files that you can restore later, if needed.

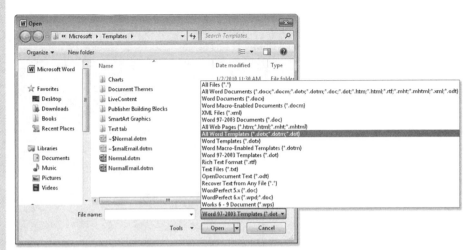

Figure 8.6
Filter the Open dialog box's file listing to show only templates.

Accessing Workgroup Templates

As mentioned earlier in the chapter, user templates are stored on a per-user basis. Each Windows user has his or her own template storage location.

If you need to make user-created templates publicly available, store them in the workgroup templates folder. When you start a document from My Templates (in the New dialog box), all the templates from both your personal template folder and the workgroup templates folder appear integrated on the same list. Users of these templates cannot tell that they are coming from two different places.

First, find out if you have a workgroup templates folder set up. If you don't, define one. Follow these steps:

1. Choose File, Options. The Word Options dialog box opens.

2. Click Advanced.

3. Scroll down to the General section and click the File Locations button. The File Locations dialog box opens.

> **tip**
>
> You can use that same procedure to change the default location for user templates if you like; choose User Templates in step 5 instead of Workgroup Templates.

4. Look at the Workgroup Templates line to see what folder has been defined for workgroup templates. In Figure 8.7, a location has not yet been defined.

5. (Optional) Change the assigned folder by doing the following:

    a. Double-click Workgroup Templates, or click Workgroup Templates and then click Modify.

    b. Navigate to the folder you want to use. (It can be either a local or network location.)

    c. Click OK.

Figure 8.7
Note the location defined for workgroup templates, and change it if desired.

6. Click OK to accept the new location.

7. Click OK to close the Word Options dialog box.

Next, move all the templates you want to share into that folder. You can do so from Windows Explorer. For example, to move templates from your personal template storage to the workgroup storage, follow these steps:

1. In Windows, open Computer (Windows Vista or 7) or My Computer (Windows XP).

2. Navigate to the location where your user templates are stored:

   - **In Windows Vista or 7**—Users\ *username*\AppData\Roaming\Microsoft\Templates.

   - **In Windows XP**—Documents and Settings\ *username*\Application Data\Microsoft\ Templates, where *username* is the name with which you have logged into Windows.

3. Select the desired template files. Hold down Ctrl as you click each one to select multiple files.

4. Cut the files to the Clipboard by pressing Ctrl+X (or use any other method you prefer).

5. Navigate to the folder you specified for workgroup templates.

6. Paste the files from the Clipboard by pressing Ctrl+V (or use any other method you prefer).

As you create new templates, as described later in this chapter, save them in either the personal or the workgroup location, depending on whether or not you want to share them.

Modifying a Template by Modifying the Current Document

You can also modify a template by editing a document based on it. When you add a style or macro to a document, for example, you're prompted for a storage location. You can choose to store it either in the current document or in the current template. If you choose to store it in the template, the template is modified when you save your work.

A message might appear asking whether you want to save your changes to the document template, or the changes might be saved behind the scenes. You can specify whether you want changes to Normal.dotm to be made "silently" or not by doing the following:

1. Choose File, Options. The Word Options dialog box opens.

2. Click Advanced.

3. Scroll down to the Save section and mark or clear the Prompt Before Saving Normal Template check box (see Figure 8.8).

4. Click OK.

caution

It is convenient to have changes silently saved to Normal.dotm, but some macro viruses infect Normal.dotm by making changes to it that you might not be aware of. Forcing Word to prompt you before making changes to that file is an extra layer of security.

Mark this check box to make sure you are aware of changes made to the Normal template.

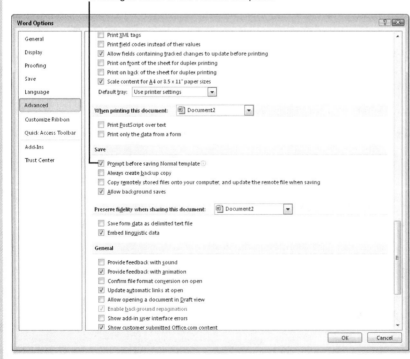

Figure 8.8
Choose whether or not to be prompted when changes are made to Normal.dotm.

Protecting Templates

You can protect templates from changes, just like you can regular documents. See "Protecting a Document" in Chapter 21, "Protecting and Securing Documents," for information about password-protecting and encrypting templates, making them read-only, and preventing them from being copied or emailed using Information Rights Management (IRM).

Creating Your Own Templates

One way to create a template is to save a modified template or document under a different name. That way, you can base the new template on an existing one and save yourself some time.

To create a template, you must first decide on the type to use. Review the template types explained in "About Templates" at the beginning of this chapter. Word 97–2003 templates are best when compatibility is an issue with earlier Word versions. Use the Word Template type for a template that will not need to include macros; use the Word Macro-Enabled Template type for one that will.

Follow these steps to create a template:

1. Open the template or document on which you want to base the new template, and then make any changes to it.

2. Choose File, Save As. The Save As dialog box opens.

3. Open the Save as Type list and choose the desired template type.

4. Navigate to the location in which you want to save the template. Refer to the locations listed in the preceding section, "Modifying Templates."

5. Click Save. The template is created.

When you choose to create a new document based on My Templates, the New dialog box appears. As you saw in Figure 8.5, by default this dialog box consists of a single tab: Personal Templates.

If you have a lot of templates to manage, consider creating additional tabs in this dialog box and grouping the templates into categories. To do this, create subfolders within the Templates folder, each with the name you want to assign to a tab, and then place the templates in the subfolders.

Follow these steps to create an additional tab and move some templates onto it:

1. Using the Windows Explorer, navigate to the folder where user templates are stored:

   ▪ **For Windows Vista or 7**—Users*username*\AppData\Roaming\Microsoft\Templates.

   ▪ **For Windows XP**—Documents and Settings*username*\Application Data\Microsoft\Templates, where *username* is the name with which you have logged into Windows.

2. Right-click an empty area of the window and choose New, Folder. A new folder appears.

3. Type a name for the new folder and press Enter.

4. Drag and drop one or more of the templates onto the icon for the new folder to move them into that folder.

Now return to Word and start creating a new document based on a user template. The New dialog box will now have an additional tab for the subfolder you created, and the template(s) you placed in that subfolder will appear on that tab.

Changing a Document's Template

Most of the time, you'll start a document based on the template you want it to use. If you change your mind later, though, you can switch templates without having to re-create the document. You can also make additional templates available, so you can use any macros or building blocks from them, without changing the primary template assigned to the document.

Follow these steps to apply a different template to the document:

1. If the Developer tab does not appear, do the following to display it:

   a. Choose File, Options.

   b. Click Customize Ribbon.

   c. On the list at the right side, mark the Developer check box.

   d. Click OK.

2. On the Developer tab, click the Document Template button. The Templates and Add-Ins dialog box opens, shown in Figure 8.9.

Figure 8.9
Use the Templates tab to change the template assigned to the document.

3. On the Templates tab, click Attach. The Attach Template dialog box appears.

4. Select the desired template from the Attach Template dialog box. (Navigate to the location containing the template.)

5. Click Open to return to the Templates tab.

6. (Optional) If you want the style definitions to update automatically to match the new template's definitions, mark the Automatically Update Document Styles check box.

7. Click OK.

If you use the Templates and Add-Ins dialog box frequently, consider adding a shortcut to it in the Quick Access toolbar. To do so, display the Developer tab, right-click the Document Template button, and choose Add to Quick Access Toolbar.

Applying Global Templates

A *global template* is a template that makes its features available to all documents, not just when it is specifically applied. Some examples of global templates include Normal.dotm and Building Blocks. dotx; their content is available no matter what template is assigned to the current document.

For more information about building blocks, see "Working with Building Blocks," p. 89.

You can also make other templates available globally. For example, if you have a template that has some handy macros stored in it, you can designate that template to be global and have access to those macros in all documents.

To make a template global, follow these steps:

1. Do one of the following:

- On the Developer tab, click Document Template. If the Developer tab is not visible, do the following to display it:

  a. Choose File, Options.

  b. Click Customize Ribbon.

  c. On the list at the right side, mark the Developer check box.

  d. Click OK.

  or

- If you have previously placed a Document Template shortcut on the Quick Access toolbar, click it. The Templates and Add-Ins dialog box opens, as shown in Figure 8.9.

2. In the Global Templates and Add-Ins section of the Templates tab, click Add. The Add Template dialog box appears.

 caution

Automatically updating document styles works only if the styles in the new template have the same names as the styles already applied to the text. If the new template uses different names for styles, you'll need to do a Find-and-Replace operation to replace all instances of the old style name with the new style name. See "Finding and Replacing" in Chapter 2, "Typing and Editing Text," for more information on Find-and-Replace operations.

3. Select the template to add globally and click OK. It appears on the list.

4. (Optional) To enable or disable global templates, mark or clear their check boxes on the list. Or to remove a template from the list completely, select it and click Remove.

5. Click OK.

 tip

It is usually better to disable a global template than to remove it because it can be more easily reenabled later.

Global templates that are set to load at startup reside

- **In Windows Vista or 7**—Users*username*\\AppData\\Roaming\\Microsoft\\Word\\Startup

- **In Windows XP**—Documents and Settings*username*\\Application Data\\Microsoft\\Word\\Startup, where *username* is the name with which you have logged into Windows.

You cannot remove these startup templates from the list in the Templates and Add-Ins dialog box (although you can disable them from there). To remove one of these, you must delete it from the Startup folder outside of Word.

Enabling Global Templates at Startup

If you find yourself reenabling the same global template(s) every time you start up Word, here's a shortcut. Copy the template into the Startup folder for Word: Users*username*\\AppData\\Roaming\\Microsoft\\Word\\Startup (Windows Vista or 7) or \\Documents and Settings*username*\\Application Data\\Microsoft\\Word\\Startup (Windows XP). Doing so forces the template to load globally at startup. You can disable it if needed from the Templates and Add-Ins dialog box on a case-by-case basis.

Preventing a Template from Loading at Startup

Some third-party applications such as Adobe Acrobat set up Word templates to load at startup to provide tighter integration with other programs. In the case of Adobe Acrobat, the automatically loaded template provides a macro for creating a new PDF document using Acrobat.

If you see items in the Templates and Add-Ins dialog box that you don't recognize and don't want, and they appear to be marked by default at startup, here's how to get rid of them:

1. Exit from Word.

2. In Windows, navigate to the folder containing the startup templates:

    In Windows Vista or 7—Users*username*\\AppData\\Roaming\\Microsoft\\Word\\Startup.

    In Windows XP—Documents and Settings*username*\\Application Data\\Microsoft\\Word\\Startup, where *username* is the name with which you have logged into Windows.

3. Delete the unwanted templates, or copy them elsewhere, or rename them so that they do not have a template file extension anymore (and therefore Word won't recognize them as templates).

4. Restart Word and then confirm that the templates no longer automatically load.

Automatically Changing the Template of All Documents Opened

Suppose your organization has been using a certain template for all documents, but now you've been given a new template and a directive to switch over all your documents to this new template.

One way to do that is to open each document and then manually switch the template assigned to the document and save/close it. An easier way, however, is to create a special macro called AutoOpen. Whatever commands you place in AutoOpen run automatically whenever you open a document. Save the AutoOpen macro in Normal.dotm.

Macro recording is covered in Chapter 23, "Macros and Add-Ins," but here's a quick overview:

1. Make sure you have already created a Document Template button on the Quick Access toolbar.

2. Click the Macro Recording button on the status bar (the document with the red circle).

   If you do not see this button on the status bar, right-click the status bar and click Macro Recording.

3. In the Record Macro dialog box, type AutoOpen as the macro name (see Figure 8.10).

Figure 8.10
Record an
AutoOpen
macro.

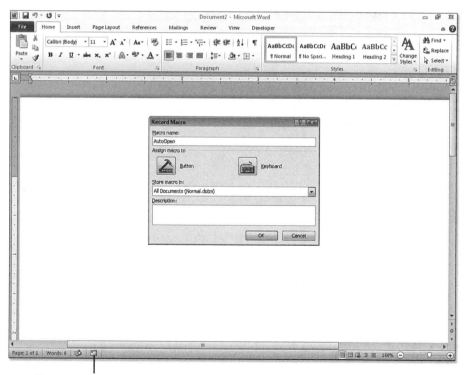

The Record Macro Button

4. In the Store Macro In list, make sure All Documents (Normal.dotm) is selected.

5. Click OK to begin the recording.

6. Click the Document Template button on the Quick Access toolbar.

7. Click the Attach button, select the template to attach, and click Open.

8. Mark the Automatically Update Document Styles check box.

9. Click OK.

10. Click the Stop Macro button (the blue square that replaced the document with the red dot in the bottom-left corner of the Word window).

The macro is now created. To try it out, open a document that uses some other template, and then note whether the document's template changes.

To see what template a document is using, choose File, Properties, Advanced Properties. On the Summary tab of the dialog box that appears, you can find the template's name near the bottom of the dialog box.

To stop the macro from running automatically at startup, delete or rename the AutoOpen macro.

➡ *For information about deleting and renaming macros, see "Renaming and Deleting Macros," p. 848.*

Troubleshooting Problems with Normal.dotm

Normal.dotm is the default template for Word documents. When Normal.dotm develops problems, those problems carry over to many documents, so it's important to know how to resolve them quickly.

Normal.dotm Is Missing

Depending on the situation, it might be perfectly normal that you can't find Normal.dotm anywhere on your hard disk. If you have not made changes to the default settings in Word, such as changing the default font, Normal.dotm will not appear in a file listing. In its default state, it is built into Word. It appears as a separate file only if you have changed it in some way.

To force it to appear, make some sort of change to the default settings. For example, on the Home tab, open the Font dialog box, change the font, and click the Default button. When prompted to change the default font, click Yes.

Normal.dotm will then appear in the default location for user templates. To browse to its folder, you might need to turn on the display of hidden files. See the next section for details.

Can't Find the Application Data or AppData Folder

The path for personal templates stored on your hard disk is as follows:

- **Windows Vista or Windows 7**—Users*username*\AppData\Roaming\Microsoft\Templates

- **Windows XP**—Documents and Settings*username*\Application Data\Microsoft\Templates

However, if you try to navigate to this folder in Windows, you might not be able to find it. That's because the Application Data or AppData folder is hidden by default.

To display hidden folders, follow these steps:

1. From any file management window:

    - **In Windows Vista or 7**—Choose Organize, Folder and Search Options.

    - **In Windows XP**—Choose Tools, Folder Options.The Folder Options dialog box opens.

2. Click the View tab.

3. Click Show Hidden Files, Folders, and Drives.

4. Click OK.

Simply changing the template does not automatically change the formatting. For example, suppose the Heading 1 style is defined as 18-point Arial in the current document, and you apply a template that defines Heading 1 as 20-point Times New Roman. The existing Heading 1 text will not change automatically, but if you reapply Heading 1 to the text, it will change at that point. In addition, any new headings you create with the Heading 1 style will have the new definition.

To force the existing Heading 1 text to change, mark the Automatically Update Document Styles check box in the Templates and Add-Ins dialog box as you are applying the new template.

If that doesn't help, you can force all the styles in the document to update themselves in each instance by selecting the entire document (Ctrl+A) and then pressing Ctrl+Q.

I Want the Original Version of Normal.dotm

If you make changes to Normal.dotm that you later decide were ill advised, or if Normal.dotm gets corrupted, you might want to go back to the original Normal.dotm that came with Word.

To revert to the original Normal.dotm, simply delete your customized copy of it. The next time you restart Word, it creates a fresh copy of Normal.dotm.

Creating Text Box Layouts

Word is obviously well suited to writing ordinary documents such as reports, letters, and memos, but it also has some other uses that most people never get a chance to explore. In this chapter, you'll learn about some of the interesting things Word can do with nonstandard layouts.

Text box layouts are layouts in which text is not typed directly onto the page, but instead placed in floating text boxes. This type of page layout has many advantages, and in fact that's the standard operating mode for most professional-quality desktop publishing programs, including Adobe InDesign and QuarkXPress, as well as consumer-level publishing programs such as Microsoft Publisher and presentation programs such as PowerPoint. You can move around each text box on the page freely, so the text need not follow a strict top-to-bottom flow. Figure 8.11 shows an example of a page layout constructed with text boxes.

Figure 8.11
Text boxes make it possible to place text precisely where you want it on the page.

Inserting a Text Box

Word 2010 includes a variety of text box building blocks for quickly inserting preformatted boxes with sample text. (Yes, it's the same building blocks feature as is used with AutoText, headers and footers, and page numbering.)

To insert a preset text box, display the Insert tab, click Text Box, and then click one of the presets on the menu (see Figure 8.12). Then click inside the text box and edit the sample text as desired.

Figure 8.12
Select a text box preset.

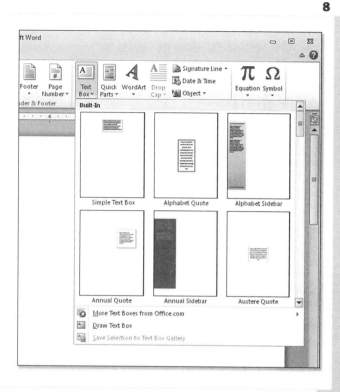

If none of the presets are to your liking, you can draw your own text box anywhere on the page, and then format it and place text in it later. To draw a text box, follow these steps:

1. From the Insert tab, click Text Box and then click Draw Text Box. The mouse pointer changes to a crosshair.

2. Drag to draw a text box on the page. When you release the mouse button, the text box appears and the Format tab appears. The default text box style is a thin solid black border and a white fill.

3. Click inside the text box and type text into it.

 caution

Text boxes can hold almost anything that the document itself can hold—text, graphics, tables, fields, and so on. There are a few exceptions, however. Text boxes cannot contain multiple columns or column breaks, page breaks, drop caps, comments, footnotes, endnotes, or markings for indexes and tables of contents.

To select a text box, click it. When a text box is selected, it has its own indent markers on the ruler; set those as you would in any document (see Figure 8.13).

When a text box is selected, a Format tab appears containing options for formatting the text box. The following sections explore those options.

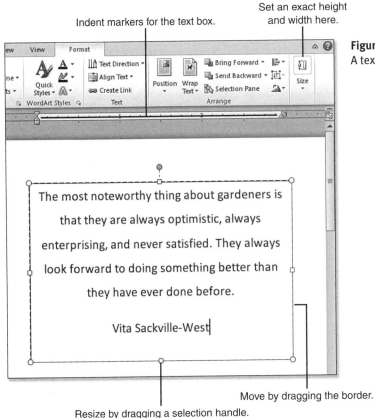

Indent markers for the text box.

Set an exact height
and width here.

Figure 8.13
A text box has its own ruler settings.

Move by dragging the border.

Resize by dragging a selection handle.

Moving and Resizing a Text Box

To move a text box, select it by clicking it so that a border
with selection handles appears around it (see Figure 8.13).
Then to move the text box, drag it by its border (but not by a
selection handle), or to resize it, drag any selection handle. If
you need the text box to be a precise size, enter values in the
Height and Width boxes on the Format tab.

Another way to enter height and width values is via the
Layout dialog box:

1. Right-click the border of the text box and choose More
   Layout Options. The Layout dialog box appears.

2. Click the Size tab.

 note

Absolute is the default for both
height and width for drawn text
boxes, but for some of the preset
ones, the width value is set to
Relative and set at a percentage of
the page width. (A relative width
enables the same building blocks
to be used on different paper sizes
and take up the same proportional
amount of space.)

3. Enter values in the Height and Width sections. If the Absolute option button is not already selected in each section, select it, so absolute measurements are entered (see Figure 8.14).

4. Click OK.

Figure 8.14
Specify a height and width in the properties for the text box.

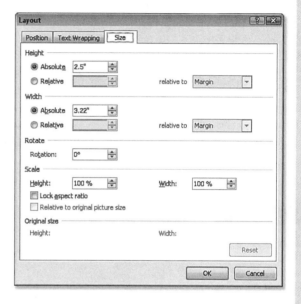

Applying and Removing Text Box Borders and Fills

Word 2010 provides a variety of style presets that can be applied to text boxes. There are six different styles, and each is available in seven different colors. (These are the same as the presets you can apply to drawn shapes, as you learn in Chapter 11, "Working with Drawings, WordArt, and Clip Art.")

Select the text box. Then open the Shape Styles list from the Format tab and make your selection, as shown in Figure 8.15.

 tip

To copy formatting from one text box to another, use the Format Painter button on the Home tab.

➥ *To learn about Format Painter, see "Copying Formatting with Format Painter," p. 173.*

If you're using text boxes for document layout, rather than as decorative aids, you probably don't want to do much with their formatting; in fact, you probably want most text boxes to be invisible (no border, no fill).

By default, drawn text boxes have visible borders; here's how to turn off the border on a text box:

1. Select the text box.

2. Display the Format tab.

3. Open the Shape Outline button's list and choose No Outline.

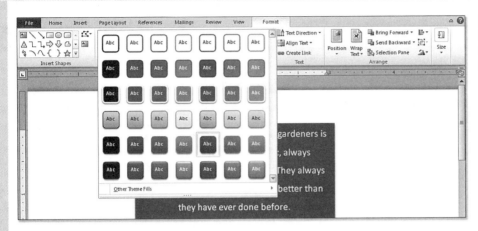

Figure 8.15
Select a formatting style for the text box.

And here's how to remove the fill, if one is applied:

1. Select the text box.

2. Display the Format tab.

3. Open the Shape Fill button's list and choose No Fill.

Need more control? There's a whole lot you can do to fine-tune the text box's line and fill. Display the Format tab, and use the Shape Fill, Shape Outline, and Shape Effects controls. These controls work the same for text boxes as they do for AutoShapes, so I won't cover them here; instead, flip over to Chapter 11 for the details.

To learn about line, fill, shadow, and 3D options, see "Creating and Modifying WordArt," p. 446.

Changing the Text Box Shape

Text boxes are rectangular by default, but you can convert them to any of a variety of shapes— rounded rectangles, circles, ovals, parallelograms, diamonds, and more.

Here's how to change the shape of a text box:

1. Select the text box.

2. On the Format tab, click Edit Shape, Change Shape and then click the desired shape (see Figure 8.16).

Even though the text box may have an asymmetric shape, the text within it still conforms to a rectangular area. For example, in a parallelogram in Figure 8.17, the lines do not begin at different positions to hug the borders of the shape; instead, the text is confined to a small area in the center that does not overlap borders.

Figure 8.16
Select a shape
for the text box.

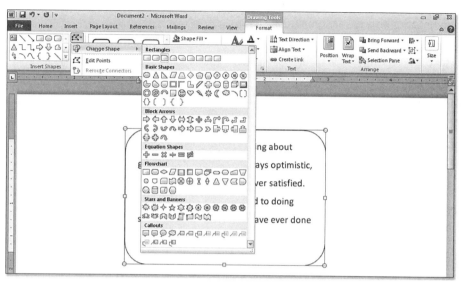

Figure 8.17
A text box with a parallelogram shape.

Setting Text Box Margins and Vertical Alignment

By default, a text box has 0.1-inch left and right internal margins and 0.05-inch top and bottom internal margins. These margins allow the text to fill the text box completely but not quite touch the border lines.

Vertical alignment is the placement of the text within the text box vertically. If there is not enough text to fill the entire text box vertically, where will the blank space occur? Text boxes have a default vertical alignment of Top, so any blank space appears at the bottom.

To change either of these settings, use the Format Shape dialog box. Follow these steps:

1. Right-click the border of the text box and choose Format Shape.

2. Click the Text Box tab.

3. Change the Left, Right, Top, or Bottom internal margin settings (see Figure 8.18).

4. Change the vertical alignment setting if desired. The choices are Top, Middle, and Bottom.

5. Click OK.

Figure 8.18
Set internal margins and vertical alignment for the text box.

Wrapping Text Around a Text Box

When a text box overlaps with regular document text, it interacts with it according to the Wrap Text setting you specify. These are the same wrap text settings as for shapes, photos, clip art, and all other types of content. These wrap settings are covered in detail in "Setting Text Wrap" in Chapter 10, "Working with Photos," but here's a quick summary of the process:

1. Select the text box, and display the Format tab for it.

2. Click the Wrap Text button, opening a menu of wrap choices. See Figure 8.19.

3. Click the desired wrapping style:

- **In Line with Text**—Treats the graphic as a large character of text, running it along with the text. When you edit the text, the graphic shifts along with it. You can drag and drop the graphic only into places where text could go.

- **Square**—Wraps text around both sides of the text box in a rectangular shape.

- **Tight**—For a rectangular text box, this is the same as Square. For a text box with some other shape (as covered in the preceding section), it wraps the text around the shape.

- **Through**—Same as Tight except somewhat tighter if it's an irregular-shaped object like a piece of clip art.

Figure 8.19
Select a wrap text setting.

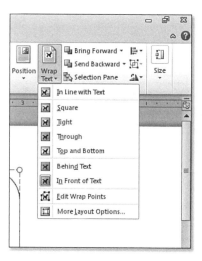

- **Top and Bottom**—The text wraps around the text box above and below it, but the space to the left and right of the text box remains empty.

- **Behind Text**—The text box is placed behind the text, so the text runs over the top of it. This one is not recommended for text boxes.

- **In Front of Text**—The text box is placed on top of the text, so the text runs behind it. Usually not a great choice because the text is obscured.

You can also choose More Layout Options for a dialog box with a few other choices, or choose Edit Wrap Points to manually edit the points around which the text wraps.

 To edit wrap points or use advanced wrapping options, see "Setting Text Wrap," p. 386.

Linking Text Boxes

In magazine and newspaper publishing lingo, all the text for a particular article is called a *story*. When a story fills up one text box and continues to another, the two text boxes are said to be *linked*.

A story-based layout with text boxes in Word is accomplished by creating multiple text boxes and linking them with the Create Link command, as follows:

1. Create all the text boxes needed for the story.

2. Click the border of the first text box and then click the Create Link button on the Drawing Tools Format tab. The mouse pointer turns into an upright pitcher.

> **note**
>
> If the text for the story is already typed, it should all appear in the first text box. All other text boxes must be empty or it won't work. Many people find it easier to create the story in a separate document and then cut and paste it into the set of linked text boxes after the links have been configured.

3. Position the mouse pointer over the center of the text box that will be linked next in the chain. The mouse pointer turns into a tilted pitcher (see Figure 8.20).

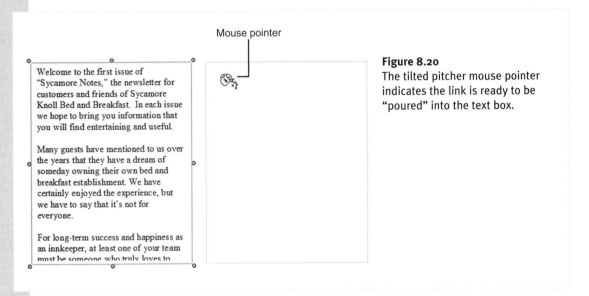

Mouse pointer

Welcome to the first issue of "Sycamore Notes," the newsletter for customers and friends of Sycamore Knoll Bed and Breakfast. In each issue we hope to bring you information that you will find entertaining and useful.

Many guests have mentioned to us over the years that they have a dream of someday owning their own bed and breakfast establishment. We have certainly enjoyed the experience, but we have to say that it's not for everyone.

For long-term success and happiness as an innkeeper, at least one of your team must be someone who truly loves to

Figure 8.20
The tilted pitcher mouse pointer indicates the link is ready to be "poured" into the text box.

4. Click to create the link.

5. If there are more text boxes to link, click the second text box and then link it to the third, then the third to the fourth, and so on until all text boxes are linked.

6. Type the story, starting in the first text box.

Alternatively, paste the story into the first text box, and it will flow into the others automatically.

Unlike in some other desktop publishing programs, Word does not have indicator to show overflow text, so if there is nowhere for excess text to go (for example, no subsequent linked text boxes), it is simply truncated. The text still exists, though, and if you enlarge the text box or link another box to it, the truncated text will reappear.

Breaking the Link

If a story does not run as long as you expected, you might want to delete the unneeded boxes or break the link to the unused boxes so they can be used for some other story.

To break a link, do the following:

1. Select the text box that should be the last box in the chain. (All boxes after this one will be unlinked.)

2. On the Drawing Tools Format tab, click Break Link.

Changing the Text Direction

One advantage of a text box is that you can set the text to run vertically in it. This enables you to create interesting special effects, such as a newsletter title that runs vertically along the left side of the page.

To create this effect, right-click the text box border and choose Format Text Box. On the Text Box tab, set the Text Direction, as shown in Figure 8.21.

Figure 8.21
Vertical text in a text box.

This text is rotated 270 degrees.

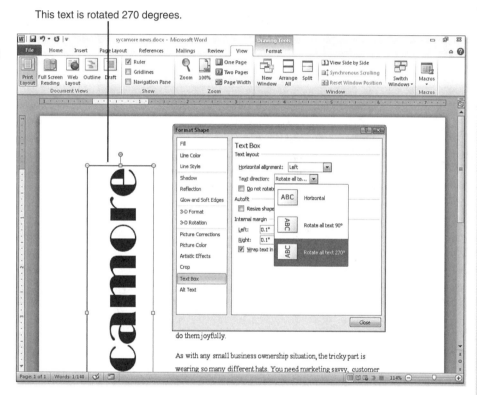

Word supports three text directions: Horizontal, Rotate All Text 90°, and Rotate All Text 270°. To select one of these options from the Ribbon, click the Text Direction button on the Format tab.

Tips for Creating Text Box Layouts

In desktop publishing programs such as Publisher, Adobe InDesign, and QuarkXPress, it is easy to place the text boxes in the same spots on every page because you can place nonprinting guidelines on each page. Word does not have guidelines per se, but it does have a nonprinting grid you can toggle on and off.

To toggle the grid, on the View tab, mark or clear the Gridlines check box. Gridlines appear in Print Layout view only. Figure 8.22 shows gridlines displayed.

Gridlines

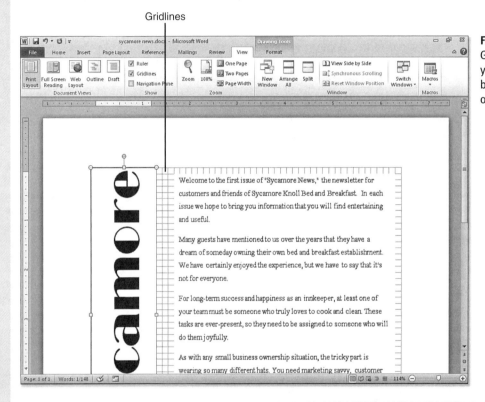

Figure 8.22
Gridlines help you align text boxes and other content.

In addition, here are some other ways to ensure consistent placement of objects between pages:

- Use the Shape Height and Shape Width controls on the Format tab to make sure that each text box is the same size, and then use the Align and Distribute controls (also on the Format tab) to place them evenly on the page.

  ➥ *To learn about Align and Distribute, see "Aligning and Distributing Objects," p. 433.*

- Create one text box the way you want it and then copy it to create the others, ensuring consistent size and shape. To copy a text box, hold down Ctrl as you drag its border (not a selection handle).

- Create one page the way you want it, with all the text boxes in place, and save that page as a building block. On the Insert tab, click Quick Parts and then choose Save Selection to Quick Part

Gallery. Make sure to change the Options setting to Insert Content in Its Own Page. You can then insert that page as many times as needed to duplicate the page layout.

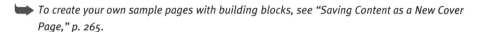 To create your own sample pages with building blocks, see "Saving Content as a New Cover Page," p. 265.

- Create temporary content to serve as guides. For example, if you want guides for creating three equal-sized columns, set Columns to 3 (Page Layout tab), set the paragraph background shading to a color, and then press Enter enough times to fill an entire page. The result is three empty-but-shaded columns. Then drag your text boxes on top of those, and remove the shading when finished.

Working with Frames

A text box is technically a graphic object, not part of the main document. That's fine in most cases, and in fact it provides some formatting benefits. For example, as you saw earlier, you have access to all the same line and fill formatting options as with AutoShapes, including 3D and shadow effects.

However, there are certain special-purpose cases in which the fact that text box text resides in the graphics layer can be problematic. One is that you can't use any automatically numbered reference elements in a text box, such as footnotes, comments, and captions. You also can't use certain fields that automatically number things based on their position in the document, such as AUTONUM and AUTONUMLGL. That makes sense if you think about it—if each text box is a separate graphical unit, it has no relationship to the document's main body.

 note

Here's a complete list of the fields that work only in frames, not in text boxes: AUTONUM, AUTONUMLGL, AUTONUMOUT, TC, TOC, RD, XE, TA, and TOA.

The solution in these cases is to convert the text boxes into frames. Frames are part of the text layer, so they can use all the aforementioned reference elements, but the frames are sectioned off from the main text (which can wrap around them).

Frames can be used only in legacy format documents—that is, documents in Word 97–2003 format. Before you can convert a text box to a frame, you must save in that format.

To convert a text box to a frame, follow these steps:

 caution

With a frame, you give up some of the formatting functionality of a text box, and you lose the ability to link. A linked text box cannot be converted to a frame. You must remove the link first.

1. Make sure you have saved the document in Word 97–2003 (.doc) format. This procedure will not work in a Word 2007 or 2010 document.

2. Right-click the text box's border and choose Format Text Box.

3. Click the Text Box tab, and then click the Convert to Frame button.

4. A warning appears; click OK. The text box becomes a frame.

You cannot convert from a frame to a text box; you must create a new text box and then cut and paste the text from the frame into it.

The most immediately apparent difference between a frame and a text box is that on a frame, the selection handles are all squares, whereas on a text box, the corner ones are circles. The squares indicate that the frame is an inline object in the document, part of the text.

To format a frame, right-click its border and choose Format Frame. The Frame dialog box opens, as shown in Figure 8.23. From here, you can do the following:

- Set the text wrapping around the frame. However, it is limited to None (same as Top and Bottom for a text box) or Around (same as Square for a text box).

- Set the size of the frame, either to exact measurements or to Auto (to change the frame size based on the contents).

- Set the horizontal and vertical positions of the frame, in relation to the margin, column, or page.

- Specify whether the frame should move with the text. For example, if you add more text above the frame, should the frame shift down or should it stay static?

- Specify whether to lock the frame's anchor. The anchor marks the position on the page.

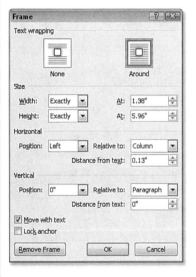

Figure 8.23
Set frame properties in the Frame dialog box.

The Frame dialog box also contains a Remove Frame button. Use this to place the frame's text into the main document as regular text and delete the frame. The text from the frame is placed at the location of the frame's anchor point.

Creating Banners

Word is perhaps not the best program for creating large-format items such as posters and banners because it doesn't have any special features in that regard. Microsoft Publisher, if available, is a more satisfactory solution. However, Word will serve in a pinch, and this section explains how to make that happen.

The challenge when working with large-format items is that most people don't have a large-format printer, so they end up printing pieces of the document on separate sheets and then knitting them together with tape or staples. Most printers have a "dead" area of about 1/4-inch around all sides of a printed page, so when creating pages designed to be pasted together, you'll need to figure in at least 1/2-inch of overlap area between them (1/4-inch on each page where two pages come together). In practice, however, it is better to leave even more space than that for overlap to simplify the connections.

Each panel of a multisheet banner is a separate page in Word. The pages can be Landscape in orientation for a banner that is 8.5 inches high or Portrait for a banner that is 11 inches high.

> ➠ *To switch between portrait and landscape page orientation, see "Setting Page Orientation,"*
> *p. 259.*

The best way to create a banner in Word is to start with a Microsoft-provided template and then modify it as dictated by the needs of your project. The Microsoft templates have divider lines that show where the copies will join, taking the guesswork out of the overlap. Once you've used the template a few times and have an idea of how things work, you can create your own from-scratch versions. Search the Office Online templates for the word *banner* to locate appropriate templates to use.

> ➠ *To review how to create a document by using a template, see "Starting a New Document Based*
> *on a Template," p. 291.*

Figure 8.24 shows a birthday banner in Print Preview, created from a template. Notice that each panel is a separate page, and each page has dotted vertical lines on it showing where the pages should be overlapped. You can either fold the pages or cut along the dotted lines to prepare them.

Figure 8.24
A multisheet banner created in Word.

When it comes time to create your own banner designs, here are some tips:

- For graphic elements that repeat on each page, such as the bar below the letters in Figure 8.24, place them in the page header and footer rather than copying them onto every sheet individually.

- Use the drawing tools in Word to draw the vertical dotted lines that will guide your cutting or folding. To make it less obvious if you don't cut the lines quite right, use a very light color for the lines, such as pale gray.

- Use text boxes to place the text on the banner rather than placing the text directly onto the page. To make sure the text boxes are the same size and position on every page, use the Clipboard to copy a text box from one page and paste it on another page.

- Try to make page breaks wherever there are natural breaks in the text, such as between letters or words.

- Do not attempt a patterned background; it's too hard to get the pieces lined up. In fact, it's best to just stick with a plain background. Use colored paper if you want.

Addressing Envelopes

There are two ways to print envelopes in Word: You can print a single envelope at a time (or multiple copies, but all addressed to the same person), or you can do a mail merge and print lots of envelopes at once, all addressed to different people. The latter is a huge topic all its own, and it's covered separately in Chapter 14. In this chapter, you'll learn about creating single envelopes, storing addresses for them, and placing them in letter documents.

Adding an Envelope to a Letter

Ready to generate an envelope for the letter you've just typed? Word can do it automatically. It even pulls out the delivery address from the letter and places it on the envelope.

Follow these steps to create an envelope layout:

1. In the letter you've composed, select the complete delivery address.

2. On the Mailings tab, click Envelopes. The Envelopes and Labels dialog box appears, with the recipient's address in the Delivery Address box (see Figure 8.25).

3. If your return address does not already appear in the Return Address box, type it there. (Word remembers it after you enter it initially.)

   Or, if you are going to print on an envelope with a preprinted return address, mark the Omit check box.

4. Change the envelope size if needed. (This is covered in the next section.)

5. Click Add to Document. Word creates a new section above the main letter, with an appropriate page size for the envelope size you chose and with the delivery and return addresses filled in.

 note

If you don't need the envelope to be stored with the document, click Print to send the envelope directly to the printer instead of adding it to the document.

Figure 8.25
Word identifies the recipient address and places it in the Delivery Address box.

Figure 8.26
Choose an envelope size.

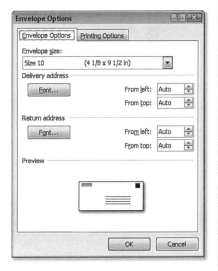

Setting the Envelope Size

The default envelope size is Size 10, which is a regular business envelope in the United States (4 1/8 inches × 9 1/2 inches). To change to a different size, click the Options button in the Envelopes and Labels dialog box. Then in the Envelope Options dialog box, select a different Envelope Size setting from the list provided (see Figure 8.26).

If none of the sizes matches your envelope, choose Custom Size from the bottom of the Envelope Size list. The Envelope Size dialog box opens, in which you can enter the exact dimensions of the envelope you have.

Changing the Address Position

Usually the default address positions work well; Word places the return address in the upper-left corner of the envelope, about 1/2 inch from the top and left edges, and places the delivery address in the center horizontally and slightly lower than center vertically.

To change the position of either of these addresses, click the Options button in the Envelopes and Labels dialog box, and then change the From Left and From Top values as needed.

Changing the Envelope Font

If you add the envelope to the document, you can then select the addresses and change their font formatting afterward.

However, if you choose not to add the envelope to the document—that is, if you send it directly to the printer with the Print button—then there is no opportunity to change the font after the fact, so you must set the desired font within the Envelope Options dialog box.

From the Envelopes and Labels dialog box, click Options, displaying the Envelope Options dialog box (refer to Figure 8.26). Then in the Delivery Address area, click Font. The Envelope Address dialog box opens, which looks very much like the Font dialog box you worked with in Chapter 4, "Applying Character Formatting." Change the font, style, size, color, and so on, and then click OK to accept the changes. Then do the same thing for the return address.

Printing an Envelope

To quickly print the envelope, click the Print button in the Envelopes and Labels dialog box. (You can reopen the dialog box by clicking the Envelopes button again on the Mailings tab if needed.) One copy of the envelope (only) prints on the default printer. It happens immediately; the Print dialog box does not appear.

Do you need more control than that? Perhaps you need multiple copies of the envelope, or a different printer than the default? For this, you must have added the envelope to the document. Just click the envelope (moving the insertion point onto its page) and choose File, Print. Under Settings, choose Print Current Page from the first drop-down list. Change the Printer if needed, increase the number of copies if needed, and then click Print.

 note

Sometimes when you insert an address from Outlook using the Envelopes and Labels dialog box, the address appears with extra vertical space between each line. To get rid of this extra space, you need to add the envelope to the document. Then select the paragraphs of the address and open the Paragraph dialog box (on the Home tab, click the dialog box launcher icon in the Paragraph group) and set the Before and After spacing to 0 Inches.

Controlling How Envelopes Feed into Your Printer

Word recommends an envelope feed orientation based on the default printer's driver information. That recommendation appears in the Feed area of the Envelopes and Labels dialog box.

Sometimes, however, the default envelope feed orientation won't work for some reason. For example, perhaps it is based on having an envelope tray that feeds the envelopes in centered, but you don't have such a tray so you're feeding the envelopes in at the left edge of the paper guide. Or perhaps the default orientation is to feed the envelope in head-first, but the printer's paper carriage width isn't wide enough for a large envelope.

To change the envelope printing orientation, follow these steps:

1. In the Envelopes and Labels dialog box, click the picture in the Feed area. The Envelope Options dialog box opens with the Printing Options tab displayed.

2. Click a picture that best represents the feed orientation needed (see Figure 8.27).

3. Click the Face Up or Face Down button, as appropriate. (This setting doesn't change which side of the page Word prints on, except if you have a duplex-capable printer, but it does change the graphic shown to help you remember how to place the envelopes in the paper tray.)

4. If you're feeding the envelope in sideways, if the return address prints to the right, click Clockwise Rotation.

5. (Optional) Select a different paper tray in the Feed From list if needed.

6. Click OK.

Figure 8.27
Choose an envelope feed orientation.

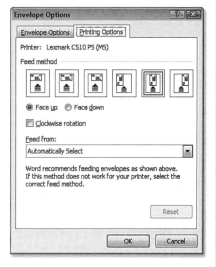

Storing and Retrieving Addresses

After you've entered a return address, Word offers to save it as the default return address. If you click Yes, it fills in that same return address automatically for all future envelopes.

You can also select an address from the Address Book that is used in Windows Mail or Microsoft Outlook. To do so, follow these steps:

1. Click the Insert Address icon above either the Delivery Address or Return Address box in the Envelopes and Labels dialog box.

2. If prompted to select a mail profile, choose the desired profile and click OK.

3. In the Select Name dialog box, addresses appear from your Outlook contact list or from the mail system associated with the profile you chose in step 2.

   Depending on the mail programs installed, you might have more than one address book available. Select from the Address Book drop-down list at the top-right corner of the dialog box.

4. Click OK. The address is filled into the Delivery Address or Return Address box.

Adding Graphics to an Envelope

There's no special feature for adding envelope graphics, but all the regular graphics tools can be used to place a graphic on an envelope that has been added to the document. You can use clip art, logo graphics, WordArt, and so on. Here's a quick list of cross-references for learning about various graphic types:

- **Graphics from files**—See "Inserting Pictures from Files," p. 384.

- **Clip art**—See "Finding and Inserting Clip Art," p. 451.

- **WordArt**—See "Creating and Modifying WordArt," p. 446.

- **Shapes**—See "Drawing a Shape," p. 417.

After inserting a graphic on the envelope and positioning it appropriately, you might find it useful to save the graphic (and optionally the return address with it) as a building block. You can then insert that building block into future envelope layouts, saving yourself the trouble of reimporting the graphic each time. See "Creating a Building Block" in Chapter 2, "Typing and Editing Text," for more information.

Using E-Postage with Word

If you use a third-party postage service such as Stamps.com, it can be accessed via Word's Envelope feature. Such systems save you trips to the post office by enabling you to print government-approved postage directly onto your envelopes. You then pay your monthly postage bill by credit card through the service.

First, of course, you must sign up for a service. When you mark the Add Electronic Postage check box (or try to) in the Envelopes and Labels dialog box, and you haven't yet installed postage software on your PC, a message appears offering to open the Microsoft Office website so you can find out more about e-postage. Click Yes to visit that page and find a link for signing up.

Once you've signed up and the postage software is installed, the Envelopes and Labels dialog box will allow you to mark the Add Electronic Postage check box, and the E-Postage Properties option will become available. (Click E-Postage Properties to set up options such as certified or registered mail or insurance.)

The exact steps for adding e-postage depend on the service you are using. For example, Stamps. com's service checks the delivery address you entered to make sure it is valid, makes corrections if needed, and prompts you for the weight and mailing date. Just follow the self-explanatory prompts to complete the postage purchase.

Creating Labels

As with envelopes, there are two ways of printing labels in Word. You can print individual labels (or a sheet containing multiple copies of the same label), or you can do a mail merge that creates one label apiece for a whole list of addressees. The latter is covered in Chapter 14. In this chapter, you'll learn how to create and print individual labels only.

To print labels, you need special label paper. There are many brands and sizes of labels; most come in full 8.5-inch × 11-inch sheets, with perforated peel-off labels. Word recognizes the model numbers for many popular brands and sizes, and you can set up custom labels in situations where none of Word's presets are appropriate.

 caution

Make sure you buy the type of label sheets designed for your printer type. Labels designed for inkjet printers cannot withstand the heat generated by the laser printing process, and might become curled or wrinkled—or worse yet, peel off or melt inside the printer—if used with a laser printer. Laser labels will work okay in inkjet printers, but the ink might not stick to them quite as well because laser label paper tends to be less porous.

Printing a Full Page of the Same Label

One common use of the Labels feature is to create return address labels for packages and other mailings. You can get really creative with these and include graphics, photos, colors, fancy fonts, and so on, or you can go strictly utilitarian.

To print a basic label, follow these steps:

 tip

To use the address that's currently stored as your default return address, mark the Use Return Address check box.

1. On the Mailings tab, click Labels. The Envelopes and Labels dialog box opens with the Labels tab displayed (see Figure 8.28).

2. In the Address box, type the address to appear on the label. (It doesn't really have to be an address; you can put any text you want here, such as THIS END UP or FRAGILE or HAVE A NICE DAY.)

   You can also select an address from your Address Book; see "Storing and Retrieving Addresses" earlier in this chapter.

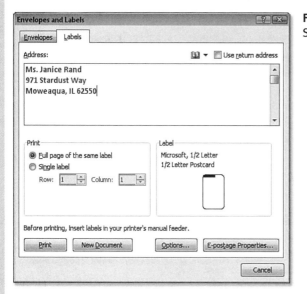

Figure 8.28
Set up a label for printing.

3. In the Print area, choose Full Page of the Same Label.

4. (Optional) Change the label size or type if needed. To do so:

   a. Click the sample in the Label area. The Label Options dialog box opens.

   b. In the Printer Information area, select Continuous Feed Printers or Page Printers.

   c. Select the label manufacturer from the Label Vendors list. This sets up the model numbers.

 note

A continuous feed printer uses a tractor-feed style of label, usually one label per row. Most continuous feed printers are dot matrix. The model numbers are different for this type of label than for page printers. Most page printers are inkjet or laser.

   d. Select the model number from the Product Number list. In the Label Information area, confirm that the height and page size matches up with the label sheet's actual content.

   If you can't find the right number, see "Creating a Custom Label Specification" below.

   e. Click OK.

5. Click Print to send the print job directly to the printer (make sure your label sheet is loaded) or click New Document to create a new document containing the label sheet (which you can then edit as needed before printing).

Printing a Single Label

Printing a single label is similar to printing a full sheet, except for one thing: When you're printing a single label, you're probably reusing a label sheet that is already missing one or more labels. So follow the steps in the preceding section, but in step 3, choose Single Label. Then enter the Row and Column numbers that describe the first available label on the sheet.

 caution

Some label sheets don't feed through the printer very well when some of the labels are missing. If you find that paper jams occur frequently when reusing a label sheet, try using a different printer. Inkjet printers are often more forgiving of paper feed issues than laser printers are, for example.

Creating a Custom Label Specification

If you're using a generic label brand and you don't know the equivalent model number for a well-known brand, you have a choice: You can browse through the product numbers for a well-known brand such as Avery until you find one that matches up with what you've got, or you can create a new custom label specification.

 tip

Avery is the most popular manufacturer of labels; you will probably find what you want in the Avery Standard set.

To create a new label specification, follow these steps:

1. From the Labels tab of the Envelopes and Labels dialog box, click Options. The Label Options dialog box opens.

2. Select an existing label that closely matches the label you want to create. (It doesn't have to be exact.)

3. Click the New Label button. The Label Details dialog box opens.

4. Type a name for the new label in the Label Name box.

5. Change any of the label measurements or specifications as needed. Refer to the Preview area for what each measurement represents (see Figure 8.29).

6. Click OK to create the new label specification. The new label appears at the top of the Product Number list in the Label Options dialog box, and the Label Products box changes to Other/ Custom.

7. Click OK to accept the new custom label as the layout to use.

8. Continue printing normally.

Fine-Tuning the Label Appearance

Use the New Document button in the Envelopes and Labels dialog box to create a new document containing the sheet of labels for printing. You can then save it for later use like any other document.

A side benefit of creating a new document is that you can customize the labels before printing them. For example, you can change the font, size, color, or other attributes of the text.

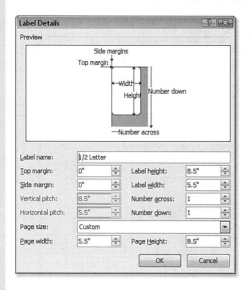

Figure 8.29
Create a new custom label specification.

The new document that holds the labels is laid out as a table. You can choose whether to display or hide the table gridlines by displaying the Table Tools Layout tab and clicking View Gridlines.

You can do anything with the labels that you can do with table cells, as covered in Chapter 9, "Creating and Formatting Tables." For example, you might add a colored background to the table cells. Here's how to do that:

1. Select the entire table by clicking the table selector box (the four-headed arrow box in the table's upper-left corner).

2. Right-click the table selector box and choose Borders and Shading.

3. Click the Shading tab.

4. Open the Fill list and choose a color.

5. Click OK. All the labels now have a shaded background.

That's just one example. Check out Chapter 9 to learn what else you can do with table formatting. Don't change the row heights or column widths, though, and don't add cell border lines, because those things can interfere with the appearance of the printed labels.

Sometimes the small differences in the way various printers feed their paper can cause text to be offset on a label. To make an adjustment, follow these steps:

1. From the Labels tab of the Envelopes and Labels dialog box, click Options.

2. Confirm that the correct label product and product number are selected, and then click Details. An information dialog box appears for the chosen label.

3. Change any of the measurements listed for the label. For example, to scoot everything to the right, increase the Side Margin setting, or to start the labels slightly higher on the page, decrease the Top Margin setting.

4. Click OK.

Rather than making a change to the overall specification for that product number, you might instead choose to create a new custom label specification that mirrors the label number but uses the different offset. Follow the steps in "Creating a Custom Label Specification" earlier in this chapter.

Creating Folded Note Cards

First, the bad news: Word is not the ideal program for creating special-paper projects like folded note cards. It doesn't have any of the friendly built-in helpers for such tasks like Microsoft Publisher does, so you have to either start with a template (if one is available that meets your needs) or set everything up manually. Nevertheless, sometimes Word is the only thing available and must be made to serve.

A folded note card is a printing challenge because certain fold types require some of the text to appear upside-down. For example, one of the most common layouts is a *quarter-fold* card, in which you fold a regular 8.5-inch × 11-inch sheet of paper twice (see Figure 8.30).

Figure 8.30
A quarter-fold note card is printed with half the text upside-down so it will look right when folded.

Special note card paper is available that works in *half-fold* layout, meaning the sheet of paper is folded only once. This results in a card that is more like a store-bought greeting card. (The paper packs usually come with envelopes of the correct size for use with the cards.)

Custom paper size presents one challenge to this half-fold type of layout. There are various sizes of cards available, and most of them don't conform to any of the preset paper sizes in Word. (Their envelopes are often nonstandard sizes too.)

Depending on the fold location, other issues arise as well; for a top-fold card, half the content must be printed upside-down, and for both top- and side-fold cards, half the content must be printed on the opposite side of the paper.

The following sections explain how to address these challenges to create folded note cards in Word.

Using Card Templates

Many greeting card templates are available in Word via Office Online, and these are great for helping you get started. Certain templates are designed for certain sizes of greeting card paper manufactured by Avery, and the Avery model numbers are indicated in the template names where applicable. Other templates are designated half-fold or quarter-fold for regular paper. Search for templates using the keywords *greeting card*, as you learned earlier in this chapter.

➡ *To review how to create a document by using a template, see "Starting a New Document Based on a Template," p. 291.*

The templates are especially advantageous for quarter-fold cards because they already have placeholders for the upside-down parts. Rather than having to make upside-down text yourself, you edit what's there.

Specifying the Paper Size and Type

To specify the paper type and size, display the Page Layout tab and choose Size, More Paper Sizes. In the Paper Size list, select the paper size if it happens to appear there, or choose Custom Size from the bottom of the list and enter the exact size of the card sheet.

➡ *For more information about custom paper sizes, see "Setting Paper Size," p. 260.*

Paper *type* cannot be controlled in Word, but some printers enable you to set a paper type in their driver. This can be useful on printers that treat paper with different coatings differently, such as printing in a higher resolution on glossy paper than on matte, or allowing for different feed roller positions for very thick cardstock paper. To explore the printer's paper settings, do the following:

1. Choose File, Print.

2. Under Printer, select the desired printer.

3. Click the Printer Properties hyperlink. The Printer Properties dialog box opens for that printer.

4. Look for options for controlling the paper type, and set them to match the paper used for the card.

5. Click OK and continue printing normally.

Creating Upside-Down Text

Technically, Word cannot produce upside-down text. That is, nothing that Word considers to be "text" can be upside-down.

There are ways around every limitation, though, and in this case the solution is provided by WordArt. You can create a WordArt text object and then rotate the object 180 degrees. It's not really text—it's a graphic that looks just like text—but your audience will never know the difference.

WordArt is covered in detail in Chapter 11, but here's a quick preview of how to use it to create upside-down text for a card:

1. On the Insert tab, click WordArt and then click the first sample on the list (plain outlined text). Some dummy text appears in its own frame.

2. Type your own text in the WordArt frame to replace the dummy text.

3. Change the font, size, and text attributes (such as bold and italic) as needed.

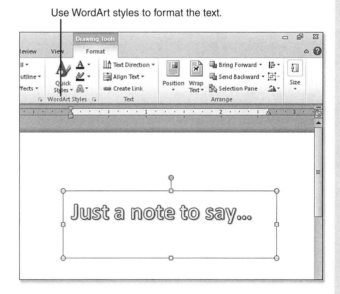

Use WordArt styles to format the text.

Figure 8.31
Enter and format the text that should appear upside-down on the card as WordArt.

4. On the Format tab, use the controls in the WordArt Styles group (Text Fill, Text Outline, and Text Effects) to change the text's appearance.

5. Click the Rotate button and then click Rotate Right 90° (see Figure 8.32). Do this once more so that the text is upside-down.

> *For more information about WordArt formatting, see "Creating and Modifying WordArt," p. 446.*

 tip

To rotate the WordArt text some amount other than 90 degrees, drag the green circle on the WordArt frame to rotate the text a custom amount.

Rotate it 90 degrees twice in succession to make it upside down.

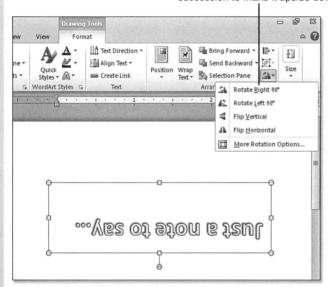

Figure 8.32
Rotate the WordArt from the Format tab.

CREATING AND FORMATTING TABLES

Creating a Table

A *table* is a grid of rows and columns that define *cells* at their intersections. Each cell is its own separate area, somewhat like a text box.

The most obvious use for a table is to organize multiple columns of data in tabular form, as in a spreadsheet. For example, in Figure 9.1, information about fish is displayed in a table. Some cells contain pictures; others contain text.

You can also use tables for page layout, a technique popular in web page design. In Figure 9.2, a table has been used to structure a newsletter layout, as an alternative to newspaper-style columns or text boxes. Word facilitates tabular layout by enabling you to merge and split certain cells, creating uneven numbers of rows and columns to accommodate nonstandard designs.

There are three ways to insert a table in a document: the Table menu, the Insert Table dialog box, and the Table Drawing tool. The following sections look at each of these methods.

Name	Description	Picture
Largemouth Bass *Micropterus salmoides*	The largemouth bass is usually green with dark blotches that form a horizontal stripe along the middle of the fish on either side. The underside ranges in color from light green to almost white. The dorsal fin is almost divided, with the anterior portion containing 9 spines and the posterior portion containing 12-13 soft rays.	
Smallmouth Bass *Micropterus dolomieu*	The smallmouth bass is generally green with dark vertical bands rather than a horizontal band along the side. There are 13-15 soft rays in the dorsal fin, and the upper jaw never extends beyond the eye.	
Guadalupe Bass *Micropterus treculi*	The Guadalupe bass is generally green in color and may be distinguished from similar species found in Texas in that it doesn't have vertical bars like smallmouth bass, its jaw doesn't extend beyond the eyes as in largemouth bass, and coloration extends much lower on the body than in spotted bass.	

Figure 9.1
Tables are commonly used for organizing multicolumn data.

Cox Family Newsletter

Upcoming events
- Brandon Cox, 8th grade graduation ceremony May 2nd
- Kelly Cox, softball tournament May 14-16
- Cinda Cox, Daisy Puppy School awards ceremony, June 3.

Summer Vacation Plans

This summer promises to be a very busy one for the Cox family! School is out for Brandon and Kelly on May 15th, and on May 17th the entire family is leaving for a two-week Mexican Riviera trip aboard the Star Galley, a wonderful kid-friendly cruise ship. Everyone is excited about the swimming, hiking, and other activities, as well as the legendary good food about the ship.

When we return from the trip, we'll barely have time to unpack our bags before the yearly awards ceremony at Daisy Puppy School, where Cinda has been training our Shetland Sheepdog, Riley. Congratulations to Cinda and Riley for completing Puppy Obedience Camp Levels I and II.

Figure 9.2
Tables can be used to create multicolumn page layouts.

Inserting a Table from the Table Menu

To access the Table menu, click the Table button on the Insert tab. The main feature of the Table menu is a grid of squares, as shown in Figure 9.3. Drag across the grid to select the number of rows and columns desired; when you release the mouse button, Word places a new table in the document with those specifications.

The tables inserted via this method have their cell widths set to Auto. The table itself occupies the full width of the page (between the margins), and the cells are equally sized to use that space. But when you start typing text into a cell, the cell begins expanding to hold that text, and all the other cells decrease in size to pick up the slack.

If you want some other type of cell-sizing behavior, use the following method of table creation instead.

Figure 9.3
Create a table by dragging across the squares on the Table menu's grid.

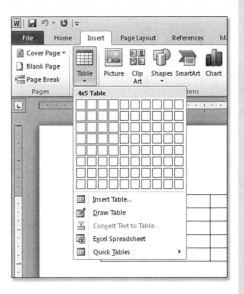

Inserting a Table via the Insert Table Dialog Box

The dialog box method of table creation takes longer, but it enables you to specify how you want the text and the cell width to interact. Three AutoFit settings are available:

- **Fixed Column Width**—This can be set to Auto, which starts with a fixed column width such that the table fills the width of the page but enables a column to enlarge based on the text you enter. It can alternatively be set to a specific value in inches (at increments as small as 1/100).

- **AutoFit to Contents**—This setting changes the cell widths so that whatever text you place in them fits on a single row. If a column contains nothing, it appears very narrow.

- **AutoFit to Window**—The table width changes depending on the size of the window in which it is being viewed. This setting is great for tables that will be displayed on web pages, because one never knows the size of the browser window a web page visitor will be using.

To use the dialog box method, follow these steps:

1. On the Insert tab, click Table and then choose Insert Table from the menu. The Insert Table dialog box opens (see Figure 9.4).

2. Enter the number of rows and columns desired in their respective boxes.

3. Select an AutoFit behavior setting.

4. (Optional) Mark the Remember Dimensions for New Tables check box to preserve these settings.

5. Click OK to create the table.

Figure 9.4
Use the Insert Table dialog box to create a new table.

Drawing a Table

Drawing a table is useful when you want unequal-sized rows and columns or a different number of rows in some columns than in others (or vice versa). This method turns your mouse pointer into a pencil, which you can use to create the table's overall borders and individual row and column dividers.

To draw the table, follow these steps:

1. On the Insert tab, click Table and then choose Draw Table. The mouse pointer turns into a pencil.

2. Drag to draw a box representing the outer borders of the table. When you release the mouse button, the cursor remains a pencil.

3. Drag to draw the rows and columns within the box you just drew (see Figure 9.5).

   To draw row and column dividers, draw straight lines. To draw a table within a table, draw a rectangle within a cell.

 note

To draw additional lines later, click inside the table; then click the Draw Table button again to reenter drawing mode.

4. (Optional) If you need to erase a line you drew, click Eraser on the Design tab and then click the line to erase. To go back to drawing mode, click Draw Table on the Design tab.

5. When you are finished drawing lines, press Esc or click the Draw Table button on the Design tab.

Figure 9.5
Use the mouse pointer as a "pencil" to draw the table.

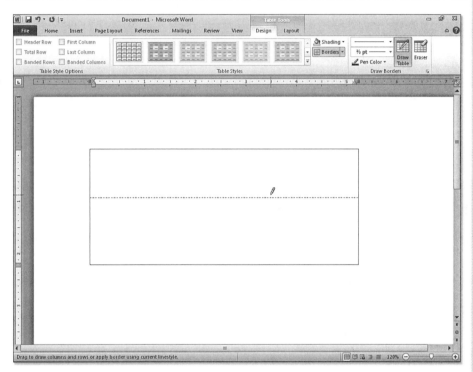

Entering Data in a Table

To type data into a cell, click in the cell and type. To move to the next cell, press Tab; to move to the previous cell, press Shift+Tab.

Depending on the AutoFit setting of the table, as you type text into a cell, one of two things will happen:

- The text will wrap to additional lines, and the cell will get taller.

- The cell will try to widen itself as much as possible, taking space away from other cells as it is able, before it starts wrapping to additional lines.

 tip
The Tab key doesn't work normally in a table cell because it's used to move around in the table, but there's a workaround. To create a tab character in a table cell, press Ctrl+Tab.

➡ *To learn about column and row sizing, see "Sizing a Table," p. 349.*

Table 9.1 summarizes the keyboard shortcuts available for moving around in a table.

Table 9.1 Keyboard Shortcuts for Table Navigation

To Move To:	Press This:
Next cell (or to start a new row if already in the last cell)	Tab
Previous cell (in same row)	Shift+Tab
First cell in the row	Alt+Home
Last cell in the row	Alt+End
First cell in the column	Alt+Page Up
Last cell in the column	Alt+Page Down
Previous row	Up arrow
Next row	Down arrow

Editing a Table

Tables are flexible; you can add and remove rows and columns, merge and split cells, move pieces around, and more.

Selecting Cells

As in most areas of Word, before you can format or modify a cell (or something within a cell), you must select it.

When a cell is selected, the entire cell appears highlighted, even if it is empty. To select a cell, position the mouse pointer at the bottom-left corner of the cell so that the mouse pointer turns into a black diagonally pointing arrow, and then click (see Figure 9.6). Any formatting you apply when the entire cell is selected affects all the content within it.

Figure 9.6
A selected cell.

There is also a keyboard method for selecting the entire cell: Position the insertion point at the end of any content within the cell and then press Shift+right arrow.

One other method for selecting a cell is found on the Layout tab. Open the Select menu and choose Select Cell (see Figure 9.7).

Holding down the Shift key and pressing an arrow key extends the selection area by one character or line in the arrow direction, so why is it that pressing Shift+right arrow at the end of a cell selects the entire cell?

Figure 9.7
The Select menu enables you to quickly select various portions of the table.

It happens because of a hidden end-of-cell marker that appears at the end of each cell's content. To see these markers, toggle on the Show/Hide (¶) feature on the Home tab (see Figure 9.8). When the insertion point is at the end of the cell content, and you extend the selection one character to the right, you select the end-of-cell marker, which in turn selects the entire cell.

Figure 9.8
Nonprinting
end-of-cell
markers appear
in each cell.

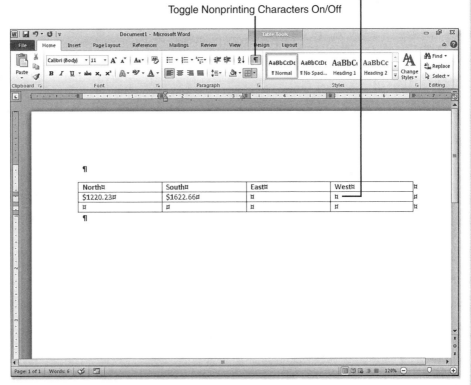

On the other hand, when the *content* of the text is selected, only the content is highlighted; a portion of the cell background appears behind it in an unhighlighted state. You do not have to select all the content in the cell; this makes it possible to apply different formatting to certain characters or objects within the cell, but not others. To select text in a cell, drag across the text. To select a graphic or other object in a cell, click that object.

Dragging across cell content selects only the content, not the cell—until you drag to include more than one cell. When you drag across multiple cells, the cells themselves become selected.

To select noncontiguous cells, hold down the Ctrl key as you select each of the cells or ranges to include.

Selecting Rows, Columns, or Tables

To select a row (or multiple rows), do one of the following:

- Click anywhere in the row. On the Layout tab, open the Select menu and choose Select Row.

- Drag across all the cells in the row, including the end-of-row marker to the far right of the row. This marker is another nonprinting character; it looks just like the end-of-cell markers (refer to Figure 9.8), but it is outside the rightmost cell in the row. Drag up or down to select additional rows.

- Position the mouse pointer to the left of the row so that the mouse pointer changes to a white arrow, and then click to select the entire row. Drag up or down to select additional rows (see Figure 9.9).

- Click in the first (leftmost) cell in the row and hold down the Shift key as you press the right-arrow key repeatedly until the entire row is selected. Press the up- or down-arrow key to select additional rows.

Click to the left of a row to select it

End-of-row marker

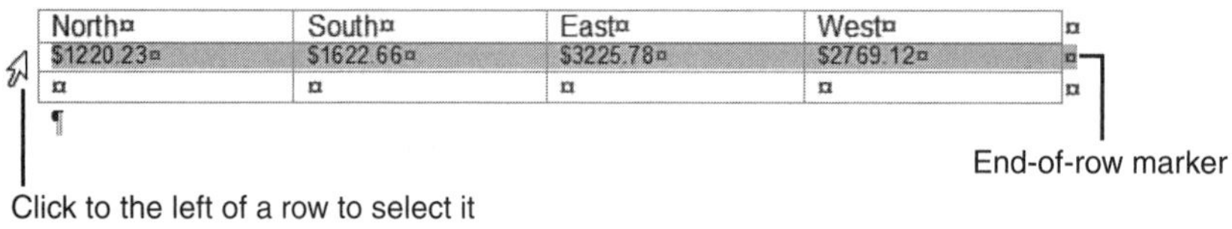

Figure 9.9
Select a row by clicking to its left or dragging across all its cells.

To select a column (or multiple columns), do one of these:

- Click anywhere in the column. On the Layout tab, open the Select menu and choose Select Column.

- Drag across all the cells in the column. There is no end-of-column marker to worry about. Drag to the right or left to select additional columns.

- Position the mouse pointer above the column so that the mouse pointer changes to a black down-pointing arrow, and then click to select the entire column (see Figure 9.10). Drag right or left to select additional columns.

■ Click in the first (topmost) cell in the column and hold down the Shift key as you press the down arrow repeatedly until the entire column is selected. Use the left- or right-arrow key to select additional columns.

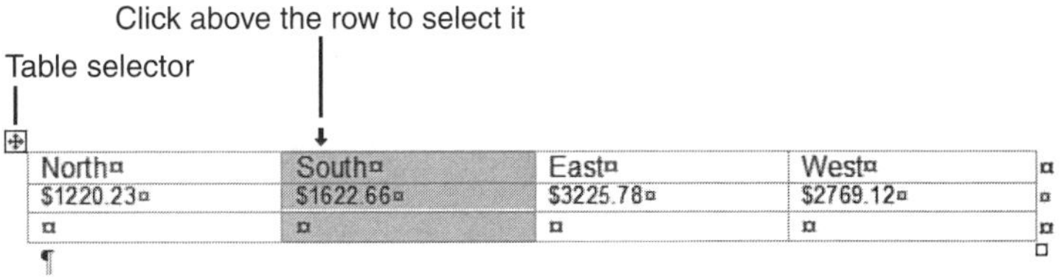

Click above the row to select it

Table selector

Figure 9.10
Select a column by clicking above it or dragging across its cells.

North¤	South¤	East¤	West¤	¤
$1220.23¤	$1622.66¤	$3225.78¤	$2769.12¤	¤
¤	¤	¤	¤	¤

To select the entire table, click the table selector icon, shown in Figure 9.10, or press Alt+5 (using the 5 on the numeric keypad with Num Lock turned off). As another alternative, you can open the Select menu on the Layout tab and choose Select Table.

Inserting Rows, Columns, or Cells

To insert a single row or column, right-click a cell within a row or column adjacent to where you want the insertion to appear, and then point to Insert and click the option that best describes what you want. There are also buttons on the Layout tab for inserting rows and columns (see Figure 9.11).

> **tip**
>
> Another way to select is by turning on the Extend Selection feature (Ctrl+Shift+F8). When it is on, you can then use the arrow keys to extend a selection in any direction. (You don't have to hold down Shift with the arrows.) To turn off Extend Selection, press Esc.

You can also insert individual cells, shifting the existing cells down or to the right. To do this, follow these steps:

1. Right-click the cell where you want to insert a new cell and choose Insert, Insert Cells.Alternatively, move the insertion point into the cell where you want to insert a new cell and click the dialog box launcher for the Rows & Columns group on the Layout tab.

2. In the Insert Cells dialog box, shown in Figure 9.12, click the insertion type you want. You can choose to shift the existing cells either down or to the right. (You can also use this dialog box to insert an entire row or column, although it's somewhat of a long way around for that.)

3. Click OK.

Inserting a new cell adds another row or column to the table if needed to hold the shifted content; if there is already an extra row at the bottom or column at the right, the content simply shifts into it and no new rows or columns are created.

Right-click a cell and select from the Insert submenu.

Buttons for inserting rows and columns.

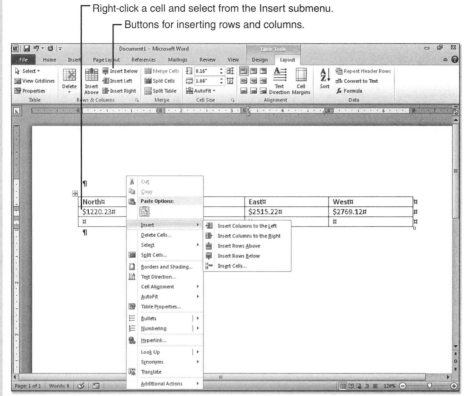

Figure 9.11
Insert a row or column by right-clicking and selecting from the Insert submenu.

Figure 9.12
Choose what should happen to the existing cells to make room for the new cell.

Deleting Rows, Columns, or Cells

A lot of people are surprised that the Delete key on the keyboard does not work to delete rows, columns, and cells. That's because Delete is not really a removal tool—it's a clearing tool. It clears whatever content is there, but it leaves the structure in place. Therefore, if you select a cell and press Delete, all the cell's content is deleted, but the cell remains.

The Layout tab's Delete button opens a menu of deletion choices. Move the insertion point into the row, column, or cell to affect and then select the deletion command from the menu, as shown in Figure 9.13.

Figure 9.13
Choose the portion of the table to delete.

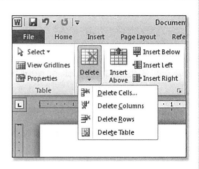

If you choose Delete Cells, a Delete Cells dialog box opens, in which you can choose whether the remaining cells should be shifted to the left or up. (It's just like the Insert Cells dialog box from Figure 9.12, except it's deleting instead of inserting.)

The Cut feature of the Clipboard can also be used to remove entire rows or columns. (It doesn't work for individual cells; it just clears them.) To delete an entire row or column, select it and then press Ctrl+X or click the Cut button on the Home tab.

 note

Cutting isn't really deleting, but if you cut something and then never paste it, the effect is the same.

Deleting an Entire Table

To delete an entire table, display the Layout tab, click the Delete button, and choose Delete Table (refer to Figure 9.13).

There are also some less direct methods. Just like with individual rows, columns, and cells, you can't delete an entire table with the Delete key; selecting the entire table and pressing Delete simply clears all the content out of the table. There's an exception to that, however. If you select a larger block of the document than just the table—for example, the table plus the end-of-paragraph marker before or after it—and then press Delete, Word deletes the entire block, including the table structure.

The Cut feature of the Clipboard also works on entire tables. Select the entire table and press Ctrl+X or click the Cut button on the Home tab. (You can also right-click the table selector icon and choose Cut to cut the entire table.) You can then paste the entire table from the Clipboard to another location in the document, if you want.

Moving and Copying Rows and Columns

To move or copy a row or column, you have a choice of two techniques: using a drag-and-drop operation or using the Clipboard (Cut/Copy/Paste).

Here's the drag-and-drop method:

1. Select the row(s) or column(s) to move or copy.

2. Position the mouse pointer over the selection, so that the pointer becomes a white arrow.

3. (Optional) Hold down the Ctrl key if you want to copy (rather than move).

4. Drag to the left or right for columns, or drag up or down for rows, to move the selection to a new position.

Here's the Clipboard method:

1. Select the row(s) or column(s) to move or copy.

2. Cut or copy the selection to the Clipboard using one of these methods:

   - **Ribbon method**—Click Cut or Copy on the Home tab.

   - **Keyboard method**—Press Ctrl+X for Cut or Ctrl+C for Copy.

   - **Right-click method**—Right-click the selection and choose Cut or Copy.

3. Click where you want the selection to go. If you're moving/copying a row, click in the leftmost cell of the row that should appear below the selection; if you're moving/copying a column, click in the column that should appear to the right.

4. Paste the selection from the Clipboard using one of these methods:

   - **Ribbon method**—Click Paste on the Home tab.

   - **Keyboard method**—Press Ctrl+V.

   - **Right-click method**—Right-click and choose Paste.

tip

When moving a row, position the mouse pointer over the leftmost cell in the row.

caution

Individual cells cannot be moved in the same sense as a row or column is moved, but you can move the cell content with either a drag-and-drop or cut-and-paste operation. Be careful, though, that you do not overwrite existing content. If the destination cells are not empty, the previous content is deleted—not moved over. (You're not working with cells here, but cell content.)

Merging and Splitting Cells

Merging cells erases the dividers between them; *splitting* a cell adds a divider, creating two cells out of one. Using merging or splitting, you can create all sorts of interesting tables with unequal numbers of rows and columns, much like in the drawn tables you learned about at the beginning of the chapter. (In fact, the table-drawing tools provide one method of merging and splitting.)

To merge two or more cells, select the cells and click the Merge Cells button on the Layout tab (see Figure 9.14), or right-click the selection and choose Merge Cells.

When you're merging multiple nonempty cells, the resulting merged cell contains all the content from all the merged cells, separated by paragraph breaks.

Click here to merge the selected cells.

Figure 9.14
Merge the
selected cells.

When you're merging cells that contain different formatting settings, the resulting merged cell takes on the cell formatting from the leftmost or topmost cell in the merged range. This rule applies only to cell-wide formatting, though, not character formatting. For example, text that's bold will continue to be bold after the merge.

Another way to merge cells is to use the Eraser feature, found on the Design tab. Click Eraser, and the mouse pointer becomes an eraser. Then click the divider line between any two cells to merge them (see Figure 9.15).

The mouse pointer becomes an eraser.　　　　Eraser

Figure 9.15
Use the Eraser
tool to merge
cells.

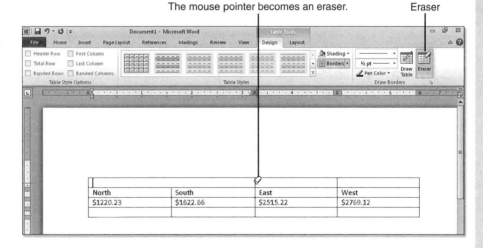

Merging cells is simple because there are no options involved; cells are either merged or they are not. With splitting, however, you must specify how many pieces you want the cell split into vertically or horizontally.

To split a cell, follow these steps:

1. Click in the cell to be split and then click the Split Cells button on the Layout tab. Alternatively, you can right-click the cell and choose Split Cells.

2. Enter the number of columns and rows in which to split the selected cell. For example, to split it into four columns, enter 4 as the number of columns and 1 as the number of rows (see Figure 9.16).

3. Click OK to perform the split.

Figure 9.16
Enter information about the desired split.

You can also split using the table-drawing tools. This works just like it did when you were drawing the table initially (if you used that method to create the table). To split a table by drawing, follow these steps:

1. On the Design tab, click Draw Table. The mouse pointer turns into a pencil.

2. Drag to draw divider lines where you want splits to occur.

3. Click the Draw Table button again, or press Esc, to turn drawing mode off.

Splitting a Table

Splitting a table adds a blank paragraph (non-table) between two rows. To split a table, click in the row that should become the first row in the second table and then click the Split Table button on the Layout tab.

To rejoin a table that has been split, delete the paragraph marker between the tables.

Creating a Nested Table

A *nested table* is a table within a table. Nested tables can be useful when you are using a table for page layout and then want to use a table for data organization within the layout. For example, in Figure 9.17, a table-based newsletter contains a mini-calendar table within its right column.

To create a nested table, click inside a cell and then insert a new table as you would normally, using any method you learned earlier in the chapter.

If the table to be nested already exists, you can paste it into a cell. Don't use a regular paste operation for this, though, because Word will assume you want to merge the two tables. Instead, follow these steps to paste one table into another:

 tip

If you have a table such as the nested calendar in Figure 9.17 that you might want to reuse, consider saving it as a building block. To do so, select the table, display the Insert tab, and click Quick Parts. On the menu that appears, click Save Selection to Quick Part Gallery. Set up a building block entry for it in the Quick Parts gallery; you can then access it from the Quick Parts menu for reuse.

1. Cut or copy the table to be nested onto the Clipboard.

2. Place the insertion point in the cell in which you want to paste the table.

3. Right-click at the insertion point and choose Paste as Nested Table.

Figure 9.17
A table can be nested within another table.

Nested table

Sizing a Table

By default, a newly inserted table is as wide as possible, given the margin and indent settings at the location where it is placed. So, for example, if you place it on an 8.5-inch × 11-inch page with 1-inch margins on each size, the table will be 6.5 inches wide. The columns are equal in size, so in an eight-column table that's 6.5 inches wide, for example, each cell is 0.83 inches (approximately 13/16 inches) wide.

The default height of a table is determined by the number of rows, with a single-height line for text in each row. For example, if the default font size is 11-point, each row's height will be such that one line of 11-point text can fit into it.

Changing the AutoFit Setting

The AutoFit setting determines how (or whether) the table's size will change as the content is added to it.

There are three possible AutoFit settings for a table, and you can switch among them from the AutoFit button on the Layout tab, as in Figure 9.18, or by right-clicking the table and choosing AutoFit:

- **AutoFit Contents**—Each cell is as wide as it needs to be to hold its content. Empty columns are very small (one character wide). Text wraps to additional lines in a cell, but only after the cell has expanded as much as it can, given the widths of the other columns and the overall table size.

- **AutoFit Window**—The table resizes itself depending on the size of the page on which it is displayed. This is useful for web pages and also for nested tables. For example, the calendar in Figure 9.17 would dynamically change its width as the column in which it resides changes width if you set it to AutoFit to Window.

- **Fixed Column Width**—Each cell stays at its current size until you manually change it.

The table's AutoFit setting forms the basis of its initial width settings, but there are numerous ways of manually adjusting those widths.

Figure 9.18
Choose an AutoFit setting to govern the table's sizing.

Resizing by Dragging

The easiest way to resize a row or column is simply by dragging; position the mouse pointer over the right border (for width) or bottom border (for height) and drag (see Figure 9.19). To change the width of the entire column or the height of the entire row, make sure that nothing is selected in the table when you begin dragging.

Dragging a column border changes the spacing between the cells it lies between, but no other cells are affected, nor is the overall size of the table. If you want all the other cells to stay the same size, and the overall size of the table to change with the resizing, hold down the Shift key as you drag.

If a cell is selected in the table when you drag, the resizing affects only the row containing the selected cell. The adjustment affects only the two cells that the border lies between. To resize the whole row, hold down Shift.

Specifying an Exact Size

If you need precise sizes for rows or columns, click in a cell and then use the Height and Width boxes on the Layout tab. The Height value affects the entire row; the Width value affects the entire column (see Figure 9.20).

Figure 9.19
Resize a column by dragging.

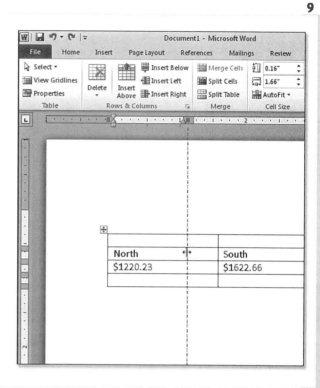

Width

Figure 9.20
Enter height
and width val-
ues for the row
and column of
the current cell.

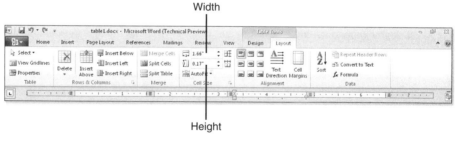

Height

You can also change row and column sizes from the Table Properties dialog box. Follow these
steps:

1. Right-click the row or column to affect and choose Table Properties.

   Alternatively, you can click in the row or column to affect and then either click the dialog box
   launcher for the Cell Size group on the Layout tab or click the Properties button in the Table
   group on the Layout tab.

2. In the Table Properties dialog box, click the Column tab. The width information for the selected
   column appears (see Figure 9.21).

Figure 9.21
Set a specific size for each column.

3. Change the column width if needed.

4. To change another column, click the Next Column or Previous Column button and change the width for it. Do this for all the columns you need to change.

5. Click the Row tab. The height information for the current row appears. By default, the Specify Height check box is not marked, which enables the row to dynamically resize itself depending on its content.

6. If you want to specify an exact height for the row, mark the Specify Height check box and enter a value.

7. Set the Row Height Is value to either At Least or Exactly. At Least allows the height to grow larger than the specified value but not smaller. Exactly forces the row to be exactly the specified value, even if the text is truncated (see Figure 9.22).

8. Mark or clear the Allow Row to Break Across Pages check box as desired.

9. To change another row, click the Next Row or Previous Row button and then change the height for it. Repeat until all rows have been set.

10. Click OK.

Figure 9.22
Set a specific size for each row, or allow the rows to auto-size.

Distributing Column Widths Evenly

Tables start out with uniform-sized rows and columns, but as you have seen, you can make changes to those values. To go back to even spacing, click the Distribute Columns or Distribute Rows button on the Layout tab (see Figure 9.23). As an alternative method, you can select the entire table and then right-click the table and choose Distribute Rows Evenly or Distribute Columns Evenly from the shortcut menu.

Make row heights equal.

Figure 9.23
Set row heights or column widths to use the available space equally.

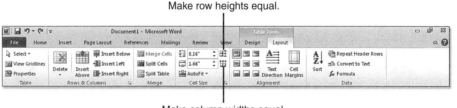

Make column widths equal.

Resizing the Entire Table

To resize the table as a whole, drag one of its outside borders. You'll get different results, though, depending on where you drag:

- **Left border**—Changes the width of the leftmost column.

- **Right border**—Changes the width of the rightmost column.

 tip

Holding down Shift while dragging the bottom-right corner constrains the resizing so that the table's aspect ratio (height-to-width ratio) is preserved.

- **Bottom border**—Changes the height of the bottom row.

- **Bottom-right corner**—Changes the height and width of the table overall, with all rows and columns adjusted proportionally.

Formatting a Table

Now that you've learned about the structural aspects of table creation and editing, let's look at some ways of making the table more attractive and readable.

Applying Table Styles

Table styles are similar to the character and paragraph styles you learned about in Chapter 6, "Creating and Applying Styles and Themes." They quickly apply named sets of formatting. The main difference is that a table style contains table-specific features such as cell border formatting, cell shading, and special designations for the first and last row and column.

➡ *To learn more about styles, see "Understanding Styles," p. 217.*

To apply a table style, click anywhere in the table and then select one of the table styles from the Design tab (see Figure 9.24). For more choices, click the down-arrow button to open a larger menu.

Table Styles

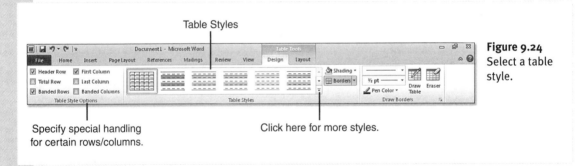

Figure 9.24
Select a table style.

Specify special handling for certain rows/columns.

Click here for more styles.

After applying a table style, use the check boxes in the Table Style Options group of the Design tab to turn on/off certain formatting extras. Each of these designates certain rows or columns to receive different formatting. For example, Header Row formats the first row differently; Total Row formats the last row differently. The Banded options make every other row or column different, for easier reading.

Not all styles support banded rows and columns. If nothing seems to be happening when you turn on Banded Rows or Banded Columns, try selecting a different table style.

If you're happy with the current table style except for wanting bands, modify the style. To do so, open the Table Styles list (from the Design tab) and choose Modify Table Style. Assign a new name in the Name box, and then open the Apply Formatting To menu and choose one of the band options (such as Banded Rows or Banded Columns). Change the formatting as desired, and then click OK.

Setting the Default Table Style

To set a style as the default for new tables, right-click the desired style on the Table Styles list and choose Set As Default.

In the Default Table Style dialog box, choose either This Document Only or All Documents Based on the Normal.dotm Template to specify the scope of the setting. Then click OK to make the style the new default.

Creating or Modifying Table Styles

To create a table style, you can either start with an existing one and give it a new name, or start from scratch with a new definition.

To create or modify a table style, follow these steps:

1. Open the Table Styles list on the Design tab and select the style that is closest to the one you want.

2. Open the Table Styles list again and choose Modify Table Style. The Modify Style dialog box opens.

3. In the Name box, type a new name. (It is better to create a new style than overwrite the definition of an existing one, and in some cases Word will not let you modify a built-in style.)

4. To make whole-table changes, set the Apply Formatting To value to Whole Table and then make formatting changes using the controls provided. You can choose a different font, size, and color; change the borders; change the cell shading and alignment; and more (see Figure 9.25). You will learn more about these formatting types in upcoming sections of this chapter.

5. To make changes to only certain rows or columns, select the desired scope from the Apply Formatting To list (for example, Header Row), and then make formatting changes.

6. (Optional) To store the style in the template (for reuse in other documents), click New Documents Based on This Template.

7. Click OK. The new custom table style is created.

Custom table styles, when they exist, appear at the top of the Table Styles list in the Custom section (see Figure 9.26).

 note

When you apply a table style, any direct (manual) formatting applied to the table is wiped away. This is by design. To change styles but keep the manual formatting, instead of clicking a style on the Table Styles list, right-click it to display a menu. Then on that menu, choose Apply and Maintain Formatting.

 note

If the formatting you want to apply does not appear in the dialog box, click the Format button to open a menu of more choices. For example, from the Format menu, you can choose Banding to fine-tune the bands to include more than one row or column per band.

Border Thickness   Border Sides   Alignment
Border Style   Border Color   Fill Color

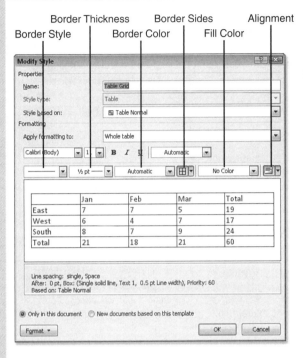

Figure 9.25
Create your own table style definition.

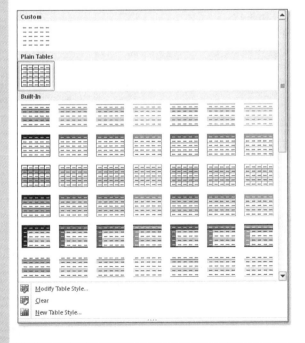

Figure 9.26
You can access custom styles from the Styles list on the Design tab.

To better understand the formatting controls in the Modify Style dialog box, review the information in the following sections. The formatting can be applied manually, as explained in these sections, or integrated into the style.

Changing the Cell Background Color

To apply a solid-color background (fill color) to one or more cells, use the Shading drop-down list on the Design tab (see Figure 9.27). As in other areas of Word, you can choose between theme colors, tints of the theme colors, standard colors, or More Colors (to open a color selection dialog box).

➡ *To learn more about how Word uses colors, see "Changing Font Color," p. 158.*

Figure 9.27
Select a solid-color shading.

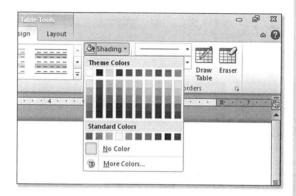

To apply a patterned background to a cell, you must use the Borders and Shading dialog box, as follows:

1. Select the cell(s) to affect.

2. Right-click the selection and choose Borders and Shading.

3. Click the Shading tab.

4. Open the Style list and select the pattern to apply to the background.

5. Open the Color list and select the basic color for the background.

6. Open the Fill list and select the color for the pattern (see Figure 9.28).

7. Click OK to apply the patterned background.

> **caution**
>
> Avoid strongly contrasting patterns as backgrounds for cells containing text, because it makes the text difficult to read. A patterned background would be more appropriate for an empty row that separates two rows of text, for example, or as a background for a cell that contains a picture.

You can also use the Borders and Shading dialog box method to apply a solid-color background if you prefer it to the Ribbon method. For a solid-color background, set the Style setting to Solid (100%).

Pattern Background   Pattern

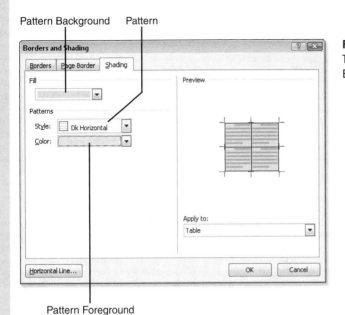

Pattern Foreground

Figure 9.28
To apply a patterned background, use the Borders and Shading dialog box.

Working with Cell Borders

The term *border* in the context of a table has two subtly different meanings. In one definition, the border is the visible line around one or more sides of a cell. When you set a cell to "No Border," you are setting the lines around it to not be visible when printed. This is the definition generally adhered to when formatting tables with the Design tab, and in this section of the chapter, *border* has that meaning.

Another definition of *border* is the boundary around the four sides of the cell, whether or not it is visible. Using this definition, every cell has a border on every side. It's convenient to talk about cell borders this way when discussing resizing a cell by dragging, for example, because the ability to drag a border is not dependent on its having a visible line.

Nearly everything you learned about paragraph borders in Chapter 5, "Formatting Paragraphs and Lists," applies also to table cells. The same attributes apply to both paragraph and table borders: line style, line thickness, and line color.

➡ *To learn more about how borders work, see "Applying Paragraph Borders," p. 209.*

One easy way to apply borders—that is, visible lines—to a table (or parts of a table) is to use the tools on the Design tab, as shown in Figure 9.29.

Figure 9.29
Tools for formatting table borders.

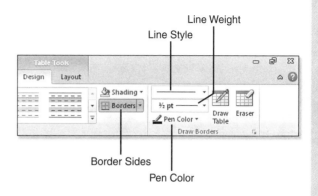

Select the border style, width, and color, and then apply the border sides. If you apply the sides first, the settings you later choose for style, width, and color will not be automatically applied; you will need to reapply the sides to put them into effect.

The Borders button opens a list of various border sides, shown in Figure 9.30. (Look back at Table 5.1 in Chapter 5 for a review of these.) Keep in mind that in a table, the borders refer to the selected cells as a group, not to the individual cells. For example, Outside Borders places the border around the selection, not around each cell, and Top Border places the border across the top of the selection, not at the top of each cell.

Figure 9.30
Select the border sides to apply to the table.

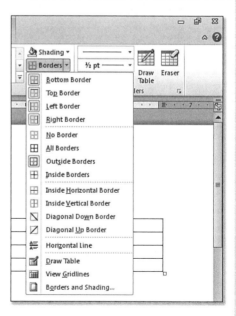

You can also use the Borders and Shading dialog box to apply borders, just as you did for paragraphs in Chapter 5. Follow these steps:

1. Select the cell(s) to affect.

2. On the Design tab, open the Borders list and choose Borders and Shading. The Borders and Shading dialog box opens.

3. Click the Borders tab if does not already appear (see Figure 9.31).

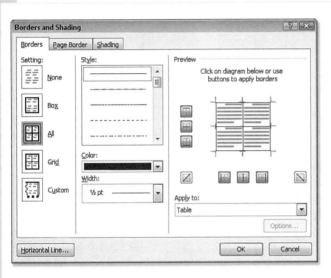

Figure 9.31
You can format cell borders from the Borders tab of the Borders and Shading dialog box.

4. Select a border type from the Setting icons along the left side of the dialog box:

   - **None**—Turns off all borders.

   - **Box**—Places an outside border in which all sides are the same thickness.

   - **All**—Places the same border around all sides of all cells in the selected range.

   - **Grid**—Places a thicker outside border and a thinner inside border.

   - **Custom**—Enables you to select and format each side individually. (You can start with any of the other settings, and when you start to change individual sizes, the setting changes to Custom automatically.)

5. On the Style list, select a line style.

6. On the Color list, select a line color. (Color selection works the same here as with any other colored object.)

> *For an explanation of Word's color choices, see "Changing Font Color," p. 158.*

7. On the Width list, select a line thickness.

8. (Optional) If you want to remove the border on certain sides, click the corresponding button in the Preview area. (There is a button for each of the four sides.)

9. Click OK to accept the new border.

Setting Cell Margins

Each cell has internal margins—that is, an amount of space between the border on each side and the text you type into the cell. In this sense, a cell is very much like a text box.

➡️ *For an explanation of text boxes and their internal margin settings, see "Creating Text Box Layouts," p. 307.*

You can set the internal margins for all cells at once, or for individual cells.

Setting Overall Internal Margins for the Table

The overall internal margins for the table provide a baseline; you can then make changes for individual cells later.

To set the overall internal margins for the table, follow these steps:

1. On the Layout tab, click Cell Margins. The Table Options dialog box opens.

2. Enter margin settings in the Default Cell Margins section for each side (see Figure 9.32).

3. (Optional) To place spacing between cells, mark the Allow Spacing Between Cells check box and enter an amount of space.

   This setting enables you to add extra space for the margins where two cells meet. The extra spacing is contextual; although it applies to the entire table, it applies to certain cells depending on their position. For example, with overall margin settings of 0.1 inches on all sides but an Allow Spacing Between Cells setting of 0.1 inch, the topmost, leftmost cell in the table would have a top and left internal margin of 0.1 inch and a bottom and right internal margin of 0.2 inches.

4. Mark or clear the Automatically Resize to Fit Contents check box.

   When selected, the table cells can resize as you type to accommodate long text entries or large graphics.

5. Click OK.

Figure 9.32
Set cell margins from the Table Options dialog box.

Setting Internal Margins for an Individual Cell

Depending on a cell's content, you might need for it to have different internal margins than the rest of the table. To customize the internal margins for a certain cell, or a range of cells, follow these steps:

1. Select the cell(s) to affect.

2. On the Layout tab, click the Properties button. The Table Properties dialog box opens.

3. Click the Cell tab and then click the Options button. The Cell Options dialog box opens.

4. Clear the Same as the Whole Table check box. Individual internal margin settings become available for Top, Bottom, Left, and Right (see Figure 9.33).

Figure 9.33
Change the internal margins for individual cells.

5. Mark or clear the check boxes as desired:

   - **Wrap Text**—If needed, allows text to wrap to additional lines in the cell.

   - **Fit Text**—If needed, reduces the size of the font to fit the text in the cell.

6. Click OK.

Setting Text Alignment Within a Cell

Regular paragraphs in a document have only one dimension in which they can be aligned: horizontally. Table cells, on the other hand, have both a vertical and horizontal alignment setting. There are nine combinations possible in all, and each is represented by a button in the Alignment group of the Layout tab. Select the cell(s) to affect and then click one of those buttons (see Figure 9.34).

You can also set alignment from the shortcut menu for any cell. Select the cell(s) to affect and then right-click the selection. Point to Cell Alignment and then select an alignment from the submenu.

Figure 9.34
Choose a vertical and horizontal alignment for selected cells.

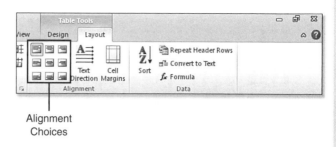

Alignment
Choices

Changing Text Direction

Text in a table cell can be oriented in any of three directions: horizontal (left to right), vertical (top to bottom), or vertical (bottom to top), just like in a text box. To toggle between these orientations, click the Text Direction button on the Layout tab.

Repeating Headings on Each Page

When a table runs more than one page in a document, it can be a challenge to keep track of what each column represents when looking at the later pages. One solution to that is to repeat the heading row on each page by manually copying it, but then when you edit the table so that it contains more or fewer rows, that repeated heading row gets thrown out of place.

> **⚠ caution**
>
> Changing the text direction to a vertical one increases the height of the rows, and when you go back to horizontal orientation, the rows don't automatically go back to their earlier, smaller heights. To put the rows back to their original sizes, drag the bottom-right corner of the table frame up, or set the Height size to the original height. (With 11-point text, the original height is approximately 0.19.)

To solve this problem, Word enables you to set the header to be repeated on subsequent pages automatically whenever a table crosses a page break. To set this up, follow these steps:

1. Click in the header row.

2. On the Layout tab, click Properties. The Table Properties dialog box opens.

3. Click the Row tab, and then mark the Repeat As Header Row at the Top of Each Page check box.

4. Click OK.

Orienting the Table on the Page

So far in this chapter, we've been working *inside* a table, but now let's consider how the table interacts with the rest of the document. By default, a table takes up the full width of the page (or the full width of whatever you place it into), but you can resize it to a smaller width. When a table is less than full width, it can interact with the rest of the document as a graphic object would. It can be set for a certain horizontal alignment (like a paragraph), and text can be set to wrap around it in various ways.

Setting Table Alignment

The paragraph's alignment does not have an effect unless the paragraph is narrower than the space available to it. Because by default it exactly fills the available space, and most people don't change that, table alignment is not that important for most users.

If you need to set the table alignment, however, it's fairly easy to do so. Follow these steps:

1. Click anywhere in the table.

2. On the Layout tab, click Properties. The Table Properties dialog box opens.

3. Click the Table tab, and in the Alignment section, click Left, Center, or Right (see Figure 9.35).

4. (Optional) If you chose Left as the alignment, enter an amount of indentation from the left. (This is like the left indent for a paragraph.)

5. Click OK.

Figure 9.35
Set alignment for the table as a whole.

Setting Table Text Wrap

Table text wrap allows the regular paragraphs of the document to wrap around the table if the table is narrower than the maximum document width. It is somewhat like the text wrapping around graphic objects or text boxes.

➤ *To set text wrapping around a photo or other graphic, see "Setting Text Wrap," p. 386.*

To set the text wrap for a table, follow these steps:

1. Click anywhere in the table.

2. On the Layout tab, click Properties. The Table Properties dialog box opens.

3. Click the Table tab, and in the Text Wrapping section, click Around (see Figure 9.35).

4. (Optional) Click Positioning, opening the Table Positioning dialog box (see Figure 9.36).

Figure 9.36
Fine-tune the positioning setting.

5. Set the horizontal position for the table. You can choose a setting from the drop-down list (Left, Right, Center, Inside, or Outside) or type a number representing an amount of off-set in inches, in which case Left positioning is assumed.

6. In the Horizontal section, set the Relative To setting to define what that setting is in relation to (Column, Margin, or Page).

7. In the Vertical section, set a Position and Relative To values. As with the Horizontal section, you can either choose a relative amount from the drop-down list or type a numeric value in inches. The measurement can be in relation to Paragraph, Margin, or Page.

8. In the Distance from Surrounding Text area, enter spacing amounts to separate the edge of the table from the text that wraps around it.

9. If the table should be anchored to the surrounding text, mark the Move with Text check box; if it should remain fixed on the page and the text should be able to move past it, clear that check box.

 note

Inside and Outside are special settings that float the table to the left or right depending on whether the page is odd numbered or even numbered. It's designed to facilitate two-sided layouts. On an odd-numbered page, Inside aligns to the left and Outside to the right; on an even-numbered page, it's the opposite.

 note

When working with a relative setting such as Left or Right, there is no real difference between Margin and Page, but when using specific numeric values, the difference is apparent; 1" from the margin is very different from 1" from the edge of the page.

10. If the table should be allowed to overlap other content on the page, mark the Allow Overlap check box.

11. Click OK twice to close both dialog boxes.

Creating a Table Caption

Long, complex reports often have multiple tables in them, numbered for reference. You can manually number the tables and create your own captions for them, but it is much easier to allow Word to manage the table-captioning process. That way, if you insert a new table earlier in the document, the tables that follow it are automatically renumbered.

To add a caption to a table, follow these steps:

1. Select the entire table, and then right-click the table and choose Insert Caption. The Caption dialog box opens (see Figure 9.37).

   Alternatively, you can click the Insert Caption button on the References tab.

2. Leave the Label setting at Table.

3. In the Position list, choose where you want the captions to appear for tables. (Usually tables have captions above them.)

> **note**
>
> The Caption text box in the Caption dialog box shows you a sample of the caption that will appear based on the other settings in the dialog box.

Figure 9.37
Set up a caption for tables in the document.

4. The caption will read *Table 1*. If you want some other word than *Table*, click New Label and specify another word instead.

   Alternatively, to omit using a word at all before the number, mark the Exclude Label from Caption check box.

5. Click the Numbering button. The Caption Numbering dialog box opens (see Figure 9.38).

6. Select a format from the Format list.

7. (Optional) To include a chapter number with the caption, mark the Include Chapter Number check box, and then choose what style designates a chapter and what separator character should be used.

Figure 9.38
Control the numbering style for table captions.

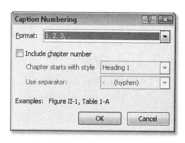

8. Click OK to return to the Caption dialog box.

9. Click OK. The caption appears in the document, immediately above (or below) the table.

10. Click to the right of the caption and type a text description if desired. For example, after *Table 1*, you might type a colon and then *Regional Management Team*, as in Figure 9.39.

This part is inserted automatically by captioning

Figure 9.39
A completed table caption with a manually typed description.

Table 1: Regional Management Team

Division	Sales	Customer Service	Operations
North	Tom Brown	Dick Burrow	Harry Rushmore
South	Sue Murphy	Sheila Walker	Roy Wallace

This part was manually typed

Sorting Tabular Data

One reason people like to store data in table format is that it makes the data easier to search and sort. Word's Sort feature works with regular paragraphs too, but when it's used with a table or other delimited data it has some additional functionality, such as the ability to sort by multiple columns at once.

 For information about delimited data, see "Converting Text to a Table," p. 374.

Sorts can be either ascending (0 to 9, then A to Z) or descending (Z to A, then 9 to 0).

> **note**
>
> *Delimited* data is text that is separated into columns. For example, comma-delimited data consists of regular paragraphs (one per row) in which the data for each column is separated by commas, like this: *data1,data2,data3*. Data can also be tab-delimited (as with the columns created via tab stops in Chapter 5), or it can be delimited using some other character.

Sorts can be performed assuming a particular column contains text, numbers, or dates. This distinction helps you sort based on meaning rather than based purely on the first character:

- **Text sort**—No meaning assigned; sort is based purely on the first digit. For example, a list of 1, 5, and 10 would be listed in this order: 1, 10, 5.

- **Number sort**—Sort is alphabetical, except when numbers are involved; then it is based on the number chronology. For example, a list of 1, 5, 10 would be sorted in that same order.

- **Date sort**—Sort is alphabetical except when dates are involved; then it is based on date chronology. For example, a list of 10/1/11, 10/2/10, and 12/2/09 would be sorted from earliest to latest date.

To sort the data in a table, follow these steps:

1. Click anywhere in the table and then click the Sort button on the Layout tab. The Sort dialog box opens, as shown in Figure 9.40.

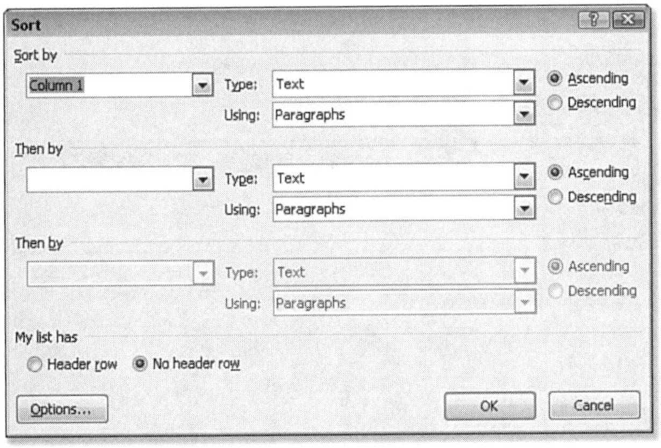

Figure 9.40
Set up a sort specification for the table.

2. If the first row contains header labels, select the Header Row option button; otherwise, click No Header Row.

3. In the Sort By list, select the column by which to sort. If you chose Header Row in step 2, the text from that row appears as labels here; otherwise, generic names appear (Column 1, Column 2, and so on).

4. Open the Type list and select Text, Number, or Date.

5. Click Ascending or Descending.

6. (Optional) Set up a secondary sort in the Then By section. The secondary sort takes effect only in the event of a tie in the primary column. You can also enter a third level in the subsequent Then By section.

7. (Optional) To make the sort case-sensitive, click the Options button, mark the Case Sensitive check box, and click OK.

8. Click OK to perform the sort.

Sorting Delimited Data That's Not in a Table

What if your data is not in a table, but instead is delimited with commas, tabs, or some other character? You have a couple of options.

One option is to convert the delimited data into a table with the Convert Text to Table feature, covered later in this chapter.

Another is to perform the sort and specify the delimiter character. Select the paragraphs to sort and then go through the preceding steps. In step 7, clicking the Options button opens the Sort Options dialog box. One of the choices in this dialog box is Separate Fields At. You can specify Tabs, Commas, or Other as the delimiter character; then click OK and perform the sort normally.

Performing Math Calculations in a Table

Word is no substitute for a powerful spreadsheet program such as Excel, but it does have some basic math functions built into it. You can use these to perform operations such as sum, average, count, and round. You can also type your own math formulas for the cells, with or without functions.

One little hiccup in using math in a Word table is that the cells don't have names, at least not in the same sense as in Excel. There are no visible letters designating columns or numbers designating rows.

There's a secret to that, though; they actually *do* respond to those same names as in Excel. The columns have names starting with A at the left, and the rows have numbers starting with 1 at the top. So, for example, the second cell in the second row is B2. Those labels don't appear anywhere in Word, though, so you have to count across or down to determine how many positions away from A1 a particular cell lies and then reference its name accordingly. You can also refer to all the cells in a certain direction with ABOVE, BELOW, LEFT, and RIGHT. For example, =AVERAGE(LEFT) averages everything to the left of the current cell.

Math formulas in a Word table begin with equal signs, just like in Excel. They can use the traditional math operators:

- Addition (+)

- Subtraction (−)

- Multiplication (*)

- Division (/)

Table 9.2 includes some examples.

Table 9.2 Basic Math Formulas for Word Tables

Formula	Description
=SUM(ABOVE)	Sums the contents of all the cells above the current one (same column)
=SUM(LEFT)	Sums the contents of all the cells to the left of the current one (same row)
=A1+A2+A3	Sums the contents of cells A1, A2, and A3
=SUM(A1:A3)	Same as above, but uses the SUM function
=A1*(A2+A3)	Multiplies A1 by the sum of A2 and A3

You can't just type a formula into a cell; you must use the Formula dialog box to set it up. Follow these steps to do so:

1. Position the insertion point in the cell where you want to place the formula.

2. Click Formula on the Layout tab to open the Formula dialog box (see Figure 9.41).

Figure 9.41
Create a math formula.

3. In the Formula box, a default function might appear, depending on the position of the cell within the table. Accept it, modify it, or delete it and type a different formula or function entirely. Table 9.3 lists the available functions and their syntax. Table 9.4 lists the valid comparison operators you can use for logical functions such as IF, NOT, and AND.

 tip

You can use the Paste Function list to select from among the available functions. The chosen function is added to the current content of the Formula text box.

4. (Optional) Choose a number format from the Number Format list. A number of currency, percentage, and other numeric formats are available.

5. Click OK.

Table 9.3   Math Functions for Word Tables

Function	Purpose	Examples
ABS()	Displays the absolute value of a number.	Absolute value of A1: =ABS(A1)
AND(x,y)	Displays 1 if both x and y are true, or 0 (zero) if either is false).	Check whether A1 and B1 are both greater than zero: =AND(A1>0,B1>0)
AVERAGE()	Averages the numbers in the named range.	Average the values in the cells above the current one: =AVERAGE(ABOVE)
COUNT()	Counts the number of numeric values in a list.	Count the number of numeric values in the cells to the left of the current one: =COUNT(LEFT) Count the number of numeric values in the range A1 through A6: =COUNT(A1:A6) or =COUNT(A1,A2,A3,A4,A5,A6)
DEFINED(x)	Displays 1 if x is a valid expression or 0 if it is not.	Check the formula in A1 for errors: =DEFINED(A1)
FALSE()	Displays a zero.	FALSE()
IF(x, y, z)	Evaluates the expression x, and executes the instructions in y if it is true or in z if it is false. The instructions in y and z can refer to a cell, a number, or TRUE or FALSE.	Display the content of A3 if A1>0; otherwise, display the content of A2: =IF(A1>0,A3,A2) Display TRUE if A1>0; otherwise, display FALSE: =IF(A1>0,TRUE,FALSE)
INT	Displays the numbers to the left of the decimal place only (does not round).	Display only the integer portion of the number in cell A1: =INT(A1)
MAX()	Displays the largest number in the list range.	Display the maximum value in cells A2 through A4: =MAX(A2,A3,A4) or =MAX(A2:A4)
MIN()	Displays the smallest number in the list range.	Display the minimum value in cells A2 through A4: =MIN(A2,A3,A4) or =MIN(A2:A4)

Table 9.3   Continued

Function	Purpose	Examples
MOD(x,y)	Displays the remainder after dividing x by y a whole number of times.	Display the remainder after dividing A1 by A2: =MOD(A1,A2) For example, if A1 contains 6 and A2 contains 4, the result would be 2 (because 4 goes into 6 one time with a remainder of 2).
NOT(x)	Displays 1 if x is false, or 0 if x is true.	Display 1 if A1 is not greater than or equal to 10: =NOT(A1>=10)
OR(x,y)	Displays 1 if either x or y is true; otherwise, displays 0.	Display 1 if either A1 is less than 0 or A2 is greater than 6: =OR(A1<0,A2>6)
PRODUCT()	Multiplies a list of numbers.	Multiply the values in A1 and A2: =PRODUCT(A1,A2) Multiply the values in A1 through A3: =PRODUCT(A1:A3) Multiply the value in A1 by 7: =PRODUCT(A1,7)
ROUND(x,y)	Rounds the value of x to y number of decimal points.	Round the number in A1 to a whole integer (no decimal place): =ROUND(A1,0) Round the number in A1 to the number of decimal places specified in A2: =ROUND(A1,A2)
SIGN(x)	Displays 1 if x is a positive number or −1 if x is a negative number.	Check the positive/negative status of the number in A1: =SIGN(A1)
SUM()	Adds numbers in the specified range.	Add the numbers above the current cell: =SUM(ABOVE) Add the numbers to the left of the current cell: =SUM(LEFT) Add the numbers in cells A1 through A4: =SUM(A1:A4) or =SUM(A1,A2,A3,A4)
TRUE	Displays a 1.	TRUE()

Table 9.4 Comparison Operators

Operator	Meaning
>	Greater than
>=	Greater than or equal to
<	Less than
<=	Less than or equal to
=	Equal to
<>	Not equal to

Editing the Number Format

If none of the number formats are right, you can create your own by typing the codes into the Number Format text box. Here's a quick look at what you can do:

- **Literal symbols**—Type the actual symbols you want to use, in the spots where you want them. For example, precede the number with a currency symbol such as $ or follow it with a percentage symbol.

- **Commas and decimal points**—Add or remove these items as desired.

- **Required digits**—Represent these with 0. The numbers will have at least that many places, using leading zeros if needed. For example, applying 000 as the number of required digits would make the number 1 appear as 001.

- **Optional digits**—You don't have to specify these explicitly except when setting up commas between every three numbers, like this: #,##0.

- **Decimal places**—Set these up with 0s (required digits) after a decimal point. For example, 0.000 would ensure one digit before the decimal place and three after it.

- **Negative number handling**—After the main spec, add a semicolon and then indicate how you want negative numbers handled. For example, you could precede the negative number format with a minus sign or surround it in parentheses.

Setting the Order of Operations

When including multiple math operators in a formula, keep in mind the default order of operation. Word processes multiplication and division first, followed by addition and subtraction. If you need to change that order, enclose the portions to be calculated first in parentheses.

For example, in the formula

=A1+A2*5

the A2*5 portion is calculated first, and then the result is added to A1. If you want the addition done first, write it this way:

=(A1+A2)*5

Referencing Values Outside the Table

Formulas and functions can include references to numbers that exist elsewhere in the document, not just in cells within that table. To reference a number, set up that number as a bookmark and then reference the bookmark.

➡ *For more information about bookmarks, see "Working with Bookmarks," p. 593.*

To create a bookmark and then reference it in a formula, follow these steps:

1. Select the number to be bookmarked in the document.

2. On the Insert tab, click Bookmark. The Bookmark dialog box opens.

3. In the Bookmark name box, type a name (keep it short, with no spaces) and click Add. The Bookmark dialog box closes.

4. In the table, begin creating the formula as you normally would. In the spot where you want the bookmark to be referenced, open the Paste Bookmark list and select the bookmark (refer to Figure 9.41).

5. Finish creating the formula as you normally would.

Getting Data into or Out of Tabular Format

As you've seen so far in this chapter, one way of creating a table is to insert it from scratch and then type your data into it. But there are other ways to place tabular data into your document, as you'll learn in the next several sections.

Converting Text to a Table

Any text can be converted to a table in Word. The key question is, how many columns will it have?

When you convert regular paragraphs to a table, the table consists of a single column only, and each paragraph is in its own row. If you want more columns, you must make sure that the text is properly delimited before the conversion.

Delimited text is text that is broken into sections by some consistently used symbol. The most common delimiter characters are tabs and commas. For example, if you have set up a multicolumn layout with tab stops, those paragraphs are *tab-delimited*.

Data exported from a database program is usually in comma-delimited format. For example, the following is a comma-delimited data table consisting of four rows and four columns:

```
First Name,Last Name,City,State
  Chuck,Perkins,Decatur,IL
  Mildred,Perryman,Moweaqua,IL
Francis,Zindel,Moweaqua,IL
```

Word recognizes common delimiter characters, so when you convert delimited text to a table, Word is able to create the appropriate number of columns to hold it. If there is an inconsistent number of delimiters in the various rows you've selected for inclusion in the table, Word goes with the largest number. So, for example, if you accidentally type two commas between two values rather than the customary one comma, Word takes that as an invitation to insert two columns, and all the other rows become off by one. That's the most common mistake people make when creating delimited text for table conversion, so pay sharp attention to the delimiter usage.

After preparing the data with delimiters, follow these steps to convert it to a table:

1. Select the text to include in the table.

2. On the Insert tab, click Table and then click Convert Text to Table. The Convert Text to Table dialog box opens (see Figure 9.42).

3. Confirm that the number of columns is what you expected. If it is not, your delimiters are off; click Cancel and fix them.

4. Set an AutoFit behavior for the new table. The options here are the same as when creating a table via Insert Table.

> For more information about AutoFit options, see "Inserting a Table via the Insert Table Dialog Box," p. 337.

Figure 9.42
Convert the selected text to a table.

5. Select the delimiter character. Word has probably already made the correct choice, but confirm that it is accurate.

6. Click OK. The text is converted to a Word table.

Converting a Table to Regular Text

You can also go the opposite direction: convert a table to regular text paragraphs. Again, you're faced with a delimiter character—what character will substitute for the column breaks? The traditional choice is tabs or commas, but you can use any character you wish.

To convert a table to text, follow these steps:

1. Select the entire table.

2. On the Layout tab, click Convert to Text. The Convert Table to Text dialog box opens (see Figure 9.43).

3. Select the delimiter character to be used.

4. If there are nested tables in the selected table, mark or clear the Convert Nested Tables check box to decide their disposition.

5. Click OK to convert the table to text.

Figure 9.43
Convert the table back to regular text.

Pasting Tables from Other Office Applications

Several other Office applications utilize row-and-column data organization in various ways. For example, PowerPoint has its own custom table format (similar to that of Word), and Excel has spreadsheets.

Using the Office Clipboard, you can copy and paste data between Office applications seamlessly, creating new Word tables on the fly to hold the new data.

To paste from Excel, follow these steps:

1. In Excel, select the cells to be copied and then press Ctrl+C (or click Copy on the Home tab) to copy them to the Clipboard.

2. Switch to Word, position the insertion point in the desired location, and press Ctrl+V (or click Paste on the Home tab) to paste the selection into Word.

3. A Paste Options icon appears next to the pasted selection; click it to open the Paste Options menu (see Figure 9.44).

4. Click the desired paste option. You can choose to retain the original formatting, match the document's formatting, paste as a picture or text only, or create a dynamic link to the original data.

For even more pasting options, instead of step 2, click the down arrow on the Paste button and choose Paste Special. A Paste Special dialog box opens; from here you can choose to paste in a variety of formats. One of these options, Microsoft Excel Worksheet Object, keeps the data in actual Excel cells, so you can edit it later using Excel's own commands. This is called *embedding* (see Figure 9.45).

Figure 9.44
Choose Paste Options after pasting the selection.

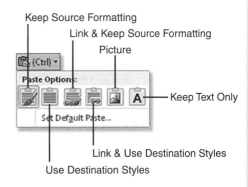

Keep Source Formatting
Link & Keep Source Formatting
Picture
Keep Text Only
Link & Use Destination Styles
Use Destination Styles

Figure 9.45
Pasting as a Microsoft Excel Worksheet Object creates an embedded worksheet in Word.

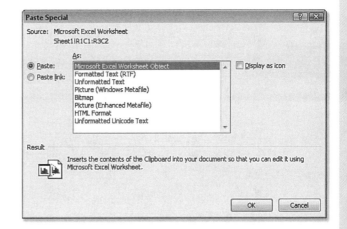

For more information about pasting and linking, see "Linking to Data in Other Files," p. 604.

The procedure is basically the same to paste from PowerPoint (and other applications); select the table in PowerPoint, copy it to the Clipboard, paste it into Word, and then set any paste options desired.

Embedding Excel Worksheets as Tables

Word's table feature enables you to perform some basic calculations with formulas and functions, as you saw earlier in this chapter. However, it isn't as robust as Excel in this regard. If you want the full Excel functionality, consider embedding an Excel worksheet into the document.

One way to embed an Excel worksheet is to copy data from an existing Excel file and then paste it with Paste Special, choosing Microsoft Excel Worksheet Object as the type. (See the preceding section for help with that.)

If the file does not already exist, however, you might find it easier to embed a new blank worksheet in the Word document. Follow these steps to do that:

1. Click in the Word document where you want the embedded worksheet to appear.

2. On the Insert tab, click Table and then click Excel Spreadsheet. A blank spreadsheet appears in the document, and Excel's commands and tabs appear.

3. Create the worksheet as you would in Excel; when you are done, click outside the worksheet's area to return to Word.

The resulting Excel object can be formatted, aligned, and otherwise handled like any other object. Right-click it and choose Format Object to open a dialog box with controls for size, layout, border, and other formatting options.

10

WORKING WITH PHOTOS

Understanding Digital Photography

Word tends to treat all picture files more or less the same—it imports them and places them on the page where you specify. All digital images are not created equal, though. There are many types, and some of those types are radically different from others.

This chapter focuses on one specific type of image: the *digital photograph*. A digital photo is a computer representation of an analog source. It could be a photo of a person captured with a digital camera, or it could be a picture of a magazine clipping captured with a scanner. Digital photos can also be acquired from online sources or purchased on CDs.

A digital photograph is a type of *bitmap image*. The word *bitmap* comes from the fact that the picture consists of a grid (map) of tiny individual pixels of different colors, with the exact color for each pixel described as a string of binary digits (called *bits*). Figure 10.1 shows a zoomed-in example. (Another name for this type of image is *raster*.)

When a photo is taken on a digital camera, the camera uses a light-sensitive grid called a *charge-coupled device (CCD)* to measure the amount of red, green, and blue for each pixel. These values are then written to a file and stored inside the camera, and then they're eventually transferred to a computer or printer. When a hard-copy photo is scanned, a similar process takes place inside the scanner.

 note

There are actually two meanings for the term bitmap. One is generic, meaning any picture that is composed of a grid of colored dots. The other is a specific Microsoft-developed file format called Windows Bitmap, with a .bmp extension.

Figure 10.1
A photo consists of a grid of tiny colored pixels.

How large is the resulting file for that digital photo? It could be anywhere from less than 20KB to over 10MB. The exact size depends on these factors:

- **The color model**—The way the color of each pixel is described, such as CMYK or RGB.

- **The color depth**—The number of bits used to describe each color, such as 24-bit or 32-bit.

- **The file format**—The format in which the file is saved, such as JPEG or TIF.

- **The resolution**—The number of pixels that comprise the image horizontally and vertically.

The following sections look at each of these factors in greater detail.

Understanding Color Models

A photo can use any of several color models. The most common of these are Red/Green/Blue (RGB) and Cyan/Magenta/Yellow/Black (CMYK).

RGB is the dominant color model used for onscreen display. Use RGB as the color model when creating web pages and other documents that will be distributed online. RGB works so well for onscreen use because it matches the way monitors display colors. RGB defines colors using a 24-bit system that uses 8 bits each for red, green, and blue. Each of the three colors has a value ranging from 0 to 255.

CMYK is the color model used for high-quality printouts. Use CMYK as the color model when creating brochures, newsletters, and other documents that will be printed. Cyan, magenta, yellow, and black are the four colors used in color printers. A CMYK image is a 32-bit image, with 8 bits each for cyan, magenta, yellow, and black. Only a few graphics file formats support CMYK; TIF is one of them.

Most digital cameras and scanners save their images as RGB by default, but there may be a setting you can adjust in the software that will change this mode if your camera will capture in TIF format. If not, you can open the picture in a graphics-editing program such as Photoshop or PaintShop Pro and convert the image between models. You might need to save the file in a different file format to get CMYK color.

What happens if you don't convert the image? Not much, really, except a minor loss of color quality. You can certainly print RGB color images, and you can use CMYK images on web pages. The colors might not be quite as accurate, however, as if you had used the correct color model for the situation. CMYK and RGB have a slightly different *gamut*—that is, set of colors they include. If your image contains some colors that are out-of-gamut for the color model, the closest possible color is substituted.

Understanding Color Depth

An image's color depth (also called *bit depth*) is the number of bits required to uniquely describe each possible color a pixel can be. In 1-bit color, each pixel is either black or white; in 4-bit color, there are 16 possible on/off combinations for bits, so there are 16 color choices. 8-bit color has 256 color choices (2 to the 8th power), and so on.

As noted in the preceding section, a color RGB image uses 24 bits to describe each pixel, and a CMYK image uses 32 bits. As you might guess, CMYK has more colors to choose from and is generally more accurate in expressing colors, but the file sizes are also larger.

Some scanners and digital cameras have a grayscale feature that takes the color depth down to 8-bit black-and-white. An 8-bit grayscale image captures 256 levels of gradation between white and black. A grayscale image usually has a much smaller file size than a color one because it requires fewer bits to describe each pixel.

Some scanners also have a black-and-white mode (separate from grayscale), which captures pictures in a 1-bit mode. Each pixel is either black or white and requires only 1 bit to describe it. The resulting files are extremely small (1/24 the size of a full-color RGB image) but not very attractive. Standalone fax machines often use this mode for sending and receiving faxes; that's why pictures tend to fax poorly.

 note

Scanners typically advertise higher bit depths than 24 or 32. The extra bits are for color correction. The scanner collects extra data and then throws out the bad bits to account for "noise" or error in the scanning process.

Depending on the file format, an RGB image might actually have more than 24 bits. For example, some file formats (such as Photoshop's native PSD format) support alpha channels, which are extra sets of 8 bits used for special purposes such as transparency or clipping. Such file formats tend to produce larger files than their strictly-24-bit counterparts like JPEG.

In some cases, the file format might specify *fewer* than 24 bits as the maximum. The Graphics Interchange Format (GIF) is like that, for example; it is limited to 8-bit color (256 colors in total).

Understanding File Formats

The file format is the standard by which the information about each pixel is recorded. Different file formats can produce very different file sizes and quality levels. These differences are mainly due to two factors: the color depth supported (as described in the preceding section) and the type and amount of compression used.

Compression is an algorithm (a math formula) that decreases the amount of space a file takes up on disk by storing the pixel color data more compactly. Some file formats do not support compression at all; others support one of these types:

- **Lossless compression**—The image is compressed but no image quality is lost. The compression is performed via a completely reversible compression algorithm.

- **Lossy compression**—The image is compressed by recording less data. Either less information about each pixel is recorded, or some of the pixels are removed (and then resimulated when the image is displayed). The image is somewhat reduced in quality as a result.

Some file formats are always compressed; others give you a choice. The ones that give you a choice may also give you a sliding scale of compression level to choose from. You can set the compression level for a file when you resave it in a graphics-editing program.

The TIF format is interesting in a number of ways. It produces very large files, but it also supports a high color depth (up to 48-bit), and it supports a number of lossless compression types, including LZW compression (the most common), Huffman encoding, Packbits, and FAX – CCITT 3. It is also one of the few file formats that Word supports that allows you to save in the CMYK color model. (Adobe Photoshop's .PSD format also does this, but Word does not accept that format.)

Table 10.1 lists some of the most popular file formats for photos as well as their support for compression and color depth.

Table 10.1 Popular Photo Formats Supported in Word 2010

Extension	Compression	Maximum Color Depth
JPEG or JPG	Lossy, adjustable (1 to 99)	24-bit
GIF	Lossless	8-bit
PNG	Lossless	48-bit
BMP	None	24-bit
TIF or TIFF	Lossless	48-bit

Understanding Image Resolution

The final factor affecting an image's size is its *resolution*. Resolution has several meanings, depending on whether the image is already stored in digital form and how it is being captured.

For an image that is already a saved file, resolution is the number of pixels vertically and horizontally that comprise the image, such as 800 (wide) by 600 (high). You can change the resolution on a saved image by using a graphics-editing program to resample the image, either adding or removing pixels. When a graphics program adds pixels, it creates them by *interpolation*. It takes the numeric values of two adjacent pixels, averages them, and then inserts a pixel between them with the averaged values.

Digital cameras, because they tend to capture images of a consistent height-width ratio, often express the resolution as the total number of pixels (height times width). A million pixels is a *megapixel*, so a 3-megapixel camera captures images in which the number of pixels vertically times the number of pixels horizontally is somewhere around 3 million.

For an image that is being input into a computer via a scanner, you specify the resolution you want in dots per inch (dpi). The original size of the hard-copy image you are scanning, combined with the dpi setting you choose, determines the overall number of pixels that will comprise the image. For example, if you scan a 3-inch × 5-inch photo at 200 dpi, it will have a resolution of 600 × 1000 when saved as a file.

How Word Handles Pictures

Pictures in Word get special treatment; they have their own set of controls on the Format tab (which appears when a picture is selected). You can apply many special effects, such as picture styles, soft edges, reflection, artistic effects, and color correction. You will learn about these effects later in this chapter.

However, these new picture-formatting capabilities are available only in Word 2010's native file format, not in the older Word 97-2003 format. If you are working with a document created in Word 2003 or earlier, commands for working with pictures are limited to those commands that were available in previous Word versions.

 note

Word 2007 uses the same format as 2010. For simplicity, in this book I refer to it as Word 2010 format, but it would more accurately be called 2007/2010 format.

To determine whether Word is considering your document to be a native Word 2010 document or a backward-compatible one, look at a picture's selection handles, and check out the Format tab. Figure 10.2 shows a picture in a Word 2010 document. It has pale blue selection handles, and the Format tab features a Picture Styles area.

Figure 10.3 shows a picture in a backward-compatible document. It has dark blue-gray selection handles, and the Format tab contains only controls for formatting features from earlier Word versions.

If you want to work with a picture using the backward-compatible version of the Format tab shown in Figure 10.3, use File, Save As, Word 97-2003 Document format to save the file; the picture's type changes automatically. To go the other direction—that is, to gain Word 2010 functionality for a picture in a backward-compatible document—choose File, Info and click the Convert button to upgrade the file to Word 2010 format.

III

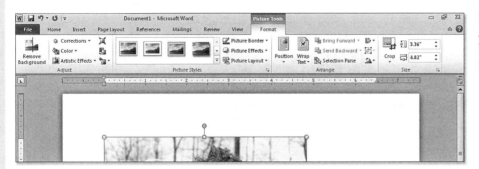

Figure 10.2
A picture in a Word 2010 format document.

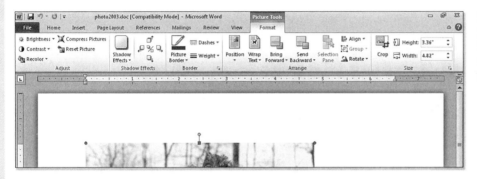

Figure 10.3
A picture in backward-compatible mode.

The tools and dialog boxes are somewhat different for Word 2010 pictures versus backward-compatible ones. In the following sections, I'll point out the differences where applicable.

Inserting Pictures from Files

To insert a picture from a file stored on your hard disk (or other disk), follow these steps:

1. On the Insert tab, click Picture. The Insert Picture dialog box opens.

2. (Optional) By default, all supported file types are shown, as in Figure 10.4. To narrow down the files shown to a specific type, select the type.

   Under Windows Vista or Windows 7, type is set from the drop-down list button to the right of the filename. Under Windows XP, it's set from the Files of Type drop-down list.

3. Navigate to the folder containing the file and select it.

4. Click Insert.

 note

If you are using Windows XP, to see thumbnail images, open the Views button's menu and choose Thumbnails. If you are using Windows Vista or Windows 7, thumbnails automatically appear for the picture icons.

Figure 10.4
Select a file to insert.

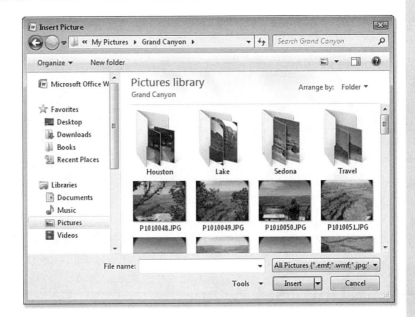

You can also create a dynamic link between the picture and the document, so the copy in the document stays up-to-date when the original changes. To do so, click the down arrow next to the Insert button in step 4 and choose either Link to File or Insert and Link. Link to File creates a link that is automatically updated each time the document is opened; if the picture file is not available, an error appears. Insert and Link creates a link but also retains a static copy of the picture, so if the original is not available, the last available version appears.

To learn more about linking, see "Linking to Data in Other Files," p. 604.

Word accepts pictures in these formats:

■ Windows Metafile (.wmf)

■ Windows Enhanced Metafile (.emf)

■ Compressed Windows Enhanced Metafile (.emz)

■ Compressed Windows Metafile (.wmz)

■ JPEG File Interchange Format (.jpg, .jpeg, .jfif, .jpe)

■ Macintosh PICT (.pct, .pict)

■ Compressed Macintosh PICT (.pcz)

■ Portable Network Graphics (.png)

- Tag Image File Format (.tif, .tiff)

- Graphics Interchange Format (.gif, .gfa)

- Windows Bitmap (.bmp, .dib, .rle, .bmz)

- CorelDRAW (.cdr)

- Computer Graphics Metafile (.cgm)

- Encapsulated PostScript (.eps)

- WordPerfect Graphics (.wpg)

note

Graphic import filters are registered in the Windows Registry in HKEY_LOCAL_MACHINE\Software\Microsoft\Shared Tools\Graphics Filters\Import. The actual filter files are stored in Program Files\Common Files\Microsoft Shared\GRPHFLT.

To use a picture that's in some other file format, open the file in a graphics-editing program and then do one of the following:

- Save it in one of the supported formats.

- Copy it to the Clipboard and paste it into Word.

Setting Text Wrap

By default, a picture is placed into the document as an inline image at the insertion point. An *inline image* is a graphic that is treated as a character of text would be treated. As far as Word is concerned, the inline image is just a really big, funny-looking letter. When you edit the surrounding text, the picture scoots over to make room, just like text would scoot (see Figure 10.5).

Employee Fishing Trip
By Cynthia Hicks

On August 18, seventeen   employees of ACME Industries traveled to Coldwater Dam to enjoy a day of sport fishing. While nobody came home with a record-setting catch, almost everyone caught a few fish and had a great time enjoying the sun and the outdoors.

Figure 10.5
A picture is an inline image by default.

You can drag an inline image to a different location, but it will continue to be treated as a text character, so you can drag it only into a spot where you could drag text; you can't drag it to the far left or right of the paragraph, for example. That's the nature of an inline image.

If you need more flexibility than that, you need to change the picture's Wrap Text setting so that it is no longer an inline image, but rather a free-floating object. You can then drag the picture anywhere on the page, regardless of the text. If there happens to be text in the spot where you drag the picture, the text and the picture interact according to the Wrap Text setting you chose. For example, if you chose Square, the text wraps around the picture's rectangular border, as in Figure 10.6.

Figure 10.6
Text now wraps around the picture.

Employee Fishing Trip

By Cynthia Hicks

On August 18, seventeen employees of ACME Industries traveled to Coldwater Dam to enjoy a day of sport fishing. While nobody came home with a record-setting catch, almost everyone caught a few fish and had a great time enjoying the sun and the outdoors.

To set text wrap for a picture, follow these steps:

1. Select the picture.

2. On the Format tab, click Wrap Text, and then click the desired text-wrap setting.

   Alternatively, right-click the picture, point to Wrap Text, and click the desired wrap setting (see Figure 10.7). This method does not work with backward-compatible pictures.

Figure 10.7
Set the picture's text-wrap setting.

These are the same text-wrap options as for text boxes, which you learned about in Chapter 8, "Working with Templates and Nonstandard Layouts." All the wrap options allow the image to be free-floating except In Line With Text; that option takes the picture back to being an inline image.

For more control, choose More Layout Options from the menu in Figure 10.7, opening the Layout dialog box. From here, you can choose a basic wrapping style using buttons that correspond to the regular menu options, and you can fine-tune the setting by specifying which sides to wrap around and what distance should be left between the text and the picture (see Figure 10.8). Depending on which wrapping style you choose, some of the options might not be available.

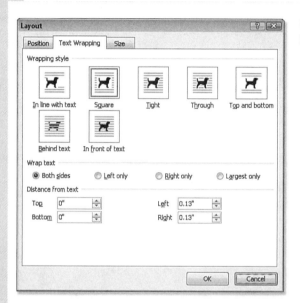

Figure 10.8
Specify text-wrap settings.

Setting Picture Position

Often a picture's position within a document is significant because it needs to stay with certain text or stay in a certain location in relation to the margins. The following sections explain some methods of positioning a picture.

Manually Positioning a Picture

A floating picture (that is, one with any text-wrap setting other than In Line With Text) can be positioned anywhere on the page simply by dragging it there. Position the mouse pointer over the center of the picture (or actually anywhere on it other than a selection handle) and drag.

Working with Anchors

Each floating picture has an anchor. An *anchor* is a marker that indicates how a floating paragraph relates to the document text. A picture anchors itself to whatever paragraph is nearest to its top edge. When you drag a picture around on a page, its anchor moves too, re-anchoring itself to whatever paragraph is nearest. You can view the anchor symbol by turning on the display of nonprinting characters (Show/Hide ¶ on the Home tab). Figure 10.9 shows an anchor.

Figure 10.9
Each picture has
an anchor.

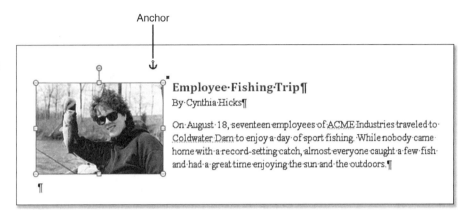

The anchor is actually part of the paragraph. When the paragraph moves, the anchor moves too, and so does the picture connected with it. For example, if you select the paragraph containing the anchor and cut it to the Clipboard, the picture disappears with it. If you then paste that paragraph in a new location, the picture is pasted there too. If the paragraph floats to another page because of text additions or deletions, the picture floats with it.

Changing a Picture's Anchor Point

You can manually change which paragraph a picture is anchored to by dragging the anchor symbol to another paragraph. If you subsequently drag the picture to place it somewhere else, though, the picture re-anchors itself to the nearest paragraph, regardless of the anchor reassignment you made.

Locking an Anchor

If you do not want a picture to re-anchor itself to the nearest paragraph when you drag the picture, lock the anchor point. That way the picture remains anchored to the current paragraph even if you move the picture.

To lock the anchor, follow these steps:

1. Select the picture and then display the Format tab.

2. Click Position, and choose More Layout Options. The Layout dialog box opens.

3. Click the Position tab.

4. Mark the Lock Anchor check box.

5. Click OK. The anchor now shows a lock symbol, indicating it has been locked.

To unlock the anchor, repeat these steps and clear the Lock Anchor check box.

Choosing a Position Preset

Position presets are a combination of location settings and text-wrap settings; they determine where on a page the picture appears and how it interacts with surrounding text.

To select a position preset, follow these steps:

1. Select the picture.

2. On the Format tab, click Position.

3. Click one of the position presets.

The positions on the Position menu are grouped according to text-wrap type: Inline with Text or With Text Wrapping (see Figure 10.10). (If you want some other text-wrap setting than that, apply the position preset first and then change the text-wrap setting as in the preceding section.)

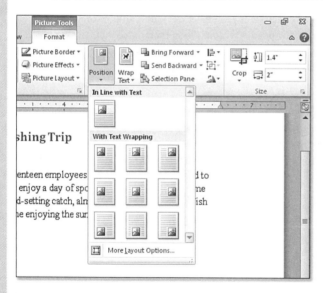

Figure 10.10
Select a picture position preset.

These picture presets set the horizontal and vertical alignment in relation to the document margins. The pictures will stay in place no matter how the text moves around them as a result of text editing you might do.

Specifying a Custom Position

For more alignment choices, choose More Layout Options from the menu shown in Figure 10.10, opening the Layout dialog box. Then click the Position tab and use the controls there to fine-tune the picture's position (see Figure 10.11).

Figure 10.11
Set custom picture position settings.

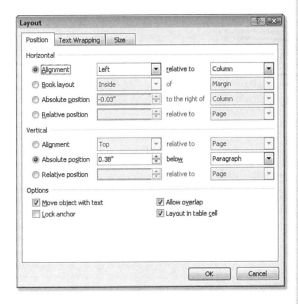

For horizontal positioning, choose one of these settings:

- **Alignment**—You can set a position (Right, Left, Centered) and what it should be in relation to (Margin, Page, Column, and so on). Most of the presets use this option. Using this setting ensures that if settings in the document change (such as margin settings), the picture will adjust itself accordingly.

- **Book Layout**—Use this setting for a two-sided layout in which you want the picture to float to the right or left depending on whether the page is an odd- or even-numbered one. The picture can be set to float either inside or outside the margin or page.

- **Absolute Position**—Use this if the picture should be locked to a certain spot on the page and be unaffected by margins, columns, or any other document-layout settings.

- **Relative Position**—Use this setting to specify a percentage relative to some other element. For example, you could set a position of 25% relative to the page to position the object 25% of the way across the page.

For vertical positioning, the same settings are available, except there's no Book Layout and the alignments are Top, Centered, and Bottom instead of Right, Left, and Centered.

Resizing Pictures

To size a picture in a Word document, drag one of its selection handles.

If you need the image to be a specific size, use the Height and Width boxes on the Format tab (see Figure 10.12). These boxes are linked—changing one dimension also changes the other by a proportional amount.

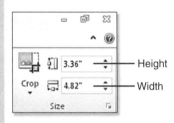

Figure 10.12
Set a height and width on the Format tab.

For even more control over the size, click the dialog box launcher for the Size group on the Format tab. Depending on the picture type, this either opens the Layout dialog box (for a Word 2010 document) or the Format Picture dialog box (for a backward-compatible document). The main difference is the dialog box name; the options are similar. Figure 10.13 shows the 2010 version.

You can set a specific size for Height and Width, or you can increase or decrease the size by percentages in the Scale section (see Figure 10.13).

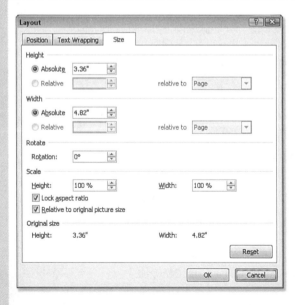

Figure 10.13
Set a precise size for an image.

The Lock Aspect Ratio check box enables you to scale the picture proportionally. When it is marked, if you enter a certain value in the Height box, the Width setting changes by the same percentage.

The Relative to Original Picture Size check box makes the scaling occur in relation to the original size (listed at the bottom of the dialog box), rather than any interim sizing that has been done.

To go back to the picture's original size, click the Reset button.

Cropping Pictures

To *crop* a picture is to trim off one or more edges so your audience can focus in on what's most important in the image. For example, in Figure 10.14, all the extraneous background has been trimmed to show the dogs more clearly.

Figure 10.14
Cropping helps the reader focus on what's important in the image.

The easiest way to crop a picture is to use the Crop tool on the Format tab. Follow these steps:

1. Click the picture.

2. Click the Crop button. The selection handles on the picture change to black lines.

3. Drag a selection handle on the image inward to crop the image. Repeat on other sides as needed.

4. Press the Esc key or click the Crop button again to finish cropping.

You can uncrop a picture at any time by reentering cropping mode (steps 1–2) and then dragging the selection handle outward again. You cannot uncrop if you have compressed the picture, however, as discussed in the next section, because compression deletes the cropped areas of the picture.

New in Word 2010 are several additional options accessible from the Crop button (see Figure 10.15):

- **Crop to Shape**—Enables you to select a shape from Word's collection of drawn objects and crop the image to fit in that shape.

- **Aspect Ratio**—Enables you to crop to an exact height-to-width ratio. This is often useful when you need a picture to conform to a certain size of box, such as on a form or in a newspaper layout.

- **Fill**—After you define the crop area, if you choose Fill, it resizes the picture to fit the space you allocated. The picture's aspect ratio is maintained, and if any blank space remains on the right and left, it is cropped out.

- **Fit**—Same as fill, except it fills to the right and left sides, and if any blank space remains at the top or bottom, it is cropped out.

To experiment with Fill versus Fit on your own, try this: Insert a picture, and then use the Crop tool to set a crop area. Then choose Crop, Fit to see what happens. Press Ctrl+Z to undo that change, and then choose Crop, Fill to see the difference.

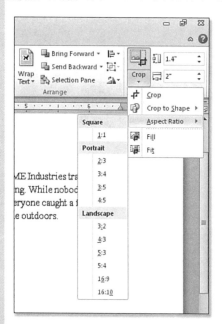

Figure 10.15
Access cropping options by clicking the arrow under the Crop button.

Compressing Pictures

The larger the original image's file size, the larger the size will be of the Word file in which you insert it. Resizing or cropping the picture in Word does not decrease the file size; it stays the same, as if the picture were being used at full 100% size. If file size is an issue (for example, if you plan to distribute the document via email or the Web), consider taking some steps to decrease it as much as you can.

There are two ways of decreasing the file size. One is to resize or crop the image file in a third-party graphics-editing program *before* importing it into Word; another is to use the Compress Pictures feature in Word.

Compress Pictures combines a variety of techniques to decrease the file size, including removing cropped-out areas of pictures and resizing the image file to a particular number of pixels per inch based on the document's planned usage.

The dialog box appearance and options available vary depending on whether you are working in a Word 2010 or a backward-compatible document.

To compress pictures for a Word 2010 document, follow these steps:

1. Select one of the pictures to be compressed. If you do not want to compress all the pictures in the document, do one at a time, or select only the pictures you want to compress.

2. Click Compress Pictures on the Format tab. The Compress Pictures dialog box opens (see Figure 10.16).

Figure 10.16
Compress the pictures in the document to decrease the file size.

3. (Optional) If you want to compress all picture(s), clear the Apply Only to This Picture check box.

4. Set the compression options:

   - **Delete Cropped Areas of Pictures**—When this is enabled, your crops (if any) become permanent when compression is performed with Compress Pictures.

- **Target Output**—Select an image quality, in pixels per inch, depending on the intended use. A lower ppi results in a smaller file size but poorer image quality. If the image is already at a low ppi, this setting does not increase its ppi; this setting only decreases ppi.

5. Click OK to perform the compression.

To compress pictures for a backward-compatible document, follow these steps:

 tip

If you just want to delete the cropped areas, but not change the photo compression, choose Use Document Resolution and mark the Delete Cropped Areas of Pictures check box.

1. Select one of the pictures to be compressed. If you do not want to compress all the pictures in the document, do one at a time, or select only the pictures you want to compress.

2. Click Compress Pictures on the Format tab. The Compress Pictures dialog box opens (see Figure 10.17).

Figure 10.17
Configure compression settings for a backward-compatible document.

3. Select the option button that indicates what you want to compress: Selected Pictures or All Pictures in Document.

4. Set the compression options:

- **Change Resolution**—This is equivalent to Target Output. Your only choices are Web/Screen (96 dpi), Print (200 dpi), or No Change.

- **Compress Pictures**—This enables the pictures to be compressed. If you turn off this option, no compression will take place (but cropping can still take place; see the next option).

- **Delete Cropped Areas of Pictures**—This is the same as for a Word 2010 document; when enabled, your crops (if any) become permanent.

5. Click OK to perform the compression now.

Setting the Brightness, Contrast, and Color Mode

You can adjust a picture's brightness, contrast, and image mode (color, grayscale, and so on) in a third-party graphics-editing program before importing the picture into Word; usually that's how the professionals do it. Most photo-editing programs have great tools for applying such effects.

If you don't have access to an editing program, though, or you forgot to make the corrections before importing into Word, you can use Word's relatively modest tools to accomplish these effects.

Adjusting Brightness and Contrast

To adjust brightness or contrast, click the Corrections button on the Format tab and select a sample that represents the effect you want (see Figure 10.18).

Figure 10.18 Choose a contrast or brightness preset adjustment from the Corrections button's menu.

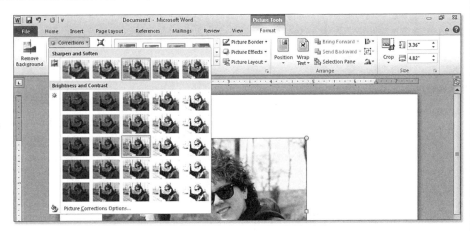

Alternatively, you can click the dialog box launcher for the Picture Styles group on the Format tab, click Picture Corrections, and use the Brightness and Contrast sliders to make adjustments.

For a backward-compatible document, the controls are somewhat different. The Brightness and Contrast settings are separate drop-down lists on the Format tab, and instead of samples, there are percentage-based presets to choose from. To access a dialog box with sliders for fine-tuning, choose More Picture Corrections from either the Brightness or Contrast button's drop-down list.

Sharpening or Softening a Picture

New in Word 2010 is the ability to adjust the sharpness or softness of a picture. This setting emphasizes or deemphasizes hard lines in the picture by subtly changing the pixel colors in areas where there is a sharp contrast between one color and another. Notice in Figure 10.18 that Sharpen and Soften presets appear on the Corrections menu, along with brightness and contrast presets.

Alternatively, you can click the dialog box launcher for the Picture Styles group on the Format tab, click Picture Corrections, and use the Sharpen/Soften slider to make a change.

This feature is not available for backward-compatible documents.

Changing the Color Mode

The image mode is controlled on the Color or Recolor button's menu (Format tab, Adjust group). The options available depend upon whether it is a Word 2010 or a backward-compatible document.

For a backward-compatible document, the button name is Recolor, and only four modes are available:

- **Automatic**—The default image.

- **Grayscale**—Color images are converted to grayscale; no change if the image is already grayscale or black and white.

- **Black & white**—Color and grayscale images are converted to black and white, with each pixel being converted to either black or white.

- **Washout**—The image remains in color, but all colors are lightened dramatically so the image looks like a watermark of itself.

There is one other option on the Recolor menu: Set Transparent Color. It enables you to click on a color on the photo that should become transparent, allowing anything under it to show through.

For a Word 2010 document, the button name is Color, and the options are much more varied, as shown in Figure 10.19:

- **Color Saturation**—Samples represent various degrees of color saturation, from nearly monochrome to very vibrant.

- **Color Tone**—Samples represent various degrees of tint adjustment, measured in *temperature*. A low-temperature picture is slightly blue-tinted; a high-temperature picture is slightly orange-tinted.

- **Recolor**—Samples represent a variety of color washes and black-and-white or washed-out modes.

- **More Variations**—Opens a color picker with theme and standard colors, from which you can pick additional colors for colored washes to place over the image. Some of the washed-out effects can be used when creating watermarks, for example.

  ➡ *To learn more about watermarks, see "Applying a Page Watermark," p. 277.*

- **Set Transparent Color**—Enables you to click on a color on the photo that should become transparent, allowing anything under it to show through.

- **Picture Color Options**—Opens the Format Picture dialog box with the Picture Color tab displayed. This tab contains sliders and presets for saturation, tone, and recoloring, all in one place.

  ➡ *For a more detailed discussion of setting a transparent color, see "Setting the Transparent Color," p. 467.*

Figure 10.19
Recoloring options for pictures in Word 2010 documents.

Removing a Picture Background

With some pictures, setting a transparent color might not work very well because the background is a pattern or gradient. There might be more than one shade of color that needs to be removed.

New in Word 2010, you can tell Word to remove the background from a photo and then help it "find" the background by adjusting the amount of tolerance for variance in color.

To remove a picture background:

1. Insert the picture into the Word document, and select the picture.

2. On the Picture Tools Format tab, click Remove Background.An overlay appears over the image with the areas that it plans to remove shown in bright pink. A Background Removal tab also appears (see Figure 10.20).

3. Use the Mark Areas to Keep and/or Mark Areas to Remove tools on the Background Removal tab to correct any mistakes that Word has made.

4. Click Keep Changes. The background removal is finalized.

To reverse the background removal, use Undo (Ctrl+Z). If you can't do that, delete and reinsert the image.

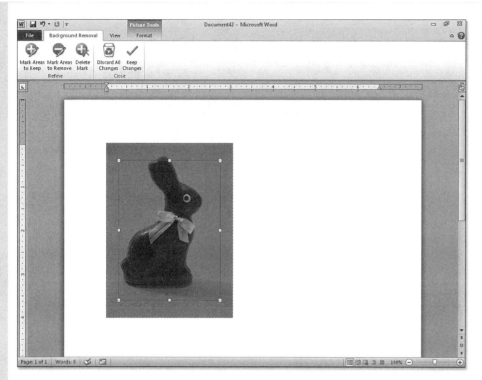

Figure 10.20
Remove the
background
from a photo.

Applying Artistic Effects

Artistic effects are new in Word 2010. They enable you to apply special transformations to a picture, like you might do in a graphics editing program like Photoshop.

To use these, select the picture and then, click the Artistic Effects button on the Format tab. After that, click the effect you want. (You can try out an effect by hovering the mouse pointer over it without clicking.) If you don't like the effect, use Undo (Ctrl+Z) to remove it immediately after applying it.

Some of the artistic effects are very interesting. For example, in Figure 10.21, an effect has been applied that makes the picture look like it is a pencil sketch. To fine-tune the preset you have applied, reopen the Artistic Effects menu and choose Artistic Effects Options. This opens the Artistic Effects tab of the Format Picture dialog box. From here, you can make subtle changes. The controls that appear change depending on the effect you have chosen.

CHAPTER

Figure 10.21
Apply artistic effects to photos for special looks like this one.

Applying Picture Styles and Effects

You can apply a variety of picture styles to your pictures. These are *presets* that combine several types of formatting, including border style and shape, shadow, edge softening, glow effects, 3-D rotation, and reflection. Most of these effects are available only in Word 2010 format documents. However, rudimentary versions of some of the effects, such as shadows and borders, are also available for pictures in backward-compatible documents.

Applying a Picture Style

To apply a picture style, click the down arrow in the Picture Styles group of the Format tab and select one of the samples on the menu (see Figure 10.22).

You cannot save your own picture styles (unfortunately), but you can modify a picture style by changing its effects.

To fine-tune the picture style, use the Picture Effects drop-down list in the Picture Styles group of the Format tab to specify various combinations of effects, such as Shadow, Reflection, Glow, Soft Edges, Bevel, and 3-D Rotation.

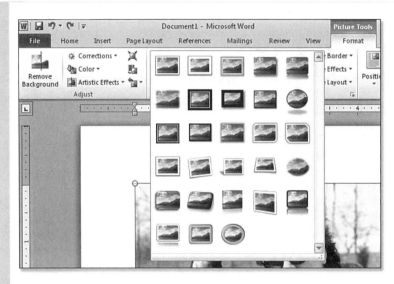

Figure 10.22
Select a picture style.

Applying a Picture Preset

Word 2010 has a number of picture shapes and textures, known as *presets*. They add special effects to the picture, such as beveled edges, contours, and different surface textures and lighting. You can access these from the Preset option on the Picture Effects menu, shown in Figure 10.23.

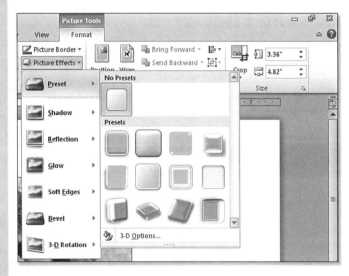

Figure 10.23
Choose a picture preset.

For more options, choose 3-D Options from the menu and then click 3-D Format. You can then set amounts for top and bottom bevel, color depth, contour color, surface material, lighting, and angle.

> ➡ *3-D Format effects are covered in greater detail later in the book. See "Formatting Drawn Objects," p. 434.*

Applying a Shadow Effect

A *shadow* is a shaded background behind the image that makes it look like it is raised off the page. A shadow has these adjustable attributes in Word 2010 documents:

- **Color**—The shadow color
- **Transparency**—How transparent or opaque the shadow is
- **Size**—How far past the edges of the image the shadow extends
- **Blur**—How sharp or fuzzy the edges of the shadow are
- **Angle**—Which sides of the image are shadowed
- **Distance**—How far away from the image the shadow is

Shadow effects are very different for Word 2010 versus in backward-compatible documents. For Word 2010 documents, all the previously listed attributes are fully adjustable. Backward-compatible documents have some limits. For example, for the angle, you must choose from among presets, and for transparency, there is only one option: semi-transparent. Blur is not available for backward-compatible documents.

Because the effects are applied differently, let's look at the shadows for the two picture types separately.

Applying a Shadow in a Word 2010 Document

For a Word 2010 document, use the Shadow option on the Picture Effects drop-down list on the Format tab to select a shadow preset (see Figure 10.24).

If none of the presets are exactly what you want, choose Shadow Options from the menu, opening the Format Picture dialog box. On the Shadow tab, adjust the shadow options, as in Figure 10.25. Start with one of the presets if desired. Then change the shadow color, and drag each of the sliders to control the shadow's properties.

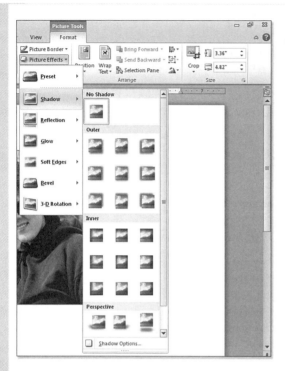

Figure 10.24
Choose a shadow preset.

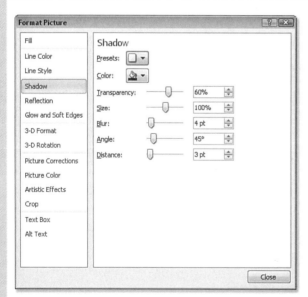

Figure 10.25
Fine-tune the shadow settings here.

Applying a Shadow in a Backward-Compatible Document

In a backward-compatible document, start by choosing a shadow style and direction from the Shadow Effects button on the Format tab. To select a different shadow color or to toggle semi-transparency on/off for the shadow, open the Color submenu (see Figure 10.26).

To fine-tune the shadow positioning, click one of the Nudge Shadow buttons to the right of the Shadow Effects button. You can nudge the shadow in any of four directions. The center button toggles the shadow on or off entirely.

Figure 10.26
Choose a shadow style and color.

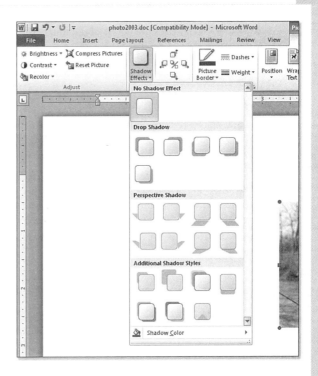

Applying Reflection

Reflection creates a reflected effect for the picture; a faint, flipped version of the picture appears below it. Choose a reflection type from the Reflection menu, via the Picture Effects menu on the Format tab. Choose Reflection Options to fine-tune the effect in the Format Picture dialog box. The settings you can adjust are

- **Transparency**—How transparent or opaque the reflection is

- **Size**—How far past the edges of the image the reflection extends

- **Distance**—How far away from the image the reflection is

- **Blur**—How sharp or fuzzy the edges of the reflection are

Applying Glow

Glow is an extra border around a picture with soft edges applied to it so that it looks like there is a colored light behind the picture. Choose a glow setting from the Glow list on the Picture Effects menu of the Format tab. To select a color that isn't on the menu, choose More Glow Colors and then click a color to use. To remove the glow, open the menu and choose No Glow.

Choose Glow Options to fine-tune the effect in the Format Picture dialog box. The settings you can adjust are

- **Color**—The color of the glow effect

- **Size**—How far past the edges of the image the glow extends

- **Transparency**—How transparent or opaque the glow effect is

Applying Soft Edges

The Soft Edges feature blurs the edges of the picture. The Soft Edges option appears on the Picture Effects menu on the Format tab. You can select a certain number of points to blur; a higher number blurs more of the picture. To remove the effect, open the menu and choose No Soft Edges. Choose Soft Edges options to fine-tune the effect in the Format Picture dialog box. There is only one adjustment you can make there: Size. It controls how far into the image the soft edge effect extends.

> **caution**
>
> Soft Edges is incompatible with some of the Preset settings; when a preset is applied that specifies a certain treatment for the edges of the image, applying a Soft Edges setting will have no effect.

Applying a Beveled Edge and Other 3-D Formatting

A *bevel* is an effect applied to the edges of a picture to make it look raised or sunken in relation to the page. It is also known as a 3-D format, because its purpose is to simulate 3-D.

You can choose a bevel preset from the Picture Effects menu on the Format tab, the same as the other effect you have learned about so far in this chapter. See Figure 10.27.

You can also choose 3-D Options from the menu to display the Format Picture dialog box. On the 3-D Format tab, you can adjust various aspects of the effect, including

- **Bevel**—You can adjust the Top and Bottom values, increasing or decreasing the size of the beveled edge effect. The Bottom setting does not do anything obvious unless the picture is also 3-D rotated (covered later in this chapter).

- **Depth**—This does nothing for the bevel per se, but if the picture is 3-D rotated, it changes the color and depth of the 3-D sides.

- **Contour**—This changes the size and color of the bevel outline.

Beveled Edges

Figure 10.27
Choose a bevel
preset for a
picture.

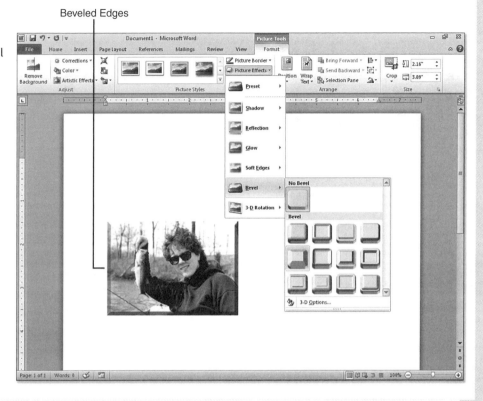

- **Surface**—You can adjust the Material and Lighting settings to control how the object on which the picture projects is composed. For example, you could make it look like the picture is on a steel plate that is lit with a bright light. These effects are usually used on drawn objects, not photos, but they are available for pictures, too.

Rotating a Picture

The procedures for rotation are different depending on the picture's type. If it's in a Word 2010 document, many more rotation options are available, including 3-D rotation; in a backward-compatible document, rotation is limited to two-dimensional spinning.

Manually Rotating a Picture

The basic manual type of rotation is the same for all picture types. When a picture is selected, a rotation handle (a circle) appears above it. Drag that handle to rotate the picture. This works for all images *except* backward-compatible images that have a Text Wrapping setting of In Line with Text (see Figure 10.28).

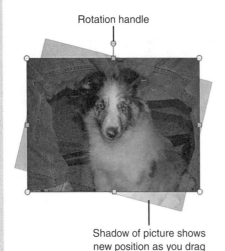

Rotation handle

Figure 10.28
Rotate a picture by dragging its rotation handle.

Shadow of picture shows
new position as you drag

Rotating a Picture by a Specified Amount

If eyeballing it isn't producing the desired results, consider rotating a picture by entering a specific rotation amount.

There are presets for rotating to the left or right 90 degrees; you can use one of these twice to rotate the picture 180 degrees (that is, to turn it upside-down). Here's how to use one of the presets:

1. Select the picture and display the Format tab.

2. Click the Rotate button on the Format tab.

3. To rotate 90 degrees left or right, select Rotate Left 90° or Rotate Right 90°.

If you need some other amount, follow these steps instead:

1. Select the picture and display the Format tab.

2. Click the Rotate button on the Format tab.

3. Click More Rotation Options. For a Word 2010 document, the Size tab of the Layout dialog box opens; for a backward-compatible document, the Size tab of the Format Picture dialog box opens.

4. Type a number of degrees in the Rotation box, or use the up/down buttons to specify the value.

5. Click OK.

Applying 3-D Rotation

3-D rotation is available only with Word 2010 documents (not in backward-compatible documents). This is a far cry from ordinary rotation! With ordinary rotation, the image does not change; it's just rotated wholesale. With 3-D rotation, however, the image is actually distorted to simulate rotation along the X, Y, and Z axes. Figure 10.29 shows some examples.

Figure 10.29
3-D rotation examples.

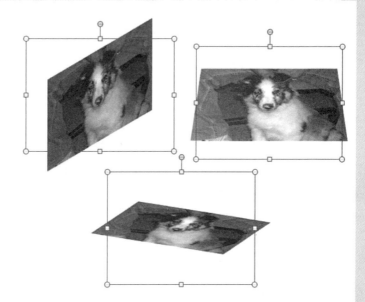

To apply a 3-D rotation preset, follow these steps:

1. Select the picture and display the Format tab.

2. Click the 3-D Rotation option on the Picture Effects menu.

3. Click one of the rotation presets.

Here's how to create a custom 3-D effect:

1. Select the picture and display the Format tab.

2. Click the 3-D Rotation option on the Picture Effects menu.

3. Click 3-D Rotation Options. The Format Picture dialog box opens with the 3-D Rotation tab displayed (see Figure 10.30).

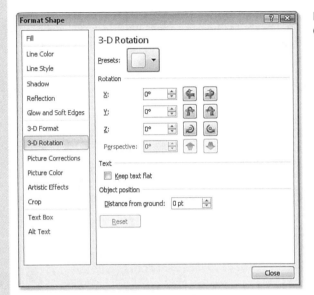

Figure 10.30
Create a custom 3-D effect.

4. (Optional) To use one of the presets as a starting point, choose it from the Presets list.

5. Use the buttons in the Rotation section to enter amounts of rotation on the X, Y, or Z axes. The up/down arrow buttons increment/decrement the value by 10 degrees per click; you can also type specific values in the text boxes.

6. Click Close to accept the rotation settings.

Applying a Picture Border

A *border* is a line around the perimeter of the picture. Some of the picture styles include borders; others don't, but you can apply the border manually after applying the style; still others, especially the ones that involve 3-D, preclude the use of a border.

Three options can be set for a border from the Format tab: Picture Border (color), Dashes (style), and Weight (thickness).

The interface is somewhat different for Word 2010 versus backward-compatible documents. For a Word 2010 document, all the options are available from the Picture Border button's menu. Submenus appear for Weight and Dashes. A backward-compatible document has separate buttons on the Format tab for Picture Border, Dashes, and Weight. Figure 10.31 shows the version for Word 2010 documents.

Applying Picture Layouts (SmartArt)

In Word 2010 documents, you can apply picture layouts to your photos. Picture layouts are, essentially, SmartArt effects that apply to single pictures. In other words, you are creating a Picture-type SmartArt diagram with a single object in it. Figure 10.32 shows some examples.

Figure 10.31
Set border options for the picture in a
Word 2010 document.

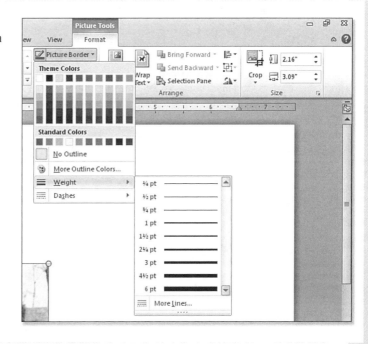

Figure 10.32
Some picture layout examples.

To apply one of these layouts, on the Format tab click the Picture Layout button and then choose a preset. See Figure 10.33.

After you apply a layout, the SmartArt Tools tabs become available (Design and Format), and you can edit the picture as you would any SmartArt diagram.

➡️ *To learn more about working with SmartArt, see Chapter 13, "Working with SmartArt and Math Formulas."*

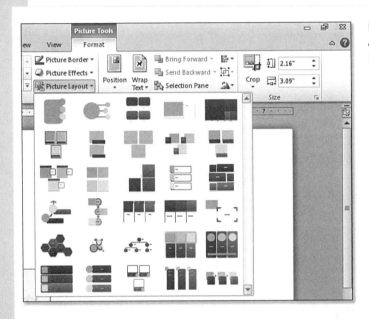

Figure 10.33
Apply a picture layout (SmartArt) preset.

Using Figure Captions

In a document that contains multiple pictures, you might find it useful to number them using Word's Figure Captions feature. Using the Figure Captions feature is preferable to manually numbering the graphics because the numbers automatically change if you add or remove graphics as you edit the document. Figure captions work just like table captions (see Chapter 9, "Creating and Formatting Tables"), but it's a separate numbering set.

 note
You can add figure captions to other objects besides pictures; you can include charts, diagrams, and just about any other object as a figure.

To add a caption to a picture (or other object), follow these steps:

1. Right-click the picture and choose Insert Caption. The Caption dialog box opens (see Figure 10.34).

2. Leave the Label setting at Figure.

3. In the Position list, choose where you want the captions to appear for figures. (Usually figures have captions below them.)

4. The caption will read *Figure 1*. If you want some other word than *Figure*, click New Label and specify some other word(s) instead.

Figure 10.34
Set up a caption for figures in the document.

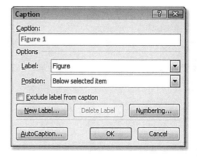

Alternatively, to omit using a word at all before the number, mark the Exclude Label from Caption check box.

5. Click the Numbering button. The Caption Numbering dialog box opens (see Figure 10.35).

Figure 10.35
Control the numbering style for figure captions.

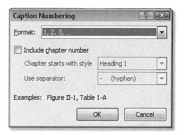

6. Select a format from the Format list.

7. (Optional) To include a chapter number with the caption, mark the Include Chapter Number check box and then choose what style designates a chapter and what separator character should be used.

8. Click OK to return to the Caption dialog box.

9. Click OK. The caption appears in the document, immediately above (or below) the picture.

10. Click to the right of the caption and type a text description if desired.

Automatically Captioning Certain Object Types

If you frequently insert certain graphic types and you always want to caption them, you can save some time by turning on AutoCaption.

From the Caption dialog box, click AutoCaption. Then in the AutoCaption dialog box, mark the check boxes for the file types that you want to automatically assign captions to. Use the Use Label and Position settings to fine-tune the labeling specs.

You might be surprised that many of the file types on the list are not graphics formats, but various other types of objects. This points to an important fact: All types of objects can have captions, not just pictures.

WORKING WITH DRAWINGS, WORDART, AND CLIP ART

Understanding Vector Graphics

The term *clip art* comes from way back in the days before computers were common. People who needed line art for sales and marketing materials would buy enormous clip art books. These books consisted of nothing but page after page of line drawings of just about any business subject imaginable, all crammed together with dozens of images per page. When they found an image they liked, they clipped it out of the book with scissors and used it in their layout paste-up. (There was no desktop publishing back then, of course.) As computers and desktop publishing became popular, the term *clip art* stuck around and began to refer to a line-art drawing saved in a file.

Usually, clip art images are *vector graphics*, not bitmaps. Vector graphics are very different from the photos you worked with in Chapter 10, "Working with Photos." Whereas a bitmap image records a numeric color value for every pixel in the image, a vector drawing expresses the image as a set of mathematical equations, somewhat like what you learned in Geometry class in high school. For example, a vector drawing of a circle consists of a math formula describing the circle (its shape and diameter) plus information about its border color and fill color. Because the graphic is constructed on the fly for each usage, its edges appear smooth (see Figure 11.1).

Math formula describes
the size and shape

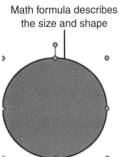

Figure 11.1
A vector graphic has smooth edges that remain smooth even when resized.

It doesn't take very much space to store that information, so vector drawings have small file sizes compared to bitmap pictures. The benefits don't stop there, though. Vector drawings also have a huge advantage over bitmaps when they are resized. When a bitmap image is resized, it loses a certain amount of quality, especially when enlarged. Resized bitmap images tend to get the "jaggies"—that is, jagged edges on curves and lines—when they are used at different sizes (see Figure 11.2). Vector drawings are not subject to this problem because each time they are resized, their math formula is simply recalculated and they are redrawn.

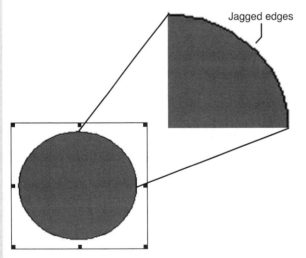

Jagged edges

Figure 11.2
A bitmap circle has jagged edges, which only get worse if the circle is resized.

Vector drawings will never replace photos because they are not realistic-looking. You can't save scanner or digital camera output in vector format. Vector graphics can't have complex shading, and it's difficult to construct anything reasonably lifelike with them. Think about the people in 3-D vector-based games such as *The Sims*, for example. They're fun to play with, but you would never mistake any of those images for photos of real humans. Vector drawings are best for cartoons, drawings, diagrams—and, of course, clip art.

Vector graphics are used for almost every object type that can be created using the tools contained within Word. For example, vector graphics are used to compose drawn shapes, WordArt, clip art, charts, and SmartArt diagrams. In this chapter, you will learn about the first three of those; the next two chapters cover the latter two.

Drawing Lines and Shapes

The drawing tools in Word create simple vector graphics. Although Word is probably not going to end up being your all-time favorite drawing tool for professional illustrations, it will do nicely for basic lines and shapes. And by combining and layering lines and shapes, you can even create some surprisingly complex drawings.

Word's drawing tools are vector based. As you learned at the beginning of this chapter, a *vector* graphic is a line-based drawing that's created via a math formula, like in geometry. Unlike a bit-map image, a vector graphic can easily be modified and resized without loss of quality. Each line and shape in a vector-based drawing has its own selection handles, so you can move, resize, and reshape it as needed.

Drawing a Shape

Word provides dozens of predrawn shapes from which you can choose, including stars, arrows, circles, and polygons.

To draw a shape in a document, follow these steps:

1. On the Insert tab, click the Shapes button and then click the desired shape (see Figure 11.3). The mouse pointer changes to a crosshair.

2. (Optional) Hold down Shift to constrain the dimensions of the shape, such as to force a rectangle to be a square or to force an oval to be a circle.

3. Drag to draw the shape. An outline shows the shape; release the mouse button when the shape is as you want it.

 note

Earlier versions of Word referred to pre-drawn shapes as AutoShapes, and some parts of the program still do too, although the term "shape" is more common in Word 2010.

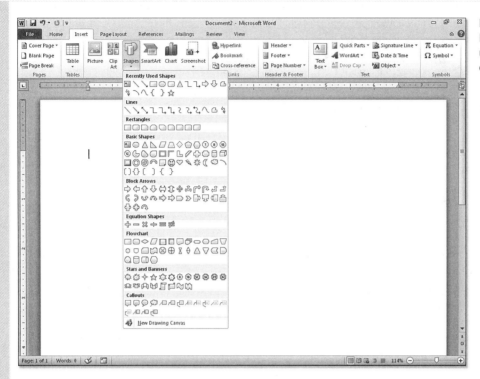

Figure 11.3
Draw a shape using Word's drawing tools.

Finding More Shapes

There's a fine line between a Microsoft Drawing object (a collection of shapes) and a piece of clip art. You will see this demonstrated later in the chapter, in "Editing Clip Art," when you learn how to convert a clip art image to a set of shapes.

Microsoft's clip art collection includes some clips that are, technically speaking, drawing shapes rather than clip art images. They include shapes that look like various types of office furniture and computers (useful in space planning drawings), simple conceptual pictures such as light bulbs and padlocks, and more.

From the Insert tab, click the Clip Art button. Then in the Search For box in the Clip Art task pane, type the keyword **AutoShape** and click Go. (AutoShape is a keyword assigned to most of the shapes in the Clip Organizer.) Click the shape you want to insert into the document.

Here's an easy way to tell whether an object is a shape or a piece of clip art: select the object and look at the Format tab. If it's the Drawing Tools Format tab, it's a drawing. If it's the Picture Tools Format tab, it's clip art or a photo.

Drawing a Straight or Curved Line

Word's palette of shapes includes several types of lines, pointed out in Figure 11.4.

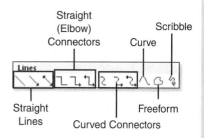

Figure 11.4
Tools for drawing lines.

- **Straight lines**—Click and hold down the mouse pointer at the beginning, point and drag to the end point; and then release the mouse. A straight line can be plain or have arrows at one or both ends.

- **Straight (elbow) connectors**—Click and drag to draw an elbow connector. You can adjust the bend in the connector by dragging the yellow diamond.

- **Curved connectors**—Click and drag to draw a curve. You can adjust the shape of the curve by dragging the yellow diamond in the center.

> **note**
> Connectors can be used by themselves but are traditionally used to join other shapes such as in a flow chart.

- **Curve**—This freeform curve is drawn differently from the others, as shown in Figure 11.5. Click the beginning point, click to create a second point, and then click again to create additional points. Between points, drag the mouse pointer to adjust the curvature of the line. When you are finished, double-click to end the shape.

Figure 11.5
Draw a curve by clicking.

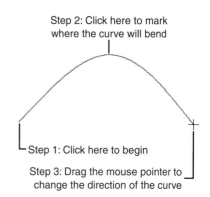

■ **Scribble**—This line is completely freeform. You can draw straight or curved segments, or a combination of them. Hold down the mouse button and drag to draw the line; when you release the mouse button, the line is completed.

Drawing a Freeform Polygon

A *polygon* is a shape that consists of line segments. A rectangle is a polygon, as is a star, a triangle, an octagon, and so on. The line segments do not need to be the same length or at any particular angle.

Word's drawing tools include a Freeform tool that creates custom polygons. (It's pointed out in Figure 11.4.) Here's how to use it:

1. Open the Shapes menu on the Insert tab and click the Freeform button.

2. Click to place the start point. (Don't hold the mouse button down.)

3. Click somewhere else to place the next point. A straight line appears between the two points.

4. Repeat step 3 to create more points. Then do one of the following:

    ■ To end the shape and leave it open (that is, not joining the startpoints and endpoints together), double-click instead of clicking for the final point.

    ■ To end the shape and close it, click on the endpoint. You don't have to be precise; if you click reasonably near the endpoint, the shape closes itself.

Working with the Drawing Canvas

A *drawing canvas* is a defined rectangular area in which you can place the lines and shapes. Using a drawing canvas is optional. If you use one, the drawing canvas functions as the backdrop on which all the lines and shapes sit. If you choose not to use one, the lines and shapes sit directly on the document page. Figure 11.6 shows a blank drawing canvas.

One advantage of using a drawing canvas is that you can apply a background fill (solid or a special effect) to the canvas, so your drawing will have a colored background separate from the document background. Another is that you can assign an automatically numbered caption to a drawing canvas, so a group of lines and shapes together can be considered a single figure for numbering purposes. (To do that, right-click the canvas and choose Insert Caption.)

To create a new drawing canvas, follow these steps:

1. On the Insert tab, click the Shapes down arrow, opening the menu of shapes.

2. At the bottom of the menu, click New Drawing Canvas.

3. Use the Shapes menu to create lines and shapes within the drawing canvas as desired.

 tip

If you always (or nearly always) want to use a drawing canvas whenever you use the drawing tools, you can set up Word to make canvas-insertion the default whenever you draw. To do this, choose File, Options, click Advanced, and then mark the Automatically Create Drawing Canvas When Inserting AutoShapes check box in the Editing Options area. (The reference to AutoShapes is a holdover from earlier Word versions, where shapes were known as AutoShapes.)

Figure 11.6
A blank drawing canvas, ready for a drawing.

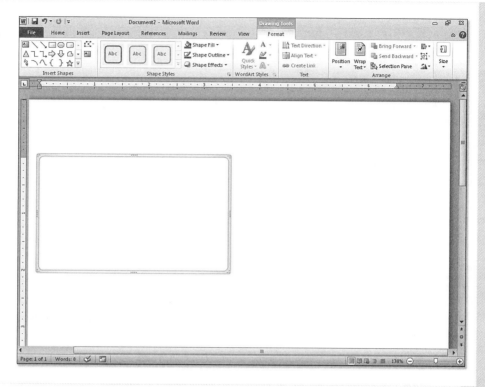

To delete a drawing canvas, select the outer border of the canvas (not any particular drawn item within it) and press the Delete key on the keyboard.

If you forget to create a drawing canvas and then later wish you had, it's not too late. Create a new drawing canvas, and then cut and paste the drawn objects into it (Ctrl+X and Ctrl+V).

Resizing the Canvas

By default, the drawing canvas occupies almost the entire space between the margins horizontally, and it is about 3.5 inches high. To resize it, drag one of its selection handles.

To size the drawing canvas so that it is exactly the size needed to hold the current content, right-click its border and choose Fit (see Figure 11.7).

To expand the drawing canvas slightly (by about 1/2 inch) so that the content has a little more space around the edges, right-click the drawing canvas border and choose Expand.

> **caution**
>
> In Word 2007, you could right-click anywhere within the canvas to get the menu shown in Figure 11.7; in Word 2010, you have to click on the drawing canvas's outer border for it.

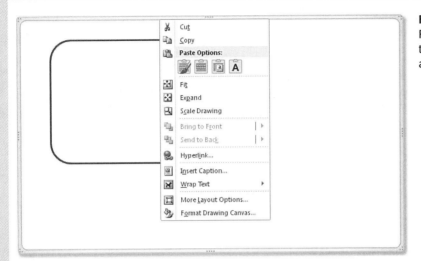

Figure 11.7
Right-click the border of
the drawing canvas to
access sizing options.

The size of the canvas is constrained by the size of the content within it. You can't make the canvas smaller than its content. However, you can resize the canvas and its content together using the Scale feature:

1. Right-click the canvas border and choose Scale Drawing.

2. Drag a selection handle to resize the canvas and the drawing together.

3. When you are finished, right-click again on the border and choose Scale Drawing again to toggle that mode off.

Formatting the Canvas

In terms of formatting, the drawing canvas is a lot like a shape or other object. You can place a border around it, and you can apply a background fill. See "Formatting Drawn Objects" later in this chapter to review the techniques for applying borders and fills to objects.

Adding Text to a Shape

Shapes can function as text boxes, and you can create some very interesting effects by adding text to unusual shapes such as starbursts and arrows.

To add text to a shape, right-click the shape and choose Add Text or click the shape and start typing. An insertion point appears in the shape; just type your text as you would in a text box and then click outside the shape when you are done.

Formatting text in a shape is the same as formatting text in a text box. You can set all the usual paragraph and character formatting, and you can adjust the vertical and horizontal alignment and internal margins.

➡ *To review the procedures for formatting text in a text box, see "Creating Text Box Layouts," p. 307.*

Modifying Drawn Objects

There are lots of ways you can modify drawing objects (lines and shapes). Some of these involve formatting, such as applying fill colors and border styles, and that type of modification is covered later in the chapter. This section, however, looks at modification from a structural standpoint— changing the contours and angles of the shapes and lines.

Modifying a Straight Line

A straight line has only two selection handles—one at each end. Drag one of those selection handles to change the line's length or to point it in a different direction.

Adding and Removing Arrow Heads

Each end of a line can be modified to include an arrow or not. Further, you can choose between different arrowhead styles. Follow these steps:

1. Right-click the line and choose Format Shape. The Format Shape dialog box opens, with the Line Style tab displayed.

2. In the Arrow Settings section, choose a Begin Type and an End Type setting.

3. For each end for which you've chosen an arrow, choose a Begin Size and an End Size setting (see Figure 11.8).

4. Click OK.

Modifying an Elbow or Curved Connector

An elbow connector is a line that turns at a 90-degree angle at some point and then turns again the opposite way so it ends up going the same direction again. A curved connector is a two-segment curve.

You can drag either end to change the position and size, just like with any other line. The angled parts or the joint where the two segments meet remain centered.

An elbow connector has a yellow diamond in the center; you can drag the diamond to move the angles (see Figure 11.9). If you drag the diamond all the way in one direction or the other, one of the angles disappears and the line becomes a simple two-segmented right angle line.

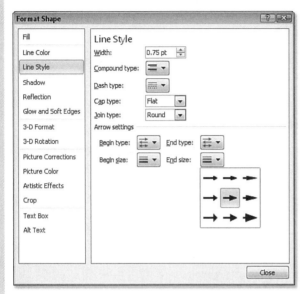

Figure 11.8
Select arrow types and sizes for each end of the line.

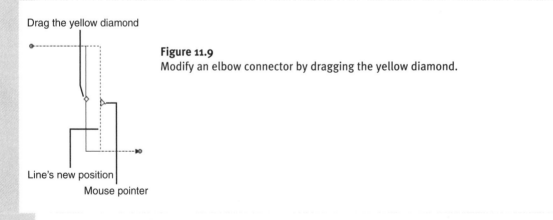

Drag the yellow diamond

Figure 11.9
Modify an elbow connector by dragging the yellow diamond.

Line's new position

Mouse pointer

A curved connector also has a yellow diamond, but dragging it does something different—it changes the position of the point where the two curves join, and one or both curves change their shape in proportion (see Figure 11.10).

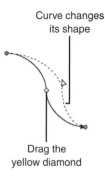

Curve changes
its shape

Figure 11.10
Modify a curved connector by dragging the yellow diamond.

Drag the
yellow diamond

Modifying Curves and Scribbles

A true curve—as opposed to a curved connector—has a variable number of bends in it. The same goes for a scribble. It may be a mixture of curves and straight lines, and it has a variable number of segments. Such lines do not have a yellow diamond for changing their shape; instead, you must edit their points.

To edit a curve or scribble, follow these steps:

1. Select the line.

2. On the Format tab, click Edit Shape and then click Edit Points. Small black squares appear on the curve for each point.

3. Drag a point to reposition it. As you drag, the curve of the adjacent segments changes (see Figure 11.11).

4. Drag other points as needed; press Esc when you're finished.

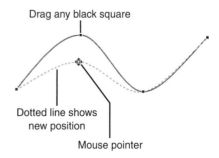

Drag any black square

Figure 11.11
Modify a curve by editing its points.

Dotted line shows
new position

Mouse pointer

Scribbles, being freeform, have more flexibility. When you click a point on a scribble, notice that two small white squares appear near it. These squares represent the ends of directional lines that can control the contours of the segment without moving it. Drag one of these squares to reshape the segment, while keeping the points at both ends of the segment stationary (see Figure 11.12).

Dotted line shows new curve

Mouse pointer

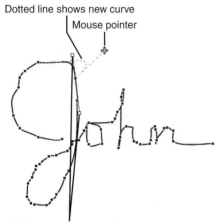

Figure 11.12
Drag the directional lines for a point to change the segment's curve without moving the startpoint or endpoint of the segment.

White squares are handles
for changing the curve

Modifying Shapes

Some shapes have one or more yellow diamonds on them when selected. You can drag these diamonds to modify the shape. Dragging diamonds does not change the shape's basic self—an arrow is still an arrow—but rather changes the proportions. For example, in Figure 11.13, the yellow diamond on a block arrow shape is used to change the thickness of the line and the size of the arrowhead.

 note
Some shapes, such as the curved ribbon-style arrows, have multiple diamonds, each one controlling a different dimension of the shape.

Drag the yellow diamond

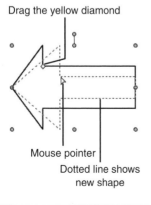

Figure 11.13
Modify a shape by dragging its yellow diamond.

Mouse pointer

Dotted line shows
new shape

Rotating and Flipping Objects

The easiest way to rotate an object is to drag the rotation handle (the circle at the top of the shape), as shown in Figure 11.14.

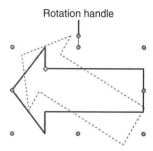

Rotation handle

Figure 11.14
Rotate a shape by dragging its rotation handle.

You can also rotate a shape with the Rotate menu on the Format tab. Choose one of the presets there or choose More Rotation Options to open the Layout dialog box's Size tab. Then enter a rotation amount in degrees in the Rotation box. These skills were covered in detail in "Rotating a Picture" in Chapter 10.

Flipping creates a mirror image of the object. From the Format tab, click Rotate and then click Flip Horizontal or Flip Vertical.

➡️ *To learn about 2-D rotation, see "Rotating a Picture," p. 407.*

➡️ *To learn about 3-D rotation, see "Applying 3-D Rotation," p. 409.*

Sizing and Positioning Objects

Now that you know how to create the lines and shapes you need for your drawings, let's look at ways to size and position those objects.

Sizing Objects

You can size drawn objects (lines and shapes) the same way you did for the other object types you've seen so far in this book. The quickest way is to drag a selection handle. Lines have only two selection handles—one at each end—but shapes have multiple handles. To keep the shape proportional as you drag, hold down the Shift key.

To specify an exact size for a drawn object, enter precise values in the Height and Width boxes on the Format tab. Depending on your display size and screen resolution, the Size controls may appear directly on the Format tab, or you may need to click the Size button to display them, as in Figure 11.15.

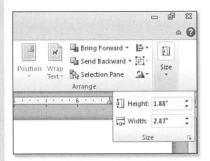

Figure 11.15
Resize an object with the Height and Width controls.

For other size-adjustment options, right-click the object and choose More Layout Options. Then on the Size tab, enter absolute or relative heights and widths, or in the Scale section, enter a percentage by which to resize (see Figure 11.16).

 caution

More Layout Options is not available on the right-click menu for shapes within a drawing canvas; you have to use the Format tab method, or remove them from the canvas.

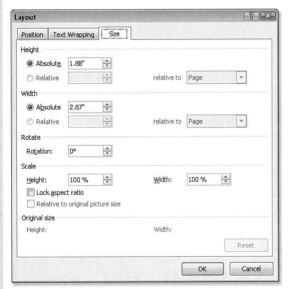

Figure 11.16
More resizing options are available on the Size tab of the Layout dialog box.

Setting Position and Text Wrapping

The same position presets are available for shapes as for pictures. Use the Position drop-down list on the Format tab to select a position if desired.

➡ *To review the available position presets, see "Choosing a Position Preset," p. 390.*

The text-wrapping options are the same as for clip art, covered later in this chapter. Drawn shapes are more like clip art than pictures in this regard because they sometimes have irregular edges around which text can tightly wrap. Choose text-wrap options from the Wrap Text button on the Format tab. You can edit the wrap points the same as with clip art, or you can stick with standard text wrap styles.

➡ *To learn more about text-wrapping options, see "Setting Text Wrap Properties for Clip Art," p. 462.*

Anchoring Lines to Shapes

When you are creating drawings that illustrate connections, such as flowcharts, you might want certain lines and shapes to remain connected. Figure 11.17 shows an example of a flowchart. Suppose you wanted to move the shapes around, perhaps to compress the spacing between them. Wouldn't it be nice if the connecting lines stayed connected?

> **note**
>
> You can create a flow chart like the one in Figure 11.17 using any shapes you like, but certain shapes are traditionally used in specific situations. For example, a rectangle usually indicates an action, and a diamond usually denotes a decision point. Many good tutorials are available online for flow charting; a quick search for "flow chart tutorial" using any search engine will turn them up.

Figure 11.17
A flowchart uses connectors to join shapes.

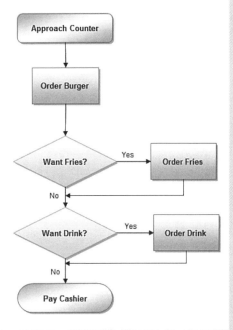

To create connections between lines and shapes, anchor the line to a shape at one or both ends. Follow these steps:

1. *Using a drawing canvas*, draw the two shapes that you want to connect. For best results use the shapes in the Flowchart group.

2. Choose one of the line tools on the Insert Shapes menu: Straight Connector (line), Elbow Connector, or Curved Connector.

 note

It is important that you use a drawing canvas for this (choose Insert, Shapes, New Drawing Canvas); otherwise, the connectors will behave like ordinary lines, and will not snap to the shapes.

3. Click to place the connector line so that its beginning point is on the border of one of the shapes. Then slowly drag it to move it until you see red selection handles light up on the border of the shape; this indicates the valid connection points. Drop the line so that its beginning point touches one of those red handles. The beginning point is now anchored.

4. Drag the other end of the line slowly over the second shape, until the red selection handles appear for it. Then drop the end of the line onto one of those points. The connector now connects the two shapes.

 tip

Lines are not required to be anchored to shapes; you can have lines anywhere on your drawing that are not connected to anything.

When both ends of a line are successfully anchored to shapes, red circles appear at each end of the line (see Figure 11.18). When an end is not anchored, a pale blue circle appears at that end instead.

Red circles indicate connections

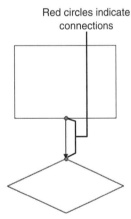

Figure 11.18
Line selection handles appear in red when a line is anchored to a shape.

Here are a few tips for working with flowchart layouts:

- **Adding text to a shape**—Usually a flowchart contains text in each shape. To add text, click a shape and start typing. See the section "Adding Text to a Shape," earlier in the chapter.

- **Changing an anchor point**—To change the point to which an end of a line is anchored, drag its endpoint. You can reanchor a line to a different point on the same shape or to a different shape entirely, or you can drag it away from any shape to make it free-floating.

- **Toggling connection points**—To toggle between the other possible connection points for a connector line, right-click the line and choose Reroute Connectors. (If nothing happens when you do that, there are no other possible connection points.)

- **Changing the connector type**—If you decide you want a different connector type, right-click the connector and point to Connector Types, and then pick a different type from the submenu: Straight Connector, Elbow Connector, or Curved Connector. Then drag one end of the line or the other as needed. You might not see the effect of the change until you reposition one end or the other of the line.

- **Aligning shapes**—Your flowchart will look nicer if all the shapes are uniformly aligned. See "Aligning and Distributing Objects" later in the chapter to learn how to make that happen.

Layering Objects and Text

A Word document has two main layers. On the *text layer* is the regular document text and any inline images. (And remember, by default pictures are inserted as inline images.) The *graphics layer* contains everything else: text boxes, drawings, pictures, and anything else that's set for a text wrapping other than inline.

 note

Layering drawn shapes works only if you are not using a drawing canvas. Drag the shapes outside the drawing canvas if the layering tools do not work.

Within that graphics layer, it is possible to stack objects. For example, you could create a drawing that consists of overlapping shapes and lines, and you could then use that drawing as a backdrop mat for a photo. Figure 11.19 shows an example.

Word's layering options enable you to move objects in stacking order within the upper layer, but that's not all. They also enable you to move graphics objects behind the text layer itself, effectively creating an extra graphics layer behind the text layer. (The original graphics layer stays on top of the text layer, so you can have graphics both on top of and behind the text.)

When you overlap one graphic object with another, by default they are stacked according to the order in which they were originally drawn, with the oldest one on the bottom.

To move an object one position within the graphics layer, select the object and then choose either Bring Forward or Send Backward (on the Format tab), respectively. To bring an item all the way forward or back in the stack of objects (but still within the graphics layer), choose Bring Forward, Bring to Front or Send Backward, Send to Back on the Format tab. Figure 11.20 shows the Send Backward button's menu.

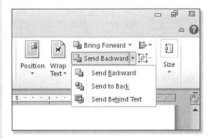

Figure 11.19
Several over-lapping drawn shapes form a background for this picture.

Figure 11.20
The Bring Forward button and Send Backward buttons have their own menu.

To move an object behind the text layer, open the Send Backward button's menu and choose Send Behind Text. To move it back above the text layer again, open the Bring Forward button's menu and choose Bring in Front of Text.

Grouping Shapes

When creating complex drawings that have multiple shapes and lines in them, it can be a challenge to select, move, and resize all the pieces at once. To make it easier, consider grouping the pieces into a single unit. You can then move, size, cut, copy, and paste the group object.

> **note**
> Depending on the object's text-wrapping setting, you might not see any immediate difference in using Send Behind Text or Bring in Front of Text. To see the difference most obviously, set Wrap Text to Through.

To create a grouping, select all the pieces (lassoing them by dragging a box around them works well) and then right-click the group and choose Group, Group. The individual selection handles disappear, and a single set of selection handles appears for the entire group.

 note

The lasso works only within the drawing canvas.

If you find you need to work with one of the pieces separately, right-click the group and choose Group, Ungroup.

After making changes, you can reestablish the group by right-clicking one of the objects and choosing Group, Regroup.

You can lasso the individual shapes in the drawing canvas, but the lasso must start *inside* the drawing canvas. If there are shapes tight against the edges of the canvas, making it hard to position the mouse pointer, expand the canvas temporarily. To do so, right-click it and choose Expand. When you're done, you can shrink it again; right-click, and choose Fit. You can't lasso multiple objects outside a drawing canvas.

Aligning and Distributing Objects

Drag-and-drop can be a frustrating, inexact way of positioning objects in relation to one another. When creating stacked groupings of objects, you might instead prefer to use the Align and Distribute commands for more precision.

Two or more objects can be *aligned* with one another at the top, bottom, middle, right edge, left edge, or horizontal center.

Single objects can be aligned, but only in relation to some portion of the page. For example, you can align an object with any of the margins or with the edge of the page.

To align objects, follow these steps:

1. Select the objects to align. (Hold down Ctrl and click on each object.) For Align to Page or Align to Margin, you need only select one object. For Align Selected Objects, you must select at least two.

2. On the Format tab, click Align and then choose the desired alignment relationship: Align to Page, Align to Margin, or Align Selected Objects (see Figure 11.21).

   This step doesn't perform alignment; it just sets the stage.

3. Click Align again and then select one of the alignments, such as Align Center or Align Left.

Distributing means spacing objects equally. You can distribute three or more objects in relation to one another, or you can distribute two or more objects in relation to the margins or page.

Objects can be distributed either vertically or horizontally. Distribution is based on the amount of whitespace between the objects, not the centers of the objects, so objects of unequal size are still distributed with equal amounts of whitespace between them.

To distribute objects, follow these steps:

1. Select the objects to be distributed. (Hold down Ctrl and click on multiple objects.) For Align Selected Objects, you must select at least three.

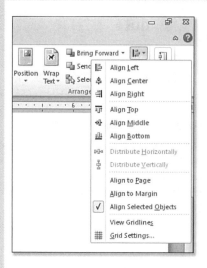

Figure 11.21
Choose the type of alignment you want to do.

2. On the Format tab, click Align and then choose the desired distribution relationship: Align to Page, Align to Margin, or Align Selected Objects.

   If you choose the latter, the objects are distributed between the rightmost and leftmost objects, or topmost and bottommost ones, but the overall space occupied by the group of objects will not change. If you choose Align to Page or Align to Margin, the distribution spreads out the objects to fill the available space on the page or between the margins.

3. Click Align again and then select one of the distributions: Distribute Horizontally or Distribute Vertically.

Formatting Drawn Objects

Once you get the objects sized, shaped, and placed where you want them, the next step is to think about their formatting. In the following sections, you'll learn how to change the colors, borders, shadows, and other effects associated with drawn objects.

Applying Quick Styles

Quick Styles offer a way to quickly apply a complete set of formatting to a drawn object: color, border, and shadow. You can choose among six designs from each of seven colors from the Shape Styles drop-down list on the Format tab. Select a shape and point to a Quick Style to see a preview of the Quick Style applied to the shape (see Figure 11.22).

The only problem with Quick Styles is that they're limited to the choices provided. If you want something other than what's provided, see the following sections to fine-tune.

Figure 11.22
Apply a Quick Style to a shape.

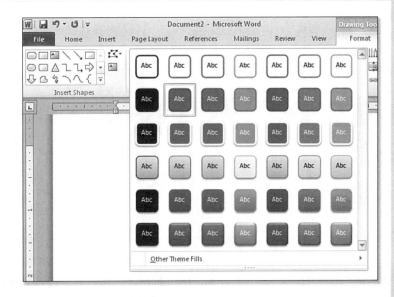

Formatting Borders

Most of what you've learned earlier in this book about borders also applies to drawn objects. You can apply a border with any style, thickness, and color desired.

Shape borders are called *outlines* in Word 2010 terminology. To format a shape border, open the Shape Outline menu from the Format tab, as shown in Figure 11.23, and select one or more of the following:

- **Color**—Choose a theme color, a tint or shade of a theme color, or a standard color, or click More Outline Colors to select from a dialog box. This works the same as for font color (see "Changing Font Color" in Chapter 4, "Applying Character Formatting") and for text boxes (see "Applying and Removing Text Box Borders and Fills" in Chapter 8, "Working with Templates and Nonstandard Layouts").

- **Weight**—Choose a line thickness, from 1/4 pt to 6 pts, or click More Lines to specify some other weight in the Format Shape dialog box.

- **Dashes**—Choose a line style. Choices include solid lines and various types of dotted and dashed lines. If desired, click More Lines to choose from a wider variety of styles in the Format Shape dialog box.

Applying Solid Fills

You've learned about theme colors and fixed colors in several other places in this book, but let's quickly review.

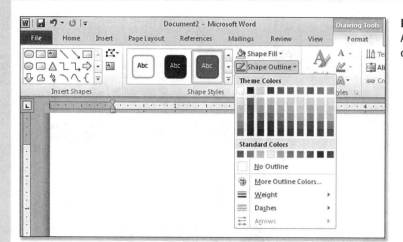

Figure 11.23
Apply border formatting to a drawn object.

A fixed color does not change, regardless of the theme applied. A few basic fixed colors are provided on the menu, but you can also choose More Colors to open a dialog box containing a variety of fixed color choices.

Theme colors are colors provided by the formatting theme you have applied (on the Page Layout tab). Choosing a theme color does not actually apply a color to the selection; it creates a link to one of the theme's color placeholders. Then whatever color happens to be assigned to that placeholder trickles down to the selection. That way, you can have elements in your document that change color automatically when you switch themes.

➡ *To change themes, see "Applying a Theme," p. 247.*

Each theme color can be applied at full strength or as a tint. A *tint* is a scaled-back version of a color, derived by blending the color with white. Tints are described in percentages, such as Lighter 40%, Lighter 80%, and so on. Shades are the darker versions of the colors, derived by blending the color with black. They have names such as Darker 25%.

To apply a solid color fill to a drawn object, follow these steps:

1. Double-click the object to select it and to display the Format tab.

2. Open the Shape Fill drop-down list (see Figure 11.24).

3. Do one of the following:

   ▪ Click No Fill to remove any color, making the shape transparent.

   ▪ Click a theme color (top row).

   ▪ Click a tint or shade of a theme color.

   ▪ Click a standard (fixed) color (bottom row).

   ▪ Click More Fill Colors to select a different fixed color.

Figure 11.24
Select a shape fill color, either a fixed color or one from the current theme.

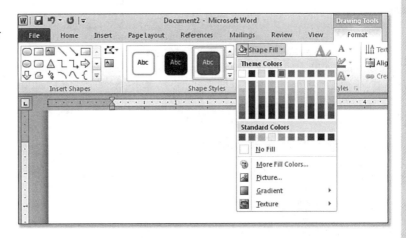

If you go with the latter choice, you can select a color from the Colors dialog box. On the Standard tab, you can click any of the colored hexagons, as in Figure 11.25.

Figure 11.25
Select one of the standard colors from the Standard tab.

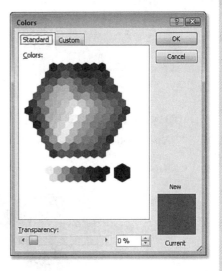

On the Custom tab, you can define a color precisely using its numeric value from either the RGB or the HSL color model (see Figure 11.26). These numeric color models can be useful when you are trying to match a color exactly; for example, many corporations have official colors to be used in all company correspondence and publications.

RGB stands for Red/Green/Blue; colors are defined with values ranging from 0 to 255 for each of those three colors. Equal amounts of each color result in varying shades of black-gray-white.

HSL stands for Hue/Saturation/Luminosity. These are also 0 to 255 values, but H is for all hues (0 and 255 are both red; the numbers in between are the other colors of the rainbow), S is for saturation (the intensity of the color, as opposed to neutral gray), and L is for the lightness/darkness (white to black). You can click any spot on the color grid to select that color, or you can drag the vertical slider up/down.

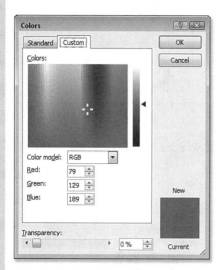

Figure 11.26
Define a color numerically on the Custom tab.

Applying a Picture Fill

A picture fill places a bitmap image inside a shape. It enables you to use any shape as a picture frame, as in Figure 11.27.

Figure 11.27
Picture fills allow any shape to be used as a picture frame.

There are several ways of setting up a picture inside a shape. One is to apply a picture preset, as you learned in Chapter 10. This works only with documents in Word 2010 format, though, so it's somewhat limited. You can't do it in a backward-compatible document, for example, and it doesn't work with all pictures. You are also limited to the shapes provided in the Picture Presets list.

A more flexible way is to insert a shape in the document and then fill the shape with the picture. This works in all types of documents, both 2010 and backward-compatible, and you can use any shape or draw your own custom shape.

To apply a picture fill to a shape, follow these steps:

1. Select the shape. Double-click it to display the Format tab if needed.

2. Click Shape Fill and then click Picture. The Insert Picture dialog box opens.

3. Navigate to the folder containing the picture to use, select it, and click Insert. The picture is inserted into the shape.

The drawback to the preceding method is that the aspect ratio is not locked, so the picture might appear distorted. You can fix this by changing the dimensions of the shape.

Applying a Gradient Fill

A *gradient* is a gradual blending of colors. A gradient can be single-color (one color plus either black or white), two-color (one color blending into another color), or preset (special combinations such as rainbow or gold).

Several common one-color gradients are available from the Shape Fill menu. Here's how to use one of these:

1. Apply a solid color fill to the shape.

2. Click Shape Fill, and then point to Gradient. The Gradient menu appears (see Figure 11.28).

3. Click one of the gradient presets.

If you would like a different one-color effect, or if you want a two-color effect or custom gradient, use the Format Shape dialog box.

When you set up a multicolor gradient, you work with *stops* on a gradient scale. Each stop represents a certain color, and the stop's position on the scale determines how much of the shape's area, percentage-wise, that color will occupy. For example, in Figure 11.29, there are five stops. To add another stop, click the + button; to remove a stop, select it and click the – button.

For each stop, you set the Color, Position, Brightness, and Transparency using the controls shown in Figure 11.29. To set them for different stops, click on the marker for the stop you want to affect. You can also drag markers along the slider to change their positions. For an evenly spaced gradient, space the markers evenly.

The Transparency setting adjusts the amount of transparency that is associated with that position in the gradient. You can use this setting to make certain areas of an object more transparent than others. For example, you could define the same color for all the gradient stops but set different levels of transparency for each stop to make an object seem like it is fading away.

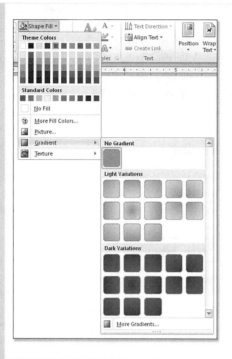

Figure 11.28
Select a gradient effect from the menu.

Each marker is a stop.

Figure 11.29
Gradient stops determine the colors and their distri-bution.

Sample shape filled with this five-stop gradient.

The Rotate with Shape option determines if the gradient rotates when you rotate a shape.

The type setting, also shown in Figure 11.29, determines the direction of the flow from one color to another. Your choices are

- **Linear**—A linear gradient, like the one shown on the sample shape in Figure 11.29, travels from one point to another. You can set it to travel vertically (as shown in Figure 11.29), horizontally, or diagonally, or you can set a specific angle.

- **Radial**—A radial gradient radiates out from a point. You can set it to radiate from the center of the object or from any of its corners.

- **Rectangular**—This gradient is similar to Radial, except that it radiates as a rectangle, rather than as a curve.

- **Path**—This gradient follows the shape of the object. Try applying it to a starburst, for example; the color radiates out from the center of the star.

You can define your own colors and stops for a gradient, or you can start with one of the Preset Colors settings. These are different from the single-color presets in the Format tab because they are color combinations with predefined stops. You can also start with one of these sets of combinations as a shortcut.

To create a custom gradient, follow these steps:

1. Right-click the shape to be filled and choose Format Shape. The Format Shape dialog box opens.

2. Click Fill, and then click the Gradient Fill button. Controls for creating a custom gradient appear, as in Figure 11.29.

3. (Optional) Select a preset from the Preset Colors drop-down list. If you select a preset, Word predefines three or more stops for you in the Gradient Stops section.

4. Open the Type drop-down list and select the type of gradient that you want: Linear, Radial, Rectangular, or Path.

   - If you chose Linear, Radial, or Rectangular, open the Direction drop-down list and choose a direction swatch.

   - If you chose Linear, increment the value in the Angle text box as needed to adjust the angle.

5. Mark or clear the Rotate with Shape check box.

6. On the Gradient Stops slider, select the first marker. (You can do them in any order; I usually start with the leftmost one and work to the right.)

7. Do the following to modify the stop:

   a. Open the Color drop-down list and select the color for that position.

   b. (Optional) Increment the Stop Position value, or drag the marker to a different position on the slider.

   c. (Optional) Increment the Brightness setting, or drag its slider.

   d. (Optional) Increment the Transparency setting, or drag its slider. Zero percent is no transparency, whereas 100 percent is complete transparency.

8. Select the next stop on the Gradient Stops slider bar, and repeat step 7.

9. (Optional) Add or remove stops.

- If you need to create more stops, click the Add (+) button and then repeat step 7 for each new stop.

- If you need to delete a stop, select it and then click the Remove (–) button.

10. Click Close to close the dialog box.

Applying a Texture Fill

A *texture* is a small bitmap image with edges that blend cleanly so that it can be tiled to occupy any size object. Textures come with Office 2010 (and earlier versions, too) and have effects such as wood, cloth, paper, and marble. Figure 11.30 shows an example of a wood texture.

Figure 11.30
A texture fill makes the object appear to be made of a material such as wood or cloth.

To apply a texture fill to an object, follow these steps:

1. Double-click the object to display the Format tab.

2. On the Format tab, click Shape Fill, point to Texture, and click the desired texture (see Figure 11.31).

You can use any bitmap graphic as a texture, but not all produce good results. A texture is much like any other small graphic; the main difference is that it is created with tiling in mind, so the right and left edges blend in with each other, as do the top and bottom edges.

It is possible to create your own textures, but it's much easier to download already-made textures from online sources. Microsoft Office Online has some textures available in its clip art collection, for example, and many websites are devoted to providing free and low-cost backgrounds and textures.

To use a texture graphic you have acquired, follow these steps:

1. Double-click the object to display the Format tab.

2. On the Format tab, click Shape Fill, point to Texture, and click More Textures. The Format Shape dialog box opens with the Fill tab displayed.

3. Click the Picture or Texture Fill button.

 note

The difference between a texture and a picture fill is that the texture fill tiles the image to fill the shape, whereas the picture fill crops or stretches a single copy of the image to fill the shape.

 caution

If you search for the keyword "texture" in the Clip Art task pane or the Clip Organizer, the results will include many graphics that are not true textures, in that they do not have the matched edges for tiling.

4. Click the File button. Select the texture file to use and click Insert to return to the Format Shape dialog box.

5. Mark the Tile Picture As Texture check box.

6. Click Close.

Figure 11.31
Apply a texture from the Texture submenu.

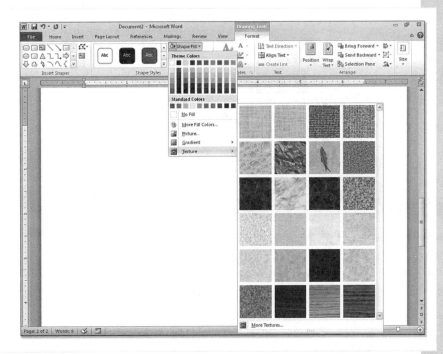

Applying a Pattern Fill

A *pattern* is a simple, repeating overlay of a one-color design over a background of another color. For example, Figure 11.32 shows one that looks like bricks. There are also patterns with dots, dashes, lines, and so on.

Figure 11.32
An example of a pattern fill.

To set up a pattern fill, follow these steps:

1. Right-click the shape and choose Format Shape. The Format Shape dialog box opens.

2. Click the Fill tab.

3. Click the Pattern Fill option button. The controls change to show pattern options. See Figure 11.33.

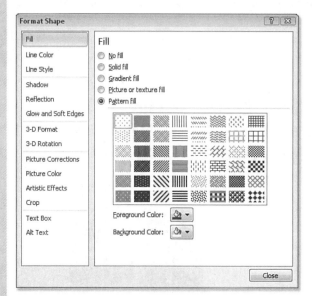

Figure 11.33
Apply a pattern fill from the Format Shape dialog box.

4. Click the desired pattern.

5. Open the Foreground Color menu and select the foreground color. As with other color selectors, you can select a theme color, a tint or shade, or a standard color.

6. Open the Background Color menu and select the background color.

7. Click Close to close the dialog box.

 note

If you do not see any patterns, set the Foreground color to something other than the background color, and they will appear.

Applying Shadows

The shadow effect for a drawn object is the same as for pictures. From the Format tab, choose Shape Effects, Shadow, and then click one of the presets, or click Shadow Options for the full array of controls via the Format Shape dialog box. See Figure 11.34.

➡ *For more detail about applying shadows, see "Applying a Shadow Effect," p. 403.*

Figure 11.34
Choose a
shadow style
and color.

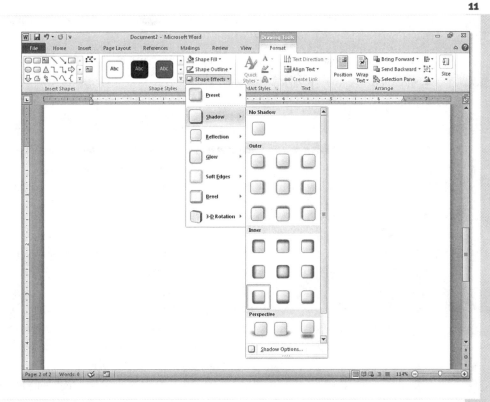

Applying 3-D Effects

A 3-D effect adds depth to a drawn object, turning your flat drawings into something with perspective. Figure 11.35 shows an example.

Figure 11.35
An example of a 3-D effect.

3-D effects apply to drawn shapes the same way they do to pictures. For information about 3-D effects, see the following sections in Chapter 10:

- "Applying a Beveled Edge and Other 3-D Formatting," p. 406

- "Rotating a Picture," p. 407

- "Applying 3-D Rotation," p. 409

Combining 3-D and Shadow in a Backward-Compatible Document

In a Word 97–2003 document, you can't apply both a 3-D effect and a shadow to the same object. This is by design; you can't simultaneously use both 3-D and shadows for WordArt and drawing objects. Applying both to a single object works just fine in Word 2010 documents because of the differences in how the tools are applied.

However, if you are forced to work in backward-compatible mode, there are ways to simulate a shadow by making a duplicate copy of the object and coloring it gray (or whatever color you want the shadow to be). Follow these steps to try it out on a simple shape:

1. Draw a shape.
2. Select the shape, press Ctrl+C to copy it, and then press Ctrl+V to paste the copy. (Alternatively, hold down Ctrl and drag the shape to create a copy.)
3. Select the top copy of the shape and apply the desired formatting to it, including a 3-D effect.
4. Select the bottom copy, and apply a plain gray fill. Remove its border.
5. Drag the bottom copy to position it in relation to the top copy so it looks like its shadow.

Creating and Modifying WordArt

WordArt is a unique combination of a drawn object and text. It enables you to format text as if it were a graphic, applying most of the same special effects to it that you apply to drawn lines and shapes, plus some additional effects that are WordArt-specific. WordArt is great for company logos, headings, decorative graphics on flyers and advertisements, and so on. Figure 11.36 shows some WordArt examples.

To create WordArt, start with one of the preset designs (called WordArt Quick Styles) and then modify it. Follow these steps to create WordArt with a preset:

1. On the Insert tab, click WordArt. A menu of presets appears (see Figure 11.37).

2. Click one of the presets. A text box containing some sample text (*Your Text Here*) appears.

3. Replace the sample text with the text you want.

If you decide you want a different preset format, on the Drawing Tools Format tab, open the WordArt Styles gallery, and make a different selection.

 note

The WordArt feature has changed substantially in Word 2010 from Word 2007, and has lost a few features (while gaining several others). For example, you can no longer use a picture or texture fill in the letters. If you want the old capabilities back, save your document in backward-compatible format and recreate the WordArt; the WordArt tools available will be similar to those in earlier Word versions.

Figure 11.36
Some WordArt examples.

Figure 11.37
Select a WordArt preset.

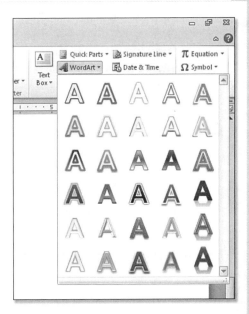

Editing and Formatting WordArt Text

To edit the text, click inside the WordArt and use regular text editing techniques (such as Backspace and Delete). This is a big change from earlier Word versions, where you could edit WordArt text only in a separate dialog box.

You can also use regular formatting tools on the WordArt text:

- **Size**—Home tab, Font Size drop-down list

- **Font**—Home tab, Font drop-down list

- **Attributes**—Home tab, Bold, Italic, and Underline buttons

- **Font Color**—Home tab, Font Color list, or Format tab, Text Fill list

 caution

One of the most common mistakes beginners make with WordArt is to use too much text, which ends up looking crowded. WordArt is best with a simple word or two.

➥ *See Chapter 4, "Applying Character Formatting," for more details.*

Applying WordArt Effects to Regular Text

WordArt has become much more integrated into the main text editing functions of Word in Word 2010 than it has ever been before, to the point where many of the WordArt effects can be applied to normal text in your document, not just to a separately floating WordArt object.

On the Home tab, in the Font group, notice that there is a Text Effects button/list. Its menu system (see Figure 11.38) contains most of the same effects that you can apply to WordArt (except for Transform, Bevel, and 3-D Rotation). You can use this menu system to format document text with such effects as Outline, Shadow, Reflection, and Glow, without having to pull out the text separately as an official piece of WordArt.

Changing WordArt Text Wrap

The default wrap position for WordArt in Word 2010 is In Front of Text. That means it floats over the top of the text in your document, obscuring it wherever the two cross. You can modify this by changing the Wrap Text setting on the Format tab, the same as with any other object.

➥ *To review the procedures for changing text wrapping, see "Setting Text Wrap," p. 386.*

Transforming the WordArt Shape

The *shape* of the WordArt is the form into which the text is poured. WordArt starts out flat and straight, but you can mold it into many different shapes.

To change the WordArt shape, select the WordArt and then on the Drawing Tools Format tab, choose Text Effects, Transform, and click one of the transformations. See Figure 11.39.

 tip

Sometimes it is hard to tell whether a transformation is appropriate for the text until you see it in action. If you hover over a transformation on the Transform menu, the selected WordArt will appear previewed with that shape.

Figure 11.38
Many WordArt–type effects can be applied to regular text via the Home tab.

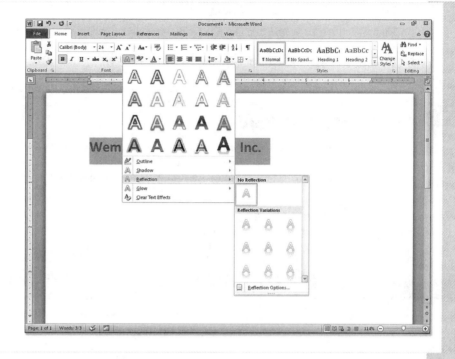

Figure 11.39
Transform the WordArt shape.

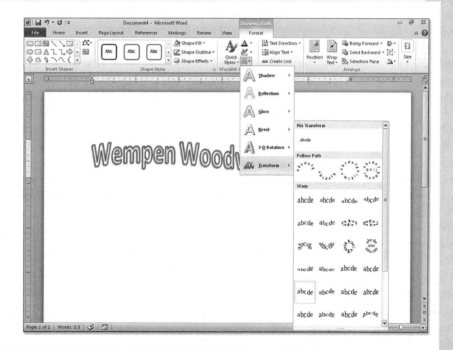

Changing the Fill and Outline

Fill and Outline for WordArt is like it is for drawn objects, except you can only fill with solids or gradients (not textures, patterns, or pictures). Use the Text Fill and Text Outline drop-down lists in the WordArt Styles group on the Format tab.

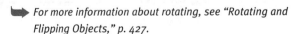 For more information about fills and outlines, see "Formatting Drawn Objects," p. 434.

Creating Vertical WordArt

You can optionally make the WordArt text run vertically on the page, with the Text Direction command. On the Drawing Tools Format tab, click Text Direction, and then choose Horizontal (the default), Rotate All Text 90°, or Rotate All Text 270°. See Figure 11.40.

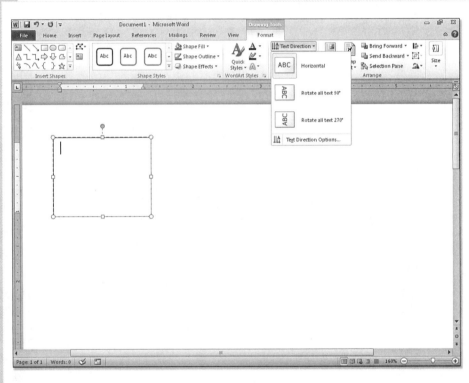

Figure 11.40
Make WordArt vertical.

Unlike in previous versions of Word, Word 2010's WordArt feature does not allow you to have vertically stacked letters (that is, text where each letter is normally oriented but they are arranged vertically). If you want to do that, save the document as a Word 97-2003 document and then re-create the WordArt using the backward-compatible WordArt tools.

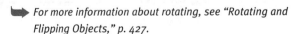 For more information about rotating, see "Rotating and Flipping Objects," p. 427.

> **caution**
>
> If you apply a vertical text direction to some WordArt and it gets all bunched up and unreadable, adjust the size of the WordArt frame to straighten it back out again.

Setting WordArt Alignment

There are two types of alignment you can set for WordArt: vertical and horizontal. Horizontal alignment is the same as with regular paragraphs and text boxes: Left, Center, or Right. Vertical alignment refers to the position of the text within the WordArt frame: Top, Middle, or Bottom.

To set vertical alignment, use the Align Text button on the Drawing Tools Format tab, as shown in Figure 11.41. To set horizontal alignment, use the alignment buttons on the Home tab, as you would for any other text.

Figure 11.41
Change vertical alignment from the Align Text button.

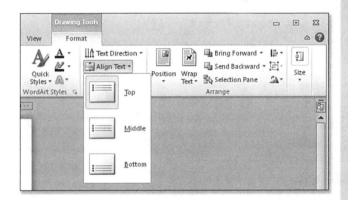

Finding and Inserting Clip Art

By purchasing Word (or Office), you gain access to a huge online repository of artwork from Microsoft. This artwork library consists of four types of files: clip art, bitmap photos, sounds, and movies (mostly animated GIF bitmaps). In this chapter, we are most concerned with the clip art, but you will also learn how to import the other types, through the Clip Art interface, and how to organize artwork of all file types using the Clip Organizer.

Most casual users will find that the Microsoft artwork library has more than enough clip art for their needs, but other clip art collections are available, either online or on CD/DVD. You can integrate these clip collections with the Clip Organizer in Word so that all artwork is available from a single interface.

 To learn more about integrating third-party clips with Word's Clip Organizer, see "Using the Clip Organizer," p. 458.

> **note**
>
> Most of the Microsoft-provided clip art is in one of two formats: Windows Metafile (.wmf) or Enhanced Metafile (.emf). These are both vector-based graphic formats that can be opened in almost any vector-based drawing program.

> **note**
>
> Most of the clips are available via the Internet, so make sure the PC is online before beginning a clip art search; otherwise, the search results will be very meager.

Clip art is organized by keyword, so you can search for a word and see all clips that contain that keyword. A clip can have multiple keywords assigned to it, so you might find the same clip by searching for *dog*, *animal*, *puppy*, and *pet*, for example.

➡ *To learn more clip art keywords, see "Using the Clip Organizer," p. 458.*

To find and insert a clip, follow these steps:

1. On the Insert tab, click Clip Art. The Clip Art task pane opens.

2. In the Search For box, type the keyword to search for.

3. Open the Results Should Be list and choose the types of clips you want. See Figure 11.42.

   For clip art only (most common), select only Illustrations. To also find Microsoft-provided stock photos, choose Photographs, too.

Figure 11.42
You can search for only certain types of clips.

4. Make sure the Include Office.com Content check box is marked if you have an Internet connection available.

5. Click Go. Word finds and displays clips that match the keyword you specified.

6. Click a clip to place it into the document at the insertion point.

Each found clip has its own menu. To see it, point at the clip and then click the down arrow that appears to its right (see Figure 11.43). The default command for a clip is Insert, so you can insert a clip either by clicking the clip or by opening the menu and choosing Insert.

Using a Clip in Another Application

You can copy clip art into other applications, even non-Microsoft programs. For example, suppose you are working with a desktop publishing program such as Adobe InDesign, and you want to use a clip art image from Word in a document there. Copy the clip to the Windows Clipboard and then paste it into that application.

Figure 11.43
Each clip has its own menu.

There are several ways to copy a clip to the Windows Clipboard:

- Insert the image in a Word document and then move or copy it to the Clipboard (with the Cut or Copy button on the Home tab).

- Find the image using Word's Clip Art task pane, but do not insert it. Instead, open the clip's menu and choose Copy (refer to Figure 11.43).

- From outside of Word (Word doesn't even need to be open), open the Microsoft Clip Organizer. You'll find it in the All Programs, Microsoft Office, Microsoft Office 2010 Tools subfolder on the Start menu. From the Clip Organizer window, search or browse to find the desired clip and then open its menu and choose Copy.

> **note**
>
> If you paste a vector clip into a bitmap graphics program such as Paint Shop Pro or Paint, it is converted to a bitmap image, and its edges become less smooth.

 To learn more about using the Clip Organizer, see "Using the Clip Organizer," p. 458.

Getting Clip Information

As you are browsing the found clips, you might have some questions about them. How large are the files? What format are they in? What keywords are associated with them? What are the filenames?

To get basic information about a clip, such as a few keywords, the size, and the file format, simply point at the clip in the Clip Art task pane. A ScreenTip appears with that information (see Figure 11.44).

Figure 11.44
ScreenTips provide basic information about a clip.

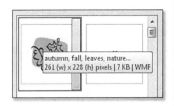

For more complete information, open the clip's menu and choose Preview/Properties. The Preview/ Properties dialog box appears, as shown in Figure 11.45. Its information includes the filename, path, image type, resolution, file size, and more. The left and right arrow buttons in the Preview/ Properties dialog box move between found clips. You can use them to browse the properties of several clips without having to close and reopen the dialog box.

➡ *To learn about editing clip keywords, see "Changing a Clip's Keywords and Caption," p. 455.*

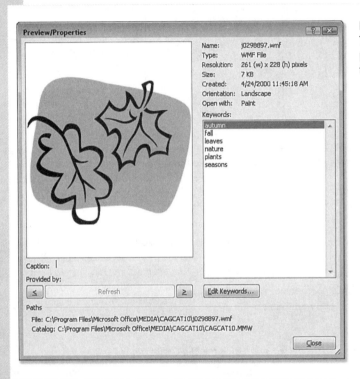

Figure 11.45
The Preview/Properties dialog box provides extended information about the clip.

Making a Clip Available Offline

Clips from the web can be inserted into your documents, but you can't edit their keywords, and they aren't available as standalone files on your hard disk.

To make a web clip fully your own, so you can edit its keywords and work with it offline, do the following:

1. Open the clip's menu and choose Make Available Offline. The Copy to Collection dialog box opens.

2. Click the desired category. (Use Favorites, or click the New button to create a new collection.)

3. Click OK. The dialog box closes, and nothing obvious seems to have happened, but the clip is now available offline.

To check to make sure the clip is available offline, rerun the same search as the one that originally found the clip, but with the Include Office.com Content check box cleared. It will still find that image. Then mark the check box and rerun the search. This time, the search will find two copies of the image—one near the top of the list (the local copy), and the other one farther down in the samples, the original from the web.

If you decide you no longer want that clip to be available offline, select the clip (in the Clip Art task pane), open its menu, and choose Delete from Clip Organizer. This deletes only your offline copy; the web-based copy from Microsoft still reappears when you do searches for which the keyword is a match. If the command is unavailable, the clip is not available offline.

 tip

Knowing a clip's filename can be especially useful if the clip is stored on your hard disk (rather than being in an online collection only). The clips are just ordinary graphics, and you can use them in other programs or copy them to other computers, but you have to know their names— and the clip names are usually fairly cryptic. For example, in Figure 11.45, the clip name is j0298897.wmf.

Changing a Clip's Keywords and Caption

After making a clip available offline, you can change its keywords. Adding keywords can be an effective way of narrowing a search so that only the exact clip (or clips) you want appears. For example, if you have a few clips that a certain client wants you to use in his documents, you could add that client's name as a keyword.

A *caption* is descriptive text that appears with the clip. Captions can indicate what a clip is used for in your organization, for example. Suppose you have three versions of a particular clip, each for a different type of document; the caption could indicate which is which.

You can change keywords and captions only for clips stored on your own hard disk or network. The ones in the web collection are shared with all other users of Office worldwide, so it makes sense that you could not modify the keywords for those clips. (If you want to modify the keywords for one of those web collection clips, save it offline first, as described in the preceding section.)

To change a clip's keyword list or caption, follow these steps:

1. From the Clip Art task pane, open the clip's menu and choose Edit Keywords.Alternatively, from the Preview/Properties dialog box for the clip, click the Edit Keywords button (refer to Figure 11.45).

    The Keywords dialog box opens, as shown in Figure 11.46.

2. Do any of the following:

    ▪ To add a keyword, type a word in the Keyword box and click Add.

    ▪ To replace one keyword with another, select the word to replace and then type a replacement in the Keyword box and click Modify.

    ▪ To delete a keyword, select the word and click Delete.

 caution

The Keywords dialog box opens for any clip, but the buttons for adding and removing keywords are disabled. You must make a clip available offline before you can edit its keywords or caption.

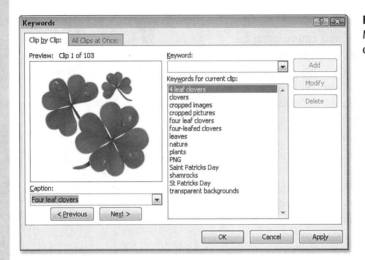

Figure 11.46
Modify the keywords and caption for a clip if desired.

3. (Optional) Type a caption for the clip in the Caption box.

4. Click OK.

You can modify the keywords for more than one clip at a time, provided all the clips you select are keyword-editable (that is, available offline). To edit keywords for multiple clips, follow these steps:

1. In the Clip Art task pane, select the clips to affect. As you click an image, it is added to the document. (You can delete it from the document later if you need to.) Hold down the Ctrl key as you click each clip to select.

2. Right-click any of the selected clips and choose Edit Keywords.

3. Click the All Clips at Once tab.If the tab is unavailable, you have selected one or more clips that cannot be edited.

4. Any keywords that the selected clips have in common appear on the Keywords Shared by Selected Clips list. If desired, select one of these and click Delete.

5. (Optional) To add a keyword to all the selected clips, type it in the Keyword box and click Add.

6. Click OK.

You can also edit keywords from the Clip Organizer window, which you'll learn about later in this chapter.

➡ To learn about the Clip Organizer, see "Using the Clip Organizer," p. 458.

Browsing Clips via Office Online

You can access Microsoft's clip art collection from outside of Word, via a web interface. Some people prefer to browse clips this way, picking the clips they like without having a particular document in mind for their immediate use. You can select as many clips as you want and have them transferred to your local hard disk and then use them in Word later (or not).

Here's how to reach the Office Online clip art collection and search for clips:

1. Click the Find More at Office.com hyperlink at the bottom of the Clip Art task pane. A separate web window opens in which you can search for clips.

2. Type a keyword in the Search Images and More box.

3. Click Search to see clips matching your search criteria. The search results appear.

4. Point to a clip. A menu pops up.

5. Click Add to Basket. A selection basket appears at the right showing that you have marked that clip to be acquired.

6. Repeat steps 4 and 5 for each clip you want.

7. When you have selected all the clips you want, click the Download link in the Selection Basket section (see Figure 11.47). If the selection basket disappears, click the Selection Basket link at the top right to redisplay it.

 note

The clips available via Office Online include not just clip art, but also photos, sounds, and movies.

 tip

You can also access the online clip art by clicking Clips Online from the Clip Organizer window (shown later in the chapter, in Figure 11.48).

Figure 11.47
Use Microsoft's Office website to transfer batches of clip art to your hard disk at once.

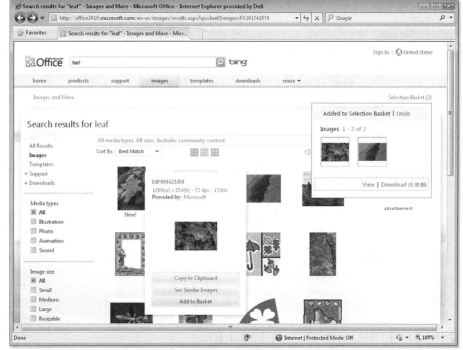

8. If a Save As dialog box appears, click Save.

9. If prompted to accept a service agreement, click Accept. If prompted to install an ActiveX control, do so. A Windows Explorer window opens at this point, showing the clips stored on your hard disk in the Collections\Selection Basket folder for the logged-in user. The Clip Organizer window also opens, showing the new clips in the Clip Organizer.

10. Close the Clip Organizer window, or leave it open to explore in the next section.

11. Close the web browser window.

Using the Clip Organizer

The Microsoft Clip Organizer is a separate program you can access from outside of Word. It's very much like the Clip Art task pane, but with more features and flexibility.

From outside of Word, choose Start, All Programs, Microsoft Office, Microsoft Office 2010 Tools, Microsoft Clip Organizer.

The Clip Organizer has two panes. On the left is the Collection List, a series of folders and subfolders for managing clips. The main collections are listed here:

- **My Collections**—Collections you create yourself or that have been created on your behalf. There are some subfolders within this collection, including Favorites, Unclassified Clips, and Downloaded Clips.

- **Office Collections**—Collections for the clip art that Office 2010 installs on your local hard disk. This collection has many subfolders that break down the clips by subject.

- **Web Collections**—Collections available online via Microsoft Office Online. There are also many subfolders here, breaking down clips by subject.

On the right, the clips in the selected collection appear in thumbnail form. For example, in Figure 11.48, the Academic category is shown in the Office Collections folder.

Browsing Clips by Category

With the Clip Organizer, you can browse freely by category without having to enter a keyword. Click a plus sign to expand a category, and then click a folder to select it. When you've drilled down to the lowest-level folder, the clips within that folder appear (refer to Figure 11.48).

 tip

As you use the Clip Organizer and its collections, errors and wasted space can accumulate and can cause clip art searches to be slower than normal. To correct any problems, use the Tools, Compact command in the Clip Organizer window. Do this periodically (every few months or so) as preventive maintenance.

 note

A yellow star in the bottom right corner of a thumbnail image indicates animation. These clips are animated GIFs rather than regular clip art. You must include Videos in the Results Should Be setting in order to find these. The animation runs when the clip is displayed on a Web page; when the clip is displayed in a regular document, it appears to be a normal graphic image. You can preview the animation from the clip's Preview/Properties dialog box.

Figure 11.48
Browse clips by category from the Clip Organizer window.

Searching by Keyword in the Clip Organizer

You can also search by keyword using the Clip Organizer. Click the Search button in its toolbar to change the left side of the window to a Search pane. Then indicate the keyword you want to search for, the collection(s) in which to search, and file type(s), just like with the Clip Art task pane in Word (see Figure 11.49). To return to the Collection List, click the Collection List button in the toolbar.

Figure 11.49
Search for clips by keyword from the Clip Organizer window.

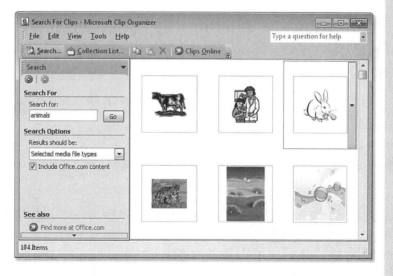

Working with Found Clips in the Clip Organizer

After locating a clip you want, open its menu to choose what to do with it. The menu is similar to the one for a clip in the Clip Art task pane in Word, but it's not identical. Here's what you can do:

- **Copy**—Copies the clip to the Clipboard; you can then paste it into any program that supports the Windows Clipboard.

- **Paste**—This command appears only if there is a compatible image currently on the Clipboard, and only when displaying a folder in My Collections. It pastes the image into the currently selected collection folder.

- **Delete from Clip Organizer**—This is available only for offline clips. This command does not delete the clip from your hard disk, but removes it from being indexed by Clip Organizer. If the clip is listed in more than one collection folder, the command removes it from all of them.

- **Make Available Offline**—This is available only for online clips. It creates a copy of the clip in the My Collections group.

- **Copy to Collection**—This is available only for clips in My Collections. It enables you to copy the clip to another collection folder.

- **Move to Collection**—This is available only for clips in My Collections. It enables you to move the clip to a different collection folder. (See "Moving Pictures Between Collections" later in this chapter.)

- **Edit Keywords**—This command is available for all clips, but you can actually perform the edits only for offline clips. (See "Changing a Clip's Keywords and Caption" earlier in this chapter.)

- **Preview/Properties**—This opens the image's Preview/Properties dialog box, as you saw back in "Getting Clip Information" earlier in this chapter.

Creating and Deleting Clip Collection Folders

You can use the Clip Organizer to organize all types of graphics files, not just clip art. If you want to use it extensively to manage your collections of artwork, consider creating extra collection folders to keep the clips neatly organized.

You can create collection folders only within the My Collections group. Follow these steps to create a new folder:

1. In the Collection List, click My Collections.

2. Choose File, New Collection. The New Collection dialog box opens.

3. In the Name box, type the desired name.

4. (Optional) If you want the collection to be subordinate to one of the existing folders in My Collections, select the existing folder.

5. Click OK to create the new collection folder.

To delete a folder, right-click it in the Collection List and choose Delete "*foldername*".

Adding Pictures to the Clip Organizer

You can add images from other locations on your hard disk to the Clip Organizer, making them more readily available in Office programs. You don't need to do this to use a picture in a document; you can use the Insert, Picture command at any time. What I'm talking about here is an optional extra step that allows the picture to be accessed via the Clip Art feature as well.

Follow these steps to tell the Clip Organizer to include a certain picture in its listing:

1. (Optional) Select the collection folder in which you want to place the clip(s).

2. Choose File, Add Clips to Organizer, On My Own. The Add Clips to Organizer dialog box opens.

3. Browse to and select the desired file(s).

4. Click Add to add the clip(s) to the collection folder you chose in step 1.

Alternatively, if you did not choose a collection folder in step 1, click Add To. Select the desired folder and then click OK.

Scanning Directly into the Clip Organizer

The Scanner and Camera Wizard was a featured part of Office 2003, but was removed from the main interface of most of the Office 2007 and 2010 applications. (You can't access it from inside Word, for example.) A remnant of the feature remains available, though, from the Clip Organizer.

If you have a scanner attached to your computer, you can use it to acquire an image to be placed in the Clip Organizer. From the Clip Organizer window, choose File, Add Clips to Organizer, From Scanner or Camera. In the Insert Picture from Scanner or Camera dialog box, select the scanner (if it is not already selected) and choose a resolution: Web Quality (low) or Print Quality (high). See Figure 11.50.

Then click Insert to scan, or Custom Insert for more settings. A folder under My Collections, with the same name as your scanner device, appears, holding the new scan.

Figure 11.50
Scan directly into the Clip Organizer with the Scanner and Camera Wizard.

Moving Pictures Between Collections

After creating new collection folders and importing images into the Clip Organizer, you might find that the clips are not organized quite as you would like them to be.

You can either move or copy a clip between collection folders. (A clip can exist simultaneously in multiple collections.)

To copy a clip into another collection folder, drag the clip from the right pane and drop it on the desired folder at the left. Alternatively, display the clip's menu and choose Copy to Collection. In the Copy to Collection dialog box, select the new location and click OK.

To move a clip from one folder to another, hold down the Shift key and drag the clip from the right pane and drop it on the desired folder at the left. Alternatively, display the clip's menu and choose Move to Collection.

Setting Text Wrap Properties for Clip Art

By default, a clip-art image is placed into the document as an inline image at the insertion point. An inline image is treated as a character of text; it moves when you edit the surrounding text, and it cannot be moved outside the text area. You can drag an inline image to a different location, but only within existing text paragraphs (see Figure 11.51).

Hop on down to the

Gibson City
Family Easter Egg Hunt
and Picnic

Figure 11.51
By default, clip art is inserted inline.

Most people prefer to use clip art as floating images, which can be dragged anywhere on the page. Text interacts with a floating image according to its text wrap setting, such as Square, Tight, Top and Bottom, and so on (see Figure 11.52).

Hop on down to the
Gibson City
Family Easter Egg Hunt
and Picnic

Figure 11.52
This clip art image is set to Square text wrapping.

Clip art uses the same Format tab as do photographic images (see Chapter 10). Select a clip's text wrap setting from the Wrap Text button's menu on the Format tab, as shown in Figure 11.53.

> **note**
>
> As with photos, a Layout dialog box is available in which you can fine-tune the text wrap settings. Choose Wrap Text, More Layout Options.

➡️ *To review text wrap settings in more detail, see "Setting Text Wrap," p. 386.*

Figure 11.53
Select a text wrap setting from the Format tab.

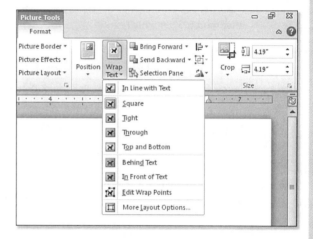

Wrapping Text Tight Against Clip Art

There are some differences when working with clip art versus photographs, in that most clip art has a transparent background. This means that text can actually wrap around the image itself, not just its frame. The Tight text wrap choice makes this possible, as shown in Figure 11.54.

Figure 11.54
Tight text wrapping allows the text to wrap around the picture itself, not just its rectangular frame.

Bring the whole family! Once again the Greater Metropolitan Gibson City Board of Realtors is sponsoring the Gibson City Family Easter Egg Hunt and Picnic on April 18th from 12:00 noon to 4:00 p.m. in the Forest Hills City Park.

Bring your own picnic lunch, or purchase a box lunch on-site for $5 per person, and enjoy live music from Zeke and the Merry Men on the Stellar Pavilion Stage from 12:00 to 1:00 p.m. Then get ready for an exciting Easter Egg Hunt for kids ages 2 to 10 at 1:30 p.m., followed by family activities including sack races, egg tosses, and more.

Editing Text Wrap Points

Sometimes the Tight text wrapping results in some odd-looking text wraps. When that happens, you can switch to Square wrapping (the easiest fix), but if the tight wrapping is important, you might instead choose to edit the wrap points. Wrap points are the markers that define the clip's wrap boundaries when Tight is used. These points are usually invisible, but you can display them and modify them.

To edit the wrap points for a clip, follow these steps:

1. Select the clip art image in the document. Make sure its Wrap Text setting is set to something other than In Line with Text.

2. Open the Wrap Text menu on the Format tab and choose Edit Wrap Points. A dotted red line appears around the image, with black circles indicating the wrap points.

3. Drag a wrap point to change it. The red outline moves along with the wrap point to show the new boundary for the image (see Figure 11.55).

4. When you are finished editing the wrap points, press Esc.

Drag a wrap point away from the image to prevent text from wrapping into that area

Figure 11.55
Manually edit the image's wrap points by dragging.

Modifying a Clip Art Image

Now let's look at some ways you can change a piece of clip art. Many of these techniques are the same for clip art as for photographs, so to avoid duplication, I'll reference the appropriate sections in Chapter 10 as needed. Some techniques, though, are unique to clip art.

Setting Clip Size and Position

Clip art can be dragged to any position on the page. Just make sure the text-wrapping setting is something other than In Line with Text, and then drag the clip art where you want it.

To resize a clip, drag one of its selection handles. To resize the clip proportionally, drag a corner handle. To resize in one dimension only, drag a side handle.

The other techniques for changing size and position are the same for clip art as they are for backward-compatible photographs. See the following sections to review them:

- To use and modify anchor points for positioning, see "Working with Anchors," p. 388.

- To specify a custom position with an exact measurement, see "Specifying a Custom Position," p. 391.

- To resize a picture using the Format tab or the Format Picture dialog box, see "Resizing Pictures," p. 392.

Cropping and Color-Adjusting Clip Art

You can crop clip art just as you do a photograph, using the Crop tool on the Format tab (see "Cropping Pictures" in Chapter 10). However, realistically speaking, you will probably not have much occasion to crop a piece of clip art. Clip art usually stands alone as a self-contained unit, without a lot of extraneous material in it. Cropped clip art can look like a mistake if not done strategically.

You can also set a clip-art image's brightness, contrast, and color mode using the same procedures as for photographs (see "Setting the Brightness, Contrast, and Color Mode" in Chapter 10).

Applying Clip Art Background Fill

Most clip art has a transparent background. The frame around the clip art is rectangular, but within that frame, the image can be any shape. And as you saw earlier in the chapter, text can wrap around that image shape when you use the Tight style of text wrapping.

You can change that transparent background to a solid-color background, though, with a varying degree of transparency. That way, the clip appears to be a rectangular object, and text wrapping applies to the rectangle. Figure 11.56 shows some clip art with a solid background.

Figure 11.56
Apply a background to a piece of clip art.

Follow these steps to apply a background fill:

1. Select the clip art. Make sure the Wrap Text setting is set to In Line with Text.

2. On the Home tab, open the Shading button's menu and select a color. You can choose a theme color, a tint or shade of a theme color, or a standard color (see Figure 11.57). (Click More Colors to select a color from a wider palette.)

➡ *To review theme colors versus standard colors, see "Changing Font Color," p. 158.*

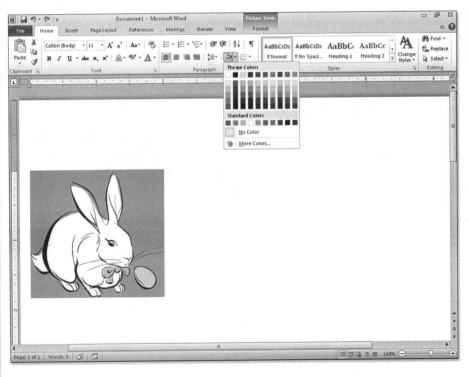

Figure 11.57
Choose a background fill color for clip art.

Applying a Fill Effect to Clip Art

Word offers special fill effects such as gradients, textures, and patterns for some objects, but not for clip art. However, you can simulate background fill effects for clip art by layering transparent-background clip art over a shape with the desired fill.

Here's how to do it:

1. Create a rectangle using the Shapes button on the Insert tab (see "Drawing a Shape" previously in this chapter).

2. Apply the desired fill effect to it (see "Formatting Drawn Objects" previously in this chapter).

3. Set the Wrap Text setting for the rectangle to Square.

4. Insert the clip art into the document.

5. Set the clip's Text Wrap setting to Square.

6. Place the clip art on top of the rectangle. If needed, move the rectangle behind the clip art (with the Drawing Tools Format, Send Backward, Send to Back command).

7. Select both the rectangle and the clip art (holding down Ctrl as you click each one).

8. Right-click the selection and choose Group, Group. The clip art and the rectangle are now a single object.

9. If desired, apply a different Wrap Text setting to the grouped object (see "Setting Text Wrap" in Chapter 10).

Setting the Transparent Color

When you are working with true clip art (WMF or EMF format), the background is usually transparent, as you just saw. This makes it easy to set up tight text wrapping around the image.

However, not every picture that the Clip Art task pane finds is real clip art. If you set the Results Should Be setting to All Media Types, you'll get an assortment of other files as well, including photos in JPG format and animated bitmaps in GIF format. And these usually do not have transparent backgrounds. Therefore, when you set text to wrap around them, the text wraps around the outer frame rather than around the image.

For example, consider the bunny in Figure 11.58. This is a JPG image provided by Microsoft Office Online, and inserted via the Clip Art task pane. It has a white background, which would be great if we were using it on a white page, but in this example, the page happens to be shaded. Because this is a bitmap image, setting the background fill to No Fill has no effect.

Bring the whole family! Once again the Greater Metropolitan Gibson City Board of Realtors is sponsoring the Gibson City Family Easter Egg Hunt and Picnic on April 18th from 12:00 noon to 4:00 p.m. in the Forest Hills City Park.

Figure 11.58
This JPG file has a white background that Word can't take away with its background fill setting.

Bring your own picnic lunch, or purchase a box lunch on-site for $5 per person, and enjoy live music from Zeke and the Merry Men on the Stellar Pavilion Stage from 12:00 to 1:00 p.m. Then get ready for an exciting Easter Egg Hunt for kids ages 2 to 10 at 1:30 p.m., followed by family activities including sack races, egg tosses, and more.

To solve this problem, use the Set Transparent Color feature in Word. Word enables you to select one color of a bitmap image to "hide," and if you choose the image's background color, the background becomes transparent. Follow these steps:

1. Select the picture.

2. On the Format tab, click Color and then choose Set Transparent Color. The mouse pointer turns to a pen.

3. Click the background of the picture. All instances of that color in the picture become transparent.

Figure 11.59 shows our bunny with its background set to transparent. Only one color can be transparent in an image at once; if you set a different transparent color, the first one goes back to normal.

Setting the transparent color has no effect on text wrap. A Tight text wrap will still not wrap around the image in Figure 11.59, even though the white background is no longer visible. You can modify this behavior somewhat by editing the wrap points (Wrap Text, Edit Wrap Points), but a rectangular image has only four wrap points, so there's only so much you can do with it. For example, in Figure 11.60, the wrap points have been moved a bit to make the text wrap as tightly as possible around the picture, but it's nowhere near as accurate as with real clip art.

 caution

All instances of that color in the image become transparent, not just the ones around the outer edges of the image. If you were to look very closely at the rabbit in Figure 11.59, you would see that the little white dot in his eye is now transparent too.

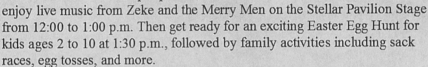 *To make more than one color transparent to remove a picture's background, see "Removing a Picture Background, p. 399.*

Figure 11.59
The JPG image's white background has been made transparent.

Bring the whole family! Once again the Greater Metropolitan Gibson City Board of Realtors is sponsoring the Gibson City Family Easter Egg Hunt and Picnic on April 18th from 12:00 noon to 4:00 p.m. in the Forest Hills City Park.

Bring your own picnic lunch, or purchase a box lunch on-site for $5 per person, and enjoy live music from Zeke and the Merry Men on the Stellar Pavilion Stage from 12:00 to 1:00 p.m. Then get ready for an exciting Easter Egg Hunt for kids ages 2 to 10 at 1:30 p.m., followed by family activities including sack races, egg tosses, and more.

Figure 11.60
Adjust wrap points to make text wrap around the JPG image.

Applying a Border

Usually a border around clip art is unnecessary, and even undesirable. A border runs around the rectangular frame of the image rather than the image itself, so applying a border draws attention to the rectangular frame and disables the ability to wrap text tightly around the image. In some cases, however, a visible border on a clip art image might be useful. For example, if you have applied a fill color to the clip art background that is similar to the page background, a border might help call attention to the image.

> **tip**
>
> A border clings tightly to the rectangular frame of the clip art, and it touches the clip on each side. If you want a little more spacing than that between the clip art image and its border, combine a bordered shape (such as a rectangle) with a borderless clip art image, similar to what's described in "Applying a Fill Effect to Clip Art," earlier in this chapter.

Applying a border to clip art is the same as applying one to a photo. Use the Picture Border button on the Format tab.

➡ *To review applying borders to photos, see "Applying a Picture Border," p. 410.*

For more line choices, choose More Lines from either the Dashes or the Weight submenu (from the Picture Border menu). This opens the Format Picture dialog box. From here, you can use the Line Style controls to select a line type, thickness, color, and so on. The combinations and choices here are more extensive than on the tab's menus (see Figure 11.61).

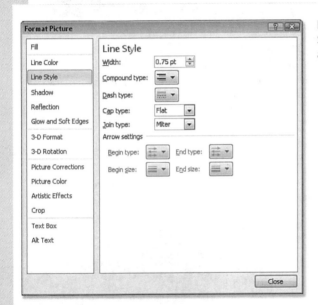

Figure 11.61
Select properties for the border around the clip art.

Applying Shadow Effects

To apply shadow effects, open the Picture Effects button's menu on the Format tab and then select a shadow effect from the Shadow submenu. See "Applying a Shadow Effect" in Chapter 10 for details.

The main difference is that when you're applying a shadow effect to a clip art image with a transparent background, the shadow clings to the image, not to the rectangular frame. If the image has a border around it, the shadow also clings to the border. For example, in Figure 11.62, a shadow has been applied to a clip with a visible border and a transparent background.

If you want the shadow to cling to the rectangular frame rather than to the image, apply a background fill to the image. (Make it the same color as the page background if you don't want it to be obvious.)

Figure 11.62
Shadows cling to the image and to the border.

Rotating Clip Art

You can rotate clip art in either 2-D or 3-D. A 2-D rotation simply spins the clip around a center point; a 3-D rotation alters its proportions so it appears to be shown at an angle. Both types of rotation are covered in Chapter 10.

➡ *To learn about 2-D rotation, see "Rotating a Picture," p. 407.*

➡ *To learn about 3-D rotation, see "Applying 3-D Rotation," p. 409.*

Flipping Clip Art

Flipping creates a mirror image of a clip. From the Format tab, click Rotate and then click Flip Horizontal or Flip Vertical.

One of the most common reasons to flip is to create a mirror-image pair of clips, such as for a masthead or logo. For example, Figure 11.63 shows two copies of a clip—one flipped and one regular.

Flipped copy

Original

Figure 11.63
Flipping an
image mirrors it.

Hop on down to the
Gibson City
Family Easter
Egg Hunt
and Picnic

Editing Clip Art

Because clip art is vector based, you can edit it on a shape-by-shape basis. You can reduce even the most complex clip art to a series of simple shapes, and you can move, resize, delete, recolor, or otherwise modify each of those shapes.

However, you cannot modify a clip in its native format; you must convert it to a Microsoft Drawing object. This is simple to do: Right-click the clip and choose Edit Picture. (If a warning appears, asking you to confirm the action, click Yes.) If the Edit Picture command is not available, try setting the clip art's Wrap Text setting to In Line with Text.

When in Edit Picture mode, the Format tab changes to show drawing tools, and each part of the clip art image becomes a separately selectable and editable object. For example, in Figure 11.64, a carrot has been removed from the picture.

Selection handles around
each individual shape

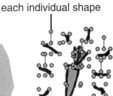

Figure 11.64
A clip art image consists of many individual shapes, all of which you can move and modify.

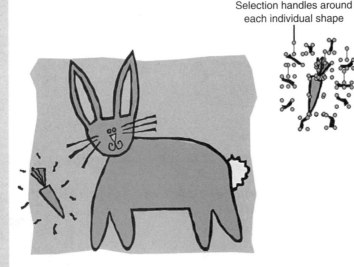

Selecting and Moving Clip Art Shapes

To select a clip art shape, click it. Selection handles appear around it. To select more than one shape at once, hold down Ctrl as you click additional shapes. This can be tricky; if you click a background shape, all the others may be deselected. Watch the mouse pointer for a plus sign, indicating that the item being pointed at will be added to the selection group. Another way is to drag a lasso around the shapes to be selected. To do this, drag an imaginary box that encompasses the pieces you want to select.

To move a clip art shape, position the mouse pointer over it. The pointer turns into a four-headed arrow as you click, and then drag. To delete a shape, select it and press the Delete key on the keyboard.

Recoloring Clip Art Shapes

After you have split apart a clip art image into individual shapes, you can recolor any of the shapes individually. To recolor a shape, select it and use the Shape Fill button on the Format tab. You can choose any solid color or any fill effect (gradient, texture, pattern, and so on). This works just like applying a color fill to any drawn shape.

➡ *For more information about fill effects, see "Formatting Drawn Objects," p. 434.*

Editing Clip Art Shapes

To edit a clip art shape, right-click the shape and choose Edit Points. Black handles appear around the shape. (Zooming in helps you see them better.) Drag these handles to change the shape's contours and dimensions. This is very much like editing the wrap points for an image, as you did earlier in this chapter (see Figure 11.65). When you are finished changing the shape, press Esc to return to normal editing mode.

Figure 11.65
Change a shape by dragging the shape handles that form it.

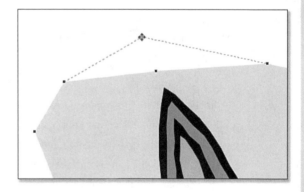

Moving and Resizing a Modified Clip

After you've broken down a piece of clip art into individual lines and shapes, it stays that way; there's no putting it back together again as a real piece of clip art. It's a drawing now, not a clip art image, technically speaking.

You can still move and resize the drawing, but the techniques for doing so are a little different.

When clip art is split into pieces and becomes a drawing, all those pieces are placed on a *drawing canvas*, to keep them together in an orderly way. You can also manually create a drawing canvas on which to draw your own lines and shapes (Insert, Shapes, New Drawing Canvas), but most people do not bother with a canvas unless their drawings are going to be very complex.

➡ *To learn more about drawing canvases, see "Working with the Drawing Canvas," p. 420.*

To enlarge the drawing canvas, position the mouse pointer over the bottom-right corner of the canvas, so the mouse pointer becomes a double-headed arrow, and then drag outward. This does not resize the drawing; it only resizes the canvas. You can also right-click the drawing canvas border and choose Fit to resize the canvas to exactly fit the drawing, or right-click the border and choose Expand to enlarge the drawing canvas slightly.

To change the size of the drawing itself, right-click the frame and choose Scale Drawing. This turns on the scaling feature. You can now drag the border of the frame to resize the drawing within it. To go back to being able to adjust the frame separately from the drawing, right-click the frame again and choose Scale Drawing again to toggle scaling off.

To move the drawing canvas, set Wrap Text (on the Drawing Tools Format tab) to anything except In Line with Text, and then drag the canvas frame as if it were any other graphics object.

To move pieces of the drawing within the drawing canvas, simply drag and drop them. If you want to work with multiple shapes at once, you might find it useful to group them. To do so, first select the pieces to group; then right-click the selection and choose Group, Group. The same skills work here as for lines and shapes that you draw yourself.

Life Outside the Drawing Canvas

A piece of clip art is never quite the same after you convert it to a Microsoft Drawing object, but you can almost get it back to normal by grouping all the pieces and then dragging the item outside the drawing canvas. Follow these steps:

1. In the drawing canvas, drag a lasso around all the pieces of the drawing, selecting them all. Then right-click and choose Group, Group.

2. Select the group object and press Ctrl+C to copy it.

3. Click outside the drawing canvas and press Ctrl+V to paste.

4. Select the drawing canvas and press Delete, deleting the canvas from the document.

If you decide you want the drawing canvas back after all, here's how to get it:

1. Select the drawing and use Cut (Ctrl+X) to cut it to the Clipboard.

2. On the Insert tab, open the drop-down list for the Shapes button and choose New Drawing Canvas. A new drawing canvas appears.

3. Use Paste to paste the drawing into the new canvas.

WORKING WITH CHARTS

Understanding Charts

A *chart* is a graphical representation of numeric data. Charts can summarize data and help people make sense out of it. (Some people call them graphs, and in fact, so did Microsoft up until the 2007 version of Word; the program that was used to create charts was called Microsoft Graph.)

To work with charts in Word, you should have a general grasp of Word's charting vocabulary. Here are some of the key terms to know, many of which are pointed out in Figures 12.1 and 12.2:

- **Data point**—An individual numeric value, represented by a bar, point, column, or pie slice.

- **Data series**—A group of related data points. For example, in Figure 12.1, all the bars of a certain color are a series.

- **Category axis (X axis)**—The horizontal axis of a two-dimensional or three-dimensional chart.

- **Value axis (Y axis)**—The vertical axis of a two-dimensional or three-dimensional chart.

- **Depth axis (Z axis)**—The front-to-back axis of a three-dimensional chart.

- **Legend**—A key that explains which data series each color or pattern represents.

- **Floor**—The bottom of a three-dimensional chart.

- **Walls**—The background of a chart. Three-dimensional charts have back walls and side walls, which you can format separately.

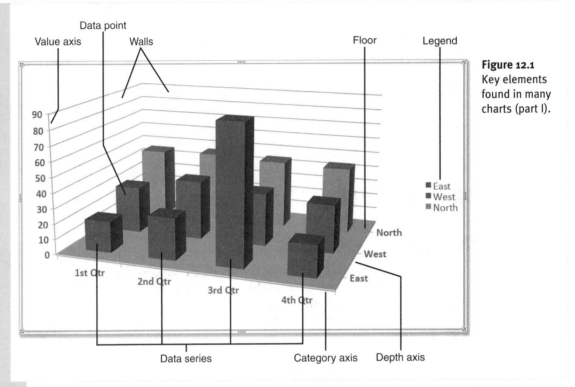

Figure 12.1
Key elements found in many charts (part I).

- **Data labels**—Numeric labels on each data point. A data label can represent the actual value or a percentage.

- **Axis titles**—Explanatory text labels associated with the axes.

- **Data table**—A table containing the values on which the chart is based.

- **Chart title**—A label explaining the overall purpose of the chart.

It is also important to understand the various areas of a chart. Each chart's complete package, including all its auxiliary pieces such as legends and titles, is the *chart area*. Within the chart area is the *plot area*, which contains only the chart and its data table. (Sometimes the chart title is overlaid on top of the plot area, but the chart title is not part of the plot area.) Figure 12.3 shows the chart area and plot area.

Figure 12.2
Key elements
found in many
charts (part II).

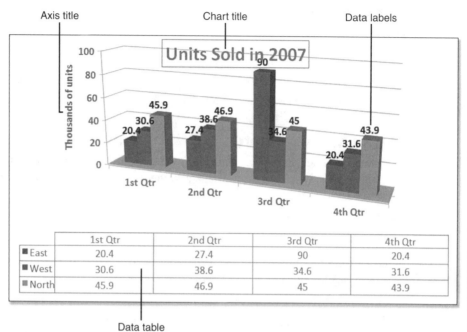

Axis title · Chart title · Data labels

Data table

	1st Qtr	2nd Qtr	3rd Qtr	4th Qtr
■ East	20.4	27.4	90	20.4
■ West	30.6	38.6	34.6	31.6
■ North	45.9	46.9	45	43.9

Figure 12.3
Chart area ver-
sus plot area.

Chart area · Plot area (shaded)

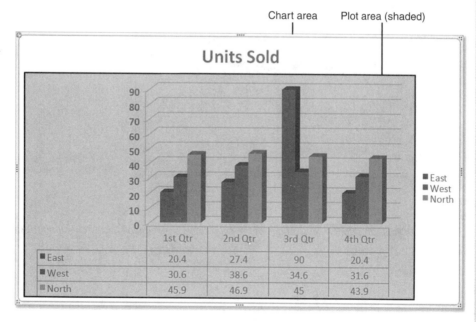

Creating a New Chart

If you create a chart in a native-format Word document, you have full access to the same powerful charting features as you do in Excel and PowerPoint. There is no need to create a chart in Excel and then import it to Word, because the capabilities are the same. Charts created in legacy Word documents (that is, Word 97–2003 format) use Microsoft Graph, the older charting tool.

The following sections review chart creation in both Word 2010 and legacy-format documents.

Creating a Chart in a Word 2010 Document

For maximum power and flexibility, create charts in Word 2010 documents rather than Word 97–2003 ones. This way you can take advantage of the powerful new charting features that Word 2010 offers.

Follow these steps to create a new chart:

1. On the Insert tab, click Chart. The Insert Chart dialog box opens.

2. In the left pane, click the desired chart type (such as Column or Pie). Then in the right pane, click the desired chart subtype (see Figure 12.4).

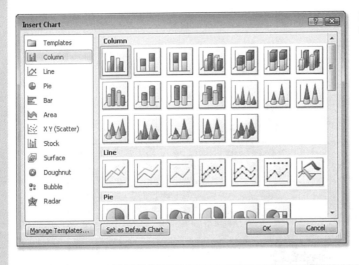

Figure 12.4
Create a new chart.

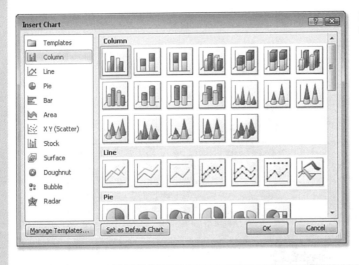 For detailed descriptions of the chart types and subtypes, see "Changing the Chart Type," p. 486.

3. Click OK. Microsoft Excel opens, displaying a sheet containing dummy data for the chart. (Word remains open in its own window, and the two windows are arranged side by side.)

4. Change the data in Excel as needed. Edit both the numbers and the labels.

   You can add or delete rows and columns as needed; the chart automatically reflects them.

    For more information about changing the data range, see "Modifying Chart Data," p. 482.

5. Switch to the Word window to view the chart. (Minimize or close the Excel window if desired, or leave it open for later editing.)

 caution

Don't bring the raw data from Excel to Word; that's awkward, and the charting feature does not accept that very gracefully. Instead, make the chart in Excel using Excel's charting tools, and then copy and paste the chart from Excel into Word. The charting tools are nearly identical between Word and Excel, so you should have no difficulty with them.

Obviously there's a lot more to charting than the simple creation process. You'll probably want to change chart types, format charts, add optional elements such as labels, and so on. You will learn all these things in the rest of this chapter.

Creating a Legacy Chart

Microsoft Graph is the same charting tool found in Word 97 through 2003. The interface has been slightly updated, but the options and features are the same.

In a Word 97–2003 document, follow these steps to create a new chart:

1. On the Insert tab, click Chart. A sample chart appears, with a floating datasheet. The toolbars and menus for the previous version of Excel appear, too (see Figure 12.5).

2. Change the data in the datasheet as needed. Edit both the numbers and the labels. You can also add or delete rows and columns. (To delete a row or column, right-click the row or column heading and press Delete.)

3. When you are finished, click away from the chart or the datasheet to return to Word.

tip

To import data from an Excel worksheet for use in your chart, choose Edit, Import File and browse for an Excel file.

If you prefer the charting tools offered by Microsoft Graph, you are free to continue using them in Word 2010. Here's how:

1. On the Insert tab, click Object. The Object dialog box opens.

2. On the Create New tab, select Microsoft Graph Chart.

3. Click OK.

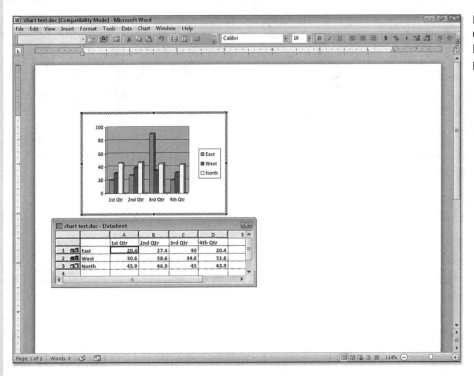

Figure 12.5
Create a new
backward-com-
patible chart.

Working with Chart Templates

Each of the chart types and subtypes that you can select from the Insert Chart dialog box (refer to Figure 12.4) represents a chart template. These templates are built in and cannot be modified.

However, you can create your own chart templates and start new charts based on them. This feature is available only for Word 2010 charting, not in Microsoft Graph.

Creating a Chart Template

To create a chart template, set the chart type, layout, and formatting as desired (as explained in the remainder of this chapter), and then follow these steps:

1. On the Design tab, click Save As Template. The Save Chart Template dialog box opens.

2. Type a name for the template in the File Name box.

3. Click Save.

 note

The default location for storing user-created chart templates if you have Windows XP is Documents and Settings*username*\Application Data\Microsoft\Templates\Charts. Under Windows Vista and Windows 7, it is \Users*username*\AppData\ Roaming\Microsoft\Templates\ Charts. Chart templates have a .crtx extension.

Starting a New Chart Based on a User Template

You can use any of your saved templates as the basis for a new chart, rather than starting with one of the built-in templates.

To start a new chart based on one of your saved templates, follow these steps:

tip

To see a template's name, hover the mouse pointer over it.

1. On the Insert tab, click Chart. The Insert Chart dialog box opens (refer to Figure 12.4).

2. Click Templates. The My Templates list appears.

3. Click the desired template (see Figure 12.6).

Figure 12.6
Select a stored user template.

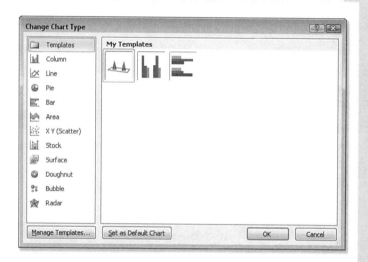

4. Click OK to start a new chart based on the chosen template.

Managing Stored Chart Templates

You can modify or delete user-created chart templates at any time. To work with them, from the Insert tab, click Chart. Then from the Insert Chart dialog box, click Manage Templates.

A file management window opens showing the folder containing the user-created charts. From here you can do the following:

- **Rename a template**—Right-click it and choose Rename. Then type the new name and press Enter.

- **Delete a template**—Click it and press Delete, or right-click it and choose Delete.

- **Back up your user templates**—Drag and drop the templates to another location or disk. To ensure that you are copying rather than moving, hold down Ctrl as you drag.

Modifying Chart Data

The whole point of a chart is to present data, so obviously the most important thing to get right in a chart is to show the correct numeric values. If your numbers aren't right, all the formatting in the world can't save you.

Editing the Data

When you create a chart, an Excel window opens in which you can enter the data. That Excel data is an embedded datasheet in your Word document, and it's known as the *data source*.

To change the numbers or labels in the chart, select the chart, and then on the Design tab, click Edit Data. The datasheet opens in an Excel window (see Figure 12.7). You might want to maximize the Excel window, as shown in Figure 12.7, for a better view.

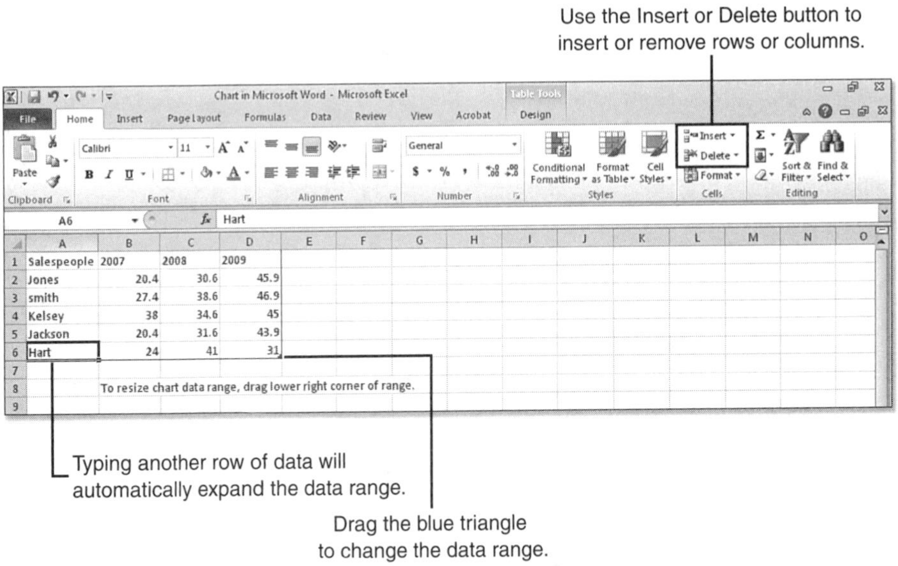

Use the Insert or Delete button to
insert or remove rows or columns.

Figure 12.7
Edit the data-sheet.

Typing another row of data will
automatically expand the data range.

Drag the blue triangle
to change the data range.

To make a change, click a cell and then type a replacement value and press Enter, just like you would in any spreadsheet.

You can also add and delete rows and columns from the sheet:

- To add a row at the bottom of the list or a column at the right, click in the first blank row or column and type new entries. The data range expands automatically.

- To add a row or column between existing rows or columns, select the row where the new row should appear or the column where the new column should appear, and then click Insert on the Home tab.

- To delete a row or column, select it by clicking its letter or number, and then on the Home tab, click Delete.

- To hide a row or column, select it, and then right-click it and choose Hide.

In the next section, you will learn how to use the Hidden and Empty Cell Settings dialog box to control what happens to a hidden row or column. It can be made to be included in the chart or not, as you prefer. Hiding a row or column is a good alternative to deleting it entirely if you think you might want to display it in the chart later. Another way to keep data in a datasheet but exclude it from the chart is to change the data range, as you'll learn next.

Changing the Charted Data Range

Notice in Figure 12.7 that a blue box surrounds the data range, and a blue triangle appears in the bottom-right corner of the last cell in the range. You can drag that triangle to expand or constrict the range to be included, as long as the range is a contiguous block on the spreadsheet.

Sometimes, however, you might want to change a chart so that it does not show all the data you have entered in the datasheet. For example, suppose you want to exclude a certain series from the chart temporarily, print a copy, and then include that series again. You don't want to delete the data altogether because you'll need it again later. In cases like this, you adjust the data range, telling Word to pull a subset of the entered data for the chart.

If you just want to redefine a smaller contiguous range, drag the blue triangle so that the range excludes some of the rows at the bottom or some of the columns at the right.

If you need more sophisticated range editing, follow these steps:

1. Click the chart to select it.

2. Display the Design tab, and click Select Data. The Excel window appears, along with the Select Data Source dialog box (see Figure 12.8).

3. Adjust the series (columns) as needed:

   - To redefine the overall range for the chart (provided that the desired range is in one contiguous block in the sheet), click in the Chart Data Range box, and then drag across the range and press Enter.

   - To remove a certain series from the chart, click its name in the Legend Entries (Series) box and click Remove.

   - To re-add a series that you've removed, click the Add button in the dialog box. Then click on the column heading in the worksheet and press Enter.

   - To reorder the series, click a series name in the dialog box and then click the Up or Down arrow button.

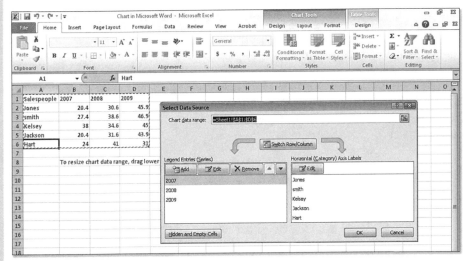

Figure 12.8
Change the
range included
in the chart.

4. If needed, change the range from which the category labels are being pulled by doing the following:

   a. In the Horizontal (Category) Axis Labels section, click Edit. The Axis Labels dialog box opens.

   b. On the worksheet, drag across the range containing the labels.

   c. Click OK in the dialog box, or press Enter.

5. Specify how to deal with hidden and empty cells by doing the following:

   a. Click the Hidden and Empty Cells button. The Hidden and Empty Cell Settings dialog box opens.

   b. Choose how to show empty cells: as gaps, as zero, or spanned with a line.

   c. Mark or clear the Show Data in Hidden Rows and Columns check box.

   d. Click OK.

6. Click OK. The datasheet becomes available for manual edits. Make any additional changes to it as desired, and then close it and return to the chart in Word.

Switching Between Rows and Columns

By default, a chart displays datasheet rows as series and datasheet columns as categories. You can flip this rather easily, though, by clicking the Switch Row/Column button on the Design tab.

Controlling How the Chart and Document Interact

A chart is an object, in the same way that a photo, clip art image, or diagram is an object. Therefore, you can make it interact with the document text in all the standard ways, such as setting its positioning and text wrap. These settings were covered in detail in Chapter 10, "Working with Photos," but the basics are briefly repeated here for convenience.

Setting Text Wrapping

Text wrapping controls how the document text interacts with the chart. Text wrapping for a chart is identical to that for a picture:

1. Select the chart.

2. On the Format tab, click Wrap Text. A menu of text wrap choices appears.

3. Click the desired text wrap setting.

> *For detailed descriptions of text wrapping choices and their effects on the surrounding text, see "Setting Text Wrap," p. 386.*

Positioning a Chart

Position presets are available for charts, the same as for other graphics objects. These presets set the chart frame to precise relative or absolute positioning within the document page.

To apply a position preset to a chart, follow these steps:

1. Select the chart.

2. On the Format tab, click the Position button, and click one of the position presets.

To set an exact position for the chart, follow these steps:

1. Select the chart.

2. On the Format tab, click the Position button and then click More Layout Options. The Layout dialog box opens.

3. On the Position tab, set the desired layout. You can choose layout by Alignment, by Book Layout, or by Absolute Position.

4. Set any options desired, such as Move Object with Text or Lock Anchor (see Figure 12.9).

5. Click OK to accept the new position setting.

> **note**
>
> If no options are available on the Position tab, set the text wrapping to something other than In Line with Text.

> *For more detailed descriptions of the position choices, see "Setting Picture Position," p. 388.*

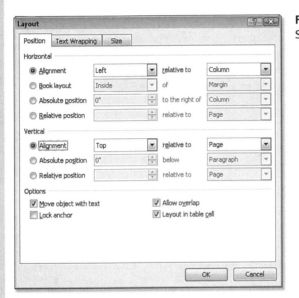

Figure 12.9
Select a position preset.

Changing the Chart Type

The chart's type is the single most important design setting you can apply to it. The same data can convey different messages when presented using different chart types. For example, if you want to show how each person's work contributes to the whole, a pie chart is ideal. If you would rather concentrate on the numeric value of each contribution, you might prefer a bar or column chart.

To change the chart type, follow these steps:

1. Select the chart.

2. On the Design tab, click Change Chart Type. The Change Chart Type dialog box opens. It is just like the Insert Chart dialog box shown in Figure 12.4, except for the name.

3. Select the desired category in the left pane, or scroll through the list in the right pane to browse the types. You'll find more details in Table 12.1.

4. Select the desired chart type in the right pane.

5. Click OK to change to the new chart type.

Word 2010 offers 11 chart categories, and several types within each category. The categories are listed in Table 12.1.

 caution

Each chart type and subtype is designed to serve a specific purpose. Choosing an inappropriate chart type can prevent your message from getting across to your audience, and in some cases it can actually make the data misleading or incomprehensible. For example, if you change a multiseries bar chart to a pie chart, you lose all the data except the first series because pie charts are single-series charts by definition.

Table 12.1   Chart Categories

Category	Sample	Notes
Column		The default chart type; useful for measuring one numeric value against another. Multiple data series are handled via different bar colors. There are several types of column charts, and each presents a different look at the data. For example, a stacked column chart makes each bar into a mini pie chart, showing how each series contributes to the total height of the bar.
Line		Represents each numeric value as a point and connects the points within a series with a line. Multiple series are handled via different line colors and styles.
Pie		Shows how the parts contribute to the whole with- out focusing on the actual numeric values. Most types of pie charts are single-series only.
Bar		Identical to the column chart type, except it's horizontal.
Area		Similar to a line chart, except the space under the line is filled in. When multiple series are shown, a larger area in front can potentiallytially obscure a smaller area behind it, so care must be taken in arranging the series and applying 3-D effects.
X Y (Scatter)		Represents each numeric value as a data point but does not necessarily connect them (although some types do draw lines). This enables you to spot trends in the data, such as clusters of points in a certain area. For example, suppose you are plotting hours studied (X axis) and test scores (Y axis). Each data point represents a student's score, and you can observe whether, generally speaking, there is a correlation between higher scores and more hours of study.
Stock		Represents financial information such as stock prices. This type of chart is useful primarily for showing high-low-close-open data for a stock or other tradable commodity.
Surface		A 3-D sheet, such as what might be created if you stretched a canvas over the tops of a 3-D column chart. It is useful for finding the highest and lowest points among intersecting sets of data. For example, if your data represents the profit made on certain sizes of certain products, you could see which product/size combination resulted in the greatest profit.
Doughnut		Very much like a pie chart, except it can hold multiple series, each in a concentric ring of the doughnut. For example, you could show how each member of a sales team contributed to the total sales in each of several months.
Bubble		Similar to a scatter chart, except it adds an additional element: bubble size. You might use a bubble chart to show how many users bought certain products on certain days, for example. Days might be the horizontal axis (category), products the vertical axis, and the bubble size might represent the number of users.
Radar		Shows changes in data of frequency relative to a center point. Lines connect the values in the same data series.

Each chart type has at least 2 subtypes to choose from, and some have up to 19 subtypes. Don't let them overwhelm you, though; even though there are many subtypes, they fall into predictable categories.

Here are some of the major ways in which the chart subtypes can be differentiated:

- **2-D vs. 3-D style**—Some types show the shapes as flat 2-D objects; others show them as 3-D with sides and tops. The chart categories with available 3-D types are column, line, pie, bar, area, surface, and bubble.

- **Clustered, stacked, or 3-D**—When there are multiple series in a bar, column, or area chart, some types cluster the series, some stack them on a single bar (or other shape), and some add a third axis to the chart (front-to-back) and place each series on a separate axis.

- **Different shapes**—For bar and column charts, you can choose rectangular bars, cylinders, cones, or pyramids.

- **Regular or 100 percent**—For bar and column charts, a stacked bar can be regular (that is, the bar height represents the sum of the values), or each bar can be the same height (100 percent). A 100 percent bar is essentially a rectangular pie chart; it does not represent actual values, but rather the contribution of each series toward the whole.

- **Regular or exploded**—Pie and doughnut charts can optionally have one or more pieces set apart from the rest of the chart (exploded) to emphasize them.

- **Points, lines, or both**—A scatter chart can show data points without lines, lines without data points, or both.

- **Curved or straight lines**—When a scatter chart has lines, the line segments can be either curved or straight.

- **Wireframe or filled**—Radar and surface charts can appear with each series as a different color fill, or they can appear in wireframe view (with transparency set for each series).

Working with Chart Elements

After choosing an appropriate chart type and subtype, the next task is to decide which additional elements to include in the chart. In other words, besides the data points, what do you want your chart to include? Possibilities include legends, walls, floors, gridlines, titles, data labels, and so on. Each of these can be displayed/hidden, positioned, and formatted.

Applying a Chart Layout

Chart layouts are preset combinations of chart elements that serve as shortcuts to adding and formatting these elements. For example, one of the chart layouts places the legend across the top, adds data labels, removes the walls and floors, removes the gridlines, and adds a chart title.

 note

The main problem with chart layouts is that there aren't very many of them and you can't create your own. So take them for what they're worth, but you'll probably need to do some additional tweaking after applying one.

To apply a chart layout, select the chart and then select a layout from the Chart Layouts group on the Design tab (see Figure 12.10).

Click a layout...

Figure 12.10
Apply a chart layout to the chart.

...or click here for more choices.

Adding a Chart Title

A *chart title* is a text box that floats above the chart and describes its purpose. The chart title can be placed in either of two locations: Centered Overlay (which places the title within the chart's plot area) or Above Chart (which places the title above the plot area). Figure 12.11 shows the difference.

Figure 12.11
Centered Overlay (top) versus Above Chart (bottom) for chart title placement.

To create a chart title, first place the box, and then edit the placeholder text within it:

1. Select the chart.

2. On the Layout tab, click Chart Title. A menu appears.

3. Click Centered Overlay Title or Above Chart. The title appears in the chosen location.

 note

You cannot change the chart title box's size, but if you increase or decrease the font size, the box grows or shrinks automatically.

4. Click in the chart title's text box, delete the placeholder text, and type your own text.

5. To format the chart title's frame, choose More Title Options from the Chart Title menu and use the Format Chart Title dialog box to apply your selections. Click Close when you're finished.

6. To format the text in the chart title, select the text and then use the Home tab's controls in the Font group.

➡ *For detailed descriptions of the options in the Format Chart Title dialog box, see "Formatting Individual Chart Elements," p. 507.*

➡ *For more information about text formatting with the Home tab, see "Changing Text Font, Size, and Color," p. 145.*

Working with Legends

The *legend* is the key that explains what each of the colors or patterns represents in a multiseries chart. It's critical to understanding the chart unless some other means of explanation is provided (as in a data table, or in individual labels for each pie slice or bar).

You can place the legend either outside or inside of the chart's plot area, and you can place it on any of the four sides or in the top-right corner. The Legend menu offers some presets, but you can also choose to display the Format Legend dialog box for additional options.

To turn off the legend or select one of the presets, follow these steps:

1. Select the chart.

2. On the Layout tab, click Legend. A menu appears.

3. Select one of the presets on the menu, or select None.

Not all of the possible combinations of legend position are represented by the presets. To specify the desired position and choose whether it should overlap the chart, follow these steps:

1. Select the chart.

2. On the Layout tab, click Legend. A menu appears.

3. Click More Legend Options. The Format Legend dialog box opens (see Figure 12.12).

4. Select a legend position.

5. If you want the legend outside the plot area, mark the Show the Legend Without Overlapping the Chart check box. Otherwise, clear the check box to make the legend overlap the chart.

6. To format the legend box's frame, use the Format Legend dialog box to apply your selections for fill, line, shadow, and so on.

> ➡ *For detailed descriptions of the options in the Format Legend dialog box, see "Formatting Individual Chart Elements," p. 507.*

7. Click Close.

8. To format the text in the legend, select the text and then use the Home tab's controls in the Font group.

> ➡ *For more information about text formatting with the Home tab, see "Changing the Text Font, Size, and Color," p. 145.*

Figure 12.12
Select the legend position.

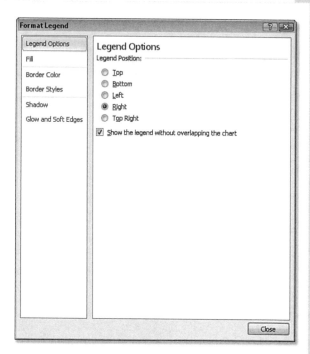

Using Data Labels

You can make data labels appear on (or near) each data point. A data label can contain any combination of these:

- The series name (duplicated from the legend, if present)

- The category name (duplicated from the category axis labels, if present)

- The numeric value represented by the data point

- The percentage of the whole that the data point represents (only on pies, doughnuts, and 100 percent bars)

Data labels can be applied to any chart type, but they're especially useful on pies, and in fact they are often used as an alternative to a legend, as in Figure 12.13. This works especially well when presenting charts in black and white because then the audience does not have to match up the colors or patterns of the slices to the legend key. It makes the meaning of each slice or point more obvious.

Figure 12.13
Data labels can substitute for a legend.

To apply data labels, you can choose from one of the presets or define your own labels.

The preset data labels use the data point values only and place them in your choice of locations. To use one of the presets, do this:

1. Select the chart. (Optional: To affect only a certain data series or data point, select it.)

   ➡ *To learn how to select only a certain data series or data point, see "Selecting Chart Elements," p. 507.*

2. On the Layout tab, click Data Labels.

3. Select one of the presets from the menu. (The menu varies somewhat depending on the chart type.)

To use other data in the labels, such as the series name, category name, or percentage, you must use the Format Data Labels dialog box. Follow these steps:

1. Select the chart. (Optional: To affect only a certain data series or data point, select it.)

2. On the Layout tab, click Data Labels.

3. On the menu, select More Data Label Options. The Format Data Labels dialog box opens (see Figure 12.14).

4. In the Label Contains section, mark or clear check boxes for the types of information to appear.

5. In the Label Position section, select a position for the label.

6. (Optional) Mark the Include Legend Key in Label check box, and then choose a separator character for it. The legend key indicates which series a value belongs to.

7. Click Close to apply the new settings.

Figure 12.14
Customize the data labels for the chart.

Applying Axis Titles

Axis titles are text labels that appear on the axes to indicate what they represent. For example, a chart might have a value axis of 0 to 100, but what does that represent? Dollars? Millions of dollars? Units sold? Errors recorded? An axis title can help clarify what's being measured. Figure 12.15 shows a 3-D chart with three axes, all with titles.

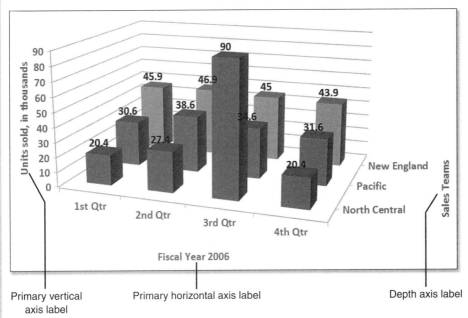

Figure 12.15
Add axis titles
where needed
to clarify the
meaning of the
data.

Each of the three dimensions of a chart (or two dimensions, depending on the chart) has its own separate setting for axis titles. On the Layout tab, click Axis Titles to open a menu, and then select from the submenu for the desired axis, choosing either preset or custom settings. For example, in Figure 12.16, the choices for the primary vertical axis appear.

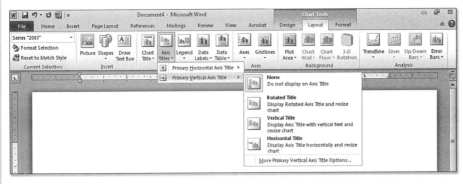

Figure 12.16
Different pre-
sets are avail-
able for each of
the axis titles.

As you can see in Figure 12.16, for vertical axes you can choose whether you want the text to appear Rotated, Vertical, or Horizontal. Rotated text actually rotates each letter 90 degrees, whereas Vertical text makes the letters appear normally oriented but runs them vertically (stacked). In Figure 12.15, both the primary vertical axis label and the depth axis label are rotated.

Modifying Axis Properties

Several types of modifications are available for the various axes in a chart. For example, you can make the axis scale run in a different direction (for example, right-to-left instead of the default left-to-right on a horizontal axis), and you can turn off the text on an axis. For numeric axes, you can also add automatic "thousands" or "millions" labels.

Applying an Axis Preset

For some of the most popular changes, presets are available. To change an axis's properties using presets, follow these steps:

1. Select the chart.

2. From the Layout tab, click Axes. A menu opens listing the various axes available in the current chart.

3. Point to an axis on the menu to display its submenu (see Figure 12.17) and choose a setting.

Figure 12.17
Select a preset for the desired axis.

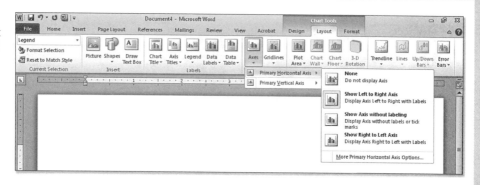

Adjusting the Axis Scale

One of the most dramatic ways you can change an audience's interpretation of a chart is by adjusting the axis scale. For example, in Figure 12.18, both the charts use the same data but different vertical axis scales. In the top chart, the difference between bars appears minimal, but in the bottom chart, it's dramatic.

Word is actually pretty smart about adjusting the axis scale automatically; the chart at the bottom in Figure 12.18 shows the default for this data in Word. In cases where Word does not correctly deduce what you want, however, you can make manual changes.

To adjust the axis scale, follow these steps:

1. Select the chart.

2. From the Layout tab, click Axes. A menu opens, listing the various axes available in the current chart.

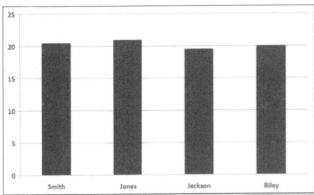

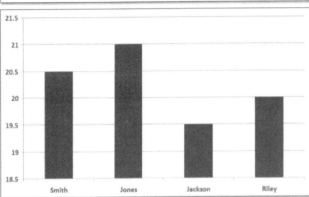

Figure 12.18
Set the desired values for an axis's scale to modify the chart's appearance.

3. Point to the desired axis, and then choose the More command for it. For example, for the primary vertical axis, choose More Primary Vertical Axis Options. The Format Axis dialog box opens.

4. To change the range of numbers represented on the axis, click Fixed for Minimum, Maximum, or both, and then enter the desired value(s). For example, in Figure 12.19, the minimum value on the axis is set to 10 and the maximum to 25.

5. To change the unit of measure shown on the axis (with numbers and gridlines), click Fixed next to Major Unit, Minor Unit, or both, and then enter the desired value(s).

6. (Optional) To reverse the scale, mark the Values in Reverse Order check box.

7. (Optional) To use a logarithmic scale, mark the Logarithmic Scale check box and then enter a Base setting.

8. (Optional) To change the unit of display on the axis, open the Display Units list and choose a unit (for example, Thousands or Millions).

 note

Specifying a unit is somewhat like adding an axis label, except that in addition to adding the label for the unit, it converts the numbers on the scale. For example, if your scale is currently 0, 1000, 2000, 3000, and so on, and you set the Display Units to Thousands, the scale changes to 0, 1, 2, 3.

Figure 12.19
Adjust the axis scale's minimum and maximum values, as well as major and minor units.

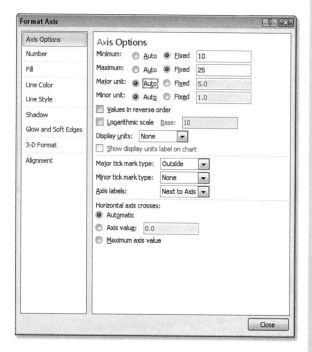

9. (Optional) Use the Major Tick Mark Type and Minor Tick Mark Type settings to change the way tick marks appear on the chart for the major and minor units. This does not affect the gridlines, only the small marks that appear on the axis line.

10. (Optional) In the Horizontal Axis Crosses section, choose Axis Value and then specify where the vertical and horizontal axes will meet. This setting makes it possible to have a chart that has data on both sides of the horizontal axis, as in Figure 12.20.

11. Click Close when you are finished.

Changing the Axis Number Type

On axes that contain numeric values, you can indicate what type of number formatting to use. For example, the numbers can appear as currency (with dollar signs), as percentages, or as any of several other number types.

To set the number type, follow these steps:

1. Select the axis.

2. On the Format tab, in the Current Selection group, click Format Selection. (Alternatively, right-click the axis and choose Format Axis.) The Format Axis dialog box opens.

   If you have selected the wrong chart area, you can select the correct area from the drop-down list in the Current Selection group.

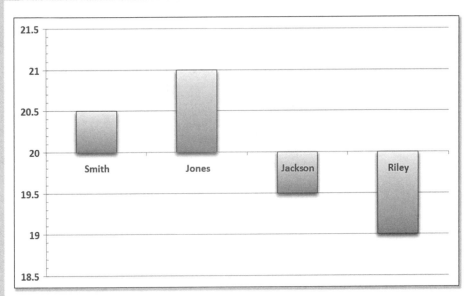

Figure 12.20
When the Horizontal Axis Crosses value is set to 20, values that are less than 20 hang down below the horizontal axis.

3. Click Number. The Number options appear.

4. On the Category list, select the type of number formatting you want.

5. Adjust the settings that appear for the chosen category. For example, for currency you can set the number of decimal places and the currency symbol.

6. Click Close.

Using Gridlines

Gridlines are horizontal or vertical lines that appear on the chart's walls to help the audience's eyes track across from the values on the axes to the data points.

Word uses major horizontal gridlines by default in most chart types. The positioning of these gridlines is determined by the Major Units measurement set in the preceding section, in the Format Axis dialog box. The gridlines can be turned on/off, and you can optionally turn on/off minor horizontal gridlines or vertical gridlines.

To toggle gridlines on or off, use the presets from the Gridlines button on the Layout tab. As you can see in Figure 12.21, vertical and horizontal gridlines have separate submenus, on which you can toggle major and minor lines.

To control the type of gridlines, choose the "More" option from the menu. (For example, in Figure 12.21, choose More Primary Horizontal Gridlines Options.) Then in the Format Gridlines dialog box (see Figure 12.22), set the properties for the line.

 tip

There are other ways to format gridlines, which you will learn about in "Formatting Individual Chart Elements" later in this chapter. On the Format tab, you can use the Shape Styles group to apply shape outlines and effects that change the gridline color, thickness, shadow, and more.

Figure 12.21
Toggle major or minor gridlines on/off for vertical and horizontal axes.

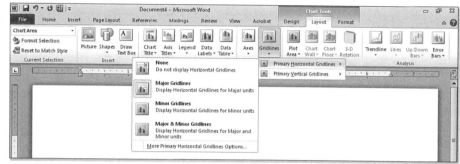

Figure 12.22
Format the gridlines by specifying a line thickness here.

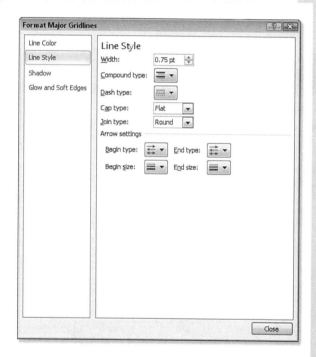

Adding Trendlines

A *trendline* is a line superimposed over a two-dimensional chart (usually a scatter chart) that helps express the relationship between a pair of values. Trendlines are often used in statistics and scientific research to show overall trends of relationship between cause and effect.

To understand the value of a trendline, let's look at an example. Suppose a coach asked his basketball players to practice shooting free throws as many hours a day as they could for a one-week period. Different students approached this assignment with varying degrees of dedication; some players did not practice at all, whereas others practiced as much as 3 1/2 hours per day. At the end of the week, each player made 100 free-throw attempts and recorded his or her number of successes.

To prove a positive relationship between practicing and success, the coach plotted this data in a Word chart. The relationship is not mathematically perfect because we're dealing with humans, not machines. However, an overall trend is apparent (see Figure 12.23).

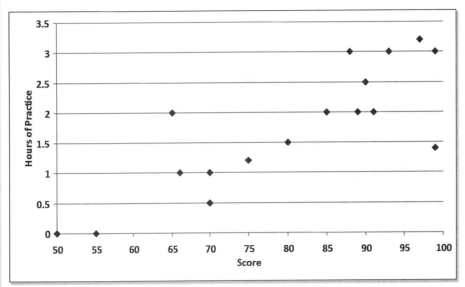

Figure 12.23
This scatter chart shows the relationship between two variables.

To quantify this trend, add a trendline to the chart. The simplest and most straightforward type of trendline is a linear one (a straight line). In Figure 12.24, a linear trendline has been applied. The trendline helps the data analysis in two ways. First, the line itself shows where the expected score will be for any number of hours of practice (or fractions thereof). Second, it shows a statistical equation that represents the relationship. In the formula shown in Figure 12.24, for example, you could plug in a number of practice hours for Y and then solve for X to determine the expected score.

To add a trendline, follow these steps:

1. Select the data series for which you want to add a trendline.

2. On the Layout tab, click Trendline.

3. On the Trendline menu, select the desired trendline type. (If you are not sure what type you want, choose Linear Trendline.)

Figure 12.24
Adding a linear
trendline to
the chart helps
quantify the
relationship.

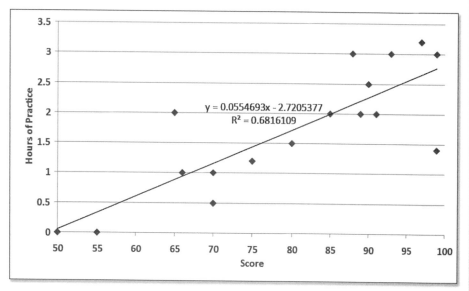

If you do not select the data series in step 1, and if it is a multiseries chart, a dialog box prompts you to select the series to receive the trendline. Make your selection and click OK. For more trendline options, choose More Trendline Options in step 3, and select the series to which they apply if prompted. Then in the Format Trendline dialog box, shown in Figure 12.25, change any of these options:

- **Trend/Regression Type**—Select a type here. More types are available in this box than were on the Trendline menu. Table 12.2 lists the trendline types.

- **Trendline Name**—This is useful when you have more than one trendline per chart. Automatic makes the trendline name the same as the data series name; Custom lets you enter a new name of your choosing.

- **Forecast**—This lets you extend the trendline forward or backward to predict values that are outside the data range.

- **Set Intercept**—This changes the tilt of the trendline so that its left end points to a different number on the vertical axis.

- **Display Equation on Chart**—This toggles the equation on/off.

- **Display R-Squared Value on Chart**—The R-squared value is a measurement of the reliability of the equation in predicting the outcome. Statisticians appreciate it, but most people don't know what it is. Toggle it on/off here.

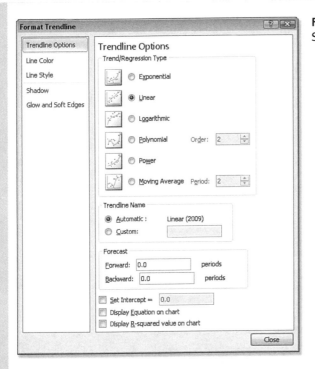

Figure 12.25
Set trendline options.

Table 12.2 Trendline Types

Trend/Regression Type	Useful For...
Exponential	Data that is increasing or decreasing at an accelerating or decelerating rate. Cannot be used with zero or negative data.
Linear	Data that is increasing or decreasing at a relatively steady rate.
Logarithmic	Data that rapidly increases or decreases and then levels out.
Polynomial	Data that fluctuates between high and low values.
Power	Data that increases or decreases at a constant rate. Cannot be used with zero or negative data.
Moving Average	Data that contains interim fluctuations that should be discounted when determining the trend overall.

Adding Error Bars

When sampling a population for research purposes, how can you be certain that you didn't get unusual data? For example, what about the basketball player who is naturally so good at free throws that he can shoot 90 percent without practice? With a small sample, you can't be sure that your data isn't being skewed by unusual cases, but as the sample size grows, so does your confidence in your results.

Even though the formula from the trendline in the preceding section can provide a prediction of a value, in reality that value may be off. The actual value might turn out to be higher or lower than that. For example, what if someone practices free throws for 1.5 hours? The chart in Figure 12.24 indicates that the expected score would be somewhere around 77, but that's just a guess. The amount by which a guess could be off—in either direction—is its *margin of error*. That margin of error is shown on a chart by using *error bars*.

For example, in Figure 12.26, the margin of error for each data point appears to be about 3 points horizontally and 1 hour vertically. In other words, given a player's number of hours practicing, his score could have been 3 points higher or lower, and given a player's score, his practice time could have been 1 hour more or less.

The amount of certainty in the results is described as the *amount of error*. In other words, how confident are we that, given a player's practice time, we can predict his score within a certain margin of error? Are we 90 percent confident? 95 percent? As the desired confidence level goes up, so does the margin of error required to achieve it, and the point spread grows.

 note

You can use error bars on area, bar, column, line, scatter, and bubble charts.

 caution

Don't confuse margin of error with amount of error; they're two different things. The margin of error is the point spread. The amount of error is the confidence level that the point spread is accurate.

Figure 12.26
Error lines show the range of statistically probable values if the data were resampled.

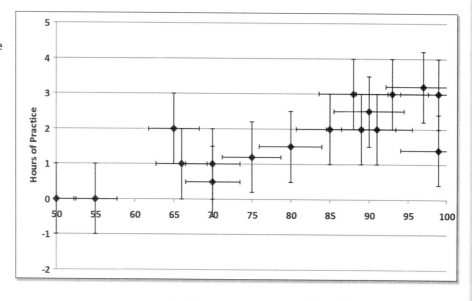

Amount of error can be measured in several ways: by standard error, standard deviation, or a specific percentage. We won't get into the differences between these calculation methods here—that's something for a college-level Statistics course to delve into—but let's assume you know which method you want to use. If you don't, go with a fixed percentage, because that's the easiest to understand.

To apply error lines to a chart, do this:

1. Select the data series for which you want to add an error bar.

2. On the Layout tab, click Error Bars. A menu appears.

3. On the menu, select the calculation type for amount of error:

   ■ Error Bars with Standard Error

   ■ Error Bars with Percentage (by default 5 percent error, or 95 percent confidence)

   ■ Error Bars with Standard Deviation (by default 1 standard deviation)

If you did not select a series in step 1, a dialog box opens from which you can choose a data series (if it is a multiseries chart). Make your selection and click OK to continue. If you do not see the dialog box, choose More Error Bars Options.

To fine-tune the error bars, click Error Bars again and choose More Error Bars Options. Then in the Format Error Bars dialog box, set the error amount desired. You can enter a certain percentage, fixed value, or number of standard deviations (see Figure 12.27).

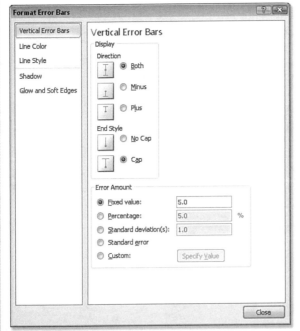

Figure 12.27
Fine-tune the amount of error to be expressed in the error bars and the method by which it will be calculated.

Adding Up/Down Bars

Up/down bars are specific to stock charts. They are filled rectangles that run between the open and close value, as in Figure 12.28. When the open value is higher, the bar is dark; when the close value is higher, the bar is light. Up/down bars let you see at a glance the overall change in the stock that day, disregarding the fluctuations that occurred throughout the trading day. For example, you can see in Figure 12.28 that on 1/8/2007, the stock's price fluctuated a great deal (by nearly $5), but the net loss was only about 50 cents from opening to closing.

Figure 12.28
Up/down bars make the fluctuation between the high and the close values more obvious.

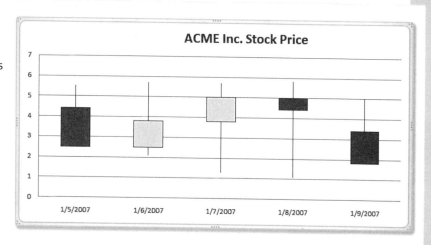

To turn up/down bars on or off, click Up/Down Bars on the Layout tab and choose Up/Down Bars from the menu that appears.

Adding and Formatting a Data Table

A chart does a nice job of summarizing data, but sometimes it's useful to see the original data in addition to the chart. You can copy and paste the data from the Excel sheet into the document as a table below the chart, but it's much easier to simply turn on the display of a *data table*. A data table repeats the data on which the chart is based, as in Figure 12.29.

Optionally, you can set a data table to show legend keys, as in Figure 12.28, or simply show the data. If you display the legend keys, the legend itself becomes superfluous and can be removed if desired.

To turn on/off the data table, follow these steps:

1. Select the chart.

2. On the Layout tab, click Data Table.

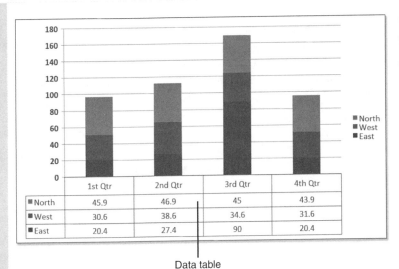

Data table

3. On the Data Table menu, choose one of the following options:

- None

- Show Data Table

- Show Data Table with Legend Keys

In the data table's options, you can choose which borders should be visible in the data table. From the Data Table menu, choose More Data Table Options, and then clear the check boxes for the borders to hide: Horizontal, Vertical, or Outline.

Applying Chart Styles

The Chart Styles list on the Design tab applies colors from the current color theme to the chart in various combinations and with various effects (see Figure 12.30).

Chart Styles do *not* change the color set (color theme). The colors for the entire document are set on the Page Layout tab, as you learned in Chapter 6, "Creating and Applying Styles and Themes." Chart Styles simply combine the color placeholders defined by the theme in different ways. For example, some Chart Styles use the same theme color for all the bars, lines, or slices in a chart, but in different tints, whereas others use different colors from the theme for each item.

To change the theme colors, see "Working with Themes," p. 246.

Figure 12.30
Apply the theme's colors to the chart in different ways with Chart Styles.

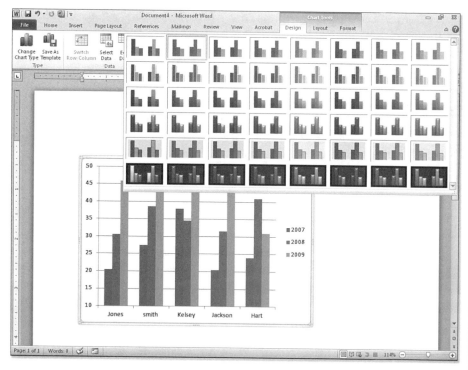

Formatting Individual Chart Elements

Now let's look at the formatting options available for individual pieces of the chart—data series, data points, legends, titles, and so on. Each of these has its own Format dialog box. Some of the options in this dialog box do not change no matter what type of element; others are unique to a particular element.

Selecting Chart Elements

Each chart element can be separately formatted, and many of them have special options you can set depending on the element type. We'll look at some of these in the remainder of this chapter. However, before you can format a chart element, you must select it.

Clicking on an element is one way to select it. Hover the mouse pointer over an element, and wait for a ScreenTip to appear to make sure you are in the right spot (see Figure 12.31). Then click to select the element.

Some elements can be selected either individually or as part of a group. For example, you can select a group of bars in the same series in a bar chart either together or separately. When you click once on such items, the entire group becomes selected; click again on the same item to select only that one object. You can tell when an element is selected because a rectangular box appears around it. When a data series is selected, a separate rectangular box appears around each bar (or other shape).

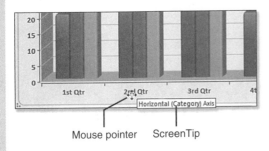

Figure 12.31
To select a chart element, position the mouse pointer over it and click.

Mouse pointer   ScreenTip

It can be difficult to tell what you are clicking when several elements are adjacent or overlapping, so Word provides an alternate method of selection. On the Format or Layout tab, in the Current Selection group, a drop-down list is available. Choose the desired element from that list to select it (see Figure 12.32).

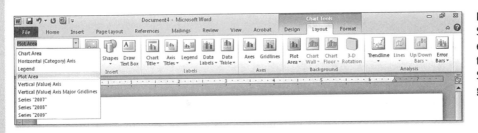

Figure 12.32
Select chart elements from the Current Selection group's list.

Clearing Manually Applied Formatting

Word's charting dialog boxes are *nonmodal*, which means they can stay open indefinitely; their changes are applied immediately, and you don't have to close the dialog box to continue working on the document. Although this is handy, it's all too easy to make an unintended formatting change.

To clear the formatting applied to a chart element, select it and then, on the Format tab, click Reset to Match Style. This strips off the manually applied formatting from that element, returning it to whatever appearance is specified by the chart style that has been applied.

Applying a Shape Style

Shape Styles are presets that you can apply to individual elements of the chart, such as data series, data points, legends, the plot area, the chart area, and so on. A Shape Style applies a combination of fill color, outline color, and effects (such as bevels, shadows, or reflection).

To apply a Shape Style:

1. Select an element of the chart, as you learned in a preceding section.

2. Open the drop-down list in the Shape Styles group of the Format tab and click the desired style (see Figure 12.33).

Applying Shape Outlines and Fills

> **note**
> Like the overall Chart Styles on the Design tab, the Shape Styles use the theme colors in various combinations. If you need to change the theme colors, do so from the Page Layout tab, as described in "Working with Themes" in Chapter 6.

The Shape Styles group on the Format tab contains Shape Fill and Shape Outline drop-down lists, from which you can apply manual formatting to the selected chart element. These work the same as with drawn lines and shapes, which Chapter 11, "Working with Drawings, WordArt, and Clip Art," covered in detail.

➡ *To learn about applying fill and outline formatting, see "Formatting Drawn Objects," p. 434.*

Click a shape style.

Figure 12.33
Apply Shape Styles to individual elements of a chart.

Click here for more shape styles.

Applying Shape Effects

The Shape Effects menu (Format tab, Shape Styles group) enables you to apply various special effects to a chart's elements that make them look shiny, 3-D, textured, metallic, and so on. As shown in Figure 12.34, there are a number of presets available for 3-D effects that make the element look like it is raised, indented, shiny, rounded, and so on.

You can also create your own effects by combining the individual effects on the Shape Effects menu. The available submenus and effects depend on the element selected; for data series and points, there are fewer options than for the chart area as a whole, for example.

Each effect on the Shape Effects menu also has an Options command that opens the Format dialog box for the selected element. The following sections look at these in more detail.

Applying Shadow Effects

Shadow effect presets are available from the Shape Effects, Shadow submenu. Choose outer or inner shadows, or choose shadows with perspective (see Figure 12.35).

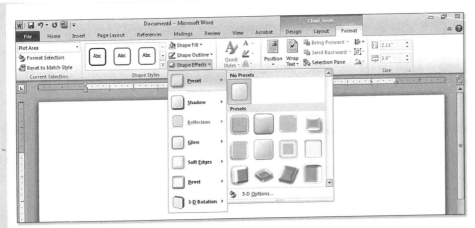

Figure 12.34
Shape Effects can be manually applied to individual chart elements.

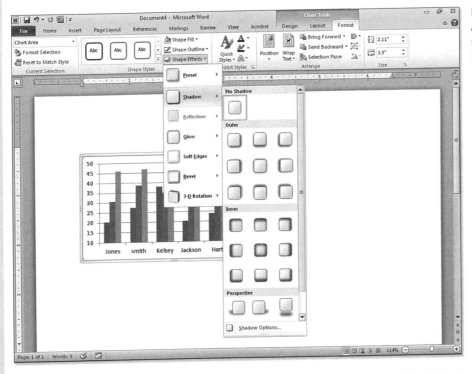

Figure 12.35
Apply preset shadow effects here.

For additional shadow fine-tuning, choose Shadow Options from the menu to open the Shadow settings in the Format dialog box. (The exact name of the dialog box depends on the chart element chosen.) From here, you can change the shadow color and adjust its transparency, size, blur, angle, and distance (see Figure 12.36).

Figure 12.36
Fine-tune shadow effects.

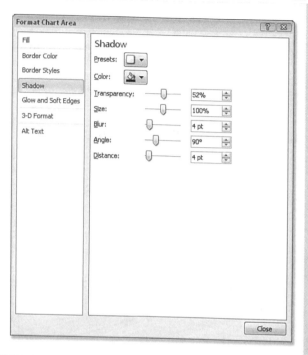

To review the shadow settings available, see *"Applying a Shadow Effect," p. 403.*

Applying Reflection Effects

Reflection is unavailable on the Shape Effects menu when you're working with chart elements. Reflection is not totally off-limits for charts, though; you can make text reflected via the Text Effects list in the WordArt Styles group, as you will see later in this chapter.

Applying Glow Effects

A glow effect places a fuzzy "halo" of a specified color around the object. The samples on the Glow submenu show each of the theme colors in a variety of glow sizes. To change these colors, change to a different color theme for the entire document (on the Page Layout tab).

You can also specify a fixed color; from the Glow submenu, choose More Glow Colors and then pick a standard color, a theme color, or a custom color, as you would with any other object. Choose Glow Options for settings that will further fine-tune the glow effect.

To review the Glow settings available, see *"Applying Glow," p. 406.*

Applying Soft Edge Effects

Soft Edges is just what it sounds like. It makes the edges of the selected element fuzzy. You can choose a variety of degrees of softness from the Soft Edges submenu: 1 pt, 2.5 pt, 5 pt, 10 pt, 25 pt, and 50 pt.

➡ *To review the Soft Edges settings available, see "Applying Soft Edges," p. 406.*

Applying Bevel Effects

Beveling changes the shapes of the edges of the object. Beveling can make the object appear to have rounded corners, for example. Another name for beveling is 3-D Format.

Apply one of the preset bevel effects from the Bevel submenu, or select 3-D Options to open the 3-D Format options, shown in Figure 12.37. From here you can change the height and width of the effect at the top and bottom of the object, change the color of the depth and contours, and change the surface material, lighting, and lighting angle.

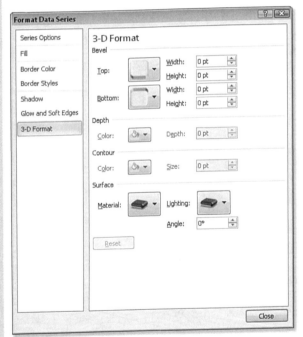

Figure 12.37
Fine-tune the bevel on the chart element from the 3-D Format settings.

➡ *To review the Bevel settings, see "Applying a Beveled Edge and Other 3-D Formatting," p. 406.*

Changing the Shape of a Series

When specifying the chart's type and subtype for a bar or column chart, you choose the shape of the data bars for the entire chart. These can be bars, cylinders, cones, or pyramids.

You can also change the shape used on a series-by-series basis if desired. When you do this, a couple of extra shape types are available that you can't get with the Change Chart Type method: partial cones and partial pyramids. Instead of showing a full cone or pyramid of the size that the data point represents, the bar displays as a full-height cone or pyramid "sawed off" so that its top marks the data point position (see Figure 12.38).

Figure 12.38
The partial pyramid setting makes all pyramids the same size and then cuts off the tops of lower values.

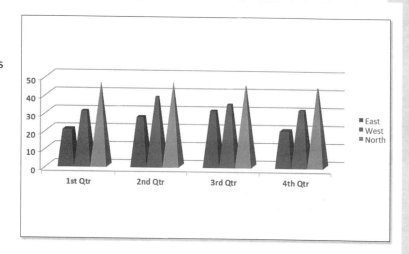

To change the bar shape for the entire chart, see "Changing the Chart Type," p. 486.

You can also change the shapes of an individual series by doing the following:

1. Select a data series.

2. Right-click any bar in the data series and choose Format Data Series to open the Format Data Series dialog box.

3. Click Shape to display the Shape options.

4. Select the desired shape.

5. Click Close. The change is applied to only the selected series.

Adjusting Data Spacing

When working with chart types that involve multiple series of data in a bar, column, or similar style of chart, you can adjust the amount of blank space between the series. To do this, change the data spacing for any series, and all the others will fall into line:

1. Select any data series, and then right-click any data point within it and choose Format Data Series.

2. In the Format Data Series dialog box, click Series Options.

3. Drag the slider to adjust the Gap Depth setting. This is the amount of whitespace between bars from front to back in a 3-D chart. Figure 12.39 shows this setting at its minimum No Gap setting.

4. Drag the slider to adjust the Gap Width setting. This is the amount of whitespace from side to side between bars or series. Figure 12.39 shows this setting at its maximum Large Gap setting.

5. Click Close to close the dialog box.

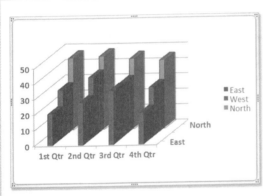

Figure 12.39
Adjusting the spacing between the bars by changing the gap settings.

Formatting Chart Text

Text in a chart is an odd hybrid of regular text and WordArt, and its formatting options reflect that. There are two ways to format text in a chart: use regular formatting techniques from the Home tab, or apply a WordArt Style to the entire chart (preset or custom).

Changing the Font, Size, and Text Attributes

Most of the text formatting that applies to regular text also applies to chart text. On the Home tab, you can choose a different font, size, and color, just like with any other text.

 note

The Font Color button on the Home tab's Font group is the same as the Text Fill button on the Format tab's WordArt Styles group. You can set the font color in either place; making a change to one also makes the change to the other.

You can also format the text in the selected element using a special version of the Font dialog box, enabling you to specify less-common font formatting such as character spacing. To do this:

1. Select the desired chart element.

2. On the Home tab, click the dialog box launcher icon in the Font group. The Font dialog box opens. It's a different version than for regular text, as shown in Figure 12.40.

3. Choose the font, style, size, color, and effects desired from the Font tab.

   In addition to the regular font-formatting options, an Equalize Character Height option is available. When enabled, this option forces all the characters to the same height.

Figure 12.40
Format chart text using a special version of the Font dialog box.

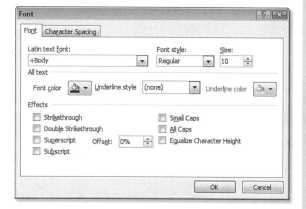

4. (Optional) Adjust the character spacing on the Character Spacing tab if desired. Normal spacing is the default, but you can set it to Expanded or Condensed and specify a number of points by which to adjust. You can also indicate that you want kerning for text at or above a certain size.

5. Click OK.

   ➤ *To review font formatting and character spacing, see "Changing the Font and Size," p. 147, and "Adjusting Character Spacing and Typography," p. 168.*

Applying a WordArt Style

WordArt Styles enable you to change the fill and outline for chart text and to apply special effects to it such as Glow and Reflection.

You can affect all the text in the entire chart at once by selecting the Chart Area before applying a WordArt Style, or you can affect only certain text by selecting that element first.

From the Format tab, click the Quick Styles button to see the available presets, as in Figure 12.41; point at a preset to see a preview of its application in the chart. If you have a wider window than that shown in Figure 12.41, you might instead see a WordArt Styles gallery in the WordArt Styles group.

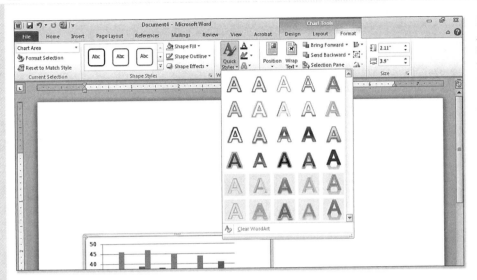

Figure 12.41
Apply WordArt
Styles presets
to quickly for-
mat all the text
in the chart at
once.

If none of the presets meets your needs, use the Text Fill, Text Outline, and Text Effects lists to create your own custom WordArt effect:

- **Text Fill**—Works just like Shape Fill. You can apply any color (theme or fixed) or any type of fill
  effect, such as a gradient or picture.

- **Text Outline**—Works just like Shape Outline. If you do not want an outline around your text,
  choose No Outline.

- **Text Effects**—Similar to Shape Effects. You can apply a Shadow, Reflection, or Glow effect to the
  text in the chart.

To review the Shape Fill and Shape Outline settings, see "Formatting Drawn Objects," p. 434.

13

WORKING WITH SMARTART AND MATH FORMULAS

What Is SmartArt?

SmartArt replaces and improves upon the Diagrams feature in 2003 and earlier versions of Word. Using SmartArt, you can create a variety of graphical conceptual diagrams.

There are eight main categories:

- **List diagrams**—These diagrams show a list of items in a graphical format that helps to emphasize their importance.

- **Process diagrams**—These diagrams show the progress made toward a goal and are useful for step-by-step procedures (see Figure 13.1).

- **Hierarchy diagrams**—These diagrams show an organization's structure, or when run horizontally, can be used for tournament brackets. Figure 13.2 shows a simple organization chart, which is a type of hierarchy.

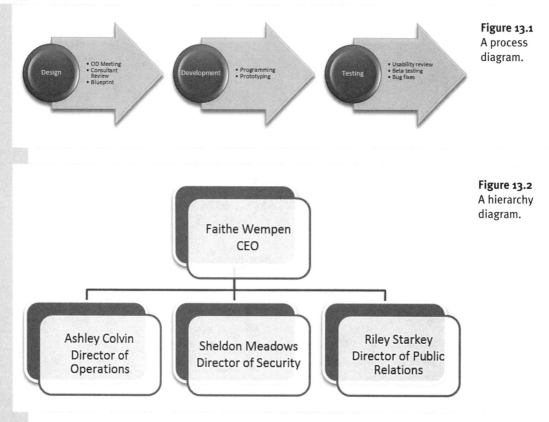

Figure 13.1
A process
diagram.

Figure 13.2
A hierarchy
diagram.

- **Cycle diagrams**—These diagrams show a repeating process. They are like process diagrams except the beginning and the end connect (see Figure 13.3).

- **Relationship diagrams**—These diagrams show how one item relates to another. For example, a relationship diagram can show that one group is a subset of a larger group or how one process depends upon another. Figure 13.4 shows a Venn diagram relationship, which indicates overlap between groups.

- **Matrix diagrams**—These diagrams show relationships of components to a whole, such as how the various departments make up a business unit (see Figure 13.5).

Figure 13.3
A cycle diagram.

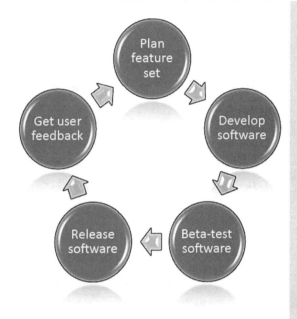

Figure 13.4
A relationship diagram.

Figure 13.5
A matrix diagram.

- **Pyramid diagrams**—These diagrams show the progression of items from largest quantity to smallest quantity, such as the relationship of the number of workers to the number of executives in a company (see Figure 13.6).

- **Picture diagrams**—These diagrams include placeholders for photos in their designs. Some of these are unique to this category, but most of them appear in other categories as well.

In some ways, SmartArt diagrams are similar to the charts that you learned about in Chapter 12, "Working with Charts." Both use a complex system of interrelated lines and shapes to create meaning out of data, and both can be formatted either with Quick Styles or with shape and WordArt formatting. The main difference is that whereas charts present numeric data, SmartArt presents text-based data.

> **note**
>
> Charts and SmartArt, as well as drawn objects (from Chapter 11, "Working with Clip Art, Drawings, and WordArt"), are all based on a drawing engine called Escher 2.0, which is incorporated into all Office products. Therefore, no matter which Office product you are working with, the drawing, charting, and SmartArt tools are consistent in interface and capability.

Figure 13.6
A pyramid diagram.

Inserting a SmartArt Diagram

SmartArt diagrams are considered illustrations, and they are inserted from the Illustrations group of the Insert tab. Follow these steps:

1. On the Insert tab, click the SmartArt button. The Choose a SmartArt Graphic dialog box opens.

2. Click the desired category of diagram, or click All to see all the diagrams at once (see Figure 13.7).

Figure 13.7
Create a new diagram by selecting the layout type you want.

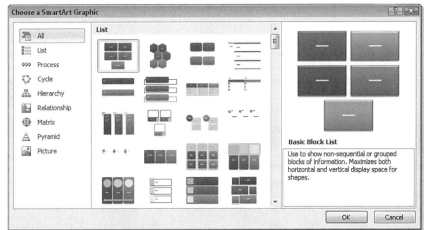

3. Click the desired diagram layout, and then click OK. A text pane appears to the left of the empty diagram layout.

4. Click in a [Text] placeholder and type the desired text. Repeat for each [Text] placeholder.

   The basic layout and options might be okay, but the real power of SmartArt comes from its customization features. In the next several sections of the chapter, you'll learn how to make the SmartArt diagram your own by changing its layout, formatting, and text in various ways.

 caution

Spell check does not work on the text in a SmartArt diagram in Word. However, full spell-check features are available for SmartArt in PowerPoint (both dialog box and red underlines), and the dialog box-based spell check is available for SmartArt in Excel.

Changing the Diagram's Layout

The *layout* is what you selected in Figure 13.7 when you created the chart; it determines the size, shape, and arrangement of the shapes that comprise the diagram. Before you spend a lot of time on the formatting and appearance of a diagram, it's wise to make sure that you have the right layout for your needs. Preset layouts are available on the Design tab, and you can customize the layout by adding or removing shapes, changing the diagram flow direction, and more.

Choosing a Different Layout

To change the layout of a diagram, use the Layouts group controls on the Design tab.

To change to a different layout within the same major category (for example, to change from one Process diagram style to another), open the list of layouts and click the desired style, as in Figure 13.8.

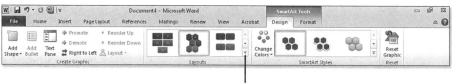

Figure 13.8
Choose a different layout type from within the same major category.

Click here for more layout choices.

To change to a different layout in a different major category, open the Layouts gallery (by clicking the arrow pointed out in Figure 13.8) and choose More Layouts from the bottom of the list. This reopens the Choose a SmartArt Graphic dialog box (refer to Figure 13.7), from which you can choose any layout, even one that is radically different from the existing one. (You might need to move some text around after changing to a different layout.)

Changing the Flow Direction

Most diagram types can be reversed so that they flow from right to left instead of left to right—or in the case of a cycle diagram, counterclockwise instead of clockwise.

To reverse the flow, click the Right to Left button in the Create Graphic group of the Design tab. Click it again to return to the original flow direction.

Adding Shapes

Each diagram type starts out with a default number of shapes in it, but you can easily add more shapes to it.

You insert new shapes in relation to an existing shape. The new shape can either be of the same level of importance (that is, the same outline level) as the existing shape, or be superior or subordinate to it. On most diagram types, there is only one level of shape, but on hierarchy charts, many levels are possible.

To add a shape, follow these steps:

1. Select the existing shape to which the new shape should be related.

2. To insert a new shape at the default level, click the left (graphical) portion of the Add Shape button on the Design tab.

   The default level for a single-level chart is a shape of the same level as the others. The default level for a hierarchy chart is the level that is subordinate to the topmost level.

   Alternatively, to specify the level at which to insert the new shape, click the arrow on the right side of the Add Shape button and then select the desired relationship, as in Figure 13.9.

Figure 13.9
Select a level and position at which to insert the new shape.

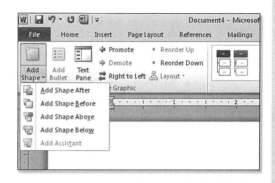

- **Add Shape After**—Inserts a shape of the same outline level either below or to the right of the selected shape.

- **Add Shape Before**—Inserts a shape of the same outline level either above or to the left of the selected shape, depending on the layout flow.

- **Add Shape Above**—Inserts a shape of a superior level to the selected shape, either above it or to its left. If no superior level is available, this option is unavailable.

- **Add Shape Below**—Inserts a shape of a subordinate level to the selected shape, either below it or to its right. If no subordinate level is available, this option is unavailable.

- **Add Assistant**—Available only for hierarchy charts, this option adds a shape that is subordinate to the selected shape but not part of the regular layout.

 note

Here's an alternative way to display the list of available shape insertion types: Right-click an existing shape and point to Add Shape.

Removing Shapes

To remove a shape from the diagram, select the shape and press the Delete key on the keyboard, or right-click the shape and choose Cut. No warning appears; the shape is simply deleted. You can use Undo (Ctrl+Z) to reverse a deletion immediately afterward, however.

 note

In a hierarchy chart, if you delete a shape that has subordinate shapes, the first (leftmost or topmost) subordinate that formerly reported to it moves up into its vacated position.

Promoting or Demoting a Shape

Promoting or demoting individual shapes helps fine-tune a multilevel diagram. It is most obviously useful in a hierarchy chart such as an organization chart, but it can be useful for adding detail to other chart types as well.

Each time you select a shape and click Demote on the Design tab, it moves down one level in significance. If there is no subordinate level, a bullet point is created beneath the preceding shape (that is, the shape that was formerly to its left or above it) at its former level. Figure 13.10 shows an example of a demoted item that has become a bullet point. You can click in the bullet point's text box and type more bullet points there if desired.

Figure 13.10
Items demoted past the lowest level of a shape in a diagram become bullet points.

Each time you select a shape and click Promote on the Design tab, it moves up one level. You can do this for bullet points, too; select some bulleted text and click Promote to move it into its own shape in the diagram.

Adding Bulleted Lists

Demoting an item that is already at the lowest level of significance in a chart turns the item into a bulleted list, as you just learned. However, you can also create bulleted lists subordinate to any level in the diagram, without having to do any demotion.

To create a bulleted list subordinate to a shape, select the shape and then on the Design tab, click Add Bullet. A text box is created below the shape, and a bullet character is applied to it. Type the desired text. Press Enter to type another bullet item if desired.

To create a multilevel bulleted list, press the Tab key at the beginning of the bulleted paragraph to indent it one level in outline significance. Press Shift+Tab to promote a bullet level within the outline.

 tip

Sometimes it can be easier to see the outline levels if you have a text-based outline to work with. The text pane appears by default; you can click the Text Pane button on the Design tab to toggle it on/off. In the text pane, you can type, edit, and promote/demote outline levels without having to worry about the graphical aspect of the diagram. For more information, see "Using the Text Pane" later in this chapter.

Positioning Organization Chart Branches

One of the drawbacks to a large organization chart (a type of hierarchy chart) is the space it takes up. When there are many levels and each level has many items, the chart can spread out horizontally to the point at which it's not very readable.

The SmartArt organization chart layout has several positioning alternatives available, and you can apply them on a branch-by-branch basis on an organization chart. For example, you can stack all the subordinate boxes vertically or make them branch off from one or both sides of a center pillar.

To change the positioning of subordinate items on a branch of an organization chart, follow these steps:

1. Select the shape for which you want to change the subordinates.

2. On the Design tab, click Layout and then click the desired layout (see Figure 13.11).

Figure 13.11
Choose the desired positioning for the selected branch of the organization chart.

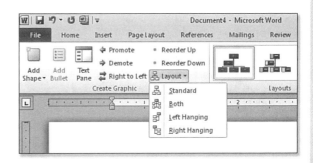

Working with Diagram Text

Diagrams exist to convey text messages in graphical ways. The text in the diagram is the star of the show; the boxes, arrows, and other flourishes are just supporting players. In this section, you'll learn how to add, edit, and format a diagram's text.

Adding and Editing Text

Each shape in the diagram starts out with a plain [Text] placeholder. That placeholder does not print, so you're free to leave some shapes without any text in them if that's appropriate for your message.

To replace the [Text] placeholder with some real text, click the placeholder (it immediately disappears when you do) and type the desired text. You can do this in the shape itself or in the text pane.

To edit text, click to move the insertion point inside the shape and then edit as you would any other text—use Backspace or Delete to remove characters, or select the text and press Delete to remove blocks of characters.

Formatting Diagram Text

As with chart text (covered in Chapter 12), diagram text is a blend of regular text and WordArt text. As a result, the formatting you can apply to diagram text includes both standard text formatting and WordArt formatting.

Changing the Font by Applying a Font Set

The default font in a SmartArt diagram comes from the font theme, which is chosen on the Page Layout tab. SmartArt diagrams use whatever font is specified as the secondary font (the one for body text).

To change the fonts globally throughout the entire document, including on the diagrams, select a different font set from the Theme Fonts drop-down list on the Page Layout tab (see Figure 13.12).

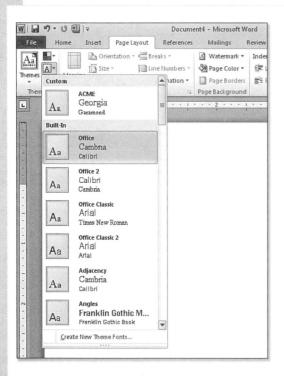

Figure 13.12
Select different font sets to change the appearance of the chart.

If you want to change the font only on the one individual SmartArt diagram, see the following section.

Changing the Font, Size, and Text Attributes Manually

Most of the standard text-formatting controls are available for diagram text. Use the Font group on the Home tab, or right-click the text and use the Mini Toolbar, as in Figure 13.13.

 note

The Font Color button on the Home tab's Font group is the same as the Text Fill button on the Format tab's WordArt Styles group. You can set the font color in either place.

Figure 13.13
You can format text in a diagram via the Mini Toolbar that appears when you right-click it.

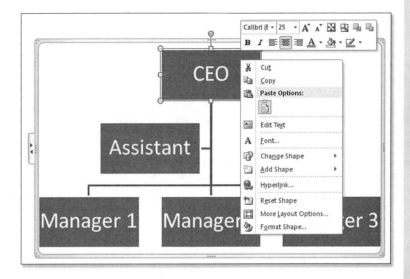

You can also format diagram text via a special version of the Font dialog box that includes most of the usual text attributes (with the exception of Emboss, Engrave, and Hidden) plus Equalize Character Height, which sets all the characters to the same height. To access the Font dialog box, right-click the selected text and choose Font, or click the Home tab and then click the Font group's dialog box launcher icon. This is the same dialog box as for charts, and it works the same way (see Figure 13.14).

Figure 13.14
Fine-tune the diagram text's formatting using the Font dialog box.

The Character Spacing tab in the Font dialog box works just like it does for regular text. Normal spacing is the default, but you can set it to Expanded or Condensed and specify a number of points by which to adjust. You can also indicate that you want kerning for text at or above a certain size.

> ➡ *To review font formatting and character spacing, see "Changing Text Font, Size, and Color," p. 145, and "Adjusting Character Spacing and Typography," p. 168.*

Applying WordArt Quick Styles to Text

WordArt Styles enable you to change the fill and outline for diagram text and apply special effects to it such as Glow and Reflection. They work similarly in SmartArt and in charts, so if you mastered their use in Chapter 12, you're ahead of the game.

From the Format tab, open the WordArt Styles list to see the available presets; point at a preset to see a preview of its application in the diagram.

If none of the presets meets your needs, use the Text Fill, Text Outline, and Text Effects lists to create your own custom WordArt effect:

- **Text Fill**—Applies the selected color to the text. You can apply any color (theme or fixed) or any type of fill effect, such as gradient or picture.

- **Text Outline**—Applies a colored outline to the text. If you do not want an outline around your text, choose No Outline.

- **Text Effects**—Applies a special effect to the text, such as Shadow, Reflection, Glow, or Bevel. These are the same as the Shape Effects you learned about in Chapters 11 and 12.

> ➡ *To review fill and outline settings, see "Formatting Drawn Objects," p. 434.*

> ➡ *To review Shape Effects, see "Applying Shape Effects," p. 509.*

Using the Text Pane

Each diagram has a text pane. It appears by default and can be displayed or hidden in either of these ways:

- On the Design tab, click the Text Pane button.

- Click the left/right arrow button at the left edge of the diagram frame (see Figure 13.15).

To close the text pane, you can also click its Close button (the X in the upper-right corner).

In the text pane, you can create an outline for the diagram, much like you do with Outline view in Word or PowerPoint.

Here are some things you can do in the text pane to modify the diagram's text:

- **Add a shape**—Click at the end of the text in a bullet and press Enter, and then type the text for the new shape.

Figure 13.15
Use the text pane to more easily edit the diagram's text.

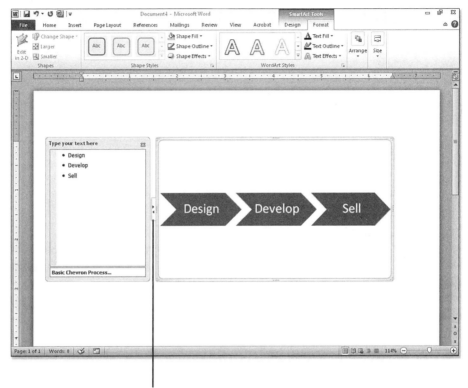

Click here to display/hide the text pane.

- **Demote a shape**—Click anywhere within a bulleted list item and press Tab or click the Demote button on the Design tab.

- **Promote a shape**—Click anywhere within a bulleted list item and press Shift+Tab or click the Promote button on the Design tab.

- **Format text**—Right-click the text in the text pane and use the Mini Toolbar that appears. Alternatively, you can select the text in the text pane and use the Home tab's Font group controls, or you can right-click the text and choose Font.

Setting Text Positioning Within a Shape

Within each shape is a *text area*, which is a rectangular area in which the text appears. The text area varies depending on the shape, but generally it lies completely within the shape so that text does not hang outside the shape's outline.

This text area functions much like a text box does. (See "Creating Text Box Layouts" in Chapter 8, "Working with Templates and Nonstandard Layouts," for a full description of text box formatting.) To access the text box controls for a text area, follow these steps:

1. Select the shape.

2. Right-click the shape and choose Format Shape. The Format Shape dialog box opens.

3. Click Text Box. The text layout options appear (see Figure 13.16).

4. In the Text Layout section, set the vertical alignment and text direction.

5. In the Internal Margin section, specify the amount of blank space that should be maintained between the edge of the shape and the text.

6. Click Close.

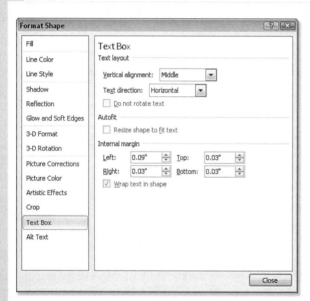

Figure 13.16
Adjust the internal margins and vertical alignment of the text within the shape.

Formatting a Diagram

Now comes the fun part—formatting the diagram. You can apply any of the many Quick Styles to the diagram as a starting point and then fine-tune the settings by applying fills, outlines, and effects to individual diagram elements.

Applying SmartArt Styles

To quickly apply formatting presets to the entire diagram, select it, and then open the SmartArt Styles list from the Design tab and choose the desired style.

As you can see in Figure 13.17, the drop-down list has two sections: Best Match for Document and 3-D. The Best Match for Document styles format uses non-3-D features such as gradients, lines, fills, and spacing; the 3-D styles add 3-D rotation and depth to that mix to create fancier effects.

Figure 13.17
Select a SmartArt Style for the diagram.

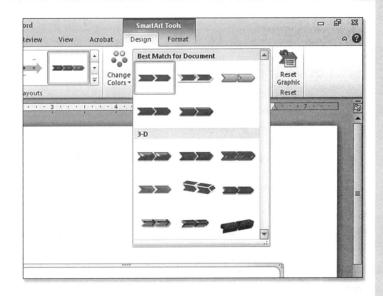

Applying a 3-D Style to a Diagram Slows Down Word's Performance

On a PC with less RAM and CPU speed than average, editing a chart in a 3-D style can cause frustrating delays as the chart redraws itself. To avoid this problem, on the Format tab click the Edit in 2-D button. The chart appears temporarily without its 3-D effects. Then when you are finished editing it, click Edit in 2-D again to toggle it back to 3-D view.

Some Shape Effects Don't Show Up on a 3-D Diagram

When 3-D rotation is applied, some of the other shape effects don't show up properly. For example, you can't have both a shadow and a 3-D rotation applied to the same diagram. Removing the 3-D rotation causes the other effects you've applied to appear.

Changing the Theme Effects for the Entire Document

When you insert a new SmartArt diagram, its default settings (colors and effects) depend on the theme applied to the document.

To format all the SmartArt in the entire document the same way, leave them all at their defaults and then select a different theme from the Page Layout tab, as you learned in Chapter 6, "Creating and Applying Styles and Themes."

The theme provides different settings in three areas: colors, fonts, and effects. If you like the current colors and fonts but just want to apply different effects to graphical objects such as SmartArt, choose a different effect set from the Theme Effects list (also on the Page Layout tab). These effects apply not only to the selected SmartArt, but to every graphical object in the document that does not have manual formatting applied to it—SmartArt, charts, drawn shapes, and so on (see Figure 13.18).

> **caution**
>
> If you have applied manual formatting to a diagram or to one or more shapes within it, changing to a different theme or set of effects will have no effect on it. Right-click the frame of the graphic and choose Reset Graphic to reset the whole diagram so that the theme can affect it, or right-click an individual shape and choose Reset Shape to reset a particular shape.

➡ *To review how to apply themes, see "Working with Themes," p. 246.*

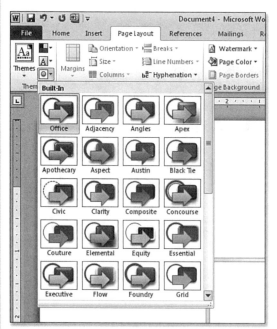

Figure 13.18
Apply effects to all the SmartArt, charts, and drawings in the document at once from the Theme Effects menu on the Page Layout tab.

Changing Diagram Colors

To change a diagram's colors overall, use the Change Colors list in the SmartArt Styles group of the Design tab. As shown in Figure 13.19, you can select various combinations of the theme colors here. The entire document can use a single color, or you can choose one of the Colorful options to make each piece of the diagram a different theme-supplied color.

Figure 13.19
Select a SmartArt Style for the diagram.

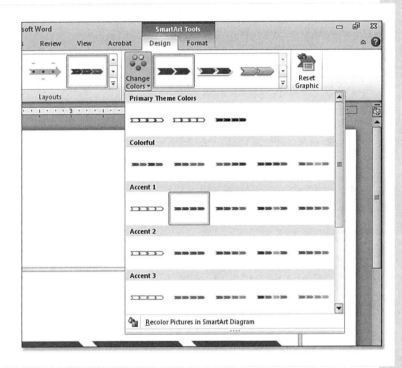

To review how to change the theme colors for the document, see "Working with Themes," p. 246.

Formatting an Individual Shape

You can format each shape in the diagram separately from the diagram as a whole. For example, if you don't like the color assigned to a certain shape, you can change it to a different theme color or to a fixed color of your choosing. You can also apply various fill effects separately to each shape, such as 3-D rotation, beveled edges, shadows, and glows.

Applying a Shape Style

The easiest way to reformat an individual shape is with a Shape Style. As you learned in Chapter 12 in "Applying a Shape Style," these are presets that you can apply to individual elements. A Shape Style applies a combination of fill color, outline color, and effects.

To apply a Shape Style, follow these steps:

1. Click a shape to select it. To select multiple shapes to affect, hold down Ctrl as you click on each one.

2. Open the drop-down list in the Shape Styles group of the Format tab and click the desired style.

Applying Shape Outlines, Fills, and Effects

For maximum control over a shape's formatting, use the Shape Fill, Shape Outline, and Shape Effects drop-down lists in the Shape Styles group of the Format tab. These work the same way for SmartArt diagrams as they do for drawings, covered in Chapter 11, and charts, covered in Chapter 12. You can use solid colors, tints, gradients, or even picture fills for each shape.

➡ *To learn about applying fill and outline formatting, including special fills such as pictures and gradients, see "Formatting Drawn Objects," p. 434.*

➡ *To learn about applying shape effects, see "Applying Shape Effects," p. 509.*

Some Shape Effects Don't Show Up on a 3-D Diagram

When 3-D rotation is applied, some of the other shape effects don't show up properly. For example, you can't have both a shadow and a 3-D rotation applied to the same diagram. Removing the 3-D rotation causes the other effects you've applied to appear.

Changing the Shape Geometry

Not happy with the type of shape used in the diagram? For example, would you rather have rectangles than chevrons or stars rather than circles? It's easy to change to any shape you like. (Microsoft calls the shape's "shape" its *geometry*.)

All the same shapes that you worked with in Chapter 11 are available for use in a diagram. Figure 13.20 shows a diagram that was originally composed of chevrons but now uses four different shapes instead.

To change a shape, follow these steps:

1. Select the shape.

2. On the Format tab, click Change Shape in the Shapes group. A menu of shapes appears (see Figure 13.21).

3. Click the desired shape.

 caution

When selecting the shape geometry for pieces of a diagram, keep in mind that the more similar to a rectangle the chosen shape is, the more efficiently text fits inside it. Oddly pointed shapes such as stars typically have a small text area.

Figure 13.20
Each shape in the diagram can be different.

Figure 13.21
Each shape in the diagram can be different.

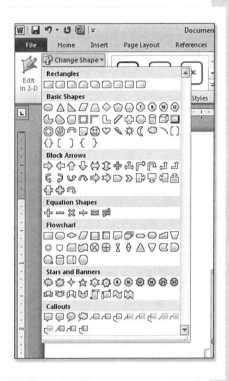

To go back to the default shape, right-click the shape and choose Reset Shape.

Sizing, Positioning, and Rotating a Shape

You can do all these things to a shape:

- **Resize**—Drag a selection handle to resize the shape.

- **Move**—Drag its border (but not on a selection handle) to move it. A shape cannot be moved outside the diagram frame.

- **Enlarge**—Click the Larger button on the Format tab to enlarge the shape and shrink the other shapes to make room for it. The positioning between them remains constant. There is also a Larger button on the Mini Toolbar, which appears when you right-click the shape.

- **Shrink**—Click the Smaller button on the Format tab to shrink the shape and enlarge the other shapes so that the overall diagram continues to be the same size. Again, the positioning between them remains constant. There is also a Smaller button on the Mini Toolbar.

- **Rotate or Flip**—Drag its rotation handle (green circle) to rotate it. Or, on the Format tab, in the Arrange group, click Rotate, and choose a flipping or rotation option. (The Arrange group might be collapsed into an Arrange button, depending on the width of the Word window.)

 note

To rotate by a precise amount, choose More Rotation Options from the Rotate menu. In the Layout dialog box that appears, set a Rotation amount in degrees.

> *To learn more about rotating and flipping, see "Rotating and Flipping Objects," p. 427.*

> *To learn more about sizing and positioning drawn objects, see "Sizing and Positioning Objects," p. 427.*

Controlling Diagram Size and Positioning

Diagrams are objects, just like charts and graphics, and they have the same sizing and positioning options. Here's a quick review; you can find full details for object sizing and positioning in Chapter 10, "Working with Photos."

Resizing a Diagram

When a SmartArt diagram is selected, a light blue border appears around it. This border has dotted tabs in the corners and on three sides; you can drag any of these to resize the diagram's frame (see Figure 13.22).

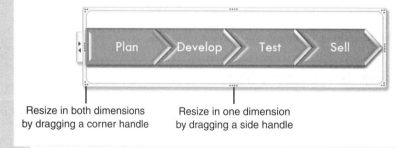

Figure 13.22
Resize a diagram by dragging the dotted areas on its frame.

Resize in both dimensions by dragging a corner handle

Resize in one dimension by dragging a side handle

For more precise sizing of the diagram, use the Size controls on the Format tab. Enter precise values in the Height and Width boxes of the Size group.

Positioning a Diagram

Position presets are available for diagrams, the same as for other graphics objects. These presets set the diagram frame to precise relative or absolute positioning within the document page.

To apply a position preset to a diagram, follow these steps:

1. Select the SmartArt diagram.

2. On the Format tab, in the Arrange group, click Position. Then click one of the position presets.

To set an exact position for the diagram, you must set Wrap Text to something other than In Line with Text. So first do this:

1. On the Format tab, in the Arrange group, click Wrap Text.

2. Click any of the text wrap settings other than In Line with Text.

> 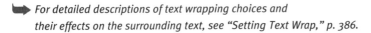 *For detailed descriptions of text wrapping choices and their effects on the surrounding text, see "Setting Text Wrap," p. 386.*

Next, open the Layout dialog box and choose specific positioning as follows:

1. On the Format tab, in the Arrange group, click Position, More Layout Options. The Layout dialog box opens.

2. On the Position tab, set the desired layout. You can choose layout by Alignment, by Book Layout, by Absolute Position, or by Relative Position.

3. Set any options desired, such as Move Object with Text or Lock Anchor.

4. Click OK to accept the new position setting.

> *For more detailed descriptions of the position choices, see "Setting Picture Position," p. 388.*

note

Resizing the frame also resizes the diagram within it proportionally, but only if the resizing forces a change in the content. For example, suppose you have a short, wide diagram with lots of extra blank space above and below it. Decreasing the height of the SmartArt frame does not change the diagram; it simply tightens up the excess space. However, decreasing the width of the frame does shrink the diagram, and increasing the width enlarges the diagram. The reverse would be true for a tall, thin diagram that has extra blank space on the sides.

How to Convert SmartArt to Regular Drawing Objects

If you're having trouble positioning, sizing, or formatting a shape in your SmartArt in a certain way, here's a workaround: Take the shapes out of the SmartArt frame and make them regular drawing objects instead. You lose the automation of the SmartArt feature, but you gain formatting flexibility.

Continued...

In PowerPoint, you can simply select a shape in a SmartArt diagram, cut or copy it to the Clipboard, and then paste it outside the diagram frame. However, if you try that in Word, instead of the shapes, you get a plain bulleted list containing the text that was in the pasted shapes. This happens because in PowerPoint, the default paste format is graphical, but in Word, the default paste format is HTML text.

To get around this problem, use Paste Special to paste the cut or copied shapes. Follow these steps:

1. Select the shape(s) in the diagram.

2. Press Ctrl+C to copy or Ctrl+X to cut the shape(s).

3. Click outside the diagram frame.

4. On the Home tab, open the Paste button's menu and click Paste Special. The Paste Special dialog box opens.

5. In the As list, select Microsoft Office Graphic Object.

6. Click OK.

Creating Math Formulas with the Equation Editor

Mathematics has its own language, complete with special symbols and syntax and even special types of line breaks, dividers, and superscript/subscript requirements. It's no wonder, then, that most word processing programs are inadequate for expressing complex mathematical equations.

Here are some of the reasons it's difficult to express math concepts in a word processing program:

- Special symbols are often required that are not found on a standard keyboard, such as sigma (Σ) and pi (Π).

- Math formulas often involve complex combinations of superscript and subscript, sometimes with multiple levels.

- The proper size for certain symbols and characters can depend on the usage. For example, parentheses or brackets that span a complex, multiple-line equation must be very tall.

- Fractions need to be expressed with the numerator above the denominator—on separate lines, but part of a single unit. This can be nearly impossible to simulate with regular paragraphs or tables.

Figure 13.23 illustrates some of these issues. Notice that the symbols ϖ and ∞ are used, along with some subscript characters and a fractional expression. Notice also that the two sets of parentheses are different sizes and that fractions are represented with their numerators and denominators on split lines.

Figure 13.23
Math formulas like this one can be a challenge to create as regular text.

$$f(x) = a_0 + \sum_{n=1}^{\infty} \left(a_n \cos\frac{n\pi x}{L} + b_n \sin\frac{n\pi x}{L} \right)$$

Fortunately, the Equation Editor feature in Word makes creating complex equations like the one in Figure 13.23 a snap. By using a combination of regular typing, symbols, and placeholder boxes, the Equation Editor can build virtually any mathematical expression you would ever need.

Inserting a Preset Equation

In algebra and trigonometry, certain key equations seem to come up repeatedly, such as the Pythagorean theorem and the quadratic formula. There's no need to re-create them each time you need them; Word provides them as equation presets.

To insert an equation preset:

1. On the Insert tab, open the Equation button's drop-down list.

2. Click one of the presets.

The equation appears in its own object frame in the document. You can edit it if desired, as explained later in the chapter.

Creating a New Blank Equation Object

If none of the presets matches your needs, create a new, blank equation object instead by clicking the Equation button (click its face, not its down arrow) or by pressing Alt+=. An equation frame appears, along with a text placeholder (see Figure 13.24).

Figure 13.24
A new blank equation frame.

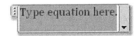

Creating a Basic Equation

To create a simple equation, just start typing it in the equation frame. You can use any number, letter, or symbol from the keyboard, plus you have access to a variety of math symbols from the Symbols group on the Design tab.

Basic math symbols are shown by default on the Symbols group's palette, as shown in Figure 13.25.

Figure 13.25
Select symbols from the Symbols group.

Click here for more symbols.

For access to even more symbols, open the palette of symbols, and click the down arrow on the Basic Math heading, opening a menu as shown in Figure 13.26. From there, choose one of the other collections of symbols. Some of the categories are small and basic; others have dozens of choices and their own subsections.

Click here to open the menu.

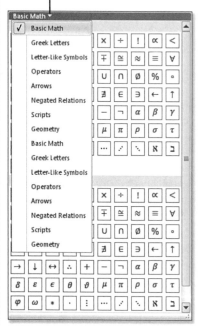

Figure 13.26
Additional collections of symbols are available by selecting another category.

Inserting and Filling Structures

Structures are symbols or combinations of text placeholder boxes that help you create math expressions that cannot be easily expressed on a single line of text.

A *stacked fraction* is one of the simplest and most common examples. It consists of two placeholder boxes, one on top of the other, with a horizontal line between them (see Figure 13.27).

Figure 13.27
Structures contain one or more placeholder boxes.

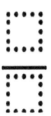

To insert and fill a structure:

1. In the equation, position the insertion point where you want the structure to be inserted.

2. On the Design tab, click one of the buttons in the Structures group to open its menu.

3. Click on the desired structure to insert it.

4. Click in a placeholder and type or insert the content. Repeat this for each placeholder.

<aside>
🔍 **note**

Structures can be nested. You can place one structure inside the placeholder box for another structure, creating complex nests of structures and equations.
</aside>

For example, here are the steps for a simple superscript:

1. In the equation, position the insertion point where you want the structure to be inserted.

2. On the Design tab, click Script.

3. In the Subscripts and Superscripts section of the menu, click Superscript. Two placeholder boxes appear: one regular-sized and one smaller and slightly raised.

4. Click in the first placeholder box and type or insert the content that should precede the characters in superscript.

5. Click in the second placeholder box and type or insert the content that should appear in superscript.

All the other structures work the same way, although some of them might appear intimidating and complex. Just click in the placeholders and fill in the content.

Switching Between Professional and Linear Layout

The default type of equation layout is Professional, which shows structures spread out on multiple lines wherever appropriate. Professional layout makes math formulas that are easy to read and understand.

When space is an issue in a document, however, you might be loathe to give up two or more lines of a page to show an equation. For situations like that, it's helpful to switch the equation's view to Linear. Using a Linear view runs the equation on a single line, changing the symbols where needed to alternatives that can be expressed in a linear fashion (see Figure 13.28).

$$(x + a)^n = \sum_{k=0}^{n} \binom{n}{k} x^k a^{n-k}$$

Figure 13.28
The same equation in Professional versus Linear view.

$$(x + a)\wedge n = \sum\_(k = 0)\wedge n\ \llbracket (n \vert k)\ x\wedge k\ a\wedge(n - k) \rrbracket$$

To switch between Linear and Professional views, use the corresponding buttons in the Tools group on the Design tab. Alternatively, click the down arrow at the bottom-right corner of the equation's frame and choose the desired view from the menu that appears.

Formatting an Equation

In some ways, formatting an equation is like formatting the text in a text box. There are a few quirks, though. Here's a quick summary:

- **Font**—Cambria Math is used for formulas by default. Although you can change this (right-click the equation and choose Font, or select the font from the Home tab), note that font changes do not take effect unless the font you choose supports mathematical symbols. Because Cambria Math is the only font that ships with Word 2010 that fully supports all math symbols used in the new Equation Editor, it is in effect your only choice.

- **Size**—By default, the baseline font for an equation is 11 point. Some characters can be larger or smaller than that depending on their context. You can select the equation's frame and then choose a different font size from the Home tab to adjust the overall size of the equation up or down proportionally from there.

- **Color**—If desired, use the Font Color button on the Home tab to change the color of the text used for the equation. Keep in mind, however, that equations are nearly always utilitarian objects, not decorative.

- **Bold**—You can apply boldface to individual characters or to the entire equation.

- **Strikethrough**—You can apply strikethrough to individual characters or to the entire equation.

- **Italics**—Letters in an equation are italicized by default, as are some symbols. It is usually best to leave these at their default, because people expect to see those items italicized, and the italics help them make sense of the equation.

- **Underline**—You cannot apply underline to individual characters; you can apply it only to the equation as a whole.

- **Horizontal justification**—The equation frame is an inline object and cannot be floated freely in the document. However, you can set its horizontal justification. Click the down arrow at the bottom-right corner of the equation frame, and on the menu that appears, point to Justification and choose a justification option (see Figure 13.29). Alternatively, you can use the Paragraph controls on the Home tab.

Figure 13.29
Set horizontal justification for the equation.

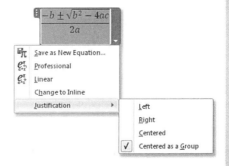

Switching Between Inline and Display Mode

An equation is a graphics object—sort of. It's not a completely free-floating object, like a drawn shape or a photo, but it does have some independence from the surrounding text.

An equation can interact with the text in the document in either of two ways:

- **Inline**—The equation is treated as an inline image and runs in with the text like any other character. Most of the font-formatting options available for a regular paragraph apply to it.

- **Display**—The equation is its own separate object, with positioning controlled by the Justification setting on the equation's menu. It appears on a separate line from the surrounding text.

To switch back and forth between these, click the down arrow at the bottom-right corner of the equation to open the equation's menu, and then choose Change to Display or Change to Inline. (The wording changes depending on the mode currently in use.)

III

Need More Text Wrap and Position Control Over an Equation?

Because an equation is not a truly independent object, it does not have Position and Wrap Text settings the way a piece of SmartArt does. If you want to wrap text around an equation, you must place it in a container, such as a text box, that allows text wrapping.

To place an equation in a text box:

1. Draw the text box.

2. Select the equation and press Ctrl+X to cut it to the Clipboard.

3. Click inside the text box and press Ctrl+V to paste the equation there. Now the equation is part of the text box and can be moved around with it.

4. Resize the text box to match the size of the equation, and move it where you want it.

5. Set the text wrapping for the text box to whatever you want it to be for the equation.

6. Remove the text box's visible border to make it blend into the background so the equation gets the attention.

Saving an Equation to the Equation Gallery

After spending the time to create an equation, you can save it for later reuse by creating a building block for it in the Equation Gallery. The Equation Gallery is a section of the Building Blocks template that you've worked with in other chapters; it serves as a repository for custom user equations.

To save the current equation, follow these steps:

1. Select the equation.

2. On the Design tab, click the Equation button and then choose Save Selection to Equation Gallery.

3. In the Create New Building Block dialog box, a linear version of the equation appears in the Name box. Change this to a friendly text name that helps you remember the equation's purpose.

4. Leave all the other options in the dialog box set at their defaults, as in Figure 13.30, or change them if desired.

5. Click OK.

 tip

The equations appear on the list in alphabetical order, so to force one to the top of the list (above the Word-supplied presets), begin it with a number rather than a letter. To take this one step further, you can create a set of custom equations and specify the order in which they appear on the menu by preceding each one's name with a number representing the desired position.

➡ *To review the options available in the Create New Building Block dialog box, see "Working with Building Blocks," p. 89.*

The custom equation now appears on the Equation menu, along with all the preset equations that come with Word.

Figure 13.30
Set equation options.

PERFORMING MAIL AND DATA MERGES

Understanding Mail Merges

Mail merge combines a main document with a list of database records to create customized copies of the main document for each record.

The most common type of mail merge, of course, is a mailing. Mail merging was originally developed to create form letters, like the kind you probably get in your mailbox every day that address you by name and suggest that you buy some can't-live-without product.

Word's mail merge feature can actually do much more than generate form letters, however. You can use it to generate envelopes, labels, personalized copies of business reports or children's stories, auction catalogs—just about anything that combines fixed text with variable text.

Let's start by looking at the files involved in a mail merge. A mail merge uses two files:

- The **main document** is a Word document. It contains all the text that should remain the same from copy to copy.

- The **data file** contains the variable data to be merged. It can be a Word document (with the data in a table), an Excel worksheet, an Outlook contact list, a Windows Mail address book, a delimited text file, or any of several other data types.

> *To learn more about delimited text files, see the sidebar "Understanding Delimited Data" on p. 555.*

To set up a mail merge, you insert merge fields that reference the data file into the main document. For example, if the data file has a FirstName field, you might have a line in the main document that looks like this:

Dear <<FirstName>>:

When you perform the merge, you can send the results either to a new file or directly to the printer. The result is a separate copy of the main document for each of the database records, with that record's information inserted:

Dear Joe:

You can set up a mail merge main document manually, but Word provides several features that partially automate the process. The features that Word provides are different depending on the document type you want to produce:

- **Letters**—Create a personalized form letter for each recipient. Each letter will print on a separate sheet of paper.

- **E-mail messages**—Create an email message for each recipient with customized information inserted from the recipient's contact information.

- **Envelopes**—Create an envelope for mailing a letter to each recipient. This is similar to Letters except for the paper size and type.

- **Labels**—Create sheets of mailing labels in which each label contains the mailing address of a different recipient. This is similar to Envelopes except instead of the recipients being on separate sheets, they are combined.

- **Directory**—Create a listing of database entries, such as a product catalog. This is like Labels except there is not a defined area in which each record's data appears; instead, you can set up the layout any way you like.

- **Normal Word Document**—This option enables you to use mail merge features in an ordinary Word document—that is, one that is not one of the listed special types.

Word provides the tools you need for setting up merges on the Mailings tab, shown in Figure 14.1. You can go your own way with them, or you can use a step-by-step Mail Merge Wizard to guide you.

The Mailings tab has five groups to it. The first one, Create, has buttons for creating individual envelopes and labels, which you learned about in Chapter 8, "Working with Templates and Nonstandard Layouts." The Create group has no role in mail merging.

The other four groups on the Mailings tab, shown in Figure 14.1, correspond to the stages of setting up a mail merge. They appear from left to right in chronological order:

- **Start Mail Merge**—In this group, you choose the type of document and select the data source.

- **Write & Insert Fields**—In this group, you insert field codes and set up rules that sort and filter the records to be included.

■ **Preview Results**—In this group, you view and proofread the merge, so you can make any changes needed to it.

■ **Finish**—In this group, you save the results to a file, print them, or email them.

Figure 14.1
The Mailings tab contains buttons and lists for setting up mail merges.

This chapter covers all the controls in each of these groups in detail. Because many beginners find mail merges intimidating to set up, though, Word also offers a Mail Merge Wizard utility. The following section shows how to use this wizard to do a simple mail-merged letter.

Performing a Letter Merge with the Mail Merge Wizard

The Mail Merge Wizard guides you through the process of setting up a mail merge for letters, email messages, envelopes, labels, or a directory. Mail merge beginners find it useful because it prompts you for each step of the process; mail merge experts seldom use it because it is a bit clunky and because creating your own merges on the fly is faster.

Because the rest of this chapter covers each step of the mail merge process more thoroughly, I won't go into detail for each step here. Instead, the following steps take you through a simple Letters type of merge using the Mail Merge Wizard and your Microsoft Outlook contact list. After you've completed the rest of this chapter, you can come back to the Mail Merge Wizard with a more complete understanding of its options.

To use the Mail Merge Wizard to create a set of mail-merged letters based on the addresses in your Microsoft Outlook contact list, follow these steps:

1. Start a new blank document. Then on the Mailings tab, in the Start Mail Merge group, click Start Mail Merge, and then click Step by Step Mail Merge Wizard. The Mail Merge task pane appears.

2. In the Mail Merge task pane, click Letters (see Figure 14.2, left). Then at the bottom of the task pane, click Next: Starting Document.

3. In the Select Starting Document section of the task pane, leave Use the Current Document selected (see Figure 14.2, center). Then click Next: Select Recipients.

4. Click Select from Outlook Contacts (see Figure 14.2, right).

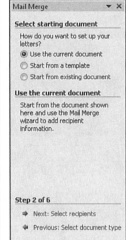

Figure 14.2
The first three screens of the Mail Merge Wizard.

5. Make sure the correct one is selected by doing the following:

   a. Click Choose Contacts Folder.

   b. In the Select Contacts dialog box, click the desired contact folder. The name of the folder depends on your mail setup and on whether you are using Outlook or Windows Mail.

   ➡ *For more information about selecting a data source, see "Choosing an Existing Data Source," p. 556.*

6. (Optional) If you don't want to send the letter to every contact in the data source, do the following:

   a. Click Edit Recipient List.

   b. In the Mail Merge Recipients dialog box, clear the check box next to each entry you want to exclude.

   c. Click OK.

   ➡ *For more information about excluding certain records, see "Filtering and Sorting the Data," p. 570.*

7. At the bottom of the task pane, click Next: Write Your Letter.

8. Position the insertion point at the top of the document and then click Address Block (see Figure 14.3, left).

 note

To save you some time, Word has some built-in merge blocks that combine the data from multiple fields. To make up a standard postal mailing address, Word combines fields such as first name, last name, address, city, state, and ZIP into a single field called ‹‹AddressBlock››. Similarly, it combines fixed text such as "Dear" with first or last name fields to create the ‹‹GreetingLine›› field.

You are free to use individual fields in the mail merge if you prefer or if the address and greeting blocks aren't delivering the results you want. To access the full list of available fields in the Mail Merge Wizard, choose More Items instead of Address Block or Greeting Line.

9. In the Insert Address Block dialog box, select any options to fine-tune the formatting of the recipient address, and then click OK. An <<AddressBlock>> code appears in the document.

➡ *For more information about address blocks, see "Inserting Address Blocks," p. 565.*

10. Press Enter a few times after the <<AddressBlock>> code and then click Greeting Line.

11. In the Insert Greeting Line dialog box, choose a greeting style and then click OK. A <<GreetingLine>> code appears in the document.

➡ *For more information about greeting lines, see "Inserting Greeting Lines," p. 567.*

12. Finish composing the letter as you would any other letter. When you are finished, at the bottom of the task pane, click Next: Preview Your Letters.

13. In the Preview Your Letters section of the task pane, use the << and >> buttons to move between previews of the letters. To exclude a recipient, click Exclude This Recipient when that person's preview appears (see Figure 14.3, center).

Figure 14.3
The second three screens of the Mail Merge Wizard.

14. At the bottom of the task pane, click Next: Complete the Merge.

15. To send the letters to the printer, click Print (see Figure 14.3, right). A Merge to Printer dialog box appears; click OK to print the letters from there.

Or, to open the letters in a new document for further editing, follow these steps:

a. Click Edit Individual Letters. The Merge to New Document dialog box appears.

b. Click OK. The letters open in a new document.

16. Save the main document if you think you will want to perform this same merge again. Otherwise, close the main document without saving.

The ⟨····⟨····AddressBlock····⟩····⟩ Puts Too Much Space Between the Lines

The <<AddressBlock>> field actually inserts three or more paragraphs, one for each line of the address. Each of these paragraphs has the default setting of having 10 points of space after it. That's where that extra space is coming from.

To fix it, follow these steps:

1. Right-click the <<AddressBlock>> code and choose Paragraph.

2. In the Paragraph dialog box, mark the Don't Add Space Between Paragraphs of the Same Style check box.

3. Click OK.

Another way is to insert the fields manually that comprise the address rather than relying on the <<AddressBlock>> field. You can do this from the Insert Merge Field button on the Mailings tab. Then instead of pressing Enter to create paragraph breaks between the lines of the address, use Shift+Enter to create line breaks.

If there's still too much space between lines, it's probably because the between-line spacing in the paragraph is set to 1.15 instead of 1. Select the paragraph(s), and on the Home tab, open the Line Spacing button's menu, and click 1.0.

Now that you've seen a bit of what mail merge can do via the semiautomated wizard process, let's take a closer look at each step of the process.

First we'll look at the Envelopes and Labels choices, because they have additional options you can set.

Selecting a Main Document Type

A mail merge starts with your selection of the type of main document. To do this, click the Start Mail Merge button on the Mailings tab and select a type from the menu (see Figure 14.4).

As listed at the beginning of this chapter, there are several main document types to choose from. The type you select changes the paper size and view that Word uses for the main document:

- **Letters**—Regular 8.5-inch × 11-inch page size, Print Layout view.

- **E-mail messages**—Regular 8.5-inch × 11-inch page size, Web Layout view.

- **Envelopes**—Opens an Envelope Options dialog box in which you set the size.

- **Labels**—Opens a Label Options dialog box in which you set the size.

- **Directory**—Same page size and view as Letters.

Figure 14.4
Select the type of main document.

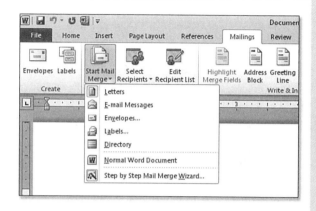

Setting Envelope Options

When you select Envelopes from the Start Mail Merge button's menu, the Envelope Options dialog box appears, shown in Figure 14.5. From here you can select the envelope size from the Envelope Size list. Many standard sizes are provided; you can also choose the Custom Size option and enter your own dimensions for it.

Figure 14.5
Select the envelope options.

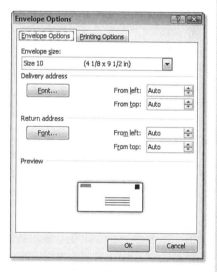

You can also set the font to be used for the delivery and return addresses on the envelopes. Click the Font button in either the Delivery Address or the Return Address area to set its font size, typeface, and color.

➡ *For details about setting the envelope font, see "Changing the Envelope Font," p. 324.*

The From Left and From Top settings in the Delivery Address and Return Address sections enable you to fine-tune the positioning of those addresses on the envelope. The default setting of Auto places the return address 1/2-inch from the top-left corner, and it places the delivery address in the horizontal center of the envelope, slightly lower than the vertical center. In most cases, the Auto setting is appropriate, provided you have correctly identified the envelope size.

Finally, you can choose how the envelopes feed into the printer—or rather, how Word perceives that they do. We covered this in Chapter 8, where you learned about printing individual envelopes. Refer to the section "Controlling How Envelopes Feed into Your Printer" in Chapter 8.

Setting Label Options

When you select Labels from the Start Mail Merge button's menu, the Label Options dialog box appears, shown in Figure 14.6. From here you can select the label type, which in turn tells Word the size of each label and how many rows and columns of labels appear on each sheet.

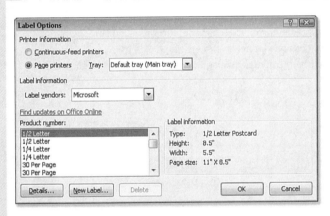

Figure 14.6
Select the label options.

To print labels, you need special label paper. There are many brands and sizes of labels; most come in full 8.5-inch × 11-inch sheets, with perforated peel-off labels. Word recognizes the model numbers for many popular brands and sizes; you can also set up custom labels if none of Word's presets are appropriate.

From the Label Options dialog box, first select the type of printer you have: continuous-feed or page printer. This makes a difference because the label products available are different for each type. A *page printer* accepts individual sheets of paper. A *continuous-feed* printer uses a tractor feed to pull connected sheets through the printer. Most ink-jet and laser printers are page printers, and most dot matrix printers are continuous feed. There are special labels-only printers, however, that use ink-jet technology to print on continuous-feed labels.

 caution

Make sure you buy the type of label sheets designed for your printer type. Labels designed for ink-jet printers cannot withstand the heat generated by the laser printing process and might become curled or wrinkled—or worse yet, peel off or melt inside the printer—if used with a laser.

After selecting the printer type, choose a label brand. The most common brand is Avery, but Word supports many other brands as well. Selecting a label brand filters the Product Number list to show only the product numbers for that brand. Select the product number that matches what you have.

If you're using a generic label brand and you don't know the equivalent model number for a well-known brand, you have a choice: You can browse through the product numbers for a well-known brand such as Avery until you find one that matches up with what you've got, or you can create a new custom label specification by clicking New Label and creating a new definition in the Label Details dialog box.

➡ *For complete steps for creating a new label specification, see "Creating a Custom Label Specification," p. 329.*

Selecting a Data Source

Word can pull data for a mail merge from a variety of data source types. Because Word is part of the Office suite, it's only natural that mail merge readily accepts data from Outlook, Excel, Access, Microsoft Works Database, and even other Word files (provided the data is in a table). It accepts data from a variety of other non-Microsoft sources too, including dBASE, Paradox, and Lotus 1-2-3, as well as from delimited data files. Or, if the data source you need does not already exist, you can create a new data source via Word's own interface.

Understanding Delimited Data

A delimited data file is one that represents multiple columns without actually having column lines. The break between columns is represented by a consistent character between entries, such as a comma or tab. Rows are represented by paragraph breaks.

For example, here's a plaintext delimited version of a table with three rows and three columns, with names in each cell:

- Tom,Dick,Harry
- Barbie,Ken,Skipper
- Mary Ann,Ginger,Gilligan

Delimiters enable plaintext files to serve as databases. Almost all database programs can import and export delimited text files, which makes it possible to exchange data with almost any database program.

Delimited files also make it possible to do a Word mail merge based on virtually any data from any database program. If Word does not directly support mail merging from that database program, export the data to a delimited text file, and then use the delimited text file for your Word merge.

How Can I Use a Fixed-Width Data File?

Word cannot use a fixed-width data file in a mail merge; it accepts only delimited or tabular data files.

However, Excel can import fixed width data. In Excel, on the Data tab, click From Text and then select the file containing the data. Excel walks you through a wizard that enables you to select the column widths and import the data. Save your work in Excel, and then use that new Excel file as your data source for the mail merge in Word.

Choosing an Outlook Contact List as a Data Source

Because Outlook is the default email and contact management program for Office, Word makes it easy to use it as the data source for a mail merge. The fields are already mapped between the two programs so that Outlook's address fields fit into the <<AddressBlock>> field, for example. There's little you need to do in the way of setup if you're planning to use an Outlook file for the merge.

You saw earlier in the chapter, in "Performing a Letter Merge with the Mail Merge Wizard," how to choose Outlook as a data source from the wizard. To do it without the wizard, follow these steps:

1. From the Mailings tab, click Select Recipients.

2. On the Select Recipients menu, click Select from Outlook Contacts. The Select Contacts dialog box opens.

3. Click the desired Outlook contact file.

   If there are multiple choices, as in Figure 14.7, and you do not know which one to pick, look for the one with Contacts in the name, the largest number in the Count column, and Outlook in the Location column.

4. Click OK to accept the chosen Outlook contact file. The Mail Merge Recipients dialog box opens.

5. Clear the check boxes for any entries you do not want to include in the merge, and then click OK.

 For more information about excluding certain records, see "Filtering and Sorting the Data," p. 570.

> 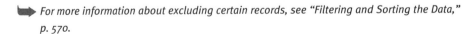 **note**
>
> When you have selected a valid Outlook contact file, the Edit Recipient List button becomes available on the Mailings tab. If the Edit Recipient List button remains unavailable, try again to select the Outlook contact list.

Choosing an Existing Data Source

Outlook is only one possible program from which you can draw data. Word can accept data from a variety of data sources, including Excel worksheets, Word tables, plaintext files, and files from various database programs including Paradox and dBASE. You can also pull data from server-based SQL and Oracle databases.

Figure 14.7
Select the Outlook data file.

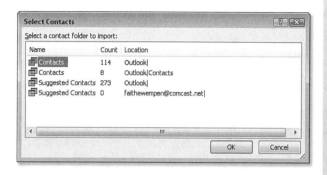

Choosing an Excel Data Source

An Excel worksheet works well as a data source for a mail merge, provided you set it up according to these guidelines:

- The first row of the file should contain the field names.

- The records should appear, one per row, immediately below the field names.

Some people set up an Excel worksheet with a sheet title in cell A1, a few blank rows, and then the data after that. Word cannot interpret such a layout as a valid data file for a merge, though, so you need to edit the Excel file beforehand to omit any rows at the top that are extraneous to the data. Figure 14.8 shows an Excel file that is correctly set up.

Figure 14.8
This Excel file is properly config-ured to be used in a Word mail merge.

In addition, if you are planning on using the <<AddressBlock>> field to create an address block in the main document, rather than inserting individual fields, the field names in the first row of the worksheet should be similar to the field names used in Outlook: First Name, Last Name, Address, City, State/Province, ZIP/Postal Code, and Country/Region. The closer you get to that naming con-vention, the more flawlessly the data maps to Word's <<AddressBlock>> field.

To select an Excel file as a data source, follow these steps:

1. From the Mailings tab, choose Select Recipients, Use Existing List. The Select Data Source dialog box opens.

2. Select the Excel file to use as a data source and click Open. The Select Table dialog box opens.

3. Select the worksheet that contains the data. If you are not sure, try Sheet1$ (see Figure 14.9).

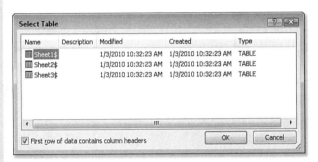

Figure 14.9
Select the sheet that contains the data to be used in the mail merge.

4. Click OK. The Excel file is now connected as the data source for the mail merge.

5. (Optional) To confirm that the field names have been set up properly, click the Insert Merge Field button on the Mailings tab. The field names should appear here.

If generic names appear there instead, check the file in Excel to make sure the field names appear in row 1.

Choosing a Word Data Source

A Word file can serve as a data source if one of these conditions is true:

 tip

You can rename the tabs in an Excel workbook by double-clicking a tab and typing a new name (in Excel). The names you assign appear in the Select Table dialog box if you have assigned any; otherwise, the sheet names appear generic, as in Figure 14.9.

- The Word document begins with a table, and that table contains the records, one per row, with the field names in the first row. In this case, the Word file is treated like an Excel worksheet.

- The Word document contains the records, one per paragraph, with the fields delimited by a consistent character such as a tab or comma. In this case, the Word file is treated like a delimited text file (discussed later in the chapter).

To choose a Word document, follow these steps:

1. From the Mailings tab, choose Select Recipients, Use Existing List. The Select Data Source dialog box opens.

2. Select the Word document file to use as a data source and click Open.

3. If the records are delimited, rather than in a table, a dialog box might appear prompting you to specify the delimiter character. This happens only if Word cannot figure out the delimiters on its own. If needed, enter the information required and click OK.

Choosing a Delimited Text Data Source

In a data source file in which the fields are delimited, you might need to specify which character is used as the delimiter. Word prompts you if needed. Other than that, it's pretty straightforward:

1. From the Mailings tab, choose Select Recipients, Use Existing List. The Select Data Source dialog box opens.

2. Select the text file to use as a data source and click Open.

3. If a Text File Connection Parameters dialog box appears prompting you to specify the delimiter characters, specify the characters used for field and row delimiters, and then click OK.

   This happens only if Word cannot figure them out on its own.

Setting Up an Oracle or SQL Database as a Data Source

Word can connect to a variety of database server types, including SQL and Oracle. You set up a data source once, and then you can reuse it without having to go through its configuration again.

To set up a SQL or Oracle database, follow these steps:

1. From the Mailings tab, choose Select Recipients, Use Existing List. The Select Data Source dialog box opens.

2. Click the New Source button. The Data Connection Wizard dialog box opens (see Figure 14.10).

Figure 14.10
Choose the type of data source you want to set up.

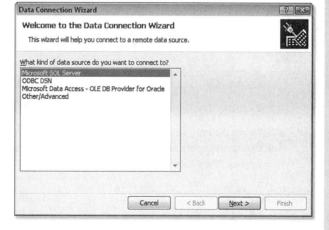

3. Select the type of server to which you want to connect (Microsoft SQL Server or Microsoft Data Access – OLE DB Provider for Oracle) and click Next.

4. Type the server name in the Server Name box.

5. If the server is on your own network, you might be able to connect to it using Windows Authentication (the default Log On Credentials setting). If not, choose Use the Following User Name and Password and then enter the username and password required to log into the server.

6. Click Next to continue. Word logs into the server.

7. When prompted, select the data table or query from which you want to pull records, and then click Next.

8. At the Save Data Connection File and Finish screen, enter a filename in the File Name box for the shortcut to the database.You can optionally enter a description and a friendly name.

9. Click Finish to connect to the data source and close the dialog box.

In the future, you can select the shortcut you just created from the Select Data Source dialog box (step 1) and bypass the other steps.

Using an ODBC Data Source

ODBC (Open Database Connectivity) is a widely used standard for connecting to databases. Data sources that use ODBC use SQL to connect, but they go through an ODBC driver installed in Windows. Using ODBC, you can access Excel workbooks, Access databases, dBASE databases, and other types of sources if you have ODBC drivers for them, stored either on a server or on a local or network client. For example, if your company's customer database is stored in Access on the main server, you could access it via ODBC for your mail merge.

Follow these steps to connect to an ODBC data source:

1. From the Mailings tab, choose Select Recipients, Use Existing List. The Select Data Source dialog box opens.

2. Click the New Source button. Choose ODBC DSN from the list of server types and click Next.

3. Select the type of ODBC data source to which to connect. The items on the list depend on the ODBC drivers set up on your PC; by default, Windows and Office provide dBASE, Excel, and Access. Then click Next.

4. As prompted, specify the data file you want to use and the specific data table within it.

5. At the Save Data Connection File and Finish dialog box, enter a filename in the File Name box for a shortcut to be created for this data source (see Figure 14.11).

You can optionally enter a description and a friendly name.

 note

You can also specify Excel and Access files as data sources by choosing them directly from the Select Data Source dialog box, as you would any file. In fact, that's what you did earlier in the chapter, in the section "Choosing an Excel Data Source." It's basically the same process except the method described in the following steps sets up an .odb shortcut to the file for easier access.

Figure 14.11
Name the shortcut to the database so you can reuse it in the future.

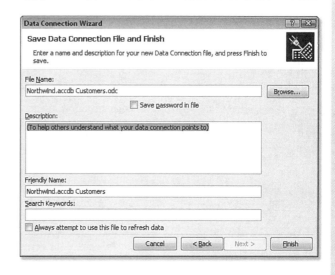

6. Click Finish to connect to the data source and close the dialog box.

In the future, you can select the shortcut you just created from the Select Data Source dialog box (step 1) and bypass the other steps.

Creating a New Data Source in Word

If the data source does not already exist, you might find it easier to create it from within Word than to fire up some outside program to create it. Word makes it easy to create a simple Access database to hold mail merge data for a personal contacts mailing list, even if you do not have Access installed on your PC and don't know anything about that program. It's all just fill-in-the-blanks.

To create a new data source, follow these steps:

1. From the Mailings tab, choose Select Recipients, Type New List. The New Address List dialog box appears.

2. If desired, customize the field names that appear in the columns. To do so, see "Customizing Fields" later in this chapter.

caution
You can open this database in Access if you have Access installed. Do not change the table name or structure, though, or the connection to your main document in Word will no longer work.

3. Enter the first record into the top row of the grid provided. To omit a field, simply leave it blank.

4. To start a new record, click New Entry. Another blank row appears (see Figure 14.12).

5. Continue adding records until you are finished; then click OK. The Save Address List dialog box appears.

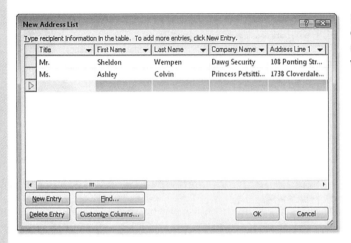

Figure 14.12
Create a new data source by entering records in the rows and columns provided.

6. Type a filename to use, and change the location if needed.

7. Click Save. Word creates a new Access database containing a single table with the data you just entered.

   ➡ To add more records to the address list, or edit it, see "Editing the Data Source," p. 563.

You can use the new database in future mail merge projects by choosing it as an existing data source, as you learned in "Using an ODBC Data Source" earlier in this chapter.

Customizing Fields

The fields provided for a new data source are typical for a personal mailing list, including name, address, and phone number. Perhaps you do not need or want all those fields, or maybe you need some different fields instead or in addition. For example, if you are creating a new data source to store inventory or events, the default fields need to be almost totally changed.

Here's how to customize the fields in the New Address List dialog box:

1. From the New Address List dialog box (from step 1 in the preceding section), click Customize Columns. The Customize Address List dialog box opens (see Figure 14.13).

2. Delete any fields you don't want. To delete a field, select it, click Delete, and click Yes to confirm.

3. Rename any fields as desired. To rename a field, select it, click Rename, type the new name, and click OK.

4. Add any new fields as desired. To add a field, click Add, type the new field name, and click OK.

5. Reorder any fields as desired. To move a field, select it and then click Move Up or Move Down.

6. Click OK to return to the New Address List dialog box. (If you're done, you can click the OK button for that dialog box, too.)

Figure 14.13
Change the columns (fields) that appear in the Customize Address List dialog box.

Editing the Data Source

Normally when you pick database records for your mail merge, you are not editing the data source; you're simply changing your usage of it. For example, if you exclude a certain person from a mailing, that person's record still exists in the database. To edit the database, you would normally go through the database program's own interface.

However, if you created the database from within Word, as in the preceding sections, Word might be the only means you have of accessing that database, particularly if you do not have Access installed. If so, you might need to delete or add records to the database from Word.

To edit the data source from within Word, follow these steps:

1. From the Mailings tab, click Edit Recipient List. The Mail Merge Recipients dialog box opens.

2. In the Data Source box (bottom-left corner), select the data source (probably an .mdb file) and then click Edit. The Edit Data Source dialog box opens. It is just like the New Address List dialog box (refer to Figure 14.12) except for the name.

3. Do any of the following:

   ■ To create a new entry, click New Entry and fill in the fields.

   ■ To delete a record, click the gray box to its left to select it, and then click Delete Entry and click Yes to confirm.

   ■ To change the columns, follow the steps in the section "Customizing Fields" earlier in this chapter.

4. Click OK to accept the changes to the data source.

5. Click OK to close the Mail Merge Recipients dialog box.

 tip

Some of the templates that Microsoft provides have "merge" in their names, meaning they are special versions designed for mail merging. For example, try starting a new document with Median Merge Letter, one of the templates installed locally on your hard disk (File, New, Sample Templates). It contains placeholders with suggestions for inserting merge fields. Those placeholders are "dead." In other words, they do not reference actual merge fields. You must delete them and replace them with real merge fields, as you'll learn in the next section.

Preparing the Main Document

The main document is the file in which you place all the boilerplate text and the merge codes that will personalize each copy. Depending on the type of merge you are doing, the main document can be an envelope, a label sheet, a letter, an email message, or just about anything else. It's just an ordinary Word document except for the presence of the merge fields.

To prepare the main document, do the following:

- Confirm that the margins, page size, and page orientation are correct for the document you want. These were set automatically when you chose the document type from the Start Mail Merge button's menu, but it's worth checking.

- If needed, apply a template or change the paragraph styles to suit the needs of the project. Choose a different formatting theme if desired.

- Type the boilerplate text, leaving blank spots or reminders for the fields that you'll insert. To avoid forgetting to insert a merge field later, you might want to type something like FIELD HERE in the spot where it will go and then apply a bright-colored highlight to it (from the Home tab or the Mini Toolbar).

Inserting Merge Fields

Now that the two essential pieces are in place—the main document and the data source—it's time to join them. To do this, you'll insert merge fields that reference the data source into the main document.

Inserting Single Fields

The most straightforward way to go is to insert individual fields, one at a time. When you insert a field, Word places a code with double angle brackets into the document, like this: <<City>>.

To insert fields into the main document one at a time, follow these steps:

1. Position the insertion point where you want to place the field.

2. On the Mailings tab, click Insert Merge Field. A list of available fields from the data source appears (see Figure 14.14).

3. Click the desired field. A code appears for it in the document.

4. Repeat these steps to insert additional fields in the document as needed.

 note

The field names come from the data source, so they will change depending on the data source you've selected and might not be the same as shown in the examples in this chapter.

Figure 14.14
Insert a merge field from the Mailings tab.

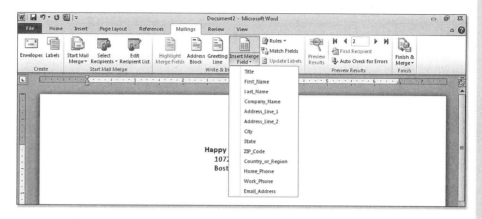

As you insert fields, make sure you leave the appropriate spaces and punctuation between them. For example, press the spacebar once between a <<First_Name>> and a <<Last_Name>> field.

Inserting Address Blocks

One of the most common uses for mail merge is to enter a mailing address block, like this:

Joe Smith
120 Main Street
Any Town, IN 46822

You can set up a mailing address block by inserting fields one at a time, as you learned in the preceding section, but it is time-consuming to do so. Assuming the first and last name are in separate fields, and so are the city, state, and ZIP code, you end up having to insert six separate fields just to create a simple address block.

Word offers a shortcut for setting up address blocks in the <<AddressBlock>> field. This field pulls the needed data from each of the applicable fields and creates a nicely formatted address block in a single step.

To insert an <<AddressBlock>> field, follow these steps:

1. Position the insertion point where you want the block to appear.

2. On the Mailings tab, click Address Block. The Insert Address Block dialog box opens (see Figure 14.15).

3. In the Insert Recipient's Name in This Format box, select the sample that best represents how you want the name to appear.

4. If you do not want the company name, clear the Insert Company Name check box.

5. In the Insert Postal Address area, specify how you want to (or don't want to) insert the country/region. The default setting is to include the country only if it is different from the value set in the drop-down list (United States in Figure 14.15).

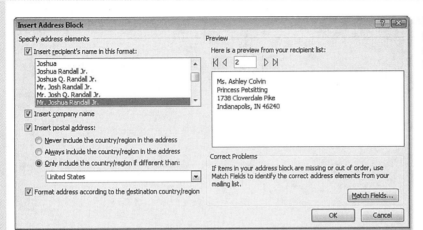

Figure 14.15
Specify options for the address block to be inserted.

6. Preview the addresses in the Preview area by clicking the right and left arrow buttons.

7. Click OK to insert the address block.

How does Word know what fields to use in the address block? It attempts to match up the fields in your data source with the various placeholders in an address block. If the data source uses common naming conventions, it usually does a pretty good job. If it makes any mistakes, click the Match Fields button in the dialog box to make adjustments.

The ⟨··⟨····AddressBlock····⟩··⟩ Isn't Using the Correct Fields

Word does a pretty good job of figuring out which fields in the data source should be used for the <<AddressBlock>>, the <<GreetingLine>>, and other special fields, but it's not perfect, especially if the field names in the data source are cryptically named.

Remapping the data source's field names to the placeholders in Word solves such problems. To do this, follow these steps:

1. From the Mailings tab, click Match Fields. The Match Fields dialog box opens. Word's internal names appear on the left, and the fields in the current data source to which they are mapped appear on the right (see Figure 14.16).

2. For any mappings that do not seem correct, open the drop-down list and select the proper field to map to that placeholder.

3. Click OK to accept the changes.

4. Update all fields in the document by selecting the entire document (Ctrl+A) and pressing F9. If the <<AddressBlock>> field does not change, delete it and reinsert it.

Figure 14.16
Specify which fields in your data source match up with Word's Address List.

Match Fields

In order to use special features, Mail Merge needs to know which fields in your recipient list match to the required fields. Use the drop-down list to select the appropriate recipient list field for each address field component

Unique Identifier	Customer ID
Courtesy Title	Title
First Name	First
Middle Name	Middle Name
Last Name	Last
Suffix	Suffix
Nickname	Nickname
Job Title	Job Title
Company	Company
Address 1	Address
Address 2	(not matched)
City	City
State	State

Use the drop-down lists to choose the field from your database that corresponds to the address information Mail Merge expects (listed on the left.)

☐ Remember this matching for this set of data sources on this computer

OK   Cancel

Inserting Greeting Lines

A *greeting line* is the line at the beginning of a letter that usually starts with "Dear." It's similar to an address block in that Word builds it automatically by drawing from multiple fields in the database.

To insert a greeting line, follow these steps:

1. Position the insertion point where you want the block to appear.

2. On the Mailings tab, click Greeting Line. The Insert Greeting Line dialog box opens (see Figure 14.17).

Figure 14.17
Specify options for the greeting line to be inserted.

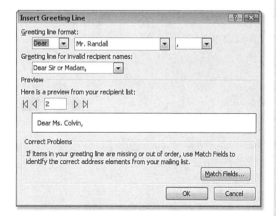

Insert Greeting Line

Greeting line format:

Dear ▾ | Mr. Randall ▾ | , ▾

Greeting line for invalid recipient names:

Dear Sir or Madam, ▾

Preview

Here is a preview from your recipient list:

◁◁ ◁ 2 ▷ ▷▷

Dear Ms. Colvin,

Correct Problems

If items in your greeting line are missing or out of order, use Match Fields to identify the correct address elements from your mailing list.

Match Fields...

OK   Cancel

IV

3. Set up the greeting the way you want it by selecting from the drop-down lists provided.

4. Specify a greeting line for invalid recipient names. Word will use this setting if the field from which it is drawing the name is blank or unreadable.

5. Click OK to insert the field code.

As with address blocks, you can remap the fields that Word uses from the data source. To do so, click the Match Fields button in the Insert Greeting Line dialog box. For more help with this, see "The <<AddressBlock>> Isn't Using the Correct Fields" in the "Troubleshooting" section earlier in the chapter.

 tip

For business letters, it is customary to start with Dear; to use the person's title and last name, as in Mr. Jones; and to finish with a colon (not a comma). For personal letters, it is customary to start with Dear, use the person's first name, and finish with a comma.

Setting Up Fields on Labels

If you set up your mail merge using the Letters, E-Mail Messages, or Envelopes document type (from the Start Mail Merge button's menu), each record in the data source is used for a separate copy of the document. For example, you create a single letter in the master document, and then the merge process generates as many customized copies as needed for the data in the data source.

However, if you set up your mail merge for labels, there will be more than one record per page of the document. A label layout consists of a table, and each record is in its own cell.

If you use the Mail Merge Wizard, the cells of the table are populated with the <<AddressBlock>> field automatically. However, if you are setting up labels manually, you need to enter them yourself. This is not difficult; you simply create one label's layout and then update all the other fields.

Follow these steps to set up the fields in a label layout:

1. Begin the mail merge by choosing the document type (Labels) from the Start Mail Merge button and then setting up the type of labels you want, as you learned earlier in this chapter.

2. Select or create the data source, as you learned earlier in this chapter.

   After you've selected a data source, a <<Next Record>> field appears automatically in each cell of the table (except the first cell).

3. (Optional) To make the table cells easier to see, do the following:

   - On the Home tab, click the Show/Hide (¶) button to toggle on the display of hidden characters.

   - On the Layout tab, click View Gridlines.

4. Click in the top-left cell in the table and insert the field(s) you want. It is easiest to simply insert the <<AddressBlock>> field, but you can manually create the address block if you prefer.

5. Click the Update Labels button. The <<AddressBlock>> field, or whatever fields you entered in step 4, are copied to the remaining cells (see Figure 14.18).

6. Continue with the merge, as described in the rest of this chapter.

Update Labels Button

Figure 14.18
Enter the field(s) in the top-left cell, and then click Update Labels to populate the change in the rest of the cells.

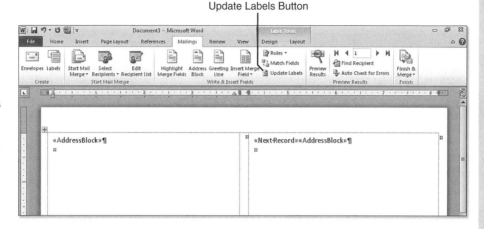

Setting Up Fields in Directories

A directory is a free-form type of mail merge document, in which you can place many records on a page if you like. It's somewhat like a set of labels except there are no table cells to tell Word where to break things off. Instead, you must insert a <<Next Record>> field manually where you want one record to stop and the next one to begin.

For example, suppose you want a listing of people's names and phone numbers, as in Figure 14.19. This merge consists of three fields: first name, last name, and phone number.

 For information about setting tab stops and dot leaders, see "Working with Tab Stops," p. 191.

To create a directory merge, you need to enter the desired fields once in the document, and then enter a <<Next Record>> field. Follow these steps:

1. Insert the fields to be displayed for each record.

2. Position the insertion point to the right of the last field.

3. On the Mailings tab, click Rules. Then click Next Record on the menu that appears. Word inserts a <<Next Record>> field. Figure 14.20 shows the fields that were used for Figure 14.19, for example.

4. Continue with the merge, as described in the rest of this chapter.

 note

The merge shown in Figure 14.19 was created by inserting the name fields, pressing Tab, and inserting the phone number field. Then the tab stop was changed to a right-aligned stop and placed at the right margin, and a dot leader was added.

note

If you preview the merge results before performing the actual merge, you will not see the directory as it will actually be; instead, you'll see one record only. This is the normal behavior for a directory type of merge. The only way to see the full directory is to perform the merge to a new file or to the printer.

Anna Bedecs...(317)555-3432
Thomas Axen...(317)555-7890
Martin O'Donnell..(217)555-5289
Ming-Yang Xie..(765)555-0098
Sven Mortensen...(765)555-7890
Peter Krschne..(765)555-4431
Andre Ludick..(317)555-7890
Helena Kupkova..(317)555-8799
Jean Philippe Bagel..(342)555-3421
Alexander Eggerer..(211)555-8754
Bernard Tham...(317)555-4533
Michael Entin...(765)555-3251
John Rodman..(504)555-1551
Karen Toh..(342)555-3241
Soo Jung Lee..(149)555-2521

Figure 14.19
A directory merge places information from multiple records on a single page.

«First_Name» «Last_Name»...«Business_Phone»«Next Record»

Figure 14.20
The merge fields used for the listing shown in Figure 14.19.

Filtering and Sorting the Data

If the data source was created specifically for this mail merge project, it might contain exactly the records you want and no others. If that's your situation, you can skip this whole section on filtering. (Stick around, though, if you want the records sorted in a certain way.)

Most of the time, however, people do mail merges using generic databases that are designed for more than just a single mail merge. For example, you might draw recipients from your Outlook contact list or a SQL database containing the personnel listings for your entire company. To avoid wasting paper and generating a lot of unneeded copies of the merge, apply a filter to the data set so that it contains only the records you want.

Excluding Individual Records

If your data source does not contain many records, you might find it easier to manually mark the records to exclude than to set up a formal filter that defines exclusion criteria.

To exclude records, follow these steps:

1. On the Mailings tab, click Edit Recipient List. The Mail Merge Recipients dialog box opens.

2. Clear the check box for the records you want to exclude (see Figure 14.21).

3. Click OK.

Applying a Filter

Applying a filter is useful when the records that you want to include have something quantifiable in common. For example, perhaps you want only addresses in a certain range of ZIP codes, or only people whose last names begin with a certain letter, or perhaps you want only the records that have complete mailing addresses. The following sections explain some techniques for filtering.

Figure 14.21
Exclude any records you do not want to use.

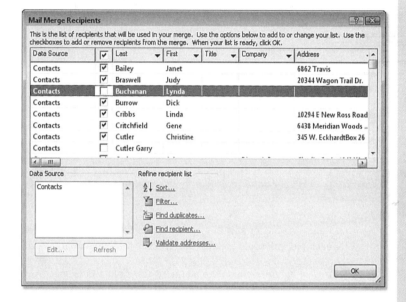

Filtering for Blank or Nonblank Entries

One of the most basic filters is to include only records in which a certain field is blank or nonblank. For example, for an email merge, you might include only records for which the E-Mail field is non-blank, or for a merge that prints labels to send cards to only your friends, not your business contacts, you might include only records for which the Company field is blank.

To filter for blank or nonblank entries, follow these steps:

1. From the Mailings tab, click Edit Recipient List. The Mail Merge Recipients dialog box opens.

2. Click the down arrow to the right of a field name to open a menu, and then click either (Blanks) or (Nonblanks) from the menu (see Figure 14.22).

 caution

Be careful to click the arrow, not the field name. If you click the field name, the list becomes sorted by that field and the menu does not open.

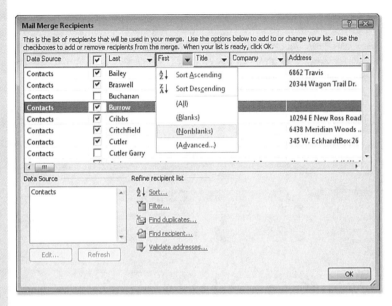

Figure 14.22
Filter a particular field based on its blank or nonblank status.

3. Repeat step 2 for each field you want to filter by. You can filter by multiple fields this way. For example, you could include only records that have nonblank Address, City, State, and ZIP fields.

To turn off a filter, reopen the menu for that field and choose (All).

Creating an Advanced Filter

An advanced filter is one in which you actually specify criteria for inclusion based on certain values or ranges. It consists of one or more *criteria*. A criterion consists of a field name, a comparison operator, and a value. For example, in "ZIP equals 46240," *ZIP* is the field name, *equals* is the comparison operator, and *46240* is the value.

Advanced filters can have multiple criteria, joined with either And or Or. If you use And, both of the rules must be true for a record to be included; if you use Or, at least one of the rules must be true.

To set up an advanced filter, follow these steps:

1. From the Mailings tab, click Edit Recipient List. The Mail Merge Recipients dialog box opens.

2. Click the Filter hyperlink. The Filter and Sort dialog box appears.

3. On the Filter tab, open the Field drop-down list and select the field for the first rule.

4. Open the Comparison drop-down list and choose the comparison operator.

5. In the Compare To box, type the value to which to compare. Figure 14.23 shows an example in which the ZIP code must equal 46240.

Figure 14.23
Create filtering criteria in the Filter and Sort dialog box.

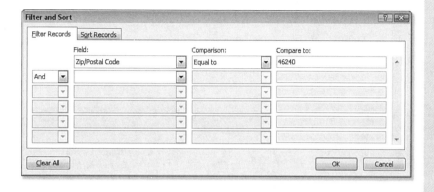

6. (Optional) Set the And/Or indicator for the second line and enter an additional rule. Keep entering additional rules as needed.

7. Click OK to apply the filter. The list in the Mail Merge Recipients dialog box changes to show only the records that the filter selects.

8. Click OK to accept the filtered list.

Sorting the Records

Usually when you create a mailing, the order in which the items print is not an issue because you're just going to drop them in the mailbox and they'll get all mixed up there anyway. However, with large bulk mailings, some mail processing services ask that clients provide the items for mailing in a certain order, usually by ZIP code. To have the items print in a certain order, you can set up a sort.

To perform a simple sort, click a field's column heading in the Mail Merge Recipients dialog box. Each time you click, it toggles between an ascending and descending sort. Alternatively, you can open the field's menu (by clicking its arrow) and choosing Sort Ascending or Sort Descending.

You can perform advanced sorting in the Filter and Sort dialog box. You can set up a sort as part of creating the filter, as in the preceding section's steps; just click the Sort Records tab and enter the sort criteria before closing the Filter and Sort dialog box.

If you just want to sort (no filtering), or if you have already closed the dialog box, follow these steps:

1. From the Mailings tab, click Edit Recipient List. The Mail Merge Recipients dialog box opens.

2. Click the Sort hyperlink. The Filter and Sort dialog box appears with the Sort Records tab displayed (see Figure 14.24).

3. Open the Sort By drop-down list and select the field by which you want to sort.

4. Click Ascending or Descending to set the sort order. Ascending is 0 to 9, then A to Z; Descending is Z to A, then 9 to 0.

5. (Optional) Specify additional sorts in the subsequent rows. The additional sorts take effect only in the event of a tie for the first sort. For example, if two records have the same ZIP code, perhaps you want the tiebreaker to be last name.

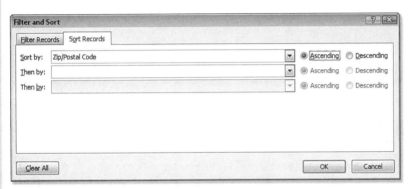

Figure 14.24
Set up one or more fields by which to sort.

6. Click OK to accept the sort condition(s).

Finding a Recipient

In a large database, it can be a challenge to find a particular record by scrolling through and browsing. To access the Find feature within the Mail Merge Recipients dialog box and use it to locate a certain record, follow these steps:

1. From the Mailings tab, click Edit Recipient List. The Mail Merge Recipients dialog box opens.

2. Click the Find Recipient hyperlink. The Find Entry dialog box opens.

3. Type the text string you want to find.

4. Choose one of the option buttons: All Fields or This Field. If you choose This Field, open the drop-down list and select the field to search.

5. Click Find Next. The list jumps to the first occurrence of that string.

6. Click Find Next again to find the next instance, and so on until you have found the record you are seeking.

Finding Duplicate Entries

Large databases can sometimes contain duplicate entries due to data entry errors and lack of synchronization between sources. To ensure that none of these duplicates gets into your mail merge, you can use the Find Duplicates feature:

1. From the Mailings tab, click Edit Recipient List. The Mail Merge Recipients dialog box opens.

2. Click the Find Duplicates hyperlink. The Find Duplicates dialog box opens, showing groups of records that appear to be very similar or identical (if any).

3. Clear the check box for the items you do not want to be included in the mail merge (see Figure 14.25).

4. Click OK to return to the Mail Merge Recipients dialog box and continue the merge.

Figure 14.25
Evaluate entries that Word finds to be similar, and deselect any that appear to be duplicates of another.

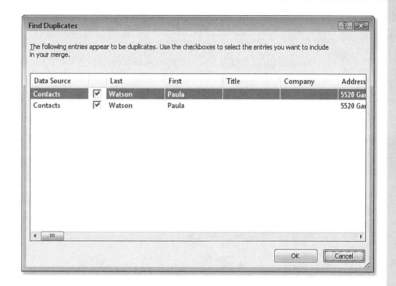

Validating Addresses

Address validation looks up addresses in an actual postal mailing database online and determines whether each one is deliverable. This feature is not included with Word, but Word does provide a link for accessing a third-party data validation service, such as Stamps.com.

If you have subscribed to such a service, you can access it from the Mail Merge Recipients dialog box by clicking Validate Addresses. If you have not signed up for a service, a message appears offering to take you to the Microsoft Office website, from which you can browse for available third-party services.

Previewing and Printing the Merge

After setting up the main document and performing any needed sorting or filtering on the data set, the next step is to preview the merge. Previewing is optional, but it can save you from printing stacks of documents that contain merge errors. With paper and ink costs as high as they are these days, previewing can be a real benefit.

To preview the merge results, click the Preview Results button on the Mailings tab. This button is an on/off toggle between the field codes and the merge results.

While you're looking at the preview results, you can use the arrow buttons in the Preview Results group on the Mailings tab to scroll from one record to another (see Figure 14.26).

 note

As noted earlier, if you are previewing a directory merge, or other merge type in which you have inserted the ⦃⦃·Next Record···⦄···⦄ code yourself to separate records that will appear on a page together, you might see only one record at a time with Preview Results, not the entire page as it will actually be. To preview the page more accurately, merge to a new document (Finish & Merge, Edit Individual Documents).

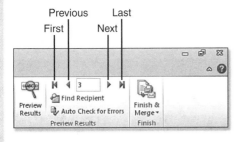

Figure 14.26
Preview merge results.

Checking for Errors

To save on paper, it's important to check the merge for errors before you print. But if you have thousands of records, it can be a chore to sort through them manually.

To automate the process of checking for common errors, such as empty fields or invalid field names, follow these steps:

1. On the Mailings tab, click Auto Check for Errors. The Checking and Reporting Errors dialog box opens.

2. Click Simulate the Merge and Report Errors in a New Document.

   You can use the other options in this dialog box to go ahead and complete the merge if you prefer.

3. Click OK. If there are any errors, they appear in a report in a new document. Otherwise, a dialog box appears, telling you there are no errors; click OK to clear it.

4. If Word finds errors, correct them.

Merging to a New Document

To save paper, I always merge to a new document rather than directly to a printer. That way if there are errors that the Error Check did not catch, such as a missing ZIP code or improper spacing between fields, I'll notice them before printing.

Merging to a new document also has the side benefit of enabling you to edit individual copies before printing. For example, perhaps for one certain person you want to add a personal note in an extra paragraph at the end of the letter.

 note

The numbers you enter in the range in Figure 14.27 refer to the record numbers—that is, the records in the order you specified in the sort, or the default order from the data source if you did not specify a sort.

To merge to a new document, follow these steps:

1. From the Mailings tab, click Finish & Merge, Edit Individual Documents. The Merge to New Document dialog box appears (see Figure 14.27).

2. Click All to merge all records, or specify a range of records if you don't want to do them all at once. (For example, perhaps you want only the first 100 records in the new file, and then you'll perform the merge again to put the next 100 in another new file, and so on.)

3. Click OK. Word performs the merge and places it in a new document.

Figure 14.27
Merge all records or enter a range.

Merging to a Printer

If you're feeling confident about your merge, you can send it directly to the printer, without creating a new document. You might do this for a merge that you've already completed successfully before, such as a merge you perform every month to send letters to the same group of people.

To merge directly to the printer, follow these steps:

1. From the Mailings tab, click Finish & Merge, Print Documents. The Merge to Printer dialog box appears. It is identical to the Merge to New Document dialog box in Figure 14.27 except for its name.

2. Click All to merge all records, or specify a range of records if you don't want to print them all at once.

3. Click OK. The Print dialog box opens.

4. Set any print options as desired (including selecting the printer to use), as you learned to do in Chapter 3, "Correcting and Printing Documents."

5. Click OK to print.

Merging to Email

Merging to email sends the messages via your default email program, using the email address in whatever field you specify from the data source. (You must make sure, therefore, that your data source has an email address for every record you select.)

Follow these steps to merge to email:

1. From the Mailings tab, click Finish & Merge, Send E-mail Messages. The Merge to E-Mail dialog box appears (see Figure 14.28).

Figure 14.28
Merge to email by specifying the field containing the email addresses and the subject line and mail format.

2. Make sure the field containing the email addresses is selected from the To drop-down list.

3. Enter the subject line to use in the Subject Line box.

4. Select a mail format from the Mail Format list.

   If your document includes formatting, such as colors, different font sizes, and so on, make sure you choose HTML as the mail format.

 caution

Before performing step 6, make sure your emails are just the way you want them. Word will send them immediately after the next step, with no opportunity to check them.

5. In the Send Records section, choose All, or choose the current record or a range of records.

6. Click OK. Your email program opens, the emails are created, and they are placed in your Outbox folder for sending.

7. In your email program, perform a Send/Receive operation to send the messages if they are not sent automatically.

Creating Custom Merges with Word Fields

The simple mail merges you've learned about so far in this chapter insert data by referencing fields in the specified data source. Nine times out of ten, that's all you'll need for a mail merge. But wouldn't it be nice to be able to do something a little more complex for that tenth time?

Suppose you are creating a letter to all your customers, but you want the letter to say different things depending on the values in certain fields of your database. For example, perhaps you want customers who have not ordered from you in more than six months to receive a special promotional offer. Or perhaps you want to be able to enter a different promotional offer each time you run the merge and be prompted to enter the offer in a dialog box. All that and more is possible by using fields.

There are two types of fields: merge fields and Word fields. Throughout this chapter, you've been using *merge fields*—that is, fields that come from the data source you specify for a mail merge. These fields exist only because of the data source connection. *Word fields*, on the other hand, are preprogrammed into Word itself and can be used in any type of document, not just merge documents.

You will learn about fields in Chapter 16, "Working with Fields and Forms," including how to insert and modify them and how to control their syntax. For now, though, let's look at a few specific fields that are useful when doing merges. They're so useful for merges, in fact, that they appear on a special menu on the Mailings tab. Click Rules to see the list, as shown in Figure 14.29.

Figure 14.29
Certain Word fields that are especially useful in mail merges appear on the Rules menu on the Mailings tab.

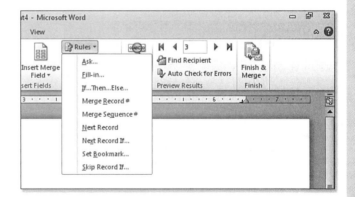

Collecting Information with a Fill-In Field

A {FillIn} field prompts the user for an entry and then places it in the document. You can set it up to ask you only once per merge or to ask you separately for each copy.

For example, suppose you have a standard form letter in which you offer customers a certain percentage of discount if they bring the letter with them into your store on certain dates. You can reuse the same main document time after time and set it up to ask you each time how much discount you want to offer and what the date range should be.

To insert a {FillIn} field, follow these steps:

1. Position the insertion point where you want the field to appear.

2. On the Mailings tab, click Rules, and then choose Fill-In. The Insert Word Field: Fill-In dialog box opens.

3. In the top part of the dialog box, enter the prompt that will appear to the user.

4. (Optional) In the bottom part of the dialog box, shown in Figure 14.30, enter a default value that will be used if the user does not fill in the dialog box (for example, if he clicks Cancel or closes the dialog box without typing anything).

Figure 14.30
Create a {FillIn} field.

5. (Optional) If the value should be the same for every record in the merge, mark the Ask Once check box. Otherwise, Word will ask you repeatedly, once for each record.

6. Click OK to insert the field.

Whenever you open the document or initiate the merge, Word updates the field and prompts the user for the entry.

{FillIn} fields are useful when the value that the user enters does not need to be stored for reuse. In the aforementioned example, the user enters a discount amount to offer to the customers, but that discount amount does not need to be stored for calculations; it is simply placed in the document. If you need to store the user's entry as a variable and then perform a calculation on it or reprint it later in the document, use an {Ask} field instead, as described in the following section.

Collecting and Storing Information with an Ask Field

An {Ask} field is like a {FillIn} field, except the value that the user enters is stored in a bookmark for later reuse. So, for example, you could prompt for a certain value, such as a discount percentage, and then have that value be repeated in several places in the document.

You will learn about bookmarks in Chapter 15, "Copying, Linking, and Embedding Data." A *bookmark* is a named location or text entry in the document. Bookmarks have a variety of uses. You can create bookmarks to mark certain paragraphs and then set up hyperlinks that jump directly to those paragraphs, for example.

➤ *To learn about bookmarks, see "Working with Bookmarks," p. 593.*

When you use an {Ask} field to prompt the user for an entry, Word stores that entry in a bookmark. The bookmark in this case is like a variable you might set in computer programming. You can then insert that bookmark's content in various places in the document by using a {Ref} field.

For example, at the beginning of the mail merge, you might use an {Ask} field to prompt the user for a salesperson's name and to store that name in a bookmark called *Employee*. Then that person's name can be set to appear in the body of the letter and on the signature line.

To insert an {Ask} field and then reference its bookmark in the document, follow these steps:

1. Move the insertion point to the beginning of the document. Do not select text.

2. Create the bookmark. To do so:

   a. On the Insert tab, click Bookmark.

   b. In the Bookmark dialog box, type the name you want to use.

   c. Click Add.

3. Create references to the bookmark as needed in the document. To do this:

   a. Move the insertion point to where you want the bookmark's content.

   b. On the Insert tab, click Quick Parts, and then click Field.

   c. On the Field Names list, click Ref.

   d. In the Bookmark Name list, click the bookmark name (see Figure 14.31).

   e. Click OK.

4. Move the insertion point to the beginning of the document.

5. On the Mailings tab, click Rules and then click Ask. The Insert Word Field: Ask dialog box opens.

6. On the Bookmark list, select the bookmark you created earlier.

7. In the Prompt box, type the text that should appear in the user prompt.

8. In the Default Bookmark Text box, type the default text to use if the user does not enter text. Figure 14.32 shows the completed dialog box.

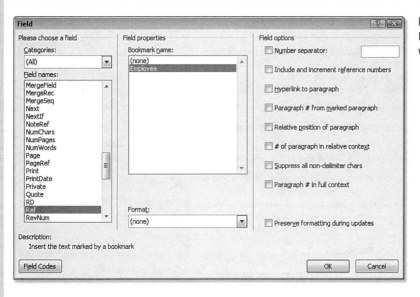

Figure 14.31
Reference a bookmark
with the {Ref} field.

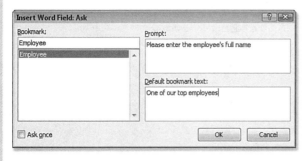

Figure 14.32
Create an {Ask} field that prompts the user to fill
in the value for a bookmark.

9. Click OK.

10. To test the field(s) in the document, select the entire document (Ctrl+A) and press F9 to update
    all the fields.

> To learn more about updating fields, see "Updating a Field," p. 633.

Setting Up Conditions with an If…Then…Else Field

You can use the {If} field (aka the If…Then…Else field) to insert different text in each copy of the
merge depending on the value of a certain field. For example, suppose you're going to send the
mail merge letter to customers in several countries, and depending on the country, you would like

to offer a different promotion. In the spot where the sentences will appear with the promotional offer, you can insert an {If} field and specify the value of the Country field as the condition in choosing one block of text or another to be inserted.

To create an {If} field that displays different text based on a condition, follow these steps:

1. Position the insertion point where you want the conditional text to appear.

2. On the Mailings tab, click Rules and then click If...Then...Else. The Insert Word Field: IF dialog box opens.

3. In the Field Name list, select the field that will provide the criterion.

4. In the Comparison list, select the comparison operator, such as Equal To or Greater Than.

5. In the Compare To box, type the value to which to compare the field.

> **caution**
>
> Make sure you preview the merge before sending it to a printer but after inserting an {If} field to make sure the results are as you intended.

6. In the Insert This Text box, type the text string to display if the comparison is true. (Leave it blank if you want nothing to display if true.)

7. In the Otherwise Insert This Text box, type the text string to display if the comparison is false. (Leave it blank if you want nothing to display if false.) Figure 14.33 shows a completed example.

8. Click OK to insert the field.

Figure 14.33
Use an {If} field to set up different scenarios based on the entry in one of the fields.

Using a Field to Set Bookmark Text

Earlier in the chapter, you saw how to use {Ask} to set a bookmark's value based on input from the user. A related field, {Set}, is used to set a bookmark without user input. You could use this to set an initial value for a bookmark, for example. (Then later in the merge, you could allow the user to change that value with a Fill-In or Ask.)

To insert a {Set} field into a document:

1. From the Mailings tab, click Rules and then click Set Bookmark. The Insert Word Field: Set dialog box opens.

2. On the Bookmark list, click the bookmark name for which you want to set a value.

3. In the Value box, type the value to which to set the bookmark.

4. Click OK.

One important usage for the {Set} field is within an {If} field. You might want a bookmark to be set one way if an {If} statement is true and another way if it is false. For example, if a letter recipient is female, you might want the pronouns in the document to be feminine (her/hers); otherwise, the pronouns should be masculine (him/his).

However, to nest a {Set} within an {If}, you must manually edit the field code, and you must manually create the {If} statement. (You can't use the Rules button's If...Then...Else insertion method.) Therefore, you might want to postpone this topic until after you've read Chapter 16. Then read the section "Nesting Fields" to learn how to nest one field inside another.

Assigning Numbers to Merge Records

Sometimes when creating a large number of merged copies, you need to sequentially number the copies as Word generates them, so that each copy has a unique identifying number. There are two ways of doing this in Word: Merge Record # {MergeRec} and Merge Sequence # {MergeSeq}.

The {MergeRec} field assigns a number to each copy based on the actual number of the record within the data source. If you skipped over any records in the data source, the numbering skips, too. For example, if a filter excluded the first 100 records, {MergeRec} would begin with 101.

The {MergeSeq} field assigns a number to each copy based on the records that were included in the merge, not the records in the original data source. So even if you skipped over 100 records, {MergeSeq} would always begin with 1.

To insert either of these, select it from the Rules menu on the Mailings tab: Merge Record # or Merge Sequence #. There are no options for either of these; they simply insert a code.

Advancing to the Next Record (or Not)

As you saw earlier in the chapter, in the section "Setting Up Fields in Directories," you can insert a {NextRecord} field to force the merge to continue to the next record without starting a new copy of the main document. To do this, on the Mailings tab, choose Rules, Next Record.

Two related fields, {NextRecordIf} and {SkipRecordIf}, enable you to set up conditions whereby you either process or skip the next record in the merge according to certain conditions you specify. Each of these has its own command for insertion on the Rules menu, and each opens a dialog box in which you can set up a criterion based on the contents of a field in the data source. Neither of these is commonly used; if you want to skip certain records based on the content of a certain merge field, it's easier to simply set up a filter for the data source that excludes certain values for that field.

COPYING, LINKING, AND EMBEDDING DATA

Understanding Types of Data Sharing

Windows and Office both have some great data-sharing features that enable you to move data easily from one application to another. You can embed Excel charts in Word, store PowerPoint slides in Access databases, insert web bookmarks and hyperlinks into email messages, and much more. There are so many data-sharing possibilities, however, that it can sometimes get confusing. In this chapter, you'll learn about the various ways of sharing data and their advantages and drawbacks.

For basic data sharing, most people use the Clipboard, along with its associated commands (Cut, Copy, Paste), or drag-and-drop. These methods move or copy the content from one location to another without creating a connection between the locations.

> *To review data sharing via the Clipboard or drag-and-drop, see "Moving and Copying Text and Objects," p. 64.*

The ordinary copy-and-paste operation has its limitations, however. For example, suppose you have a chart in Excel that you want to use in Word. If you copy and paste that chart into Word, and then the data changes in the Excel worksheet on which it was originally based, the copy of the chart in Word does not update automatically. Copy-and-paste creates a one-time snapshot of the chart.

For more active connectivity between a source and destination, a variety of sharing techniques are available:

- **Hyperlinking**—You can create a text-based link to the original source document. When you click the link, the original document opens for viewing.

- **Bookmarking**—You can create an invisible marker in a document; then you can hyperlink to that marker rather than to the document as a whole.

- **Object linking**—You can create a link between the pasted copy and the file containing the original object, so that the pasted copy changes when the original does.

- **Object embedding**—You can insert various types of content into a document without converting that content to Word format. This makes it possible to edit the embedded object in its native program later.

- **Inserting with field codes**—You can use the InsertText and InsertPicture field codes to link external files to a Word document. This special-purpose technique has some benefits but also some drawbacks compared to object linking.

This chapter looks at each of these techniques with an eye toward better and more convenient content integration.

Working with Hyperlinks

A *hyperlink* is a pointer to another file or to an email address. You can assign the hyperlink to either text or a graphic. When you click the text or the graphic, the referenced file opens or a new message is started to that email address. That's called *following* the hyperlink.

Hyperlinks are most common on web pages, but any Word document can have hyperlinks in it. In fact, you might find that the easiest way to join a set of related documents is to place hyperlinks in each document that connect to the other documents in the set.

 note

Hyperlinks are actually {Hyperlink} fields; you can see this by selecting the hyperlink and pressing Shift+F9 to toggle field codes on/off. Chapter 16, "Working with Fields and Forms," covers fields in detail.

Automatically Creating Hyperlinks by Typing

Because Word is able to identify web and email addresses as such, it automatically turns them into hyperlinks as you type them. This works with any text strings that start with http:// or www or that are structured as an email address.

If you do not want certain instances to be hyperlinks, here are some ways to circumvent the process on a case-by-case basis:

- Immediately after the automatic conversion, press Ctrl+Z to undo the last action.

- At any time, right-click the hyperlink and choose Remove Hyperlink.

Turning Off Automatic Hyperlink Creation

By default, Word converts all web and email addresses to live hyperlinks. If you find yourself frequently undoing an automatic hyperlink conversion, you might want to turn that feature off.

Follow these steps to disable automatic hyperlink creation:

1. Choose File, Options. The Word Options dialog box opens.

2. Click Proofing and then click AutoCorrect Options. The AutoCorrect dialog box opens.

3. On the AutoFormat As You Type tab, clear the Internet and Network Paths with Hyperlinks check box.

4. Click OK.

5. Click OK to close the Word Options dialog box.

Following a Hyperlink

To *follow* a hyperlink is to activate it, so that the document, web page, or other referenced item opens.

In Word, clicking a hyperlink does not follow it. This is by design, because you might need to click in the hyperlink's text to edit it. Hold down Ctrl as you click on a hyperlink to follow it in Word.

If you like, you can turn off the Ctrl requirement for following a hyperlink, but there's a drawback to that: You can no longer click inside a hyperlink to edit its text. Instead, you must right-click the hyperlink and choose Edit Hyperlink and edit its text in the Edit Hyperlink dialog box.

 note

If a security notice appears when you follow a hyperlink, click OK to continue. This notice appears when the location being referred to is not on Windows' list of trusted sites. If you know the site you're going to is valid, then it's perfectly safe to ignore this warning. To prevent the notice from appearing in the future for hyperlinks to that location, add that location to the Trusted Locations list, as you'll learn to do in Chapter 21, "Protecting and Securing Documents."

 To set up a new trusted location, see "Specifying Trusted Locations," p. 802.

Disabling Ctrl+Click to Follow Hyperlinks

In Word, you must Ctrl+click to activate a hyperlink; regular clicking will not work. This is by design because you might need to click in a hyperlink and edit its text, and you couldn't do that if clicking were set up to activate the hyperlink. (You could still right-click it and choose Edit Hyperlink, however, to edit the text.)

Continued...

If you would rather have regular clicking activate hyperlinks in Word anyway, follow these steps:

1. Choose File, Options. The Word Options dialog box opens.

2. Click Advanced.

3. In the Editing Options section, clear the Use CTRL+Click to Follow Hyperlink check box.

4. Click OK.

Creating a Text Hyperlink

The most common type of hyperlink is flagged in Word as a bit of underlined text. You've seen this hundreds of times on web pages, but you can create this same type of hyperlink in any Word document. That hyperlink can point to another Word document, to a web page, to an executable file, or virtually anywhere else.

You can either turn some existing text into a hyperlink or insert brand-new text as you are creating the hyperlink. Either way, follow these steps:

1. (Optional) If the text that you want to use already exists in the document, select it.

2. On the Insert tab, click Hyperlink. The Insert Hyperlink dialog box opens (see Figure 15.1). You can also reach the Insert Hyperlink dialog box by using the keyboard shortcut Ctrl+K or by right-clicking on the selected text and choosing Hyperlink from the shortcut menu.

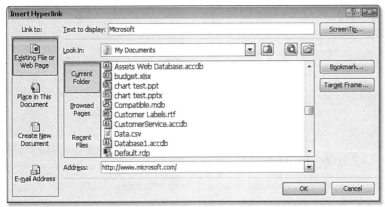

Figure 15.1
Create a hyperlink to a file, web page, bookmark, or email address.

3. If you selected any text in step 1, it appears in the Text to Display box. Add or change text here if desired.

4. Do one of the following:

- **Create a hyperlink to a web address**—Enter the web URL for the site to which you want the text to link in the Address text box.

- **Create a hyperlink to a file on your hard disk**—Use the folder list under the Look In box to browse to the desired location, and select the file.

 note

A *ScreenTip* is text that appears in a box when the user points at the hyperlink in a web browser. If you do not specify a ScreenTip, the hyperlink's address is the ScreenTip.

5. (Optional) To add a ScreenTip to the hyperlink, click the ScreenTip button, type the text, and click OK.

6. Click OK. When you return to your document, the text you highlighted is now a different color (blue, by default) and underlined, indicating that it is now an active hyperlink.

The exact color of the hyperlinks depends on the theme colors.

Hyperlinking to an Executable File

You can use hyperlinks to run applications. This is a fairly uncommon usage, but it can come in handy. For example, in training materials, you might include a hyperlink as a shortcut to opening the application on which you want to train the users.

To create a hyperlink to run an application, specify the application's executable file instead of a web page or data file in step 4 of the preceding steps. An executable file usually has an .exe extension, or less frequently a .com or .bat extension.

To determine the correct name and location for an application's executable file, right-click its shortcut on the Start menu and choose Properties. Then look in the Target field on the General tab of the Properties dialog box. If you know the executable file's name, you can easily find it in Windows Vista or Windows 7 by typing the name into the Start menu's search field. If the executable file appears in the results, you can create a shortcut from it, rather than traversing through the rest of the Start menu, looking for it.

Adding a Hyperlink to an Image

A graphic can function as a hyperlink, such that when the user clicks the image, the specified web page or document opens. The process for building a graphical hyperlink is similar to that of building a text hyperlink:

1. Select any clip art, picture, drawing object, or WordArt in the document.

2. On the Insert tab, click Hyperlink to display the Insert Hyperlink dialog box (or use the Ctrl+K or right-click method if you prefer).

3. Type the address for the link in the Address box, or browse for and select the file to which to hyperlink.

4. (Optional) If you want a custom ScreenTip, click ScreenTip, type the text, and click OK. Otherwise, the ScreenTip shows the complete path to the chosen file.

5. Click OK to complete the hyperlink.

The picture will not look different. If you hover the mouse pointer over the picture, however, the ScreenTip you specified will appear. To test the hyperlink, Ctrl+click the image.

Creating an Email Hyperlink

Besides referencing other files and web pages, hyperlinks can start the user's email editor and begin a blank email message with the recipient name filled in automatically. This is useful for providing a hyperlink through which someone can email you to comment on your web page.

Follow these steps to create an email hyperlink:

1. Select the text or choose an image for the hyperlink.

2. On the Insert tab, click Hyperlink to display the Insert Hyperlink dialog box (or use the Ctrl+K or right-click method if you prefer).

3. In the lower-left corner of the Insert Hyperlink dialog box, click E-Mail Address.

4. Enter the email address to which the hyperlink should send a message, as shown in Figure 15.2.

Figure 15.2
Hyperlinking to an email address.

Notice how the phrase mailto: is automatically added to the beginning of your email address.

5. (Optional) To pre-enter the subject line for the message, type the text in the Subject box.

6. (Optional) If you want a custom ScreenTip, click ScreenTip, type the text, and click OK. Otherwise, the ScreenTip shows the email address.

7. Click OK to complete the link.

Creating and Hyperlinking to a New Document

When creating groups of hyperlinked documents, it's best to create all the documents first, and then create the hyperlinks. If you forget to create one of the documents, though, it's easy to create it on the fly as you create the hyperlink. The Create New Document option in the Insert Hyperlink dialog box does just that.

Follow these steps to create a new document and a hyperlink to it:

1. Select the text or choose an image for the hyperlink.

2. On the Insert tab, click Hyperlink to display the Insert Hyperlink dialog box (or use the Ctrl+K or right-click method if you prefer).

3. Click Create New Document.

4. In the Name of New Document text box, type the name to be used for the new document. Do not type the path—just the name.

5. If the path listed under Full Path is not correct, click the Change button, browse to a different path, and click OK.

6. (Optional) If you want a custom ScreenTip for the hyperlink, click ScreenTip, type the text, and click OK. Otherwise, the ScreenTip shows the complete path to the new document.

7. Click Edit the New Document Now if you want the document to open for editing in Word now, or click Edit the New Document Later if you don't want it to open.

8. Click OK to complete the link.

Editing a Hyperlink

You can change a hyperlink's text, address, ScreenTip, or any other aspect of it. However, changing the underlined text in a hyperlink does not change its underlying address; they are two separate settings.

The easiest way to change a hyperlink's displayed text is simply to move the insertion point into the hyperlink text and edit it with Backspace, Delete, or any of the other editing techniques you use with regular text. Or, if you prefer, you can use the dialog box method described in the following steps.

Here's how to edit a hyperlink:

1. Right-click the hyperlink and choose Edit Hyperlink. The Edit Hyperlink dialog box opens. It looks just like Figure 15.1 or 15.2, depending on the hyperlink type.

 tip

There's one minor way in which editing hyperlink text is different from editing regular text: You can't delete individual characters from the beginning of the hyperlink text by using the Delete key. Clicking in front of the hyperlink text and pressing Delete once selects the entire hyperlink; pressing Delete again deletes the entire hyperlink. If you want to delete characters at the beginning of the hyperlink text, click after them and then use the Backspace key, or select only the characters to delete and then press Delete or Backspace.

2. Make any changes desired:

   ▪ Change the text to display.

   ▪ Click the ScreenTip button and change the ScreenTip text.

   ▪ In the Address (or E-Mail Address) box, change the address to which the hyperlink refers.

   ▪ If it's an email address hyperlink, change the subject.

3. Click OK to accept the changes.

Removing a Hyperlink

Removing a hyperlink doesn't remove the text; it just converts it to regular text. To remove a hyperlink, right-click the hyperlink and choose Remove Hyperlink from the menu. Simple, eh? If you already have the Edit Hyperlink dialog box open, you can also click the Remove Link button there to remove a hyperlink.

Changing Hyperlink Underlining and Color

Hyperlink text appears underlined and in whatever color the theme has assigned for hyperlinks (or visited hyperlinks).

You can remove the underlining from the hyperlink by selecting it and clicking the Underline button on the Home tab to toggle underlining off. However, be cautious when stripping off the underline from a hyperlink, because that makes it difficult for your readers to discern that a hyperlink is present.

The one quirk in hyperlink formatting is color. If you select a hyperlink and then try to change its font color, you'll discover that it won't work. The color remains whatever the theme has assigned for hyperlinks of its type.

There are two ways to change the hyperlink's color. One is to manually strip off all existing formatting from it and apply your own. Do the following for each hyperlink:

1. Select the hyperlink and press Ctrl+spacebar. All formatting is removed, but the hyperlink remains.

2. Click the Underline button on the Home tab to reunderline the hyperlink text. (This is optional but recommended, because hyperlinks that are not underlined are difficult to discern in a document.)

3. Apply the desired color.

 note

A *visited hyperlink* is one that you have clicked on (opened). Visited hyperlinks appear in a different color to help you keep track of which links you have used. This is perhaps not all that helpful in a Word document with a couple of stray hyperlinks in it, but on a page with a huge listing of links, it's invaluable.

 note

Your color choice actually is applied, but it's not visible because the hyperlink formatting sits on top of it. If you were to remove the hyperlink, the text would take on the color formatting you selected.

The other way is to change the color that the theme assigns to hyperlinks. This method affects all the hyperlinks in the entire document at once:

1. On the Page Layout tab, open the Theme Colors list and choose Create New Theme Colors.

2. In the Create New Theme Colors dialog box, open the Hyperlink list and select a different color for (unvisited) hyperlinks.

3. Repeat step 2 for Followed Hyperlink. You can choose the same color as in step 2 or a different color (see Figure 15.3).

Figure 15.3
Change the colors assigned to hyperlinks.

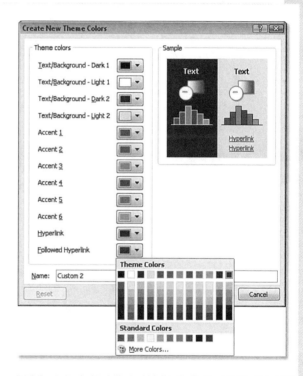

4. In the Name box, replace the default name with a name of your choosing.

5. Click Save.

Working with Bookmarks

Hyperlinks are great all by themselves, but they point to entire files, not specific parts of the file. If the referenced document is long, your audience will wonder what specific part of its contents you wanted them to view within it.

 note

Bookmarks are actually {Bookmark} fields; you can see this by selecting the bookmark and pressing Shift+F9 to toggle field codes on/off. Chapter 16 covers fields in detail.

A *bookmark* provides a more specific way of referring to document content. You can create a named bookmark to indicate a certain spot in the document, and then you can reference that bookmark's name in a variety of referencing activities, including cross-references and hyperlinks. You can also quickly jump to a bookmark using the Go To feature, as you learned in Chapter 2, "Typing and Editing Text."

➡ *To review the Go To command and how to use bookmarks with it, see "Using Go To," p. 81.*

Creating a Bookmark

You can create a bookmark to any portion of a document—a heading, a body paragraph, a specific word or phrase, or a graphic object of any type. The bookmark can be a single spot in the document (that is, a single character marker), or it can encompass multiple paragraphs and objects.

Does it matter how large the selection is that you bookmark? It depends on how you plan to use the bookmark. If you are going to use it only for navigation, such as with a Go To operation or a cross-reference, it makes no difference because it will always jump to the beginning of the bookmarked area regardless of the area's size. However, if you plan to use the bookmark for text insertion operations, such as with the {IncludeText} field covered later in this chapter, make sure you incorporate everything within the bookmark that you want to be included in the insertion.

➡ *For information about the {IncludeText} field, see "Inserting Text with {IncludeText}," p. 609.*

To create a bookmark, follow these steps:

1. Position the insertion point where you want the bookmark to be inserted.

   To bookmark a paragraph, position the insertion point at the beginning of that paragraph. To bookmark a graphics object, select the object.

2. On the Insert tab, click Bookmark. The Bookmark dialog box opens.

3. In the Bookmark Name box, type a name for the bookmark (see Figure 15.4).

   The name can be up to 40 characters and can include letters, numbers, or a combination of the two, but no spaces and no symbols.

4. Click the Add button. The bookmark is now created.

 tip

Many of the uses for a bookmark, such as a Go To operation or a cross-reference, work with all the headings in the document automatically, so you do not usually have to create bookmarks for the headings in your document to reference them.

Figure 15.4
Create a bookmark.

Jumping to a Bookmark

One use for a bookmark is to quickly locate a certain location in the document. To jump to the book-marked location in the document, follow these steps:

1. On the Insert tab, click Bookmark.

2. In the Bookmark dialog box, click the desired bookmark and click Go To.

3. Click Close.

Here's an alternative method:

1. Click the Select Browse Object button in the Word window, or press Ctrl+Alt+Home.

2. On the palette of icons that appears (see Figure 15.5), click Go To. The Find and Replace dialog box opens with the Go To tab displayed.

3. In the Go to What list, select Bookmark.

4. Open the Enter Bookmark Name list and click the desired bookmark.

5. Click the Go To button to jump to that bookmark in the document.

6. Click Close.

Inserting a Hyperlink to a Bookmark

A hyperlink to a bookmark is like a saved Go To operation. Rather than having to go through the Go To process each time, you can simply Ctrl+click the hyperlink to that bookmark.

Choose Bookmark here.

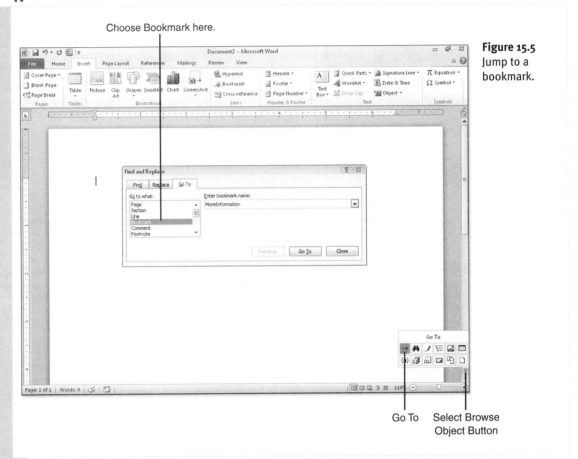

Figure 15.5
Jump to a bookmark.

Go To   Select Browse
               Object Button

Hyperlinking to a Bookmark in the Same Document

Most of the time, the bookmarks to which you will want to refer are in the same document as the reference. This is considered a "Place in This Document" type of hyperlink, and there is a special button for it in the Insert Hyperlink dialog box.

To create a hyperlink to a bookmark that's in the same document, follow these steps:

1. Position the insertion point where you want the hyperlink to be inserted, or select the text that you want to use as the hyperlink.

2. On the Insert tab, click Hyperlink. The Insert Hyperlink dialog box opens.

3. Click Place in This Document. A list of all the headings and bookmarks in the document appears.

4. Click the desired bookmark (see Figure 15.6).

 tip

You can also use this same procedure to create a hyperlink to the top of the document, or to any of the headings, by selecting one of those items instead in step 4.

Figure 15.6
Create a hyperlink to a bookmark in the same document.

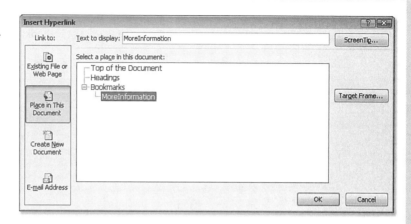

5. Check the text in the Text to Display box, and edit it if needed.

6. Click OK to insert the hyperlink.

Hyperlinking to a Bookmark in Another Document

You can also create hyperlinks to bookmarks in other documents. When the hyperlink is followed, not only does the referenced document open, but the display jumps to the referenced bookmark.

Follow these steps to create a hyperlink to a bookmark in another document:

1. Start creating a new hyperlink as you normally would:

    a. Select text or position the insertion point.

    b. On the Insert tab, click Hyperlink.

    c. Change the text in the Text to Display box if needed.

    d. Set up a ScreenTip if needed.

2. Click Existing File or Web Page, and then browse for and select the desired document. (You must have already saved the document containing the book-mark for it to appear on this list.)

3. Click the Bookmark button. The Select Place in Document dialog box opens, listing all the bookmarks in the selected document (see Figure 15.7).

4. Click the desired bookmark.

5. Click OK to return to the Insert Hyperlink dialog box.

6. Click OK to insert the hyperlink.

 tip

Word uses standard HTML syntax to reference bookmarks, so if you happen to know the bookmark name, you don't have to do steps 3–5. Instead, you can click at the end of the filename in the Address text box and then type a # sign followed by the bookmark name.

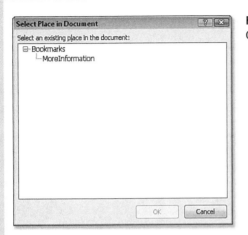

Figure 15.7
Create a hyperlink to a bookmark in another document.

Inserting a Cross-Reference to a Bookmark

A *cross-reference* is a dynamic reference to a location. For
example, suppose that on page 10 of your document, you
want to refer to a certain definition in a paragraph that is currently on page 4 of your document. You could say "Refer to
the definition on page 4," but then what if you add more text
to the document later, or delete some text, such that the definition is no longer on page 4? With a cross-reference, rather
than a manual reference, you don't have to worry about the
reference becoming out-of-synch. Create a bookmark at the
definition's location and then create a cross-reference to that
bookmark.

 note

Cross-references are actually {Ref}
or {Pageref} fields; you can see
this by selecting the cross-reference
and pressing Shift+F9 to toggle field
codes on/off. Chapter 16 covers
fields in detail.

You can create cross-references to many types of content, not just bookmarks. In Chapter 18,
"Citing Sources and References," you'll learn more uses for a cross-reference, but for now let's take
a quick look at how to cross-reference a bookmark:

1. Create the bookmark, as described earlier in this chapter.

2. Position the insertion point where you want to insert the cross-reference, and then type any supporting text that should go along with it. For example, you might type something like this:

   ```
   For more information, see "Creating Special Effects" on page
   ```

3. On the Insert tab, click Cross-Reference. The Cross-Reference dialog box opens.

4. Open the Reference Type list and select Bookmark.

5. Open the Insert Reference To list and select the type of information you want to appear as the
   reference. For the example given in step 2, you would want Page Number, for instance. Or for a
   bookmark, you could choose Bookmark Text to insert the literal text that the bookmark marks.

6. (Optional) If you want the cross-reference to function as a live hyperlink to the bookmark, make sure the Insert as Hyperlink check box is marked.

7. Select the bookmark from the For Which Bookmark list (see Figure 15.8).

8. Click Insert. The designated information is inserted as a code in the document.

9. Click Close.

Figure 15.8
Create a cross-reference to a bookmark.

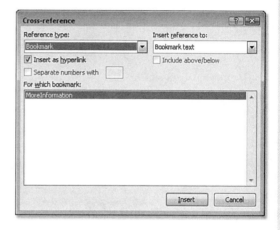

 For more information about cross-referencing, see "Creating Cross-References," p. 717.

Embedding Data

With a simple cut-and-paste operation that moves content between applications, the cut-and-pasted data retains no memory of the application from which it came. The receiving application converts the incoming data into the best possible format it can, given its capabilities. For example, Excel cells are converted to a table grid in Word. There's no going back; you must edit the inserted content in Word or not at all.

Sometimes, however, you might want the data to retain its connection to the source application. For example, you might want to be able to edit the inserted Excel cells in Excel in the future, because Excel has superior calculating features and can do things that can't be done in a Word table.

> **caution**
>
> Embedded data does not retain a connection to the original data file from which it came, so changes made later to the original data file are not reflected in the Word copy and vice versa. If you need a connection like that, what you want is *linked data*, covered later in this chapter.

For situations such as this, what you want is *embedded data*. Embedded data remembers its roots, and you can reopen it in that same application later. You can embed existing data from another program, or you can create a new embedded object in Word using the tools from almost any other application installed on your PC.

There are two different ways to embed existing data, depending on whether you want to embed an entire file or just a snippet of data.

Embedding an Entire Existing File

When you embed an entire existing file in a Word document, you are in effect storing a complete copy of that file within the Word file, so the file size grows dramatically. There are advantages, however, to make up for the larger file size. When embedding an entire file, you do not necessarily have to *show* the entire file in Word, but the entire file remains available. So, for example, if you embed an Excel workbook that has multiple sheets, you can choose which sheet (or which portion of a sheet) you want to display in Word, and you can change your mind at any time later. You might want to display one sheet, print your work, and then display a different sheet, for example.

To embed an entire file in Word, insert it as an object by following these steps:

1. Position the insertion point where you want the object to appear.

2. On the Insert tab, click Object (the button face, not the arrow adjacent to it). The Object dialog box opens.

3. On the Create from File tab, click Browse.

4. Locate and select the desired file and click Insert. The complete path to the file appears in the File Name box (see Figure 15.9).

5. Click OK to insert the file.

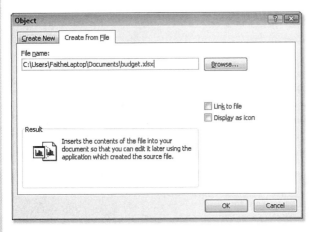

Figure 15.9
Create an embedded object from an entire existing file.

The embedded object appears in the document. When you select the object, small black square selection handles appear around it, the same way a backward-compatible graphic would appear.

When you double-click the embedded object, the object opens in its native application for editing. If the native application is a Microsoft Office product or other supported product, the Ribbon or the toolbars for that product appear within the Word 2010 window, as in Figure 15.10. If the native application is not fully supported, the object opens in a separate window for that application.

To return to Word if you're working with a supported Microsoft Office product's content, click the Word document in an area away from the object. Word's Ribbon reappears, and the object goes back to being a "picture."

To return to Word if you're working with an unsupported product's content, open the File menu in that application and look for a command that includes *Return to* in it, such as Exit and Return to Document 1 (where "Document 1" reflects the Word document's filename).

Excel Ribbon

Figure 15.10
An embedded Excel worksheet opened for editing in Word.

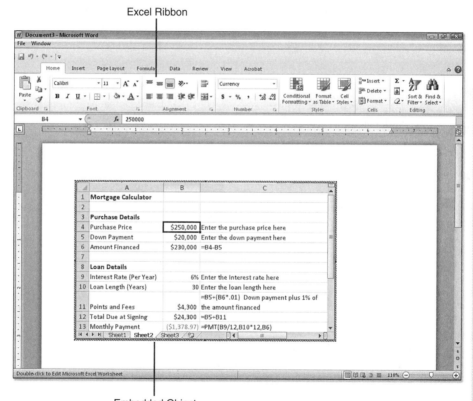

Embedded Object

Changing the View of the Embedded File

When an embedded file is selected, it can be resized like any other object, but it will be resized as an image would. Drag a selection handle, and the displayed content will enlarge or shrink to fit the new frame size. So, for example, suppose you have an embedded Excel worksheet that shows a 10×0 cell block. If you click once on the embedded object and then drag its bottom-right selection handle inward, the 10×10 block will shrink proportionally, but it will still show 100 cells. Each cell will simply be smaller.

However, when an embedded file is *activated* (by double-clicking it), as in Figure 15.10, resizing its frame has a different effect—it makes less or more of the file appear in the window. For the earlier 10×10 cell block example, you might double-click the object and then drag the bottom-right selection handle inward so only an 8×8 block of cells is visible. Then click away from the object to return to Word.

For Excel workbooks that contain multiple sheets, only one sheet can be shown at once, but you can switch freely among them with the worksheet tabs when the object is activated. If you need to show multiple sheets at once, copy the object and set a different sheet to display in each copy.

Embedding a Data Selection

Sometimes embedding an entire data file is overkill. Why embed a huge file and grow your Word document's file size dramatically when all you really want is a few worksheet cells or a single chart or graphic?

To embed a portion of a file, use the Paste Special command rather than Insert Object. As you learned in Chapter 2, Paste Special provides a means of setting options for a Paste operation, and that's exactly what you need here.

Follow these steps to embed some data from another program into Word:

1. Open the other program and then open or create the data.

2. Copy the desired data to the Clipboard.

3. Switch to Word and position the insertion point where you want the pasted selection to appear.

4. On the Home tab, open the Paste button's menu and choose Paste Special. The Paste Special dialog box opens.

5. On the As list, select a document type that ends with the word *Object*. (There will probably be only one choice.) For example, in Figure 15.11, it's Microsoft Excel Worksheet Object.

6. Click OK. The selection is pasted as an embedded object.

 note

If there is no data type on the As list that ends in *Object*, you cannot create an embedded object using Paste Special for this data.

Figure 15.11
To embed, use Paste Special and make sure you choose an "Object" data type.

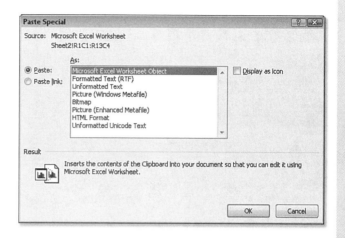

Embedding a New Object

When you want to embed a new object of some other type than Word, you can do so from within Word so that the object is saved within the Word document rather than in a separate file. This can save some time and effort, because you don't have to open the other application separately.

You can create a new embedded object using almost any application installed on your PC. The only requirement is that the application must conform to the Windows Object Linking and Embedding (OLE) standards. Most productivity applications do.

To create a new embedded object, follow these steps:

1. In Word, position the insertion point where you want the new object to appear.

2. On the Insert tab, click Object and then click Object from the resulting menu. The Object dialog box opens.

3. On the Create New tab, scroll through the Object Type list and select the desired object type. The object types listed depend on the applications installed on your PC. For example, Figure 15.12 shows the creation of a new Microsoft Excel Worksheet object.

4. Click OK to insert the new object. The tools and menus for the selected object type appear.

5. Create the object and then return to Word.

To re-edit the object at any time later, double-click it.

 caution

If you think you might want to reuse the object in other programs or documents, do not embed it as a new object in a Word file; instead, create it separately outside of Word and then embed it as an existing file, as you learned earlier in this chapter.

 tip

You can insert legacy objects from earlier versions of Office using these steps. For example, to insert an equation using the old-style equation editor, so that the equation is usable in Word 97–2003 documents, choose Microsoft Equation 3.0 as the object type.

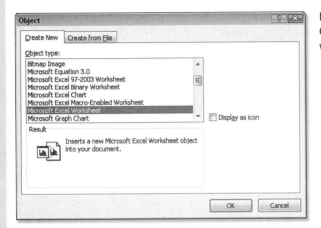

Figure 15.12
Choose the type of new embedded object you want to insert.

Linking to Data in Other Files

The terms *linking* and *embedding* are sometimes thrown around loosely as if they were a single action, as in Object Linking and Embedding, but they are actually quite different.

As you just learned in the preceding section, *embedding* creates a static copy of an object within Word, retaining its memory of the application from which it came. Embedding can be done with whole files, snippets of existing files, or brand-new content that is not related to an existing file.

Linking, on the other hand, can be done only with existing saved files. Linking inserts a dynamic link to the original data file. That way, if the original data file changes, the version in Word also changes, and vice versa. Linking is quite handy when you need to create connections between files that are not finalized yet, because you are always assured of having the most recent data.

However, linking is not always appropriate or even helpful. It has some definite drawbacks. The biggest one is that files containing links are slower to open and save. Whenever a file that contains a link is opened or saved, the linked data is updated, which takes time. You can minimize this impact by setting the links to be manually updated, but then you run into the potential problem of forgetting to update them and losing the benefit of dynamic updates.

 To learn how to set a link to be manually updated, see "Managing Link Update Settings,"
p. 607.

You must also take care not to move the linked files, or the Word document will not be able to find them. This causes an error when the document is opened. Before you distribute a file that contains links via email or on a network where not everyone has access to the folders containing all the files, you should disable or remove the links in it, because the recipients will not have access to the linked file.

> **note**
>
> Links are actually {Link} fields; you can see this by selecting the linked content and pressing Shift+F9 to toggle field codes on/off. Chapter 16 covers fields in detail.

 To learn how to remove a link, see "Breaking a Link," p. 608.

Creating a Link

As with embedding, there are two different procedures for creating a link, depending on whether you want to link to an entire file or only a portion of it.

Linking to an Entire File

The procedure for linking an entire file is similar to that of embedding an entire file, except you indicate that you want the file to be linked. Follow these steps:

1. Position the insertion point where you want the object to appear.

2. On the Insert tab, click Object and then click Object from the resulting menu. The Object dialog box opens.

3. On the Create from File tab, click Browse.

4. Locate and select the desired file and click Insert. The complete path to the file appears in the File Name box (see Figure 15.13).

5. Mark the Link to File check box. This step is important; if you don't do it, you'll get an embedded file, not a linked one.

6. Click OK to insert the linked file.

Figure 15.13
Create a link with Insert Object.

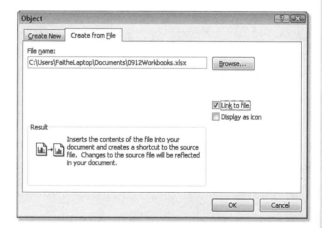

A linked file functions much like an embedded file in a Word document; when selected, it appears with square black selection handles and can be formatted as a graphic. The main difference is in the editing; when you double-click it to activate it, the original data file opens for editing in its own window, rather than using embedded tabs and menus within Word.

Linking to a Portion of a File

The procedure for linking a portion of a file is similar to embedding a portion of a file. One difference is that with linking, the data you are copying must be saved in another file, so you must make sure you've saved your work in the other application before linking it into Word.

To link to a portion of a file, follow these steps:

1. Open the other program and then open or create the data.If you're creating a new data file, make sure you save it before proceeding; otherwise, there will be no filename to link into Word.

2. Copy the desired data to the Clipboard.

3. Switch to Word and position the insertion point where you want the pasted selection to appear.

4. On the Home tab, open the Paste button's menu and choose Paste Special. The Paste Special dialog box opens.

5. Click Paste Link. The As list changes to show only the formats in which a link is possible (see Figure 15.14).

6. On the As list, select the desired content type.

note

You have a wider choice of content types here than with embedding. The content can be based in a variety of formats, any of which will maintain the link to the original data. For example, Formatted Text (RTF) pastes Excel data cells in as a Word table. Pay attention to the explanation in the Result area of the dialog box to find out what each available option does.

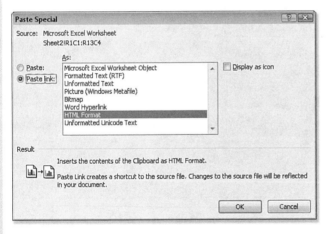

Figure 15.14
Create a link with Paste Special.

7. (Optional) If you would prefer that the link be an icon in the Word document, rather than a full display of the data, mark the Display as Icon check box. (Or, if you would prefer it to be a text hyperlink, do not mark the check box, but choose Word Hyperlink as the As type.)

8. Click OK to create the link.

You don't need to edit the linked file from within Word. If you chose its native application as the content type (in step 6), you can open it separately in its native application, or if Word happens to be open already, you can double-click the linked file in Word to open it in its native application in a separate window.

Managing Link Update Settings

Whenever you open or save a Word document containing a link, the link is updated automatically. Linked data is also updated automatically on the fly whenever both files happen to be open at the same time.

As mentioned earlier, updating links takes time, especially in a document with multiple links. To minimize the performance impact, you might choose to set the links for manual updating.

To change a link's update settings, follow these steps:

1. Right-click the object in Word and point to Linked Worksheet Object (or whatever type of object it is, if not a worksheet) to open a submenu. Then click Links. The Links dialog box opens.

   The exact name of the command to open the submenu varies depending on the object. For Excel data, it is Linked Worksheet Object.

2. Select the link from the list of links (if there is more than one link in the document).

3. In the Update Method for Selected Link section, click Manual Update (see Figure 15.15).

4. Click OK.

 note

The Locked check box locks the link so that it cannot be updated, either manually or automatically. You might use this to prevent an error from occurring if the linked data is taken offline, for example, or to preserve a certain version of the data in the document. (Of course, another way to preserve the current version would simply be to break the link entirely. See "Breaking a Link" later in this chapter.)

Figure 15.15
Specify manual updating for one or more links.

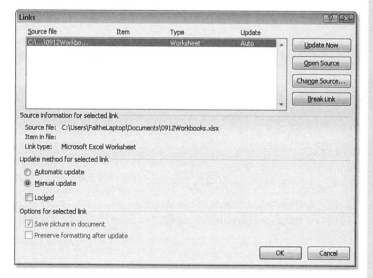

Manually Updating a Link

After setting a link to manual updates, you must update it yourself. To do so, right-click the linked content and choose Update Link. An alternative method: Display the Links dialog box (shown in Figure 15.15), click the link, and click Update Now.

Changing the Linked File's Location or Range

If the linked file changes its location or name, or if you need to refer to a different portion of it (for example, a different range of cells from a worksheet), use the Links dialog box shown in Figure 15.15 to make that change. Follow these steps:

1. Right-click the object in Word and point to Linked Object to open a submenu. Then click Links. The Links dialog box opens.The exact name of the command to open the submenu varies depending on the object. For example, for Excel data, it would be Linked Worksheet Object.

2. Select the link from the list of links (if there is more than one link in the document).

3. Do any of the following:

   - To check that the link's source file is still available, click Open Source. If it opens, the link is functional. Close the source file.

   - To change the path or name of the source file (for example, if it has been moved or renamed), click Change Source, browse for the new filename and location, and click Open.

   - To change the portion of the source file that is linked, click Change Source. Then after selecting the file and location, click the Item button and specify the portion of the file to be linked. For Excel data, for example, you can specify a cell range or a bookmark name.

4. Click OK to close the Links dialog box.

Breaking a Link

When you no longer need the dynamic link between the source and the Word document, you should break the link for better performance. (Remember, links slow down the file's saving and opening.)

To break a link, follow these steps:

1. Right-click the object in Word and point to Linked Object to open a submenu. Then click Links. The Links dialog box opens.The exact name of the command to open the submenu varies depending on the object. For example, for Excel data, it would be Linked Worksheet Object.

2. Select the link from the list of links (if there is more than one link in the document).

3. Click Break Link. At the confirmation box, click Yes.

4. If there are no more links, the Links dialog box closes automatically. If other links remain, break them too if desired, or click OK to close the Links dialog box.

Inserting Content with {IncludeText} and {IncludePicture}

In Chapter 16, you'll learn a lot about *fields*, which are codes that insert objects, values, or data into a Word document. You've already seen several types of fields in this chapter: {Hyperlink}, {Ref}, {Pageref}, {Link}, and {Bookmark}. Each inserts or marks content in a certain way.

Now let's look at two more fields that are useful for inserting external content: {IncludeText} and {IncludePicture}. These are non-OLE alternatives, and the links do not automatically update. Use them if the data is unlikely to change very often but you still want to maintain a link.

Inserting Text with {IncludeText}

The {IncludeText} field inserts a linked copy of external text into the document. It is not intended to replace OLE linking; instead, it's used for special-purpose insertions involving field codes. It is designed to provide a flexible block of text that you can combine with other fields. For example, if you have defined a certain number in one document as a bookmark, you could then use it in a field calculation in another document by using {IncludeText} to bring in that bookmark's content.

There are two ways of inserting an {IncludeText} field. You can use the Insert Text from File command, or you can use Insert Field. Each has its advantages and drawbacks.

Creating an {IncludeText} Field with Insert Text from File

This first method inserts entire files rather easily, and it enables you to browse for the file you want to insert. However, it does not allow you to browse for bookmark names, so you must know the exact name of the bookmark you want (if you don't want the entire file). It also does not enable you to use special switches in the field code. Here are the steps to follow:

1. Position the insertion point where you want the inserted text to appear.

2. On the Insert tab, click the arrow on the Object button, and then click Text from File. The Insert File dialog box opens.

3. Navigate to and select the file you want to include.

4. (Optional) To include only a bookmarked range, click the Range button, type the bookmark name, and click OK.

5. Open the drop-down list on the Insert button and choose Insert as Link (see Figure 15.16).

Creating an {IncludeText} Field by Inserting a Field Code

An alternative method provides dialog box options for including any of several switches, such as for XSL transformation or namespace mappings, but it does not enable you to browse for the path and name of the file. To use this method, follow these steps:

1. Position the insertion point where you want the inserted text to appear.

2. On the Insert tab, click Quick Parts and then click Field. The Field dialog box opens.

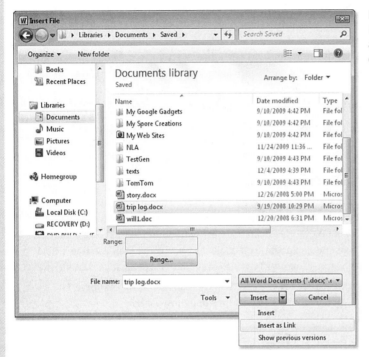

Figure 15.16
Insert a link to a text file to create an {IncludeText} field automatically.

3. In the Categories list, choose Links and References (or choose All).

4. On the Field Names list, click IncludeText.

5. In the Filename or URL text box, type the complete path and name of the file (see Figure 15.17). If the path includes spaces, enclose it in quotation marks. Replace single backslashes with double ones.

6. (Optional) If you want to enter a bookmark name, do the following:

   a. Click the Field Codes button. A Field Codes text box appears, showing the syntax that will be used for the field code.

   b. Click at the end of the existing code string and type a space. Then type the bookmark name.

   c. Click Hide Codes to return to the regular view of the dialog box.

7. (Optional) For any of the special-purpose field options, mark the check box and enter the desired value. Or, if you are more comfortable working directly with the switches, click Field Codes and enter the syntax manually. Table 15.1 explains the available switches.

8. Mark or clear the Preserve Formatting During Updates check box to indicate how you want formatting handled when the field is updated. When the check box is marked, the main document's formatting prevails; when it's cleared, the formatting is brought in with the text being inserted.

9. Click OK. The text is inserted.

Figure 15.17
Use IncludeText to insert text from a file.

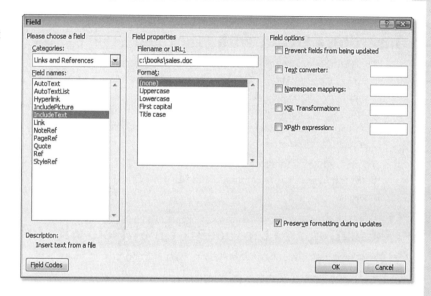

Table 15.1   Switches for the {IncludeText} Field

Switch	Purpose	Arguments
\!	Prevents Word from updating fields in the inserted text unless the field results have changed in the original location.	None
\c className	Specifies a converter to use; necessary only for WordPerfect 5.x for Windows or 6.x files.	WrdPrfctWin or WordPerfect6x
\n mapping	Specifies a namespace for XPath queries.	The namespace
\t file	Specifies an XSLT file for formatting XML data.	The .xsl filename
\x path	Specifies the XPath for returning a fragment of data in an XML file.	An element of an XML file

Updating an {IncludeText} Field

After inserting the field, you can update it by right-clicking it and choosing Update Field or by selecting it and pressing F9.

To view the code on which the field is based, right-click it and choose Toggle Field Codes, or select it and press Shift+F9.

Text that has been inserted using {IncludeText} is directly editable in Word—unlike text brought in with Insert Object. However, the next time you update the field, any changes made to the text are wiped away as a fresh copy is loaded from the original source. To save your changes to the original source, press Ctrl+Shift+F7.

Inserting a Picture with {IncludePicture}

The {IncludePicture} field links to a picture from an outside source. Like {IncludeText}, it's not meant as a replacement for an OLE link; rather, it has some special-purpose uses. For example, you might set up a field with a logical condition and then use two different {IncludePicture} operations to insert one picture or the other based on the condition.

There are two methods of creating an {IncludePicture} field: the Insert Picture command and the Insert Field command.

 caution

A linked picture inserted with {IncludePicture} is updatable, but there's no way of updating it via Word's user interface. You have to use the shortcut key F9 to do it. Why? Well, an object must have a "context" that determines which right-click menu command set appears for it. A linked picture is a field-inserted object, but it is also an inline image. The designers of Word had to pick which context menu would be the most useful for you to have, and they went with the one for inline images. That's why there's no Update Field command on the right-click menu for a picture linked with {IncludePicture}.

Creating an {IncludePicture} Field with Insert Picture

In Chapter 10, "Working with Photos," you learned how to insert a picture from a file. The resulting picture is a static image; it is not linked to the original.

 *To review the procedure for inserting a picture from a file, see "Inserting Pictures from Files," p. 384.*

To use an {IncludePicture} link for it instead of inserting a static copy, there's just one little change: Instead of clicking the Insert button in the Insert Picture dialog box, open the Insert button's drop-down list and choose Insert and Link, the same as with Figure 15.16. This method is simple and lets you browse for the file easily, but it does not allow options to be set for the import and linkage.

Creating an {IncludePicture} Field by Inserting a Field Code

By using the field code insertion method, you can specify various options and switches for the {IncludePicture} field. However, it's not quite as easy a method as Insert Picture.

Before starting an {IncludePicture} insertion, make sure you know the full path and name of the file you want to insert, because you can't browse for it when inserting the field. The full path includes the drive letter and folder, like this: C:\Books\Xfer.tif.

To insert a graphic by inserting an {IncludePicture} field code, follow these steps:

1. Position the insertion point where you want the inserted picture to appear.

2. On the Insert tab, click Quick Parts and then click Field. The Field dialog box opens.

3. On the Field Names list, click IncludePicture.

4. In the Filename or URL text box, type the complete path and name of the file. If the path includes spaces, enclose it in quotation marks. Replace single backslashes with double ones.

5. (Optional) Mark any of the Field Options check boxes for any special options desired:

- **Graphic Filter**—You can specify a certain filter file to use (.flt file), but Word can usually determine this automatically for you. Marking this check box includes the \c switch with the filter you specify as the argument.

- **Data Not Stored with Document**—Marking this check box includes the \d switch, which creates a link only; it does not insert the graphics data into the document. This reduces the document file size, but if the original file is not available, the graphic does not display.

- **Resize Horizontally from Source**—Marking this check box includes the \x switch, which resizes the graphic horizontally based on the source image.

- **Resize Vertically from Source**—Marking this check box includes the \y switch, which resizes the graphic vertically based on the source image.

6. Click OK. The picture is inserted.

 tip

To update all the field codes in the document at once, press Ctrl+F9.

The resulting inserted picture does not obviously appear to be a field, unlike the inserted text with IncludeText. It is not shaded gray, and if you right-click it, no special field-related commands appear. However, the picture *is* a field, and it *is* updatable; select it and press F9 to update it.

WORKING WITH FIELDS AND FORMS

Understanding Fields

Fields are the often-underappreciated placeholders that work behind the scenes in a document. They help perform the magic involved with many of the most powerful features in Word, such as mail merging, indexing, automatic generation of tables of contents, automatic figure numbering, cross-referencing, page numbering, and more.

There are many different types of fields, each with a specific purpose, but they break down into three main categories. You can use fields to do the following:

- Insert text or graphics into the document, such as page numbering, dates and times, text from other documents, graphics from external files, document properties, or calculated values.

- Mark a location for later use, such as with a bookmark, table of contents marker, or indexing code.

- Perform an action, such as running a macro or opening a hyperlink in a web browser.

Many people use fields in Word without even realizing it because so many of Word's features automatically insert and modify fields. For example, when you insert a date or time and set it to be automatically updated, Word inserts a {Date} or {Time} code. And when you create an OLE link to an object, Word inserts a {Link} code.

Throughout this book, you've been learning about fields in an indirect way. Whenever a feature has been discussed that used a field, you've learned to insert that field via a button or dialog box, but you haven't looked too deeply yet at what's really going on behind the curtain. Table 16.1 lists some of the Word features that employ fields and cross-references them to where those skills are covered in the book.

Table 16.1   Word Features That Use Fields

Field	Purpose	Covered in
{AutoText}	Inserts an AutoText entry	"Working with Building Blocks," p. 89
{Bookmark}	Creates a bookmark marker	"Working with Bookmarks," p. 593
{Date}	Inserts an automatically updated date	"Inserting a Date or Time Code," p. 271
{Hyperlink}	Inserts a hyperlink	"Working with Hyperlinks," p. 586
{IncludePicture}	Inserts a non-OLE linked picture from an external file	"Inserting a Picture with {IncludePicture}," p. 612
{IncludeText}	Inserts non-OLE linked text from an external file	"Inserting Text with {IncludeText}," p. 609
{Index}	Generates an index	"Generating the Index," p. 749
{Link}	Inserts an OLE-linked object	"Creating a Link," p. 605
{NoteRef}	Inserts the number for a footnote	"Working with Footnotes and Endnotes," p. 708
{Page}	Inserts an automatically updated page number	"Adding and Formatting a Page-Numbering Code," p. 269
{PageRef}	Inserts the number of the page containing the specified bookmark	"Inserting a Cross-Reference to a Bookmark," p. 598
{Ref}	Inserts the text marked by a bookmark	"Inserting a Cross-Reference to a Bookmark," p. 598
{Seq}	Inserts an automatically numbered caption	"Using Figure Captions," p. 412
{Symbol}	Inserts a symbol from a specified font	"Inserting Symbols and Special Characters," p. 54
{Time}	Inserts an automatically updated time	"Inserting a Date or Time Code," p. 271
{TA}	Marks a table of authorities entry	"Creating Citations and Tables of Authorities," p. 737
{TC}	Marks a table of contents entry	"Creating a Table of Contents," p. 723
{TOA}	Inserts a table of authorities	"Creating Citations and Tables of Authorities," p. 737

Table 16.1 Continued

Field	Purpose	Covered in
{TOC}	Inserts a table of contents	"Creating a Table of Contents," p. 723
{XE}	Inserts a marker for an index entry	"Marking Index Entries," p. 741
{=}	Inserts a formula or calculated field	"Performing Math Calculations in a Table," p. 369

This chapter delves into the technical nitty-gritty details that govern fields and shows you how you can select, insert, modify, and format fields to accomplish a variety of document-creation and formatting tasks. Even if you don't end up working manually with fields very often, this is not wasted study! The more you understand about how fields really work, the better you will be able to troubleshoot problems that may occur or to tweak an individual field's options to fit an unusual formatting need.

Inserting Fields

You can insert many fields via the regular Word user interface, as listed in Table 16.1. However, you can also insert a field using the Insert Field command, a more direct route that provides access to more of the field's optional switches and parameters.

To insert a field, follow these steps:

1. Position the insertion point where you want the field to be inserted.

2. On the Insert tab, click Quick Parts and then click Field. The Field dialog box opens.

3. (Optional) On the Categories list, select a category to narrow the list of field names.

4. On the Field Names list, click the desired field name. Lists and check boxes appear for the available options for that field. For example, in Figure 16.1, the options for the Date field are shown.

5. Select any options as needed, and then click OK.

Specifying Field Properties and Options

As you insert a field (as in the preceding section), the Field dialog box prompts you to select the properties and options you want. *Field properties* are settings from which you must make a selection (or accept the default). For example, in Figure 16.1, the date format is a property. If you do not choose one, Word uses a default property. *Field options* are optional parameters; to omit them, simply leave their check boxes blank.

If you are interested in the codes behind these user-friendly dialog box controls, click the Field Codes button to display the Field Codes text box. It shows the code that Word inserts for the properties and options you have selected so far (see Figure 16.2).

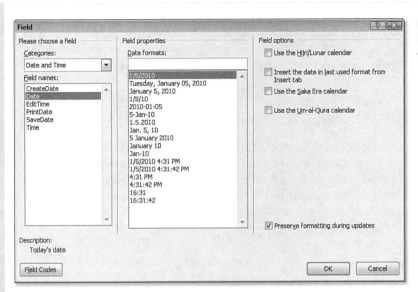

Figure 16.1
Insert a field from the Field dialog box.

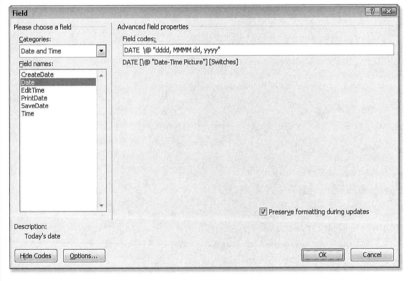

Figure 16.2
View the codes behind the properties and options you have selected.

To delve even further into the field's coding, click the Options button to display the Field Options dialog box. Each available switch and option for the field is listed and described on the Field Specific Switches tab. To add one of them, select it and click Add to Field (see Figure 16.3).

> **note**
>
> The Field Options dialog box doesn't do anything that the check boxes and lists in the Field dialog box don't do, but the description of each option in the Description area of the Field Options dialog box can help you figure out what a particular option does.

Figure 16.3
Work directly with the field's optional switches and properties in the Field Options dialog box.

Manually Typing Field Codes

If you know exactly what you want in terms of field codes, you might find it easier and quicker to simply type them into your document.

Field codes are bracketed with curly braces, like this: {Date}. However, you can't manually type the curly braces, because Word won't recognize the code as a field. Instead, you must press Ctrl+F9 to get the ball rolling.

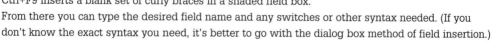

> **tip**
>
> You can add a button to the Quick Access toolbar that starts a new blank set of field braces. Choose File, Options, and click Quick Access Toolbar. Select All Commands from the Choose Commands From list. Then select Insert Field Chars and click Add.

Ctrl+F9 inserts a blank set of curly braces in a shaded field box. From there you can type the desired field name and any switches or other syntax needed. (If you don't know the exact syntax you need, it's better to go with the dialog box method of field insertion.)

Here are some tips for getting the syntax right:

- Field names are not case-sensitive.

- If a property or argument contains spaces, you must enclose it in quotation marks. For example, {Username "John Doe"} would be correct. {Username John} would also work because John does not have spaces in it, but {Username John Doe} would be incorrect.

- If you need a real quotation mark, use "\".

- If you're specifying a path, use double backslashes rather than single—for example, { IncludeText C:\\Docs\\Myfile.doc}. This is necessary because single backslashes indicate switches and special codes.

- Leave one space between the field name and each property or switch.

- Leave one space between the backslash (\) in the switch and its parameters.

- Leave one blank space to the right of the left bracket and to the left of the right bracket.

Common Syntax Errors in Field Codes

When manually typing the code for a field, it is easy to make a mistake. Word fields have different syntax than you might be used to in Excel functions or VBA, for example.

Here are some of the most commonly broken syntax rules. If you're having a problem with a field code, check to make sure you are following all these rules:

- Spaces are required between the outer braces and the codes inside them:
  - Right: { Date }
  - Wrong: {Date}

- Spaces are required between each argument and switch in the code, and between the switch and its parameter:
  - Right: { Date \@ "hh:mm" }
  - Wrong: { Date\@"hh:mm" }

- Text strings must be in quotation marks if they contain spaces:
  - Right: { Set CompanyName "ACME Corporation" }
  - Wrong: { Set CompanyName ACME Corporation }

- Do not use colons, semicolons, commas, or any other characters to separate arguments or parameters. (This is not an Excel function!)
  - Right: { If { Date \n "MM/dd" } = 12/25 "Merry Christmas!" "Have a nice day!" }
  - Wrong { If { Date \n "MM/dd" } = 12/25; "Merry Christmas!"; "Have a nice day!" }

- When nesting fields, do not manually type the curly braces for the inner field; insert them with Ctrl+F9.

Toggling Between Data and Field Code Views

By default, a field displays its result in the document rather than its code. (Exception: Fields that do not generate results, such as bookmarks and index markers, do not display at all by default.)

To toggle between displaying the field result and the field code, do either of the following:

- Select the field and press Shift+F9.

- Right-click the field and choose Toggle Field Codes.

Note that this toggles only the selected field. To toggle more than one field at once, select a contiguous area of the document that includes multiple fields and press Shift+F9. To toggle all the field codes in the entire document at once, press Alt+F9, or select the entire document (Ctrl+A) before pressing Shift+F9.

Field codes in the document appear just like they do in the Field dialog box (refer to Figure 16.2). They appear with a gray background, which helps you remember they are fields, but that gray background does not print and does not appear in Print Preview or Full Screen Reading view.

 note

There is one minor difference between what appears in the Field dialog box and what appears with codes displayed inline in the document. If the Preserve Formatting During Updates check box was marked in the Field dialog box, the * MERGEFORMAT switch appears inline. It does not appear in the Field dialog box's version of the code string.

Editing Field Code Strings

When a field code string is displayed in the document (Shift+F9), you can edit it manually just like any other text. The trick is knowing what to type. Many fields have fairly complex code strings with various properties and options.

Most people aren't able to remember all the syntax rules for each field type, of course, so Word provides an easier way to edit a field code string: Right-click the field code and choose Edit Field. The Field dialog box reappears, as in Figure 16.1, and you can make any changes needed via a friendly dialog box interface.

 tip

After creating a custom field code string, save it to the Quick Parts gallery for easy reuse. To do so, on the Insert tab click Quick Parts, and then click Save Selection to Quick Part Gallery. Store it in any gallery you like. (You might want to create a new category called Custom Fields, for example.)

Nesting Fields

When you're using fields that require input, such as the logical condition ones like {Compare} and {If}, you might want that input to come from other fields. To manage this, you can nest one field inside another.

For example, you might want to test whether today is a certain day of the week. If it is Friday, this message should appear: "Time cards are due today by 5:00 p.m." Otherwise, this message should appear: "Time cards are due on Fridays by 5:00 p.m." Here's the complete syntax for that:

```
{ If { Date \@ "dddd" } = "Friday" "Time cards are due today by 5:00 p.m." "Time
cards are due on Fridays by 5:00 p.m." }
```

The main thing to remember when nesting fields is that you can't type the braces for the nested fields; you must insert the braces with Ctrl+F9. Let's go over the general process.

First, you would start the outer field:

1. Press Ctrl+F9 to insert a new blank set of braces.

2. Type the desired field name and then any portion of the field's properties or switches that should come before the nested field.

3. Press Ctrl+F9 to insert another new blank set of braces, and in the new set, type the field to be nested.

4. Click to move the insertion point to the right of the closing bracket for the nested field, and continue typing the outer field.

5. Press F9 to update the field and display its result.

Here's another example. The {Set} field creates a bookmark. It requires two pieces of information: the bookmark name and the text that should be placed within it. So, for example, if you want to create a bookmark called CompanyName and set its value to Microsoft, the field should read as follows:

```
{ Set CompanyName "Microsoft" }
```

That's fine, but what if the company name changes? You can instead use the {FillIn} field to ask the user to specify the company name:

```
{ Set CompanyName { FillIn "Enter the company name" } }
```

Now suppose you want to enter that company's name in the Title field of the document's properties. Create another nested set of fields like this:

```
{ Title { Ref CompanyName } }
```

> **tip**
>
> When you're inserting a date or time via the Field dialog box, the examples that appear in the Date Formats list show today's date. If you are more comfortable choosing based on the generic syntax, such as M/d/yyyy, click the Field Codes button and then click the Options button; the list of formats that appears in the Field Options dialog box shows the generic codes.

Selecting the Right Field

A big part of using fields successfully in Word is knowing which fields are available and which are most applicable to a particular situation. The following sections explain the types of fields available.

Date and Time Fields

In Chapter 7, "Formatting Documents and Sections," you learned that you can click Date & Time on the Insert tab to insert a date or time code via a dialog box interface. If you mark the Update

Automatically check box in this dialog box, Word inserts a {Date} field rather than the actual date or time. If you toggle the field code on an inserted date (Shift+F9), it might look something like this:

```
{ Date \@ "M/d/yyyy" }
```

The main switch for the {Date} field is \@, which is followed by the syntax for the date or time format you want.

The {Date} field has a few other switches, but you'll probably never use them:

- \h is for the Hijri/Lunar calendar.

- \l is used to insert the date with the last format chosen using the Date and Time dialog box.

- \s is used for the Saka Era calendar.

You might be surprised to find that inserting a time with the Date and Time dialog box does *not* insert a {Time} field. Instead, it inserts a {Date} field with time-based formatting. For example:

```
{ Date \@ "HH:mm" }
```

So what's the {Time} field for? It's basically the same as {Date}, except with fewer options. You can't specify a certain alternative calendar via switches, for example. Strictly speaking, the {Time} field is redundant. It doesn't need to exist, except that people expect it to and might not think to use a {Date} field to express a time.

> *To learn how to create custom date and time formats, see "Constructing a Custom Date or Time Format," p. 636.*

Besides the {Date} and {Time} fields, there are several other date/time-related fields from which you can choose. All of them pull their information from the file's properties, not from the PC's clock/calendar.

- {CreateDate} displays the file creation date. It never changes, because the document's creation date never changes.

- {PrintDate} displays the date on which the document was last printed. It updates itself automatically when you print the document.

- {SaveDate} displays the date on which the document was last saved. It updates itself automatically when you save the document.

- {EditTime} displays the total amount of time spent editing the document. It does not update automatically.

Document Information Fields

As you learned in "Inserting a Document Property" in Chapter 7, each document has a set of properties. Some of those properties are editable, such as Author; others are automatically calculated by Word, such as FileSize. You can insert these document properties into the document using the document information fields.

Most of these fields have an obvious one-to-one correlation with a certain property. For example, the {Author} field inserts the author's name, the {Comments} field inserts any comments that have been placed in the document properties, and so on. The field properties vary depending on the nature of the information being inserted. Fields that insert text have properties for setting text case; fields that insert numbers have properties for choosing a number format. Some fields also have additional options. For example, in Figure 16.4, the {FileSize} field's result can be expressed in either kilobytes or megabytes.

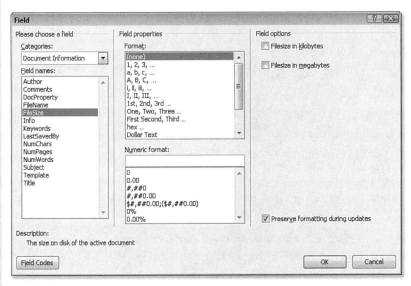

Figure 16.4
Document information fields insert various document properties.

If you do an item-by-item check of fields versus properties, you will find that not every document property has a corresponding field. The {DocProperty} field helps overcome this problem. It is a generic inserter for whatever document property you specify. Its list of available properties includes every property available for the document (except custom properties).

For example, suppose you want to insert the company name from the Company property. There is no Company field, so you would use {DocProperty} like so:

```
{ DocProperty Company }
```

Document Information Content Controls

There is another way of inserting document properties into the document text—content controls. A *content control* is an XML-based tag that pulls information from a data source—in this case, your document file's properties.

To insert document information via a content control, on the Insert tab click Quick Parts, Document Property; then click the desired piece of information, such as Author.

Content controls are not fields; they are a type of link. Content controls automatically update when their data changes; for example, if you change the author name of the file, an Author content control updates immediately in the document; in contrast, an {Author} field does not.

User Information Fields

These three simple fields pull user information from Word. They are somewhat like the document information fields. However, this data is not stored with the document, but with the logged-in user on the PC:

- {UserAddress} inserts the user's address, if set up in the program. To set up an address, choose File, Options, and click Advanced. In the General section, enter the address into the Mailing Address box.

- {UserInitials} inserts the user's initials, if set up in the program. To set up initials, choose File, Options, click General, and enter the initials into the Initials box.

- {UserName} enters the user's name, if set up in the program. To set up the name, choose File, Options, click General, and enter the name into the User Name box.

Numbering Fields

The numbering fields have one thing in common: They help you automatically number various types of items in your document. Each is automatically updated whenever you add more numbering fields or rearrange existing fields. For example, if you switch the positions of two figure captions, they also switch numbering.

Most of the numbering fields are inserted via Word's user interface in various contexts, but a few are available only via the Field dialog box. The numbering fields are listed here:

- {AutoNum} inserts an automatic number. You can specify the formatting you want for it (Arabic, Roman, letters, and so on). Use this to number anything you like. Each {AutoNum} code in the document shows an incremented value.

- {AutoNumLgl} inserts an automatic number in legal format, with or without a trailing period.

 note

The {AutoNum}, {AutoNumLgl}, and {AutoNumOut} fields are sequenced together, so the same list continues regardless of which of the three field codes you use. There are no switches or properties; the list is completely automatic.

- {AutoNumOut} inserts an automatic number in outline format.

- {BarCode} inserts a delivery point bar code based on the text found in a bookmark. Generally, the bookmark points to a ZIP Code field and changes for each mail merge record with the {Set} field.

- {ListNum} inserts numbering for a list. This is somewhat like {AutoNum}, but rather than there being three separate fields for regular numbers, legal numbers, and outlines, there are field properties that define which type of list to use. The valid values for this property are LegalDefault, NumberDefault, and OutlineDefault. Another difference is that you can set the level in the list, and you can set a start-at value, so you can have some control over the list.

- {Page} inserts the number of the current page. You most commonly use this in headers and footers, but you can use it anywhere in the document.

- {RevNum} counts the number of times the document has been saved. Each time it is saved, the {RevNum} counter is incremented.

- {Section} displays the section number where the field is placed.

- {SectionPages} displays the total pages in the section where the field is placed.

- {Seq} inserts an automatic sequence number. This is the field used for figure captions and other automatically numbered items. A bookmark is created to indicate what type of item is being sequenced. For example, to automatically number figures, each figure has a caption like this: Figure {Seq Figure}. Optional switches can be added for formatting—for example, {Seq Figure \? ARABIC}.

Equation and Formula Fields

These math-related fields are mostly covered elsewhere in Word; you will seldom have reason to insert them manually via the Field dialog box. Here's a quick round-up of them:

- {=} is a formula field. Do not try to construct its syntax manually; instead, click the Formula button in the Field dialog box and construct the formula via the Formula dialog box.

- {Advance} offsets the position of the subsequent text by a specified number of points in a specified direction. You might use this to fine-tune the positioning of text on a page when trying to make printed text line up correctly on a preprinted form, for example.

- {Eq} inserts an equation using the legacy-style Equation Editor (that is, the version from Word 97–2003). Word does not recommend that you construct the syntax manually; click the Equation Editor button in the Field dialog box to open the legacy Equation Editor.

 caution

For the {Advance} field, the expected entries for the field options are not obvious in the Field dialog box. For more information, click Field Codes, and then click Options to see a complete list of the switches and get information about each one.

- {Symbol} inserts a symbol, by character number, from a specified font. If no font is specified, the font assigned to the paragraph where the field resides takes precedence. Usually it is preferable to use the Symbol insertion controls on the Insert tab to insert a symbol because you can browse for the desired symbol more easily (that is, you don't have to know its number).

Index and Table Fields

These fields mark entries for tables of contents, indexes, and tables of authorities; then they generate those items. (The "Table" in this category's name refers to tables of contents, tables of authorities, and tables of figures, not to ordinary Word tables.)

These codes are hardly ever inserted manually. A user would use the Table of Contents, Table of Authorities, or Index feature in Word to insert the markers and generate the listings. However, it is useful to know what the various codes mean, in case you see them in documents and need to decide whether to keep or delete them.

These are the codes for indexes:

- {XE} marks index entries. Various properties and options are available for defining an entry, but these are best created with the Mark Index Entry dialog box (covered in Chapter 19, "Creating Tables of Contents and Indexes").

- {Index} generates the index.

For tables of contents, these codes apply:

- {TC} marks table of contents entries. Usually tables of contents are generated automatically based on heading levels, but you can use this field to manually mark some text to be included.

- {TOC} generates the table of contents.

For tables of authorities:

- {TA} marks the table of authorities entries.

- {TOA} generates the table of authorities.

> *To create an index, see "Marking Index Entries," p. 741 and "Generating the Index," p. 749.*

> *To create a table of contents, see "Creating a Table of Contents," p. 723.*

> *To create a table of authorities, see "Creating Citations and Tables of Authorities," p. 737.*

Link and Reference Fields

This category contains fields that insert linked content from other locations, as well as fields that automatically number pages and footnotes. (Automatic numbering of other items, such as list numbering or figure caption numbering, is handled by fields in the Numbering category, covered previously in this chapter.)

Several of the linking-type fields were covered in Chapter 15, "Copying, Linking, and Embedding Data." Here's a quick review of those:

- {Hyperlink} inserts a hyperlink. Hyperlinks are more commonly inserted via the Hyperlink command on the Insert tab.

- {Link} inserts an OLE link to an object. OLE links are more commonly inserted via Paste Special or the Insert Object command.

- {IncludePicture} inserts a non-OLE link to an external picture. Picture links are more commonly inserted via the Insert Picture dialog box by selecting Insert and Link from the Insert button's drop-down list.

- {IncludeText} inserts a non-OLE link to an external text file. Text links are more commonly inserted via the Insert Text from File command by selecting Insert as Link from the Insert button's drop-down list.

The following fields insert numbering codes:

- {NoteRef} inserts the number of a footnote or endnote. These numbers are automatically updated as content changes in the document. These are normally placed via footnote and endnote insertion.

- {PageRef} inserts the page number on which the specified bookmark appears. This code is inserted when you create a cross-reference that refers to a page number.

And these fields insert text strings of various types:

- {Quote} inserts a literal text string that you specify. For example, {Quote "Hello world"} displays the text Hello world.

- {Ref} inserts text marked by a bookmark. You learned about this one in Chapter 15, in the section "Inserting a Cross-Reference to a Bookmark."

- {StyleRef} inserts the text from a paragraph that has the specified style applied. For example, if you have the title of your document set up with a style called DocTitle, the field {StyleRef DocTitle} inserts that title later in the document.

There are also two AutoText-related fields:

- {AutoText} inserts the specified AutoText entry as an updatable link. This is different from inserting AutoText items from the Building Blocks feature, as in "Working with Building Blocks" in Chapter 2, because the latter inserts an unlinked, nonupdatable copy.

- {AutoTextList} creates a shortcut menu based on AutoText entries in the active template. You specify some placeholder text to appear in the field. When the user right-clicks the field, a pop-up list appears of AutoText entries to choose from to fill in that field.

Creating a Pop-Up List

The {AutoTextList} field generates a pop-up list based on the style applied to the field and the items in the AutoText gallery that share that same style. Here's a quick exercise to see how it works:

1. Create a new paragraph style called Popup (or anything else you want to call it).

2. Type the text for the first entry you want on your pop-up list into the document and then apply the Popup style to it.

3. Select the entire entry, and on the Insert tab, click Quick Parts and click Save Selection to Quick Part Gallery.

4. In the Create New Building Block dialog box, set the Gallery to AutoText and save it there.

5. Repeat steps 2–4 for each item you want to appear on the pop-up menu.

6. Position the insertion point where you want the field and then press Ctrl+F9 to start a new, blank field. Within the field's curly braces, type the following: AutoTextList **"Right-click here" \s Popup**

7. Press Shift+F9 to toggle the field codes off.

8. Right-click the field, and a menu appears showing your AutoText choices.

9. Click one of the choices on the menu to fill in the field.

Document Automation Fields

The document automation fields are used to set up code strings that automate processes in the document. Some programmers prefer to use document automation fields rather than Visual Basic for Applications for some basic automation tasks like filling in a form with user information or determining whether one value equals another. Here are a few simple examples.

The {Compare} field compares two values and returns a 1 if the comparison is true or 0 if it is false. It is a programming construct, useful for setting up logical conditions. For example, you might count the number of words in the document with the {NumWords} field and then compare that value to 1000:

```
{ Compare {NumWords} >= 1000 }
```

This {Compare} field returns a 1 if the word count is 1000 or above; otherwise, it returns a 0.

The 1 and 0 are all well and good, but it might be nicer to show some meaningful text based on the condition. For that, we need an {If} field. Here's an {If} field's syntax:

Expression1 Operator Expression2 TextTrue TextFalse

Suppose, for example, that if {NumWords} is at least 1000, we want to print "OK" in the document; otherwise, we want to print "Need More Words". Here's the {If} field to accomplish that:

```
{ IF {NumWords} >= 1000 "OK" "Need More Words" }
```

Here are the other available document automation fields:

- {DocVariable} inserts the value of a VBA Word document variable. (This is not the same as the document's properties, which you can insert with document information fields covered previously in this chapter.)

- {GoToButton} inserts a button that, when clicked, jumps the insertion point to a specified bookmarked location.

- {MacroButton} inserts a button that, when clicked, runs a specified macro.

- {Print} sends a print instruction to the printer; you can use it to automatically print a document, for example. It is usually combined with some other field, such as {If}, rather than standing alone.

Mail Merge Fields

Chapter 14, "Performing Mail and Data Merges," covers the Mail Merge feature in Word, which is a robust tool for merging the data from one file or database with a document in another file. Most of the fields involved in mail merging are automatically inserted when you work through the mail merge, or you can insert them using the Rules list on the Mailings tab.

- {AddressBlock} inserts data pulled from multiple fields to form a standard postal mailing address.

- {Ask} prompts the user to enter a value to be stored in a bookmark. You can then insert the content of that bookmark anywhere in the document via the {Ref} field.

- {Compare} compares two values and shows a 1 or 0, depending on whether they match. You learned about this field earlier in the chapter in the "Document Automation Fields" section.

- {Database} inserts the results of a database query in a Word table.

- {Fill-in} prompts the user to enter a value and then displays it in the field. This is different from {Ask} in that it does not store the value in a bookmark for later reuse.

- {GreetingLine} inserts a greeting line in a mail merge document. You can optionally use the \e switch to specify what name to use if the name is blank. For example, you might want something like *Dear Valued Customer*.

- {If} prescribes two different actions to take based on the outcome of a logical test. This is like {Compare} except you can specify the output in each situation rather than accepting the default 1 and 0 outputs.

- {MergeField} inserts a mail merge field. It requires a field name property, like this: {MergeField FirstName}.

- {MergeRec} numbers each merged record in a mail merge. If a filter excludes any records, they are still numbered, and the numbered records have gaps in the numbering.

- {MergeSeq} also numbers each merged record in a mail merge, but it does not number records excluded by a filter.

- {Next} goes to the next record.

- {NextIf} goes to the next record in a mail merge only if a condition is met.

- {Set} assigns new text to a bookmark.

- {SkipIf} skips the next record in a mail merge only if a condition is met. It is the opposite of {NextIf}.

Updating and Editing Fields

Now that you know about the fields you can insert, let's look at how you can edit the properties of a field and update its values after insertion.

Updating a Field

Most fields are not automatically updated each time you open or save the document. (In this way, they differ from OLE linked objects, which are automatically updated by default.)

To update a single field, select it (or click anywhere in it) and press F9, or right-click the field and choose Update Field. If you have toggled the display of the field code string on, updating the field toggles it back to displaying the results.

To update multiple fields at once, select them as part of a contiguous selection range and press F9. To update all the fields in the entire document, select the entire document (Ctrl+A) and press F9. If the update takes too long, you can abort it by pressing Esc.

You can't update all fields. Certain fields are not affected by performing an update because they do not pull information from a source that can be changed. For example, the Print, MacroButton, GoToButton, and Eq fields are like that.

In addition, certain fields are not affected by performing a manual update because they automatically update themselves. Examples include Date, Time, Page, and Seq. Date and Time update each time you open or print the document (or open it in Print Preview), and item-numbering fields such as Page and Seq update whenever there is a change in pagination or item sequencing, respectively.

Before we get into specifics, it's worth noting that a lot of keyboard shortcuts are involved in working with fields, and some of them are the only way to accomplish a particular action. Table 16.2 includes a quick summary of these shortcuts.

Table 16.2 Summary of Keyboard Shortcuts for Fields

Description	Shortcut
Save changes to the source file (only for {IncludeText})	Ctrl+Shift+F7
Update the selected field(s)	F9
Toggle field code display	Shift+F9
Insert a blank set of field braces	Ctrl+F9
Run macro (only for {MacroButton})	Alt+Shift+F9
Unlink a field	Ctrl+Shift+F9
Go to the next field	F11
Go to the previous field	Shift+F11
Lock a field from changes	Ctrl+F11
Unlock a locked field	Ctrl+Shift+F11

Field Doesn't Update

Remember, most fields do not update automatically. To manually update a field, right-click it and choose Update Field, or select it and press F9.

If neither of these methods works, check to make sure the field is not locked. Try unlocking it by selecting the field and pressing Ctrl+Shift+F11. Also examine the field's code and make sure that the \! switch is not present. (That switch locks the field against changes.)

Check to make sure that it's actually a field. When you right-click it, does the Update Field command appear on the shortcut menu? If not, perhaps it's not a field; it might have gotten unlinked (perhaps you accidentally pressed Ctrl+Shift+F9 on it to unlink it), or it might not have been a correctly constructed field in the first place.

If all else fails, delete the field and re-create it.

Locking Fields Against Updates

Some fields can be *locked*, so they are never updated even when someone issues an Update Field command on them. For example, if you use a field to enter the current date on the day the document was created, you would not want that field to update every time you open the document.

Some fields have a Prevent Fields from Being Updated check box in the Field dialog box. Marking this check box adds a \! switch in the code string for that field. You can type the switch into the code string manually if you find that easier than going back to the Field dialog box.

If the field you want to lock does not have that \! switch as part of its syntax, here's another way: Click in the field and press Ctrl+F11. To confirm that the field has been locked, right-click it; the Update Field command is unavailable on the menu that appears.

To unlock a field that has been locked this way, click in it and press Ctrl+Shift+F11.

Updating Fields for Printing

By default, Word does not automatically update fields before printing. This is intentional, because it gives you more control over your data. If you would like to change this behavior so that all links are updated before printing, open the Word Options dialog box (File, Options), click Display, and mark the Update Fields Before Printing check box.

 tip

You do not have to turn on Update Fields Before Printing for dates and times to update; they update automatically when you view the document in Print Preview or when you print.

Finding and Moving Between Fields

Sometimes it can be difficult to know where the fields are actually located in a document, especially when some of the fields do not contain visible content, such as a bookmark or index marker.

There are several ways to surmount this obstacle. One way is to select the entire document and toggle the field codes (Shift+F9). It doesn't take you to the codes, but it makes them easy to see.

Another way, which you can actually combine with the preceding one, is to go to the next field code by pressing F11 or to the previous one by pressing Shift+F11. Word jumps to the beginning of the next or previous field. You might not see anything there (if the field is hidden), but after jumping to that spot, right-click the spot and choose Toggle Field Codes or press Shift+F9, and the field appears.

A third way is to use the Select Browse Object feature, covered in Chapter 2, "Typing and Editing Text," to move from one field to the next. Click the Select Browse Object button (or press Ctrl+Alt+Home) and choose Browse by Field to go to the next field.

 To review Select Browse Object as a method of finding objects, see "Using Select Browse Object," p. 80.

Converting Fields to Plaintext

If you decide at some point that you will never want to update a particular field again, you can convert it to regular text (that is, *unlink* it). Doing so copies its current value into the document and then deletes the field placeholder.

 note

Unlinking has no effect on a marker type of field, such as a bookmark or index entry.

Before unlinking a field, update it one last time (F9) if needed. Then select it (or select multiple fields to operate on at once) and press Ctrl+Shift+F9. You can reverse an unlink with an Undo operation, but otherwise it's a one-way route. To restore the field, you need to reinsert it from scratch.

Formatting Fields

When a field inserts data from another source, such as from a bookmark or an external text file, the formatting of the original is inserted, too. For example, suppose you bookmark the text *The New Deal* in one section of your document, and you create a bookmark for it called NewDeal. Now when you insert that bookmarked text elsewhere in the document with the {Ref NewDeal} field, the inserted text appears bold and in italic.

That's the basic default for the formatting, but there are some ways to circumvent that, as you'll learn in the next several sections.

Preventing the Formatting from Changing

What happens if you change the formatting of the original and then update the field? That depends on a switch. Ordinarily the formatting would change, but you can prevent it from changing by using the * MERGEFORMAT switch. For example:

```
{ Ref NewDeal \* MERGEFORMAT }
```

You can also employ MERGEFORMAT to lock in any manual formatting you have applied to the field.

Specifying Font Formatting for a Field

To apply specific font formatting to the text displayed in a field, toggle on the field code display and then format the first character in the field name the way you want the field result to be. (Font formatting in this context includes font, size, color, and attributes such as bold, italic, and underline.)

For example, with the {Ref} example from the preceding section, suppose you want to format that field's result as italic. Select the "R" in "Ref" and click the Italic button Mini Toolbar that appears. Then add * charformat to the end of the code string. (This part is not required if the field has no arguments.)

```
{ Ref NewDeal \* charformat }
```

Then update the field (F9) to see the change.

Specifying a Numbering Type

Numeric fields can use any of several types of characters to represent the numbers, such as Arabic (1, 2, 3), Roman (I, II, III), and so on. To specify the type of numbering, use the * switch followed by the appropriate code. The easiest way to set a numbering type is in the Field dialog box; it provides a list of the available types. Alternatively, you can use switches in the field code, as in Table 16.3. (Note that the codes are case-sensitive; alphabetic is different from ALPHABETIC, for example.)

Table 16.3 Codes for Numbering Types

Numbering	Switch	Example	Notes
1, 2, 3	* Arabic	23	
a, b, c	* alphabetic	w	After the 26th letter, the letters start repeating: 27 would be aa, 28 would be ab, and so on.

Table 16.3 Continued

Numbering	Switch	Example	Notes
A, B, C	* ALPHABETIC	W	Same as preceding except uppercase.
i, ii, iii	* roman	xxiii	
I, II, III	* ROMAN	XXIII	
1st, 2nd, 3rd	* Ordinal	23rd	
First, Second, Third	* Ordtext	twenty-third	
One, Two, Three	* Cardtext	twenty-three	
Hex	* Hex	17	Hexadecimal numbering. Each place is 16, so 23 would be 1 × 16 plus 7.
Dollar Text	* DollarText	Twenty-three and 00/100	Converts numerals to written-out words for the numbers. This is the format traditionally used for writing checks.

Constructing a Custom Numeric Format

A numeric field's number format (aka the *numeric picture*) controls the appearance of the number in cosmetic ways, such as its number of decimal places, its presence of currency symbols or percent signs, and so on.

The easiest way to set the number format is in the Field dialog box; a list of available types is provided. It is much easier to construct the codes this way than to build them manually. Alternatively, you can use the \# switch, followed by the numbering format in quotation marks. For example:

```
{ FileSize \# "#,##0" }
```

If you want to build the numbering format code manually, consult Table 16.4 for the symbols to use.

Table 16.4 Codes for Numeric Pictures

Character	Purpose	Notes
#	A number if present; otherwise, a blank space. Rounds off extra fractional digits.	Use this to limit a number to a maximum number of decimal places, like this: #.##. Any places not needed do not appear.
0	A number if present; otherwise, a zero.	Use this to force a number to a minimum number of decimal places, like this: 0.00. Any places not needed appear as zeros.
$	Places a literal dollar sign in the field result.	

Table 16.4 Continued

Character	Purpose	Notes
+	Places a plus or minu s sign in front of any field result other than zero.	This is not a literal plus sign; it changes to a minus sign for a negative number.
−	Places a minus sign in front of negative numbers.	This is not a literal minus sign; it does not appear for a positive number.
.	Places a literal decimal point in the field result.	Use this to separate # or 0 codes to show where in the number those codes are referring to. For example, 0.0# indicates a required digit before and after the decimal point in the number and an optional second decimal place if needed.
,	Places a literal comma in the field result.	Use this to separate hundreds from thousands to the left of the decimal point: #,###.##.
		It does not necessarily conform to common usage that dictates a comma every third place; you could just as easily set up one like #,0 that would place a comma between the first and second digits.
;	Separates multiple options for a number.	You can have separate formatting sections for positive, negative, and zero numbers, in that order. For example, $###.00;($###.00),$0.00.
text	Adds literal text to the format.	Enclose in single quotes. For example, use this to include the word Dollars after the number: ###.00 'Dollars'

Constructing a Custom Date or Time Format

When you select a date or time from the Date and Time dialog box or from the Field dialog box, a list of sample formats appears. Choosing a format from one of those locations relieves you of the need to manually construct a date/time picture with switches.

However, in some cases, the format you want might not be available on the list. In such situations, you must manually construct the needed code for the switch.

For date and time fields, a \@ switch is used, followed by the desired formatting codes in quotation marks. For example:

```
{ Date \@ "MMMM d yyyy" }
{ Time \@ "hh:mm AM/PM" }
```

The code is a combination of placeholders and literal characters. The valid literal characters are colon (:), dash (-), and slash (\). They separate the parts of the date or time. Typically, colons separate hours, minutes, and seconds in times, and dashes or slashes separate months, days, and years in dates.

The valid characters for placeholders are shown in Table 16.5.

Table 16.5   Codes for Date or Time Formats

Characters	Purpose	Sample Code	Sample Result
M	Month number, 1 through 12	{ Date \@ "M" }	8
MM	Month number, 01 through 12	{ Date \@ "MM" }	08
MMM	Three-letter month abbreviation	{ Date \@ "MMM" }	Aug
MMMM	Full month name	{ Date \@ "MMMM" }	August
d	Day number, 1 through 31	{ Date \@ "d" }	5
dd	Day number, 01 through 31	{ Date \@ "dd" }	05
ddd	Three-letter day of the week abbreviation	{ Date \@ "ddd" }	Tue
dddd	Full day of the week	{ Date \@ "dddd" }	Tuesday
y	Two-digit year	{ Date \@ "y" }	10
yy	Four-digit year	{ Date \@ "yy" }	2010
h	Hour on 12-hour clock, 1 through 12	{ Time \@ "h" }	3
hh	Hour on 12-hour clock, 01 through 12	{ Time \@ "hh" }	03
H	Hour on 24-hour clock, 0 to 23	{ Time \@ "H" }	3 or 17
HH	Hour on 24-hour clock, 00 to 23	{ Time \@ "HH" }	03 or 17
m	Minutes, 0 to 59	{ Time \@ "m" }	4
mm	Minutes, 00 to 59	{ Time \@ "mm" }	04
AM/PM	AM or PM, uppercase	{ Time \@ "hh:mm AM/PM" }	03:04 AM
am/pm	am or pm, lowercase	{ Time \@ "hh:mm am/pm" }	03:04 am

Understanding Forms

Forms enable you to collect information from people via a fill-in-the-blanks interface. The forms you create in Word can be printed and completed on paper or filled out from within Word. With a little extra programming know-how, you can connect them to an XML data system or an Access database.

Word 2007 introduced a whole new class of form fields called *content controls*, which are used throughout Office 2010 applications as a means of interfacing with external data sources. These content controls have some great capabilities that were not present in Word 2003 and earlier, but they also have a few drawbacks. Therefore, Word 2010 also provides access to—and support for—legacy form controls that work in backward-compatible documents. In the following sections, you learn about both.

Designing a Form

The first step in creating a form is to create an ordinary Word document that contains all the "fixed" text used on the form. For example, before creating a Name field that the user fills in, type Name in the document and leave some space after it for the field to come later. To ensure that there is enough space for the fields, you might enter dummy characters where they will go, like this:

Name: &&&&&&&&&&&&&&&&&&&&&&&&&

Address: &&&&&&&&&&&&&&&&&&&&&&&&&

City: &&&&&&&&&&&&&& State: && ZIP: &&&&&-&&&&

If you simply type the text and placeholders into a document, though, the form might not be as tidy as you would like. Notice in the preceding example how the Name and Address text, having different numbers of characters, start the field at different spots. Adding a Tab character after the colon for each label might help with that:

Name: &&&&&&&&&&&&&&&&&&&&&&&&&

Address: &&&&&&&&&&&&&&&&&&&&&&&&&

City: &&&&&&&&&&&&&& State: && ZIP: &&&&&-&&&&

There's still an alignment issue with the State and ZIP, though. They aren't aligned with anything in particular; they're just hanging out there after City. So what if you put the whole thing into a table, like this?

Name:					
Address:					
City:		State:		ZIP:	

As you can see, a table can be a great help in creating a form on which the fields and labels align in an orderly way. If you define separate cells for each label and entry, you don't need the placeholders to define where the fields will go. Tables are not appropriate for every form project, but they're a good addition to your toolbox of techniques.

The form does not necessarily have to be in a single table; you could divide it into several tables, or you could use a combination of regular text and tables. Figure 16.5 shows an example. This is pure text and table at the moment—it contains no form fields.

Using whatever layout you find the most expedient for your situation, design the form and lay out all its pieces with placeholders, as in the preceding examples. Here are some tips:

- **Arrange fields in logical groups**—Group the information into sections based on the type of information being gathered. For example, in Figure 16.5, the contact information is in one group, and each question being asked of the applicant is in a separate group. Each group is in its own table in this example, but you don't necessarily have to use tables for yours.

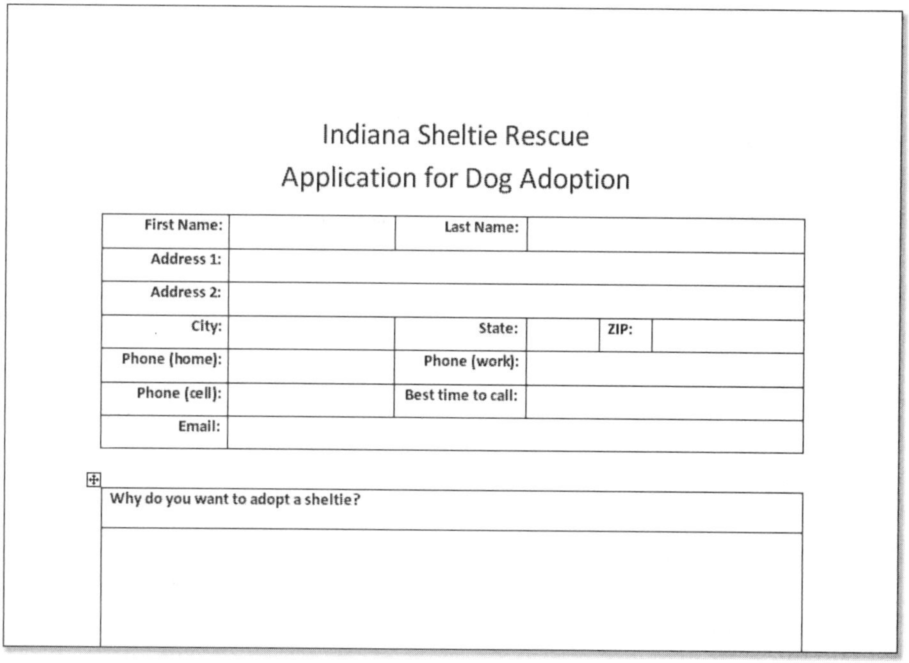

Indiana Sheltie Rescue

Application for Dog Adoption

First Name:		Last Name:			
Address 1:					
Address 2:					
City:		State:		ZIP:	
Phone (home):		Phone (work):			
Phone (cell):		Best time to call:			
Email:					

Why do you want to adopt a sheltie?

Figure 16.5 Create the skeleton of a form, to be populated with form fields later.

- **Place fields in the expected order**—People expect certain fields to be in a standard order. For example, they expect City to come before State. If you mix them up, users may have problems filling out the form.
- **Plan for different types of fields**—When you actually insert the fields, you can use not only text boxes, but drop-down lists, option buttons, and check boxes. If you think any of those will be useful, insert placeholders for them—and leave enough space for them. For example, a set of option buttons takes up more space than a drop-down list.
- **Leave enough space for user input**—Users will be frustrated if their information won't fit on the form. Leave plenty of space for names, addresses, and so on. Maximilian Theophilus Kreutzcampf will thank you for it.
- **Be clear with your labels**—Make sure it's obvious what users should put in each field. For example, suppose you have a City of Birth field, followed by a field labeled Date. Do you want the date of birth there, or the current date? Fifty percent of your users will probably guess wrong.

Saving a Form as a Template

The form isn't finished yet, of course, but now is a good time to save your work as a template. You'll want a template file, not a regular document file, because users will be creating new documents based on it.

To save the form as a template, follow these steps:

1. Choose File, Save As. The Save As dialog box opens.

2. Open the Save as Type list and choose Word Macro-Enabled Template (.dotm).If you aren't planning on storing macros in the template, you could go with Word Template (.dotx) instead.

3. In the File Name box, type the name for the template file (see Figure 16.6).

4. Click Save. The template is saved.

 tip

If you want the template to be easily accessible when starting a new document, store it in the default location for user templates: C:\Users*username*\AppData\Roaming\Microsoft\Templates.

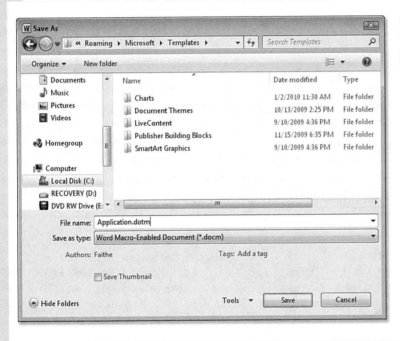

Figure 16.6
Save the document as a template. (You'll resave it after inserting the form fields.)

Differentiating Between Content Controls and Legacy Fields

Now you're ready to start inserting the form fields. There are two kinds, though—the Word 2010 form fields (aka content controls) and the legacy form fields that are a carryover from Word versions 2003 and earlier.

Content controls are a natural choice if all the users of your form are using Word 2007 or 2010. Here are some of the advantages:

- There are more types of controls, including rich text, pictures, and a calendar/date picker.

- The document doesn't have to be protected for forms, so you won't have trouble with disabled commands such as spell-checking that plague protected forms.

■ You can set a content control so that it can't be deleted or so that it unlinks itself immediately after it's filled in.

■ Their XML format makes form fields ideal for connecting with XML data sources.

There are a few things you *can't* do with content controls that the legacy form fields *can*, however:

■ You can't save the data only in a separate Word document.

■ You can't easily link a macro to a control.

■ You can't automatically format input in a predefined number format (such as currency).

■ You can't set up a form field that performs a calculation.

■ You can't limit the length of an entry.

■ You can't fill out a Word 2010 form Word 2003 or earlier.

This chapter focuses mostly on content controls, but it also provides information about the legacy form fields in case you need their capabilities or their backward compatibility.

You can combine the two types of fields in a single form. However, beware when combining the two field types, because they work differently behind the scenes. Here are some reasons to stick to one field type or the other:

■ **Saving data only**—If you want to save the data only from the form into a plaintext file (covered later in this chapter), use legacy fields only. This won't work with content control fields.

■ **Supporting Word 97–2003 users**—If the form will be filled out by people who use earlier versions of Word, use legacy fields only, and make sure you save the template as a Word 97–2003 template (.dot), not a Word 2010 .dotx or .dotm file.

■ **Preparing a database front end**—If you are creating the form as a user interface for entering data into a database, check with the database developer to find out what type of fields you should use—content controls or legacy fields. Stick only with that type. Don't mix and match, because that makes the programming of the connection difficult or impossible.

 caution

If you create a form using content controls and then use Save As to save the form in a Word 97–2003 format, a warning appears telling you that the fields will be converted to static text. That's right—static text, not legacy form fields, as you might expect. You lose all your form fields with that backward-saving, so make sure you construct the form using legacy fields if you think you will be saving in an older format later.

On the other hand, if you are creating a form to be printed or to be filled out in Word 2007 or 2010 only and saved as a new Word 2010 document, you can use both field types freely.

Displaying the Developer Tab

To work with forms, you need to work with the Developer tab. It does not appear by default. Here's how to display it:

1. Choose File, Options.

2. Click Customize Ribbon.

3. Mark the Developer check box on the list on the right side of the dialog box.

4. Click OK.

The Developer tab appears just to the right of the View tab. On the Developer tab is a Controls group that contains the buttons you need to build your form.

The Controls group contains eight buttons for Word 2010 content controls, plus one button for legacy and ActiveX controls. That latter button opens a palette of the legacy controls, as shown in Figure 16.7.

The Design Mode button in the Controls group toggles the form between Design Mode (where fields can be added and edited) and regular mode (where fields can be used to collect information).

Figure 16.7
You use the Controls group on the Developer tab to insert form fields.

Creating a Form with Content Controls

Content controls work only in Word 2007 and higher documents and templates. They look nice (friendly pale-blue frames with names, as opposed to the plain drab gray boxes in legacy forms), and they are easy for users to understand and use. You can apply formatting styles to them, and you can prevent them from being edited or deleted.

Inserting a Content Control

To insert a content control, follow these steps:

1. Position the insertion point where you want the new control.

2. On the Developer tab, make sure Design Mode is selected.

3. Click one of the content control buttons on the Controls group to insert it into the document.

There are eight content controls you can insert, summarized in Table 16.6. On the Developer tab's Controls group, point to a button to determine which content type it represents.

Table 16.6 Content Control Types

Control	Purpose
Rich Text	Holds text that the user can optionally format (bold, italic, and so on).
Plain Text	Holds plaintext that the user cannot format.
Picture	Holds a picture that the user inserts.
Building Block Gallery	Inserts a placeholder from which the user can select a building block from a gallery you specify.
Combo Box	Displays a list of values from which the user can select, and allows the user to enter other values.
Drop-Down List	Displays a list of values from which the user can select. Other values are not permitted.
Date Picker	Displays a calendar from which the user can click a date.
Check Box	Displays an on/off check box toggle. (This type is new in Word 2010.)

Configuring a Control

A content control is generic after insertion; you must provide its context via its Properties box. To view the Properties for a control, select it and then click the Properties button in the Controls group on the Developer tab.

Settings Common to All Control Types

The options available in the Properties dialog box depend on the control type, but all controls have a Title box, in which you specify the text that should appear in the thin blue bar across the top of the control. Figure 16.8 shows a photo with a title of January, for example.

The Locking settings shown in Figure 16.8 are also available for all types of controls:

- **Content control cannot be deleted**—This prevents users from deleting the control.

- **Contents cannot be edited**—This prevents users from changing what they enter in the control after the initial entry.

Style Options

By default, a field takes on the paragraph formatting of whatever paragraph you place it in. For some field types, though, you can override this formatting by applying a different style to the field entry.

For Rich Text, Plain Text, Combo Box, and List Box, you can mark Use a Style to Format Contents and then select a style from the Style list (see Figure 16.9). You can also click New Style to create a new style on the fly for it.

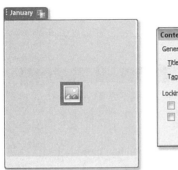

Figure 16.8
These content control options are common to all types of controls.

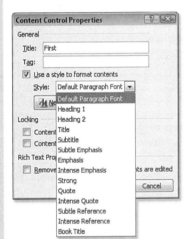

Figure 16.9
For text fields, you can specify a style to apply.

Multiparagraph Text Options

For a plaintext field only, you can choose Allow Carriage Returns (Multiple Paragraphs). This option enables users to press Enter to start a new paragraph within the field. This option is not available for rich-text fields because they always allow this.

Field-Removal Options

For both rich text and plaintext, you can choose Remove Content Control When Contents Are Edited. This option deletes the field placeholder after the user enters text into it, leaving only the text as a regular part of the document.

List Options

Combo boxes and list boxes enable you to set up the list that appears when the user activates the control. In the Drop Down List Properties area of the Content Control Properties dialog box, follow these steps:

1. Click Add. The Add Choice dialog box opens.

2. Enter the Display Name. This is the text that appears on the screen.

3. Enter the Value. This is what you enter into the database if you are connected to the form; otherwise, this is just stored with the field (see Figure 16.10).

Figure 16.10
Set up a list from which users can select.

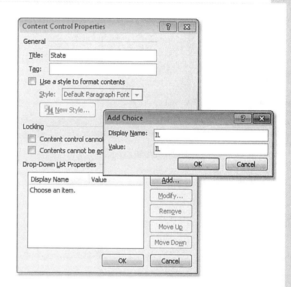

4. Click OK.

5. Repeat steps 1–4 to add more choices to the menu.

6. (Optional) Modify the list by doing any of the following:

   ▪ To modify an entry, select it, click Modify, make changes, and click OK.

   ▪ To delete an entry, select it and click Remove.

   ▪ To reorder the list, select an item and click Move Up or Move Down.

7. Click OK.

Date Options

For a date field, you can control these four settings, as shown in Figure 16.11:

- **Display the Date Like This**—Select a format from the list provided.

- **Locale**—Select a country and language.

- **Calendar Type**—Select a type based on your country. In the United States and most of Europe, the calendar is Western.

- **Store XML Contents in the Following Format When Mapped**—This setting is important only if you will be connecting to an XML data source. Select from the list of formats provided.

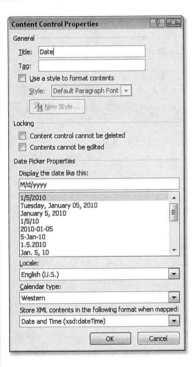

Figure 16.11
Set date options for a Date content control.

Check Box Options

For a check box, you can control how the box appears when it is checked and when it is unchecked.

To control the appearance, from the Properties box for the control, click the Change button next to Checked Symbol or Unchecked Symbol. Then select a new symbol from the Symbol dialog box that appears. You do not have to use square boxes; you can have it appear as any character or symbol you like. See Figure 16.12.

Figure 16.12
Select a different symbol to represent the marked and unmarked check boxes.

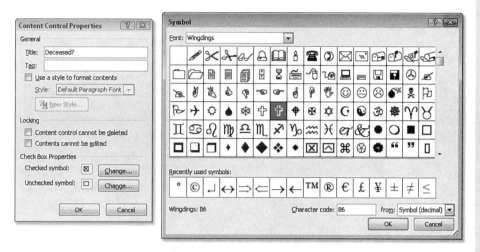

Building Block Options

The same versatile building blocks that you have learned about in other chapters are available for use in forms. For example, you can access any built-in or custom galleries such as Equations, AutoText, and Quick Parts.

The implications of this capability are significant. For example, suppose you have a set of boilerplate paragraphs that you want to be able to select among when composing letters. You could place a Building Blocks field in your template and then have easy access to those paragraphs by clicking that field whenever you are creating a new letter.

The default building block content control doesn't do anything at first; you have to set it up to be associated with a certain gallery and category. To set that up, choose a gallery and category from the Document Building Block Properties.

 To learn more about building blocks, including how to create your own categories, see "Working with Building Blocks, p. 89.

> **caution**
> Building block insertion works only if the PC on which the form is being completed has the same building blocks available.

Editing Placeholder Text

The *placeholder text* for a content control is the text that appears inside the box by default, with instructions such as *Click here to enter text*. If you like, you can customize the wording of that instruction so that it is different for each field. For example, for a control that holds first names, you could change it to *Click here and type your first name*.

> **note**
> Most of the changes you make to content control options do not require Design Mode to be on; editing the placeholder text is one of the few situations where you do need it. You can leave it on or off as desired as you work on a form.

To edit a placeholder, follow these steps:

1. On the Developer tab, click the Design Mode button to turn on Design Mode if it is not already on.

2. Click inside the control, where the placeholder text is, and edit the placeholder text there.

Creating a Form with Legacy Form Fields

Legacy form fields are the field types that were available in earlier versions of Word. You can continue to use them in Word 2010, and you *must* use them for forms to be saved in Word 97–2003 format.

Legacy form fields are accessible from the Legacy Tools button's menu in the Controls group on the Developer tab, as you saw in Figure 16.7. Table 16.7 explains each of them.

Table 16.7 Legacy Form Field Types

Form Field Type	Purpose
Text Form Field	Holds text. Unlike with content controls, you cannot format the text within the field; however, you can format the field.
Check Box Form Field	Creates an on/off check box.
Drop-Down Form Field	Displays a list containing values you specify. Users cannot add their own entries.

Yes, there are only three types of legacy form fields. The other three buttons in the Legacy Forms section of the list have other purposes. Table 16.8 describes them.

Table 16.8 Legacy Form Tools

Tool	Purpose
Insert Frame	Creates a frame. Frames are similar to text boxes; they hold static content.
Form Field Shading	Toggles form field shading on/off.
Reset Form Fields	Clears all entries in fields.

Can I Create Forms Within Email Messages?

Yes, but you can also send Word forms as email attachments in any email program, which actually might be a better way to go because of the limitations of some of the email clients that the recipients might be using.

When people receive an email with form fields (use legacy fields for this, by the way), they see the fields embedded in it. Then when they reply to the email, those fields are editable. See Chapter 22, "Developing Online-Delivered Content," for more information about how Word works with email.

Inserting a Legacy Field

To insert any legacy field, follow these steps:

1. Position the insertion point where you want the field.

2. On the Developer tab, make sure Design Mode is selected.

3. In the Controls group, click the Legacy Tools button. Its palette of tools appears.

4. Click the desired field type.

The field appears in the document as either a shaded gray box (for drop-down lists and text boxes) or as a check box (for check boxes).

Inserting a field is simple, but you will probably want to configure it after insertion. One advantage of legacy form fields is that they have some different formatting and configuration options available than content controls. Depending on what you want to do with the form, the legacy form fields might have just the option that will make your life easier.

To view the properties for a form field, right-click it and choose Properties, or click the Properties button on the Developer tab. If there is no Properties command, make sure Design Mode is marked in the Controls group and click the Properties button. Figure 16.13 shows the Properties box for a text field.

Figure 16.13
Set properties for a legacy form field.

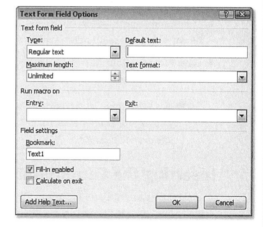

Configuring Legacy Text Field Options

There are three basic field types: Regular Text, Number, and Date. Depending on which of these types you select, different formatting options and length restrictions become available in the Options dialog box. The other three choices on the Type menu are special-purpose types, discussed later in this chapter.

If you choose Regular Text, the options shown in Figure 16.13 are available:

- **Default Text**—You can optionally specify default text to appear in the field before the user enters his or her own value.
- **Maximum Length**—This is measured in number of text characters. The default is Unlimited.
- **Text Format**—Choose among Uppercase, Lowercase, First Capital, or Title Case.

> To learn about First Capital and Title Case as formatting options, see "Changing Text Case," p. 166.

If you select Number, you can choose among these options:

- **Default Number**—This is just like Default Text; enter a default if desired.
- **Maximum Length**—This is measured in number of digits.
- **Number Format**—This drop-down list lets you specify a numeric format, some of which include currency symbols or percentage signs.

> For information about number format codes, see "Constructing a Custom Numeric Format," p. 635. You cannot construct a custom format here, but that section helps you understand the available choices.

Finally, if you choose Date, you can choose among these options:

- **Default Number**—This is just like Default Text; enter a default if desired.
- **Maximum Length**—This is measured in number of digits. It is not typically limited for dates, because dates take up only as much space as they need.
- **Date Format**—This drop-down list lets you specify a date format, including various combinations of month, day, and year.

> For information about date format codes, see "Constructing a Custom Date or Time Format," p. 636. You cannot construct a custom format here, but that section will help you understand the available choices.

Inserting the Current Date or Time

If you choose Current Date or Current Time from the Type list in the field's Options dialog box, the field changes to show the current date or time, as determined by the PC's clock. The field no longer accepts user input. It does not automatically update, but you can update it manually by selecting it and pressing F9.

 tip

For best results, set up the data to be calculated in a table, and place the calculated field in that same table. That way, you can refer to various cells by their row and column designators.

Setting Up a Calculation

If you choose Calculation as the type for the field, an Expression text box appears in the Field Options dialog box. In it, enter the formula for the calculation (see Figure 16.14). You can then use any of the calculation methods that Word supports.

> For more information about the calculations that you can perform in Word, see "Performing Math Calculations in a Table," p. 369.

Figure 16.14
Set up a Calculation field within a table, and reference cells by row (number) and column (letter).

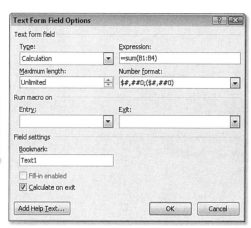

Room	$10,000
Board	$8,000
Tuition	$22,000
Miscellaneous	$5,000
Total	$45,000

Configuring Legacy Check Box Options

Check boxes are useful when you have a list of items and the user can select as many of them as he or she wants.

Check boxes have two unique options you can set for them, shown in Figure 16.15:

- **Check Box Size**—The default is Auto, which makes the check box the same size as the text that follows it. If you prefer, you can choose Exactly and enter a size in points.

- **Default Value**—This is set to Not Checked unless you specify otherwise. It determines the check box's starting state.

Figure 16.15
Set the options for a check box.

Using Option Buttons on a Form

Option buttons are sets of mutually exclusive options, such as Yes/No/Maybe. When the user selects one of them, the others in the group become deselected.

Technically, Word has no capability for option buttons on form fields. However, Word does offer an ActiveX option button. It won't work seamlessly with your other fields if you have big plans for connectivity with a database, and it won't be included if you save or print the data only in a form. However, if you are designing the form to be filled out and saved in ordinary Word documents or on paper, you are probably more concerned with the look of the form than its back-end functionality.

To create an option button set, follow these steps:

1. Position the insertion point where you want the first option button.

2. On the Developer tab, in the Controls group, click Legacy Tools, and in the ActiveX section, click Option Button (the round button, fourth from the left on the top row). A new option button and placeholder label appear.

3. Right-click the option button and choose Properties. The Properties pane opens.

4. In the Caption box, type the text that should appear next to the button.

5. In the GroupName box, type any name you like. (It must be the same for all buttons in the group, though.)

6. Repeat steps 2–5 to insert more option buttons, and make sure they all have the same GroupName.

7. Close the Properties pane.

8. Turn off Design Mode on the Developer tab and try out the buttons.

If you are interested in doing some VBA programming behind an ActiveX control so that it actually does something other than sit there and look good, right-click the control while in Design Mode and choose View Code, and then work in the Microsoft Visual Basic window that appears. (You have to know how to program in VBA for this to be much help to you.)

How Can I Program ActiveX Controls?

If you want to actually do some programming for an ActiveX field, you must know Visual Basic for Applications (VBA). To access the Visual Basic editor for a control, right-click the control while in Design Mode and choose View Code. Then work in the Microsoft Visual Basic window that opens.

Configuring Legacy List Options

A legacy list box, also called a Drop-Down Form Field, is like the list box content control. It does not allow the user to input his or her own entries like a combo box does.

The main thing to set up for a list box is the list itself. Follow these steps to create the list:

1. From the Options dialog box for the field, type the first list item in the Drop-Down Item text box.

2. Click the Add button.

3. Repeat steps 1–2 to enter the other values (see Figure 16.16).

4. (Optional) If you need to remove an item, select it and click Remove.

5. (Optional) To reorder an item, select it and click the Move up and down arrows.

6. Click OK.

> **caution**
>
> If you see a Properties pane instead of the dialog box when you attempt to open the Options dialog box for a legacy text box, check box, or list box, make sure you have chosen a control from the top row of the Legacy Controls list, and not one of the ActiveX controls.

Figure 16.16
Create the drop-down list options.

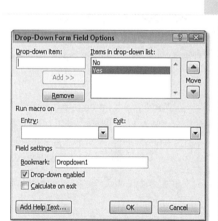

Setting a Macro to Run on Entry or Exit

If you have macros stored in the template or document, you can run one of them when the user enters or exits a particular field. For example, you might want to set up a macro that saves the file and associates it with exiting the final field on your form.

To set a macro to run on entry or exit, select the macro from the Entry or Exit drop-down list in the field's Options dialog box.

> **caution**
>
> Macro-enabled fields are possible only with legacy form fields. They work in legacy documents and templates (.dot or .doc) and in Word 2010 macro-enabled templates and documents (.dotm and .docm), but not in the regular "x" file formats (.dotx and .docx). It's not that you can't associate a macro with a field in those file formats, but that macros can't exist in those files, so there are no macros to be referenced.

IV

Enabling or Disabling a Field

In some cases, you might want to prevent users from changing the content of a field. Some would argue, "Why use a field at all if the user can't change it?" But there are reasons for that. For example, if you save the form data only to a text file, only what's in the fields is saved, so you might want some fixed values to travel along with the user-entered data.

To set up a field so that users cannot input anything into it or change its content, open its Options dialog box (right-click and select Properties) and clear the Fill-In Enabled check box.

Assigning a Bookmark to a Field

Each field has a default bookmark name so you can refer to that field whenever you reference a bookmark. See the section titled "Using a Field to Set Bookmark Text" in Chapter 14, and the section "Working with Bookmarks" in Chapter 15, to learn about the various uses for a bookmark.

To change a field's default bookmark name, open its Options dialog box (right-click and select Properties) and change the text in the Bookmark text box.

Adding Help Text

For legacy form fields, you can create help text that tells the user what to put in the field. With content controls, this isn't necessary because you can customize the placeholder text in the field, as you saw earlier in the chapter. But the unfriendly gray boxes of the legacy fields need the extra help.

You can set up help to appear in either or both of two ways: in the status bar or in a pop-up window that appears when the user presses F1 while the insertion point is inside the field. (Pressing F1 any other time opens the regular Word Help window.)

To set up help messages, follow these steps:

1. Right-click the field and choose Properties.

2. Click Add Help Text. The Form Field Help Text dialog box opens.

3. To set up F1 help:

   a. Click the Help Key (F1) tab.

   b. Select the option Type Your Own.

   c. Type the text to appear in the help message (see Figure 16.17).

   d. Click OK.

4. To set up status bar help:

   a. Click the Status Bar tab.

   b. Select the option Type Your Own.

    c. Type the text to appear in the help message.

    d. Click OK.

  5. Click OK.

Figure 16.17
Set up help text.

Creating Consistent Help Messages Across Multiple Forms

For simple forms that aren't part of an extensive form library, you'll probably want to use Type Your Own, as in the preceding steps. However, if you need to reuse the same messages over and over across many forms, consider setting up the help messages as AutoText entries and then choosing AutoText Entry in step b of step 3 or 4. That way, if you change the help message later, all the forms that use it will draw from the same updated version.

To create an AutoText entry to serve as a help message, follow these steps:

1. Type the message text in any document.
2. On the Insert tab, choose Quick Parts, Save Selection to Quick Part Gallery.
3. Type a name for the entry in the Name box.
4. Open the Gallery menu and choose AutoText.
5. Click OK to create the entry.

Now when you choose AutoText Entry from the field's Form Field Help Text dialog box, the entry you created is on the list of available entries.

Protecting a Form

You must protect a legacy form to use its fields. With content controls, protecting the form is optional but recommended.

There are several types of document protection, but the type we're interested in here makes the document uneditable except in the form fields.

To protect a form, follow these steps:

1. On the Developer tab, click Restrict Editing. The Restrict Formatting and Editing task pane opens.

2. In the Editing Restrictions section, mark the Allow Only This Type of Editing in the Document check box.

3. Open the drop-down list below the check box and choose Filling In Forms (see Figure 16.18).

Figure 16.18
Set up protection for the form so that only the fields are editable.

4. Click Yes, Start Enforcing Protection. The Start Enforcing Protection dialog box opens.

   If this button is not available, make sure you are not still in Design Mode. Click Design Mode on the Developer tab to turn it off if needed.

5. To put a password on the protection (recommended), type the desired password in the Enter New Password (Optional) box, and then retype it in the Reenter Password to Confirm box.

6. Click OK.

The Restrict Formatting and Editing task pane remains open; close it if desired by clicking the X in its upper-right corner.

To remove the protection so you can further edit the form, follow these steps:

1. If the Restrict Formatting and Editing task pane is not already displayed, click Restrict Editing on the Developer tab.

2. Click Stop Protection.

3. If you put a password on the protection, a dialog box appears prompting you for the password; enter it and click OK.

Filling Out a Form

You will probably want to test your forms as you build them to make sure they are user friendly. Filling out a form is a little different depending on the field type, so the following sections look at the processes separately.

> **caution**
>
> The form can be tested either in the template file or in a document file based on it. If you test the form in the template, though, make sure you do not save your changes with the fields filled in.

Filling Out a Form with Content Controls

To enter text in a content control, click inside the content control and then type the entry for it (see Figure 16.19).

Figure 16.19
Type in a content control.

Indiana Sheltie Rescue
Application for Dog Adoption

First Name:	First Click here to enter text.		**Last Name:**	Click here to enter text.	
Address 1:	Click here to enter text.				
Address 2:	Click here to enter text.				
City:	Click here to enter text.	**State:**	Choose an item.	**ZIP:**	Click here to enter text.
Phone (home):	Click here to enter text.	**Phone (work):**	Click here to enter text.		
Phone (cell):	Click here to enter text.	**Best time to call:**	Click here to enter text.		
Email:	Click here to enter text.				

If the form is protected, the insertion point flashes at the beginning of the document, and clicking anywhere in a protected region fails to move the insertion point; it jumps back to the beginning. The only areas you can successfully move the insertion point into are the content controls. With content controls, however, it is not mandatory that the document be protected to test a field. If the document is not protected, you can click anywhere and edit anything, not just the field entries. That's by design; it allows you to put content controls into any document.

Depending on the options set up for the content control, the content control might go away after you enter something into it, or it might become locked against further editing after the initial entry.

If either of those conditions is unsatisfactory, you can turn off their options in the content control's Properties.

Preventing Accidental Content Control Deletion

Because the form is not necessarily protected, the possibility exists that a user will accidentally delete the content control. To prevent that from happening, you can protect each control from deletion by turning on the Content Control Cannot Be Deleted option in the control's Properties dialog box. Follow these steps:

1. Unprotect the form if it is protected, and make sure Design Mode is selected on the Developer tab.

2. Select the content control and click Properties on the Developer tab. The Content Control Properties dialog box opens.

3. Mark the Content Control Cannot Be Deleted check box.

4. Click OK.

Filling Out a Legacy Form

A legacy form doesn't work properly unless it's protected. When unprotected, the form treats the fields as foreign objects, and you can't enter anything into them.

On a protected form, you can click in a field and then type the text into it, or you can press Tab to move from field to field.

If help has been set up for a field, you can press the F1 key to see the help information when the insertion point is within that field. (Pressing F1 any other time opens the general Word 2010 help window, not the specific help for that field.)

Saving and Printing a Form

After filling out the form, you will probably want to either save the form input in a file or send the completed form to the printer. The following sections explain both of those operations.

Saving Only the Form Data

In Word 2003, you could set a save option in the Save As dialog box to save only the form data in a plaintext file. You can't do that from the Save As dialog box anymore, but there's an alternative method you can use.

To save only the form data in a text file, follow these steps:

1. Choose File, Options. The Word Options dialog box opens.

2. Click Advanced.

 caution

If your form contains only Word 2007/2010 content controls, the check box in step 4 is grayed out. If the form contains a mixture of content controls and legacy form fields, the check box is available, but the resulting save captures only the data from the legacy fields.

3. Scroll down to the Preserve Fidelity When Sharing This Document section, and make sure the correct document is selected on the list.

4. Mark the Save Form Data as Delimited Text File check box and click OK.

5. Choose File, Save As. The Save As dialog box opens with Plain Text set as the file type.

6. Type a name for the file and click Save to save the text file.

In the resulting text file, the data is comma-delimited with quotation marks around text entries. For example, an address block might look like this:

"Sheri Harris","10783 Westwood Place","Anderson","IN","46282"

Printing Only the Form Data

Printing form data is similar to saving form data, in that it works only with legacy form fields, not content controls. When you choose to print only the form data, none of the other text from the form prints. However, if the form was constructed within a table, and that table had visible borders or shading, the table will print along with the data. (If you don't want the table to print, set its borders to None before printing.)

To print only the form data, follow these steps:

1. Choose File, Options. The Word Options dialog box opens.

2. Click Advanced.

3. Scroll down to the When Printing This Document section, and make sure the correct document is selected on the list.

4. Mark the Print Only the Data from a Form check box.

5. Click OK.

6. Print the document as you normally would. None of the text prints except the text in the form fields.

Tips for Creating Printed Forms

Some forms end up being used for both onscreen and on-paper data entry. That's fine, but what constitutes an effective online form might not always be the same as what constitutes an effective printed form.

Here are some things to think about when moving between printed and electronic formats:

- In an onscreen field, users can enter a lot of data in a small field because the text scrolls within the field (at least it does on a legacy form field). When that field is printed, however, there will be a limited amount of space for it. Will your users be able to adequately record their entries in the space provided?

- Drop-down fields do not work on a printed form, so you must replace them with check boxes or option buttons. (See the sidebar "Using Option Buttons on a Form" earlier in this chapter for details.)

- Check boxes might need to be larger on printed forms than on electronic ones. To change the size of a check box, right-click it and choose Properties and make the change in its Options dialog box.

- Calculated fields and fields that insert the current date/time do not work on printed forms, so remove them or change them to user-editable fields.

- Instead of using a legacy check box field, you might prefer to use a bullet character that looks like a check box. If the form will not be submitted electronically, it doesn't matter that it's not a real field. Also, more formatting options are available with a bullet character.

OUTLINING AND COMBINING DOCUMENTS

Outline Basics

Almost everyone has, at one time or another, stared at a blank page trying to get started on a long or complex writing project. Where to begin? What to include? It can be hard to wrap your thoughts around the project without a grasp of the big picture.

That's where outlining comes in. By starting with an outline, you create a structure or map that guides your writing each step of the journey and forces you to think through the entire writing process. Once the document's headings are in place, you can start filling in the body text beneath them. Suddenly the project doesn't seem so overwhelming when you're tackling it one section at a time with a clear vision of what you want to accomplish.

Word's Outline view makes it easy to create complex, multilevel outlines. (Word was the tool used to outline and write this book, in fact!) Word enables you to view the outline at various levels of detail and to easily move topics around. It even can automatically number your headings and update the numbering when you move topics.

Outlines are based on heading styles. The default heading styles are automatically applied as you promote and demote items in an outline. For example, Figure 17.1 shows part of the outline for this book's Chapter 2, "Typing and Editing Text." The top-level heading (Heading 1) is the chapter title; the second-level headings (Heading 2) are the major sections, and so on.

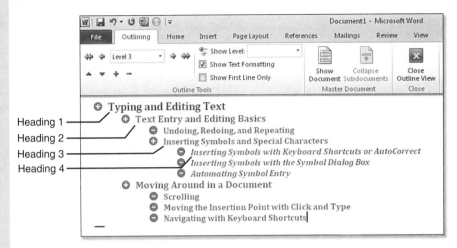

Figure 17.1
A multilevel outline based on heading styles.

In addition to the default heading styles, you can set up outlining to work with any custom styles you might have created. In "Setting a Style's Outline Level," later in this chapter, you learn how to define which outline level is associated with which style(s).

Typing an Outline in Outline View

To type or edit an outline, switch to Outline view. To do this, click Outline on the View tab, or click the Outline View button in the status bar of the Word window.

Then type the first item for the outline (see Figure 17.2).

Press Enter after each entry. Another line of the same outline level appears. At this point, you can type more lines at the same level, or you can *demote* the new line so that it is subordinate to the one above it. See the following section for information about promoting and demoting.

Once you're satisfied with the outline, you can start using it as a starting point for writing the rest of the document. You will probably want to switch to Print Layout or Draft view before adding body text. (Use the View tab or buttons to switch views, or click the Close Outline View button on the Outlining tab.) Each outline item appears as a heading in the document, with Word's default heading styles applied. Under each heading, type the appropriate body text, using Normal style or whatever style you have designated for body text in the document.

 tip

If you want to view the document's outline while you are editing it in another view (such as Print Layout), mark the Navigation Pane check box on the View tab. The Navigation pane appears in a separate pane to the left of the main document window. It has three tabs; the leftmost tab displays an outline of the document based on its headings. You can jump to a heading in the document by clicking it there.

 tip

It seems only natural to make a document's title the highest level item in the outline (Heading 1). But do you really want to waste the Heading 1 style on an item that appears only once in the document? It might be better to make all the major content headings in the document Heading 1 style, and either style the document title also as Heading 1 or create a special style just for the title (and set its outline level to 1).

Figure 17.2
Begin typing the head- ings for the outline in Outline view.

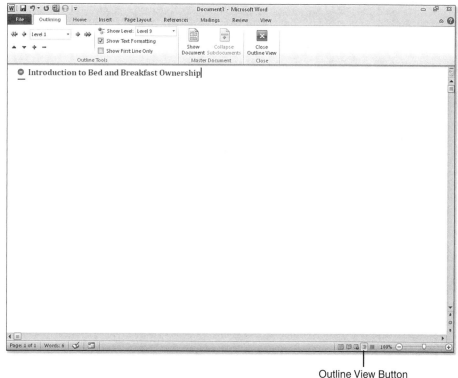

Outline View Button

Demoting and Promoting Outline Items

To demote the line, press Tab or press Alt+Shift+right arrow. It appears indented, and the line above it acquires a plus sign, indicating that it now has subordinates.

To *promote* a line so that it moves up a level in importance, click it and press Shift+Tab or Alt+Shift+left arrow.

If you prefer to use a mouse to promote and demote, click an item's plus sign (or minus sign) and then drag it to the left or right. As you drag, the item is promoted or demoted.

You can also click the buttons on the Outlining tab or use key- board shortcuts, as in Table 17.1.

 note

In Outline view, the insertion point does not have to be at the beginning of the line to use Tab or Shift+Tab to demote or promote. That's because the Tab key does not move the insertion point to tab stops in Outline view. Switch back to Draft or Print Layout view if you want to work with tab stops.

Table 17.1   Outlining Buttons and Shortcuts for Promoting and Demoting

Button	Purpose	Keyboard Shortcut
⇐⇐	Promote to Heading 1	None
⇐	Promote (one level)	Shift+Tab or Alt+Shift+Left arrow
Level 1 ▾	Outline level (select from list)	None
⇒	Demote (one level)	Tab or Alt+Shift+Right arrow
⇒⇒	Demote to body text	Ctrl+Shift+N

If you demote an item as completely as possible, it becomes *body text*. In this context, "body text" refers to an outline level, not to a particular style. You can have many different styles that all have body text set as their outline level.

➡ *To change a style's outline level, see "Setting a Style's Outline Level," p. 668.*

Checking the Styles Used in the Outline

In Outline view, there is no obvious indicator of what styles are in use. To find out, press Ctrl+Shift+S to display the Apply Styles pane and then click a line in the outline. The style is reported in the Style Name box (see Figure 17.3).

The Outline Level box on the Outlining tab lists the outline level at which the selected line is set, and if you are using the default heading styles for outlining, this corresponds to the heading level. For example, if the Outline Level box reports Level 3, the paragraph is using Heading 3 style. However, if you are using nonstandard styles for your outline, this correlation does not hold.

 note

Perhaps an easier way to see styles at a glance in an outline is to turn on the display of the Style area. To do so, choose File, Options. Click Advanced, and then in the Display section, set a positive number in inches in the Style Area Pane Width in Draft and Outline Views box (for example, 1 inch).

Creating an Outline from an Existing Document

Outlines aren't just for prewriting planning; you might also want to see an outline of a document you have already written.

To make sure the outline is accurate, first check that you have applied the appropriate heading styles to the headings. The first-level headings should be styled as Heading 1, the second-level as Heading 2, and so on. You can have up to nine levels of headings.

Figure 17.3
Demote (indent) a line by pressing Tab. Style usage can be checked from the Apply Styles pane.

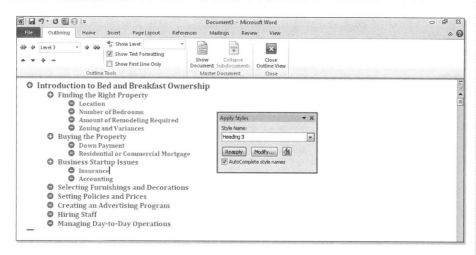

After confirming the styles on the headings, switch to Outline view. By default, the Outline view shows not only the headings, but the body text. Body text paragraphs appear with gray circles beside them. These are not bullets; they are there to help you remember you are in Outline view and to serve as selectors for the paragraphs. You can select a paragraph by clicking its gray circle, or you can move it by dragging its circle (see Figure 17.4).

Outline view makes it easy to catch style errors you might have made, such as applying the wrong style to a particular heading or accidentally styling one of the body paragraphs as a heading. If you find any style application errors, correct them by clicking that line and then choosing the desired style from the Apply Styles pane. (Press Ctrl+Shift+S to display this pane if needed.)

 tip

If you would rather use other styles than the default Heading 1s in your outline, see "Setting a Style's Outline Level" later in this chapter. Keep in mind, however, that you can redefine the formatting for all the default Heading styles, and you can apply different style sets from the Change Styles list on the Home tab. You don't have to apply different styles to achieve a different look.

Alternatively, you can promote or demote the items with Shift+Tab or Tab, respectively, or you can apply the built-in heading styles with shortcut keys: Ctrl+Alt plus the number of the heading level desired (Ctrl+Alt+1 for Heading 1, and so on). To demote to body text, press Ctrl+Shift+N.

If you do not want to see the body text in the outline, or if you want to see only certain heading levels, collapse the Outline view, as explained in the following section.

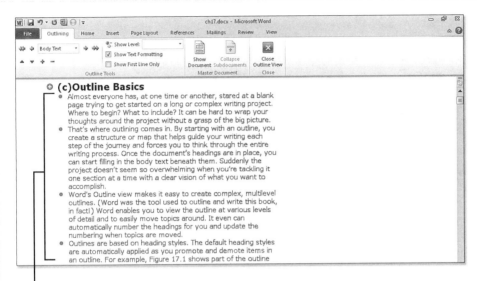

Figure 17.4
Body text
appears in an
outline with
a gray circle
to its left.

Body Text
Paragraphs

Viewing and Organizing the Outline

When the outline is fully expanded, as it is in Figure 17.4, even body text appears in it. That's useful for checking the content of a section, but it takes away the main benefit of the outline, which is to provide a high-level summary. Therefore, most of the time, you will probably want to view the outline at some level of compression.

You can collapse or expand the entire outline so that it shows only headings of a certain level and higher. For example, if you set the outline to show Level 3, anything that is not styled with a Level 3 heading or higher is hidden. To collapse the outline to a specific level, choose a level from the Show Level list on the Outlining tab (see Figure 17.5).

You can also collapse or expand individual branches of the outline.

To toggle a branch between being expanded or collapsed, double-click the plus sign to its left.

Other expansion and collapse methods operate on individual branches:

- Click the Expand button (plus sign button) or press Alt+Shift++ (plus sign) to expand everything subordinate to the item where the insertion point lies.

- Click the Collapse button (minus sign button) or press Alt+Shift+_ (underscore) to collapse everything subordinate to the item where the insertion point lies.

Figure 17.5
Choose a level to collapse or
expand the entire outline.

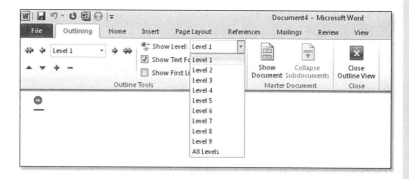

Expanding and collapsing is not the only way of changing the view of the outline, although it's the most dramatic way. Here are a couple additional settings on the Outlining tab that control outline appearance:

- **Show Text Formatting**—This on/off toggle shows or hides the different fonts and sizes used for the various heading levels.

- **Show First Line Only**—This on/off toggle makes multiple-line items (such as body paragraphs and long headings) show up as single-line items on the outline.

Rearranging Outline Topics

If you have ever tried to rearrange sections of a large document, you know how cumbersome cut-and-paste operations can be in that situation. You have to cut some text and then scroll to the section where you want to paste it, perhaps many pages away.

It is much easier to rearrange a document in Outline view because you can collapse all the body text beneath the headings and work with the document in a bird's-eye view. When you move a heading in Outline view, all the collapsed content beneath it moves automatically with it, so there's no need to scroll through pages and pages of body text to find the spot in which you want to paste.

One way to move a heading in the outline is to drag and drop it. This method works well when you need to move a heading and all its subordinate headings:

1. Click the plus sign (or minus sign) next to a heading to select it and all its subordinates. The mouse pointer becomes a four-headed arrow.

2. Drag up or down to move the heading and its subordinates to a new location.

Another way is to use the buttons on the Outlining tab. This method works well when you need to move one heading but not its subordinates, or when you need to move a block of headings (not necessarily in a neat subordinate structure):

1. Select the content to be moved up or down. You can select any number of headings or body text at any level.

2. Click the Move Up (up arrow) or Move Down (down arrow) button to move the selection up or down one position in the outline.

3. Repeat step 2 as needed until the content is at the desired position.

Setting a Style's Outline Level

As mentioned earlier, Word uses its built-in heading styles for outlines (Heading 1, Heading 2, and so on) by default. When you create an outline by typing directly into Outline view and pressing Tab and Shift+Tab to demote and promote, those heading styles are automatically applied to the outline levels. There are 10 outline levels: Level 1 through Level 9 headings, plus body text.

 To review modifying a style, see "Modifying Styles," p. 238.

If you would rather use your own custom styles than the built-in ones for headings, you must set the custom styles' outline levels so Word knows how to treat them.

To specify the outline level for a style, follow these steps:

1. Display the Styles pane. To do so, on the Home tab, click the dialog box launcher icon in the Styles group. The Styles pane opens.

2. In the Styles pane, right-click the style and choose Modify (see Figure 17.6).

   Make sure it's a user-created style you're modifying; you can't change the outline level for one of the built-in heading styles.

3. In the Modify Style dialog box, click the Format button and then choose Paragraph from its menu. The Paragraph dialog box opens.

4. Open the Outline Level drop-down list and choose the desired outline level for this style (see Figure 17.7).

5. Click OK to accept the new outline level.

6. Click OK to close the Modify Style dialog box.

> **tip**
>
> Here's another way of changing a custom style's outline level: In the Modify Style dialog box, choose a different style from the Style Based On list. The custom style takes on whatever outline level is assigned to the style on which it is based unless you set a specific outline level for it. However, with that method, all the unspecified attributes of the custom style change to match the new basis, so additional unwanted formatting changes might occur to the style's formatting.

Click here to open the Styles pane.
Right-click the style and choose Modify.

Figure 17.6
Modify the
style to set its
outline level.

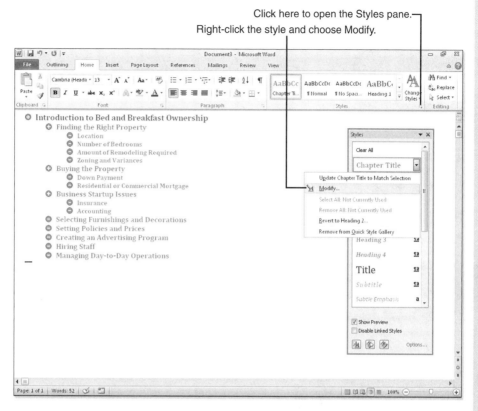

Setting an Individual Paragraph's Outline Level

You can also change the outline level on an individual paragraph-by-paragraph basis, without
affecting the style. For example, you could force a certain body paragraph to appear in the outline
by setting its outline level to one of the levels currently being shown in the outline. Here's how to
set the outline level for a paragraph without changing its style:

1. Right-click the paragraph and choose Paragraph.

2. In the Paragraph dialog box, open the Outline Level list and select an outline level.

3. Click OK.

This works on paragraphs formatted with all styles except the built-in heading styles (Heading 1
through Heading 9).

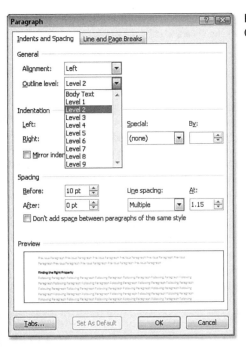

Figure 17.7
Change a style's outline level from its Paragraph properties.

Using Outline Levels to Change How Theme Fonts Are Applied

Now that you know about outline levels, let's revisit a topic from Chapter 6: font themes.

As you learned in Chapter 6, "Creating and Applying Styles and Themes," there are two fonts in a theme: one for headings and one for body text. Word decides which of those two fonts to apply to a paragraph based on the outline level assigned to its style. Anything with a style that has an outline level of Level 1 through Level 9 receives the font specified for headings; anything with a style that has an outline level of Body Text receives the font specified for body text.

Knowing this, you can rig a style to show one font or the other regardless of a paragraph's actual status as heading or body text. Suppose, for example, that you want a certain body paragraph to look different from the others. Apply an unused heading style to it, such as Heading 9, and then modify that style so that it looks the way you want it. Or better yet, create a custom style, do not base it on any other style, and then apply an outline level to it (Level 1 through Level 9). As long as a heading style is the paragraph's basis, it will use whatever heading font has been specified in the theme (unless, of course, you override the font choice manually).

Numbering Outline Items

When creating an outline that includes consecutively numbered items, you can save yourself some time by allowing Word to manage the numbering for you.

The time savings is not so much in the initial creation of the outline, but in its later editing. For example, when writing a book, the first task is to create an outline of the chapters to include: Chapter 1, Chapter 2, Chapter 3, and so on. If you manually type that text as part of each chapter title, and you rearrange the chapters, you're in for a tedious job of manually editing each title. However, if you allow Word to handle the numbering for you, you never have to deal with the numbering again; Word renumbers items automatically as you rearrange them.

To number an outline, you apply list formatting to it. You can set up list formatting in either of two ways:

- You can apply multilevel lists and create your own list definitions via the Multilevel List button on the Home tab.

- You can create and apply a list style in which to store the outline numbering format. A list style can do everything a multilevel list can do, plus it can have a name and can have a shortcut key combination assigned to it. You can also save it with a particular template.

All Levels Continue the Same Numbers on My Outline

One common problem in a document that uses custom styles is that Word numbers every paragraph equally when you apply a multilevel list, so you end up with something like this:

1) Major Heading

2) Minor Heading

3) Minor Heading

4) Major Heading

First, check to make sure the appropriate outline level has been assigned to each style. To modify a paragraph style to appear at a certain outline level, see "Setting a Style's Outline Level" earlier in this chapter.

If that doesn't work, try manually assigning a particular list level to all the paragraphs that use that style. From the Styles pane, right-click the style and choose Select All xx Instances. Then open the Multilevel List button's menu on the Home tab, point to Change List Level, and click the desired list level.

Subordinate Items Don't Restart Numbering Under a New Major Heading

Another potential problem with outline numbering is that the subordinate items don't restart the numbering after an intervening major heading, like this:

1) Major Heading

    A.   Minor Heading

    B.   Minor Heading

2) Major Heading

    A.   Minor Heading

    B.   Minor Heading

To correct this problem, modify the list style definition (or create a new multilevel list definition) and make sure that the Restart List After check box is marked and the appropriate upper level is selected.

Applying a Multilevel List

You can apply a multilevel list or list style to individual portions of an outline, but usually it's best for the entire outline to be formatted the same way for consistency.

Select the entire outline (Ctrl+A) or the portion you want to format, and then on the Home tab, open the Multilevel List button's drop-down list and click a list or list style. Each item receives the numbering format specified for its outline level.

The Multilevel List button's menu presents a gallery of list-formatting choices, including both lists and list styles (if any have been created in the current document or template). The gallery has several sections:

- **Current List**—Appears at the top of the list and shows the currently applied list type, or the default list type if none is currently applied. (You can click the Multilevel List button, rather than opening its menu, to apply the current list.)

- **List Library**—This collection of list presets always appears. Word provides several, and you can add your own lists.

- **List Styles**—If you have defined any list styles (using the Styles feature, covered later in this chapter), they appear here; otherwise, this section does not appear.

- **Lists in Current Documents**—If you have applied multilevel numbering already, the types you have applied appear here for easy reapplication. Otherwise, this section does not appear.

As shown in Figure 17.8, you can filter the Multilevel List button's menu to show only one of these four categories. Click All to open a menu and then click the category you want to show. To return to showing all the categories, reopen that menu and click All.

Creating Your Own Multilevel Lists and List Styles

You can create a multilevel list definition as either an ordinary multilevel list or a list style. The main difference between them is where they are stored:

- A multilevel list exists only in the current document. However, if desired, you can easily add it to the List Library gallery. After you do that, it is available globally, no matter what template you are using. You can't modify it, but you can delete and re-create it.

- You can set up a list style to exist either in the current document only or in the currently applied template. If you save it in the template, it is available whenever you are working with a document based on that template. You can modify a list style.

The dialog boxes for creating a new multilevel list versus a list style appear to be quite different, but if you compare them feature by feature, they come out almost identical. And in fact, when you are defining a list style, you can access a duplicate of the Define New Multilevel List dialog box, so anything you can do with a multilevel list can be saved as a list style.

Figure 17.8
Apply a list style preset from the Multilevel List button. Filter the list if desired.

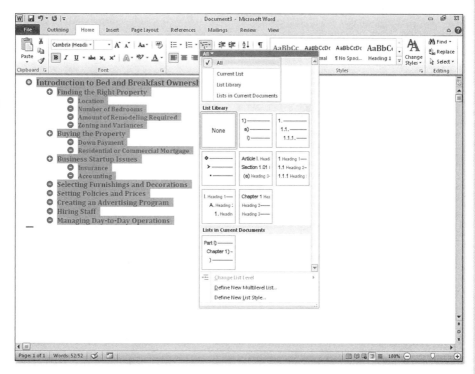

Creating a Multilevel List

To create your own multilevel list, follow these steps:

1. (Optional) To apply the new list to an outline or list or a portion thereof, select the text to which to apply it. (You can apply it later if you prefer.)

2. (Optional) If you want to base the new multilevel list on an existing one, open the Multilevel List button's menu (on the Home tab) and click the desired list to apply it to the selected text.

3. Open the Multilevel List button's menu and choose Define New Multilevel List. The Define New Multilevel List dialog box opens (see Figure 17.9).

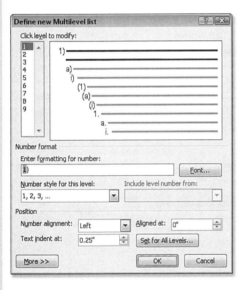

Figure 17.9
Define the formatting for a new multilevel list.

4. Click the number representing the level you want to modify.

5. In the Number Style for This Level list, select the numbering style desired. The placeholder (shaded gray) in the Enter Formatting for Number box changes to represent the new style.

6. In the Enter Formatting for Number box, type any additional text that should surround the number placeholder.

   For example, you could type **Chapter** in front of the placeholder, or add punctuation after it, such as a period, colon, or parenthesis.

7. (Optional) To change the font formatting, click the Font button, make any changes desired, and click OK. All font attributes are available to apply to outline numbering except Outline and Small Caps.

8. (Optional) To change the position (alignment, indentation, and so on), make changes to the values in the Position section of the dialog box.

   You can control every aspect of the positioning here, including the amount of indentation before and after the numbering or bullet, whether a tab character appears after the number, and whether there should be a tab stop to go with that tab character.

9. (Optional) To change the position settings for all levels at once, click the Set for All Levels button. In the Set for All Levels dialog box shown in Figure 17.10, choose an indentation and text position for the first level and then specify the amount of additional indent for each level beneath it. This creates an orderly cascade effect between levels. Click OK to return to the Define New Multilevel List dialog box when finished.

Figure 17.10
Define the formatting for all levels of outlining at once.

10. (Optional) For more options, click the More button in the bottom-left corner of the dialog box. This displays the additional options, as in Figure 17.11.

Figure 17.11
Set additional options that will affect all levels of outlining.

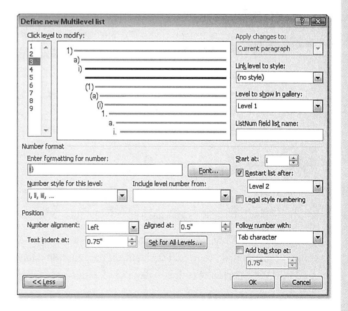

11. Set any of the additional options as needed:

- To link a particular level to a certain style, select a style from the Link Level to Style list. This enables you to create a special outline level that pertains only to a certain style, and anytime you apply that style in the document, the numbering appears with it.

- To define which levels appear when this list appears in the Gallery, choose a level from the Level to Show in Gallery list.

- To use the specified list formatting with a ListNum field list, specify a name in the ListNum Field List Name box. (Make up a unique name.) Then when you create a numbered list with the {ListNum} field, you can use the name as a parameter to specify the list's formatting.

→ *To learn more about the {ListNum} field, see "Numbering Fields," p. 625.*

- To start the numbering for a level at a number other than 1, specify a number in the Start At box.

- To use legal-style numbering, mark the Legal Style Numbering check box. This forces all the numbering to Arabic (1, 2, 3), regardless of its setting otherwise in the style or list definition.

- To specify a character to appear after the number, set the Follow Number With setting. You can use a tab, a space, or nothing.

- If you want some other character to follow the number, type that character following the number code in the Enter Formatting for Number box.

- If you include a tab character after the number, you might want to set a tab stop for it. To include a tab stop in the formatting, mark the Add Tab Stop At check box and then enter a position in inches.

12. When you are finished with the specification for the selected level, select another level from the Click Level to Modify list and then repeat steps 5–11. Repeat for each level.

13. Click OK to create the new list format.

The new list format is applied to the portion of the list that was selected when you began the creation process. You can also apply it from the Multilevel List button's menu, from the Lists in Current Documents section of the menu.

I Can't Edit a Multilevel List Definition

This is one of the inherent drawbacks of using a multilevel list definition instead of a list style. You can't edit it. You have to create a new multilevel list.

Fortunately, it's not difficult to re-create the list. Select the outline (or text that has the existing list applied to it) and then start a new multilevel list definition. It takes its default settings from the selected text; just make the changes necessary and click OK to save the new definition.

If you want to save the multilevel list definition as a list style, select the text to which it is applied. Then from the Multilevel List button's menu, choose Define New List Style. The new list style's default settings are based on the selected text.

To modify the definition of a list style, right-click the style on the Multilevel List button's menu and choose Modify. (This command is not available on the right-click menu for non-style list definitions.)

Including Numbers from Higher Outline Levels

Suppose you want each outline item to be double-numbered, including both the higher level item's number and its own, like this:

> Chapter 1, Section A
> Chapter 1, Section B
> Chapter 1, Section C

To set this up, use the Include Level Number From drop-down list in the Define New Multilevel List dialog box. For example, here's how to set up the preceding example for Level 2:

1. In the Define New Multilevel List dialog box, click 2 on the Click Level to Modify list.

2. Open the Number Style for This Level list and choose A, B, C. An A appears (shaded) in the Enter Formatting for Number box.

3. Click to move the insertion point to the left of the shaded A code, and type **Chapter** and press the spacebar once.

4. Open the Include Level Number From drop-down list and choose Level 1. The 1 code appears in the Enter Formatting for Number box, after the word *Chapter*.

5. Press the spacebar twice after the 1 code, and then type **Section** and press the spacebar once. Now the entry in the Enter Formatting for Number box looks like this: Chapter 1 Section A.

6. Open the Follow Number With list and choose Space.

7. Continue creating the list definition as usual.

Adding a Custom Multilevel List to the Gallery

A custom multilevel list, like the one you created in the preceding section, is saved with the current document only. It does not have a name (like a style would have), and you cannot transfer it between documents.

To add the list formatting specification to the Gallery (that is, the List Library area of the menu) so that it is available in all documents, do the following:

1. Open the Multilevel List button's menu.

2. In the Lists in Current Documents section, locate and right-click the list to be added.

3. Choose Save in List Library. The list formatting now appears in the List Library portion of the menu. It is also saved to the Normal.dotm template, so it will be available in future documents you create.

Creating a List Style

A list style defines a multilevel list in a slightly different way; it contains all the specifications for a regular multilevel list, but it saves them in a named style that you can then apply as you would any other style. You can also store it with a specific template.

To create your own list style, follow these steps:

1. (Optional) To apply the new list to an outline or list, or a portion thereof, select the text to which to apply it. (You can apply it later if you prefer.)

2. (Optional) If you want to save the style to a particular template, apply that template to the current document.

    To apply a different template to a document, see "Changing a Document's Template," p. 302.

3. (Optional) If you want to base the new style on an existing multilevel list, open the Multilevel List button's menu (on the Home tab) and click the desired list to apply it to the selected text.

4. On the Home tab, open the Multilevel List button's menu and choose Define New List Style. The Define New List Style dialog box opens (see Figure 17.12).

5. Type a name for the style in the Name box.

6. (Optional) To start the numbering at a number other than 1, change the value in the Start At box.

7. Select an outline level from the Apply Formatting To list.

8. Choose text formatting for that list level: Font, Size, Bold, Italic, Underline, and Color.

9. For the selected level, click either the Numbering or Bullets button.

10. Select a number type or bullet character. You can do the following:

    - Select a bullet or number type from the list of presets to the right of the Numbering and Bullets buttons.

    - Click the Insert Symbol button and select any character from any font to use as a bullet character.

    - Click the Insert Picture button and select a picture bullet.

11. (Optional) Click the Decrease Indent or Increase Indent button to change the amount of indent for the chosen outline level.

> 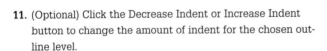 **tip**
>
> If you want to set other text formatting than what appears in the dialog box (for example, strikethrough or superscript), click the Format button and choose Font to open the Font dialog box.

12. Choose where to save the style: Only in This Document or New Documents Based on This Template.

13. Choose a different outline level from the Apply Formatting To list and then repeat steps 8–12.

14. (Optional) To further fine-tune the numbering of the list levels, click the Format button and choose Numbering. Then select additional options from the Modify Multilevel List dialog box.This dialog box is identical to the one shown in Figure 17.11, except for its name. Refer to step 11 in the section "Creating a Multilevel List" earlier in this chapter for specifics about this dialog box. When you are finished working with it, click OK to return to the Define New List Style dialog box.

15. Click OK to define the new style and apply it to the selected text.

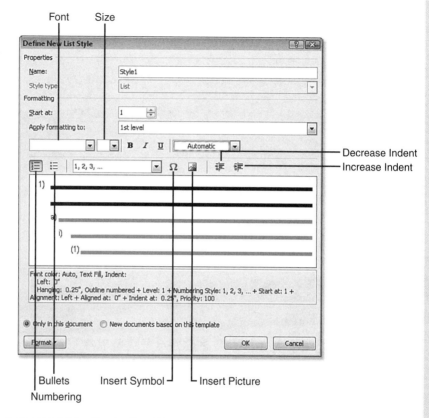

Font   Size

Figure 17.12
Define the formatting for
a new list style.

Decrease Indent
Increase Indent

Bullets   Insert Symbol   Insert Picture
Numbering

Order of Style Application Revisited

Remember from the Chapter 6 sidebar "Order of Style Application" that when multiple styles
are applied to the same text and one layer contradicts another, the formatting is determined
according to a hierarchy. Character takes top priority, followed by Paragraph, and then List, and
finally Table.

So how does that affect outline numbering? Well, suppose you have an outline consisting of a
bunch of Heading 1 and Heading 2 style headings, and you apply a list style to the entire list. (It
doesn't even need to be in Outline view necessarily.) The paragraphs still retain their Heading 1
and Heading 2 style designations; if you check them out in the Styles pane, you'll see that the
paragraph styles are intact and unmodified. The list styles are applied on top of the paragraph
styles, as separate elements. If the list style specifies anything that contradicts the paragraph
style, the list style prevails, but the paragraph style controls anything that the list style does
not specify.

Deleting a Multilevel List or List Style

Once you add a multilevel list to the List Library gallery, it's there until you remove it, in all documents regardless of their template. To remove a list from the My Lists gallery, right-click it on the Multilevel List button's menu and choose Remove from My Lists.

Theoretically, you can delete a list style like any other style (by right-clicking it in the Styles task pane and choosing Delete), except for one thing: List styles don't show up in the Styles task pane. So instead you must go through the Manage Styles dialog box to delete a list style. Follow these steps:

1. On the Home tab, click the dialog box launcher icon in the Styles group to open the Styles task pane.

2. Click the Manage Styles button at the bottom of the task pane. The Manage Styles dialog box opens.

3. Click the name of the style to delete.

4. Click the Delete button.

5. At the confirmation box, click Yes.

6. Click OK to close the Manage Styles dialog box.

Printing or Copying an Outline

Unfortunately, printing an outline leaves something to be desired in Word 2010, as with earlier versions. The Help system tells you that you can print the outline at any level of detail desired by collapsing the outline to the view you want and then printing it. However, this is not the case; the entire document prints.

So how, then, can you print an actual outline, with indented levels, just like what you see on the screen? Your best bet is to generate a table of contents, as you will learn in Chapter 19, "Creating Tables of Contents and Indexes," and then print the table of contents.

The same goes for copying an outline. When you select a collapsed outline and then copy it and paste it, the pasted copy is the full document, not just the outline, and you can't change that. The only way to get a copy of just the outline headings is to generate a table of contents.

Understanding Master Documents

When a Word document grows to be more than a certain size—usually around 100 pages or so—it starts becoming unwieldy to work with. It takes longer to save and open than normal, and sometimes there are delays in scrolling, pagination, and picture display. And the larger it gets, the more pronounced the problems become. To get around this, many people create large documents in chunks, with each chunk residing in a separate Word file. For example, as I was writing this book, I put each chapter in a separate document.

Dividing a large writing project into separate files has disad-vantages, though, especially if you are doing your own desktop publishing from within Word. Each document has its own page numbering and styles, and it can be a challenge to generate a master table of contents or index that encompasses all the files.

The Master Documents feature in Word offers a compromise between the two approaches. A master document is a regular Word document that contains active links to multiple other document files, inserted as *subdocuments*. When the links to the subdocuments are expanded, the master document appears to contain all their content, so you can view your entire project as if it were a single document.

A master document does not just help with viewing, however. You can also perform the following tasks:

> **caution**
>
> The use of master and subdocu-ments in Word has always been somewhat flaky, dating back to its first implementation. For whatever reason, Microsoft has not seen fit to give this feature the overhaul it needs. Although you can success-fully use master and subdocuments, treat the files and folders in which these documents reside with cau-tion. It's easy to gum up the works if you move or rename a master or subdocument file from its original location.

- Do a single spell-check for all subdocuments.

- Number pages consecutively across all subdocuments.

- Number captions and footnotes consecutively.

- Generate a single index for all subdocuments.

- Generate a single table of contents.

In some instances, a master document offers the best of both worlds when working with large documents—you retain the flexibility and performance of individual document files for each section, while still gaining the benefits of having a combined document.

Master Documents Make Word Crash

Since its inception, the Master Documents feature has been a bit quirky and buggy, and that fact hasn't changed with Word 2010, unfortunately. The reason is somewhat technical; it has to do with the fact that a master document's hyperlink is not a simple hyperlink but a complex set of hooks that tie the content to the master document. It's this complexity that enables master documents to do all the unique things they can do, such as integrate a single set of styles, but it's also the complexity that makes them crash-prone. There's an interesting article about this at http://word.mvps.org/faqs/general/WhyMasterDocsCorrupt.htm.

If you find yourself with a master document that makes Word crash whenever you open it, there's no good way of repairing it. Instead, convert it to a regular document (by unlinking each subdocument) and then copy and paste its content into a new blank document. Then re-create the subdocuments from that new document.

Continued...

You might also think about finding an alternative to using master documents for your project. You might insert the files with the Insert, Object, Text from File command, for example. This method does not maintain a dynamic link between the file and its source, but it does let you combine several documents into one.

If you need a dynamic link but don't need the tight integration of numbering, headers/footers, styles, and so on that a master document provides, consider using an OLE link to insert the content, as you learned in Chapter 15, "Copying, Linking, and Embedding Data."

Master Documents and Styles

Master documents enforce a consistent set of formatting across multiple subdocuments, some of which might have different formatting from the others. Toward this end, the master document imposes its own definition of each style on all the subdocuments.

Subdocuments retain their own style definitions when they are opened for editing separately from the master document. If you open a subdocument using the File, Open command, it shows its own styles. If you open a subdocument from its link in a master document, on the other hand, it shows the styles from the master document.

For example, suppose that your master document defines Heading 1 as Arial Bold, and you import another document into it as a subdocument that defines Heading 1 as Times New Roman. When viewed as part of the master document, the headings in the subdocument appear as Arial Bold, but when the subdocument is viewed as a standalone document, its headings appear as Times New Roman.

The master document redefines the definitions for any styles that it has in common with the subdocuments, but if a subdocument contains a style that the master does not contain, that custom style carries over to the master document. For example, suppose in the subdocument that you have a style called MyHead1, and it's applied to all the headings in the subdocument. The master document does not have this style. When the subdocument is imported into the master document, those headings remain MyHead1, and they do not change.

There's an exception to this rule, though. If MyHead1 is based on another style, and that style is differently defined in the master document, you might see a trickle-down change. For example, if MyHead1 is based on Heading 1, any facet of MyHead1 that is not explicitly defined carries over from the master document's definition of Heading 1.

➡ *For more information about styles, see "Understanding Styles," p. 217.*

Master Documents and Headers/Footers

The master document applies its headers and footers to all the subdocuments. If a subdocument has its own header or footer that is different, it will be suppressed when the subdocument is viewed within the master document. (However, the subdocument's own header and footer continue to be available when the subdocument is opened outside the master document.)

That doesn't mean, however, that you can't have different headers and footers for each subdocument. When Word inserts subdocuments, it separates them with continuous section breaks. (You can see this by switching to Draft view.) And as you learned in Chapter 7, "Formatting Documents and Sections," each section can have its own header and footer definition. Therefore, you can set up different headers and footers for each subdocument from within the master document.

➡ *For information about creating headers and footers that are different for each section of a document, see "Working with Multiple Headers/Footers," p. 275.*

Master Documents and TOCs and Indexes

Tables of contents and indexes work the same way in a master document as in any other document. You position the insertion point where you want the TOC or index to appear, and then you generate it using the commands on the References tab.

The main thing to watch out for when generating a TOC or index for a master document is to make sure you create it within the master document, not in one of the subdocuments. To ensure you get the insertion point positioned correctly, display the document in Outline view and then click outside any of the subdocument borders. Then switch back to Print Layout view (or whatever view you prefer to work in) and create the table of contents or index.

➡ *For information about creating a table of contents, see "Creating a Table of Contents," p. 723.*

➡ *To learn how to create an index, see "Marking Index Entries," p. 741, and "Generating the Index," p. 749.*

Master Documents and Numbered Notes or Captions

Elements such as footnotes, endnotes, figure captions, and other automatically numbered elements are automatically numbered across all subdocuments. The numbering codes continue from one subdocument to the next automatically.

➡ *To create automatically numbered figure captions, see "Using Figure Captions," p. 412.*

➡ *To create footnotes and endnotes, see "Working with Footnotes and Endnotes," p. 708.*

Creating a Master Document

There are two ways to go about creating a master document, depending on what raw material you have already created:

- If the subdocuments already exist and you need to combine them into a master document, start with a blank document to be the master document and insert the documents as subdocuments.

- If the entire text exists as a single document and you want to break sections of it into subdocuments, start with the existing document as the master document and then create subdocuments from pieces of it.

The following sections explain each of these procedures in detail.

Inserting Existing Documents into a Master Document

If parts of the document already exist in separate files, a master document can be useful in joining them without them losing their identities as separate files. After you insert them into the master document, you can edit the subdocuments within the master document or edit them as individual files—whatever works best for you.

To insert a subdocument, follow these steps:

1. Create a new document to function as the master document.

2. (Optional) Type any text into the master document that should exist outside of any subdocuments. For example, perhaps you want a cover page for the project as a whole.

3. If the master document is not already in Outline view, switch to it. This is necessary because the Master Document controls are on the Outlining tab.

4. On the Outlining tab, in the Master Document group, click Show Document. Additional buttons appear on the Outlining tab.

5. Click the Insert button. The Insert Subdocument dialog box opens.

6. Select the document to be used as a subdocument and then click Open.

 tip

To reduce the number of style conflicts between the master document and its subdocuments, apply the same template to all the subdocuments and to the master document before inserting the subdocuments.

 tip

You don't have to do step 2 now; you can do it anytime. However, sometimes it is easier to find your place in a master document's structure when there is text in it that lies outside of a subdocument, especially when the subdocuments are collapsed. It can also be easier to move the insertion point before the first subdocument later if there is already text there. Therefore, I usually type a few lines of text before the first subdocument, if for no other reason than as a placeholder.

The document appears embedded in the main document, surrounded by a nonprinting border (see Figure 17.13). The icon in its top-left corner is a selector; you can click it to select all the text in the subdocument at once.

At this point, the display is still in Outline view, but you can switch to any view you like to work with the document. Repeat the steps to insert additional subdocuments where needed.

Select entire subdocument.   Insert an existing file as a subdocument.

Figure 17.13
The document
is inserted as a
subdocument.

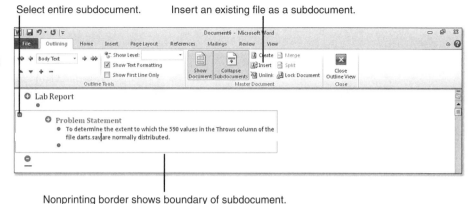

Nonprinting border shows boundary of subdocument.

Separating an Existing Document into Subdocuments

Now let's look at the other side of the coin—what if the document is *already* in one big file and you
want to split out pieces of it into subdocuments? Splitting a large document into subdocuments can
dramatically improve Word's performance because it does not have to manage so many pages at
once. And by using a master document to keep the pieces joined, you can retain all the benefits of
having a single document, such as combined pagination and indexing.

Subdocuments can be especially useful when multiple people are collaborating on a project; by
breaking a document into subdocuments, people can take their part and work separately, and
then recombine their work into the single master document when they're finished. For example, in
Figure 17.14, a lab report has been broken into subdocuments.

To break text into a subdocument, it must begin with a heading (preferably a Heading 1 style one,
but others work, too). Word uses the text of that heading as the filename for the subdocument.

You can break out individual subdocuments, or you can break a document into multiple subdocuments all at the same time. If you want to simultaneously create multiple subdocuments, the document must conform to some rules:

- The use of heading styles must be consistent. In other words, for two headings of the same
  importance in the document, you must apply the same style.

- The heading style that should delineate the subdocument breaks must be the highest level
  heading used in the selection. It does not *have* to be Heading 1, but a lower level heading works
  only if there are no Heading 1 paragraphs in the selection.

To create subdocuments, follow these steps:

1. Switch to Outline view, if you're not already there, and click the Show Document button on the
   Outlining tab if needed to make the Create button available.

Each heading and its content
is in a separate subdocument.

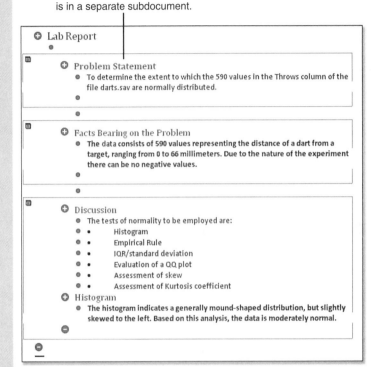

Figure 17.14
The document has had its content separated into individual subdocuments.

---

2. Click the plus sign next to a heading to select it and all the subordinate text beneath it.

(Optional) To create multiple subdocuments at once, select other headings of the same level as the one you selected above. (Hold down Shift and click on the plus signs to their left.)

3. Click the Create button. Each of the headings in the selection (and all its subordinate text) becomes its own subdocument.

 tip

To avoid having to rename files, write the headings with the names you want for the subdocument files. Then after the subdocuments have been created, you can rewrite the headings, if you like.

Word assigns subdocument filenames automatically based on the text in the leading heading in the subdocument. It can use up to 229 characters, including spaces in the name, but it does not use symbols or punctuation marks. If it finds one of those, it truncates the name at that point. So, for example, the heading *Don't Panic* would generate a subdocument called Don.docx. If you want to change a subdocument's filename, see "Renaming a Subdocument" later in this chapter.

Viewing and Collapsing Subdocuments

By default, the master document shows all the subdocuments expanded after their insertion. You can collapse them to show only their hyperlinks by clicking Collapse Subdocuments on the Outlining tab (see Figure 17.15).

When you close and reopen a master document, all the subdocuments appear collapsed. To expand them, click Expand Subdocuments on the Outlining tab.

Once you've inserted or created the subdocuments you need, there's no reason you have to stay in Outline view. Switch to any view you like for editing.

 caution

You cannot expand or collapse individual subdocuments; it's an all-or-none proposition. However, you can open individual subdocuments in their own windows, as you'll learn in the next section.

If you switch to Draft view, you notice that Word has inserted continuous section breaks between the subdocuments. You must leave these in place; they're necessary for the proper functioning of the master document. You can also view these section breaks from Outline view if you toggle off the Show Document feature on the Outlining tab. If you accidentally delete a section break, press Ctrl+Z to undo the deletion, or reinsert the section break.

Double-click a Subdocument icon to open that document.

Expand/Collapse Subdocuments toggle.

Figure 17.15
When collapsed, subdocuments appear as hyperlinks to the files.

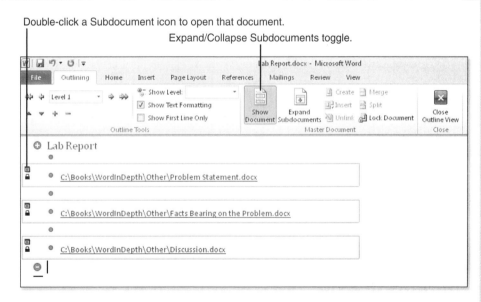

Editing Subdocuments

You can edit subdocuments within the master document, just as you would any other document content, using any view you like. When you switch to some other view, such as Print Layout, the borders disappear that delineate the subdocuments, so the master document appears to be one big seamless piece. Content can be moved and copied between subdocuments as easily as between different sections in a single document.

To edit a subdocument within the master, follow these steps:

1. Expand the subdocuments, as you learned in the preceding section.

2. Switch to Print Layout view, or your favorite view for text editing.

3. Make changes to the subdocument(s).

4. Save your work (File, Save). Changes are automatically saved to the subdocuments as well as to the master document.

If you prefer, you can open an individual subdocument for editing in its own window. This is faster and more efficient because Word does not have to keep track of the other sub-documents, and it's the best way to go when you need to make changes that affect only that one subdocument.

There are several ways to open a subdocument in its own Word window:

- Open the document file as you would any other (File, Open).

- When subdocuments are collapsed in the master document, Ctrl+click the subdocument's hyperlink.

- Double-click the Subdocument icon to the left of the sub-document in the master document, as shown in Figure 17.15.

tip

You can set up a header and footer for a subdocument, as described in Chapter 7, to be used when the sub-document is printed by itself. When the subdocument is printed as part of the master document, however, it takes on the header and footer of the master document, and any header/footer that it has on its own is ignored.

When a subdocument is open in its own window, it behaves exactly like any other regular document. There's no indication that it is a subdocument. That's because subdocuments are really just ordinary documents; they are considered subdocuments only in relationship to the master document that references them.

Changes you make to a subdocument from outside the master document are reflected in the master document when you save your work on the subdocument. You can't edit the copy in the master document while the subdocument is open in a separate window; it is locked there until you close the separate-window copy.

Modifying the Master Document's Structure

In addition to editing the individual subdocuments, you can change the way the master document organizes them. The following sections explain some of the changes you can make.

Moving a Subdocument

It's easiest to rearrange subdocuments from Outline view because you can clearly see where each subdocument starts and ends because of the gray outline around each subdocument.

To move a subdocument within the master document, use one of these methods:

- Select the entire subdocument (by clicking its Subdocument icon) and drag and drop it up or down. You can do this when subdocuments are either expanded or collapsed.

- If subdocuments are expanded, select the entire subdocument (by clicking its Subdocument icon) and then cut it to the Clipboard (Ctrl+X). Position the insertion point where you want it to go, and then paste it (Ctrl+V).

 caution

To maintain the separateness of each subdocument, make sure you drop or paste the subdocument in an empty spot, not within another subdocument. (Combining subdocuments is a separate topic, covered later in this chapter.) If you have a hard time finding an empty spot, click where you want to place the subdocument and press Enter a few times to create some extra space in the master document; then paste the subdocument.

Removing a Subdocument

To remove a subdocument from the master document completely, select its hyperlink and press Delete on the keyboard. Removing the subdocument from the master document does not delete the subdocument file; it still exists and can be inserted into any other master document or used as a standalone document.

Unlinking a Subdocument

Unlinking a subdocument converts it to regular text within the master document and removes the link to the subdocument file. The subdocument file still exists outside the master document, but it is no longer linked to the master document, so changes made in one place are no longer reflected in the other.

Here's how to unlink a subdocument:

1. Display the document in Outline view and expand subdocuments.

2. Click anywhere within the subdocument you want to unlink.

3. Click Unlink on the Outlining tab (see Figure 17.16).

Figure 17.16
Select a subdocument, and then click Unlink.

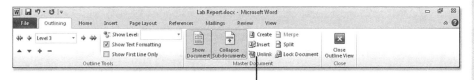

Click Unlink to convert the subdocument to
regular text within the master document.

If you do not want the subdocument anymore after you've unlinked it, delete it from any file management window (Computer, Windows Explorer, and so on).

Renaming a Subdocument

Word automatically assigns subdocument names when you use Create to create new subdocuments out of existing text. These names are derived from the heading text, so usually they are appropriate, but sometimes you end up with filenames that are too long to be practical or too short to be understandable.

> ⚠ **caution**
>
> Do not rename a subdocument file from Windows Explorer or any other file management window; the master document will lose its connection to it if you do. Rename a subdocument *only* using the procedure described in the preceding steps.

To rename a subdocument's file, follow these steps:

1. Display the master document in Outline view and collapse all subdocuments.

2. Double-click the Subdocument icon to open the subdocument in a separate Word window.

3. Choose File, Save As, and save the subdocument under a different name.

4. Close the subdocument's window. The hyperlink in the master document reflects the new name for the subdocument.

The old subdocument file still exists, but it is no longer linked to the master document; instead, the copy with the new name is linked. You can delete the old copy if you like; deleting unused subdocuments keeps your file organization tidy and prevents you from accidentally working with outdated copies.

Merging Subdocuments

As you work on your master document, you might find that you have been overzealous creating subdocuments. If it makes more sense to have fewer subdocuments, you can easily combine them.

To combine two subdocuments, follow these steps:

1. View the master document in Outline view and then expand the subdocuments.

2. Make sure the two subdocuments to be merged are adjacent to one another. Move one of them if needed.

3. Select the first subdocument, and then hold down Shift and select the other one, so that both are selected and any space between them is selected.

4. Click the Merge button on the Outlining tab. The two subdocuments are combined into a single one that has the name of the subdocument that was above the other.

   The old file for the orphaned subdocument still exists on your hard disk; you might want to delete it to avoid later confusion.

Here's an alternative method for merging two subdocuments. This one doesn't involve the Merge button; instead, it uses the Outline Tools on the Outlining tab:

1. View the master document in Outline view and then expand the subdocuments.

2. Select the text of the subdocument that should move into the other one.

3. Click the Move Up or Move Down arrow button in the Outline Tools group of the Outlining tab to move the selected subdocument up or down one position in the outline. Keep clicking the button until the subdocument has moved completely into the other subdocument's border.

4. Save the master document to save the new content into the combined subdocument.

Nesting Subdocuments

Nesting a subdocument is slightly different from merging two subdocuments. When you merge subdocuments, two files are combined into one. When you nest one subdocument inside another, the two separate files continue to exist, but one is referenced within the other. Most people don't use nested subdocuments because most projects are not so long and complex as to need that level of organization. However, when you do have an extremely complex project that needs to be divided at multiple levels, having the feature available can be a godsend.

When you nest one subdocument inside another, you are in effect creating nested masters. For example, if A is your master document and B and C are your subdocuments, and you choose to nest D and E inside of B, B is both a subdocument (of A) and a master document (of D and E). Figure 17.17 illustrates this concept.

Figure 17.17
You can nest subdocuments within other subdocuments, creating a virtual document "tree."

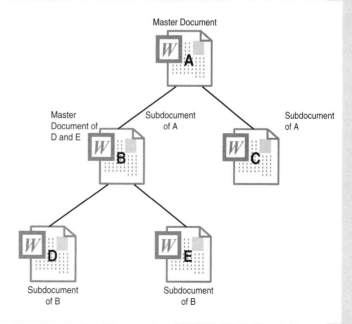

To nest one subdocument into another, follow these steps:

1. View the master document in Outline view and then expand subdocuments.

2. Select the subdocument that is to be nested within another.

3. Drag and drop the Subdocument icon for the selected subdocument inside the border of another subdocument.

The subdocument appears indented, with a gray box inside the gray box of its master.

Splitting a Subdocument

Splitting a subdocument leaves the first heading and its subordinate text under the original subdocument name and creates a new subdocument for each of the additional headings. (All the headings must be the same level.)

To split a subdocument, follow these steps:

1. Display the master document in Outline view and expand the subdocuments.

2. Ensure that the subdocument begins with a heading of the highest level. (That is, there should be no headings of a higher level later in the subdocument than that one.)

3. Add more headings of the same level as the first one in the spots where you want splits to occur.

4. Select the entire subdocument by clicking the Subdocument icon to its left.

5. Click the Split button on the Outlining tab.

6. Save the master document.

> **note**
>
> Splits and merges appear to happen immediately onscreen, but they do not actually take effect in the data files until you save the master document. That's why if you collapse the subdocuments, Word asks if you want to save your changes—it can't display accurate filenames until it updates the files.

Locking and Unlocking a Subdocument

When a subdocument is locked, you cannot modify the copy in the master document, and it does not update when the subdocument is modified outside of the master. It might be useful to lock a subdocument when its content is in flux and you want to preserve the most recent "official" version of it until you are ready to update the entire project.

To lock a subdocument, click anywhere within the subdocument in the master document and then click the Lock Document button on the Outlining tab. A lock icon appears to the left of the subdocument, indicating that it is locked (see Figure 17.18).

Lock a Subdocument

Figure 17.18
A locked sub-
document
shows a lock
icon to its left.

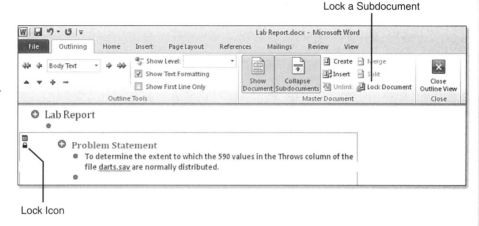

Lock Icon

How Can I Prevent Others from Editing a Subdocument?

If you are contributing a subdocument to someone else's master document, you might want to
lock your subdocument so that the person compiling the master document can't change it.

There are several ways to lock the subdocument—some more secure than others:

- Store the subdocument in a folder to which other users have only Read-Only access but
  to which you have full access. Instead of providing the document file via email or on disk,
  point users to the network location where it is stored.

- Set the Read-Only attribute in the file's properties. (Right-click the file and choose
  Properties to access them.) The users can turn off Read-Only for the file, but they have to
  know how to do it, so it slows them down.

- When saving the file in the Save As dialog box, click Tools, choose General Options, and
  mark the Read-Only Recommended check box. This opens the subdocument as Read-Only
  by default. The user can resave it without Read-Only enabled, but it's an extra step.

- Set a password for the file. To do so, from the Save As dialog box, click Tools, choose
  General Options, and enter a password in the Password to Modify box. The person assembling the master document needs to know the password to make changes to your subdocument.

And, of course, there's also the low-tech method of simply asking your coworker to show you
any changes he or she makes.

The Subdocument Won't Unlock

If you can't edit a subdocument within a master document, first make sure that the Lock Document button is not selected on the Outlining tab. Toggle it off there if needed.

If that's not the problem, next check to see if the subdocument is open for editing in a separate Word window. If it is, you won't be able to edit the copy in the master document until you close that separate window.

Finally, check to make sure the subdocument's file properties have not been set for read-only. Usually you would remember if you set that, but sometimes the read-only property gets set automatically, like when you copy files from a CD-R to your hard disk. It's worth a check.

When multiple users work on subdocuments, local and network file permissions become an issue. For example, if a subdocument is stored in a shared folder to which you have only Read-Only access, the subdocument appears locked in the master document and you can't unlock it. To fix a situation like that, you must modify the network permissions (or have your administrator do it). You can't resolve it from within Word.

Paginating and Printing a Master Document

A master document's header and footer override those of the individual subdocuments, so pagination is a simple matter. Just place a page-numbering code in the master document's header or footer, and let Word take care of the rest.

➡ *For information about using page-numbering codes in headers and footers, see "Adding and Formatting a Page-Numbering Code," p. 269.*

The print results are different depending on which view you print from:

- In Outline view, what you see is what will print. Expand or collapse the subdocuments and outline levels and then print. Word prints whatever was showing.

  ➡ *To learn about expanding and collapsing outline levels, see "Outline Basics," p. 661.*

- In any other view, the entire master document prints, including all subdocuments, with the page numbering, styles, and headers/footers defined in the master document. (Any of those settings in individual subdocuments that conflict are ignored.)

CITING SOURCES AND REFERENCES

Understanding Sources and Citations

A *bibliography* is a list of works cited in a report. Students in most high school and college classes routinely have to write research papers that contain bibliographies, and so do professional researchers and scholars.

Even if you haven't written a research paper lately, you probably have some vivid memories of your last experience in doing so. Citing sources in the proper format (that is, the format your school teaches, or the format customary in your profession) has always been one of those "tear your hair out" tasks because there are so many rules—and exceptions to the rules—regarding the proper capitalization, spacing, and indentation of listings. Entire reference manuals have been published (and have sold very well!) that do nothing but demonstrate how to format various types of entries. And with the rise of Internet research, the potential for confusion over bibliography formatting has only gotten worse because there are even more types of sources from which to draw.

One of the most valuable features in Word 2010, at least from the perspective of students and researchers, is its ability to automatically generate bibliographies or lists of works cited in any of a variety of well-known formats, including MLA and APA (the big two for academia). I sure could have used this when I was in school!

Citing sources in Word involves four steps:

1. **Select a citation style**—You can change your mind later about this, but selecting the style you think you are most likely to use will help Word present the applicable fields in which to enter information about your sources.

2. **Enter sources**—You enter each source into an internal database of sources stored in the document. You can do these all upfront, or you can enter them individually as you write the document. Even if a source is referenced multiple times in the document, it needs to be entered only once.

3. **Insert in-text references**—Each time you want to refer to one of the sources in the document, you insert a code that places either a parenthetical reference to the source or a footnote or endnote, depending on the dictates of the citation style you are using.

4. **Generate a bibliography**—When you are finished with the document, you generate a Bibliography page that presents all the sources from the internal database in a specified format. (In some citation styles, this is called a Works Cited page.)

In the following sections, you learn how to accomplish each of these steps.

Selecting a Citation Style

A *citation style* is a set of rules for formatting various types of sources. The most significant difference between them is their handling of citations. Some styles use inline citations, wherein a source is referenced in parentheses after its first usage. The complete information about the source is then presented either in a Bibliography or a Works Cited page. Other styles use numbered footnotes or endnotes. There are also formatting and alphabetization differences between styles.

Select the citation style from the Style drop-down list on the References tab (see Figure 18.1).

Table 18.1 provides a list of the citation styles that Word 2010 supports. It is not critical for you to understand the differences and subtleties of each format; the main thing is to know which style is required for your school or business.

 tip

The Citations and Bibliography tools in Word work best if you set the citation style before you begin entering sources. This is because some citation styles require more information about the source than others, and Word needs to make sure that it prompts you appropriately. However, if you change your mind later and choose a different citation style, you do not have to reenter all your source information. In most cases, Word can make the transition seamlessly without reprompting you for additional source information.

Figure 18.1
Select a citation style.

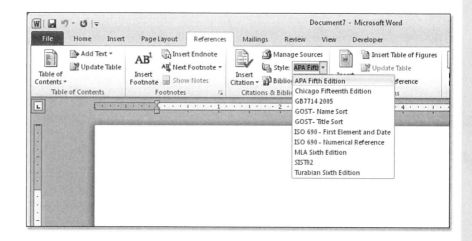

Table 18.1   Citation Styles in Word 2010

Word Calls It...	Stands For...	Used In...	Notes
APA Fifth Edition	American Psychological Association	Academic research, scientific research, professional journals	Uses inline citations and a Bibliography page
Chicago Fifteenth Edition	Chicago Manual of Style	Journalism, publishing	Uses footnotes or endnotes
GB7714 2005	N/A	China	
GOST	*gosudarstvennyy standart*, which is Russian for "State Standard"	Russia and many former Soviet-bloc countries	Can be sorted by either name or title
ISO 690 First Element and Date	International Standards Organization	Patents, industry, manufacturing	Uses inline citations
ISO 690 Numerical Reference	International Standards Organization	Patents, industry, manufacturing	Uses footnotes or endnotes
MLA Sixth Edition	Modern Language Association	English studies, comparative literature, literary criticism, humanities	Uses inline citations and a Works Cited page
SIST02	N/A	Japan	Used only in Asia
Turabian Sixth Edition	Named for its developer, Kate Turabian	Academic research, especially musicology, history, and theology	A simplified version of Chicago Manual of Style format

Entering Sources

Word 2010 stores the sources you enter in a database inside the document, so the source list is always available whenever that document is open. Sources can also be saved to a master database called Sources.xml, located in Users*username*\ AppData\Roaming\Microsoft\Bibliography, so you can reuse sources in multiple documents.

As you enter the data for a source, Word displays the field text boxes to fill in based upon the type of source being used. For example, if you are entering information about a book, it prompts you for fields including Author, Title, and Publisher, whereas for a piece of artwork, it prompts for fields such as Artist, Title, and Institution.

To add a source, follow these steps:

1. Check to make sure you have chosen the appropriate style from the Style list. See the preceding section for details.

2. On the References tab, in the Citations & Bibliography group, choose Manage Sources. The Source Manager dialog box opens.

3. Click the New button. The Create Source dialog box opens.

4. Open the Type of Source list and choose the type (for example, Book, Journal Article, or Web site). The fields change to reflect what's needed for that type of source. For example, Figure 18.2 shows the fields for a book.

caution

As mentioned in Table 18.1, some citation styles use footnotes or endnotes instead of in-text citations. However, Word does not enforce that particular convention; if you use Insert Citation, Word always inserts an inline citation, even if your chosen citation style does not use inline citations. Therefore, be aware of the rules regarding inline or footnote citations in your chosen style at least at a basic level.

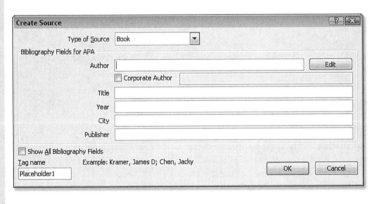

Figure 18.2
Fill in the fields provided for the selected source type.

5. Enter the author or artist's name in one of these ways:

   ▪ Type the author's full name directly into the Author or Artist box. You can type it either as *First Middle Last* or as *Last, First Middle*. (Word can figure it out based on your usage of a comma or not.) If there is more than one author, separate the names with semicolons.

- If the author is an organization, mark the Corporate Author check box and then enter the organization's name.

- Click the Edit button and enter each part of the name in the boxes provided in the Edit Name dialog box (see Figure 18.3). If there is only one author, click OK; if there are multiple authors, click Add after each one, and click OK when finished.

 tip

Multiple authors are usually ordered alphabetically by last name. If one author is more significant than the others, use the Up and Down buttons in the Edit Name dialog box to reorder them.

Figure 18.3
Specify the parts of the name explicitly in the Last, First, and Middle boxes.

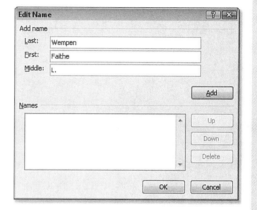

6. Fill in the other fields for the selected source type.

7. Click OK to return to the Source Manager dialog box.

8. Create more sources, or click Close when you are finished.

 note

If you want access to the other fields in the database that Word does not consider applicable to this source type, mark the Show All Bibliography Fields check box.

Editing a Source

It is uncommon to need to edit a source (unless you make a mistake when initially entering it), because a source represents a fixed point in time. A book is published, and its author, date, and title never change. However, online sources are changing this rule a bit because their content can change on a daily basis; the information you retrieve depends on the date on which you accessed it.

To edit the information for a source, follow these steps:

1. On the References tab, click Manage Sources. The Source Manager dialog box opens.

2. Click the desired source, either from the Master List or the Current List, depending on which location you want to change. If you want to change both the copy in the document and the master copy, it does not matter which you select (see Figure 18.4).

3. Click Edit. The Edit Source dialog box opens. It's the same as the Create Source dialog box from Figure 18.2.

4. Make any changes needed to the source information.

5. Click OK.

6. Change another source, or click Close.

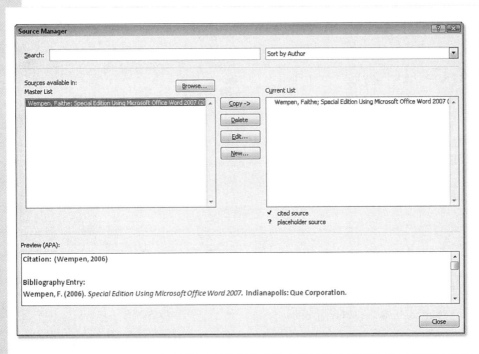

Figure 18.4
Select the source to be changed.

Deleting a Source

You can delete a source from the Master List, from the Current List, or from both places. However, if the source is cited in the current document, you must delete the citation from the Current List before you can delete the source to which it refers. (You can still remove it from the Master List without deleting the citation.)

To delete a citation, follow these steps:

1. On the References tab, click Manage Sources. The Source Manager dialog box opens.

2. Click the desired source, either from the Master List or the Current List, depending on which location you want to delete the source from (refer to Figure 18.4).

3. Click Delete. The source is removed from the list.

4. Delete other sources, or click Close.

Transferring Sources to and from the Master List

The Master List is a source database maintained separately from the current document. You can use it to quickly retrieve previously used sources for use in other documents. By default, every source you create is entered into the Master List.

To transfer sources between the Current List and the Master List, follow these steps:

1. On the References tab, click Manage Sources. The Source Manager dialog box opens.

2. Click the desired source, either from the Master List or the Current List.

3. Click the Copy button to copy that source from its current list to the other one. The button face changes to show a ← or →, depending on which side is selected (see Figure 18.4).

 tip

The most common copy direction is from the Master List to the Current List. Because the Master List's entries are automatically created, there is usually not much reason to copy a source to the Master List. However, if you accidentally delete a source from the Master List, you might want to copy that source back to it from the Current List.

Inserting Inline References to Sources

An inline reference to a source is inserted in parentheses in the text. Depending on the citation style you have chosen and the type of source you are citing, the parenthetical citation includes one or more of these items:

- Author's name (always included)

- Year

- Title

- Page number

The most common usage is the author name and date, like this:

> *A recent study has found that students who abstain from illegal drug use are 25 percent more likely to finish high school than students who do not (Smith, 2010).*

Even if the citation style requires these elements, they may be omitted if the text includes them. For example:

> *A recent study by Sally Smith (2010) found that students who abstain from illegal drug use are 25 percent more likely to finish high school than students who do not.*

> *To omit part of a citation, see "Editing a Citation," p. 703.*

To insert a citation, follow these steps:

1. Position the insertion point where you want the citation.

   Depending on the context, the citation can go at the end of the sentence (as in the first of the preceding examples) or within the sentence (as in the second example).

2. On the References tab, click Insert Citation. A menu appears listing all the sources in the current document (see Figure 18.5).

3. Click the desired source. A reference to it is inserted as a field.

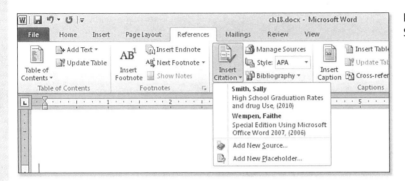

Figure 18.5
Select the source to cite.

> If the desired source does not appear on the list but you have all the information you need to enter it now, see the next section, "Creating a New Source When Entering a Citation."

> If the desired source does not appear on the list and you do not have the needed information to enter it now, see "Inserting Temporary Placeholders for Later Entry of Sources," later on this page.

Creating a New Source When Entering a Citation

Sometimes it's hard to know what sources to enter until you get to the point in the document where you need to cite them. If you did not already enter the source you want to use, follow these steps to insert the citation and create its source entry at the same time:

1. Position the insertion point where you want the citation.

2. On the References tab, click Insert Citation. A menu appears (refer to Figure 18.5).

3. Click Add New Source. The Create Source dialog box appears.

4. Enter the information for the new source, as you did in the section "Entering Sources" earlier in this chapter.

5. Click OK in the Create Source dialog box. The source is created, and a citation for it is inserted into the document.

Inserting Temporary Placeholders for Later Entry of Sources

As you are writing the document, perhaps you realize there is a source you need to cite but you don't have all the details handy to formally enter it as a source. In situations like that, you can create a temporary placeholder for the source, so you can go ahead and insert its citations. Then later, when you have all the facts you need, you can update the source listing in the Source Manager.

To insert a citation and create a temporary placeholder for the source, follow these steps:

1. Position the insertion point where you want the citation.

2. On the References tab, click Insert Citation. A menu appears (refer to Figure 18.5).

3. Click Add New Placeholder. The Placeholder Name dialog box appears.

4. Type a name for the placeholder. A good name would be something that will help you remember the source you plan to cite, such as the author's last name or an abbreviated version of the article title.

5. Click OK. A citation is inserted into the document with the placeholder in parentheses.

To complete the information for a placeholder when you have the information available, follow these steps:

1. On the References tab, click Manage Sources.

2. On the Current List, click the placeholder. Placeholders are identified by question mark icons, as shown in Figure 18.6.

3. Click Edit. The Edit Source dialog box opens.

4. Enter the information needed for the source and click OK.

5. Complete other placeholders, or click Close.

Figure 18.6
Select and edit the placeholder.

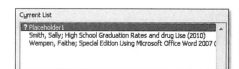

Editing a Citation

A citation is a field that pulls its information from the source on which it is based, so you cannot edit its text directly. You can, however, show or suppress certain pieces of information. For example, you can make a citation show a page range (useful when citing two or more articles in the same journal, for example), and you can suppress the usage of the author, date, or title.

To edit a citation, follow these steps:

1. Click the citation in the document. It appears in a blue box, indicating that it is a field.

2. Click the down arrow to the right of the field, opening a menu (see Figure 18.7).

3. Click Edit Citation. The Edit Citation dialog box opens (see Figure 18.8).

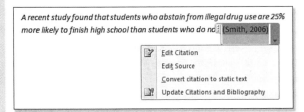

Figure 18.7
Open the menu for the citation field.

Figure 18.8
Include a page range or suppress one or more of the standard items.

4. (Optional) To add page numbers, type a range in the Pages box. Use a hyphen but no spaces to separate a range, like this: 12-24.

5. (Optional) In the Suppress area, click the check box for any elements to suppress.

 tip

Even if a certain element does not appear in the current citation style, you can still suppress it, so that if you change to a different citation style that does include that element, it will be suppressed at that point.

Converting a Citation to Plaintext

To edit a citation directly (that is, by changing its text) and not just add or suppress elements, you must convert it to plaintext so that it is no longer a field linked to a source.

As you can imagine, converting a citation to plaintext is not a good idea in most cases because it no longer updates when you change the source information or the citation style. However, sometimes it's the only way to achieve the desired effect.

To convert a citation to text, follow these steps:

1. Click the citation in the document. It appears in a blue box, indicating that it is a field.

2. Click the down arrow to the right of the field, opening a menu (refer to Figure 18.7).

3. Click Convert Citation to Static Text. The citation remains in place but is no longer a field.

Generating a Bibliography

A bibliography appears at the end of the document and lists all the sources cited. Usually sources are arranged alphabetically by the author's last name.

The formatting of the bibliography, and the facts that appear about each source, depend heavily on the citation style in use. For example, Table 18.2 shows the same entry in several different styles. As you can see, some styles use bold or italic; some use the complete name of the author; some begin with the title rather than the author's name; and so on. Some separate items with commas, some use ellipses, and some use colons.

 note

A couple of citation styles arrange bibliography entries differently. For example, GOST–Title Sort sorts by title, and ISO–690 Numerical Reference sorts chronologically by position in the document. (That style also numbers inline references rather than using author and date.)

Table 18.2   Comparison of Bibliography Formatting Among Citation Styles

Citation Style	Example
APA	Smith, S. (2010). High School Graduation Rates and Drug Use. Journal of Education Research, 23–31.
Chicago and Turabian	Smith, Sally. "High School Graduation Rates and Drug Use." Journal of Education Research (2010): 23–31.
GB7714 and ISO 690 First Element and Date	High School Graduation Rates and Drug Use. Smith, Sally. . 2010., Journal of Education Research, 23–31.
MLA	Smith, Sally. "High School Graduation Rates and Drug Use." Journal of Education Research (2010): 23–31.
ISO 690	1. High School Graduation Rates and Drug Use. Smith, Sally.
Numerical Reference	2010, Journal of Education Research, 23–31.
SIST02	High School Graduation Rates and Drug Use. Smith, Sally., 2010, Journal of Education Research, 23–31.

I've shown you the examples in Table 18.2 not to try to teach you the syntax of each style, but to illustrate how changing the citation style affects the bibliography. You can change to a different citation style either before or after the bibliography is generated; Word automatically keeps the entire document's citations and bibliography consistent with the selected style.

Word comes with two built-in bibliography layouts in its Bibliography Gallery:

- **Bibliography**—Begins with a Heading 1 styled "Bibliography" paragraph, followed by the entries in a paragraph style called Bibliography. The bibliography does not start on a new page.

- **Works Cited**—Same as Bibliography, except the text at the top is "Works Cited" instead. It does not start on a new page.

If you want, you can create additional bibliography-formatting specifications and save them to the Bibliography Gallery for later reuse.

Inserting a Bibliography from the Bibliography Gallery

The Bibliography Gallery is the list of bibliography layouts that appears when you open the Bibliography button's list on the References tab. Word calls the layouts *bibliographies*, although of course they are not real bibliographies but codes that generate bibliographies using the sources in the current document. That's important because you can save and reuse bibliographies between documents.

To create a bibliography using one of the layouts in the Gallery, follow these steps:

tip

These layouts are actually building blocks that can be renamed, deleted, and so on from the Building Blocks Organizer. See "Working with Building Blocks" in Chapter 2, "Typing and Editing Text," for details.

1. Position the insertion point where you want the bibliography to appear.

2. On the References tab, click Bibliography.

3. Click the gallery entry that best represents the bibliography you want to create. It is inserted into the document at the current position.

If you want to insert the bibliography at the beginning or the end of the document or the current section, you do not have to move the insertion point to the desired spot beforehand (step 1). Instead, you can right-click a gallery entry and select a location from the shortcut menu, as in Figure 18.9.

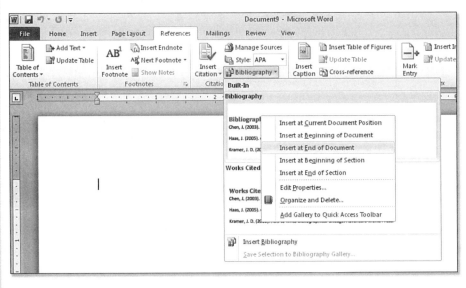

Figure 18.9
If desired, select a position for the bibliography from its shortcut menu in the gallery.

Working with a Bibliography Field

The inserted bibliography appears in a field, with a light blue box around it like any other field.

You can click the Bibliographies button at the top to open a menu, as shown in Figure 18.10. From here you can choose a different style (Bibliography versus Works Cited), or you can convert the bibliography to static text, so that it no longer updates and can be freely edited like any other text.

Click here to access the menu.

Figure 18.10
The button at the top of the bibliography provides commands for managing the field.

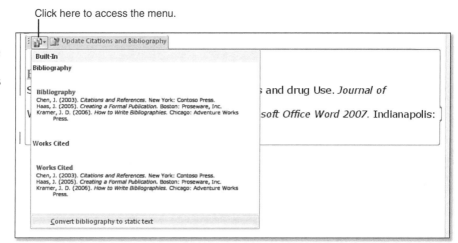

Saving a Bibliography as a New Gallery Entry

After inserting a bibliography, you can format its text. For example, you can apply a different heading style to its heading, apply a different body style to its body, or add indentation or other special formatting.

Then you can save your changed version of the bibliography as a new Bibliography Gallery entry for later reuse. To create a new entry, follow these steps:

1. Format the bibliography as you want it.

2. Select the bibliography. On the References tab, click Bibliography and select Save Selection to Bibliography Gallery. The Create New Building Block dialog box opens.

3. Change the name in the Name box to something descriptive of the format you're creating.

4. (Optional) Enter a brief description in the Description box (see Figure 18.11).

5. Click OK to create the new bibliography gallery entry.

 caution

The default name might be the text from the first entry in the bibliography at present, or it might be blank. Neither of those is a good name, though, because you will potentially apply this bibliography format in other documents that do not have these same sources.

Figure 18.11
Create a new building block entry for the bibliography.

Your gallery entries appear at the bottom of the Bibliography button's menu. (Scroll down the menu if you don't see them at first.) To access its building block properties later, right-click it and choose Edit Properties.

Removing a Bibliography from the Gallery

To remove one of your custom bibliographies from the gallery, follow these steps:

1. On the References tab, click Bibliography, and scroll down the list to locate your custom entry.

2. Right-click the entry and choose Organize and Delete. The Building Blocks Organizer dialog box opens with the chosen entry already selected.

3. Click the Delete button.

4. Click Yes to confirm.

5. Click Close.

Working with Footnotes and Endnotes

Another way of citing a source is to create a footnote or endnote for it. Footnotes and endnotes are the same except for their position: *Footnotes* appear at the bottom of the page on which the reference occurs, whereas *endnotes* appear at the end of the document or section. Figure 18.12 shows a footnote and points out some of the key features involved in footnote usage:

- **Reference mark**—Appears within the body text. This is usually a number but can also be a symbol.

- **Separator line**—The line that separates the body text from the footnote area.

- **Footnote reference**—The corresponding number or symbol to the reference mark, appearing at the beginning of the footnote.

- **Footnote text**—The footnote itself. It is different from the footnote reference and is formatted using a different style.

Figure 18.12
A footnote and
its reference
mark.

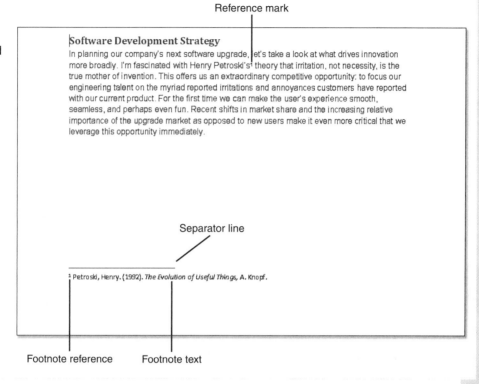

Reference mark

Software Development Strategy
In planning our company's next software upgrade, let's take a look at what drives innovation more broadly. I'm fascinated with Henry Petroski's[1] theory that irritation, not necessity, is the true mother of invention. This offers us an extraordinary competitive opportunity: to focus our engineering talent on the myriad reported irritations and annoyances customers have reported with our current product. For the first time we can make the user's experience smooth, seamless, and perhaps even fun. Recent shifts in market share and the increasing relative importance of the upgrade market as opposed to new users make it even more critical that we leverage this opportunity immediately.

Separator line

[1] Petroski, Henry. (1992). *The Evolution of Useful Things*, A. Knopf.

Footnote reference   Footnote text

An endnote has all those same pieces: reference mark, separator line, endnote reference, and endnote text. However, with an endnote, the separator line and the notes that follow it appear on the last page of the document, immediately after the last body text paragraph (not at the bottom of the page).

 note

In this section of the chapter, I'll refer to footnotes and endnotes generically as "notes" for simplicity whenever there is no difference between them in functionality.

Where Should You Place the Reference Mark?

A reference mark is usually placed either immediately after the item being referenced or at the end of the sentence. There is no hard-and-fast rule for choosing between these, but logic usually dictates the best choice.

Often the placement of the reference mark sets up reader expectations of what the note will contain. For example:

The Kemmerly Hypothesis[1] has some merit in the Johnson case, in my opinion.

Readers will expect the footnote to explain the Kemmerly Hypothesis itself, unrelated to the Johnson case.

The Kemmerly Hypothesis has some merit in the Johnson case, in my opinion[1].

Continued...

Readers will expect the footnote to elaborate on your assertion of the applicability of the Kemmerly Hypothesis to the case.

Inserting a Footnote

To insert a standard footnote, do either of the following:

- Press Ctrl+Alt+F.

- On the References tab, click Insert Footnote.

Word inserts a reference mark at the insertion point and then jumps to the bottom of the page and places a footnote reference. It then leaves the insertion point flashing there next to the footnote reference, so you can type the footnote text.

If you're working in Draft view, footnotes do not appear on the document page. Instead, a separate Notes pane appears at the bottom of the Word window, as in Figure 18.13. If the pane does not appear, click the Show Notes button on the References tab. You can drag the divider between the panes up or down to see more or less of the note area at once.

note

To move a reference mark, select it and then cut and paste it or drag it to a new location. If the new location puts it out of sequence, Word automatically renumbers the notes.

To copy a footnote, copy its reference mark (with a copy-and-paste or a Ctrl+drag-and-drop operation). Word creates a copy of the note too.

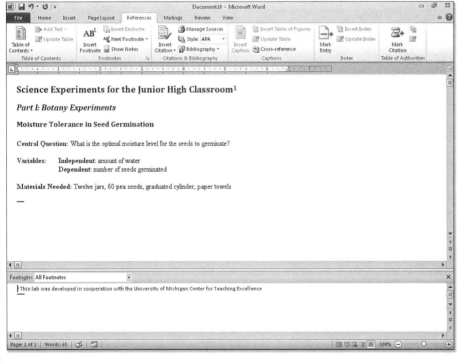

Figure 18.13
A footnote in Draft view.

Why Does the Page Footer Overlap the Footnote Area?

This can happen if the footnote area and the page footer area both are very large (more than five lines) and there's a section break on the same page. Either remove the section break or add some blank lines above the footnote text in the footnote area.

 ## Why Can't I Delete a Footnote or Endnote?

The only way to delete a footnote or endnote is to delete the reference mark for it in the body text. You cannot delete one from the Notes pane or the footnote or endnote area of the document.

Inserting an Endnote

To insert an endnote, do either of the following:

- Press Ctrl+Alt+D.

- On the References tab, click Insert Endnote.

Word inserts a reference mark at the insertion point and then jumps to the end of the document and places a new endnote reference. It leaves the insertion point flashing there so you can type the endnote text.

In Draft view, endnotes appear just like footnotes, in the separate Notes pane at the bottom of the screen (refer to Figure 18.13).

Deleting a Note

To delete a note, delete its reference mark in the body text. The footnote or endnote goes away automatically.

You can delete all the text for a footnote or endnote, but its number or symbol remains in the Notes pane (or at the bottom of the page or end of the document) until you delete the reference mark from the body of the document.

Jumping to the Note That Corresponds to a Reference Mark

When working with footnotes, it's easy enough to find the note that corresponds to the number or symbol—just scroll down to the bottom of the page. However, with endnotes, it is not always so easy because the note might be on a page far removed from its reference.

To jump to the footnote or endnote, double-click the reference mark in the body text.

Moving Between Notes

There are several ways to jump from one footnote or endnote reference mark to another within the body text.

Perhaps the easiest method is to use the Next Footnote button on the References tab. Click it to go to the next footnote, or open its menu to go to the previous footnote or the next or previous endnote.

Another way to move between notes is with the Go To command on the Home tab. This method lets you specify a certain footnote or endnote number to find:

1. On the Home tab, click the arrow beside the Find button and click Go To. (Alternatively, click the Select Browse Object icon below the vertical scroll bar and click the Go To button.) The Find and Replace dialog box opens with the Go To tab displayed.

2. On the Go To What list, click Footnote or Endnote.

3. Enter the footnote or endnote number you want to find.

   You can either enter an exact number or enter a plus or minus sign and a number to move relative to the current position (–2, for example).

4. Click Go To.

5. Click Close.

Finally, you can "page" through the footnotes or endnotes with the Select Browse Object controls below the vertical scroll bar:

1. Click the Select Browse Object button, and then click Browse by Footnote or Browse by Endnote (see Figure 18.14).

2. Click the Previous or Next button to jump to the next or previous instance of whichever you chose.

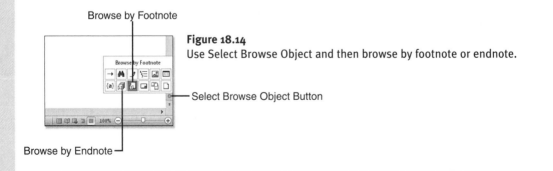

Browse by Footnote

Figure 18.14
Use Select Browse Object and then browse by footnote or endnote.

Select Browse Object Button

Browse by Endnote

Switching Between Footnotes and Endnotes

Perhaps you started out using footnotes and later decide you want endnotes instead—or vice versa. No matter; it's easy to change between them.

One way is to change each note individually:

- To change a footnote to an endnote, right-click it and choose Convert to Endnote.

- To change an endnote to a footnote, right-click the endnote text and choose Convert to Footnote.

Another way is to change all the notes in the document at once:

1. Right-click any note and choose Note Options, or click the dialog box launcher in the Footnotes group of the References tab. The Footnote and Endnote dialog box opens.

2. Click the Convert button. The Convert Notes dialog box appears. The options available depend on what type of notes you already have in the document. For example, in Figure 18.15, the only option is to convert footnotes to endnotes because the document does not currently contain endnotes.

3. Click OK and then click Close.

Figure 18.15
Convert all notes at once.

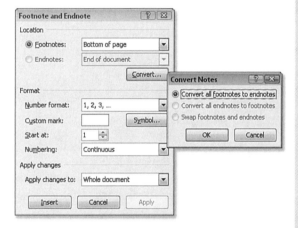

Changing the Positioning of the Notes

Notes can appear either at the bottom of the page or immediately below the text on the page. By default, footnotes appear at the bottom and endnotes appear below the text, but you can change this positioning.

To modify the text positioning, follow these steps:

1. Right-click any note and choose Note Options, or click the dialog box launcher in the Footnotes group of the References tab. The Footnote and Endnote dialog box opens.

2. In the Location section, open the drop-down list for Footnotes or Endnotes and choose the desired position (refer to Figure 18.15).

3. Click Apply.

Changing the Note Numbering or Symbols

By default, footnotes use Arabic numbering (1, 2, 3) and endnotes use lowercase Roman numbering (i, ii, iii).

To change to a different style of numbering or to a set of symbols, follow these steps:

1. Right-click any note and choose Note Options, or click the dialog box launcher in the Footnotes group of the References tab. The Footnote and Endnote dialog box opens.

2. Select a format from the Number Format list (refer to Figure 18.15).

   This setting applies to all the notes in the document or section.

   Alternatively, you can enter a custom symbol to use, or you can browse for a symbol.

   This setting applies to only the current footnote or endnote; it enables you to enter your own symbols to use for each note on an individual basis. Your own symbols override the default ones.

3. (Optional) Set a different Start At value than 1 if desired.

4. (Optional) To restart numbering with each section or page, choose how you want restarts to occur from the Numbering list. The default is Continuous, which means no restarting of numbering.

5. In the Apply Changes To list, choose the scope for your changes. Unless you have multiple sections in your document, the only choice here is Whole Document.

6. Click Apply.

Modifying Note Styles

You can format footnotes or endnotes manually, as you can any text, but it is much more efficient to modify their styles instead and let those changes populate automatically through the document.

Four styles are used for notes:

- **Footnote reference**—For the reference mark that appears in the footnote area.

- **Footnote text**—For the text of the footnote.

- **Endnote reference**—For the reference mark that appears in the endnote area.

- **Endnote text**—For the text of the endnote.

Here's a way to modify a style used in a footnote or endnote:

1. Display the Styles task pane by clicking the dialog box launcher in the Styles group of the Home tab.

2. Format the footnote or endnote reference or text the way you want the style to be.

3. Select the footnote or endnote reference or text.

4. On the Styles task pane, right-click the style and choose Update to Match Selection.

And here's another way:

1. Right-click the footnote or endnote reference mark or text and choose Style. The Style dialog box appears.

2. Select the style you want to modify.

3. Click Modify. The Modify Style dialog box appears.

4. Make any changes to the style as needed.

5. Click OK, and then click Apply.

> *To learn more about modifying styles, see "Modifying Styles," p. 238.*

 tip

If the footnote or endnote styles are not listed in the Styles task pane, access them via the Style Inspector.

How Can I Tell What Style a Footnote or Endnote Is Using?

Unless you have applied other styles, footnotes always use Footnote Reference for the number and Footnote Text for the text. Endnotes always use Endnote Reference and Endnote Text.

If you're not sure whether the correct styles are applied, try displaying the Styles task pane (from the Styles dialog box launcher on the Home tab) and noting what style is highlighted on that list.

If that doesn't work, click the Style Inspector button on the Styles task pane to display the Style Inspector window. Then click in the footnote or endnote. The style in use appears there (see Figure 18.16).

Changing the Note Separator Line

The *note separator line* is the line between the body text and the footnotes or endnotes. By default, it is a plain 1-point black line that runs one-third of the way across the page.

Word treats this separator line as a single character of text. As such, you can format it only by doing the things you can do to text: You can increase its width and thickness slightly by increasing its "font size," and you can change its color and make it bold.

Here's how to access that line for the limited formatting just described:

1. View the document in Draft view (View tab, Draft).

2. If the Notes pane is not already displayed, click Show Notes on the References tab.

 tip

For a double separator line, apply Underline formatting to the separator line.

Click here to display
the Styles pane.

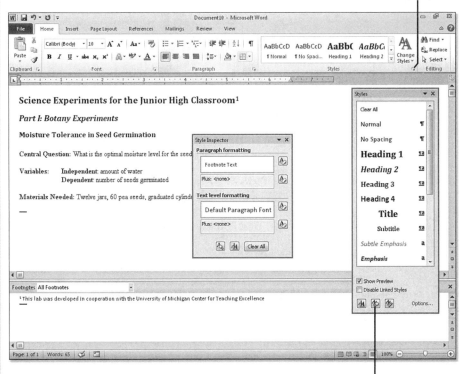

Figure 18.16
Use the Style
Inspector to
check out
style usage in
footnotes and
endnotes.

Style Inspector Button

3. In the Footnotes (or Endnotes) drop-down list on the Notes pane, select Footnote Separator (or Endnote Separator). The line appears (see Figure 18.17).

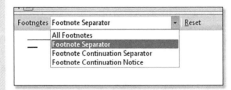

Figure 18.17
To view the line, switch to Draft mode, display the Notes pane, and then choose Footnote Separator from the drop-down list.

4. Select the line.

5. Use the Font tools on the Home tab or on the Mini Toolbar to change the line's color and thickness as desired.

Managing Footnote Continuations

When a footnote is too long to fit on one page and still be on the same page as its reference mark, Word splits the footnote and continues it on the next page. When that happens, a continuation separator and continuation notice appear. The continuation separator line is just like the regular separator line except it's longer. The continuation notice is blank by default; you can enter it in yourself—perhaps something like *(continues on next page)*.

To format the continuation separator and continuation notice:

1. Switch to Draft view.

2. On the References tab, click Show Notes to display the Notes pane if needed.

3. Open the Footnotes drop-down list and choose Footnote Continuation Separator. The separator line appears.

4. Format the separator line as desired. See the preceding section for help with that.

5. Open the Footnotes drop-down list and choose Footnote Continuation Notice. By default, nothing appears.

6. Type the text you want to use as the separation notice into the Notes pane.

7. Close the Notes pane when finished. (Click Show Notes again on the References tab.)

 note

If you want a real Word-drawn line shape as the separator, complete with all the formatting that's inherent in a shape, you won't be able to have it appear automatically on each page that has footnotes. Instead, you'll need to delete the line from the Footnote Separator in the Notes pane (refer to Figure 18.16) and then draw a line manually on each page on which a footnote occurs.

 note

Continuation is an issue only for footnotes, not endnotes.

My Footnotes Disappeared When I Saved in Web Format

Your footnotes didn't disappear; they just moved. When you save a document in Web format, footnotes are converted to endnotes, with hyperlinks that connect the footnote numbers in the body text to the notes at the end.

Creating Cross-References

Perhaps you've noticed that this book has a lot of cross-references. Whenever I'm talking about a topic that's covered in another section, a cross-reference note appears telling you which page to turn to for more information.

Unfortunately, due to the page layout process that this book has to go through, those cross-references are not automatically generated. Yes, believe it or not, there is a person with a four-year college degree whose job is to go through and manually insert the correct page numbers for each of those cross-references.

If only this book were laid out in Microsoft Word 2010, the cross-referencing process could be completely automated. (Of course, someone might be out of a job....) In Word, you can create cross-references to bookmarks, headings, sections, captions, or just about any other marker in a document. These cross-references update dynamically, so if the page on which a particular heading changes, all cross-references to that heading change, too.

You got a taste of cross-referencing in Chapter 15, "Copying, Linking, and Embedding Data," in the section "Inserting a Cross-Reference to a Bookmark," but now let's take a look at the full gamut of cross-referencing that's available.

First, here's how to insert a basic cross-reference:

1. On the References tab, click Cross-Reference. The Cross-Reference dialog box opens.

2. Select the type of item being referenced from the Reference Type list.

3. On the For Which list, select the instance of the reference type to be referenced. For example, if you chose Heading in step 2, select from a list of all the headings in the document (see Figure 18.18).

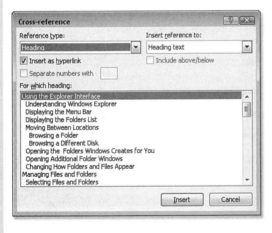

Figure 18.18
Create a cross-reference.

4. Select the way you want to refer to it from the Insert Reference To list.

5. (Optional) To make the cross-reference a live hyperlink, make sure the Insert as Hyperlink check box is marked.

6. (Optional) To includes the word "above" or "below" with the cross-reference, mark the Include Above/Below check box.

7. Click Insert to insert the cross-reference.

8. Click Close to close the dialog box.

The resulting cross-reference is a field such as {REF}. You can check this out for yourself by right-clicking it and choosing Toggle Field Codes. You can work with it the same as any other field; see Chapter 16, "Working with Fields and Forms." (See, another cross-reference! They're everywhere once you start noticing them.)

 caution

Cross-references apply only within the current document; you cannot create a cross-reference from one document to another. If you are working with a master document, and there are cross-references between subdocuments, make sure you expand all the subdocuments before printing; otherwise, the cross-references will not work.

Cross-Referencing Options

Now that you know the basics, let's delve a little further into the types of cross-references you can create. A cross-reference can refer to any of these elements:

Numbered item	Heading
Bookmark	Footnote
Endnote	Equation
Figure	Table

The cross-reference itself can consist of any of these:

- The actual text of the item being referenced.

- The page number on which the referenced item lies.

- The number of the referenced item in the chronology of the document (for example, *3* for the third paragraph).

- The caption of the item (if it has one), either with or without its numbering (for example, *Figure 3: Sales Revenue*).

- The word "Above" or the word "Below," depending on whether the cross-reference comes before or after the item being referenced in the document.

 caution

Some editing purists object to the use of above or below to refer to material that is actually on a previous or subsequent page. I'm not allowed to use those terms that way in this book, for example! Word does not enforce this rule, though; it allows you to use above/below even when the cross-reference is separated from the item it is referring to by many pages.

Cross-Reference Context

Some of the cross-reference types give you a choice of various *contexts*. The context determines how much information will appear depending on where the cross-reference lies in relation to the referenced location.

For example, suppose you want to refer to heading 3(a)(iii). The full context for that reference would appear as 3(a)(iii). But if the cross-reference were also in section 3, you might not need to include the 3; you could simply use (a)(iii). Further, if the cross-reference were in section 3(a), you could simply use (iii).

Word provides three settings for cross-reference types that might have a context. The names are different depending on the type, but here are the ones for headings:

- **Heading Number**—Provides contextual numbering

- **Heading Number (No Context)**—Provides only the lowest level of numbering

- **Heading Number (Full Context)**—Provides the complete numbering regardless of position

For numbered items and bookmarks, context is set by paragraph number. (Replace the word "heading" with "paragraph" in the preceding list.)

The other types of cross-references do not support contextual referencing.

Why Does My Cross-Reference Produce an Error?

Check to make sure you have not deleted the item being cross-referenced. For example, if you cross-reference a heading and then delete that heading, an error message displays on the cross-reference field. If that doesn't help, try pressing F9 to update the field. Still no good? Delete the cross-reference and re-create it.

Footnote and Endnote Cross-References

For footnotes and endnotes, you can choose to insert the note number (formatted or unformatted), the page number on which it appears, or the word *above* or *below*. Often it is useful to combine more than one cross-reference in the body of the text, like this:

> For more information on shellfish allergies, see note 1 on page 47.

In that example, both the numbers 1 and 47 are separate cross-references. They both refer to the same footnote, but they are set up to provide different information.

So what's the difference between a formatted and unformatted note number? An unformatted one takes on the formatting of the paragraph into which you place it; a formatted one retains the formatting applied to footnote reference numbers by the Footnote Reference style.

Caption Cross-References

Equations, figures, and tables can all have captions, and these captions can be cross-referenced. When you choose any of these three types of content, you get the following options for what to insert:

- Entire caption (Example: *Table 2: Quantities in Stock*)

- Only label and number (Example: *Table 2*)

- Only caption text (Example: *Quantities in Stock*)

- Page number

- Above/Below

 tip

You can create building blocks for cross-references you want to reuse. Just select the entire block of text, including the cross-reference within it, and on the Insert tab, click Quick Parts, Save Selection to Quick Part Gallery.

My Headings Aren't Showing Up as Headings for Creating a Cross-Reference

Make sure you have your custom heading styles set up to correspond to a heading outline level. To do this for a style:

1. Display the Styles task pane by clicking the dialog box launcher in the Styles group of the Home tab.

2. Right-click the style in the Styles task pane and choose Modify.

3. In the Modify Style dialog box, click Format and then click Paragraph.

4. In the Paragraph dialog box, set the Outline Level setting to a heading level (such as Heading 1).

5. Click OK twice.

CREATING TABLES OF CONTENTS AND INDEXES

Creating a Table of Contents

A *table of contents* (TOC) is a listing at the beginning of a document (usually) that shows all the headings of a certain level and higher and their page numbers. This book has one, and so does almost every other technical book. Don't confuse a TOC with an *index*, covered later in the chapter; an index appears at the *end* of the document (again, usually) and shows an alphabetical list of topics and their page numbers. Figure 19.1 shows a typical TOC. It contains multiple levels and uses dot leaders to align the entries with the right-aligned page numbers.

Checking Style Outline Levels

The key to generating an accurate TOC is making sure the document is properly formatted beforehand, with the correct styles in place.

As you learned in Chapter 17, "Outlining and Combining Documents," you can assign an outline level to each style (Level 1 through Level 9 or Body). Word uses each style's heading level to determine the level of the TOC to which it belongs. For example, all styles defined as Level 1 are at the top level of the TOC, and so on. So your first task is to check out the styles you've used for the document headings and make sure they are appropriately assigned to an outline level. (This is not an issue if you use Word's built-in heading styles because they are already appropriately assigned.)

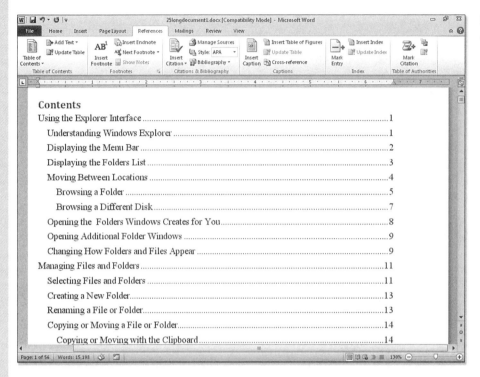

Figure 19.1
A typical TOC.

To view and change the outline level for a heading style, follow these steps:

1. Click the dialog box launcher in the Styles group on the Home tab. The Styles task pane opens.

2. Right-click the style and choose Modify. The Modify Style dialog box opens.

3. Click the Format button and choose Paragraph. The Paragraph dialog box opens.

4. If needed, change the Outline Level to reflect the style's level of importance in the outline and click OK.

5. Click OK to close the Modify Style dialog box.

Creating a TOC from a Preset

After making sure your style usage is consistent, you are ready to generate the TOC. It can be as easy or as difficult as you make it, depending on how picky you want to get with the options.

By far the easiest way to go is to choose one of the TOC presets, as shown in the following steps:

1. Position the insertion point in a new blank paragraph where you want the TOC. Typically, it goes at the beginning of the document, but this is not mandatory.

2. On the References tab, click the Table of Contents button. A menu opens.

3. Click one of the TOC presets on the menu (see Figure 19.2).

Figure 19.2
Select a preset from the menu for a quick-and-easy TOC.

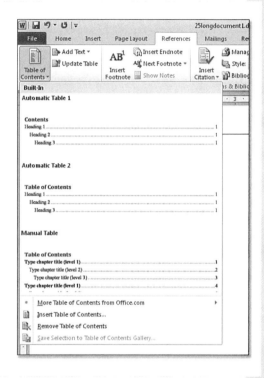

There are three presets on the Built-In section of the menu:

- **Automatic Table 1**—Places a default TOC at the insertion point, with the title "Contents."

- **Automatic Table 2**—Places a default TOC at the insertion point, with the title "Table of Contents."

- **Manual Table**—Creates a TOC using content control placeholders that turn into regular text after you type in them. This is not an automatically updating TOC, and it does not use the TOC feature; it simply creates the look of a TOC for manual use.

> *For more information about content controls, see "Creating a Form with Content Controls,"*
> *p. 642.*

The TOC appears in a content control frame (yes, it's a content control, like the ones in Chapter 16, "Working with Fields and Forms"). When you click inside the TOC, two buttons become available, as shown in Figure 19.3. The left one opens the Table of Contents menu, the same as the one on the References tab. The right one updates the TOC (as described in the next section).

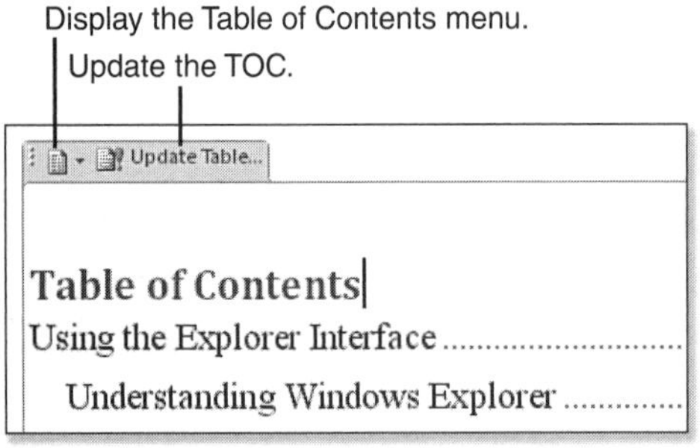

Display the Table of Contents menu.

Update the TOC.

Figure 19.3
A TOC is in a content control frame, with buttons at the top for controlling it.

| Update Table... |

Table of Contents

Using the Explorer Interface ....

Understanding Windows Explorer ....

Updating a TOC

As the document changes, the table of contents might become out of date. A TOC does not update automatically by default, so you must issue a command to update it.

To update a table of contents, follow these steps:

1. Click the Update Table button at the top of the TOC's frame (refer to Figure 19.3). The Update Table of Contents dialog box opens.

   You can also click the Update Table button on the References tab.

2. Select the type of update you want:

   - **Update Page Numbers Only**—This is the quickest update method, but it ignores any changes made to the headings or any new headings you might have added.

   - **Update Entire Table**—This method takes a little longer; it completely regenerates the TOC. Except in long documents, you will not notice much difference in the speed.

I See an "Error! Bookmark Not Defined" Message

This happens if you delete one or more of the headings or {TC} codes from the document and then update the TOC using the Update Page Numbers Only option. Do an update that re-creates the entire TOC instead to fix this.

Removing a TOC

To get rid of the TOC, you can just select it in the document and press Delete, the same as with any other content control. Here's an easier way, though:

1. On the References tab, click Table of Contents. (You can also display this same menu by clicking the Table of Contents button at the top of the TOC's frame.)

2. Click Remove Table of Contents.

Manually Marking Entries for the TOC

Besides the headings in your document, you might occasionally want some nonheading text to appear in the TOC. One way to do this is to use a unique style for that text and set that style's outline level to the desired TOC level. See "Checking Style Outline Levels" earlier in this chapter if you want to do that.

However, if you don't want to change the text's style to force its inclusion in the TOC, there are a couple of alternatives.

Including an Entire Paragraph with Add Text

If you want an entire paragraph to appear in the TOC that is styled such that it would not normally appear (for example, a body paragraph or a note), here's a simple way to mark it for inclusion:

1. Click in the paragraph to be included in the TOC.

   You do not actually have to select the text; just move the insertion point into its paragraph. The entire paragraph is included in the TOC regardless of what portion of it you select.

> **note**
>
> To reverse an inclusion so that the paragraph no longer shows up in the TOC, repeat steps 1–3 for the paragraph, but instead of choosing a level in step 3, choose Not Shown in Table of Contents.

2. On the References tab, click Add Text. A menu opens.

3. Click the level at which that text should appear. A field code is inserted that marks the entry.

4. Repeat steps 1–3 for each additional entry to include.

Using {TC} Fields to Manually Mark Entries

You can also use {TC} fields to manually create TOC entries. There's a bit of extra work involved in setting them up, and you have to change the TOC options to make sure they are included, but these fields offer excellent flexibility. Options are available with a {TC} field that aren't available with the newfangled method described in the preceding section. For example, you can specify the exact text that should appear in the TOC (not necessarily the whole paragraph), and you can specify that the page number should be suppressed for that entry.

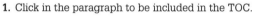
To learn more about specifying what is included in the TOC, see "Choosing Which Styles and Entries Are Included," p. 730.

To begin inserting a {TC} field, position the insertion point where you want the field and press Alt+Shift+O. This opens the Mark Table of Contents Entry dialog box shown in Figure 19.4.

From here, enter the following information:

- **Entry**—This is the literal text that appears in the table of contents.

- **Table Identifier**—If you have more than one TOC in the document, you can pick the one to which you want the entry to apply. Leave this set to the default for the main TOC.

- **Level**—Select the TOC level at which the entry should appear.

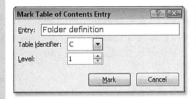

Figure 19.4
Use the Mark Table of Contents Entry dialog box to insert a legacy-style {TC} code.

 For more information about multiple TOCs in the same document, see "Working with Multiple TOCs," p. 733.

Another way to insert a {TC} field is to press Ctrl+F9 to create a new set of field brackets and then manually type the code. Here's the basic syntax:

```
{ TC "Text that should appear in the TOC"
[switches] }
```

These are the switches you can use:

- \l— That's a lowercase L, not a 1. It specifies the outline level. Examples:

  ```
  { TC "Summary" \l 3 }
  { TC "Sales Plan" \l 2}
  ```

- \n— This suppresses the page number for the entry. Example:

  ```
  { TC "Main Office" \n }
  ```

 caution

When manually typing field codes, don't forget the syntax rules for fields, as described in the "Troubleshooting" section at the end of Chapter 16, "Working with Fields and Forms."

tip

After creating a {TC} field with the correct syntax, you can copy that code, paste it into other spots, and then just change the text within the quotation marks.

Creating Custom TOCs

You can generate a TOC using your own custom settings, changing nearly every aspect of the table of contents from the text styles to the type of tab leader. Then you can save your custom TOC as a preset that appears on the Table of Contents button's menu, so you can reuse those settings in other documents.

Starting a Custom TOC

To start a custom TOC, click Table of Contents on the References tab and choose Insert Table of Contents. The Table of Contents dialog box opens, as shown in Figure 19.5.

Figure 19.5
Start a custom TOC from the Table of
Contents dialog box.

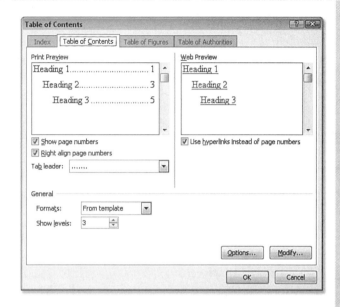

Setting Basic TOC Options

The most basic options for a TOC are found on the Table of Contents tab. Set any of these as
desired:

- **Show Page Numbers**—This toggles on/off the page numbering. Each page number is generated
  based on the page on which the heading appears.

- **Right Align Page Numbers**—When this option is disabled, the page numbers appear immediately after the text; when it's enabled, they appear at the right margin.

- **Tab Leader**—By default, a dotted leader is used when Right Align Page Numbers is turned on
  (see previous bullet). You can use other styles of leaders or not use a leader at all.

- **Use Hyperlinks Instead of Page Numbers**—This refers only to Web Preview versions of the document and versions saved to web formats. Online it is more useful for the reader to have each
  heading be a hyperlink because page numbering is relative onscreen.

- **Formats**—This drop-down list contains alternative style sets, like the ones you find on the Home
  tab when you click Change Styles. The TOC can use a different style set than the rest of the
  document. (The default, From Template, matches the TOC with the document's style set.)

- **Show Levels**—This indicates the number of heading levels that will be included in the TOC. The
  default is 3, which includes outline levels 1–3.

➡ *For more information about style sets, see "Changing the Style Set," p. 221.*

Choosing Which Styles and Entries Are Included

By default, the following are included in a TOC:

- All headings using the built-in heading styles (Heading 1, Heading 2, and so on).

- All paragraph styles that have outline levels assigned to them, up to the level indicated in the Show Levels setting, covered in the preceding section.

- All paragraphs manually marked for the TOC with the Add Text button on the References tab. (See "Manually Marking Entries for the TOC" earlier in this chapter for details.)

If you want to include other styles in the TOC, or if you want to include entries you have manually marked with the {TC} field, you must make some adjustments.

To specify which styles and entries should be included, follow these steps:

1. From the Table of Contents dialog box (refer to Figure 19.5), click Options. The Table of Contents Options dialog box opens.

2. For each style that you want to include in the TOC, type a number in the TOC Level column indicating the desired level (see Figure 19.6).

 note

If you do not want any styles to be included (only {TC} entries and outline levels, perhaps?), clear the Styles check box.

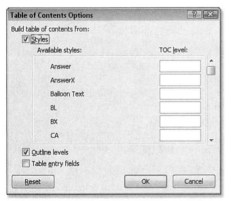

Figure 19.6
Select the styles to be included in the TOC.

3. (Optional) To include outline styles or not (that is, custom styles based on their Outline Level setting), mark or clear the Outline Levels check box. It is marked by default.

4. (Optional) To include entries marked with {TC} field codes, mark the Table Entry Fields check box.

    ⮕ *To use {TC} fields, see "Using {TC} Fields to Manually Mark Entries," p. 727.*

5. Click OK.

Why Can't I Add a New Style for TOC Entries?

From the Table of Contents dialog box, if you click Modify, a Style dialog box appears that lists TOC styles 1 through 9. There is a New button, but it is grayed out. You can't add new TOC styles.

So why is the button there, if you can't use it? It's because this same dialog box is used for other parts of the program, such as indexing, and in some of those parts you can add new styles.

Defining the Appearance of the TOC

The entries in the TOC are formatted according to special built-in paragraph styles with names that begin with "TOC". You can modify these styles as you would any other style, from the Styles pane, as you learned in Chapter 6, "Creating and Applying Styles and Themes."

There is also a TOC-specific interface for modifying TOC styles. Follow these steps to use it:

1. From the Table of Contents dialog box, click Modify. The Style dialog box appears. Only the TOC styles appear on the list (see Figure 19.7).

2. Click one of the TOC styles and review its specifications in the Preview area.

 caution

Don't confuse the styles that go into the TOC with the styles that are used to display it. The TOC includes entries for various headings in the document, but when those entries are in the TOC, they are formatted with the corresponding TOC style, not their original style. So, for example, text that is Heading 1 in the document will be TOC 1 in the TOC.

3. (Optional) If you need to change the definition of the style, click Modify.

4. Use the Modify Style dialog box to change the style definition, and then click OK.

5. Click OK to close the Style dialog box.

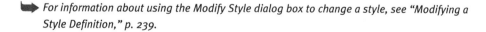 *For information about using the Modify Style dialog box to change a style, see "Modifying a Style Definition," p. 239.*

Understanding the {TOC} Field Code

When you insert a TOC, you are actually inserting a {TOC} field code. It has certain switches based on the settings you choose in the Table of Contents dialog box. You can view the field code by selecting the TOC, right-clicking it, and choosing Toggle Field Codes.

 tip

You can manually construct a table of contents code. To do so, press Ctrl+F9 to place a blank field code bracket set at the insertion point, and then type TOC followed by the desired switches, as in Table 19.1.

Figure 19.7
You can modify the TOC styles by selecting one and clicking Modify.

For example, here's a typical code:

```
{ TOC \o "1-3" \h \z \u }
```

Table 19.1 lists a few of the most common switches for the {TOC} field; for practice, decipher the preceding example from that table. You don't need to memorize these or be able to manually construct complex TOCs from them because the Table of Contents dialog box handles this for you in almost all cases; this reference is handy mostly for when you need to make small tweaks to the TOC's behavior.

Table 19.1 Common Field Code Switches for {TOC}

Switch	Purpose
\b	Uses a bookmark to specify the area of the document from which to build the TOC. (This is the one you'll need for making a partial TOC.)
\f	Builds a TOC by using {TC} entries.
\h	Hyperlinks the entries and page numbers in the TOC.
\l	Defines the {TC} field level used. Follow this by the level range in quotation marks, such as "1-3".
\n	Builds the TOC without page numbers.
\o	Uses outline levels. Follow this by the level range in quotation marks, such as "1-3".
\p	Defines the separator between the table entry and its page number. Follow this by the separator in quotation marks.
\t	Builds the TOC using style names other than the standard outline styles. Follow this by the extra style names and their levels in quotation marks, with each one separated by commas. For example, you would use the following if the style named B1 is to be included at level 1 and the style named CX is to be included at level 2: "BL,1,CX,2".

Table 19.1   Continued

Switch	Purpose
\u	Builds the TOC using the applied paragraph outline levels.
\w	Preserves tab characters within table entries.
\x	Preserves line breaks within table entries.
\z	Hides page numbers when in Web Layout view.

Creating a Custom TOC Preset

After generating the TOC exactly as you want it, you can save its specifications for later reuse. To do so, follow these steps:

1. Select the TOC.

2. On the References tab, click Table of Contents, and then choose Save Selection to Table of Contents Gallery. The Create New Building Block dialog box opens.

3. In the Name box, type the name to assign to the preset.

4. Leave the Gallery set to Table of Contents. Leave the Category assigned to General (or create/change the category if you prefer).

5. Leave Save In set to Building Blocks.dotx.

6. In the Options list, choose whether the new TOC should be on its own page:

   - **Insert Content in Its Own Paragraph**—Starts a new paragraph for the TOC but not a new page.

   - **Insert Content in Its Own Page**—Starts the TOC on a new page.

7. Click OK to create the new entry. It now appears on the Table of Contents button's menu.

To delete a custom preset, right-click it on the Table of Contents button's menu and choose Organize and Delete. Then in the Building Blocks Organizer dialog box, click Delete, click Yes to confirm, and click Close to close the dialog box.

Working with Multiple TOCs

You can have multiple TOCs in a single document. This book has that—did you notice? There is a brief TOC at the beginning that lists just the chapter titles, and then a second, more detailed TOC following it.

If you have multiple TOCs, you might want them to both cover the same content, as the ones in this book do, but at different levels of detail. Alternatively, you might want each of them to cover different content—perhaps a separate TOC for Parts I and II of a book, for example.

Adding a Second TOC for the Entire Document

To add another TOC that covers the entire document, simply position the insertion point and repeat the TOC insertion as you normally would. A dialog box appears, asking whether you want to replace the current TOC; click No, and a second TOC appears.

Adding a TOC That Covers Only Part of a Document

Things get a little trickier if you don't want the TOC to cover the entire document. You must define a bookmark that includes all the text you want to include, and then manually edit the {TOC} field's code string to specify a bookmark with the \b switch.

Here are the specifics:

1. Select all the text to be included in the TOC, and define a bookmark for it. To do so, on the Insert tab, click Bookmark. Type a bookmark name and click Add.

   ➡ *To learn about bookmarks, see "Working with Bookmarks," p. 593.*

2. To edit the code for an existing TOC, select the TOC, right-click it, and choose Toggle Field Codes. Or, to create a new TOC code, press Ctrl+F9 to insert new brackets and then type TOC followed by a space.

3. In the TOC field code, add the \b switch, followed by the bookmark name. (The bookmark name does not appear in quotation marks, because it is not literal text but an identifier.)

4. Generate (or regenerate) the TOC by right-clicking the field code and choosing Update Field.

   ➡ *For more information about field codes, including updating them and toggling their displays, see Chapter 16, "Working with Fields and Forms."*

Building a TOC Across Multiple Documents

To create a TOC that covers multiple documents, use the Master Documents feature to bring the documents together in a single container document, and then generate the TOC with all the sub-documents expanded.

➡ *To learn about master documents, see "Understanding Master Documents," p. 680.*

If you do not want to use master documents (and that's understandable, since the feature is a bit clumsy), there's an alternative: the {RD} field. RD stands for Referenced Document; it provides a way of inserting a reference to an external document within the current one.

You can either press Ctrl+F9 and type RD, or you can insert the field with the Insert, Quick Parts, Field command, as you learned in Chapter 16. Make sure you position the insertion point where you want the reference.

If you are referencing a file in the same location as the file receiving the field, you can simply place the filename in quotation marks, like this:

```
{ RD "extrainfo.docx" }
```

If you need to point to another location, use the complete path, like this:

```
{ RD "C:\\projectfiles\documents\extrainfo.docx" }
```

After inserting the {RD} field, generate the TOC as you normally would. The contents of the referenced document are included in the TOC using the same rules as applied to the TOC in the current document. For example, if you create a TOC that uses outline levels 1–2, any headings in the referenced document at those outline levels are included as well.

Creating a Table of Figures

A table of figures is just like a TOC except instead of headings, it lists figures and their captions. Many technical manuals provide a table of figures that is separate from the TOC so users can easily look up a particular diagram or schematic, for example.

Captioning Figures

A table of figures is easiest to generate if you have used Word to insert captions for each figure. You learned how to do this in Chapter 10, "Working with Photos," but here is a quick review:

1. Right-click a graphic and choose Insert Caption, or select the graphic and click the Insert Caption button on the References tab. The Caption dialog box opens.

2. In the Caption box, the numbering is already filled in. Click after the numbering and type a descriptive caption if desired (see Figure 19.8).

    For more information about the options available for captions, see "Using Figure Captions," p. 412.

3. Click OK. The caption appears adjacent to the graphic.

> **tip**
>
> You do not have to use the Insert Caption feature to create figure captions. You can simply type the desired text and then apply the Caption paragraph style to it. The captions are not automatically numbered that way, however.

Figure 19.8
Create a caption for the selected graphic.

The caption's paragraph style is Caption; you'll use that style to generate the table of figures in the next section.

Generating the Table of Figures

After ensuring that all the figure captions use a common paragraph style (for example, Caption), you can generate the table of figures. Its options are virtually identical to those for a TOC except there are no presets.

Follow these steps to generate a table of figures:

1. Position the insertion point where you want the table of figures to appear.

2. On the References tab, in the Captions group, click Insert Table of Figures. The Table of Figures dialog box opens (see Figure 19.9).

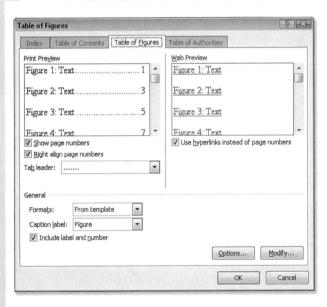

Figure 19.9
Build a table of figures.

3. Click the Options button. The Table of Figures Options dialog box opens.

4. Open the Style drop-down list and select the style used for the captions (probably Caption), as shown in Figure 19.10.

5. Click OK.

6. Set up the other options for the table of figures. They are the same as the options available for a TOC. See "Creating Custom TOCs" earlier in this chapter for a full explanation.

7. Click OK. The table of figures appears in the document.

 note

If you want to include {TC} codes in the table of figures, as described in the following section, mark the Table Entry Fields check box.

Figure 19.10
Set the style to be used for the table of figures.

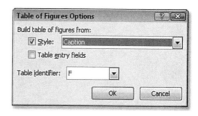

Manually Marking Captions

As you saw in the preceding steps, you must specify a single style that all the figure captions share, and the table of figures is based on that style. (It is the Caption style if you use Word's captioning feature.)

But what if there is more than one style used for the figure captions? In that case, you must insert {TC} field codes to manually mark the entries. This is similar to using the {TC} codes to mark TOC entries, covered earlier in this chapter.

The main difference is that you need to add an extra switch: \f. Then you follow the switch with a letter identifier to identify the table of figures. It can be any letter you want as long as you use the same letter for all entries that should share a common table of figures. For example:

```
{ TC "A typical network topography" \f a }
```

Then as you are compiling the TOC, make sure that in the Table of Figures Options dialog box, you mark the Table Entry Fields check box. This tells Word to include {TC} codes in the listing.

Creating Citations and Tables of Authorities

"Citation" might sound like a generic term, but it actually has a specific meaning in Word. A *citation* is a reference to a legal document, such as a case or statute. Citations are different from footnotes and bibliography entries and are used almost exclusively in the legal profession. Word makes it easy to enter citations inline in the text and then compile them into a master reference called a *table of authorities*.

Marking Citations

When citing a source for the first time in a document, you typically enter a long (full) version of it, which includes the case numbers, dates, and other information. Then in later references within the same document, you usually enter a short version, which typically consists of only the case name.

To create a citation, follow these steps.

1. Select the long version (first usage) of the first in-text citation in the document.

2. Press Alt+Shift+I or click Mark Citation on the References tab. The Mark Citation dialog box opens with the citation already filled into the Selected Text box (see Figure 19.11).

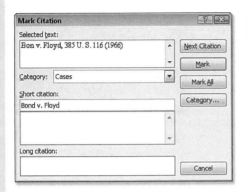

Figure 19.11
Mark a citation.

3. Edit the text as needed in the Selected Text box.

4. Open the Category list and choose the type of citation (cases, statutes, treatises, and so on).

5. In the Short Citation box, enter a shortened version of the citation, to use for subsequent references. The default is for it to be the same as the selected text.

6. Click Mark. The selected text appears in the Long Citation box.

   Alternatively, if you want Word to search the whole document and mark all references to the same citation, long and short, click Mark All.

7. To move to another citation, click Next Citation. Word jumps to the next citation.

8. Select the entire citation, and repeat steps 3–6 for it.

 tip

You can create a custom category if needed. Click the Category button, and in the Edit Category dialog box, select one of the numbers at the bottom of the list and type a new name for it in the Replace With box. Click Replace and then click OK.

note

Word looks for the next citation by looking for telltale identifiers such as "v." or "In re."

So what's actually happening behind the scenes here? Word is inserting a {TA} field code. You can see that code by clicking the Show/Hide (¶) button on the Home tab to toggle on the display of hidden text. For example, it might look something like this for a long citation:

```
{ TA \l "Bond v. Floyd, 385 U.S. 116 (1966)" \s "Bond v. Floyd" \c 1 }
```

For a short citation, the syntax is simpler:

```
{ TA \s "Bond v. Floyd" }
```

Table 19.2 explains the switches you can use with the {TA} field.

Table 19.2 Switches for the {TA} Field

Switch	Purpose
\b	Makes the page number bold.
\c	Defines the category number for the field. Follow this with a digit representing the position of the category chosen from the Mark Citation dialog box. Here's a quick reference: 1: Cases 2: Statutes 3: Other Authorities 4: Rules 5: Treatises 6: Regulations 7: Constitutional Provisions 8 and up: Undefined, but you can define them yourself
\i	Makes the page number italicized.
\l (lowercase L)	Defines the long citation. Follow it with the long citation in quotation marks.
\r	Includes the bookmark's range of pages in the page number for the field.
\s	Defines the short citation. Follow it with the short citation in quotation marks.

Generating the Table of Authorities

After you have marked all the citations, you are ready to compile the table of authorities. Follow these steps to do so:

1. Position the insertion point where you want the table of authorities to appear.

2. On the References tab, click Insert Table of Authorities. The Table of Authorities dialog box opens (see Figure 19.12).

3. Set any of these options as needed:

   - **Use Passim**—It is common when listing citations that appear repeatedly in the same document to substitute the word *passim* for the multiple page references. By default, Word uses *passim* whenever there are at least five references to the same citation. Clear this check box if you want to display the actual page numbers in each instance instead.

   - **Keep Original Formatting**—Some citations contain character formatting such as bold, italic, and underlining. That formatting carries over to the table of authorities automatically by default. If you do not want it to, clear this check box.

   - **Tab Leader**—This is the same as with a table of contents. Select the leader type or none at all.

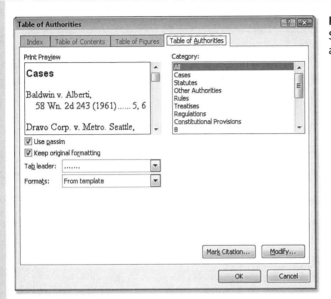

Figure 19.12
Set the style to be used for the table of authorities.

- **Formats**—This is also the same as with a table of contents. Select one of the style sets, or use From Template to match the style set that the document uses.

- **Category**—The default here is All, which generates a table containing all categories. You can narrow that down to a certain category by selecting it here.

4. (Optional) Click Modify to modify the styles used for the table of authorities, as you did with the TOC styles earlier in the chapter. There are only two styles used here: Table of Authorities and TOA Heading.

5. Click OK to generate the table of authorities.

Creating an Index

An *index* is an alphabetical listing of topics, usually at the back of a book or long document, that lists the page numbers on which the topics are covered. There's one in this book, for example, and you might have even used it already to look up a topic or two.

Creating a really good index is a skill that takes time to learn. It's not as simple as marking every instance of every word, because some words are not important to index (such as "the"), and some words are used so frequently in the document that you must decide which are the most significant

 caution

It's okay to mark index entries as you write, but there's no point in generating the index until the document is complete. If you make changes to the document that affect pagination, you will need to regenerate the index afterward.

occurrences. There are people who make a full-time living creating indexes, and there are even international conventions and seminars for indexers. Word's indexing capabilities are adequate for most people, although professional indexers might use other tools.

Creating an index is a three-step process:

1. Decide on the conventions for the index.

2. Mark the entries for the index.

3. Generate the index.

The next several sections of the chapter elaborate on those steps.

 note

Each document is indexed separately in Word, so if you are writing a publication with different chapters in separate Word documents, you need to tie them all together somehow before indexing. See "Indexing Across Multiple Documents" later in this chapter for some ideas.

Deciding on the Indexing Conventions

As you mark entries, you specify the wording of the entry and the formatting of the page numbers. Therefore, before you start marking entries, you should make some basic decisions about conventions. Here are some things to think about:

- **Page number format**—Will page numbers be bold, italic, or both?

- **Proper names**—Will proper names be listed by the person's last name, as in Smith, John? (That's usually the best way to go.)

- **Acronyms**—Will acronyms be listed by acronym or by the spelled-out version, or both? If both, will they both have the page number, or will one of them be a cross-reference to the other?

- **Verb forms**—Will you index verbs by the gerund form (Saving) or the infinitive form (Save)?

- **Verb versus noun entries**—When there's an action being performed on an object, will it be listed under the noun or the verb? For example, when saving a file, will it be under File with a subentry of Save, or will be under Save with a subentry of File?

- **Adjectives**—Most professional indexers avoid entries that start with adjectives. For example, instead of listing Multiple Tables, you might want to list that under Tables with a subentry of Multiple.

- **Word form**—You'll want to avoid multiple forms of the same word as primary entries. For example, instead of having separate entries for Install, Installation, and Installing, combine them with a common usage.

Create your list of rules that you'll follow when indexing, and keep that list handy as you proceed through this chapter.

Marking Index Entries

When you mark an index entry, you specify that the selected word or phrase should be included in the index, along with the page number. You can mark entries manually or automatically.

When you mark entries manually, you maintain complete control over which instances of a term are marked. You might not want every mention of a word to be marked, for example—just the instances where the topic is discussed in detail. Marking entries manually takes a long time in a large document, but this results in a superior index because you can follow the conventions you set in the preceding section.

When you mark entries automatically, you create an Index AutoMark file that contains the words to include in the index. Then you use the AutoMark feature to apply that list to your document, and Word automatically inserts indexing codes for all instances it finds of the words contained in the AutoMark file. AutoMarking is fast, but you lose the ability to make little adjustments to the wording as you go. For example, if you wanted to combine several word forms into a single entry, AutoMarking would not be able to accomplish that.

Manually Marking Index Codes

When you manually mark an index entry, you insert an {XE} field. You don't have to manually create the field, though; you can use the Mark Index Entry dialog box. The dialog box interface helps you set up the field code, so you don't have to remember the syntax.

To mark an index entry, follow these steps:

1. Select the text to include in the index. This is typically a single word or phrase—something concise.

   Alternatively, if you want to create a single entry for a multiparagraph section, create a bookmark that marks the entire section, and then position the insertion point at the beginning of the section.

2. Press Alt+Shift+X, or on the References tab, click Mark Entry. The Mark Index Entry dialog box opens.

3. In the Main Entry text box, the text you selected in step 1 appears. Confirm that it appears as you want it to appear in the index; change it if needed (see Figure 19.13).

4. (Optional) Apply any bold, italic, or underline formatting to the Main Entry text as desired. Select the text in the Main Entry text box, and then use these shortcut keys: Ctrl+B for bold, Ctrl+I for italic, or Ctrl+U for underline. To strip off existing formatting, press Ctrl+spacebar.

5. In the Options section, choose the option button that best represents what you want for this entry:

 note

Index entries are inserted immediately before the selected text. You do not have to select text in step 1; if you prefer, you can just position the insertion point where you want to place the index entry. If you don't select text, though, you need to type the entry in step 3; it will not be pre-filled for you.

 tip

If you selected text in step 1 that contains a colon or a quotation mark, Word adds a backslash (\) symbol before the character to indicate that it is a literal character, not a special code. If you manually type the text in step 3 for the entry, put the backslash symbol in yourself if including a colon or quotation mark.

 caution

Use manual formatting as in step 4 sparingly and strategically. In most cases, index entries should be plain text. If you selected some text in step 1 that was already marked as bold, italic, or underlined, that formatting carries over automatically; strip it off with Ctrl+spacebar if needed.

Figure 19.13
Mark an index entry.

- **Cross-Reference**—Use this for a reference to another main entry. See "Creating Cross-References" later in this chapter if you want one of these.

- **Current Page**—This is the default setting. It prints the page number on which the index entry begins.

- **Page Range**—If you choose this, you must then select a bookmark from the Bookmark list. The page range shown is the range on which the bookmarked range lies. You must have created the bookmark in step 1 (or prior to that).

6. (Optional) If you want the page number to be bold or italic, mark the Bold or Italic check boxes.

7. Click Mark. The entry is marked with an {XE} code.

8. If you have other entries to mark, leave the Mark Index Entry dialog box open, and select other text and repeat the process. The Mark Index Entry dialog box can remain open as you edit the document.

9. When you are finished marking entries, click Cancel to close the dialog box.

 caution

Be consistent with your use of bold and italic for page numbers. Professional indexers sometimes use bold and italic to give special meaning to entries. For example, if there are many entries for a particular topic, they might bold the page number for the most important entry.

 tip

You can see the indexing codes by turning on the display of hidden characters; click the Show/Hide (¶) button on the Home tab.

How Can I Use a Colon or Quotation Mark in an Index Entry?

Word interprets a colon in the main entry as a separator between it and a subentry; this enables you to enter the main entry and the subentry together in the Main Entry text box, saving some time. If you want a literal colon in the index entry, precede it with a \ symbol, like this: *10\:00 Appointment.*

The same goes for quotation marks. In an {XE} field code, the text is set in quotation marks, so you cannot use regular quotation marks within the code string. If you need a literal quotation mark in an entry, precede it with a \ symbol, like this: "\"WYSIWYG\"".

I Can't See the Index Marking Codes I Created

Index field codes show up only when hidden text is displayed. On the Home tab, click the Show/Hide (¶) button to toggle on the display of hidden text.

I Manually Created an Index Field Code and It Doesn't Work

Make sure you are following the syntax prescribed for field codes in Word. One of the most common mistakes people make is to forget to leave a space after the opening bracket and before the closing bracket. See the "Troubleshooting" section at the end of Chapter 16 for more help with field syntax.

Creating Subentries

Often it is useful to have a multilevel index, in which one major topic is placed in the alphabetical main list and beneath it multiple subtopics form their own mini-list. For example:

```
Folders
        Attributes, 22
        Creating, 18
        Deleting, 19
        Renaming, 21
```

To create a subentry, follow the steps in the preceding section, but after step 4, enter the subentry text in the Subentry box. The resulting code creates an entry that is alphabetized according to the Main Entry text, but with a page number next to the Subentry text.

You can also enter a subentry in the Main Entry text box. To do this, separate the main entry and the subentry by a colon, like this: Folders:Creating. Don't put a space on either side of the colon. To save even more time, you can copy such an entry to the Clipboard and then paste it into the Main Entry text box for each entry you want to create, changing the subentry for each one.

Occasionally you might find that you need more than two levels of subentries. You can create that by entering multiple colon-separated items in the Main Entry text box. For example:

```
Folders:Creating:In Windows 7
```

Some of My Marked Entries Don't Appear in the Index

Here are some things to check:

- Check the spelling of the entry and subentry to make sure there are no typos that are placing the entry in an unexpected location.

- If your index is in a master document, verify that all the subdocuments were expanded when you generated the index.

- If you are using the \f switch to limit an entry to a certain index, ensure that you are using the correct letter with it and that the letter is in quotation marks.

- Make sure each subentry is separated from the other entries by a colon.

- If you manually added any switches, ensure that you got the syntax right for those switches.

- If the index depends on a bookmark, double-check that the bookmark exists and is spelled correctly in the reference to it in the {Index} field code's \b switch.

Creating Cross-References

Sometimes the same content goes by two or more different names, and you aren't sure which one the user will look up in your index. In a situation like that, if it's a single entry, you might just include both entries in both places. However, if it's a complex, multilevel series of entries, you can save space in your index by creating the entries in one place and then cross-referencing them with all the other possible synonyms the user might look up.

To create a cross-reference, follow the same steps as in "Manually Marking Index Codes" earlier in this chapter, except choose Cross-Reference in step 5, and then enter the cross-reference text in the Cross-Reference text box.

 note

These cross-references for indexing are different from the cross-references you learned about in Chapter 15, "Copying, Linking, and Embedding Data." The cross-references covered there insert in-document references and have nothing to do with indexing.

There are two subtly different types of indexing cross-references. The standard "See" type points to the alternate name of a topic where the index entries for it occur. For example, since a *folder* and a *directory* refer to the same thing in PC computing, under Directory you might have a listing such as *See* Folder. A "See also" type, on the other hand, points to a related but not synonymous entry. For example, if some of the information presented in a section on files is also applicable to folders, you might have an entry like this under Folders: *See Also* Files.

A cross-reference does not insert a page number; it just inserts the literal text you specify. Therefore, it does not really matter where you insert the cross-reference code. You can insert all the cross-reference codes at the beginning or end of the document if you find that more convenient, or you can insert them throughout the document wherever they occur to you.

Marking Multiple Instances of the Same Text

To save some time, you can have Word mark all the instances of a specific text phrase in the document.

Follow the steps in "Manually Marking Index Codes" earlier in this chapter, but instead of clicking Mark in step 7, click Mark All.

Although this procedure marks every instance of a specific word or phrase, it does not mark multiple phrases at once; you have to repeat it for each individual index entry. If you want to automatically mark multiple entries at once, see the next section.

Understanding {XE} Field Codes

The {XE} index marker codes are simple. They do not have options switches; all they have is the XE code plus the index entry in quotation marks, like this:

```
{ XE "Folders" }
```

AutoMarking Index Entries

AutoMarking can save you some time if you have a large document to be indexed. Not only does it mark multiple instances of the same text, as in the earlier section, but it marks multiple words and phrases at once. There are two steps in this process: Create the AutoMark file, and then run it to create the entries in your main document.

Creating the AutoMark File

To create the AutoMark file, start a new blank document and insert a two-column table.

 caution

To prepare for AutoMarking, you must set up a list of words to be marked. Creating this list can take a significant amount of time, so you might find that AutoMarking does not save you all that much time after you've taken the trouble to compile the AutoMark file. AutoMarking also will probably not mark everything you want to include in the index, so you will likely need to go back though your document afterward and add more entries manually. It's a trade-off, and you must determine its usefulness on a case-by-case basis.

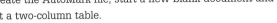 *For information about creating tables, see "Creating a Table," p. 335.*

In that table, in the left column, type words or phrases to be included in the index. In the right column, type the entry the way it should appear in the index. You can use colons to create subentries where needed, as you learned in "Creating Subentries" earlier in this chapter. Apply bold or italic as needed to the text in the right column. If you leave the right column blank for a row, Word uses the same text as in the left column.

Indexing is case-sensitive, so be sure that the left column includes all variations of words that might appear in your document in both uppercase and lowercase. However, make sure you standardize on either uppercase or lowercase in the right column so that your index contains only one main entry for that word. Further, make sure that you capture all the forms of a word in the left column, but place the same entry for each of them in the right column. For example, Figure 19.14 shows all the entries for words that appear under a single heading of Training in an index.

tip

You might want to view the AutoMark table side by side with the main document you are indexing to help you recall what words you want to include. You can manually arrange the windows or use the View tab's Arrange All button or View Side by Side button to auto-arrange the open windows.

Figure 19.14
A portion of an AutoMark file.

Trainer	Training
trainer	Training
Trainers	Training
trainers	Training
Training	Training
training	Training
Train	Training
train	Training
classes	Training
learning	Training
teaching	Training

After creating all the entries in the table, save and close the file. It does not matter what name you give it, as long as you remember what you chose.

AutoMarking the Main Document

Generating the AutoMark file is the time-consuming part; using it to mark the entries in the main document is quick and easy. Follow these steps:

1. Open the main document to be indexed.

2. On the References tab, click Insert Index. The Index dialog box opens.

3. Click the AutoMark button. The Open Index AutoMark File dialog box opens.

4. Select the AutoMark document you created in the preceding section and click Open. The entries are automatically marked with {XE} codes.

Working Directly with {Index} Field Codes

The index is generated by an {Index} field code. You can see it by selecting the index, right-clicking it, and choosing Toggle Field Codes. Table 19.3 lists the switches for the {Index} field. You do not need to change these in most cases, because they are automatically generated based on your choices in the Index dialog box. They are provided here in case you want to add one of the more obscure options that the dialog box does not control. Some of the sections later in this chapter use a few of these codes for special functions.

Each of the switches is followed by a parameter, usually entered in quotation marks (except in the case of the \b switch, where the bookmark name is not in quotation marks).

Table 19.3   Switches for the {Index} Field

Switch	Purpose
\b	Uses a bookmark to specify the area of the document from which to build the index. Follow this by the bookmark name.
\c	Defines the number of columns if more than one. Follow this by the number in quotation marks.
\d	Defines the separator between sequence and page numbers. Follow this by the separator character in quotation marks.
\e	Defines the separator character used between the index entry and the page number. Follow this by the separator character in quotation marks.
\f	Creates the index by using only the specified entry type. Follow this by a letter in quotation marks representing the entry type. It can be any letter except "i." (Using "i" places the entry in the main index and is the same as omitting the \f switch entirely.) You'll learn more about this option later in the chapter, in the "Indexing Only Selected Entries" section.
\g	Defines the separator character used in a page range. Follow this by the separator character in quotation marks.
\h	Defines the spacing or heading for each letter grouping. See "Controlling the Appearance of Index Headings" later in this chapter for details.
\k	Defines the separators between cross-references and other entries. Follow this by the separator character in quotation marks.
\l	Defines the separators between page numbers for multiple-page references. Follow this by the separator character in quotation marks.
\p	Limits the index to the specified letters. See "Indexing Only Selected Letters of the Alphabet" later in this chapter for details.
\r	Runs index subentries onto the same line as the main entry.
\s	Includes the referenced sequence number with the page number.
\y	Enables the use of yomi text for sorting index entries (applicable only for East Asian languages).
\z	Defines the language ID Word used to generate the index. The default is "1033," which is the code for U.S. English.

Generating the Index

After marking the entries for the index, you are ready to compile it. If you accept all the default formatting options, generating the index is simple. Follow these steps:

1. Position the insertion point where you want the index to appear.

2. On the References tab, click Insert Index. The Index dialog box opens (see Figure 19.15).

3. Click OK. The index appears in the document.

Figure 19.15
Create an index from the Index dialog box.

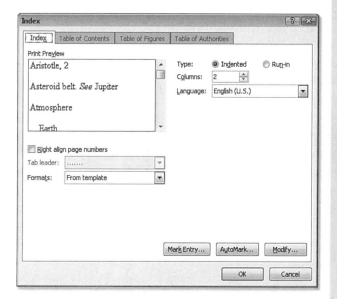

The index appears in its own section, and a section break is inserted between it and the rest of the document. Because it is in its own section, you can apply different page formatting to it, such as different margins, headers/footers, and page numbering.

If the index doesn't match what you want in content or appearance, see "Formatting the Index" later in this chapter to learn about the options available for it.

Updating the Index

If you change the document after creating the index, the index might become out of synch with the actual page numbers. To fix this, update the index.

The index is a field code, the same as a TOC or any other similar listing, so you can update it by selecting it, right-clicking it, and choosing Update Field. You can also click the Update Index button on the References tab, or click inside the index and press F9.

Spell-Checking an Index

The spell-checker does not check an index because the index is not "real" text in the document; it's a field.

To get around this, run a spell check with hidden text turned on (via the Show/Hide (¶) button on the Home tab), so that all the {XE} field codes appear. Word checks the spelling in the codes, and because they form the text in the index, the text is indirectly checked.

Another way to perform a spell-check is to select the index and press Ctrl+Shift+F9 to unlink the index field. This changes the index field to plaintext. The downside is that you can no longer update the index after doing that, because it is no longer an {Index} field. Therefore, do this as the very last step in the document-creation process.

The Page Numbering in the Index Doesn't Match the Printed Copy of the Document

This can happen if your document contains hidden text (enough to throw off the page numbering) and the hidden text is displayed when you generate the index. The onscreen version is tracked with the onscreen text (which contains the hidden text), but when you print the document, the hidden text doesn't print, so the page numbering is off.

On the Home tab, click Show/Hide (¶) to hide the hidden text and then regenerate the index.

Indexing Only Selected Entries

Not every entry marked with an {XE} code must necessarily appear in every index. By manually editing the field codes for your {XE} markers, you can define an entry as belonging to one index or another.

The switch you'll use for this is \f. Follow the switch by a letter, in quotation marks. It can be any letter except "i". Using "i" indicates it belongs in the master index, which is the same as omitting the \f switch entirely. Use the same letter for each entry that should be in the same index together. You can use any single character from the ANSI character set, including letters, numbers, and symbols.

 tip

If you need a single {XE} field to appear in more than one custom index, or the custom index plus the main one, insert separate {XE} codes for each index it should appear in. Just copy and paste the existing {XE} code, and then change the letter specified for the \f switch.

Display the {XE} field codes by toggling Show/Hide (¶) on from the Home tab. Then in each {XE} field, add the \f switch and the chosen letter, like this:

```
{ XE "Tables:Creating" \f "k" }
```

Next, modify the {Index} field code by right-clicking it and selecting Toggle Field Codes, and then add the same switch and letter to it. Or, to create a new index, create a new {Index} field by pressing Ctrl+F9 and typing **Index**:

```
{ Index \f "k" }
```

Indexing Only Selected Letters of the Alphabet

If you need to split your index into multiple sections alphabetically, you might want to create a separate index for each letter or for groups of letters. To do this, use the \p switch.

Modify the {Index} field code by right-clicking it and selecting Toggle Field Codes, and add the \p switch to it followed by the range of letters (no quotation marks). Place two hyphens between the first and last letters in the range, like this:

```
{ Index \p a--h }
```

caution

If AutoCorrect tries to convert the double hyphen into a dash, press Ctrl+Z to undo it. If you find yourself using double hyphens a lot, you might be better off disabling the dash conversion in AutoCorrect (covered in "Automating Corrections with AutoCorrect" in Chapter 3, "Correcting and Printing Documents").

Formatting the Index

Indexes, like TOCs, can be formatted in various ways. Some of those formatting options are layout related and are controlled from the Index dialog box (refer to Figure 19.15); others are style related and are controlled by modifying the Index styles. The following sections explain the details.

Setting the Index Layout

In the Index dialog box (References tab, Insert Index), you can choose from among several options that control the way the index is laid out on the page.

Type

The Type setting controls how subentries appear. The default is Indented, which places each subentry on a separate line and indents it, like this:

```
Folders
      Attributes, 22
      Creating, 18
      Deleting, 19
      Renaming, 21
```

The alternative is Run-In, which runs in subentries with the main entry, separating each part with semicolons, like this:

```
Folders: Attributes, 22; Creating, 18; Deleting, 19; Renaming, 21
```

Indented layouts are much easier to read but take up more space. If page count is an issue, using a run-in index layout can help fit the index onto fewer pages.

Columns

The Columns setting determines the number of newspaper-style (snaking) columns to be used for the index. Because most index lines are fairly short, using several columns can help fit the index on fewer pages. An average number of columns for a typical index is three. Fewer than that, and there is too much whitespace; more than that, and longer entries are broken into too many short lines.

Language

The Language setting determines the alphabetization rules. There is probably only one option on this menu—the one for the default language and country for your copy of Word.

Right Align Page Numbers

This setting places the page numbers at the right margin of the column; optionally, it adds a tab leader (in your choice of styles) between the entry and the number, like this:

```
Folders
        Attributes........22
        Creating.........18
        Deleting.........19
        Renaming.........21
```

Formats

As with TOCs, this setting enables you to apply a different style set to the index than to the rest of the document. The default setting, From Template, uses the same style set as the main document.

➡️ *For more information about style sets, see "Changing the Style Set," p. 221.*

Defining Index Styles

As with TOCs and tables of authorities, the styles for index entries come from built-in styles Index 1 through Index 9. You can modify the definitions of these styles to control the various levels of the index. (An index can have up to nine levels of subentries, which is why there are nine index styles.)

To modify an index style, follow these steps:

1. On the References tab, click Insert Index. The Index dialog box opens.

2. Click Modify. The Style dialog box appears, listing only the index styles (see Figure 19.16).

3. Click one of the styles, and then click Modify. The Modify Style dialog box opens.

 tip

If you want the new definitions of the index styles to be saved with the template so that new documents will use them too, in the Modify Style dialog box, mark the New Documents Based on This Template option button.

Figure 19.16
Redefine one or more of the paragraph styles that govern index formatting.

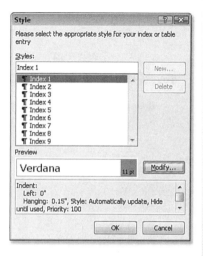

4. Make changes to the style, as you learned to do in Chapter 6.

5. Click OK to accept the changes to the style.

6. Repeat steps 3–5 to modify other styles if needed, and then click OK.

> *For information about using the Modify Style dialog box to change a style, see "Modifying a Style Definition," p. 239.*

Controlling the Appearance of Index Headings

An index can have headings for each letter—an A heading followed by all the entries that begin with A, and so on. To include such a heading, add the \h switch to the {Index} field code.

To use capital letters, follow the switch with a capital A in quotation marks, like this:

```
{ Index \h "A" }
```

To add other symbols to the heading, include them along with the capital A, like this:

```
{ Index \h "====A====" }
```

You can use any symbol character in a normal text font (such as * or $), but you cannot use letters of the alphabet. (You can't use an all-symbol font such as Symbol or Wingdings, however.)

To use lowercase letters, add *lower (*not* in quotation marks), like this:

```
{ Index \h *lower }
```

To omit the letter but include spacing, place a space in quotation marks, like this:

```
{ Index \h " " }
```

Indexing Across Multiple Documents

If you need to index multiple documents as a single unit, your best bet is to use a master document, as described in Chapter 17. Expand all the subdocuments, and then make sure the insertion point is at the end of the master document (outside of any subdocument) and generate the index. You can mark the entries in the individual documents while they are open within the subdocument, or you can prepare each one individually ahead of time outside the master document.

Another alternative if you don't like master documents, or if you have problems with them crashing, is to use the {RD} field, which stands for Referenced Document. This was mentioned earlier in this chapter, in the context of TOCs, but it works for indexes as well. An {RD} field tells Word to search another file and use its contents in any index or TOC you create in your current document. You could start a new blank document just for the index and then refer to each of your Word files with a separate {RD} code within it. Then when you generate the index, the index pulls marked entries from all the referenced files.

You can either press Ctrl+F9 and type RD, or you can insert the field with the Insert, Quick Parts, Field command, as you learned in Chapter 16.

If you are referencing a file in the same location as the file receiving the field, you can place the file-name in quotation marks, like this:

```
{ RD "Chapter1.docx" }
```

If you need to point to another location, use the complete path, like this:

```
{ RD "C:\\projectfiles\documents\Chapter1.docx" }
```

After inserting the {RD} field, generate the index as you normally would. The contents of the referenced documents are included in the index using the same rules as applied to the index in the current document.

Creating Multiple Indexes in a Single Document

Just like with TOCs, you can use bookmarks to define regions of the document to include in an index and then index only those bookmarked regions. To do this, you must manually edit the index's field code to add the \b switch.

Follow these steps:

1. Select all the text to be included in the index, and define a bookmark for it. To do so, on the Insert tab, click Bookmark. Type a bookmark name and click Add.

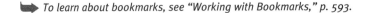 *To learn about bookmarks, see "Working with Bookmarks," p. 593.*

2. To edit the code for an existing index, select the index, right-click it, and choose Toggle Field Codes. Or, to create a new index code, press Ctrl+F9 to insert new brackets and then type Index followed by a space.

3. In the Index field code, add the \b switch, followed by the bookmark name. (The bookmark name does not appear in quotation marks, because it is not literal text but an identifier.)

4. Generate (or regenerate) the index by right-clicking the field code and choosing Update Field.

➡ *For more information about field codes, including updating them and toggling their displays, see Chapter 16, "Working with Fields and Forms."*

COLLABORATING WITH OTHERS

Exploring Word 2010 Collaboration Options

Microsoft Word 2010 offers a multitude of collaboration options, both within Word as well as on the web.

Word's built-in collaboration tools allow you to mark up and comment on documents by passing these documents back and forth between your teammates. This is called *offline collaboration*. If you're upgrading from a previous version of Word, these built-in collaboration tools should be familiar.

In addition to offline methods, Word supports several kinds of *online collaboration*, including several options new to Word 2010. Online collaboration allows you to store your documents in a controlled environment and work with your teammates to edit, comment on, and revise them.

With Word 2010, you can use free tools such as Microsoft Office Live Workspace or SkyDrive to collaborate, which require limited technical skill to set up. If you work in a large organization, your company's IT department could deploy Microsoft SharePoint Server 2010 for enterprise collaboration. Word 2010 also offers a new feature called *coauthoring*, which enables more than one person to work on a document at the same time. Finally, Microsoft Office Web Apps, Microsoft Word 2010 Mobile, and Microsoft Office Communicator 2007 R2 all offer additional collaborative features.

There's obviously no shortage of collaboration options with Word 2010. The key is choosing the right option for your specific collaboration needs.

Configuring Word's Built-in Collaboration Tools

When multiple people edit a document, it is often useful to have a clear trail of who changed what, or who made each change or remark. To facilitate this type of tracking, Word provides several tools that enable users to "mark up" a document without losing sight of the original. You can:

- Use the Comments feature to attach comments to various parts of the document, somewhat like sticky notes on a hard copy.

- Use the Tracking feature to track content and formatting changes by user, and to easily accept or reject the changes that others make.

- Use the Compare feature to look at two versions of a document side by side for a line-by-line comparison, or to see a merged version that incorporates the differences between them as tracked changes.

 caution

The collaboration features covered in this chapter assume that everyone has unrestricted access to the document. In a close-knit team environment, that might be fine, but if you need to place restrictions on the editing allowed for individual documents, see Chapter 21, "Protecting and Securing Documents."

Displaying or Hiding the Reviewing Pane

The *Reviewing pane* is a separate pane that appears alongside the main window, listing the changes that have been made to the selected text. As you can see in Figure 20.1, it shows all the tracked revisions and comments, broken down by category (Main Document Changes and Comments, Header and Footer Changes, Text Box Changes, and so forth).

To toggle the Reviewing pane on and off, click the Reviewing Pane button on the Review tab. To choose a vertical or horizontal orientation for it, click the down arrow to the right of the button and select the desired orientation.

Figure 20.1 points out two buttons on the Reviewing pane's title bar:

- **Update Revision Count**—This repolls the document for the number of revisions and updates the counter in the title bar of the Reviewing pane.

- **Show/Hide Detailed Summary**—This toggles on and off some extra information about the breakdown of the revision count (how many comments, how many deletions, and so forth).

Controlling the Use of Balloons

Tracked changes can appear as markup within the document text or as colored balloons outside the text's right margin.

Figure 20.2 shows an example of a balloon that identifies a deletion.

Figure 20.1
Display or hide the Reviewing pane.

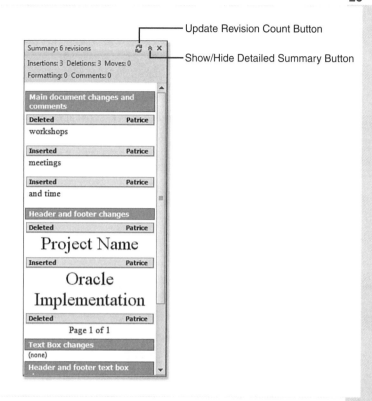

— Update Revision Count Button

— Show/Hide Detailed Summary Button

Figure 20.2
Revisions with
balloons make
your changes
easier to see.

To control the appearance of balloons versus inline revisions and comments, follow these steps:

1. On the Review tab, open the Track Changes button's menu and select Change Tracking Options. The Track Changes Options dialog box opens (see Figure 20.3).

2. At the bottom of the dialog box, select one of the following options in the Use Balloons (Print and Web Layout) drop-down list: Always, Never, or Only for Comments/Formatting.

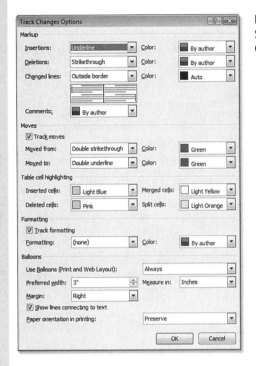

Figure 20.3
Set up balloon options at the bottom of the Track Changes Options dialog box.

3. If you chose Always or Only for Comments/Formatting, set up your preferred specs for the balloons:

- **Preferred Width**—The width of the extra space that appears to the right of the page onscreen, in which the balloons appear.

After Enabling Balloons, My Text Is Too Small

The display has to shrink the zoom when you use balloons to track changes and comments to make room for the balloon area to the right (or left) of the main page. You can improve this somewhat by making the balloon area narrower. To do so, decrease the Preferred Width setting.

- **Measure In**—The unit of measurement for the preceding setting.

- **Margin**—The side of the page on which balloons appear. The default is Right.

- **Show Lines Connecting to Text**—Connects a balloon to the comment or change to which it refers.

- **Paper Orientation in Printing**—Choose Auto (switches to Landscape if needed to make comments fit), Preserve (sticks with the page's established orientation), or Force Landscape (always prints in landscape when comments are present).

4. Click the OK button to accept the new balloon settings.

Changing the Colors and Markings Used for Revisions

In the Track Changes Options dialog box (refer to Figure 20.3), not only can you control the balloon behavior, but you can change the colors used to mark the various types of revisions.

For each revision type, you can choose a type style (such as underline or strikethrough) and a color. You can choose a fixed color, choose Auto (which is the same as saying, "don't change the color"), or choose By Author. The By Author option automatically colors each reviser's work differently, so you can see at a glance who changed what.

Here are the changes for which you can specify colors and markings:

- **Insertions**—New text, typically indicated in underlining and a different color. Your choices are Color Only, Bold, Italic, Underline, Double Underline, and Strikethrough.

- **Deletions**—Deleted text, typically indicated by strikethrough and a different color. The choices are the same as for insertions, plus a few extras such as Hidden, carets (^), hash marks (#), and double strikethrough.

- **Changed Lines**—Any line in which there is a change, typically indicated by a vertical line at the border. The settings here are Left Border, Right Border, Outside Border, and None. If you choose Outside Border, the border appears at the left for left-hand pages and at the right for right-hand pages.

- **Comments**—Notes you insert with the New Comment feature, covered later in this chapter. Here, you can set the color of the comment balloon or indicator.

- **Moves**—You can track moves from one location to another. In earlier versions, moves were not treated specially; they were just combinations of deletions and insertions. For both Moved From and Moved To, you can choose all the same options as for Insertions. In addition, for Moved From, you can choose double-strikethrough, carets (^), hash marks (#), or Hidden.

- **Table Cell Highlighting**—Changes you make to a table structure are marked by applying colors to the cells affected.

- **Formatting**—Formatting is not tracked by default, but you can enable its tracking and choose what marks and colors are used, with the same options as for insertions.

Changing the Username

If you specify any of the colors in the preceding section as By Author, Word automatically assigns a different color to each person's changes and comments. It determines whether a different person is editing the document by looking at the username that's set up in Word. If you want to simulate a different user, or if a different user sits down to make changes at the same PC, logged in as the original Windows user, you'll want to change the username so the color used will be different.

To change the username, follow these steps:

1. On the Review tab, open the Track Changes button's menu and select Change User Name.

2. In the User Name box of the Word Options dialog box, type a new name (see Figure 20.4).

3. In the Initials box, type the initials for the new name. Initials are optional to enter; the full user-name will be used in place of initials if no initials are entered.

4. Click the OK button.

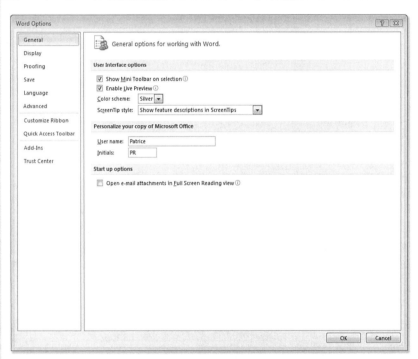

Figure 20.4
Change the username here to trigger a different color for revisions set up to be colored By Author.

Working with Comments

Comments are like little sticky notes you insert to make notes about the document. In book publishing, for example, an editor might use a comment to ask the author a question about a certain sentence or phrasing. The Comments feature in Word enables you to insert, edit, and delete comments and to browse the document by jumping from comment to comment.

 note

Comments do not replace revision marks; each has its place in the editing process. Use comments when you have a question or remark to make about the document but you are not proposing a specific change; use revision marks when you want to demonstrate your idea for a change.

Inserting Comments

You can insert comments anywhere in a document, including in the body, the header or footer, footnotes or endnotes, and so forth. Depending on whether you have enabled balloon usage, the comment appears either in a balloon or in the Reviewing pane.

To create a comment, follow these steps:

1. Select the text to which the comment refers, or position the insertion point where you want the comment marker to appear.

2. On the Review tab, click the New Comment button. A new comment balloon appears (if balloon usage is turned on), or the Reviewing pane appears with the insertion point flashing within a new comment line (if balloon usage is turned off).

   The text you selected in step 1 also becomes highlighted with the color assigned to comments for the current user, and the current user's initials and a number appear there. For example, for the first comment from Anne Smith, it would show [AS1].

3. Type the comment, and then click away from it to accept it.

 tip

If the comment applies broadly to a large section, position the insertion point at the beginning of that section. If the comment refers to a specific word or phrase, though, it is better to select that in step 1.

 note

Comments appear in the Reviewing pane, not in balloons, when you are working in any view other than Print Layout, Web Layout, or Full Screen Reading.

Viewing and Editing Comments

When balloons are turned on, you can view and edit the comments directly in the balloons.

When balloons are turned off, you can view a comment by pointing at the comment indicator in the document, but to edit it, you must open the Reviewing pane.

Click the Reviewing Pane button on the Review tab to toggle it on or off. Then just click in the desired comment in the Reviewing Pane and type your edits (see Figure 20.5).

To move between comments using the Reviewing pane, click the comment you want; the document view jumps to that comment. Alternatively, click the Next or Previous button in the Comments group of the Review tab to move between comments. (The Previous and Next buttons in the Changes group move between revisions, rather than comments.)

 caution

If you want to comment on someone else's comment, it is usually best to insert a new comment rather than typing your remarks within the original comment, so the tracking is clearer. It can sometimes be difficult to tell where one comment starts and another begins if the two are in the same balloon.

Deleting Comments

To remove a comment, right-click the comment balloon in the margin or the comment body in the Reviewing pane and choose Delete Comment. You can also delete a comment by deleting the text to which it is attached.

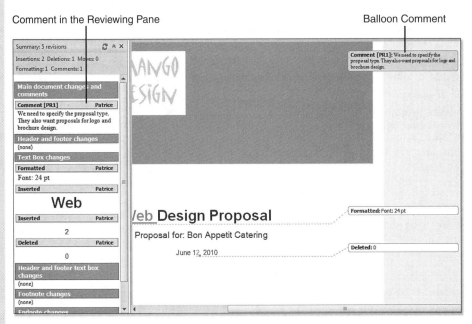

Comment in the Reviewing Pane

Balloon Comment

Figure 20.5
View and edit comments from the Reviewing pane or from balloons.

To remove all comments, click the down arrow to the right of the Delete button in the Comments group on the Review tab, and choose Delete All Comments in Document.

Using Revision Tracking

Revision tracking marks insertions, deletions, moves, and (optionally) formatting changes. Earlier in this chapter, you learned how to configure the revision tracking feature to mark what you want, and in the style and color that you prefer. Now let's look at how to actually *track* revisions.

To turn revision tracking on or off, click the Track Changes button on the Review tab. When Track Changes is on, the revision markings you specified appear in the document as you edit.

The revisions appear differently depending on whether balloons are enabled. When balloons are enabled, the insertion appears inline in the document (underlined and in color by default), and the deletion appears in a balloon (see Figure 20.6).

When balloons are disabled or are set to show only comments and formatting, both the insertion and the deletion appear inline in the text, and a change bar appears alongside the paragraph, as in Figure 20.7.

Figure 20.6
When balloons are enabled, deletions appear in balloons.

Job Description

Job Purpose:

Markets products by developing and implementing marketing and advertising campaigns; tracking sales data; maintaining promotional materials inventory; planning meetings and trade shows; maintaining databases; preparing reports.

Duties:

- Implements marketing and advertising campaigns by assembling and analyzing sales forecasts; preparing marketing and advertising strategies, plans, and objectives; planning and organizing promotional presentations; updating calendars.
- Prepares marketing reports by collecting, analyzing, and summarizing sales data.
- Implements and monitors all social media campaigns on Facebook, MySpace, Twitter, and YouTube.
- Keeps promotional materials ready by coordinating requirements with graphics department; inventorying stock; placing orders; verifying receipt.
- Supports sales staff by providing sales data, market trends, forecasts, account analyses, new product information; relaying customer services requests.
- Researches competitive products by identifying and evaluating product characteristics, market share, pricing, and advertising; maintaining research databases.
- Plans meetings and trade shows by identifying, assembling, and coordinating requirements; establishing contacts; developing schedules and assignments; coordinating mailing lists.
- Monitors budgets by comparing and analyzing actual results with plans and forecasts.
- Updates job knowledge by participating in educational opportunities; reading trade publications.
- Accomplishes organization goals by accepting ownership for accomplishing new and different requests;

Deleted: <#>Tracks product line sales and costs by analyzing and entering sales, expense, and new business data.¶

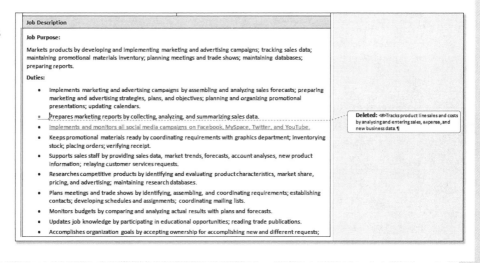

Figure 20.7
When balloons are disabled, both insertions and deletions appear inline.

Job Description

Job Purpose:

Markets products by developing and implementing marketing and advertising campaigns; tracking sales data; maintaining promotional materials inventory; planning meetings and trade shows; maintaining databases; preparing reports.

Duties:

- Implements marketing and advertising campaigns by assembling and analyzing sales forecasts; preparing marketing and advertising strategies, plans, and objectives; planning and organizing promotional presentations; updating calendars.
- ~~Tracks product line sales and costs by analyzing and entering sales, expense, and new business data.~~
- Prepares marketing reports by collecting, analyzing, and summarizing sales data.
- Implements and monitors all social media campaigns on Facebook, MySpace, Twitter, and YouTube.
- Keeps promotional materials ready by coordinating requirements with graphics department; inventorying stock; placing orders; verifying receipt.
- Supports sales staff by providing sales data, market trends, forecasts, account analyses, new product information; relaying customer services requests.
- Researches competitive products by identifying and evaluating product characteristics, market share, pricing, and advertising; maintaining research databases.
- Plans meetings and trade shows by identifying, assembling, and coordinating requirements; establishing contacts; developing schedules and assignments; coordinating mailing lists.
- Monitors budgets by comparing and analyzing actual results with plans and forecasts.
- Updates job knowledge by participating in educational opportunities; reading trade publications.

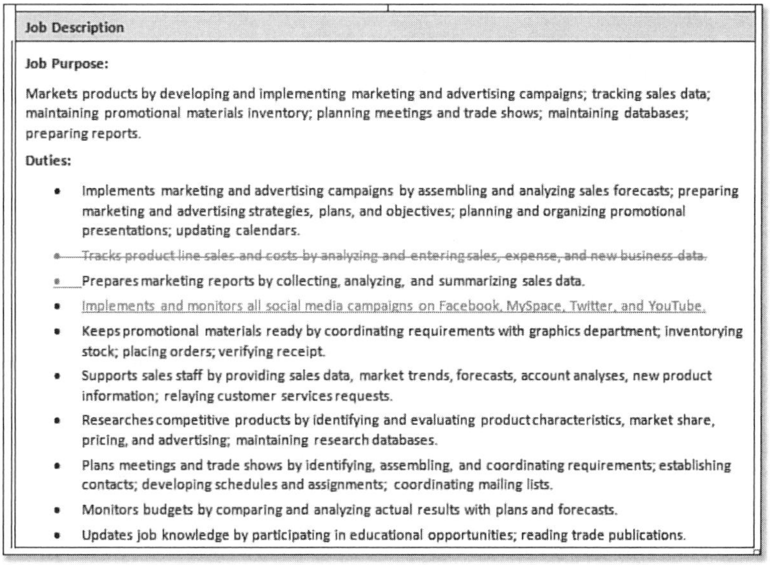

Reviewing Revisions

You can review your own revisions, but it is much more common to review someone else's revisions, or even revisions from multiple reviewers. You can then respond to the reviewing marks by accepting or rejecting each change individually or accepting or rejecting all changes as a whole (or all changes within a selected range).

Displaying or Hiding Revision Marks

Showing revision marks is not always necessary or appropriate. For example, as you are reviewing a document that someone else has written, you might want to make changes to it without being distracted by seeing the changes that other people have already made.

One way to avoid showing revision marks is to turn off the Track Changes feature and accept any existing revisions, of course, but then you lose the tracking benefits. A better way is to track changes but not show the changes onscreen. To do this, set the Display for Review list's setting to Final. To display the tracking marks again, set it to Final: Show Markup (see Figure 20.8).

Display for Review List

Figure 20.8
Show or hide revision marks, and view the final or the original version.

As you can see in Figure 20.8, the Display for Review list also has two other options: Original and Original: Show Markup. These show the document as it was before tracked revisions were made.

Displaying or Hiding Certain Types of Revisions

Perhaps you want to see revisions, but only certain types. For example, maybe someone on your team has insisted that you track formatting changes, but you don't like to see all those formatting change balloons and marks onscreen.

To choose which types of changes appear, open the Show Markup list on the Review tab and select or deselect the types of revisions you want to view (see Figure 20.9). Not only can you choose which types, but you can discriminate between reviewers if there have been more than one.

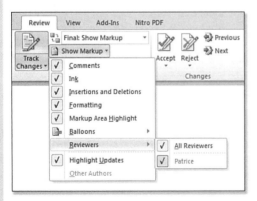

Figure 20.9
Choose which specific reviewers and revision types you want to see onscreen.

Moving Among Revisions

To move between revisions, you can use the Next and Previous buttons in the Changes group on the Review tab. Don't confuse them with the buttons of the same names in the Comments group, which are just for comments.

Simply moving between revisions does nothing to them; you're just viewing them. If you want to accept or reject them while you're moving to them, see the following section.

Accepting or Rejecting Revisions

To accept or reject an individual revision, move to it or select it and then click the Accept or Reject button on the Review tab. If you choose Accept, the revision is incorporated into the document and the revision marks are removed; if you choose Reject, the original text is restored and the revision marks are removed.

When you click the Accept or Reject button, by default each of these jumps to the next revision automatically after it performs its action. That makes it convenient to quickly move through a series of revisions because you do not have to click Next to go

 tip

Here's an even quicker way to accept or reject changes: Right-click the revision balloon in the margin, and then choose Accept Change or Reject Change from the menu.

to the next instance as a separate step. However, it does cause a problem if you want to look at the accepted/rejected revision after accepting or rejecting it, to make sure it looks right in context.

If you would prefer *not* to advance to the next revision after accepting or rejecting, open the drop-down list for the button and select the alternative version of the command that does not involve moving to the next revision. For example, in Figure 20.10, you would select the Accept button's Accept Change option. For the Reject button, the equivalent is Reject Change.

Figure 20.10
Select a type of acceptance or rejection from the button's menu.

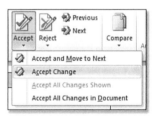

To accept all revisions in the entire document, open the Accept button's menu and choose Accept All Changes in Document. If some of the revisions are not currently displayed (for example, if you selectively turned off some of them with the Show Markup button's menu), an additional command appears: Accept All Changes Shown. This accepts all the changes currently displayed, but not the hidden ones.

The Reject button works the same way. Choose Reject All Changes in Document or Reject All Changes Shown to do a mass rejection.

Preventing Others from Tampering with Revisions

You just saw how easy it is to accept or reject revisions or to turn them off completely. That means that anyone revising your document can make changes that you aren't aware of and can accept or reject other people's changes before you even get a chance to see them.

To prevent that from happening, you can lock down the document so that all changes are tracked and tracking cannot be disabled. You'll learn more about security lockdowns in Chapter 21, "Protecting and Securing Documents," but here's a quick summary of how to do it:

1. On the Review tab, click the Restrict Editing button.

2. In the Restrict Formatting and Editing task pane, select the Allow Only This Type of Editing in the Document check box.

3. Select Tracked Changes in the drop-down list.

4. Click the Yes, Start Enforcing Protection button.

5. Type a password, and then type it again to confirm it.

6. Click the OK button.

When the document is thus protected, the Track Changes, Accept, and Reject buttons are unavailable. To turn protection off, click Stop Protection in the Restrict Formatting and Editing task pane and enter your password.

 tip

There is no way to make Accept Change and Reject Change the defaults on the Accept and Reject buttons. However, you can add those commands to the Quick Access toolbar if you like. Right-click the command and choose Add to Quick Access Toolbar. Once a command is on the Quick Access toolbar, it has an automatic shortcut key assigned to it based on its position on the toolbar. For example, if the new command is in position 6 (from left to right), press Alt+6.

 I Forgot My Password and Can't Turn Off Locked Revision Marks

How do you turn off locked revision marks if you don't know, or forgot, the password? There's not an easy way to do it. Saving as a different filename won't do it, nor will saving in Rich Text Format or HTML. If you just want to see the document without revision marks, set the Display for Review setting to Final on the Review tab. You can, however, get rid of revision marks by saving in plaintext format. Then close and reopen the file, and all the revision marks will have been accepted. You'll need to reapply all the formatting, of course; that's the disadvantage.

Comparing Documents

Tracking changes works well when multiple people are working on a single copy of the document. Perhaps they are circulating it from one person to another or accessing it at different times from a server, but there exists only one version of the document that everyone edits.

When one person saves his or her own separate copy and then makes changes to it, though, that system breaks down. Suddenly you have two versions of the document, each with some changes that the other one does not have. For situations like that, you must compare the two versions and integrate the changes from both into a single master copy.

Viewing Two Documents Side by Side

One way to compare two documents is to view them side by side in separate windows. You can choose to lock the scrolling together so that when you scroll one window, the other scrolls an equal amount, or you can allow the windows to scroll separately.

 tip

Other options for viewing two documents side by side include using a system with dual monitors or using the Windows 7 snap feature, which enables you to resize an open window by dragging it to the edge of the screen.

To view two documents side by side, follow these steps:

1. Open both documents. Display one of the two as the active document.

2. On the View tab, click View Side by Side. If only two documents are open, they immediately appear side by side. If three or more are open, the Compare Side by Side dialog box opens (see Figure 20.11).

3. Click the document to display side by side with the first one and click OK. The two documents appear side by side, each in its own copy of Word, as shown in Figure 20.12.

By default, the two windows are set for synchronized scrolling. To turn this off, on the View tab, click the Synchronous Scrolling button.

Figure 20.11
Select the document to compare with the active one.

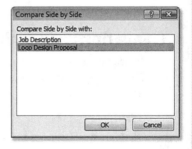

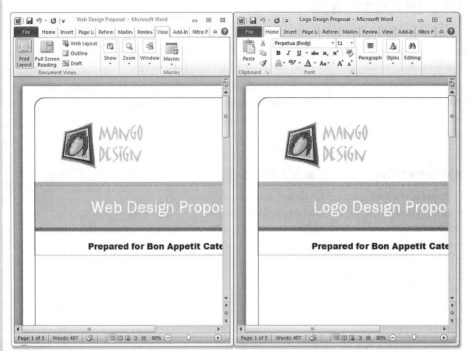

Figure 20.12
Two documents displayed side by side.

I Don't See the Synchronous Scrolling Button

Don't see a Synchronous Scrolling button? That's probably because your screen is not wide enough to show complete tabs for two document windows side by side. Instead, some of the groups appear as buttons. Click the Window button to open a menu containing the Window group's options, and you'll find the Synchronous Scrolling button there.

Comparing and Combining Documents

Instead of manually comparing the documents line by line, you might prefer to use the Compare feature in Word to automatically insert revision marks to show how one document differs from another.

There are actually two variants of the process:

- **Compare**—Generates a new copy that combines the two versions; this is also called *legal black-lining*. The major difference between this and Combine is that when the original also has revision marks in it, those revision marks are accepted in the resulting document, and the changes between it and the second document appear as a single user set of revision marks. All differences are attributed to a single new reviewer.

- **Combine**—Merges the revisions from both copies into a single document, which can be either the original or the copy, as you specify, or a brand-new document. You can repeat the Combine operation to combine revisions from multiple copies. All revision marks are kept in both copies and remain attributed to the original reviewers.

Comparing with Legal Blackline

When you compare with legal blackline, all previous unresolved revision marks in the documents are accepted, and only the differences between the two documents appear as markup. The new markup is attributed to whomever you specify in the Label Changes With text box. Other than those two things, the process is nearly identical to that of combining, covered in the next section.

Follow these steps to compare two documents:

1. On the Review tab, click the Compare button, and then click Compare in the menu that appears. The Compare Documents dialog box opens, shown in Figure 20.13.

Click to Browse for Documents

Figure 20.13
Choose the two documents to compare.

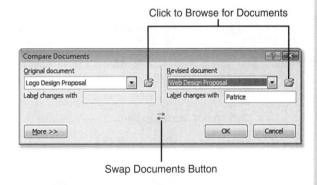

Swap Documents Button

2. Select one of the documents to compare from the Original Document drop-down list, or click the Browse button to browse for it.

3. Select the other document to compare from the Revised Document drop-down list, or click the Browse button to browse for it.

4. By default, the Label Unmarked Changes With setting is whatever username is set up in Word as the current user. Change the name if desired in the text box.

5. Optionally, click the More button and then set any of the following options, shown in Figure 20.14:

 note

It doesn't really matter which document you enter as original or revised since later in these steps you are able to specify where the revisions will be placed. If you get them in the opposite order than you want, though, you can easily swap their places by clicking the Swap Documents button.

- **Comparison Settings**—Clear the check boxes for any comparisons you want to omit. For example, you might not care about differences in whitespace or case changes.

- **Show Changes At**—By default, revisions are marked at the Word level, but you can set this to Character level if you prefer. (See the preceding sidebar for more information.)

- **Show Changes In**—Choose where the combined markup will appear. You can choose to place the revisions in the Original document, the Revised document, or a new document.

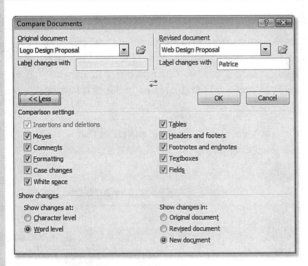

Figure 20.14
Advanced options for comparing documents.

6. Click the OK button to perform the combine operation.

7. Repeat the process if needed to combine additional documents with the newly combined one.

Combining Two or More Documents

To combine two or more documents, you combine them two at a time. In other words, you start with one and compare another to it, taking on the revisions from the second one. Then you compare that resulting version to a third, and that result to a fourth, and so on until all versions have been combined.

To combine documents, follow these steps:

1. On the Review tab, click the Compare button, and then click Combine in the menu that appears. The Combine Documents dialog box opens, which is nearly identical to the Compare Documents dialog box (refer to Figure 20.13).

2. Select one of the documents to combine from the Original Document drop-down list, or click the Browse button to browse for it.

3. Select the second document to combine from the Revised Document drop-down list, or click the Browse button to browse for it.

4. By default, the Label Unmarked Changes With setting is whatever username is set up in Word as the current user. Change the name if desired in either of the text boxes.

5. Optionally, click the More button and then set any of the following options, as shown in Figure 20.14:

> **note**
>
> Unmarked changes are differences between the two documents that are not currently marked with revision marks attributed to a particular reviewer.

- **Comparison Settings**—Clear the check boxes for any comparisons you want to omit. For example, you might not care about differences in whitespace or case changes.

- **Show Changes At**—By default, revisions are marked at the Word level, but you can set this to Character level if you prefer.

- **Show Changes In**—Choose where the combined markup will appear. You can choose to place the revisions in the Original document, the Revised document, or a new document.

6. Click the OK button to perform the combine operation.

7. Repeat the process if needed to combine additional documents with the newly combined one.

Understanding Character-Level Versus Word-Level Revisions

The default type of revision tracking operates at the Word level. That means if a word is even one letter different from another word, the entire word gets struck-through and replaced, like this:

~~differing~~different

Word-level revisions are easier to browse because most people read entire words at a time.

Character-level revisions, on the other hand, show revisions within the individual words. If not all the letters of the word change, not all are marked as changed:

Differ~~ing~~ent

Working in Full Screen Reading View

When reading a document onscreen, you might prefer to work in Full Screen Reading view (also called Reading Layout view). This view changes the pagination and layout of the document to make its text larger and more easily readable onscreen.

Full Screen Reading is not a suitable view for reviewing documents in which you must check for proper pagination and overall page attractiveness, because it flows the text and graphics into a custom two-column layout that has no relationship to the document's actual print layout. It excels, however, in situations where you need to read, highlight, and comment on the document. Figure 20.15 points out a few of its features.

Go to Previous Screen ―| |― Go to Next Screen

PARTNERSHIP AGREEMENT
of the
Dollar $ign Divas Investment Club

This AGREEMENT of PARTNERSHIP is made as of May 15, 2010 by and between the undersigned Partners.

I. Formation
The undersigned hereby form a General Partnership in, and in accordance with the laws of, the State of California.

II. Name
The name of the Partnership shall be Dollar $ign Divas.

III. Term
The Partnership shall begin on May 15, 2010 and shall continue until December 31 of the same year and thereafter from year to year unless earlier terminated as hereinafter provided.

IV. Purpose
The purpose of the Partnership shall be to invest the assets of the Partnership in stocks, bonds, and securities for the financial and educational benefit of the Partners, while employing fundamental principles and techniques of sound investment practices.

V. Meetings
Periodic meetings shall be held regularly as determined by the Partnership.

VI. Capital Contributions
The Partners will each make minimum monthly investments of $100 at regular monthly meetings. Partners may also make optional additional contributions in any $100 increment(s). Regular monthly contributions, normally collected at meetings, are due prior to the scheduled meeting in the case of any planned absence, or by the end of the third day after the meeting from anyone who was unable to attend that monthly meeting due to an emergency or illness. No Partner's capital account shall exceed twenty percent (20%) of the capital accounts of all Partners.

VII. Valuation of the Partnership
The current value of the assets of the Partnership, less the current value of the debts and liabilities of the Partnership (hereinafter referred to as the "value of the Partnership") shall be determined at a regularly scheduled date and time (hereinafter referred to as the "valuation date") preceding the date of each periodic meeting.

VIII. Capital Accounts
There shall be maintained a capital account in the name of each Partner. Any increase or decrease in the value of the Partnership on any valuation date shall be credited or debited, respectively, to each Partner's capital account on that date. Any other method of valuating

Figure 20.15
Full Screen Reading view works well when you're reviewing someone else's work.

To enter Full Screen Reading view, click the Full Screen Reading button at the bottom-right corner of the Word window, or click the Full Screen Reading button on the View tab.

To leave Full Screen Reading view, click the close (x) button in the upper-right corner of the Full Screen Reading display.

> **note**
> Don't like the two-column display in Full Screen Reading view? Switch to a single-column display by opening the View Options button's menu and clicking Show One Page.

Moving Between Screens

A *screen* in Full Screen Reading view is an onscreen page. By default, Word displays two pages at a time, side by side like in a book, as in Figure 20.15.

To move between screens, click the right and left arrow buttons at the top of the window, pointed out in Figure 20.15. Note that the left and right sides of the screen are considered different "screens," so in Figure 20.15, you are actually seeing screens 1 (left) and 2 (right).

To jump to a particular screen, heading, or other marker, click the screen number at the top of the window to display a Screen menu, shown as in Figure 20.16. You can also access the Go To and Find features from here.

Figure 20.16
Use the Screen menu to jump to a particular screen or heading in the document.

Using the Full Screen Reading Tools

Click the Tools button to open a menu (see Figure 20.17) from which you can select several of the most common Word features you might need while reading a document:

- **Research**—Opens the Research pane, and switches Full Screen Reading view to showing a single page at a time. From here you can use any of the research tools, covered in Chapter 3, "Correcting and Printing Documents."

- **Text Highlight Color**—This is the same as the Highlighter button on the toolbar, to the right of the Tools button. You can turn highlighting on/off and change the highlight color. See Chapter 4, "Applying Character Formatting," for details about highlighting.

- **New Comment**—This is the same as the New Comment button on the toolbar. It starts a new comment in a balloon (if comments are configured to appear that way) and switches to showing a single page at a time.

- **Find**—Opens the Find and Replace dialog box, which you can use to locate specific text strings, as you learned in Chapter 2, "Typing and Editing Text."

 tip

If you like seeing a single page at a time, see "Setting Reading View Options," later in this chapter, to make that the default.

Figure 20.17
The Tools menu provides quick access to popular tools for reading and revising documents.

Setting Reading View Options

The View Options button's menu in Full Screen Reading view, shown in Figure 20.18, is a rich source of viewing and editing options and features:

- **Don't Open Attachments in Full Screen**—When this is enabled, Word documents that come to you as email attachments and documents from SharePoint Services sites don't open in Full Screen Reading view by default.

- **Increase Text Size and Decrease Text Size**—These commands make the text larger and smaller, respectively, to help with readability. Graphics are not affected.

- **Show One Page and Show Two Pages**—These commands toggle between one-page and two-page viewing. A "page" in this context is the same as a "screen."

- **Show Printed Page**—When this option is enabled, the page borders appear.

- **Margin Settings**—When this option is enabled, the text runs all the way to the edges of each screen, making more text visible at once.

- **Allow Typing**—When this option is enabled, you can position the insertion point and edit text from within this view.

- **Track Changes**—Opens a submenu from which you can control revision tracking, so the edits you make (see Allow Typing) can be tracked or not, as desired.

- **Show Comments and Changes**—Enables you to toggle on/off individual types of changes.

- **Show Original/Final Document**—Opens a submenu from which you can choose whether to show revisions onscreen and whether to show the original or the revised version.

Figure 20.18
The View Options menu enables you to control the appearance and functionality of Full Screen Reading view.

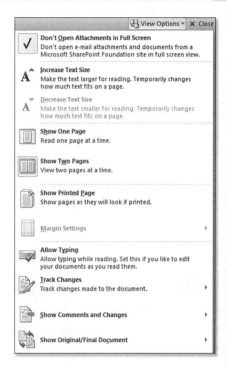

Using Microsoft Office Live Workspace

Microsoft Office Live Workspace (http://workspace.officelive.com) is a free web-based tool that offers online file sharing, storage, and collaboration. With Microsoft Office Live Workspace, you can do the following:

- Share up to 5GB of documents in your workspace.

- Collaborate on Microsoft Word, Excel, and PowerPoint documents.

- Maintain versions of your documents for future reference.

- View, edit, and share password-protected documents for added security.

At the time of this printing, Microsoft Office Live Workspace is in beta, and its features and appearance are subject to change.

What Is a Workspace?

A *workspace* is an area where a group of people can store and collaborate on related documents. You can control access to your workspace so that only certain people can view or edit workspace documents.

Controlling document access entails setting up permissions to the workspace so that users can only change documents in spaces they have been given permission to access. By controlling access, you limit unexpected document changes and deletions by those who shouldn't have access in the first place. At the same time, because you can set up read-only access to any area, those who need to see the documents can see them without changing them.

Another advantage to a workspace is that all finalized documents are stored in a common, consistent place, which in turn minimizes downtime. If one employee's computer goes down, documents stored on that computer can't be accessed by anyone until that computer is fixed. On the other hand, if documents are stored in a common workspace, access doesn't depend on a particular machine being down. Because the workspace is on the web, it is less likely to go down and cause problems.

Signing Up for Microsoft Office Live Workspace

To sign up for Microsoft Office Live Workspace, follow these steps:

1. Go to http://workspace.officelive.com, shown in Figure 20.19.

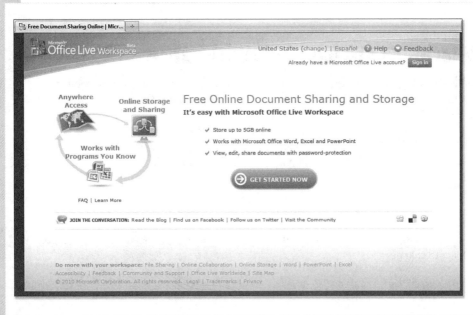

Figure 20.19
Set up a free collaborative workspace in a few minutes.

2. Click the Get Started Now button.

3. Enter your email address and click the Next button.

4. If your email is already used for other Microsoft online services, enter your Windows Live ID email address and your password. Click the Sign In button to continue.

5. If Microsoft doesn't recognize your email address, you're prompted to enter more detailed account information. Click the Finish button when you're done.

Figure 20.20 shows your initial Microsoft Office Live Workspace.

Figure 20.20
Microsoft Office
Live Workspace
offers a quick
three-step
process to get
started.

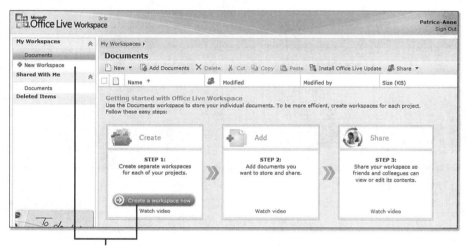

Click to Create a New Workspace

Creating Workspaces

Your Microsoft Office Live Workspace account can contain multiple workspaces and documents. To make it easier to access your content, it's a good idea to create a separate workspace for each of your projects.

To create a workspace, follow these steps:

1. In the Documents window, click the Create a Workspace Now button in the Step 1 box or click the New Workspace link. Figure 20.21 shows the Create a New Workspace pop-up box that opens.

2. Click the Blank Workspace link to create an empty workspace where you can upload your own documents. Alternatively, choose one of the workspace templates with sample documents and folders focused on a specific project type. For example, you can choose to create an Event Workspace, Meeting Workspace, or Project Workspace filled with starter documents.

Figure 20.22 shows an example of a workspace using the Project template.

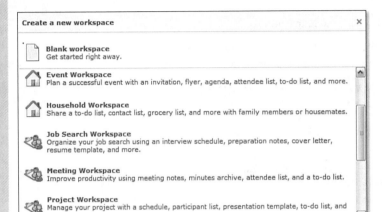

Figure 20.21
Create a workspace from scratch or start with a template.

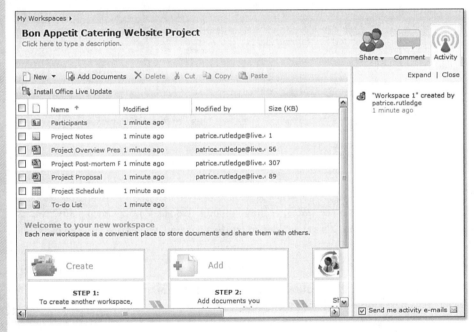

Figure 20.22
With a template, your workspace includes sample documents and folders.

Your workspace lists all available folders and documents, which you can double-click to open. In this window, you can create new lists, documents, and folders. You can also add, delete, cut, copy, and paste documents.

Note that if you choose to create a blank workspace, it will remain empty until you start adding your own folders and documents.

Adding Documents to Your Workspace

To upload your own documents to your workspace, open the workspace to which you want to add the document and click the Add Documents Now button in the Step 2 box or click the Add Documents button in the workspace menu bar.

In the Open dialog box that appears, navigate to the document you want to add and click the Open button. Your uploaded file appears in the list of files for that workspace (see Figure 20.23).

Figure 20.23
New documents you add to your workspace appear immediately in the document list.

New Uploaded Document

Sharing Workspaces

One of the benefits of using Microsoft Office Live Workspace is sharing and collaborating with your colleagues.

To share your workspace with others, follow these steps:

1. Open the workspace you want to share.

2. Click the Share This Workspace Now button in the Step 3 box or click the Share button in the upper-right corner of the screen and select Share Workspace from the menu. Figure 20.24 shows the Share Your Workspace section, which now appears at the top of your workspace.

3. Enter the email addresses of the individuals with whom you want to share your workspace. You can give them privileges as either editors or viewers depending on whether you want to allow them to actually change your documents.

4. Optionally, enter a message. If your recipients aren't aware that you're going to send them an invitation, it's a good idea to explain more about sharing your workspace.

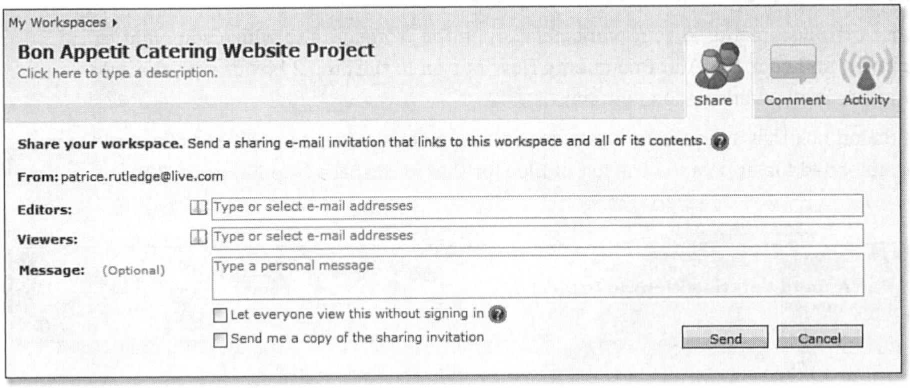

Figure 20.24 Choose to give colleagues editor or viewer access to your documents.

5. To allow recipients to view your workspace without logging in, click the Let Everyone View This Without Signing In check box. This is particularly useful if you want to give access to people outside your organization who might not want to sign up for an account to view documents.

6. Click the Send button.

Your recipients receive an email with a link inviting them to connect with you on your Microsoft Office Live Workspace.

Editing Documents in Your Workspace

To edit a Microsoft Word document in the workspace, open the workspace in which the document you want to edit is stored, and then double-click its name in the document list.

Figure 20.25 shows an open document. From this window, you can click any of the following buttons:

- **Edit**—Prompts you to run the Office Live Update, which installs the Microsoft Office Live Add-in. With this add-in, you can edit Microsoft Word, Excel, and PowerPoint in your online workspaces.
- **Save As**—Enables you to open your document or save it to your computer.

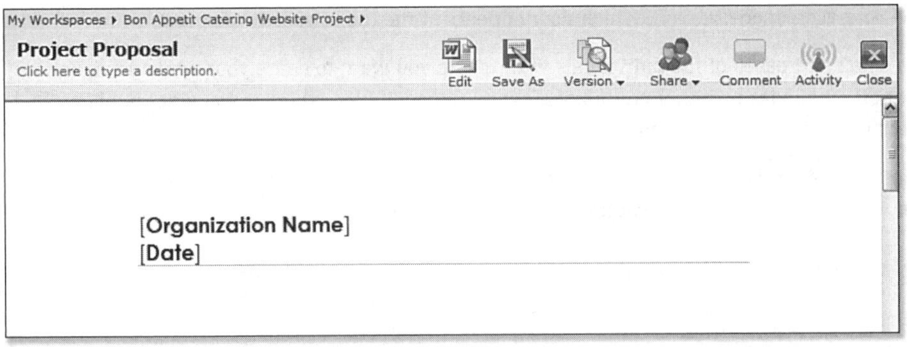

Figure 20.25 In this window, you can edit, share, version, save, or comment on a document.

- **Version**—Saves versions of your documents for future reference. Version control is particularly useful if you have numerous users making changes to a document and you want to track the changes they make. Or, you might want to track several versions of an important proposal or report. From this menu, you can save versions, add new document versions, or delete versions you no longer need.

- **Share**—Shares your workspace or screen with others. See "Sharing Workspaces," earlier in this chapter.

- **Comment**—Opens a box where you can enter a comment about the document.

- **Activity**—Opens a task pane that lists recent activity for this document.

- **Close**—Closes the window and returns to the main workspace.

Managing Workspaces

On the left side of your Microsoft Office Live Workspace screen, you can view a list of your workspaces in the My Workspaces section. To manage a particular workspace, pause the mouse over it to open a pop-up box, shown in Figure 20.26.

Figure 20.26
Manage your workspace from this easy-to-access pop-up box.

In this box, you can click any of the following links:

- **Edit Profile**—Edits the profile of the workspace owner.

- **Open**—Opens the workspace.

- **Share**—Enables you to enter the email addresses of the editors and viewers you want to invite to this workspace.

- **Rename**—Renames the workspace title.

- **Hide**—Hides the workspace from the My Workspaces section, but it doesn't delete it. To show the workspace again, click the My Workspaces link, select the check box before the workspace in the list, and click the Show button.

- **Delete**—Deletes the workspace and places it in the Deleted Items folder. Click the Deleted Items link to access this folder, where you can restore deleted items or empty all items from the folder permanently.

Collaborating with SkyDrive

SkyDrive, located at http://skydrive.live.com, is another collaboration option for Office 2010 users. Word 2010 enables you to save documents directly to SkyDrive, which offers up to 25GB of free online storage that you can use to collaborate with colleagues anywhere in the world. Be aware that as a web application, the features and appearance of SkyDrive are subject to change.

> **note**
>
> If you're looking for more storage space, SkyDrive is a good alternative to Microsoft Office Live Workspace. Be aware, however, that SkyDrive doesn't offer a versioning feature.

SkyDrive is part of Windows Live and requires a Windows Live ID to access. If you have an existing account with another Windows Live application such as Hotmail or Messenger, you already have a Windows Live ID. If you don't, you can sign up for a free Windows Live ID.

Setting Up SkyDrive

To set up SkyDrive, go to http://skydrive.live.com (see Figure 20.27), click the Sign In link, and enter your Windows Live ID. If you don't have an ID, sign up for a free account by clicking the Sign Up button.

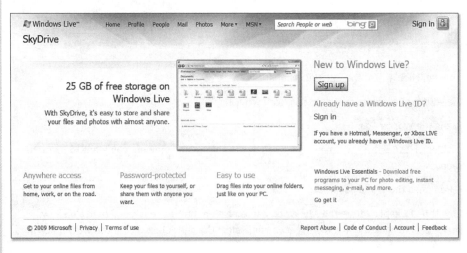

Figure 20.27
Signing up for SkyDrive takes only a few minutes.

On SkyDrive (see Figure 20.28), you can do the following:

- Create new folders by selecting Folder from the New drop-down menu. You can share folders with everyone (a public folder), only people in your network, or selected people you have provided access to. Alternatively, you can make your folder private so that only you can access it.

- Add files to your folders by clicking the Add Files link. From here, you can browse your computer and select the files you want to upload. You can upload files up to 50MB each.

Figure 20.28
Upload up to 25GB of documents to share with your network.

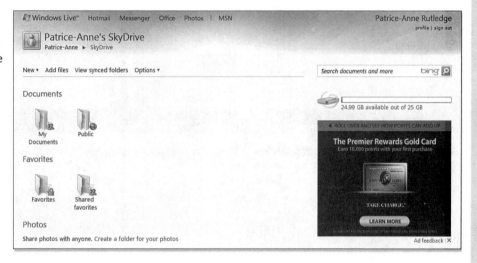

- View synced folders that you synchronized with Windows Live Sync. If you haven't synchronized files yet, you can download and install Sync on your computer.

- Open individual documents by clicking a folder icon and then clicking the document's icon. See the next section, "Working with Documents in SkyDrive," for more information.

- View your available storage in the upper-right corner of the screen.

Working with Documents in SkyDrive

Figure 20.29 shows the document window where you can view and edit a Word document in the Microsoft Word Web App as well as download, delete, move, copy, and rename documents. See "Collaborating with Microsoft Office Web Apps" later in this chapter for more information.

As a reminder, you can open a document by clicking its folder icon in the main SkyDrive window and then clicking the document icon.

 caution

SkyDrive doesn't have version control. If you require the ability to manage multiple versions of your files, consider Microsoft Office Live Workspace or SharePoint.

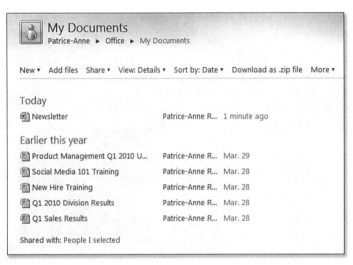

Figure 20.29
You can edit, comment on, and share documents in SkyDrive.

You can also add comments about the document or view comments made by others in your network. If you want to provide direct access to a document, send that person the URL in the Web Address field. Remember that anyone accessing this URL needs a Windows Live ID.

Saving to SkyDrive from Microsoft Word

You can also upload documents to SkyDrive directly from Microsoft Word. You must have a Windows Live ID and SkyDrive account to do so.

To save from Word, follow these steps:

1. Click the File tab and select Save & Send. In Backstage View, click Save to Web (see Figure 20.30).

Figure 20.30
Save directly to SkyDrive from Microsoft Word.

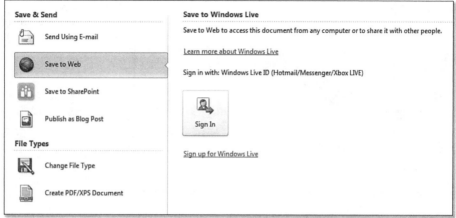

2. On the right side of the screen, click the Sign In button to open the Connecting to docs.live.net dialog box, shown in Figure 20.31.

Figure 20.31
Enter your Windows Live ID email and password to access SkyDrive.

3. Enter your Windows Live ID email address and password and click the OK button. Your SkyDrive information appears on the right side of the screen (see Figure 20.32).

 tip

Click the New Folder button to create a new folder. (The actual SkyDrive site opens.)

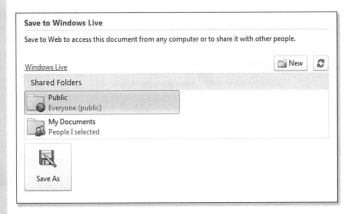

Figure 20.32
Choose the folder where you want to upload your Word document.

4. Select the folder where you want to save your document and click the Save As button.

5. In the Save As dialog box, enter a filename and click the Save button.

Coauthoring in Microsoft Word

Coauthoring is a new Office 2010 feature that enables you to work on the same document simultaneously with other colleagues no matter where they're located. You can also easily identify changes and who is making them. Coauthoring is available for Word, PowerPoint, and OneNote as well as the Excel web app and requires either Microsoft SharePoint Foundation 2010 or a SkyDrive account accessed with your Windows Live ID.

Coauthoring offers a distinct advantage over sending documents to multiple people for review and then consolidating their feedback into one master document. It also enables everyone collaborating on a document to view the content, changes, and feedback that others have provided in real time.

Other Ways to Collaborate in Microsoft Word 2010

Depending on what additional technologies your company chooses to deploy and the extensions to Microsoft Office 2010 you use, there are even more ways to collaborate on Word documents.

Collaborating with Microsoft SharePoint Workspace 2010

If you have Microsoft Office Professional Plus 2010 installed, your Office suite includes Microsoft SharePoint Workspace 2010, formerly called Microsoft Office Groove. This application is the desktop client for Microsoft SharePoint Server 2010, Microsoft's online collaboration platform.

Whereas companies of any size can easily use Microsoft Office Live Workspace or SkyDrive for collaboration, SharePoint allows larger companies to maintain their document controls, communications, and team services on a system they control. SharePoint servers are generally located in enterprise environments. These companies have a dedicated IT staff responsible for maintaining, backing up, and controlling access to the server containing the company information. Unlike Office Live Workspace or SkyDrive, a corporate IT staff normally installs and maintains SharePoint and provides access to specific individuals within your company.

SharePoint Workspace 2010 enables you to perform the following collaboration tasks:

- Work simultaneously on your Word documents with colleagues in multiple locations using Office 2010's new coauthoring feature. See "Coauthoring in Microsoft Word," earlier in this chapter, for more information.

- Check in and check out files, allowing you to securely access and review documents stored on the server.

- Create local SharePoint workspaces to collaborate on documents without access to SharePoint Server.

- Access Microsoft Office Web Apps such as the Microsoft Word Web App.

- Save to SharePoint from within Microsoft Word. To do so, click the File tab, select Share, and click Save to SharePoint (see Figure 20.33).

Figure 20.33
Access
SharePoint
directly from
Microsoft Word.

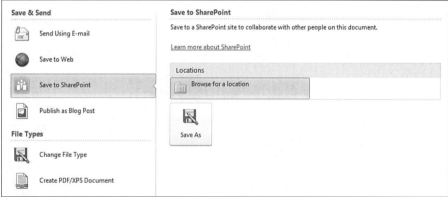

Collaborating with Microsoft Office Web Apps

Microsoft Office Web Apps are free online applications that enable you to view and perform basic editing tasks on your Word, Excel, PowerPoint, and OneNote documents. You can access Web Apps through a web browser (Microsoft Internet Explorer, Safari, or Mozilla Firefox) on either a PC or a Mac—even one that doesn't have Microsoft Office installed on it. Access to Web Apps requires Windows Live SkyDrive or SharePoint Workspace 2010. See "Collaborating with SkyDrive" earlier in this chapter for more information.

You can also access Microsoft Office Web Apps through a Smartphone. See the next section, "Collaborating with Microsoft Word Mobile 2010."

Collaborating with Microsoft Word Mobile 2010

Microsoft Office Mobile 2010 offers mobile versions of Word, Excel, PowerPoint, OneNote, Outlook, and SharePoint Workspace. It's a separate product from Microsoft Office 2010 and doesn't come with any of the Office versions. Using SharePoint Workspace Mobile, you can view and edit documents in Word Mobile and sync them back to SharePoint for collaboration on the go.

Collaborating with Microsoft Office Communications Server 2007 R2

Part of Microsoft Office Professional Plus 2010, Microsoft Office Communicator Server 2007 R2 (there is no 2010 version) furthers Office 2010 collaboration by integrating instant messaging, video conferencing, telephony, application sharing, and file transfer.

If your company deploys this technology, you'll be able to share your desktop instantly while coauthoring with a colleague anywhere in the world or start an instant messaging session with this person.

PROTECTING AND SECURING DOCUMENTS

Understanding Document Protection

As you create, edit, and manage documents, you might not always want everyone who has access to the drive to be able to open and modify all documents. Word 2010 offers a variety of ways of protecting documents. They break down into these areas:

- **Restricting access to the document entirely**—This includes using Windows file encryption, setting network access permissions, and placing a password on the file in Word.

- **Restricting what users can do to a file**—This includes restricting style usage and editing and preventing users from turning off revision marks, as well as setting a document to be read-only.

- **Marking a document as finalized**—You can mark a document as Final and add a digital signature to it to confirm that it has not been changed since being marked as such.

- **Preventing macro-based attacks**—To avoid macro viruses, you can choose to use macro-enabled file formats only when necessary, and you can set up trusted locations in which to store macro-enabled files. Files not in those trusted locations can then have higher macro security levels.

- **Protecting your privacy**—This includes removing personally identifying information from the file, such as the author name and keywords; controlling when Word does or does not go online to retrieve extra content; and participating (or not) in the Customer Experience Improvement program.

This chapter looks at each of these types of protection.

Restricting Access to a Document

The most basic type of protection for a document is to prevent others from accessing it entirely. You can do this in several ways. You can put a password on the file within Word itself, you can locally encrypt the location in which it is stored, or you can remove network access to the location.

Password-Protecting a Document in Word

You can put two separate passwords on a file: one to open it and one to modify it. That way you can give one password to certain people and the other password to others, depending on what you want them to be able to do with it. (You can also set more complex editing permissions, as you'll learn later in this chapter.)

When you password-protect a document against being opened in Word, Word encrypts it internally, and the encryption can only be decrypted by entering the correct password. This is important because then someone using a text editor outside of Word cannot browse the protected file. Password protection does not simply prevent the file from opening in Word; it actually changes the file.

When you password-protect the file against changes being saved to it, the file is not encrypted. That password simply prevents it from being saved; someone can still go into the file with a text editor and look at it (or with Word itself for that matter).

Saving with a Password

To password-protect a file, follow these steps:

1. Choose File, Save As. The Save As dialog box opens.

2. In the Save As dialog box, click Tools and choose General Options. The General Options dialog box opens (see Figure 21.1).

3. (Optional) In the Password to Open box, type a password. Passwords can be up to 15 characters long.

4. (Optional) In the Password to Modify box, type a different password. You can use one or both passwords, but if you use both, they must be different.

5. Click OK. A Confirm Password dialog box opens.

 tip

For best security, use passwords that combine lowercase and uppercase letters, numbers, and symbols.

 note

The Read-Only Recommended check box does not enforce anything; it simply opens the document by giving the user a choice of read-only or not. It is not related to password protection, even though it is in the same dialog box as the passwords.

6. Retype the password and click OK.

7. In the Save As dialog box, click Save to save the file with the password.

Figure 21.1
While saving, set a password for the file in its General Options dialog box.

Removing a Password from a File

To remove a password from a file, you must open the file, so you have to know the password. Assuming you do, here's how to remove it:

1. Choose File, Save As. The Save As dialog box opens.

2. In the Save As dialog box, click Tools and choose General Options. The General Options dialog box opens (refer to Figure 21.1).

3. Clear the password boxes. (Select the current password and press Delete.)

4. Click OK.

5. Click Save to save the file without the password.

Using Windows Encryption

If you have a drive that uses the NTFS file system under Windows 2000 or higher, you can encrypt folders so that anything you put in those folders is accessible only to the currently logged-in user.

Windows NTFS encryption is designed to prevent multiple people who share the same physical PC from accessing each other's private files. It does not prevent people accessing your PC via the network from accessing the files, as long as you are logged in as you and are sharing them.

You can encrypt individual files, but it is better to encrypt an entire folder and then place the files into it that you want to protect. Any files in an encrypted folder are automatically encrypted; when you move or copy them outside that encrypted location, they become decrypted. As long as you are logged in as the user who encrypted the folder, the encryption is invisible and unobtrusive. Encrypted folders can hold any files, not just Word documents, of course.

Encrypting a Folder

Some companies have very robust encryption systems for their files, including Windows BitLocker (included in some versions of Windows Vista and Windows 7) and USB hardware keys. For the average user, however, Windows encryption is more than adequate for preventing unauthorized access to files and folders.

To encrypt a folder in Windows XP or higher, follow these steps:

1. In any file management window (such as Windows Explorer), right-click the folder and choose Properties. The Properties dialog box opens.

2. On the General tab, click Advanced. The Advanced Attributes dialog box opens (see Figure 21.2).

3. Mark the Encrypt Contents to Secure Data check box.

4. Click OK.

5. Click OK again. A Confirm Attribute Change dialog box opens.

6. Click the way you want the encryption to apply:

   - Apply changes to this folder only.

   - Apply changes to this folder, subfolders, and files.

7. Click OK. The folder's name turns green in the file listing.

Figure 21.2
Encrypt a folder on your hard disk in which to store private files.

I Don't Have Permission to Encrypt or Decrypt a Folder

In Windows Vista and Windows 7, you must be logged in with administrative privileges to encrypt or decrypt folders. Even if you are, you might still see a warning box saying you do not have permission. Click Continue in that box, and Windows lets you finish the operation. If that doesn't work, log out from the Start menu and log back in as a user with greater privileges.

Decrypting a Folder

To decrypt a file within an encrypted folder, simply move or copy it somewhere else. You do not have to decrypt the entire folder just to decrypt the file.

If you do want to decrypt the entire folder, however, here's how:

1. In any file management window (such as Windows Explorer), right-click the folder and choose Properties. The Properties dialog box opens.

   You can tell an encrypted folder because its name appears in green.

2. On the General tab, click Advanced. The Advanced Attributes dialog box opens (refer to Figure 21.2).

3. Clear the Encrypt Contents to Secure Data check box.

4. Click OK.

5. Click OK again. A Confirm Attribute Change dialog box opens.

6. Click the way you want the decryption to apply:

   - Apply changes to this folder only.

   - Apply changes to this folder, subfolders, and files.

7. Click OK. The folder's name turns from green back to black in the file listing.

Removing Network Share Permission for a Location

If your PC is connected to a network, you can share certain folders with others on the network. One way to prevent someone from accessing a file is to remove the share permission for that folder so that people can no longer browse that location.

To check to see if a location is shared, and to remove sharing from it if needed, follow these steps from Windows 7:

1. From a file management window (such as Windows Explorer), right-click the folder and point to Share With.

2. Click Nobody.

From Windows Vista:

1. From a file management window (such as Windows Explorer), right-click the folder and choose Properties. The Properties dialog box opens.

2. Click the Sharing tab. If there is a path in the Network Path section, the folder is being shared.

3. To unshare it, click the Share button. A File Sharing dialog box opens.

4. Click Stop Sharing.

5. Click Done.

From Windows XP:

1. From a file management window (such as Windows Explorer), right-click the folder and choose Sharing and Security. The Properties dialog box opens with the Sharing tab displayed.

2. Clear the Share This Folder on the Network check box.

3. Click OK.

Restricting What Users Can Do to a Document

In addition to preventing access completely to a document, you can restrict what a user can do to it. As you saw earlier in the chapter, you can assign a password to modify the document, effectively making it read-only if the person does not know the password. There are other ways to restrict the document as well.

Recommending Read-Only

You can make the document read-only in general, unrelated to a password for modification, and you can make this restriction optional or required.

Look back at Figure 21.1; notice the Read-Only Recommended check box. When this is marked, each time the document is opened, a message appears asking if you want to open it as read-only. This gives the user the option of read-only, which prevents accidental changes from being saved to the original. If the users choose to allow the read-only attribute to be enabled, they can still modify the document onscreen, but they cannot save their changes to overwrite the original file.

Making the Document File Read-Only

You can also make a document read-only from outside of Word by setting the file's properties to read-only. There's no way to lock this on, so someone who is determined to make changes to the file can go into the properties and turn off the read-only attribute, but it does provide a layer of annoyance that slows people down from making changes and might prevent an inexperienced user from making them.

To make a document read-only from Windows, follow these steps:

1. From a file-management window, such as Windows Explorer, right-click the file and choose Properties. The Properties dialog box opens for that file.

2. On the General tab, mark the Read-Only check box (see Figure 21.3).

3. Click OK.

Figure 21.3
Set a file's properties to read-only from Windows.

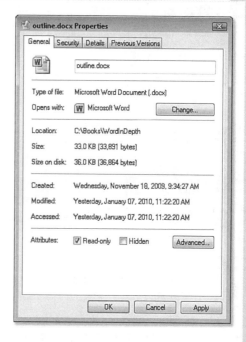

Setting a Read-Only Editing Restriction

In addition to protecting the document at a file level, you can protect it from inside Word by applying editing restrictions.

When you set a document to be read-only via editing restrictions, not only can people not *save* changes to it, but they can't *make* changes to it. You can put a password on that protection if desired, or you can leave it open so that people who know how to manage document protection settings can override it.

Follow these steps to prevent document editing:

1. On the Review tab, click Restrict Editing. The Restrict Formatting and Editing task pane appears.

2. In the Editing Restrictions section, mark the Allow Only This Type of Editing in the Document check box.

3. Open the drop-down list and choose No Changes (Read Only), as shown in Figure 21.4.

Figure 21.4
Set the document to be read-only.

4. Click Yes, Start Enforcing Protection. The Start Enforcing Protection dialog box opens (see Figure 21.5).

5. (Optional) If you don't want users to be able to disable the read-only status, enter a password in the Enter New Password (Optional) box, and then repeat it in the Reenter Password to Confirm box.

   If you omit the password, anyone can override the document's read-only status from the Protect Document task pane.

6. Click OK.

Figure 21.5
If you want, enforce the read-only status with a password.

Restricting a Document to Comments Only

You can set a document's editing restrictions so that users can enter comments (with the New Comment button on the Review tab) but otherwise cannot edit the document. To do this, follow the steps in "Setting a Read-Only Editing Restriction," but instead of choosing No Changes in step 3, choose Comments.

➡ *To learn more about comments, see "Working with Comments," p. 762.*

Restricting a Document to Form Fill-In Only

You can set a document's editing restrictions so that form fields can be filled in, but otherwise no changes can be made. Follow the steps in "Setting a Read-Only Editing Restriction," but in step 3 choose Filling In Forms.

➡ *To learn how to create forms to fill out onscreen, see Chapter 16, "Working with Fields and Forms."*

Forcing Revision Marks to Stay On

When you use revision marks to track changes, anyone editing the document can turn them off and thereby hide the changes they are making. To prevent this, you can set the editing restriction so that changes are permanently tracked on and can't be turned off without knowing the password.

To force revisions to stay on, follow the steps in "Setting a Read-Only Editing Restriction," but in step 3, choose Tracked Changes.

➡ *To learn how to track changes and accept/reject revisions, see "Using Revision Tracking," p. 764.*

Restricting Style Usage

If you are collaborating with others on a document, it might be important that only certain styles be used for formatting. For example, as I was writing this book, I used a template in which the editor had assigned certain styles for certain types of paragraphs, and I was not supposed to create any new styles. If you trust people not to create new styles, great, but if you don't, you might want to lock down the document so that styles are limited to a certain set you define.

To restrict style usage, follow these steps:

1. On the Review tab, click Restrict Editing. The Restrict Formatting and Editing task pane displays.

2. Mark the Limit Formatting to a Selection of Styles check box.

3. Click the Settings hyperlink. The Formatting Restrictions dialog box opens (see Figure 21.6).

4. Ensure that the check boxes are marked for the styles you want to allow and cleared for the styles you do not.

   You can get a head start by clicking All or None, or Recommended Minimum to get a whittled-down list that Microsoft recommends.

5. (Optional) Mark any of these check boxes:

   - **Allow AutoFormat to Override Formatting Restrictions**—When this is enabled, AutoFormat can apply styles even if you have not selected them in the list in step 4.

   - **Block Theme or Scheme Switching**—When this is enabled, users cannot apply different document themes (for example, from the Page Layout tab).

   - **Block Quick Style Set Switching**—When this is enabled, users cannot use the Change Styles feature on the Home tab to switch style sets.

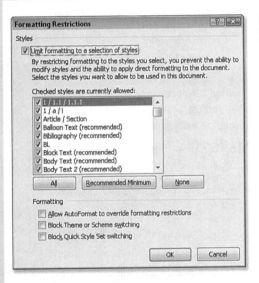

Figure 21.6
Restrict style usage to the styles you specify.

6. Click OK to accept the settings. A warning appears asking whether you want to remove unallowed style usage from the document. Click Yes or No.

7. Click Yes, Start Enforcing Protection in the Protect Document task pane to turn protection on.

Setting Up Per-User Exceptions to Restrictions

You can set up the restrictions on a document so that they do not apply to certain users. To do this for groups (if groups are defined), mark the check box next to the desired group in the Exceptions section of the Restrict Formatting and Editing task pane.

If there is not a group set up that represents the users to be excluded from restrictions, you can manually set up the individual usernames. To do this, click the More Users hyperlink in the Restrict Formatting and Editing task pane, opening the Add Users dialog box (see Figure 21.7).

Figure 21.7
Specify users to whom the restrictions should not apply.

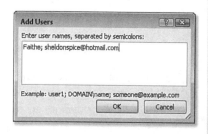

Then enter the users, separating the names with semicolons. You can use any of the following nomenclatures:

- **Username**—For local users on this PC, enter the names by which they log in.

- **Email addresses**—For email recipients, enter their email addresses.

- **Domain usernames**—For network domains, enter the domain name, a slash (\), and the username, like this: *Domain\user*.

After you enter the names and click OK, Word attempts to verify the names and addresses. (It does not really verify email addresses; it just checks them for correct form.) Names that are verified appear in an Individuals section in the task pane; you can then mark their check boxes there to select them (see Figure 21.8). (They are not selected simply because you entered them in the Add Names dialog box; selecting their check box is a necessary separate step.)

Figure 21.8
Users you add appear in the Individuals section.

Marking a Document as Final

A finalized document is read-only, and when it is being viewed, some features in Word are not available. When users try to edit it, they see a message in the status bar that the document is final.

To mark a document as final, follow these steps:

1. Choose File, Info.

2. Click the Protect Document button. A menu opens.

3. Click Mark as Final.

4. Click OK.

5. A confirmation appears; click OK.

This is not a security feature; anyone who receives an electronic copy of it can simply turn off the Mark as Final attribute by repeating steps 1-4. It is merely a way to designate a document so that no *inadvertent* changes are made to it.

Preventing Macro-Based Attacks

Macro viruses were prevalent a decade or so ago. A macro virus would travel along with a document and infect the Normal.dot template, causing various mischief in the program. One common result of macro virus infection, for example, was that any time you tried to save a file, it would save as a template (.dot) rather than a document (.doc). Macro viruses are no longer common, due mostly to the fact that Microsoft aggressively implemented macro virus protection in later versions of Word. (Excel was also vulnerable to some macro viruses.)

Word 2010 has good protection against macro viruses, taking a multiprong approach to preventing them from doing damage.

Choosing Nonmacro File Formats

The most basic way to protect against macro viruses is to use a file format that does not support viruses. Word 2010 offers two document formats: The regular .dotx does not support macros, and the macro-enabled .dotm does. When you do not need macro capability, use .dotx.

Specifying Trusted Locations

In Word 2010, macros are allowed to run in a macro-enabled document or template—or not—based on the location of the file. You can set up certain locations to be trusted; then whatever files you put in that location automatically have full macro-running privileges.

The following folders are trusted by default under Windows Vista and Windows 7:

> Program Files\Microsoft Office\Templates
> Users*username*\AppData\Roaming\Microsoft\Word\Startup
> Users*username*\AppData\Roaming\Microsoft\Templates

In Windows XP, the last two folders in this list are

> Documents and Settings*username*\Application Data\Microsoft\Startup
> Documents and Settings*username*\Application Data\Microsoft\Templates

To set up additional trusted locations, follow these steps:

1. Choose File, Options. The Word Options dialog box appears.

2. Click Trust Center.

3. Click the Trust Center Settings button. A separate Trust Center dialog box appears.

4. Click Trusted Locations (see Figure 21.9).

5. Click Add New Location.

6. Click the Browse button and browse to the desired location; then click OK.

7. If desired, mark the Subfolders of This Location Are Also Trusted check box (see Figure 21.10).

8. Click OK.

Figure 21.9
View and add trusted locations.

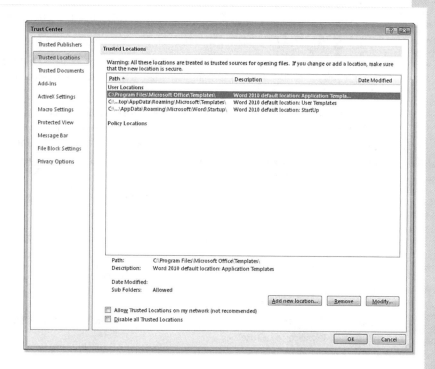

Figure 21.10
Create a new trusted location.

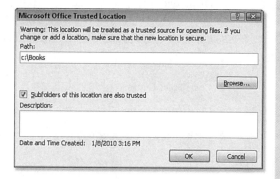

Other settings that you can optionally use for trusted locations (refer to Figure 21.9) are as follows:

- **Allow Trusted Locations on My Network**—Enables you to add trusted locations that exist other than on your local PC.

- **Disable All Trusted Locations**—Just what the name says. Only files signed by trusted publishers are trusted. (You'll learn about trusted publishers in the next section.)

- **Remove**—Removes a trusted location from the list.

- **Modify**—Opens the Microsoft Office Trusted Location dialog box.

Working with Trusted Publishers

Another way to trust a macro is to verify that it comes from a trusted publisher. Macro settings enable you to specify what should happen when a macro from a trusted publisher wants to run outside of a trusted location.

When you open a document that includes one or more signed macros, Word prompts you as to whether you want to trust macros from that signer. Information about the signer's certificate appears, including the name, the issuing authority, and the valid dates. If you choose Yes, that signer is added to your Trusted Publishers list. If this hasn't occurred yet, your Trusted Publishers list is blank in the Trust Center dialog box.

To view the Trusted Publishers list, follow these steps:

1. Choose File, Options.

2. Click Trust Center.

3. Click the Trust Center Settings button.

4. Click Trusted Publishers.

If you have a trusted publisher on your list, you can select it and then click View to view its information or Remove to untrust it.

Adjusting Macro Settings

Macro settings apply only to macros that are stored in presentations, not in trusted locations. They determine whether the macro should run and whether you should receive notification.

Follow these steps to get to the macro settings and to change them if desired:

1. Choose File, Options.

2. Click Trust Center.

3. Click Trust Center Settings. The Trust Center dialog box opens.

4. Click Macro Settings (see Figure 21.11).

5. Select the macro setting that best describes what should happen when a macro tries to run outside of a trusted location.

6. Click OK on both open dialog boxes.

Figure 21.11
Adjust macro settings for locations other than trusted locations.

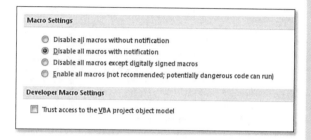

Configuring Protected View and File Blocking

Protected View is a new security feature in Word 2010 that automatically blocks certain types of files from being opened or edited, in case they contain content that might harm your computer. This includes not only macro content, but other types of active content, too. Protected View offers even more comprehensive protection than macro blocking.

Perhaps you have noticed that when you open a Word document that originated from the Internet (such as from an email attachment), Word opens the document in Protected View by default. The Ribbon does not appear, and you cannot edit the document until you turn off Protected View by clicking the Enable Editing button, as shown in Figure 21.12.

Figure 21.12
Protected View prevents the document from being edited and prevents the Ribbon from appearing.

To control Protected View's settings, follow these steps:

1. Choose File, Options.

2. Click Trust Center.

3. Click Trust Center Settings. The Trust Center dialog box opens.

4. Click Protected View.

5. Mark or clear check boxes to control what types of documents open in Protected View by default. See Figure 21.13.

6. Click OK.

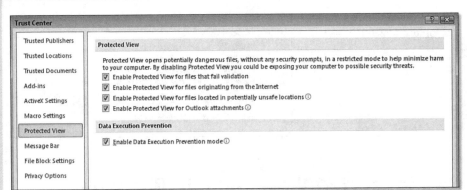

Figure 21.13
You can clear certain check boxes to allow Word to open documents normally instead of in Protected View.

You can also block certain files from opening, or open them in Protected View, based on their file type. This allows you to specify that certain file types, such as those that were generated in older versions of Word, be opened in Protected View regardless of whether they originated from a trusted location. Files from Word 6.0 and Word 95, for example, are commonly set to be blocked by default because they were generated in versions of Word that lacked macro virus protection.

To block certain file types, follow these steps:

1. Choose File, Options.

2. Click Trust Center.

3. Click Trust Center Settings. The Trust Center dialog box opens.

4. Click File Block Settings.

5. Mark or clear check boxes for file types you want to block. See Figure 21.14.

6. At the bottom of the dialog box, specify what you want Word to do with files that match the specifications you chose in step 5.

7. Click OK.

Figure 21.14
Configure file blocking to prevent certain file types from opening without protection.

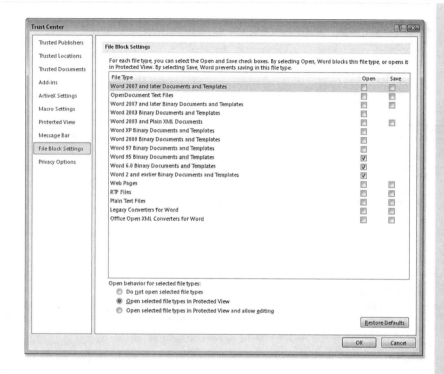

Protecting Your Privacy

When you distribute a Word document or make it available to others, a certain amount of personal information about its author travels along with it. This can include properties, headers and footers that you might have neglected to remove, comments, revisions, and other items. You can see that information, and remove it, in Word 2010.

Finding and Removing Personal Information

Inspecting a document shows you all the hidden and less-obvious pieces of personal information that might potentially travel along with a document so that you can remove them if desired.

To inspect a document, follow these steps:

1. Choose File, Info, Check for Issues, Inspect Document. If prompted to save your document, click Yes. The Document Inspector dialog box opens (see Figure 21.15).

2. Clear the check boxes for any content you do not want to check for.

3. Click Inspect. Results appear, as in Figure 21.16. For each type of content found, a Remove All button appears.

4. Click Remove All to remove a type of content.

5. When finished, click Reinspect or click Close.

Figure 21.15
Select the items you want to inspect.

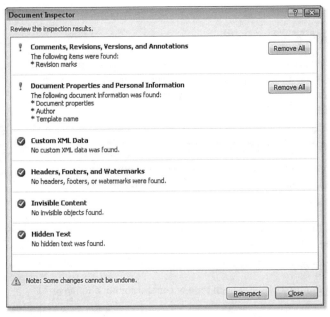

Figure 21.16
View the results of the inspection.

Setting Privacy Options

In the Trust Center's Privacy Options section are a number of settings that control how much—or little—information is sent over the Internet and with documents. You can also access the Document Inspector from there, which you used in the preceding section.

To access the privacy options, follow these steps:

1. Choose File, Options.

2. Click Trust Center.

3. Click the Trust Center Settings button. The Trust Center dialog box opens.

4. Click Privacy Options.

5. Mark or clear the check boxes for the desired options. See Figure 21.17.

6. Click OK on both open dialog boxes.

 tip

Some of the options have i symbols next to them, indicating that more information is available. Point to one of those symbols to get help on that option.

Figure 21.17
Set privacy options.

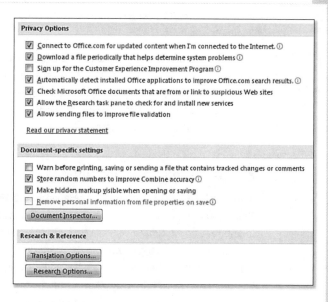

Adding a Digital Signature

Digital signatures are certifications of a document's authenticity. When sending legal or other important documents online, a digital signature can provide some measure of certainty that a document has actually come from its purported source and has not been altered since it was sent.

You can get a certificate from a certificate authority, a third-party service online, but this is not free. (It costs around $370 for secure2trust, for example.)

To find out about third-party certificates, choose File, Info, Protect Document, Add a Digital Signature, and then click Signature Services from the Office Marketplace.

You can also self-certify a document, but this is not all that secure and carries no legal authority. If you want to practice using digital signatures, though, a self-certificate does work.

To add a digital signature to a document, follow these steps:

1. Choose File, Info, Protect Document, Add a Digital Signature.

2. If you do not have a third-party signature file installed, a dialog box appears warning of that and offering to either take you to the Office Marketplace or continue. Click OK to continue.

3. In the Sign dialog box, type a description of why you are signing the document. For example, if you are approving it, you might write that.

4. If your correct name does not appear in the Signing As box, click Change and change the name.

5. Click Sign. A message appears that your signature has been added.

6. Click OK.

7. Click the Home tab, or any other tab, to return to the document. An information bar appears across the top, indicating that the document has been marked as final. (Signed documents are also marked as final.)

If you need to edit the document, click the Edit Anyway button on the information bar. This removes the signature and makes the document editable again.

To review the signatures, choose File, Info, View Signatures. A Signatures pane appears to the right of the document. In it, you can see the signatures that have been added to the document. (Multiple people may have signed it.)

Why Is My Signature Invalid?

If you sign a document without using a signature service, the signature is considered "invalid." That is not a reflection on the person signing it; it just means that the signature cannot be guaranteed as legitimate because no signature authority service was used. Signatures that are invalid are marked as such both in the signatures pane and on the File menu, next to the View Signatures button. Depending on what you are using the signing feature for, it may or may not be important to you that a signature is marked as invalid. If it is important that signatures be guaranteed, sign up for a signature service via Microsoft Marketplace.

DEVELOPING ONLINE-DELIVERED CONTENT

Web Page Development: Word's Strengths and Weaknesses

Word 2010 is a viable choice for the nonprofessional web designer who may be already familiar with Word but reluctant to learn a new application. Using Word, even people with no HTML programming language experience can create basic web pages with ease. However, Word lacks most of the high-end web design features of an application such as Microsoft Expression Web or Macromedia Dreamweaver, so someone who does web design for a living would likely not choose Word for that work.

Word makes web design easy by shielding the user from the raw coding, instead allowing the user to work in a familiar WYSIWYG (what you see is what you get) environment in which formatting can be applied with toolbar buttons and menu commands. Then when the document is saved, Word converts all that formatting to HTML coding that web browser applications can understand.

Web Technologies Supported in Word

Word 2010 is similar to earlier Word versions in its web design features. It supports all the basic HTML codes that you would expect for formatting, plus several other technologies, scripting languages, and supplemental HTML code.

Word supports all these types of web content:

- **HTML**—Hypertext Markup Language is the language of the World Wide Web. Almost every web page is built with this language. HTML, a simple formatting and organizational language, is ideal for the display of text, simple graphics, and hyperlinks. It doesn't do anything fancy like search a database or display pop-up dialog boxes. The appeal of HTML lies in its ease of use and universal acceptance.

- **CSS**—Cascading style sheets are used to define the layout of a document precisely. Style sheets are more powerful than the styles found in Word because they can also specify page layout. A style sheet can be a separate document, or it can be embedded in each HTML page. Because browsers have different capabilities in the way they interpret these styles, they interpret what they can and ignore the rest; that is, they cascade down in their interpretation and display what they are able to.

- **XML**—eXtensible Markup Language is more robust and extensible (hence its name) than HTML. You can define new tags and their uses at any time and in any way by referencing them in an associated text document. The strength of XML is its capability to use these new tags to identify specific information. This technology vastly improves the users' abilities to find specific-subject web pages and opens up the Internet to even more data mining.

- **VML**—Vector Markup Language uses text to define geometric shapes, colors, line widths, and so forth. These words are then interpreted and displayed as graphical images in browsers that understand VML (Microsoft Internet Explorer 5 and higher). No matter what size circle you want to display, you use the same amount of text to define it. VML reduces the bandwidth required to send a graphical image from a web server to a browser. This improves the browser page load time, improves image quality, and reduces Internet or intranet network congestion.

- **JavaScript and VBScript**—Both of these script-style programming languages are in common everyday use on the web right now. These languages handle simple programming tasks without having to load a separate application. The majority of browsers support JavaScript; only Microsoft Internet Explorer browsers support VBScript. These languages enable you to program interactivity into web pages.

You don't need to know how to use each or any of these technologies to build or edit web pages in Word 2010. However, if you are an experienced web page designer, it's nice to have these tools supported in Word so that you don't need to turn to some other editing program simply because you want to use one of them.

Web Page File Formats

When Word saves in Web Page format, it creates a file that contains all the HTML coding needed for display in a web browser, *plus* all the Word coding needed for full-featured editing and display in Word. Therefore, you can switch freely between Word and a web browser, and the file will look the same in both places. Microsoft calls this interchangeability of file formats *round-tripping*, and it works with Word 2000 and higher.

This beefed-up Web Page format that Word uses can display most Word features on a web page. These supplementary technologies increase the capability of HTML so that web pages can display Word-specific formatting and features that pure HTML does not support.

 note

Round-tripping applies only to web pages created in Word. If any other web page is edited in Word, it may or may not look like it originally did after it has been saved in Word.

However, round-tripping comes at a cost: The file sizes of the HTML files that Word generates are larger than those for regular HTML because they contain all that extra code for Word support. Therefore, Word 2010 also offers an alternative mode called Web Page, Filtered that saves in pure HTML without round-trip support for Word. A filtered HTML file is nearly identical to one you would create in a pure HTML editing application such as Dreamweaver.

 note

MIME is an encoding scheme for sending graphics and formatted text via email. It's been around for a long time, and most email programs support it.

Word also offers support for MHTML (MIME HTML), a file format that creates a single file out of a web page that might ordinarily require support files. For example, suppose you have a Word document that contains a graphic. If you save it in either regular Web Page format or filtered format, Word creates an HTML file (.htm) and a support folder containing a separate picture file. This can be awkward to distribute to others via email. With the Single File Web Page (.mht) format, the web page file contains both the text and the graphics with no need for support folders or files. The only drawback is that some older browsers are not able to display MHTML files.

Word Features Lost When Saving in Web Format

Some weaknesses in Word's capability to translate all its features to web pages still exist, even with the latest improvements. Here are a few Word features that do not transfer when you save in any of the Web Page formats:

- Passwords

- Word file headers/footers

- Newspaper-style column flow (although the text is unaffected)

 tip

If you plan to edit your web pages in an HTML editor application, save them as filtered web pages. Many HTML applications have trouble dealing with Word's extra formatting codes that it places in a standard web page document.

The reason for the lack of support for passwords is that typically on a website, the web server controls passwords, rather than individual documents (or pages) doing so.

The lack of support for columns and headers/footers occurs because web browsers simply have no functionality (that is, there is no HTML equivalent) to display these formatted items. When the web page is reloaded into Word, however, columns and headers and footers are restored. Because these "translation" problems are due to shortcomings in HTML or some other web technology, Microsoft cannot create a version of Word that is 100 percent compatible with web pages.

Why You Might Not Want to Use Word

When you have a choice between an application designed for a certain purpose and one designed for a more generic one, you will usually find that the specific program does its task better and with less effort. That's true with most of the higher-end full-featured web design applications.

If you are designing a commercial website that will have a lot of pages and some complex linking requirements, you will find the job much easier in an application such as Expression Web, Dreamweaver, or Visual Web Developer 2010 Express. These programs have all kinds of great shortcuts and wizards for creating, formatting, and debugging HTML code and active web content. Although Word can serve as a vessel for many kinds of web objects, such as JavaScript and VBScript, it doesn't help you generate those items in an automated manner.

Creating and Saving a Web Page in Word

In Word 2010, creating a web page is much the same as creating a Word document. You do not need to open a special environment or think differently about the contents of your page.

To begin building from a blank web page, start a new document and then switch to Web Layout view (from the View tab or the view buttons in the bottom-right corner of the screen).

Then what do you do? Just start creating your document. This is the beauty of Word: A web page is mostly the same thing as a regular document in terms of basic typing, formatting, and layout. We'll get into some specifics that are exceptions later in the chapter.

Previewing a Web Page

As you are building your web page, you can work in Web Layout view as your main editing mode and see the page very nearly as it will be when displayed on a web page.

If that's not enough and you need absolute realism, you can use Web Page Preview to examine the page (read-only) in an actual web browser.

Web Page Preview is not available as a command on any of the default tabs in Word 2010, but you can add it to the Quick Access toolbar:

1. Choose File, Options. The Word Options dialog box opens.

2. Click Quick Access Toolbar.

3. Open the Choose Commands From list and select Commands Not in the Ribbon.

4. Click Web Page Preview and click Add to place it on the Quick Access toolbar.

5. Click OK.

 note

Remember that just because your web page looks good in one browser doesn't mean that it will look good in all browsers. Unless you know that everyone will be accessing your web page with the same browser and version, it is a good idea to test your web pages with the latest versions of Internet Explorer and Firefox, as well as earlier versions if possible. It may also be helpful to try displaying the page in a variety of Mac-platform browsers. Note that if some things do not show up in one browser, you may need to remove those elements or build browser-specific pages.

Once the button is on your Quick Access toolbar, you can click it anytime to open the current Word document in your default browser. You do not have to save it as a web page before doing this.

Saving a Web Page

To save a web page, save normally, but set the file type to one of the web formats:

- Use Single File Web Page (.mht) when you are planning to send the web page via email or distribute it as a document that you want people to be able to easily download and work with. Do not use this format if you think your users may be using old web browser software.

- Use the standard Web Page format (.htm) when you are planning to round-trip the page between Word and a web browser, and if you don't mind that a separate folder for graphics and support files is required for page viewing. Don't use this format if you are planning to email the page to others or if compatibility with other HTML editing software is important.

- Use the Web Page, Filtered format (.htm) when you need the resulting file to be plain HTML with no special Word tags in it. For example, use it when you are going to integrate the page into a larger website created with Dreamweaver or FrontPage (although FrontPage does do a decent job of accepting Word web content, because it's also by Microsoft). Don't use this format if you plan to edit the page in Word in the future.

You can choose any of the formats from the Save as Type drop-down list in the Save As dialog box (File, Save As).

To save a Word document as a web page, follow these steps:

1. Choose File, Save As. The Save As dialog box opens.

2. Open the Save as Type drop-down list and select the desired format.

3. Click the Change Title button. (This button becomes available after you have selected a web format.)

4. In the Enter Text dialog box (shown in Figure 22.1), type the desired title for the page and click OK.

5. If needed, change the location. You can save directly to a web server, or you can save to a local hard disk and then upload to a web server later.

6. Click Save.

This procedure doesn't provide much in the way of flexibility, but there are many ways of setting specific options when you save. The following sections address these options.

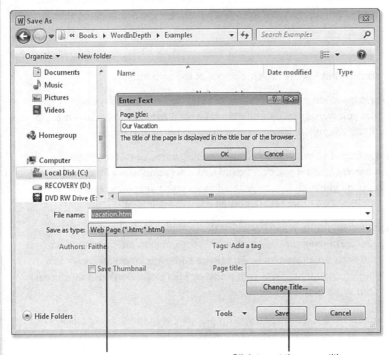

Figure 22.1
Save a file as a web page by selecting a web-based file format.

Select a Web-based format here.   Click to set the page title.

Options for Web Page Saving

Web options enable you to change the way Word saves web pages. These are more subtle options, not the big ones like filtered/unfiltered or single page/multipage. Most people won't find it necessary to change them, but you should know about them in case a situation ever arises in which they are useful.

There are two ways to open the Web Options dialog box:

- From the Save As dialog box, click Tools and select Web Options.

- Choose File, Options, click Advanced, scroll down to the General section, and click Web Options.

The following sections look at each of the tabs in this dialog box individually.

Saving for Compatibility with Specific Browsers

Under the Browsers tab for Web Options, you can set your target browser (see Figure 22.2). The target browser is based on version number and runs from Internet Explorer 3 and Netscape Navigator 3 up through Internet Explorer 6 and higher. Select your default target browser based on the audience viewing your web pages. To reach the widest audience on the Internet, use the lowest version numbers. You might choose Internet Explorer 6 as your target browser on a company intranet where everyone has standardized on Internet Explorer 6 or higher and you need these capabilities to support the content in your web pages.

Figure 22.2
Set browser-specific Save options here, balancing compatibility with feature richness.

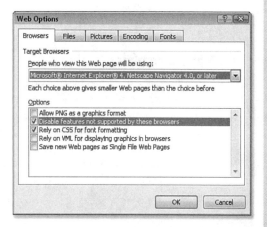

Each target browser setting enables or disables a set of supported features, including these:

- **Allow PNG as a Graphics Format**—This new format is not yet widely supported on the Internet but has advantages over GIF and JPEG files. See the following section for details.

- **Disable Features Not Supported by These Browsers**—For instance, no VML would be used in web pages designed for Internet Explorer 4 because version 4 browsers do not understand VML. If you clear this box, every web page feature built into Word is used without regard for whether a browser version can support it.

- **Rely on CSS for Font Formatting**—Only version 3 and earlier versions of Internet Explorer cannot understand CSS. I recommend leaving this option on for the greatest flexibility in changing web page formatting.

- **Rely on VML for Displaying Graphics in Browsers**—VML reduces overall web page size, but Internet Explorer versions earlier than 5 do not understand it. See the following section for more on VML.

- **Save New Web Pages as Single File Web Pages**—This format has the advantage of storing all the files in a single file. You can, of course, override this option each time you save your web page.

More About PNG and VML

The most common graphics file formats used in web pages are GIF (Graphics Interchange Format) and JPG (Joint Photographic Experts Group, also JPEG). Word automatically exports all images to these two formats when you save as a filtered web page.

Word also supports the display of two additional graphics file formats in web pages: VML (Vector Markup Language) and PNG (Portable Network Graphics).

VML Graphics

Vector images are defined by equations. As such, they scale perfectly to any size. This is in contrast to bitmap images, in which each pixel has a defined position and color value. Bitmap images scale poorly because the graphics program must interpolate pixels as the image dimensions are changed. Items created in Word using the Drawing tools are drawn as vector objects. When you save as a web page or a single file web page (.mht) in Word, the VML language defines the graphical object. The primary advantage of using VML is economy of size, especially if you're using large images. But a significant disadvantage is that only Internet Explorer version 5.0 or later can display vector objects.

PNG Graphics

PNG is basically an improved version of GIF. The idea behind this format is to solve the primary weaknesses of .gif and .jpg files: GIF can support only 256 colors, and JPG gains its small file size using a lossy compression scheme. (That is, as you make your file smaller, you lose photo clarity and resolution because image data is discarded.) Also, GIF supports transparency and animation, but JPG does not.

PNG supports 32-bit color, supports transparency, and uses a file compression scheme that does not reduce the file size at the expense of image clarity. The main reason that this format is not widely used now is that older browsers cannot read the PNG format.

Selecting Web Page File Options

From the Files tab of the Web Options dialog box, shown in Figure 22.3, you can change some file-name options and make choices about Word being your default web page editor.

The first check box asks whether you want to organize supporting files in a folder. When Word saves a web page, it sends many (although not all) supporting files—such as graphics—to a separate folder. If you deselect this check box, Word places the supporting files in the same folder as the HTML file.

The Use Long File Names Whenever Possible check box is marked by default. The only operating system that does not support long filenames is DOS (with or without Windows 3.x). Unless you have many people using this operating system (which is unlikely), leave this check box checked.

The final check box in the section, Update Links on Save, updates links to supporting graphics and components in your web page. It does not update or check hyperlinks.

Figure 22.3
Setting filenames, locations, and default editor options using Web Options in Word 2010.

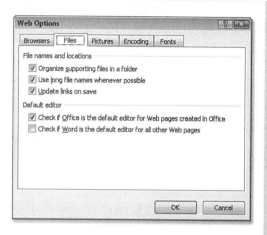

The Default Editor portion of the Files tab under Web Options enables you to decide if you want Office to be the default editor for web pages created in Office (checked by default) and Word to be the default editor for all other web pages.

Changing Page Size

The Pictures tab defines the target monitor you want for your web page.

The target monitor refers to the screen resolution you want to optimize your web pages for. This determines the "size" (width) of the page. Screen resolution is expressed in pixels, usually as width × height. The most common screen resolutions in use today on PCs are these:

- 800×600

- 1024×768

- 1280×1024

The larger the number, the more pixels (and thus more information) are displayed on the screen. If you choose a target monitor size of 800×600 for building your web pages in Word and view the resultant page at 1280×1024, much of the screen will be empty space, with most of the information crowded to the left side of the screen. On the other hand, if you design your pages at 1280×1024 and view the resultant page at 800×600, you will have to keep scrolling to the right to see all the information. The default of 1024×768 is suitable for most uses, unless you're sure that most of your audience uses other screen resolutions.

You can also change the pixels per inch of your target monitor. Again, the default of 96 is suitable for most users. Using higher values greatly increases the size of your graphics and increases your web page load time. Using a value of 120 slightly increases the detail in your web page. A value of 72 gives you smaller web graphics, but your web page will have a slightly coarser appearance.

Changing Language Encoding

The Encoding tab in the Web Options dialog box enables you to choose the language code page from those installed on your machine. Choose the appropriate code page for the language you are using to build your web page.

caution

Use common fonts for your defaults. If you use fonts in your web pages that aren't installed on your viewers' PCs, their browsers can't render your fonts and will substitute their own default fonts.

Changing the Default Fonts

You can set the default proportional and fixed-width fonts for your web page from the Fonts tab, as shown in Figure 22.4. First select a character set (a language), and then select the fonts from the drop-down lists.

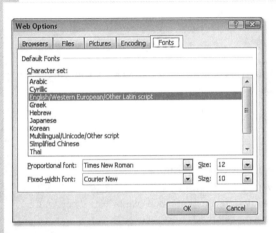

Figure 22.4
Changing the default font for your web page.

Working with Web Page Properties

When you build a web page with HTML coding, you place all the text for the web page in a section called <BODY>. There's also a <HEADER> section at the top of the file that contains some other information about the page, such as keywords that a search engine can use to index the page, and a page title.

The page title is important because it's what appears in the title bar of the web browser when the page is displayed. When you save a web page in Word, you have the option of changing the default page title by clicking the Change Title button, as you saw in Figure 22.1. But you can also change the page's title at any time, not just during the save operation, as well as specify other header information.

To work with the page's header information, do the following:

1. Choose File, Properties, Advanced Properties. (Properties is a drop-down list on the right side of the Info tab.) The Properties dialog box opens for the active file.

2. On the Summary tab, in the Title box, enter a title for the page (see Figure 22.5).

3. (Optional) Enter keywords that describe the document in the Keywords box.

4. Click OK to close the Properties dialog box.

Figure 22.5
The Properties dialog box controls the title and keywords reported to the web browsers that will display the web page.

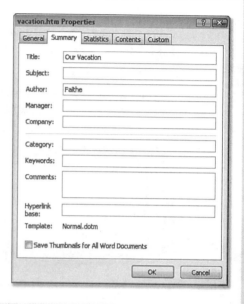

Creating Hyperlinks

A *hyperlink* is the combination of some descriptive text or an image and the location (also called the *address*) of a web page or an object. Any text or image on a web page can hold a hyperlink. Hyperlinks most commonly point to the following:

- Web pages

- Media objects such as sounds, video, or pictures

- Email addresses

The easiest way to create a hyperlink is simply to type it and let Word make it into a live hyperlink automatically. Whenever you type a string of characters that appears to be a web or email address, Word automatically converts it for you. If it doesn't for some reason, or if you want to specify some options (such as ScreenTips), see the following sections.

Creating a Text Hyperlink

Any text phrase, word, or part of a word can be included in a hyperlink. To build a hyperlink, you need some text in a document and the exact location where you want the hyperlink to lead when someone clicks it:

1. From a document in Word, highlight a text phrase. For instance, highlight *Microsoft* in the phrase *For more information, visit the Microsoft home page.*

2. On the Insert tab, click Hyperlink. The Insert Hyperlink dialog box opens, as shown in Figure 22.6.

   You can also reach the Insert Hyperlink dialog box by using the keyboard shortcut Ctrl+K or by right-clicking on the selected text and choosing Hyperlink from the shortcut menu.

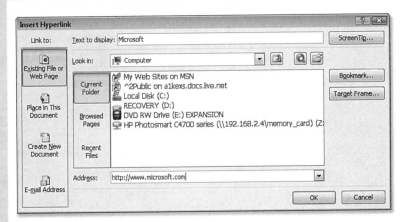

Figure 22.6
Filling in the Insert Hyperlink dialog box.

3. In the top box, labeled Text to Display, the text you high-lighted is displayed. Change it if desired.

4. In the Address text box, enter the web URL for the site to which you want the text to link.

5. (Optional) To add a ScreenTip to the hyperlink, click the ScreenTip button, type the text, and click OK. A ScreenTip is text that appears in a box when the user points at the hyperlink in a web browser. If you do not specify a ScreenTip, the URL is used as a ScreenTip.

6. Click OK. When you return to your document, the text you highlighted appears blue and underlined, indicating that it is now an active hyperlink.

 note

URL stands for *uniform resource locator*. It's the complete address to the web page or other location being referenced. Web page URLs usually begin with http:// and a great many of them (but not all) are then fol-lowed by www. Usually a company places its web pages on a server with the www designation, but some com-panies with large web presences may have separate servers for support, sales, and so on. For example, to get support from Microsoft, the URL is http://support.microsoft.com.

Adding a Hyperlink to an Image

A graphic can function as a hyperlink, such that when the user clicks on the image, a web page loads. The process for building a clickable or hot image is similar to that for building a text hyperlink:

1. Select any clip art, picture, drawing object, or WordArt within a web page.

2. Click Hyperlink on the Insert tab to display the Insert Hyperlink dialog box. (Alternatively, use any of the other previously described methods of opening the Hyperlink dialog box.) The Text to Display line is dimmed because there is no text.

3. Type the address for the link in the Address box at the bottom.

4. (Optional) If you want a ScreenTip, click ScreenTip, type the text, and click OK.

5. Click OK to complete the hyperlink.

The picture will look no different. If you view the web page using Web Page Preview, the default mouse pointer changes to a hand with a pointing finger when it hovers over the image to indicate that it is now clickable, and the ScreenTip appears.

Creating an Email Hyperlink

Besides referencing other pages, hyperlinks can start the user's email editor and begin a blank email message with the recipient name and subject filled in automatically. This is useful for providing a hyperlink through which someone can email you to comment on your web page.

Follow these steps to create an email hyperlink:

1. Select the text or choose an image for the hyperlink.

2. Click the Hyperlink button on the Insert tab to display the Insert Hyperlink dialog box.

3. In the lower-left corner of the Insert Hyperlink dialog box, click on Email Address.

4. Enter the email address, as shown in Figure 22.7.

Notice how the phrase *mailto:* is automatically added to the beginning of your email address.

Figure 22.7
Hyperlinking to an email address.

5. (Optional) Type a subject in the Subject box if you want one to be filled in each time.

6. Click OK to complete the link.

When the link is clicked, a blank, preaddressed email is opened. The email hyperlink is a convenient means for letting visitors to your web page send you feedback or questions.

Building Multicolumn Layouts with Tables

Web pages commonly use tables to create multicolumn layouts. The "traditional" organization of a web page is to place a navigation bar at the left or top and the main content to the right or below. Figure 22.8 shows an example of the left/right layout, and Figure 22.9 shows an example of the top/bottom one.

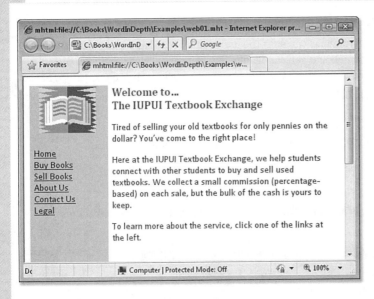

Figure 22.8
A web page that uses a table to create a layout with links to other pages at the left.

We won't go into table creation and usage here because Chapter 9, "Creating and Formatting Tables," covers the topic thoroughly. I will, however, explain in a big-picture way how to create a page like the ones in Figures 22.8 and Figure 22.9:

1. Start a new web page, switch to Web Layout view, and create a table. Size the table rows and columns as appropriate. To make a row taller, click a cell inside it and press Enter a few times.

   For example, you might want a large column at the right and a thinner one to the left that will hold navigation hyperlinks.

2. If you want any of the cells to have a colored background, right-click the cell and choose Borders and Shading. On the Shading tab, select the desired color or shading, and then in the Apply To section, open the drop-down list and choose Cell (see Figure 22.10). Click OK when you're done.

Figure 22.9
A web page that
uses a table to
create a layout
with links to other
pages at the top.

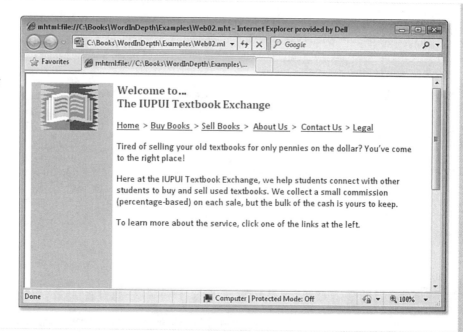

Figure 22.10
Apply shading to an individual cell if
desired.

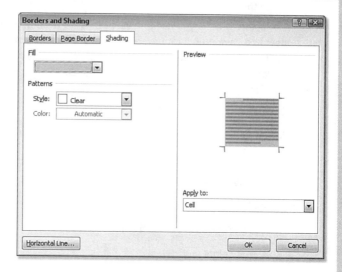

3. (Optional) Remove the borders from around all sides of the table. (With the table selected, open
the Borders drop-down list on the Paragraph group of the Home tab and select No Border.)

4. Type or insert hyperlinks in the cell that you have decided will function as your navigation bar. If you want to hyperlink to other pages you have not created yet, decide what you will name them and then go ahead and create the hyperlinks for them.

5. Type or insert the text for the main body of the page in the cell that will function in that capacity.

6. Save the page.

7. Save it again under a different name—one of the names you chose for the hyperlinks in the navigation bar.

8. Delete the main body content and enter the content for the new page. The navigation links should be able to remain the same.

9. Repeat until you have created all the pages for your site.

 tip

In the navigation bar cell, include a hyperlink to the page that you are on. Clicking it will do nothing, so it's okay to have it. The reason: You will probably copy this page and then edit the copy when you create the other pages in the website, and having the link to this page already in place will prevent your having to create it on each page later.

Creating Your Own Web Page Templates

If you will be creating a lot of web pages that share some similar elements, such as a navigation bar or a consistently sized table, creating a template can save you the time of not having to re-create those elements each instance.

A template is a file you use to base new Word documents on. Can you just open a Word document and save it under a new name? Of course. But will you occasionally have a "duh" moment when you forget to save it under a new name and overwrite the original, causing yourself hours of rework? Undoubtedly. The beauty of a template is that it doesn't allow that kind of mistake to ruin your day.

To build a new web page template, do the following:

1. Start a new, blank document (Ctrl+N) and switch to Web Layout view.

2. Create the elements that the template should contain. You might include these:

   - A company logo

   - One or more tables

   - A background texture or color

   - Font colors and styles

   - A basic text outline

   - Standard hyperlinks, such as one to your website home page

3. Save your document as a template by choosing File, Save As and choosing Word Template (.dotx) as the document type.

Attaching a Cascading Style Sheet

A *cascading style sheet (CSS)* is a file that defines formatting for a web page. It works much like a set of styles in Word. For example, suppose you define the Paragraph tag <p> in the style sheet as using 12-point font. If you then apply that style sheet to a web page, all the paragraphs on that page that use that tag will appear in 12-point font.

If you would like to use an existing CSS to format your web document, you can attach it by following these steps:

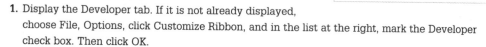 **note**

You can create cascading style sheets in any text editor, but the syntax is important and is different from regular HTML. Consult an HTML reference book to develop your own CSS.

1. Display the Developer tab. If it is not already displayed, choose File, Options, click Customize Ribbon, and in the list at the right, mark the Developer check box. Then click OK.

2. Click the Document Template button. The Templates and Add-Ins dialog box opens.

3. Click the Linked CSS tab.

4. Click the Add button.

5. Select the CSS (.css extension) and click Open to attach it.

6. Click OK to close the Templates and Add-Ins dialog box.

Blogging with Word

A *blog* is an online journal of sorts, either business or personal, which can be read on the Web or via an RSS (Really Simple Syndication) feed to a feed reader program or email program. Outlook 2010 supports RSS feeds, for example, so you can read blog posts from there as if they were email messages. Blogs are easy and inexpensive to set up, and they enable almost anyone to broadcast their opinions to the world.

Most blogging services provide web interfaces from which you can create new posts for your blog. Some email programs also enable you to generate new blog postings. So why use Word? It is primarily a matter of convenience. Word's spell-checking, research, and other proofing tools can come in handy when you are trying to make a good impression to the world, and Word's formatting features are more robust than those of most blogging services.

 note

What differentiates a blog from a web page? They do have some things in common, and blogs can be read from web interfaces. A blog is a series of dated postings and comments, with the newest listed first, whereas a web page can take any format. A blog is typically hosted on a site that provides all the formatting and layout, so all the blogger has to do is type the text and click Send.

Perhaps you're wondering about compatibility. But remember, Word 2010 is XML-based, and XML is a cousin to HTML, the language of the web. So, compatibility is not as much an issue as you might think. Word 2010 provides a blog template that you use to start a new document, and the template ensures that the entries you create conform to the strict HTML standards required for most blogging services. You don't have to worry about the coding or the server—you just focus on the writing!

Understanding the Word Blogging Interface

When you are composing a blog entry, the tabs on the Ribbon change to show only the tools that are applicable to blog entries. The usual tabs are distilled down to just three: File, Blog Post, and Insert.

On the Blog Post tab, shown in Figure 22.11, are the usual tools for editing and formatting text that you normally find on the Home tab. There are also a few proofreading tools that are normally on the References tab, and a Blog group that's unique to blogging, used for uploading your post to the blog service.

Figure 22.11
The Blog Post tab for a blog posting.

On the Insert tab, shown in Figure 22.12, are buttons for inserting a variety of types of graphical content, including charts, SmartArt, and equations. These lose their special Word 2010 functionality when you upload, though; they become regular static graphics.

Figure 22.12
The Insert tab for a blog posting.

Registering Your Blog Server in Word

Before you can post to your blog from within Word, you must register your blogging service with your copy of Word 2010 to set up the username and password required for posting.

The first time you start a new blog posting, you are prompted to register your service. You can click Register Now to begin the process, or click Register Later to begin creating your blog entry without registering. You can save the blog entry to a Word file, but you cannot post it until you register at least one blogging service.

 caution

Registering a blog in Word 2010 is not the same as creating a new blog account. This chapter assumes you already have a blog account and just need to set up Word to work with it.

When you click Register Now, the New Blog Account dialog box opens. Select your blogging service and then follow the prompts to set it up.

After you have one service registered, you can register more services by clicking Manage Accounts on the Blog Post tab and then clicking New to set up a new service.

Creating a New Blog Post

> **⚡ caution**
>
> Not all blog services work with Word's blogging tool. Word doesn't support blogging in LiveJournal or Facebook, for example. Contact your blogging provider and find out if any help is available for configuring Word.

After you've configured your blog service, creating a new post is almost as easy as creating an ordinary document.

To write a new blog post from scratch, choose File, New, Blog Post. A new blank page opens with a placeholder for the title. The default blog name appears next to *Account.* If you have more than one blog service set up, you can switch among them by clicking the blog name and then selecting from its drop-down list.

If you have already started a regular Word document and then decide you want to publish it as a blog post, choose File, Save & Send, Publish as Blog Post, Publish as Blog Post. This opens a new copy of the document as a new blog post. (The original Word document you started with also remains open, in a separate window, under its original name.)

When you are ready to publish, click the Publish button on the Blog Post tab. Or, if you click the down arrow beneath the Publish button, you can then choose either of the following:

- **Publish**—To post your text immediately.

- **Publish as Draft**—To save your text to your blog server but not post it until you log in to that server via your regular web interface and approve it.

If a username and password prompt appears, enter the info requested and click OK. After the post has been successfully sent, a yellow bar appears across the top of the document showing that it has been posted. It also shows the date and time.

Adding Pictures and Other Graphics to a Blog

You can include almost any type of picture in a blog entry that you can include in a Word document. When you save, however, Word converts every type of graphic into a static image, regardless of its original type (chart, SmartArt, and so on).

Most blogging services cannot accept graphics directly from Word. Instead, you must specify a picture-hosting service at which to store the pictures that will accompany your blog text. When you set up your blogging service, you specify whether pictures are allowed, and if so, what picture service you want to use.

The most straightforward option is simply to use your own server to host your pictures—but you can also use an image provider service. To set up the picture hosting if you have not done so already, follow these steps:

1. Choose Blog Post, Manage Accounts.

2. Click the desired blog and click Change.

3. In the dialog box for that service, click Picture Options.

4. Open the Picture Provider drop-down list and choose one of the following:

   - **My Blog Provider**—This option is available only if your blogging service permits pictures.

   - **My Own Server**—Use this option if you have server space of your own you want to use.

   - **Some other service**—Depending on your blogging service, there may be other options listed.

5. Fill in the URLs for the Upload URL and the Source URL.

6. Click OK.

7. Click OK.

note

If you don't have an image provider, click I Don't Have an Image Provider, and follow the steps on the web page that appears.

Categorizing Blog Entries

Many blogging systems enable you to categorize your entries. To add a category to an entry in Word, follow these steps:

1. Choose Blog Post, Insert Category. A Category line appears in the document.

2. Open the drop-down list for the Category line that was inserted, and choose a category.

   This list comes from your blogging service.

3. Continue composing your entry as you normally would.

tip

If you are editing an entry you started some time ago, you might want to refresh the categories to make sure the desired category is still available. To do this, choose Blog Post, Category and then click Refresh Categories.

Managing the Blog List

To add or delete blogs from Word, use the Blog Accounts dialog box. Display it by clicking the Manage Accounts button on the Blog Post tab.

From here, you can do the following:

- Click New to set up an additional site.

- Click a blog and click Change to change its settings. For example, you might need to go back and configure a URL for pictures if you did not do that initially.

- Click a blog and click Set as Default to mark the blog that should be used when you start a new blog entry.

- Click a blog and click Remove to stop using it in Word. (It does not do anything to your blogging service account or previous postings.)

Modifying a Blog Post

To modify a blog post, choose Blog Post, Open Existing. A list of posts you've made to your default blog appears. From there, select a post and click OK to open it for editing. Then republish it to save your changes.

Sending Email from Word

If you use Outlook 2010 as your email program, you have probably noticed that its email-composition window has many of the same tools as Word 2010. Even users who don't have Word installed still have that basic set of Word-like capabilities in Outlook. Therefore, there is not much benefit to composing email messages in Word. You can easily send an email that includes your Word document as an attachment; the body of the email itself can be composed in Outlook.

You can send your document as an attachment in any of several formats, including Word, PDF, XPS, and Internet Fax. To use any of those, follow these steps:

1. Choose File, Save & Send.

2. Click the button that best corresponds to what you want to do. See Figure 22.13. Each of these buttons starts a new email message in your default mail program and attaches the active document in the specified format:

   - **Send as Attachment**—Attaches it in Word format. Anyone who has Word can edit the resulting file.

   - **Send as PDF**—Saves it as a PDF file and attaches that. The resulting file cannot be edited in Word, but it retains the formatting well. Recipients need Adobe Reader or some other program that opens PDF files.

   - **Send as XPS**—Saves it as an XPS file and attaches that. The resulting file cannot be edited in Word, but it retains the formatting well. Recipients need an XPS reader, which is included in Windows Vista and Windows 7.

   - **Send as Internet Fax**—Saves it in Internet fax format and attaches that file. You can then send the resulting file with a third-party Internet Fax service (not included with Word).

3. Complete the email message and send it.

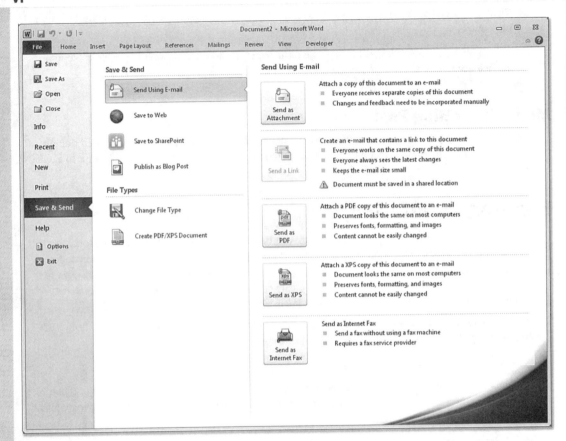

Figure 22.13
Choose to attach the document to an email in whatever format is needed

MACROS AND ADD-INS

Understanding Macros

A *macro* is a sequence of operations that Word can execute whenever you tell it to. Word's powerful macro facilities enable you to automate just about anything you would do manually in Word. You can assign a macro to a keyboard shortcut, run it from the Macros dialog box, or place a button for it on the Quick Access toolbar (or anywhere else on the Ribbon).

There are two general approaches to creating Word macros:

- Use Word's macro recorder to capture the steps in your macro as you perform them in Word. After you save the macro, you can play it back at any time using one of the options listed previously.

- Write the code of the macro yourself in the Visual Basic for Applications (VBA) programming language. Word comes with a complete programming environment, the Visual Basic Editor, which you can use to enter and edit your code, as well as powerful tools to help you debug and test your macros.

This chapter focuses mostly on recording and playing back a Word macro. To use the VBA method, you must have some background in Visual Basic programming.

What Tasks Should You Automate with a Macro?

The most common purpose for macros is to speed your work by taking a set of operations that you perform repeatedly and turning them into a one-step operation. Anytime you find yourself doing the same set of actions over and over again, you might have found a good candidate for a macro. Macros also make your work more reliable by ensuring that the steps of the macro are performed the same way, each time the macro runs. Of course, that does mean it is essential to record the macro properly. Otherwise, it performs the same *wrong* set of steps each time it runs.

Before you take the step of creating a macro, however, you might want to consider some of the other timesaving features in Word that you can use instead of macros:

- If you often need to type the same text, such as your name or address, including formatting, you might want to use Word's Building Blocks feature, which lets you save named collections of text and formatting.

  ➡️ *To learn about building blocks, see "Working with Building Blocks," p. 89.*

- To quickly apply formatting in a consistent way throughout one or more documents, you can use styles and themes.

  ➡️ *To learn how to create and apply styles and themes, see Chapter 6, "Creating and Applying Styles and Themes."*

- To create neatly formatted standard documents, such as letters, résumés, or fax cover sheets, you can use one of the document templates or wizards that come with Word, or you can create your own template.

  ➡️ *To learn about working with templates in Word, see "Creating a Document Based on a Template," p. 22.*

If none of Word's automated features alone will do the job for you, or if you want to use several of these features together, you can create a macro to carry out your commands. There is just about no end to the uses you might think of for macros. A few of the most common include the following:

- Applying complex formatting that you can't easily capture in a style, such as a mixture of different formatting types.

- Completing any task that takes several steps, such as creating a mail merge, applying complicated page setup settings, or requesting custom printing routines.

- Performing repetitive tasks in a long document. This is especially useful for documents that you have imported from other programs or that other users have created. You can record a macro that finds and replaces special characters, removes extra paragraph breaks, or applies formatting.

- Performing commands normally found in Word's built-in dialog boxes. You might want to turn a display feature—such as the display of field codes—on or off as needed. Or you might want to quickly apply a text attribute that is not on the Ribbon and doesn't have a keyboard shortcut, such as double-strikethrough.

Choosing the Macro Creation Method

When you need to create a new macro, you have a choice between recording the macro and typing the VBA code yourself. Of course, if you don't know the VBA programming language, your only option is to record the macro. You can even use the recorder as a teaching tool by recording the macro and then studying the resulting VBA code. As mentioned, this book focuses on using the macro recorder.

It's worthwhile to know a little about how the macro recorder works before recording a macro. After you turn on the macro recorder, it captures just about everything you do in Word, including typing text, applying formatting, and performing menu commands. The recorder is literal: It picks up just about every detail during the recording session. Don't be surprised, if you look at the VBA code that results from recording a macro, if Word recorded a lot more than you had in mind.

If you are, or become, proficient with VBA, you'll probably find that it is often useful to record a macro and then edit the resulting code to get it to work exactly as you want. As your VBA skills improve, you might even find that it's sometimes quicker and more accurate to type the code yourself in the first place.

Planning Your Macro

It's always a good idea to take some time to think about exactly what you want your macro to do before you begin recording. You might even want to take a few notes on paper that you can refer to while you record the macro. Think about several things before recording your macro:

- Consider how your document should be set up before the recording begins. For example, if your macro is to apply font formatting to selected text, you need to have the appropriate text selected before you start recording the macro. On the other hand, you might want to record the actual selection of the text. In many cases, the first action you record will be moving to the beginning of your document. This can ensure that the steps that follow are applied to the entire document.

- Make sure you know your keyboard shortcuts, especially the ones for moving through the document and for selecting text. Word doesn't record text selections or navigation you perform with the mouse, but you can use keyboard shortcuts to perform the same tasks. (You can still use the mouse to select Quick Access toolbar and Ribbon commands while recording.)

- Think about the exact meaning of what you want to record. For example, to move to the beginning of the next paragraph while you are recording, press the shortcut key to move to the next paragraph (Ctrl+down arrow). If you simply use the arrow keys to move to the desired location, your macro records the arrow movements, not your intention to move to the following paragraph. When you run it in a different document, it replays the arrow movements, which may not have the same result in that document.

> **tip**
>
> If you want to record a macro that performs a series of actions to selected text, select some text before you begin recording the macro. Then record your macro as you normally would. For example, you could create a macro that makes selected text bold and italic. Select some text, begin recording the macro, click the Bold and Italic toolbar buttons, and stop recording. The resulting macro toggles the bold and italic setting for any selected text.

VII

A good way to plan a macro is to take one or more "test runs" before turning on the recorder: Perform the commands and write down exactly what you did along the way. When you're satisfied that you've written down a workable list of steps, use it as a reference when recording the macro.

Recording a Macro

Ready to record? Click the Record Macro button (it looks like a table with a little red ball on it) on the status bar. The Record Macro dialog box opens (see Figure 23.1).

 note

Another way to start a new macro is to click Record Macro on the Developer tab. If the Developer tab does not appear, choose File, Options, click Customize Ribbon, and select the Developer check box in the right list pane.

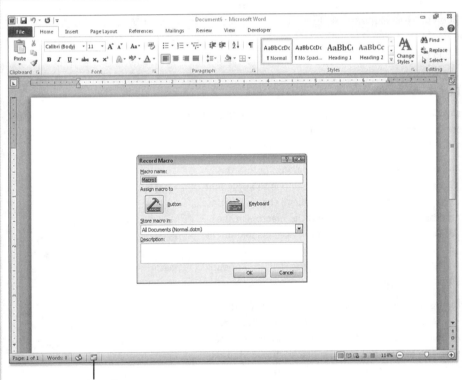

Figure 23.1
Enter the name and description of your new macro in the Record Macro dialog box.

Record Macro Button

Before you can begin recording the macro, you must give it a name and decide where you want to store it. You can also assign the macro to a keyboard shortcut or a custom Quick Access toolbar button. Although you can change all these items later, it's far more convenient to make these decisions up front and enter them correctly now.

Naming Your Macro

As you can see from Figure 23.1, Word suggests a name for your macro: Macro1, Macro2, and so on. It's usually much more useful to give your macro a more descriptive name so that it will be easy to identify when you want to use it later. Your macro name should describe the purpose of the macro and must follow these rules:

- Macro names must begin with a letter but can include numbers.

- Names can contain up to 80 letters and numbers. Spaces and other characters are not allowed (except the underscore character).

For example, the following macro names are legal:

    ApplyMyCustomFormatting
    Insert5BlankParagraphs
    TwoB_Or_Not2B

The following names are not legal:

    Create Letter
    2Spaces
    New?Document

Word does not warn you that your macro name is invalid until you click OK to start recording your macro. If your macro name contains invalid characters, Word displays a dialog box indicating Invalid Procedure Name. Simply click OK and launch the Record Macro dialog box again. Edit the name until it conforms to the naming rules. When it does, Word allows you to proceed.

At the time you name your macro, you can also enter a description. It's a good idea to enter a more specific description for your macros. For example:

> This macro goes to the top of the document and then performs a find and replace to eliminate the second space between sentences.

Deciding Where to Store Your Macro

Macros can be stored in templates and in individual documents. A macro is available for you to run only if the document or template that contains the macro is open. You can store macros in the following locations:

- **Normal.dotm**—The simplest way to create a macro that you can run at any time, in any document, is to store the macro in your Normal template. As you can see in Figure 23.1, the Normal. dotm template is selected by default as the storage place for recorded macros.

- **Active Document**—If you prefer to store the macro in the active document, click the Store Macro In drop-down list to select the document. The macro is available for you to run only when this document is the active document.

- **Other Templates**—If you store a macro in a template other than Normal, the macro is available only when that template is open or when a document based on that template is open. For example, suppose that you have created a template for writing sales proposals. If you want to record a macro that you will use only when you are working on these proposals, be sure to select the template name in the Store Macro In drop-down list. The template, or a document based on the template, must be the active document when you record the macro.

I Recorded a Macro But Now It's Not There

When you record a macro and save it in Normal.dotm, it is not actually saved there until you save Normal.dotm. So then if you start a new document, that macro might not be available until you've saved Normal.dotm. The easiest way to save it is to exit and reopen Word.

If that doesn't help, you probably saved the macro to the individual document rather than to the template. See "Copying Macros Between Documents" later in this chapter to learn how to move it over to Normal.dotm.

Assigning a Macro to a Keyboard Shortcut or Toolbar Button

If you expect to use your macro often, and you want to save time when you run it, you can assign a shortcut key or Quick Access toolbar button for running the macro. Then you can run your macro quickly by pressing the shortcut key combination or clicking the button.

Word does not require you to assign your macro to anything: You can always run the macro using the Macros button on the Developer tab. Although adding some form of shortcut can make a macro more accessible, you might prefer not to use up a key assignment or space on the Quick Access toolbar for macros you use only rarely.

For commonly used macros, however, you probably should assign a keyboard shortcut or Quick Access toolbar button.

Keyboard shortcuts are a great convenience for macros that you use often. If you use a macro only occasionally, however, you might find it difficult to remember the shortcut key. Also, if you're creating macros for other users, some users prefer shortcut keys, whereas others don't want to memorize anything.

A button on the Quick Access toolbar makes a macro readily available for use at any time. Many people prefer not to memorize shortcut keys but don't mind clicking a button.

 tip

You can print a list of the custom key assignments associated with any document or template. To do so, choose File, Print; then click the Print All Pages button to open a menu. Scroll down to the bottom of that menu and click Key Assignments. Then click Print. Word first prints all custom key assignments associated with the document itself, and then all custom key assignments associated with the template the document is based on.

Assigning a Macro to a Keyboard Shortcut

To assign a keyboard shortcut to the macro you're about to record, follow these steps while the Record Macro dialog box is open:

1. Click Keyboard in the Assign Macro To group. The Customize Keyboard dialog box appears, as shown in Figure 23.2.

Figure 23.2
Use the Customize Keyboard dialog box to assign a key combination for your macro.

2. Make sure that the correct template or document is selected in the Save Changes In drop-down list. In nearly every case, you'll want to save the keyboard shortcut in the same template or document the macro will be stored in. (Word's default setting is to store the change in the Normal.dotm template, not the current document.)

3. Click in the Press New Shortcut Key box if the insertion point is not already there.

4. Press the shortcut key combination you want to use for the macro. You can create keyboard combinations that include function keys F1 through F12, the Ctrl key, the Alt key, and the Shift key (but not the Windows key). The key combination you choose is displayed in the Press New Shortcut Key text box. Under the text box, the current assignment for this key combination is displayed, or the combination is shown as *[unassigned]*.

5. To accept the new keyboard assignment, click Assign. The new assignment appears in the Current Keys list. You can assign more than one key combination for each macro if you want to, but remember that a relatively limited number of

 caution

Word enables you to override default keyboard shortcut assignments. In fact, it doesn't even require you to confirm this with a confirming dialog box. As soon as you click Close to start recording your macro, the macro replaces the default key assignment.

To reset the keyboard shortcuts, choose File, Options, click Customize Ribbon, click the Reset button, and click Reset All Customizations.

You should be reluctant to change default key assignments. For example, if you decide to assign Ctrl+P as the shortcut key for your macro, you can no longer use that keyboard combination to print. If you store your macro in a specific document or a template you've created, the change in keystrokes will affect only the document, or documents, created with that template. In other words, the same keystrokes perform different tasks at different times, which can be terribly confusing—for you and especially for others who may use your macro.

If you store the macro in Normal.dotm, the change affects all documents—but now, Word behaves differently from the way its online documentation (and this book) says it will.

key combinations is available for everything Word has to do. Use the Remove button to delete a previously assigned shortcut.

6. To complete the assignment and continue with the recording process, click Close to begin the recording.

You cannot set up both a keyboard shortcut and a button for a macro while initially recording it, because the macro recording begins immediately when you click Close in step 6, but you can add a button for the macro to the Quick Access toolbar after the recording is finished. See "Assigning a Keyboard Shortcut to an Existing Macro" later in this chapter to learn how to do that.

Assigning a Macro to a Toolbar Button

To assign a Quick Access toolbar button to run your macro before you begin recording it, follow these steps when the Record Macro dialog box is displayed:

1. Click Button in the Assign Macro To group. The Quick Access Toolbar tab of the Word Options dialog box opens.

2. Click the macro name in the left list, and then click the Add button to move it to the right list (see Figure 23.3).

3. Click OK. The macro recording begins.

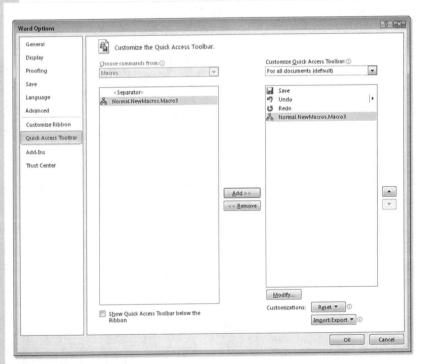

Figure 23.3
Add a macro to the Quick Access toolbar.

As noted in the preceding section, you cannot set up both a button and a keyboard shortcut for a macro while initially recording it, because the macro recording begins immediately when you click OK in step 3. However, you can add a shortcut key combination after the recording is finished. You'll learn how to do that later in this chapter.

Recording the Steps for Your Macro

If you chose to assign a keyboard shortcut or Quick Access toolbar button to your macro, Word turns on the macro recorder after specifying one or the other. If you have not assigned either one, click OK in the Record Macro dialog box to get the recording started.

When recording is enabled, a Stop Recording button (a light blue square) appears in the status bar, and the mouse pointer turns into a cassette tape symbol. If the Developer tab is displayed, you also have access to a Pause Recording button that you can use to temporarily halt the recording while you set something up, and then you can continue the recording (see Figure 23.4).

Figure 23.4
When a macro is recording, the status bar shows a Stop Recording button.

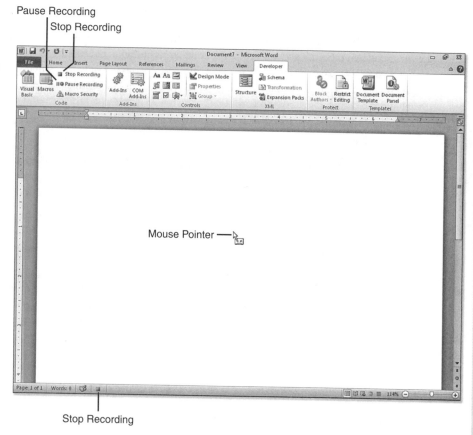

When the macro recorder is active, you can perform most normal activities in Word, and those activities are recorded as part of your macro. Some examples of actions you can record in your macro include the following:

- You can type, edit, and delete text.

- You can select text and move through the document with keyboard shortcuts. You can't use the mouse to select text or scroll while you are recording. Instead, use the arrow keys to navigate, as well as the Home, End, Page Up, and Page Down keys, as needed. To select text, press and hold the Shift key while you use the arrow or navigation keys.

note

You can still use the mouse to select Ribbon commands and Quick Access toolbar buttons while you're recording a macro.

- You can click buttons on the Ribbon or the Quick Access toolbar and fill out the dialog boxes associated with the commands.

- You can open and close documents and create new ones.

- You can choose File, Options and set or change program options.

If you want to pause your recording session and return to it later, click the Pause Recording button on the Developer tab. Any actions you perform while recording is paused are not recorded. Click Resume Recorder (same button as Pause Recording) when you're ready to resume your recording session. That button is available only on the Developer tab, so you must have displayed the Developer tab before you started recording. (You can turn it on during the recording, but the fact that you are turning it on is recorded as an activity.)

Keep a few things in mind as you record your macros:

- The macro recorder captures the actions you perform, not the keystrokes you use to complete them. So, for example, if you open the Print dialog box, the macro does not notice which method you use to do so.

- If you record a command that displays a dialog box, such as clicking a dialog box launcher for a group on a tab, the dialog box doesn't reappear when you later run the macro. Rather, Word applies whatever settings you entered using the dialog box while you were recording the macro.

- Word records *everything* in the dialog box, so if you only want to turn on italic, it's better to press Ctrl+I or click the Italic button on the Home tab of the Ribbon than it is to use the Font dialog box. Otherwise, Word also records other text attributes that apply to the current text—attributes you might not want to apply every time you run the macro.

- If you display a dialog box while you're recording, but you cancel the dialog box, Word doesn't record that command.

- Word records your actions literally. For example, if you record the File, Open command and select a file, Word records the exact filename you opened. When you run the macro, Word attempts to open the same file. If the file is not found, an error occurs, and the macro stops running.

Creating Macros That Run Automatically

In most cases, you should give your macro a name that describes its function so that you can easily remember its purpose later. There are, however, several special names you can give your macros. These names cause your macros to run automatically when certain events occur in Word:

- A macro named AutoExec runs when you start Word. For this macro to work, you need to store it in your Normal.dotm template or another always-available template.

- A macro named AutoExit runs when you exit Word. If you want a macro to run every time you exit Word, store this macro in Normal.dotm or another always-available template.

- A macro named AutoNew runs when you create a new document. If you save this macro in a specific template, such as a memo template, the macro runs each time you create a new document based on that template.

- A macro named AutoClose runs when you close a document. If you save this macro in a specific template, it runs when you attempt to close the template or any document based on the template.

- A macro named AutoOpen runs when you open the template that contains it or any document based on the template.

When you finish recording your macro, you can turn off the recorder in the following ways:

- Click the Stop Recording button on the status bar.

- Click the Stop Recording button on the Developer tab.

Running a Macro

Now that you have recorded and stored your macro, you can run it to perform the steps you have recorded. Use one of the following methods to run your macro:

- If you assigned the macro to a button on the Quick Access toolbar, you can click the button to run the macro. If you have more than one macro on the Quick Access toolbar, point at a button to see its ScreenTip to determine which is which.

- If you assigned a keyboard shortcut for the macro, press the key combination.

- To select the macro name from the list of available macros, click the Macros button on the Developer tab. The Macros dialog box appears, as shown in Figure 23.5. Select the macro name that you want to run and click Run to execute the macro.

 note

To change a macro's button on the Quick Access toolbar, choose File, Options, Quick Access Toolbar. Click the button in the right pane, and click the Modify button. Then choose an icon from the Modify Button dialog box.

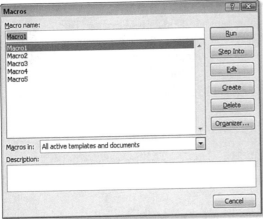

Figure 23.5
Use the Macros dialog box to select a macro to run.

Running Word Commands as Macros

Word has more than 400 built-in commands that you can run as though they were macros. Many of these commands are the same as the commands already found on Word's Ribbon and menus. In some cases, though, there are commands that aren't found on any menu or toolbar button. In other cases, these commands provide a simpler or more effective approach to operations that you can perform with other commands.

To run a built-in command as a macro, open the Macros dialog box and select Word Commands in the Macros In box. Select the desired command in the Macro Name list and then click Run.

Dealing with Macro Error Messages

When your macro runs, the statements you recorded are performed just as you recorded them. Sometimes, though, an error occurs.

The two most common problems are these:

- Missing macros (for example, trying to run a macro from a Quick Access toolbar button where the macro has been deleted or is not stored in an available template)

- Security settings preventing a macro from running

Both of these situations result in the same error message, shown in Figure 23.6.

To check that the macro is available, open the Macros dialog box (shown previously in Figure 23.5) and set the Macros In setting to All Active Templates and Documents. If the macro does not appear there, you probably have stored it somewhere else by accident. You can either re-create it or copy it from the other document or template file. (To do the latter, see "Copying Macros Between Documents" later in this chapter.)

Figure 23.6
This error means the macro cannot run, either because it is missing or because your macro security settings will not allow it.

If the macro is available, it's your security settings that need tweaking. See "Working with Macro Security," later in this chapter, for help with that.

Another common error occurs when the macro cannot execute one or more lines of its code. This is called a *runtime error*. It happens when the conditions that existed when you recorded the macro no longer exist in some way. For example, perhaps the macro specifies opening a file that does not exist anymore in the referenced location. A runtime error looks like the one in Figure 23.7.

To correct a runtime error, you can edit the VBA code for the macro (if you are able), or you can delete and rerecord the macro.

If you want to delete the macro and rerecord it, click End to stop the macro and then delete it from the Macros dialog box (refer to Figure 23.5).

Figure 23.7
A runtime error points out a problem with the macro's code.

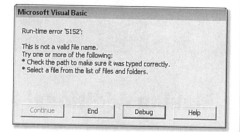

If you want to edit the code, click Debug to open the macro in the Visual Basic Editor (VBE) and then examine the code. The line that caused the error is highlighted, as shown in Figure 23.8.

At this time, the macro is still running but is suspended in a state known as *Break mode*. After making the needed correction to the code, click the Reset button in the toolbar (see Figure 23.8). Then close the Visual Basic window and try running the macro again.

> **⚠ caution**
> Occasionally, a macro runs out of control, repeating its actions over and over. This is not likely to happen with a recorded macro, but it sometimes happens when there is a programming error in a macro you have edited. In this case, you can stop the macro by pressing Ctrl+Break. Again, this puts the macro in Break mode, and you must reset the macro project.

Reset Button

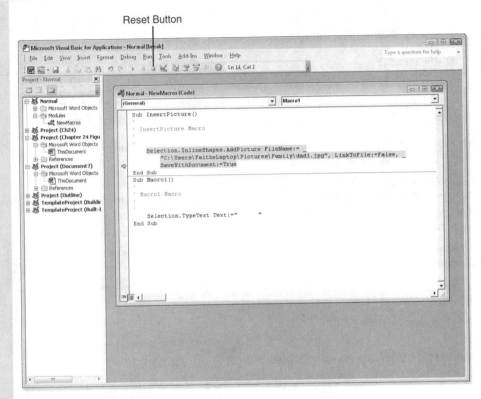

Figure 23.8
The line of
code that
caused the
error is high-
lighted.

Making Additional Macros Available

If the macro you want to use is not available in the current
document but is stored somewhere else, there are several
ways of making it available. The following sections provide
some ideas.

Opening Additional Templates to Run Macros

If you want to run a macro that is stored in a different template, you can open that template as a global template. There
are two ways to make sure that a template is loaded globally:

- **Save the template in the Word Startup folder**—To determine where that folder is located, choose File, Options.
  Click Advanced, click the File Locations button in the

 note

If a module with the same name is
already in the destination project,
Word doesn't let you copy the
module. If you still want to copy the
module, you must rename it before
copying it.

To rename a module, select it and
click Rename. Type the new name
for the module and click OK. For
example, if both the source and destination locations call the module
NewMacros, rename one of them.

General section, and then double-click Startup to see the location. Any template in this folder is opened invisibly, and as a read-only document, each time you start Word.

■ **Open a template globally**—To do this, on the Developer tab, click Document Template. In the Global Templates and Add-Ins section of the Templates and Add-Ins dialog box, click Add and then select the template to load.

Copying Macros Between Documents

Each Word document has a single VBA *project*, which is a collection of modules. A Word document can store many types of VBA code, not just macros, so it needs the capability of having multiple modules in its project. For macro purposes, however, you will work mostly with one module: the default module for storing macros, called NewMacros.

 note

You can rename modules and develop extra modules. Therefore, a template you receive from someone else might have multiple modules in them, and they might have names other than NewMacros.

Each macro is stored in the macro module as a VBA *procedure*, which is a set of step-by-step instructions to execute.

If a given document or template contains some useful macros, you might want to reuse them in some other template. One way to achieve this is to copy the macros from one project to another using the Organizer.

Follow these steps to copy one or more macros:

1. Open the source and destination templates or documents in Word.

2. On the Developer tab, click Macros, and then click Organizer. The Organizer dialog box opens (see Figure 23.9). This dialog box lets you display the modules in two templates or documents and copy modules from one list to another.

3. Under either list, if needed, display a different template:

   a. Click Close File.

   b. Click Open File.

   c. Select a different template or document.

   d. Click Open.

4. To copy a module from one list to another, select the module that you want to copy and click Copy. The macro is copied to the destination list.

 caution

After you delete a module and save the template that contained it, there is no way to recover the deleted module.

5. (Optional) To delete a module from a project, select the module and click Delete. Word asks for confirmation that you really want to delete the module.

6. When you are finished using the Organizer, click Close.

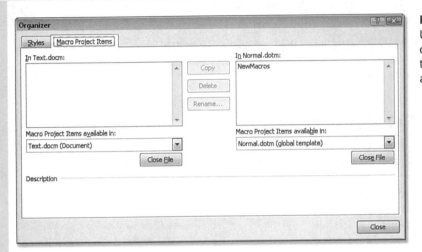

Figure 23.9
Use the Organizer to copy modules from one template or document to another.

Renaming and Deleting Macros

The Organizer copies, renames, and deletes entire modules, each of which might contain many individual macros. You might prefer to rename and delete individual macros instead.

To delete a macro, open the Macros dialog box (by clicking the Macros button on the status bar or the Developer tab) and then select the desired macro and click Delete.

To rename a macro, select the macro from the Macros dialog box and click Edit. The macro opens in the Visual Basic Editor. Find the line of code that starts with Sub and then shows the macro's name, and change the text following Sub to the desired name. Do not delete the parentheses.

Assigning a Keyboard Shortcut to an Existing Macro

As you saw earlier in the chapter, you can assign a keyboard shortcut to a macro as you create it. However, if you want both a keyboard shortcut and a Quick Access toolbar button for it, you must set up one or the other afterward.

To assign a keyboard shortcut to an existing macro, follow these steps:

1. Choose File, Options.

2. Click Customize Ribbon.

3. Click the Customize button next to Keyboard Shortcuts, near the bottom of the dialog box. The Customize Keyboard dialog box appears.

4. In the Categories list, scroll down to the bottom of the list and click Macros. A list of the macros in the current document or template appears in the Macros list (see Figure 23.10).

Figure 23.10
Assign a keyboard shortcut to an existing macro.

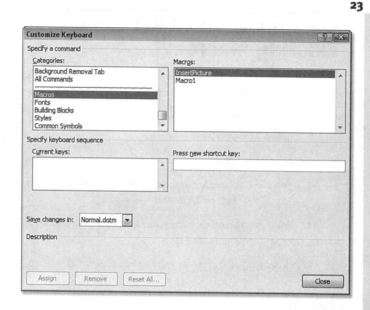

5. Click the desired macro. Any existing keyboard shortcut assigned to it appears in the Current Keys box.

6. Click in the Press New Shortcut Key box.

7. Press the shortcut key combination you want to use for the macro. You can create keyboard combinations that include function keys F1 through F12, the Ctrl key, the Alt key, and the Shift key (but not the Windows key). The key combination you choose is displayed in the PressNew Shortcut Key text box. Under the Current Keys text box, the current assignment for this key combination is displayed, or the combination is shown as *[unassigned]*.

8. To accept the new keyboard assignment, click Assign. The new assignment appears in the Current Keys list.

   You can assign more than one key combination for each macro if you want to, but remember that a relatively limited number of key combinations is available for everything Word has to do.

9. (Optional) Assign keyboard shortcuts to other macros as needed by repeating steps 5–8.

10. Click Close.

11. Click OK.

 **tip**

Click Reset All to reset all key assignments.

 tip

If you find it difficult to identify unused keyboard sequences, try sequences that begin with the Alt key; most of these are unassigned.

Alternatively, you can obtain a list of shortcut keys assigned to existing Word commands. Open the Macros dialog box. From the Macros In drop-down list, select Word Commands. This presents you with a list of Word commands. Scroll down to and select the ListCommands entry. Then click the Run button. From the List Commands dialog box, select Current Keyboard Settings. Click OK, and a new document is generated containing all the commands and associated shortcut keys and menu items.

Creating a Quick Access Toolbar Button for an Existing Macro

You can add each macro to the Quick Access toolbar. This can save you some time compared to opening the Macros dialog box and selecting the desired macro each time.

To add an existing macro to the Quick Access toolbar, follow these steps:

1. Choose File, Options.

2. Click Quick Access Toolbar.

3. Open the Choose Commands From list and select Macros. A list of the macros appears.

4. Click a macro and then click the Add button to add it to the toolbar (see Figure 23.11).

5. Add any other macros as needed; then click OK.

 tip

Although it is less common to do so, you can add buttons for macros directly to the Ribbon. See Chapter 24, "Customizing the Word Interface," to learn more about customizing the Ribbon.

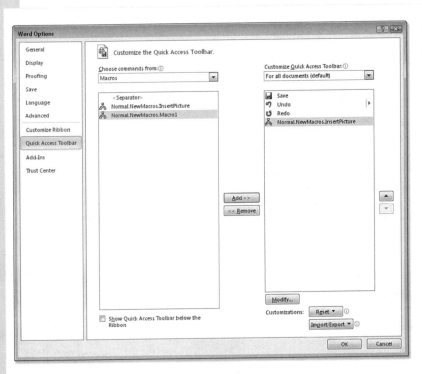

Figure 23.11
Create a button for a macro on the Quick Access toolbar.

Each macro has an identical button on the Quick Access toolbar. To tell the macros apart, point to a button to see its ScreenTip. You can also change a macro's button by selecting it from the right pane in the Word Options dialog box (see Figure 23.11) and clicking Modify.

Editing Macro Code in VBA

Macros are written in Visual Basic for Applications, a variant of the Visual Basic programming language designed for use within Office and other applications.

To write your own VBA code from scratch, you need to understand Visual Basic, and perhaps have taken a class or done some self-study in the language. However, if you just want to edit a macro, you can usually figure out what the various lines of code do and modify them in small ways or delete lines of code that are extraneous.

Opening a Macro for Editing

To open a macro in the Visual Basic Editor (VBE), follow these steps:

1. Click Macros on the Developer tab, opening the Macros dialog box.

2. Click the desired macro and then click Edit. The macro opens in the Visual Basic Editor. If there are multiple macros, each one appears in a separate section within a single window for the module. In Figure 23.12, for example, there are two macros (InsertPicture and CodeFormat) in the NewMacros module.

Figure 23.12
Use the Visual Basic Editor to change the macro code.

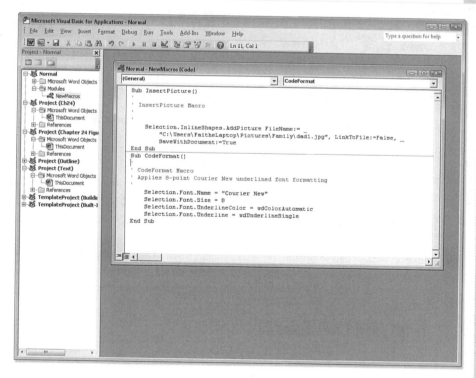

Here's a brief guide to what you see in Figure 23.12:

- Each macro's section begins with the statement Sub, followed by the macro name, and then empty parentheses ( ). For example:

```
Sub CodeFormat()
```

- Each macro ends with the statement End Sub.

- Lines with apostrophes (') at the beginning are comment lines and do not execute. These lines are there for reference purposes for someone who is examining the code. For example, in the CodeFormat macro in Figure 23.12, the following is a comment line, which came from the Description entered when recording the macro:

```
'Applies 8-point Courier New underlined font formatting
```

- Each command in a macro defines a part of the document or program and then has an equals sign and a value for that item. For example:

```
Selection.Font.Name = "Courier New"
```

Examples of Macro Command Syntax

The best way to understand macro code is to record some macros and then look at them in the Visual Basic Editor. Let's look at a few of the commands from Figure 23.12 as examples.

Inserting Graphics

The first macro in Figure 23.12, InsertPicture, contains only one command:

```
Selection.InlineShapes.AddPicture FileName:= _
    "C:\Users\FaitheLaptop\Pictures\Family\dad1.jpg", LinkToFile:=False, _
    SaveWithDocument:=True
```

This command (Selection.InlineShapes.AddPicture) has several arguments to it: FileName, LinkToFile, and SaveWithDocument. They are all run together, rather than being separated on different lines.

Instead of the plain equal sign (=), this command uses a colon and an equal sign (:=) to separate the attribute from its value. Why? That's just the way the syntax works. The only way to know this is to take a course in VBA or study a lot of macro codes that you've recorded.

Applying Character Formatting

The second macro in Figure 23.12, CodeFormat, applies four types of character formatting to text:

```
Selection.Font.Name = "Courier New"
Selection.Font.Size = 8
Selection.Font.UnderlineColor = wdColorAutomatic
Selection.Font.Underline = wdUnderlineSingle
```

Each one begins with Selection, which tells the macro you are going to be acting upon the selected text (or the insertion point location). Next comes Font, which tells the macro you will be applying font formatting. After that comes the individual attribute being set, an equals sign (=), and the value for it.

Some of the values are no-brainers. For example, the font name appears just as it does on the Font list, in quotation marks because it is a text value. And the font size appears as a regular digit.

The other two values you would have to know how to write. (That's where experimenting with recording comes in handy.) The first one, wdColorAutomatic, specifies that the underline color will be the same as the text. The second one, wdUnderlineSingle, sets the underline style.

Performing the Same Action in Different Ways

Now let's look at another pair of macros. Both of the macros make selected text bold and italic. However, they go about it in different ways, and in certain circumstances could provide different results.

The following macro, called BoldItalics1, toggles the Bold and Italic buttons on the Home tab with these lines:

```
Sub BoldItalics1()
' BoldItalics1 Macro
' Applies bold and italics from the Home tab's buttons.
'
    Selection.Font.Bold = wdToggle
    Selection.Font.Italic = wdToggle
End Sub
```

The macro appears to make the text bold and italic, but wait—does it really? Nope, it toggles the state of those features. Furthermore, it does not check their current states. If the text you selected before running the macro were already bold and italic, it would *remove* those attributes.

Here's another macro, BoldItalics2, that creates a snapshot of the text's complete character-level formatting status. When I recorded this macro, I simply opened the Font dialog box, clicked Bold Italic, and clicked OK. I did not touch any of these other options, yet they are included in the macro because the macro records everything that was in that dialog box.

```
Sub BoldItalics2()
'
' BoldItalics2 Macro
' Applies bold and italics from the Font dialog box.
'
    With Selection.Font
        .Name = "+Body"
        .Size = 11
        .Bold = True
        .Italic = True
        .Underline = wdUnderlineNone
        .UnderlineColor = wdColorAutomatic
        .StrikeThrough = False
```

```
            .DoubleStrikeThrough = False
            .Outline = False
            .Emboss = False
            .Shadow = False
            .Hidden = False
            .SmallCaps = False
            .AllCaps = False
            .Color = wdColorAutomatic
            .Engrave = False
            .Superscript = False
            .Subscript = False
            .Spacing = 0
            .Scaling = 100
            .Position = 0
            .Kerning = 0
            .Animation = wdAnimationNone
      End With
End Sub
```

Obviously, BoldItalics2 is the less efficient macro in terms of the number of lines of code needed, but because macros execute nearly instantaneously, it's not a big deal. Furthermore, BoldItalics2 is actually a better macro if what I really want is for bold and italic to be turned *on* by the macro in all cases, even if either one is already on. BoldItalics2 also removes any other formatting from the text that happened to be applied already. For example, if the selected text had been set to AllCaps, that would be removed by running BoldItalics2.

Notice in the BoldItalics2 code that a new element is being used you have not seen yet: a With statement. It defines Selection.Font as a parent category, and then everything under that within the With statement inherits that prefix. So, for example, .Italic = True is really Selection. Font.Italic = True.

If you wanted to make sure that bold and italic were turned on by the macro—not toggled—but you did not want to specify formatting for those other settings, you could simply delete the unwanted lines of code, ending up with something more efficient but still effective, like this:

```
Sub BoldItalics2()
'
' BoldItalics2 Macro
' Applies bold and italics from the Font dialog box.
'
      With Selection.Font
          .Bold = True
          .Italic = True
      End With
End Sub
```

Performing Actions Involving Logical Conditions

Some commands involve evaluating the document to see if a certain condition exists and then acting accordingly. The Replace command is an excellent example of that. In the following code, the Replace dialog box replaces all instances of "Sample" with "Example":

```vba
Sub FindReplace()
'
' FindReplace Macro
'
'
    Selection.Find.ClearFormatting
    Selection.Find.Replacement.ClearFormatting
    With Selection.Find
        .Text = "Sample"
        .Replacement.Text = "Example"
        .Forward = True
        .Wrap = wdFindContinue
        .Format = False
        .MatchCase = False
        .MatchWholeWord = False
        .MatchWildcards = False
        .MatchSoundsLike = False
        .MatchAllWordForms = False
    End With
    Selection.Find.Execute
    With Selection
        If .Find.Forward = True Then
            .Collapse Direction:=wdCollapseStart
        Else
            .Collapse Direction:=wdCollapseEnd
        End If
        .Find.Execute Replace:=wdReplaceOne
        If .Find.Forward = True Then
            .Collapse Direction:=wdCollapseEnd
        Else
            .Collapse Direction:=wdCollapseStart
        End If
        .Find.Execute
    End With
End Sub
```

Let's break this down a bit. First, there are two actions for clearing existing formatting applied in the Find and Replace dialog box:

```vba
Selection.Find.ClearFormatting
Selection.Find.Replacement.ClearFormatting
```

Next, there's a `With` statement, just like before, but this time specifying the settings in the Replace dialog box:

```
With Selection.Find
    .Text = "Sample"
    .Replacement.Text = "Example"
    .Forward = True
    .Wrap = wdFindContinue
    .Format = False
    .MatchCase = False
    .MatchWholeWord = False
    .MatchWildcards = False
    .MatchSoundsLike = False
    .MatchAllWordForms = False
End With
```

Next, the actual operation is executed. Notice that it is acting only upon the selection at this point:

```
Selection.Find.Execute
```

Then there's something you haven't seen yet: a couple of `If` statements that determine what happens based on whether the searched-for text is found.

```
With Selection
    If .Find.Forward = True Then
        .Collapse Direction:=wdCollapseStart
    Else
        .Collapse Direction:=wdCollapseEnd
    End If
    .Find.Execute Replace:=wdReplaceOne
    If .Find.Forward = True Then
        .Collapse Direction:=wdCollapseEnd
    Else
        .Collapse Direction:=wdCollapseStart
    End If
    .Find.Execute
End With
```

Finally, the macro ends up with another `Execute` statement, this time in general (not just on Selection):

```
.Find.Execute
```

Of course, these examples have just scratched the surface of what you need to know to effectively write your own VBA code or even to edit code with confidence. But they give you an idea of how to proceed as you learn more on your own.

Working with Macro Security

Back a few versions ago in Microsoft Office, macro viruses were prevalent. Some people figured out how to write executable virus code that could be stored in a macro; then whenever that macro was run as a document opened, the macro copied itself into the person's Normal.dot template, and from there it replicated itself to all new documents. (There was a variant in Excel, too.)

To counteract this, Microsoft developed macro security measures. These measures check a macro's source, author, or location and determine whether or not it is safe to run.

In the following sections, you learn how macro security works and how you can configure it to match your level of paranoia (er, *comfort with risk*).

> **note**
>
> Realistically, your chances of getting a macro virus these days are low. Because Word has included macro virus security for several versions now, people who create viruses have lost interest in making them. The last time I actually saw a Word macro virus in a file was about 10 years ago. Better safe than sorry, though.

Understanding Trusted Publishers and Locations

At first the security was simple: You could choose a level of security that applied to all macros in all files. But in Word 2010, macro security has become sophisticated, enabling you to distinguish between different locations and different macro publishers.

Word's macro security clamps down on running most macros in a document or template. (See "Setting Security Levels for Macro Running" later in this chapter for details.) However, Word relaxes its security when one of two conditions exist:

- The file containing the macro is stored in a trusted location.

- The macro has a digital signature from a trusted source.

A *trusted location* is one that Word recognizes as being your "home turf." When you place a file in a trusted location, you tell Word that it's okay to run whatever it finds in that file. This makes things much easier for amateur macro-writers who want to store their own macros in their own private templates, for example. It also makes it possible to run macros in files that friends and colleagues provide without having to go through the hassle of setting up digital signatures.

> To set up trusted locations, see "Specifying Trusted Locations," p. 802.

A *digital signature* is a code stored with the macro that compares itself to a code stored by an online or network signature

> **note**
>
> Both trusted locations and digital signatures are Office-wide features; they are not just for Word macros.

authority to determine that it is really from the author it purports to be from and that it has not been modified since that author published it. Digital signatures are somewhat complex to set up, but they're worthwhile if you are planning to distribute your macros to a wide audience, such as from a public website.

➡ *To set up digital signatures, see "Adding a Digital Signature," p. 809.*

Determining What Locations Are Trusted

Chapter 21, "Protecting and Securing Documents," deals with trusted locations in detail, but perhaps you're just curious at this point about what locations are already set up to be trusted on your system, so you can store your macro-enabled files there.

To find the trusted location list, follow these steps:

1. Choose File, Options and click Trust Center.

2. Click the Trust Center Settings button.

3. Click Trusted Locations. A list of locations appears in the Path column.

4. Click OK two times to close both dialog boxes.

Setting Security Levels for Macro Running

There are two ways to access the macro security settings in Word:

- On the Developer tab, click Macro Security.

- Choose File, Options, click Trust Center, click Trust Center Settings, and click Macro Settings.

The Macro Settings, shown in Figure 23.13, enable you to choose what happens when a file that is not in a trusted location contains macros. You can choose to enable or disable all, or you can differentiate between signed and unsigned ones.

It's up to you what settings you want to use, but I leave this set to Disable All Macros with Notification most of the time. That way I can see when a macro is trying to run, and I can then check it out and determine if it's something I want.

If you regularly run signed macros, you might choose instead Disable All Macros Except Digitally Signed Macros. Neither of the other two settings—Disable All Macros Without Notification and Enable All Macros—are optimal because each is extreme in its own direction.

Figure 23.13
Control how macros run (or don't run) when they're in files in untrusted locations.

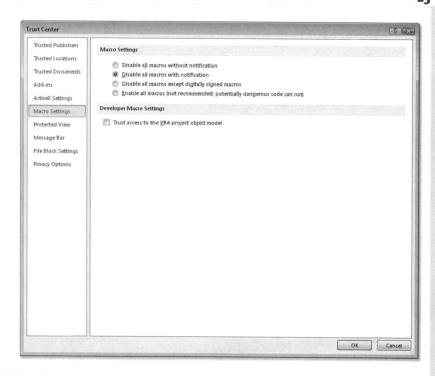

Working with Add-Ins

Add-ins are extra features that you can install for Word that extend its capabilities in some way. You can add, remove, or temporarily enable/disable the various add-ins in Word to control how it behaves.

You have already worked with some of the add-in types in this book. For example, Smart Tags (Chapter 2, "Typing and Editing Text") and templates (Chapter 8, "Working with Templates and Nonstandard Layouts") are add-ins.

One of the most powerful types of add-ins is a Component Object Model (COM) add-in. COM add-ins are supplemental programs that extend Word's capabilities by adding custom commands or features. COM add-ins can come from Microsoft or from third-party sources. They usually have a .dll or .exe extension and are written in a programming language such as Visual Basic or C++.

 note

In Word 2007 and 2010, you cannot save custom toolbars to a document or template, but you could in earlier Word versions. If you load a template containing custom toolbars, the toolbar buttons appear on an Add-Ins tab.

 caution

Many of the COM add-ins you'll find available for download on the Internet are written for earlier versions of Word, so their functionality in Word 2010 is uncertain.

To view installed add-ins, follow these steps:

1. Choose File, Options.

2. Click Add-Ins. A list of installed add-ins appears (see Figure 23.14).

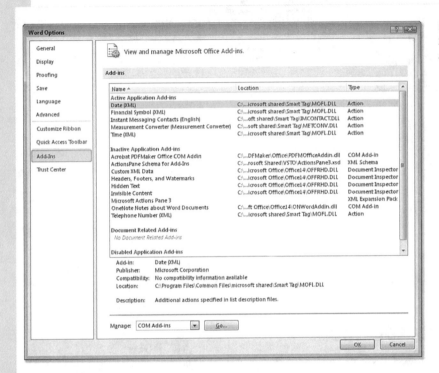

Figure 23.14
See a list of installed add-ins here.

An installed add-in can be either enabled or disabled. Having the option of disabling an add-in rather than removing it entirely is handy because it allows you to turn one off temporarily without losing it. Disabling add-ins is also helpful for troubleshooting. If you are not sure what add-in is causing Word to crash, you can disable them all and then enable them one at a time until you find the problem.

To disable or remove an add-in, you need to know what type it is, because the steps are different for the various types. To determine a type, look in the Type column.

Based on the type, open the Manage drop-down list at the bottom of the dialog box and select the desired add-in type. Then click Go to open a dialog box interface specifically for that type of add-in.

Enabling/Disabling COM Add-Ins

Choose COM Add-Ins in the Manage drop-down list and click Go to display the COM Add-Ins dialog box. It lists the available COM add-ins; you can select one and click Remove, or you can change its load behavior. You can also click Add to add more COM add-ins, although most COM add-ins come with their own setup programs that do that part for you.

Enabling/Disabling Actions

Choose Actions in the Manage drop-down list and click Go to display the AutoCorrect dialog box with the Actions controls, just like in "Working with Actions" in Chapter 3, "Correcting and Printing Documents."

Enabling/Disabling Other Add-Ins

The four remaining types of add-ins are controlled from the same dialog box. If you choose any of them and click Go, the Templates and Add-Ins dialog box opens. The dialog box contains separate tabs for each of the add-in types; add, remove, or enable/disable each type from its tab. Each of these is covered in more detail elsewhere in the book:

- **Templates**—See Chapter 8.

- **Linked CSS**—See Chapter 22, "Developing Online-Delivered Content."

Word Crashes After Enabling an Add-In

After a Word crash due to an add-in, Word will probably offer to start itself in Safe Mode the next time you start it. If it does not, hold down the Ctrl key as you click the icon or menu command to start Word to initiate Safe Mode. Then go to the list of add-ins (File, Options) and remove the one causing the problem. See "Working with Add-Ins" earlier in this chapter.

You should not use Word in Safe Mode for normal document editing because the following limitations are in effect:

- Add-ins are not loaded.

- No customizations are loaded or saved.

- You cannot save preferences.

- You cannot save templates.

- The AutoCorrect list is not loaded, and you cannot save changes to it.

- Recovered documents are not opened automatically.

- Smart Tags are not loaded, and you cannot save new tags.

- You cannot save files to the Alternate Startup Directory.

- You cannot create or open documents with restricted permission.

24

CUSTOMIZING THE WORD INTERFACE

Customization: It's Back

When Word 2007 was released, many people complained because the Ribbon was not easily customizable. You could customize the Quick Access toolbar via the Word Options dialog box, but further Ribbon customization required special utilities and an understanding of XML.

With Word 2010, Microsoft has listened to customer feedback and provided a robust way of customizing the Ribbon. You can not only make the customization changes from Word 2007, such as changing what's on the status bar and Quick Access toolbar, but you can add your own custom groups to Ribbon tabs, and you can even create your own tabs. This chapter explains all the customization options in Word 2010 so you can set up Word exactly the way you like it for maximum productivity.

Customizing the Quick Access Toolbar

The Quick Access toolbar is the row of buttons near the File tab in the top-left corner of the Word window. You can change its position (either above or below the Ribbon), add buttons to and remove buttons from it, as well as rearrange its buttons.

> ### tip
> Placing a button on the Quick Access toolbar is useful if you need access to that button no matter which Ribbon tab is displayed. If the button needs to be available only when you are working with a specific tab, you might want to add it to that tab instead; see "Customizing the Ribbon" later in this chapter.

Repositioning the Quick Access Toolbar

Depending on how it's set up, the Quick Access toolbar is either at the very top (in the title bar) or below the Ribbon. In the title bar, it's perhaps more easily accessible, but below the Ribbon there is more room for it, so you can have more buttons on it without interfering with the document name in the title bar.

To reposition the Quick Access toolbar, click the down arrow at its right end to open its menu, as shown in Figure 24.1, and choose Show Below the Ribbon (or Show Above the Ribbon, depending on its current position).

Figure 24.1
Open the Quick Access toolbar's menu with the down-pointing arrow on its right end.

Add Common Commands

The Quick Access toolbar's menu contains a list of common commands that people like to put on the toolbar. Each one of them can be toggled on or off by selecting it. A checkmark next to a command indicates that it is already on the toolbar (refer to Figure 24.1).

Add Commands from the Ribbon

Any button or control on any tab or menu on the Ribbon can be easily added to the Quick Access toolbar via its right-click menu. Simply right-click it and choose Add to Quick Access Toolbar.

Add Other Buttons

Word is such a feature-rich program that not all its features are made available by default. Some of these are less common features that there was simply no room for on the Ribbon; others are features that pertain only to certain specialty types of documents or are carryovers from earlier versions of Word. You can add these commands either to the Quick Access toolbar or to the Ribbon.

To browse the commands not already on the Ribbon and potentially add some of them to the Quick Access toolbar, follow these steps:

1. Choose File, Options.

2. Click Quick Access Toolbar.

3. Open the Choose Commands From list and select Commands Not in the Ribbon (see Figure 24.2).

4. Click a command and click Add to move it to the Quick Access toolbar.

5. Add more commands if desired.

6. Click OK.

 tip

Instead of steps 1 and 2, you can right-click any button on the Quick Access toolbar and choose Customize Quick Access Toolbar.

Figure 24.2
Add buttons to the Quick Access toolbar that have no Ribbon equivalent from here.

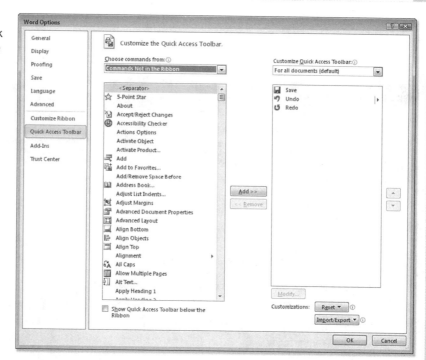

Remove Buttons

You can remove a button from the Customization options from the preceding section by clicking the command and clicking Remove (refer to Figure 24.2), but there's an easier way. You can simply right-click any button on the Quick Access toolbar and choose Remove from Quick Access Toolbar.

Customizing the Ribbon

You can customize any part of the Ribbon in Word 2010, which is a big improvement from Word 2007. You can even create your own new tabs, making it possible to consolidate the commands you use most often on a single tab for greater efficiency.

Minimizing the Ribbon

If you aren't using the Ribbon at the moment, you can hide it to get extra space on the screen to see more text at once. There are several ways to do this:

- Right-click any button on either the Ribbon or the Quick Access toolbar and choose Minimize the Ribbon.

- Click the up-pointing arrow above the Ribbon on the far right (see Figure 24.3).

- Press Ctrl+F1.

Click here to minimize the Ribbon.

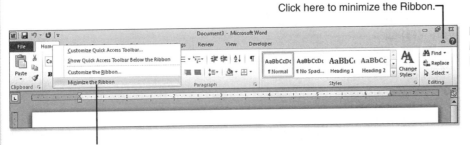

Figure 24.3
Minimize the Ribbon.

Right-click any button and
choose Minimize the Ribbon.

To redisplay it again, do any of the following:

- Right-click any button on the Quick Access toolbar and choose Minimize the Ribbon to toggle the option off.

- Click the down-pointing arrow in the upper-right corner of the Word window.

- Press Ctrl+F1.

Displaying or Hiding Tabs

If there are certain tabs you never use, you might want to hide them. For example, if you never use mail merge, there is little reason to keep the Mailings tab. Conversely, there

 caution

Some of the tabs listed in Figure 24.4 are not displayed all the time. For example, the Blog Post tab appears only when you are composing a blog post. If you disable one of these tabs and then perform an action that would normally make that tab appear, it won't appear. This can be perplexing to someone else using your computer who doesn't know you've hidden it, or even to yourself if you forgot you did.

may be nondefault tabs that you want to make available, such as the Developer tab (needed for creating forms and managing macros).

To choose which tabs display, follow these steps:

1. Right-click any button on the Ribbon and choose Customize the Ribbon. The Word Options dialog box opens with the Customize Ribbon tab displayed.

2. Mark or clear the check boxes as needed for each Ribbon tab listed in the right pane. See Figure 24.4.

3. Click OK.

Figure 24.4
Turn individual tabs on or off.

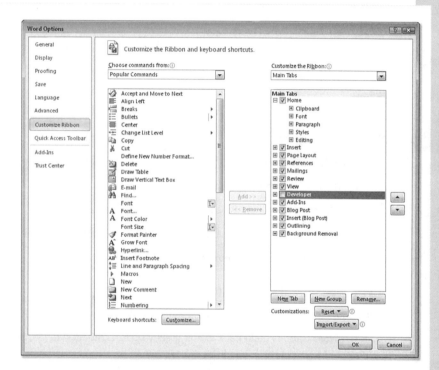

Creating or Deleting a Tab or a Custom Group

You can add any command to any tab, as long as it is in a custom group (that is, a user-created group). Therefore, you have to create the custom group before you can start customizing a tab. If desired, you can create a whole new tab and then create your custom groups on that new tab.

Creating a Custom Tab

To create your own tab, follow these steps:

1. Right-click any button on the Ribbon and choose Customize the Ribbon. The Word Options dialog box opens with the Customize Ribbon tab displayed.

2. On the Main Tabs list (right side of dialog box), click the existing tab that the new one should appear after (that is, to the right of).

3. Click New Tab. A new tab appears on the list called New Tab (Custom). By default it has one group in it: New Group (Custom). See Figure 24.5.

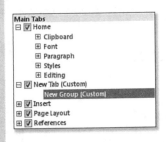

Figure 24.5
When you create a custom tab, a custom group is automatically created on it.

4. Click the new tab, and click the Rename button.

5. In the Rename dialog box, type a new name for the tab and click OK.

6. Click the new group within that new tab, and rename it the same way.

7. Click OK to close the dialog box, or leave it open for more editing.

Creating a Custom Group

Here's how to create a custom group:

1. If the Word Options dialog box is not already open, right-click any button on the Ribbon and choose Customize the Ribbon.

2. Click the tab on which you want to create the new group.

3. Click New Group. A new group is added to that tab, with the name New Group (Custom).

4. (Optional) Rename the group:

   - Click Rename.

   - Type a new name for the group.

   - Click an icon for the group. (This icon appears if the group is collapsed due to inadequate window width to display it.) See Figure 24.6.

   - Click OK.

5. Click OK to close the dialog box, or leave it open for more editing.

Figure 24.6
When you rename a group, you can also optionally change its icon.

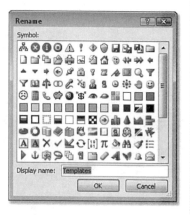

Deleting a Custom Tab or Group

To delete a custom tab or a custom group, right-click it on the Customize Ribbon tab of the Word Options dialog box, and choose Remove. You can only do this for custom tabs and groups, not the built-in ones.

🔍 **note**

All custom groups have the same name by default; Word does not number them or give them sequential names.

Adding or Removing Commands

You can't remove the standard commands on any of the built-in tabs; only the groups and commands you have placed yourself can be modified.

Adding a Command

To add a command to the Ribbon, follow these steps:

1. If the Word Options dialog box is not already open, right-click any button on the Ribbon and choose Customize the Ribbon.

2. Select the custom group to which you want to add the command.

3. On the list at the left, select the command to add.

   You might want to narrow down the list of commands by making a selection from the drop-down list first. For example, you could choose Commands Not in the Ribbon to exclude commands that are already on other tabs.

4. Click the Add button. The command appears under the group name on the right side of the window. See Figure 24.7.

5. Click OK to close the dialog box, or leave it open for more editing.

〰️ **tip**

Before you add a command to the Ribbon, consider whether it might be better to add it to the Quick Access toolbar instead. The Quick Access toolbar is always available, regardless of which tab is displayed. This can save you a step in executing the command because you never have to change tabs to get to it.

Click Add

The command appears under the custom group.

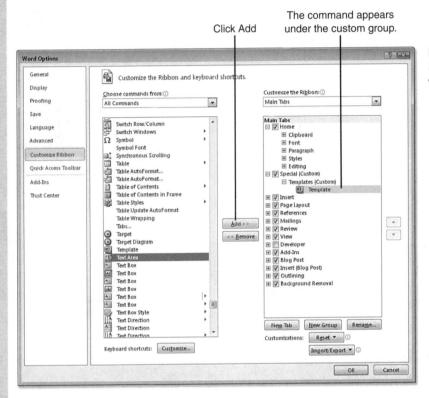

Figure 24.7
Populate a custom group with commands.

Removing a Command

To remove a command from the Ribbon:

1. If the Word Options dialog box is not already open, right-click any button on the Ribbon and choose Customize the Ribbon.

2. Right-click the command you want to remove from the list on the right side of the window.

3. Click Remove.

The command is removed from the custom group but is still available on the list on the left, for re-adding later to some other group or tab.

Renaming or Reordering Tabs

You can change the entire look of the Ribbon by renaming and/or reordering its tabs.

You can rename any tab, even the built-in ones. Just right-click the tab on the Customize Ribbon tab of the Word Options dialog box and choose Rename, and then type the new name. Word does not check whether each name is unique, so you can name them all the same thing if you like. (That wouldn't be very useful, though.)

To move a tab or group, right-click it and then click Move Up or Move Down.

Resetting Customizations

It's easy to get carried away with customizing Word and end up with an interface you barely recognize. If this happens, reset the Ribbon to its original state and start over.

To reset only one tab:

1. If the Word Options dialog box is not already open, right-click any button on the Ribbon and choose Customize the Ribbon.

2. Click the Reset button. A menu opens.

3. Click Reset Only Selected Ribbon Tab.

4. Click OK to close the dialog box, or leave it open for further editing.

To reset all customizations, including any custom shortcut keys:

1. If the Word Options dialog box is not already open, right-click any button on the Ribbon and choose Customize the Ribbon.

2. Click the Reset button. A menu opens.

3. Click Reset All Customizations.

4. Click OK to close the dialog box, or leave it open for further editing.

Exporting and Importing Customization Settings

After you get the Ribbon and other customizations just the way you like them, what happens if you need to switch to a different computer? The good news is, you don't have to recustomize everything; you can export your customization settings to a file. Then you can transfer that file to the other PC and import the customization settings there.

Exporting Customizations

To export your customization settings, follow these steps:

1. If the Word Options dialog box is not already open, right-click any button on the Ribbon and choose Customize the Ribbon.

2. Click the Import/Export button. A menu opens.

3. Click Export All Customizations. The File Save dialog box opens.

4. (Optional) Change the filename and location if desired.

5. Click Save.

6. Click OK to close the Word Options dialog box.

Importing Customizations

User interface configuration files like the one you just saved in the preceding section can be imported into Word 2010 on any other PC. Importing wipes out any customization settings on that PC, so make sure there are no customizations that you can't reproduce that you want to keep before doing this.

Here's how:

1. If the Word Options dialog box is not already open, right-click any button on the Ribbon and choose Customize the Ribbon.

2. Click the Import/Export button. A menu opens.

3. Click Import Customization File. The File Open dialog box displays.

4. Select the customization file and click Open.

5. A confirmation box appears; click Yes.

6. Click OK to close the Word Options dialog box.

Defining Shortcut Keys

Word has many shortcut keys predefined, such as Ctrl+C for Copy, Ctrl+S for Save, and so on. You can add to these assignments, and even change the assignments for key combinations. That way if any of the shortcuts are awkward for you to use, you can use keys that feel more natural for your most-used activities.

To define shortcut keys, follow these steps:

1. Right-click any button on the Ribbon and choose Customize the Ribbon.

2. Next to Keyboard Shortcuts, click Customize. The Customize Keyboard dialog box opens.

3. Select the command to which to assign the shortcut. Do this by first choosing a category at the left and then a command on the right (see Figure 24.8).

4. Look in the Current Keys box to see if there is a current key assignment for the command. That assignment is removed if you define a new assignment.

5. Click in the Press New Shortcut Key box and then press the key combination to assign.

6. By default, the assignments are stored in Normal.dotm. If you want them assigned somewhere else (such as in the current document only), select that location from the Save Changes In list.

7. Repeat steps 3–5 for other keyboard shortcuts.

8. Click Close.

9. Click OK.

Figure 24.8
Define shortcut keys.

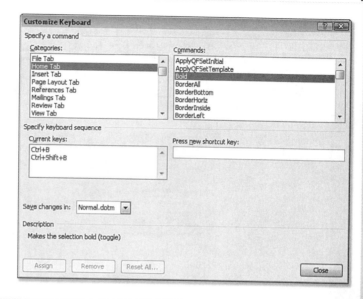

Changing Viewing Options

There are lots of ways you can change the way the Word window appears and the way documents appear within it. These can be broken down into the following broad categories:

- **View settings**—These basic settings can be adjusted from the View tab at any time. These were covered in Chapter 1, in the section titled "Working with Views."

- **Status bar content**—You can control what appears in the status bar, such as indicators for word count, page count, and macro controls.

- **Word Options settings**—You can use the Word Options dialog box to configure various settings that aren't available elsewhere.

Changing the Status Bar Content

The status bar is the bar at the bottom of the Word window, below the horizontal scroll bar. The status bar, by default, contains only a few pieces of information, such as the page count and word count, some view buttons, and a zoom slider. You can customize it by following these steps:

1. Right-click the status bar. A menu opens with check marks next to the displayed items.

2. Click an item to toggle it on or off (see Figure 24.9).

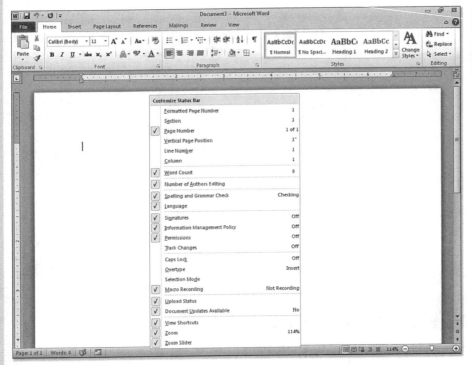

Figure 24.9
Choose what
should appear
on the status
bar.

Changing Page Display and Formatting Marks

You can change page display and formatting marks settings from the Display options of the Word Options dialog box. Follow these steps:

1. Choose File, Options. The Word Options dialog box opens.

2. Click Display.

3. In the Page Display Options section, mark or clear these check boxes (see Figure 24.10):

   - **Show White Space Between Pages in Print Layout View**—If this is enabled, the pages appear to be separated vertically; if disabled, they run together like continuous-feed paper.

   - **Show Highlighter Marks**—When this is enabled, highlighting appears both onscreen and when printed. You can disable it to hide highlighting temporarily without having to remove the highlighting.

   - **Show Document ToolTips on Hover**—When this is enabled, ToolTips (pop-up messages) appear whenever you point the mouse at something that has a tip associated with it, such as a button on the Ribbon.

Figure 24.10
Set page display and
formatting mark display
options.

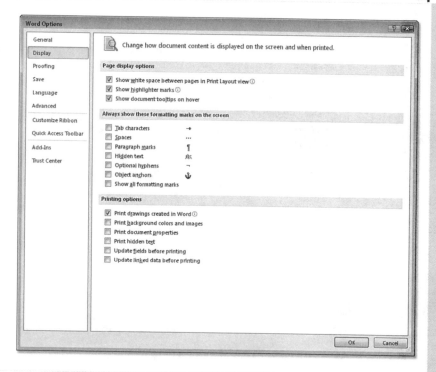

4. In the Always Show These Formatting Marks on the Screen section, mark or clear the check boxes for the various types of formatting marks.

   Note that these settings do not depend on the Show/Hide (¶) button's state (on the Home tab). For example, if you mark the check box here for Tab Characters, tab characters are always displayed, regardless of the Show/Hide (¶) button. However, if you clear that check box, tab characters are shown or hidden according to the button's status.

5. Click OK.

You can find additional display options under Advanced. Click Advanced and then scroll down to the Display section.

Setting General Options

In the General section of the Word Options dialog box are three sections: User Interface Options, Personalize Your Copy of Microsoft Office, and Startup Options (see Figure 24.11).

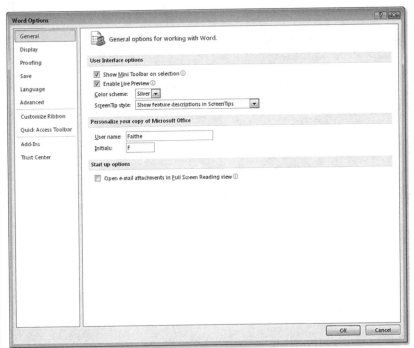

Figure 24.11
Set personalization
options.

The User Interface Options section includes a compilation of miscellaneous popular settings with no special theme to them:

- **Show Mini Toolbar on Selection**—When this is enabled and you point at some selected text, the Mini Toolbar pops up for quick access to formatting buttons (see Figure 24.12).

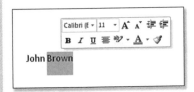

Figure 24.12
The Mini Toolbar, when enabled, appears when you point at selected text.

- **Enable Live Preview**—When this option is enabled and you point to a setting on a gallery or menu from the Ribbon, a preview of that effect shows on the selected text.

- **Color Scheme**—Here you can choose a color scheme for Office programs. This setting applies across all Office programs, not just Word. For example, the color scheme used for the figures in this book is the Silver scheme.

■ **ScreenTip Style**—From this drop-down list, you can choose to show no ScreenTips, regular ScreenTips (small amount of information, small pop-ups), or enhanced ScreenTips (full information). Figure 24.13 shows the difference between a regular and an enhanced ScreenTip.

Figure 24.13
A regular (left) and enhanced (right) ScreenTip.

■ **User Name and Initials**—Customize your copy of Word by entering this information. Your name and initials appear in various places throughout Word, including when you do mail merge and when you make comments and revisions. They also identify you as the author of the document in the document's properties.

■ **Open E-Mail Attachments in Full Screen Reading View**—When this is enabled and you open a Word document from your email program (Outlook, Windows Mail, or other program), and the document opens in Word, the document opens in Full Screen Reading view. Otherwise, it opens in Print Layout view.

Changing File Locations

Word has a variety of locations set up for saving different types of files, including documents, templates, AutoRecover files, and saved themes. You can configure these file locations in the Word Options dialog box, but different types of files are set up in different places.

To set the default AutoRecover file location and the default location for saving regular Word files, follow these steps:

1. Choose File, Options. The Word Options dialog box opens.

2. Click Save.

3. In the AutoRecover File Location box, type a path to the location where you want AutoRecover files stored (see Figure 24.14). Alternatively, you can click the Browse button and browse for a location.

4. In the Default File Location box, type a path to the location you want to appear by default in the Save As and Open dialog boxes when saving or opening Word documents. Alternatively, you can click the Browse button and browse for a location.

> **note**
>
> AutoRecover files are created automatically at the interval specified in the Save AutoRecover Information Every box. If Word crashes or terminates abnormally, the AutoRecover files are loaded so you can recover part of your unsaved work.

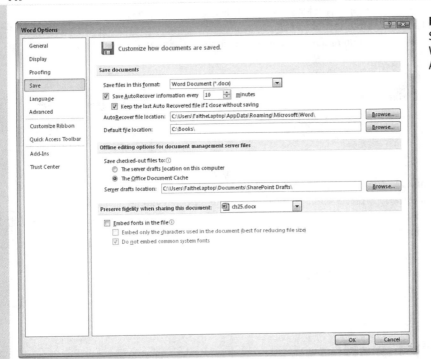

Figure 24.14
Set the locations for
Word documents and
AutoRecover files here.

5. (Optional) If you work with SharePoint server drafts and you want to set a location for those drafts on your local hard disk, enter or change it in the Server Drafts Location box. Alternatively, you can click the Browse button and browse for a location.

6. Click OK to close the Word Options dialog box.

   Alternatively, if you need to set the default locations for other types of files, continue the steps as follows:

7. Click Advanced, and then scroll down to the bottom of the window and click File Locations. The File Locations dialog box opens (see Figure 24.15).

8. Click a file type and then click Modify.

9. Browse to the desired location and then click OK.

10. Repeat steps 8–9 for each location you want to change; then click OK.

11. Click OK to close the Word Options dialog box.

Figure 24.15
Set locations for other file types here.

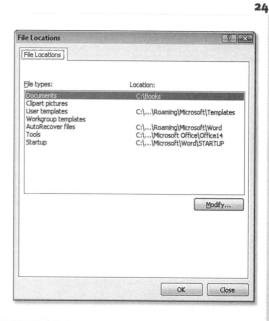

Other Customization Options

Throughout this book, I've introduced you to bits and pieces of customization as applicable to various features in Word. Here's a list of where these are covered:

- "Setting File-Handling Preferences," p. 47

- "Customizing Spelling and Grammar Options," p. 100

- "Customizing and Extending the Research Tools," p. 125

- "Setting Print Options for Word Documents," p. 135

- "Setting Options for a Certain Printer," p. 136

- "Storing Different Properties for a Single Printer," p. 138

- "Customizing the Styles Pane," p. 225

- "Configuring Word's Built-in Colaboration Tools," p. 758

- "Adjusting Macro Settings," p. 804

- "Setting Privacy Options," p. 809

- "Specifying Trusted Locations," p. 802

- "Working with Trusted Publishers," p. 804

- "Options for Web Page Saving," p. 816

- "Setting Security Levels for Macro Running," p. 858

RECOVERING FILES AND REPAIRING WORD

Recovering Document Files

So your computer just crashed, or lost power, and you haven't saved your work lately. Nearly everyone who has ever used Word has experienced this now and then. It happens. Programs crash. Data gets lost.

However, with Word 2010, not much data typically gets lost because of the very good data-recovery features built in. As in earlier versions, Word saves your work in temporary files every few minutes, and after a crash, it attempts to load those temporary files so you can recover any unsaved changes to your documents. Therefore, the most you are likely to lose is a few minutes' worth of work.

In this appendix, you'll learn how to use and configure Word's data recovery features, how to repair problems with Word and with corrupted files, and how to safeguard your work by enabling Word to create automatic backup copies of previous document versions.

Using the Document Recovery Task Pane

As you work, Word silently creates AutoRecover versions of your document in the background. These are not regular saved files, but temporary files that store the edits you have made to the file since you last saved it. They are deleted when you successfully close the file or exit the program. If the program doesn't exit normally, though, the files are still hanging around, and the AutoRecover feature can use them to help you restore your lost work the next time you start Word.

When you start Word after a crash, the Document Recovery task pane appears and lists the files that Word was able to recover. For example, in Figure A.1, four files are available.

Notice in Figure A.1 that there are actually only two documents represented; there are two versions of each document offered. One is tagged [Autosaved] and the other is [Original]. The Autosaved version is the more recent one, containing changes made since the last save.

To open one of the Autosaved versions, click it. When you are finished opening Autosaved files, click Close to close the Document Recovery task pane.

> **note**
>
> AutoRecover files are stored separately for each user. So, for example, if one user crashes Word and then shuts down the PC before attempting to recover a lost document, and then another user logs in and opens Word, the second user will not see the first user's automatically recovered documents.

It's important to note that the Autosaved version is not a "real" Word document. It's a temporary version, and it won't exist anymore after you close Word, unless you save it. You can save it under a new name with Save As, or you can replace the original copy by clicking Save.

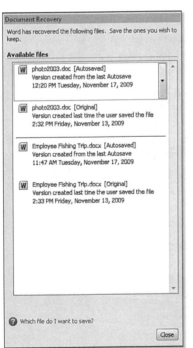

Figure A.1
Select files to recover upon startup after a crash.

Setting AutoRecover Options

By default, AutoRecover makes temporary copies of your open files every 10 minutes. If your time is very valuable and your work important, you might want to change the time to a smaller interval, such as 5 or even 3 minutes. Word slows down (very slightly) for a moment whenever it does a background save operation, but you lose less data in the event of a crash.

You can also change the AutoRecover file location. By default, it is in a user-specific location, so each user's Autosaved files are private:

- **In Windows Vista or Windows 7**—C:\Users\username\AppData\Roaming\Microsoft\Word
- **In Windows XP**—C:\Documents and Settings\username\Application Data\Microsoft\Word

If you would like one user to be able to access another user's Autosaved files, change the folder to one that's more easily accessible for all users.

To set the interval and the file location, follow these steps:

1. Choose File, Options. The Word Options dialog box opens.

2. Click Save.

tip

To turn off AutoRecover, clear the check box. But why turn it off? There's a tremendous upside to using it, and virtually no downside.

3. If desired, change the interval in the Save AutoRecover Information Every ___ Minutes box (see Figure A.2).

Figure A.2
Set AutoRecover options here.

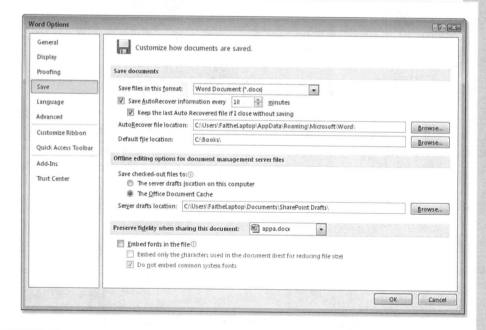

4. If desired, change the AutoRecover file location. You can either type a path or click the Browse button to browse for a location via the dialog box interface.

5. Click OK to save the changes.

Recovering Data from an Unreadable File

If Word can't open a file, and it's in the native Word 2010 format (that is, WordML format), you might be able to extract some of the text from it by deconstructing the file and browsing it as XML code.

Here's how to do this:

1. In Windows Explorer, rename the file to have a .zip extension instead of .docx.

2. Double-click the .zip file. A set of folders and XML documents appears.

3. Double-click the Word folder.

4. Double-click Document.xml. The text for the document appears in XML markup.

5. Copy the text to the Clipboard (select it and press Ctrl+C) and then paste it into a new document in Word or any text editor.

6. Clean up the text by deleting the XML codes.

 tip

You can also sometimes access an AutoRecover version of a file with the File, Info, Manage Versions, Recover Unsaved Documents command.

tip

You might need to turn on the display of file extensions in order to see what you're doing in step 1. To do so, from Windows Explorer, choose Organize, Folder and Search Options (in Windows 7). Click the View tab and clear the Hide Extensions for Known File Types check box. Click OK.

Creating Automatic Backup Copies

Have you ever made changes to a document, saved your work, and then regretted it? You're in good company. Most people have. And because it's a user error and not a program error, Word can't protect you.

However, you can configure Word to automatically save a backup copy of each document right before you save changes, so you'll always have the next-to-last version as well as the last one on hand. To set this up, follow these steps:

1. Choose File, Options. The Word Options dialog box opens.

2. Click Advanced.

3. Scroll down to the Save section and mark the Always Create Backup Copy check box.

4. Click OK.

The backup copy is stored in the same location as the original, with the same name except with "Backup of" added to the beginning. The extension on the backup files is .wbk rather than the usual .docx. When you open a backup file, it opens in Protected mode.

Dealing with Word Crashes

Word does occasionally crash, just like any other application. What do you do? The following sections provide some advice.

Sending Error Reports

Depending on the way you have set up your system, when Word crashes you might also see a prompt to send Microsoft an error report. No personal information about you is sent with these reports; Microsoft simply wants the technical codes behind the crash so it can keep track of what's wrong with the program and fix it.

Occasionally, after you agree to submit an error report, an additional dialog box appears asking for more information about the crash. Typically it asks for your permission to upload portions of the document that was open when the crash occurred. You're free to say no to this if the data is sensitive, but rest assured that the people who see it at Microsoft have no interest in your personal or business life; they just want to stop the program from crashing.

One benefit of submitting the report is that sometimes a dialog box appears afterward with a hyperlink you can click to take you to the Microsoft support site, where you can read an article that explains how to prevent that particular crash in the future. If you decline to send the error report, you don't get that information.

Checking for Program Updates

Most of the time, a crash is a one-time deal. After a crash, you should recover your documents and then reboot your PC. Usually the problem doesn't return.

If the problem does return, try updating Word. Choose File, Help, Check for Updates.

If you are using Windows Vista or Windows 7, the update utility is built into the Control Panel; the web page opens the Control Panel for you and starts Windows Update.

If you are using Windows XP, the update utility is web-based; follow the instructions on the web page to check for available updates.

Fixing Crashes Related to a Certain Document

If the problem reoccurs but only with a certain file, here are some things to try:

- Reboot. Until you've tried this, you can't assume that the document is at fault.

- If you can open the file in Word, immediately save it in a different format (such as Word 97-2003 format). Sometimes a different format clears a corruption problem with a file.

- If saving in a different format doesn't help, select all the content from the file and copy it to the Clipboard; then start a new blank document, paste the Clipboard content into it, and save the file.

  ➡️ *If you cannot open the file in Word at all, see "Recovering Data from an Unreadable File,"* *p. 884.*

Disabling Add-Ins and Extensions

Often, Word itself is not the cause of a recurring crash, but rather an add-in (an optional component, usually created by some company other than Microsoft). Add-ins are covered in Chapter 23, "Macros and Add-Ins."

If Word is able to identify a startup item that is causing a problem, it disables that item automatically the next time you start Word. This is called Automated Safe Mode. When this happens, a prompt typically appears, letting you know that the item is being disabled.

If Word starts up okay but then crashes frequently after it has been running a bit, it's possible the problem is occurring when a certain add-in or extension is executing its code in response to some action you are taking. In a situation like this, you at least have the leisure of examining what's loading and trying to disable some things. Follow these steps:

1. Choose File, Options.

2. When the Word Options dialog box opens, click Add-Ins. A list appears of all your add-ins, both active and inactive (see Figure A.3). The add-ins on your system might differ from the ones shown in Figure A.3.

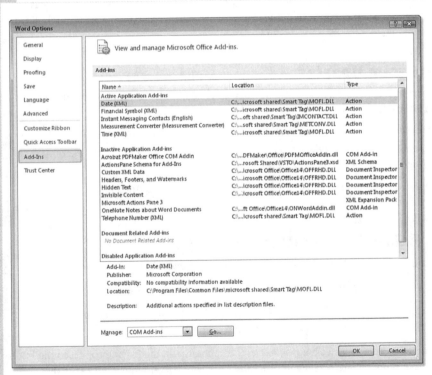

Figure A.3
Check what's loading automatically at startup.

Some of the types you might see include the following:

- **Template**—A template can contain macros, so there's a possibility of a macro causing a problem or carrying a virus. However, Word manages templates pretty tightly, so they're not a likely suspect for a crash.

- **Action**—Most of these are Actions (a.k.a. Smart Tags) provided by Microsoft. Actions are generally harmless and can be left enabled. To learn more about them, see "Working with Actions," p. 115.

- **COM Add-Ins and Word Add-Ins**—Here's what's probably causing the error. A COM add-in is a mini application that runs within Word, usually written by a third party. A Word add-in is one that's specific to Word. Poorly written add-ins can cause crashes.

- **XML Schemas and XML Expansion Packs**—These help extend Word's XML capabilities. They're not likely to cause problems.

If you have a hunch about a particular add-in causing a problem, try disabling it. Note the add-in type in the Type column (see Figure A.3) and then open the Manage list, select that type, and click Go. The dialog box that appears depends on what type you've chosen. For example, Figure A.4 shows the one for COM add-ins. (COM stands for common object model; many third-party add-ins use this format.)

Figure A.4
Check what types of add-ins are loading automatically at startup to track down a malfunctioning add-in.

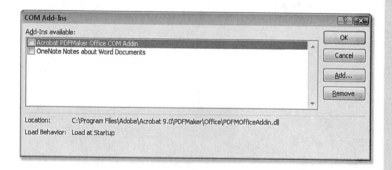

You can disable the add-in by removing the check mark from the add-in's check box or by highlighting it in the dialog box and clicking the Remove button.

CONVERTING FROM OTHER WORD PROCESSING SYSTEMS

Converting from Previous Word Versions

If you are upgrading to Word 2010 from an earlier version of Microsoft Word, you'll be pleasantly surprised at the ease with which your new program handles your old files. In most cases, they open seamlessly and automatically, with no warnings or decisions to make.

Ever since the earliest versions, Microsoft Word has standardized on the .doc extension for its files. Although Word 2007 and Word 2010 changed this to .docx for its native-format files or .docm for macro-enabled documents, all versions of Word can still open .doc files, too.

To make sure .doc files are displayed in the Open dialog box, choose All Word Documents in the Files of Type list (see Figure B.1). If this setting is set to Word Documents (.docx), only the Word 2007 and 2010 format files appear.

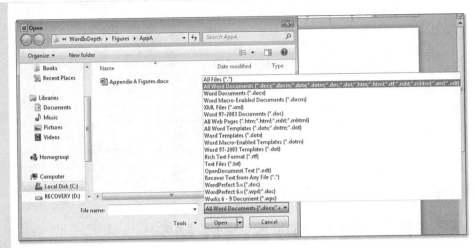

Figure B.1
Make sure
the Files of
Type setting
is All Word
Documents
to catch all
the files from
previous Word
versions.

Converting from Microsoft Works

Microsoft Works is an all-in-one suite of applications designed for casual or home use; it's like a scaled-down version of Office. New versions of it are no longer being released; the latest version, Version 9, has been out for quite a few years now.

There have actually been two different Microsoft Works products sold: the regular Works, which has its own proprietary word processor, and Works Suite, which has Microsoft Word as its word processor. If you use Works Suite, you're good to go with the instructions from the preceding section.

There have been many versions of Microsoft Works over the years, starting with an MS-DOS version; there have also been several Mac versions. They all use the same file extension: .wps. The actual file formats, however, have changed dramatically over the years. Word 2010 supports only the files from the post-2001 versions (6.0 and higher).

If your Works word processor file is version 6.0 or higher, you can open it from the Open dialog box by choosing Works 6 - 9 Document (*.wps) as the Files of Type setting.

If your Works version is lower than 6.0, you need to perform an interim save step. In your version of Works, use the Save As command to save the file in Rich Text Format (.rtf); then open the resulting file in Word 2010.

Converting from WordPerfect

Earlier versions of Word included extensive tools and help for people upgrading to Word from WordPerfect. This was deemed necessary because WordPerfect was the most popular word processor in the world for more than a decade.

However, nowadays WordPerfect is not nearly the powerhouse it once was, and people converting to Word from older versions of WordPerfect are now few and far between. Therefore, in Word 2010,

Microsoft has drastically scaled back the WordPerfect transitional features. Gone are the special WordPerfect shortcut key conversion helpers from the Help system, for example.

Word 2010 will open WordPerfect files in either 5.x or 6.x format. WordPerfect 5.x files use the .doc extension (which can be confusing because that was Word's default extension); WordPerfect 6.x files use either the .doc or .wpd extension.

To open WordPerfect files, set Files of Type to the appropriate file type. If you are not sure which WordPerfect version file you have, choose WordPerfect 6.x because that includes both of the possible file extensions.

Converting from an Unsupported File Format

Occasionally you may encounter a file created in some really old, odd word processing system. Perhaps the original program that created it isn't available anymore, so there's no way of saving it in a more compatible format.

You might not be able to preserve all the formatting from such a file, but you can at least extract the text from it. To do so, in the Open dialog box, set Files of Type to Recover Text from Any File (*.*). This enables Word to see every file type. Then select the file and click Open, and Word does its best to extract as much text as possible.

Confirming File Conversions

Word 2010 converts files silently as it opens them whenever possible. If you want to be notified when this happens, turn on the Confirm File Format Conversion on Open feature by following these steps:

1. Choose File, Options. The Word Options dialog box opens.

2. Click Advanced.

3. Scroll down to the General section and mark the Confirm File Format Conversion on Open check box.

4. Click OK.

Sharing Word Documents with Other Programs

The default file format in Word 2010 is .docx, a proprietary XML-based format that is not compatible with any other version of Word (except 2007) or any other word processor on the market. (The macro-enabled version, .docm, isn't compatible with anything else but Word 2007 either.)

If you need to share a document with someone who uses some other program, you need to use the Save As feature to save it in another file format. For Word versions from Word 97 to Word 2003, the Word 97-2003 format is your best bet; for earlier versions than that, use Word 97-2003 & 6.0/95 – RTF.

What's with the extremely long name for that format? Well, it's a hybrid file format that combines the features of all the older Word versions, all the way back to Word 95, and stores them in Rich Text Format (RTF). All that compatibility is achieved at the expense of file size; the files saved in this format are large, but they're backward-compatible. You can even open these files in Windows WordPad and nearly all versions of WordPerfect.

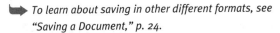 *To learn about saving in other different formats, see "Saving a Document," p. 24.*

Word 2010 does not save in WordPerfect or other word processing formats (except Microsoft Works), but most of those programs will accept Rich Text Format (RTF) files and Word 97-2003 files, so in most cases it is best to try opening the file in the other word processing program. If it won't open, you can at least see what formats the program does accept and then try to find one that Word can save as.

Setting a Default Save Format

If not everyone in your group has upgraded to Word 2007 or 2010, you will not be able to share Word documents in the default Word 2010 format with some people.

If you frequently share documents with others who use earlier versions, and you don't want to worry about whether they have the needed converter, your best bet is to set up Word to save by default in the Word 97-2003 format.

To specify a different file format as your default save format, follow these steps:

1. Choose File, Options. The Word Options dialog box opens.

2. Click Save.

3. Open the Save Files in This Format list and select the desired file format (see Figure B.2).

4. Click OK.

 note

For users of Word 2003 and earlier, Microsoft has made a Compatibility Pack available for free download that enables those versions to open Word 2010 files. You can download it from http://office.microsoft.com. You can't assume that everyone who has an earlier version of Word will do this, however, so it's usually best to save files in Word 97-2003 format if you think others who don't have Word 2007 or 2010 might want to read them.

 caution

If you need to password-protect documents—or use protection for tracked changes, comments, or forms—you should know that these documents lose their protection when saved back to Word 97-2003 and 6.0/95 - RTF format.

 note

The default format you specify affects only new files; when you resave an existing file, it is saved in its existing format.

Figure B.2
Choose a different format as your default save format.

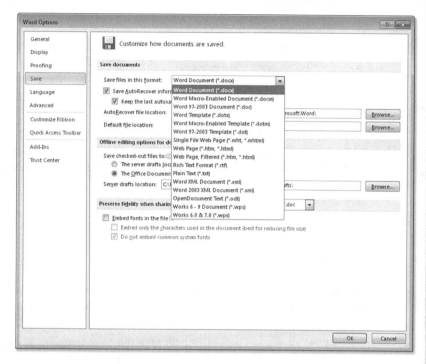

Displaying Word Files on Computers Without Any Version of Word

Microsoft Word isn't free, of course, and not all computers have it installed. If you encounter a system that doesn't have Word but needs to open Word documents, here are some options:

- Users can open Word 97-2003 documents in WordPad, the free word processing application that comes with Microsoft Windows. Some of the features of the Word document will not be visible, and you cannot save in Word format from WordPad. (However, you can save in Rich Text Format, which all versions of Word can open.)

- You can use Word 2010 to save in HTML format, which anyone using a Web browser can read.

- You can use Word 2010 to save in PDF format, which anyone with Adobe Reader can read. (Adobe Reader is free from www.adobe.com.)

 caution

The Windows XP and Windows Vista versions of WordPad cannot open Word 2010 files, so you need to save the files in an earlier format to share with these users. The Windows 7 version of WordPad can open a Word 2010 document but not all features are supported.

- You can use Word 2010 to save in XPS format, which anyone with Windows Vista or Windows 7 can read through Windows' XPS reader utility.

- You can save in a plain-text format, which can then be opened in any text application on any type of computer, including mainframes, Linux, UNIX, Macintosh, and so on. Some of those systems might not accept disks formatted in the Windows/DOS file system, but you can transfer files to such systems as email attachments or via a network gateway.

- You can provide the Microsoft Word Viewer, a free application that can be copied and distributed. This small program, available for download from http://office.microsoft.com (search for "Word viewer"), enables any Windows user to view and print any Word 97-2003 document. It supports many, although not all, Word 2010 features. For example, it supports Print Layout view, Outline view, Web Layout view, Document Map, zooming, headers, footers, footnotes, comments, and hyperlinks.

 tip

You can use Word Viewer as a helper application for viewing Word documents downloaded from the Internet. Word Viewer can also make it a little easier to work with customer and vendor organizations that have standardized on a different word processing platform.

The downside is that you can't edit text in Word Viewer. However, you can copy the text into another application through the Windows Clipboard and then paste that text into some other text-editing program.

Although Word Viewer can coexist with Word on the same computer, it works best on computers on which Word isn't installed. Even though the Word Viewer Setup program is designed to ask whether Word or Word Viewer should be the default for opening Word files, you may sometimes find that the wrong application loads if they are both installed.

SETTING UP AND MODIFYING OFFICE 2010

Installing Office 2010

Word 2010 is part of the Microsoft Office 2010 suite of programs. Although you can buy Word as a standalone product, most people either buy it as part of Office or get it preinstalled on a new computer.

Installing Office is simple. You just put the DVD into your PC and follow the prompts that appear. There are only two points at which you have significant interaction with the Setup program: You enter the product key and accept the software license terms, and you decide whether to do a standard or custom install. (Then if you choose the custom install, you pick the components to install and the folder in which you want to install them.) If you are upgrading from a previous edition of Office, you are also prompted whether to upgrade (replacing your current version) or install new (leaving the old version installed as well).

Clicking Customize opens an extra screen with three tabs: Installation Options, File Location, and User Information. These tabs are detailed in the following sections.

 note

You can keep all previous versions of all programs except Outlook; installing Outlook 2010 removes Outlook 2007 (and earlier versions) automatically.

Installation Options

On the Installation Options tab, you can choose which applications to install, what subcomponents of each one you want, and which overall shared components to install. Each item that appears in white on the list is set to be completely installed. Each item that appears in gray is set to be partially installed; click the plus sign next to such an item to see the subitems and their statuses (see Figure C.1).

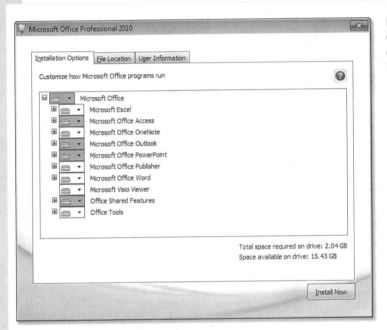

Figure C.1
On the Installation Options tab, choose which components to install.

To change the installation status of an item, click its down arrow and select the desired status from its menu. The choices are

- **Run from My Computer**—This option will be installed.

- **Installed on First Use**—This option will be installed when you issue the command to use it for the first time. You might be prompted for the Office DVD at that point.

- **Not Available**—This option will not be available.

File Location

On the File Location tab, enter the root path for storing the Office files. The default path is C:\ Program Files\Microsoft Office. This is called the root path because it's the top level under which many subfolders will be created. For example, within that folder, an Office14 folder will be created, and within that, folders for various helper files.

User Information

On the User Information tab, enter your name, company, and initials. These are optional, but if you do enter them, Word uses them to assign Author properties to the documents you create, and Word uses your initials to sign revision marks and comments you place into documents.

Modifying or Repairing Your Office Installation

After Office has been installed, you can still access its Setup program from the Control Panel and use it to modify, repair, or reinstall Office.

Follow these steps to access Setup:

1. From the Control Panel:

   - In Windows Vista or Windows 7, choose Programs, Programs and Features.

   - In Windows XP, choose Add or Remove Programs.

2. Click Microsoft Office 2010 (or Microsoft Word 2010) in the list of programs. The name varies slightly depending on the version you have and includes the version name, such as Standard or Professional.

3. Click the Change button. In Windows Vista or Windows 7, if a user account control window pops up asking for permission to continue, click Continue.

4. In the Microsoft Office window, choose the option you want:

   - **Add or Remove Features**—Opens the Installation Options list, the same as with a custom install (refer to Figure C.1). Set each component to the desired setting: Run from My Computer, Installed on First Use, or Not Available.

   - **Repair**—Repairs the current installation without adding or removing components.

   - **Remove**—Removes the entire program from your system.

   - **Enter a Product Key**—Enables you to upgrade a trial or limited version of Office by entering a product key that you purchase from Microsoft.

5. Click Continue, and then follow the prompts to complete the Setup activity you chose to perform.

> ⚑ **caution**
>
> The main reason to change the file location is to store Office on another hard disk, either because your main hard disk is nearly full or because you prefer that Windows applications be installed on their own drive. When a hard disk gets too full, Windows starts having performance issues because there is not enough extra space to create the virtual memory the system needs. Therefore, if your hard disk is nearly full, it's much better to buy a new hard disk and install Word on it than to try to squeeze it onto your existing drive.

Optional Tools and Shared Features

The steps for a custom installation in Office are fairly simple, as you just saw, and it's simple at any time to change the options that are installed. The tricky part is knowing which options you want and why.

Office 2010 comes with a variety of tools and shared features, none of which is necessary for using Word. The exact set of them depends on the version of Office you have. Most of the available tools are installed automatically in a default install, but not all of them. You might want to pick through them and remove the ones that you will never need or add the ones that look interesting that aren't already installed. Table C.1 summarizes what's available.

Table C.1 Optional Tools and Shared Features

Location in Setup	Option	Installed by Default?	Description
Microsoft Word	.NET Programmability Support	Yes	Allows Word programmability with .NET Framework version 1.1 or greater.
	Page Border Art	Yes	Graphics used for the Page Border feature (Borders and Shading dialog box).
	Quick Formatting Files	Yes	Theme files used for Quick Formats in Word.
Office Shared Features	Business Connectivity Services	Yes	Extends SharePoint and Office User Experience and Capabilities to external data and services.
	Clip Organizer	Yes	This is not actually the Clip Organizer utility itself, but rather the collections of art that are installed locally to your hard disk. There are two categories: AutoShapes and Themes, and Popular Clip Art.
	Converters and Filters	Yes	Conversion filters for various text and graphics formats. If you remove a converter for a file type and then try to open a file of that type, the open (or import) operation will fail.
	Digital Certificate for VBA Projects	Yes	A digital certificate for signing Visual Basic for Applications projects. If you remove this, you will receive security warnings when opening a VBA project that otherwise would have been signed.
	Fonts	Yes	Various fonts that come with Office 2010.
	International Support	Yes	This consists of two fonts: Japanese Font and Universal Font.
	Microsoft Office Download Control	Yes	The ActiveX control that enables clip art and templates to be automatically downloaded when selected. You'll probably want to keep this.
	Microsoft Office Themes	Yes	Provides access to the formatting themes that are consistent across applications

Table C.1 Continued

Location in Setup	Option	Installed by Default?	Description
	Proofing Tools	Yes	There are four sets of proofing tools: English, French, Spanish, and Translation Core. For each of the three languages, you can enable/disable support for Find All Word Forms, Hyphenation, Spelling and Grammar Checking, and more. For French and Spanish, you can enable translation services to English.
	Visual Basic for Applications	Yes	VBA enables you to eedit macros.
	Web Themes	Yes	There are two groups: Typical Web Themes and Additional Web Themes. Both are installed by default. Note that these are shared themes across all Office applications, not just for Word.
Office Tools	Equation Editor	Yes	Helps you create mathematical formulas with complex symbols.
	Hosted Webs	Yes	Enables the use of web folders on Office-compatible servers.
	Language Settings Tool	Yes	Provides an interface for setting language options across all Office documents.
	Microsoft Forms 2.0 .NET Programmability Support	Yes	Enables Microsoft Forms 2.0 programmability with .NET Framework version 1.1 or greater.
	Microsoft Graph	Yes	The utility that creates charts in Word, PowerPoint, and Access.
	Microsoft Office Picture Manager	Yes	The Picture Manager utility for working with graphics.
	Microsoft Query	Yes	An add-in for Excel that provides direct database connectivity.
	Optical Character Recognition (OCR)	Yes	Allows you to easily perform OCR and extract text from image documents.
	Actions .NET Programmability Support	Yes	Allows actions programmability with .NET Framework version 1.1 or greater.
	Actions Plugins	Yes	This is the main actions feature, providing intelligent recognition of data types from within Excel and Word. Various types are individually selectable.
	Microsoft SharePoint Foundation Support	Yes	Enables Office applications to interact with SharePoint Services.

INDEX

Symbols

∧ (caret codes), 78

© copyright symbol, 54

↔ double-headed arrow, 54

" (double opening/closing quote), 54

... (ellipsis), 54

— (em dashes), 54

- (en dashes), 54

= (equal to operator), 370

{=} field code, 626

> (greater than operator), 370

>= (greater than or equal to operator), 370

< (less than operator), 370

<= (less than or equal to operator), 370

<> (not equal to operator), 370

® (registered trademark symbol), 54

™ (trademark symbol), 54

← (typographical left arrow), 54

→ (typographical right arrow), 54

' (single opening/closing quote), 54

3-D effects
  drawn objects, 445-446
  paragraph borders, 211
  pictures, 406-407
  shadows combination, 446
  text, 166

3-D rotation, 409-410

A

ABS() function, 372

accepting revisions, 767-768

accessing
  building blocks, 89
  templates
    local, 23
    Office.com, 22-23

actions, 115
  add-ins, 887
  configuring, 116-117
  data assignments, 115-116
  .NET Programmability Support, 899
  performing, 116
  plugins, 899

ActiveX controls, 651

Add Clips to Organizer dialog box, 461

Add Custom Dictionary dialog box, 109

Add Fonts dialog box, 156

adding
  AutoCorrect entries
    formatted, 113-114
    text, 113
  building blocks, 90-91
  captions
    pictures, 412-413
    tables, 366-367
  commands
    Quick Access toolbar, 6
    Ribbon, 869-870
  comments, 763
  content controls, 642
  dates and times to headers and footers, 271-272

dictionaries to Word, 108-109
digital signatures, 810
document properties, 274
documents to workspaces, 781
dummy text, 89
field codes, 616-618
flagged words to dictionaries, 104
languages to spelling and grammar checker, 109-110
legacy fields, 649
page numbering to headers and footers, 269-270
pictures
  Clip Organizer, 461
  from files, 384-386
  headers and footers, 275
Quick Access toolbar
  buttons, 6, 21, 864-865
  commands, 6, 864
Quick Styles, 222
research providers, 125-126
scanned images to Clip Organizer, 461
section breaks, 255
SmartArt diagrams, 521
  shapes, 522-523
  text, 525
tables
  cells, 343
  columns, 343-344
  Insert Table dialog box, 337-338
  rows, 343-344
  Table menu, 337
text boxes, 276, 308-309
text to shapes, 422-423
watermarks, 278

types
  categories, *486*
  editing, *486*
up/down bars, 505
walls, 475

Check Box control, 643

checking
grammar
  customizing, *100*
  exceptions, *102*
  fixing errors, *97-98*
  grammar and style
    settings, *103-104*
  interactive spelling and
    grammar check, *98-100*
  Word only options, *102*
spelling
  customizing, *100*
  dictionaries. See *spell
    checking, dictionaries*
  exceptions, *102*
  indexes, *749*
  individual words, *95-96*
  interactive spelling and
    grammar check, *98-100*
  language selection, *96-97*
  multiple languages,
    109-110
  Office spelling options,
    101-102
  Proofing Errors icon, *100*
  Word only options, *102*

**Chicago Fifteenth Edition
citation style, 696**

citations
converting to text, 704
editing, 703-704
entering, 701-702
marking for table of authorities, 737-738
new sources, entering, 702
styles, 696
temporary source
  placeholders, 702-703

**Citations and Bibliography
tools, 696**

citing sources, 696
bibliographies, 705
  adding from Bibliography
    Gallery, 706

built-in layouts, *705*
deleting, *708*
editing, *707*
formatting comparison,
  705
saving, *707-708*
citations
  converting to text, *704*
  editing, *703-704*
  entering, *701-702*
  marking for table of
    authorities, *737-738*
  new sources, entering,
    702
  styles, *696*
  temporary source
    placeholders, *702-703*
cross-references, 717-718
  building blocks, *720*
  captions, *720*
  context, *719-720*
  creating, *718-719*
  footnotes/endnotes, *720*
  headings, troubleshoot-
    ing, *720*
  options, *719*
  reference items, *719*
endnotes
  adding, *711*
  cross-references, *720*
  deleting, *711*
  footnotes, compared, *708*
  jumping, *711*
  moving between, *712*
  numbering/symbols, *714*
  positioning, *713-714*
  separator lines, *715-717*
  styles, *714-716*
  switching between
    footnotes, *713*
footnotes
  adding, *710*
  continuations, *717*
  cross-references, *720*
  deleting, *711*
  disappearing, *717*
  endnotes, compared, *708*
  jumping, *711*
  key features, *708-709*
  moving between, *712*

numbering/symbols, *714*
positioning, *713-714*
separator lines, *715-717*
styles, *714-716*
switching between end-
  notes, *713*
reference marks, placing,
  709
sources
  creating for citations, *702*
  deleting, *700*
  editing, *699-700*
  entering, *698-699*
  inline references, *701-702*
  temporary placeholders,
    702-703
  transferring to/from
    Master List, *701*

Click and Type feature, 59-60

clip art
backgrounds, 465-466
borders, 469-470
captions, 455-456
Clip Organizer, 458
  browsing clips, *458*
  found clip options, *460*
  moving pictures between
    collections, *462*
  pictures, adding, *461*
  scanned images, adding,
    461
  searching by keyword,
    459
collection folders, creating,
  460
color-adjusting, 465
converting to Microsoft
  Drawing objects, 472
copying to other
  applications, 452-453
cropping, 465
envelopes, 326
fills, 466
flipping, 471
formats, 451
history, 415
hyperlinks, 589-590
information, viewing,
  453-454
keywords, 452, 455-456

How can we make this index more useful? Email us at indexes@quepublishing.com

R

FREE Online Edition

Your purchase of **Microsoft Word 2010 In Depth** includes access to a free online edition for 45 days through the Safari Books Online subscription service. Nearly every Que book is available online through Safari Books Online, along with more than 5,000 other technical books and videos from publishers such as Addison-Wesley Professional, Cisco Press, Exam Cram, IBM Press, O'Reilly, Prentice Hall, and Sams.

SAFARI BOOKS ONLINE allows you to search for a specific answer, cut and paste code, download chapters, and stay current with emerging technologies.

Activate your FREE Online Edition at
www.informit.com/safarifree

> **STEP 1:** Enter the coupon code: JNZNZBI.

> **STEP 2:** New Safari users, complete the brief registration form.
> Safari subscribers, just log in.